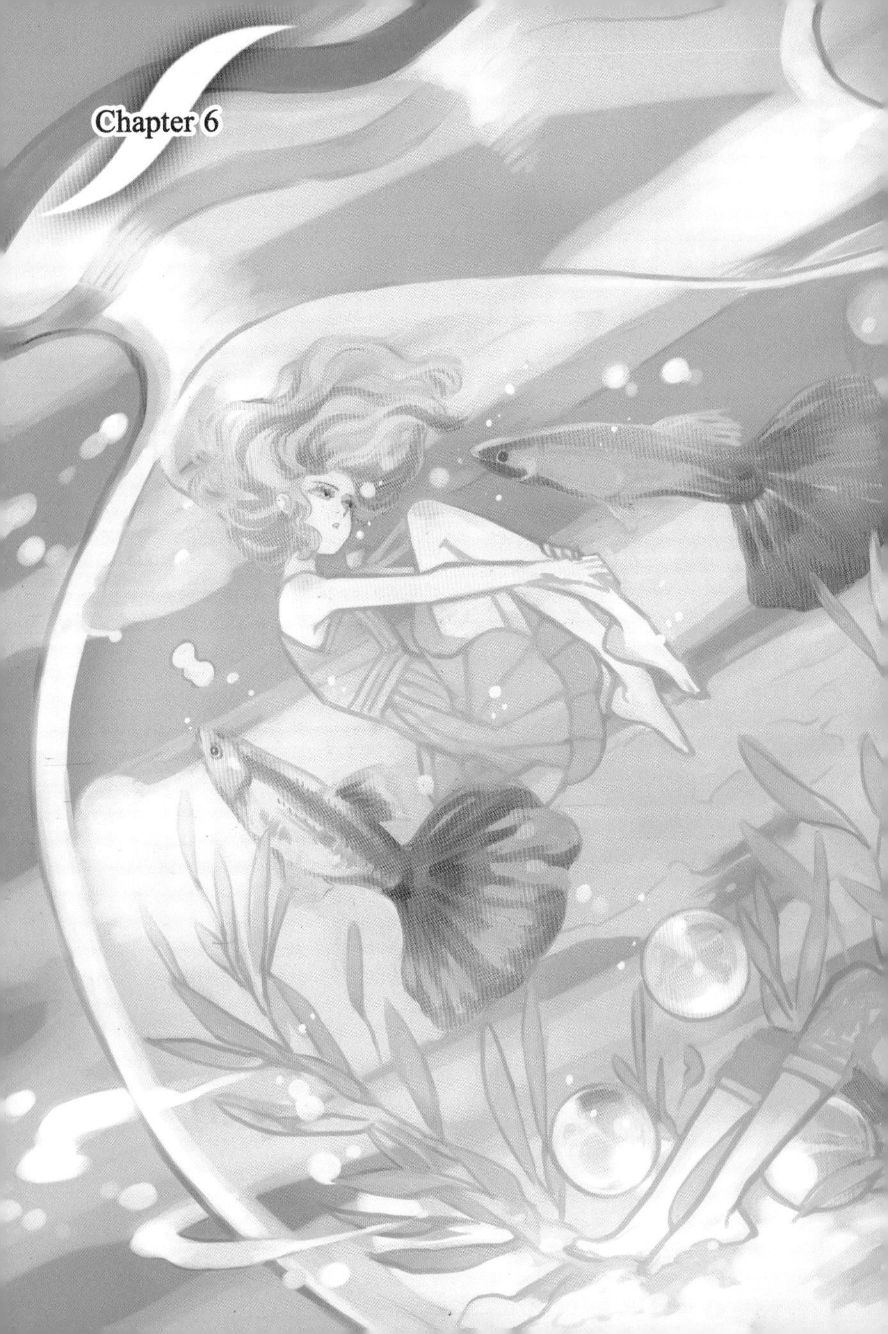
Chapter 6

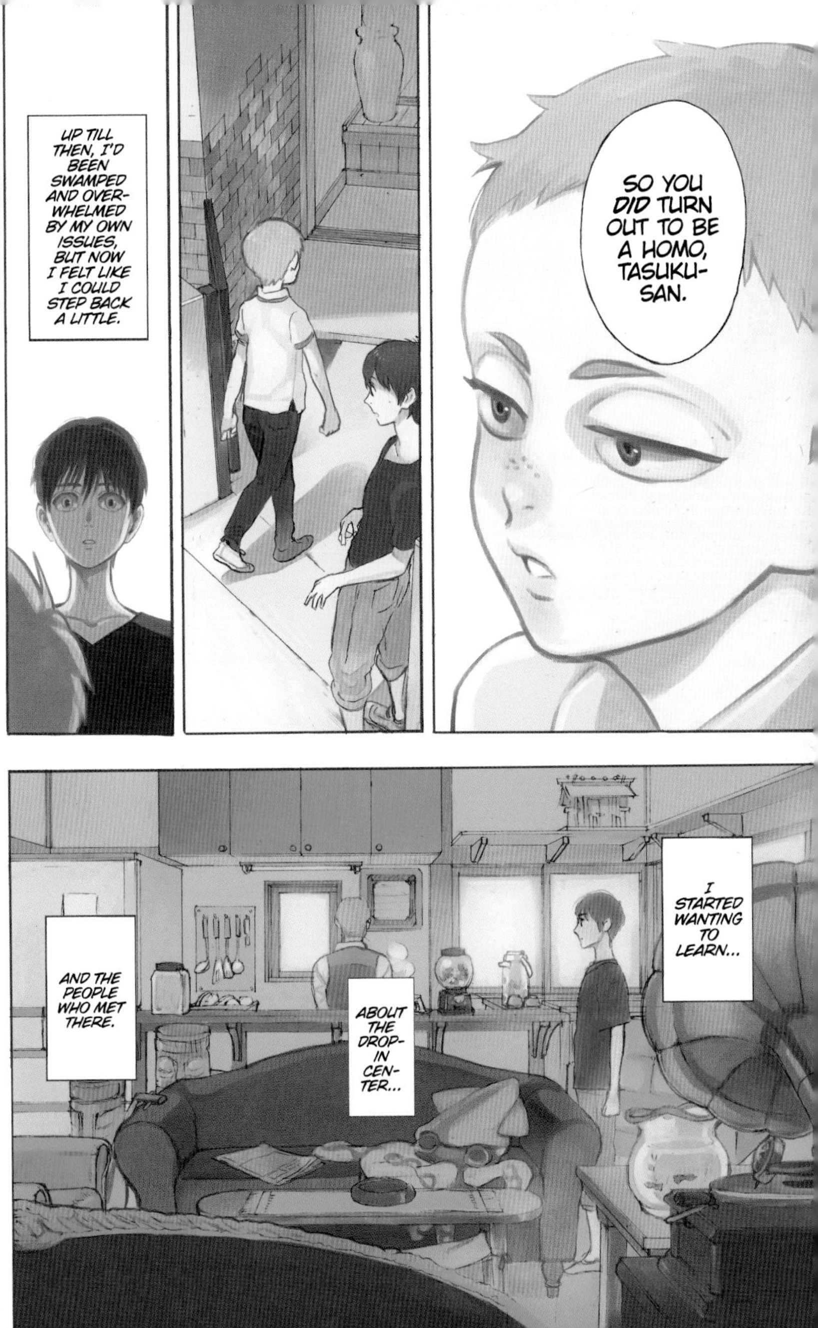
SO YOU DID TURN OUT TO BE A HOMO, TASUKU-SAN.
UP TILL THEN, I'D BEEN SWAMPED AND OVERWHELMED BY MY OWN ISSUES, BUT NOW I FELT LIKE I COULD STEP BACK A LITTLE.
I STARTED WANTING TO LEARN...
ABOUT THE DROP-IN CENTER...
AND THE PEOPLE WHO MET THERE.

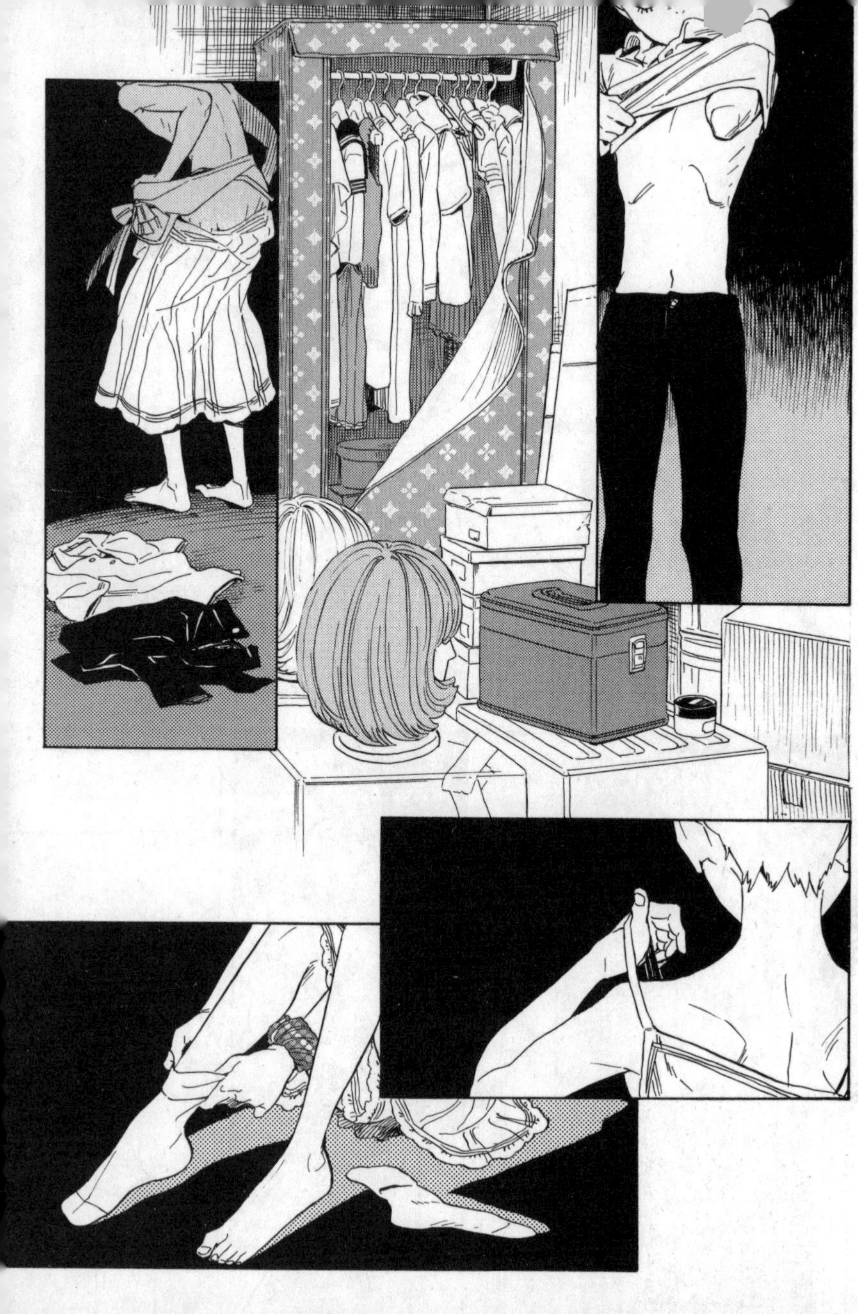

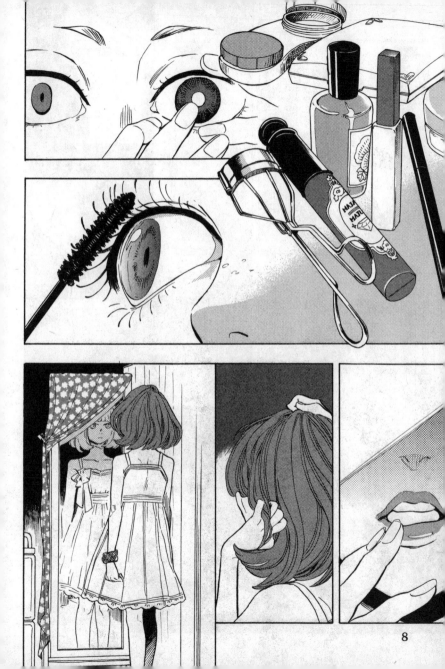

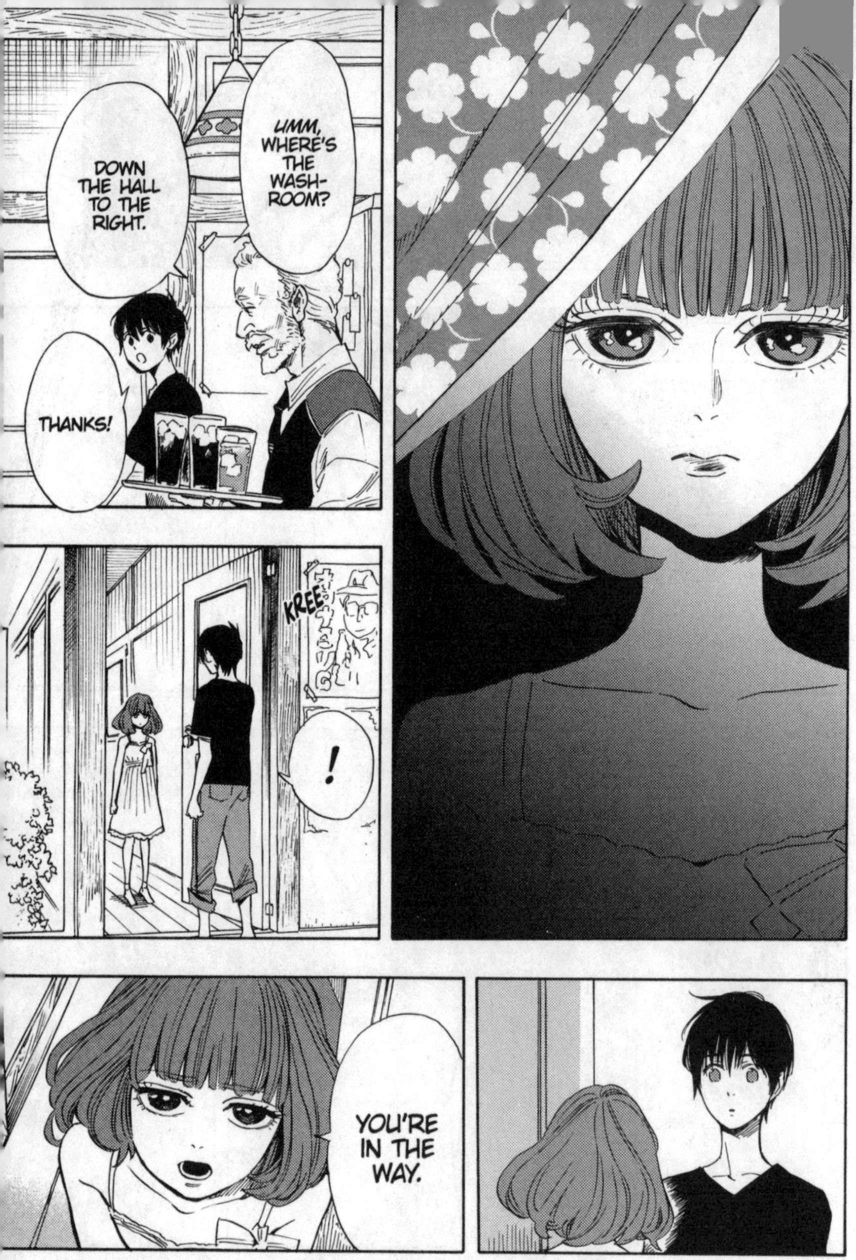
UMM, WHERE'S THE WASH-ROOM?
DOWN THE HALL TO THE RIGHT.
THANKS!
KREE
!
YOU'RE IN THE WAY.

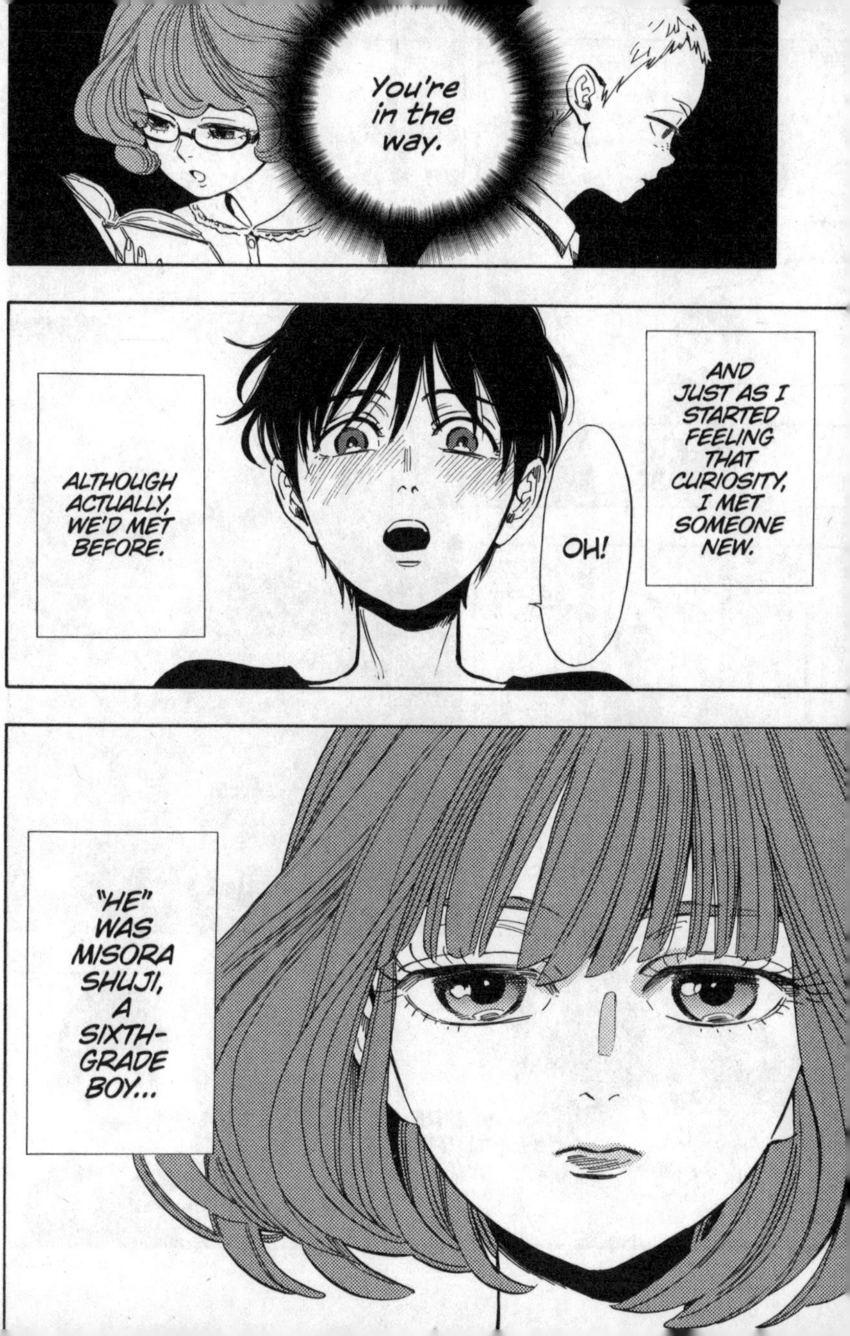
You're in the way.
AND JUST AS I STARTED FEELING THAT CURIOSITY, I MET SOMEONE NEW.
OH!
ALTHOUGH ACTUALLY, WE'D MET BEFORE.
"HE" WAS MISORA SHUJI, A SIXTH-GRADE BOY...

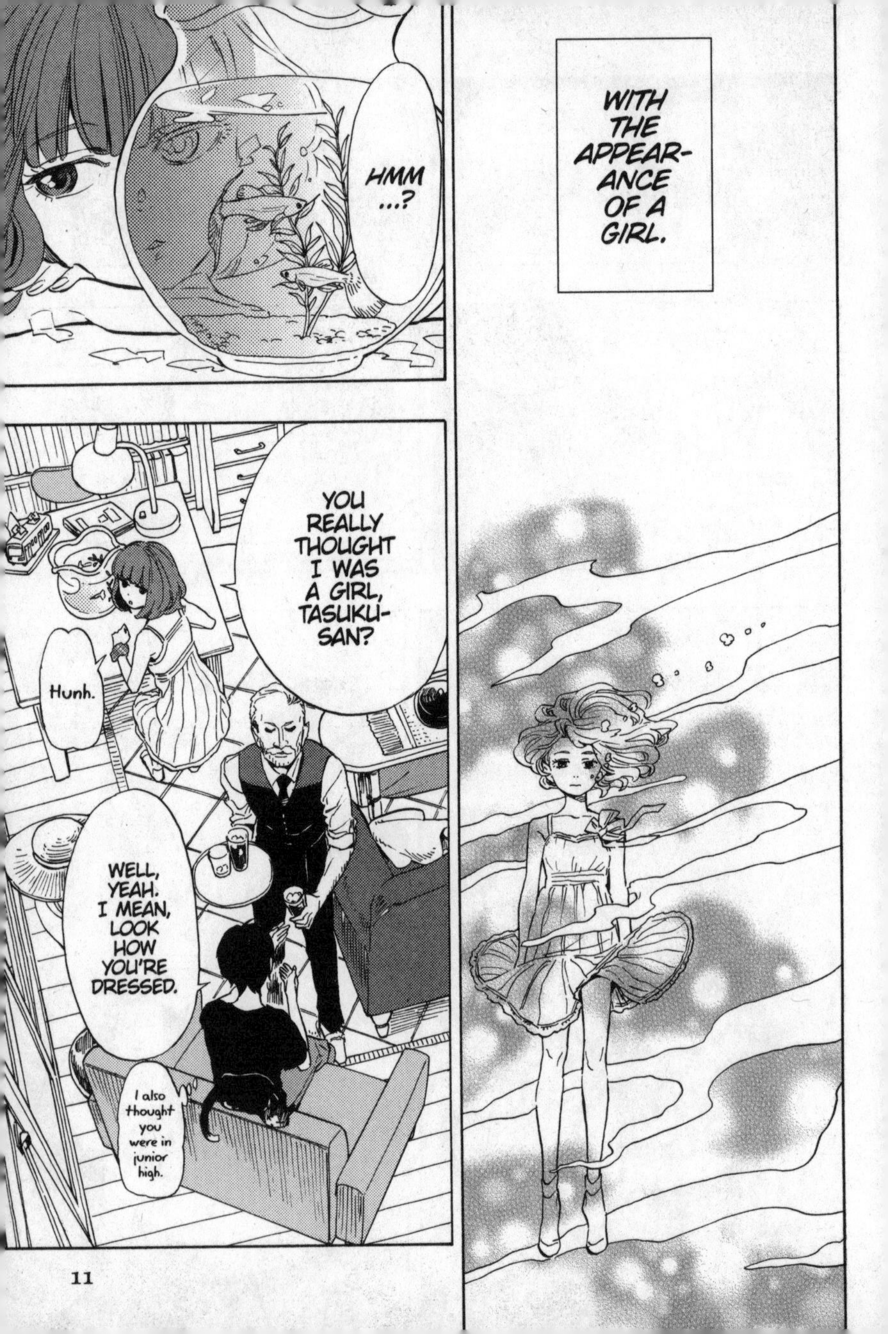
WITH THE APPEAR-ANCE OF A GIRL.
HMM ...?
YOU REALLY THOUGHT I WAS A GIRL, TASUKU-SAN?
Hunh.
WELL, YEAH. I MEAN, LOOK HOW YOU'RE DRESSED.
I also thought you were in junior high.

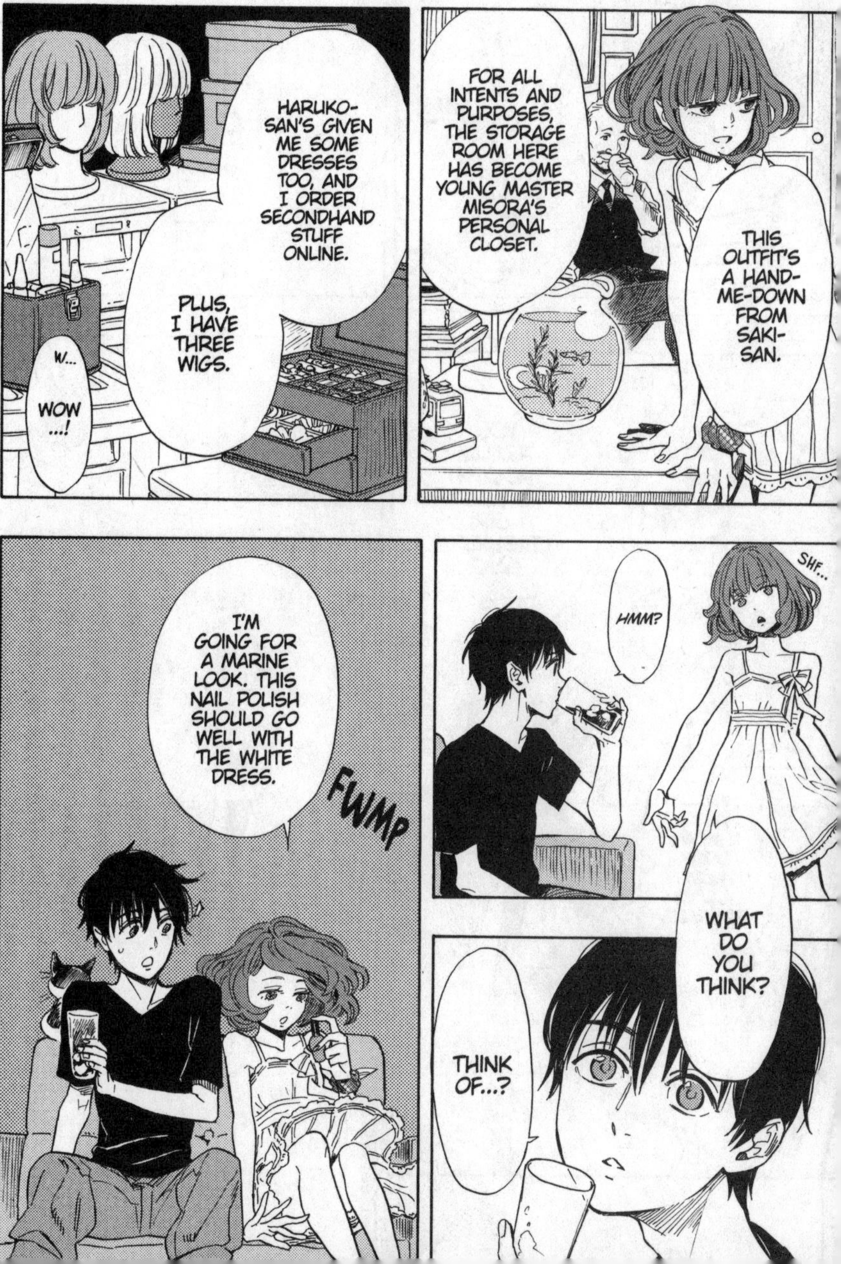
THIS OUTFIT'S A HAND-ME-DOWN FROM SAKI-SAN.
FOR ALL INTENTS AND PURPOSES, THE STORAGE ROOM HERE HAS BECOME YOUNG MASTER MISORA'S PERSONAL CLOSET.
HARUKO-SAN'S GIVEN ME SOME DRESSES TOO, AND I ORDER SECONDHAND STUFF ONLINE.
PLUS, I HAVE THREE WIGS.
W...
WOW ...!
SHF...
HMM?
WHAT DO YOU THINK?
THINK OF...?
I'M GOING FOR A MARINE LOOK. THIS NAIL POLISH SHOULD GO WELL WITH THE WHITE DRESS.
FWMP

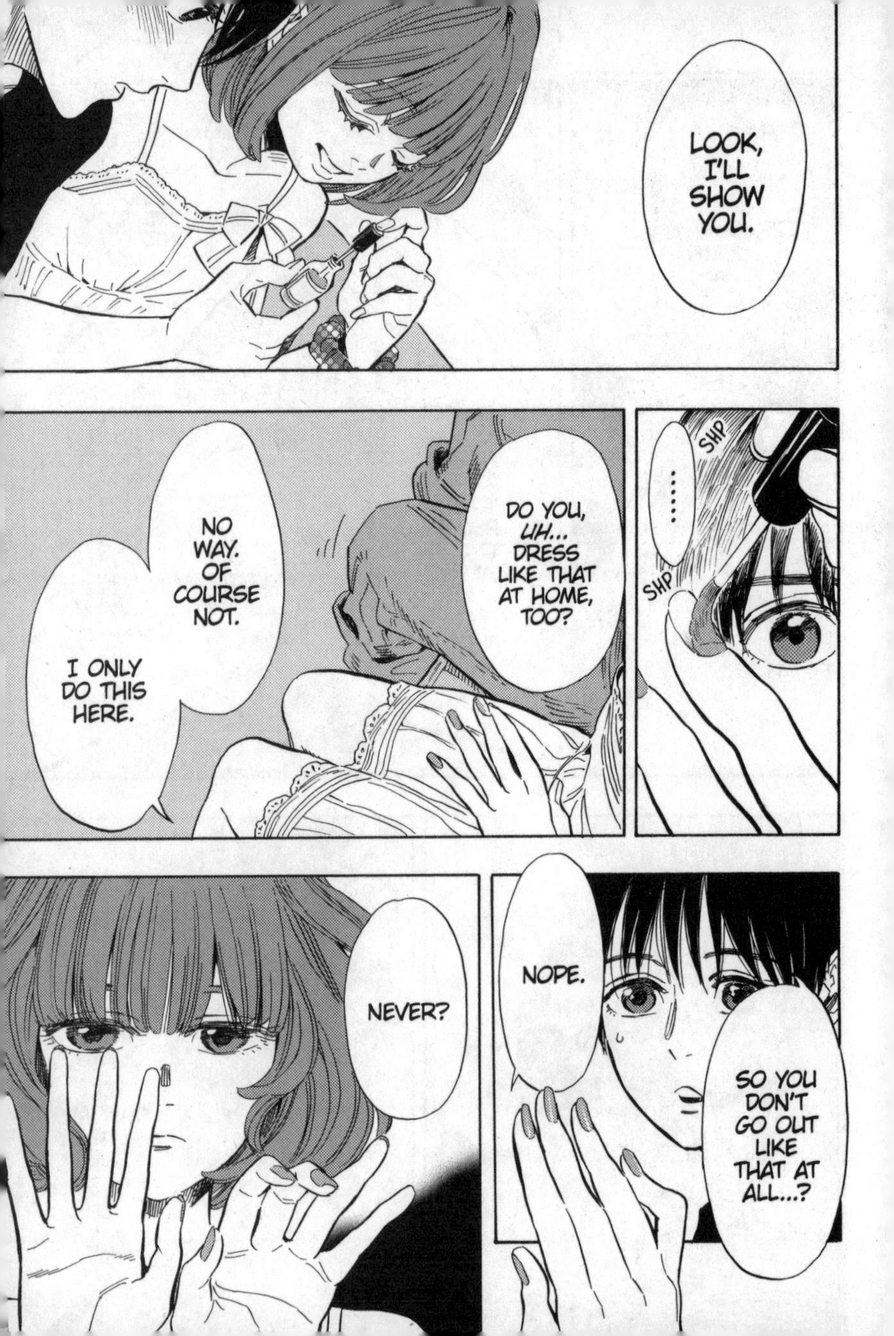
LOOK, I'LL SHOW YOU.
SHP
SHP
......
DO YOU, UH... DRESS LIKE THAT AT HOME, TOO?
NO WAY. OF COURSE NOT.
I ONLY DO THIS HERE.
SO YOU DON'T GO OUT LIKE THAT AT ALL...?
NOPE.
NEVER?

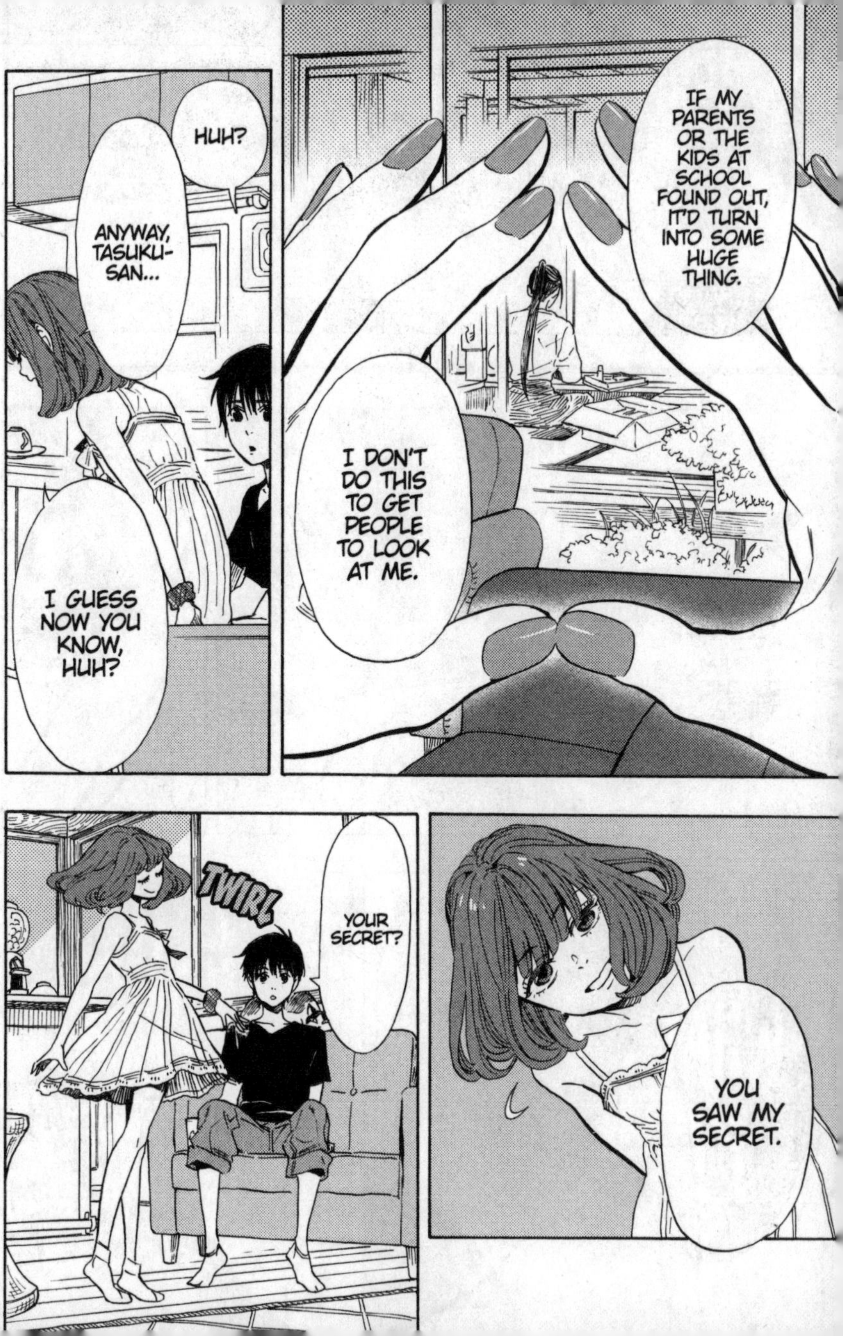
IF MY PARENTS OR THE KIDS AT SCHOOL FOUND OUT, IT'D TURN INTO SOME HUGE THING.
I DON'T DO THIS TO GET PEOPLE TO LOOK AT ME.
ANYWAY, TASUKU-SAN...
HUH?
I GUESS NOW YOU KNOW, HUH?
YOU SAW MY SECRET.
TWIRL
YOUR SECRET?

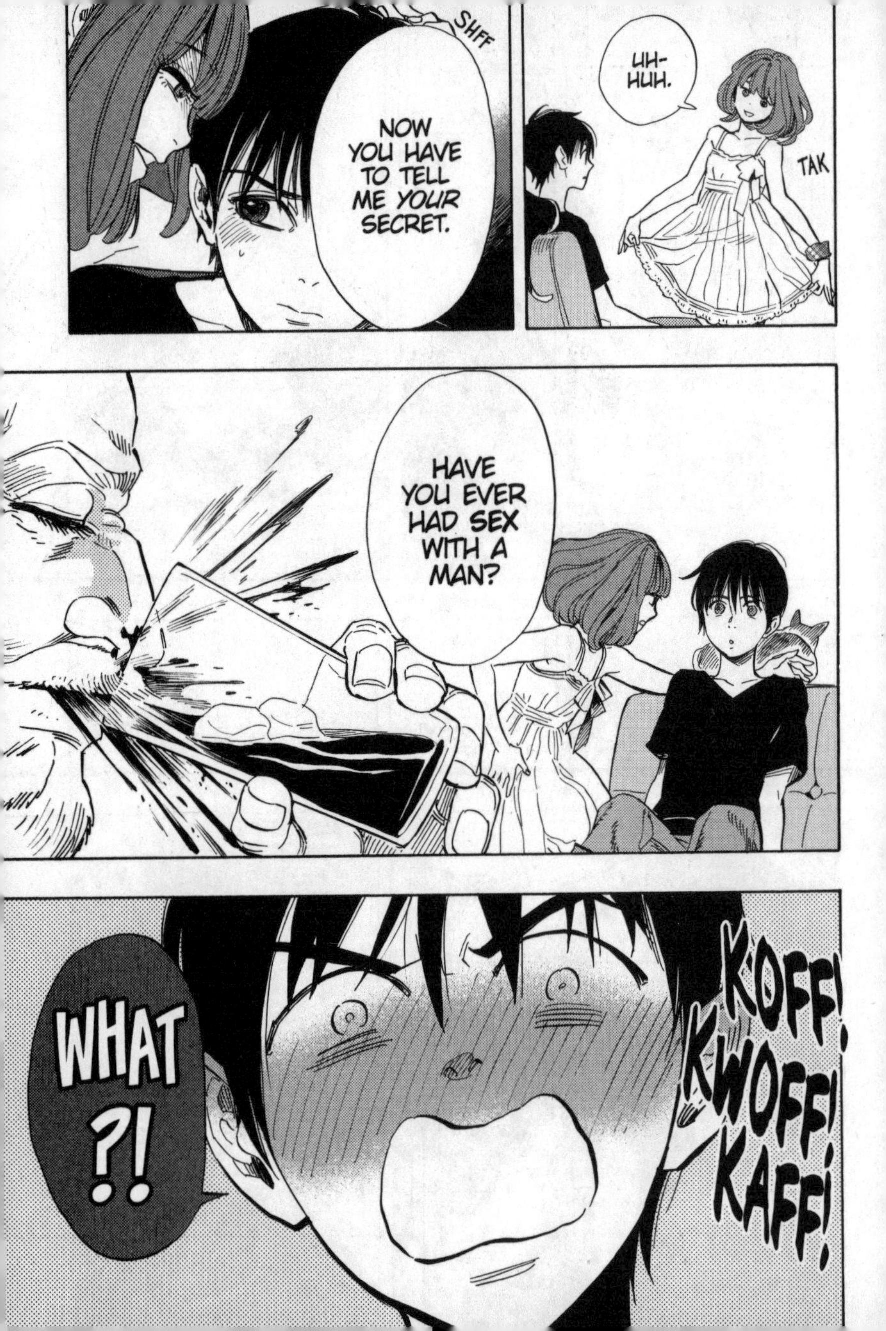
UH-HUH.
TAK
SHFF
NOW YOU HAVE TO TELL ME YOUR SECRET.
HAVE YOU EVER HAD SEX WITH A MAN?
KOFF! KWOFF! KAFF!
WHAT?!

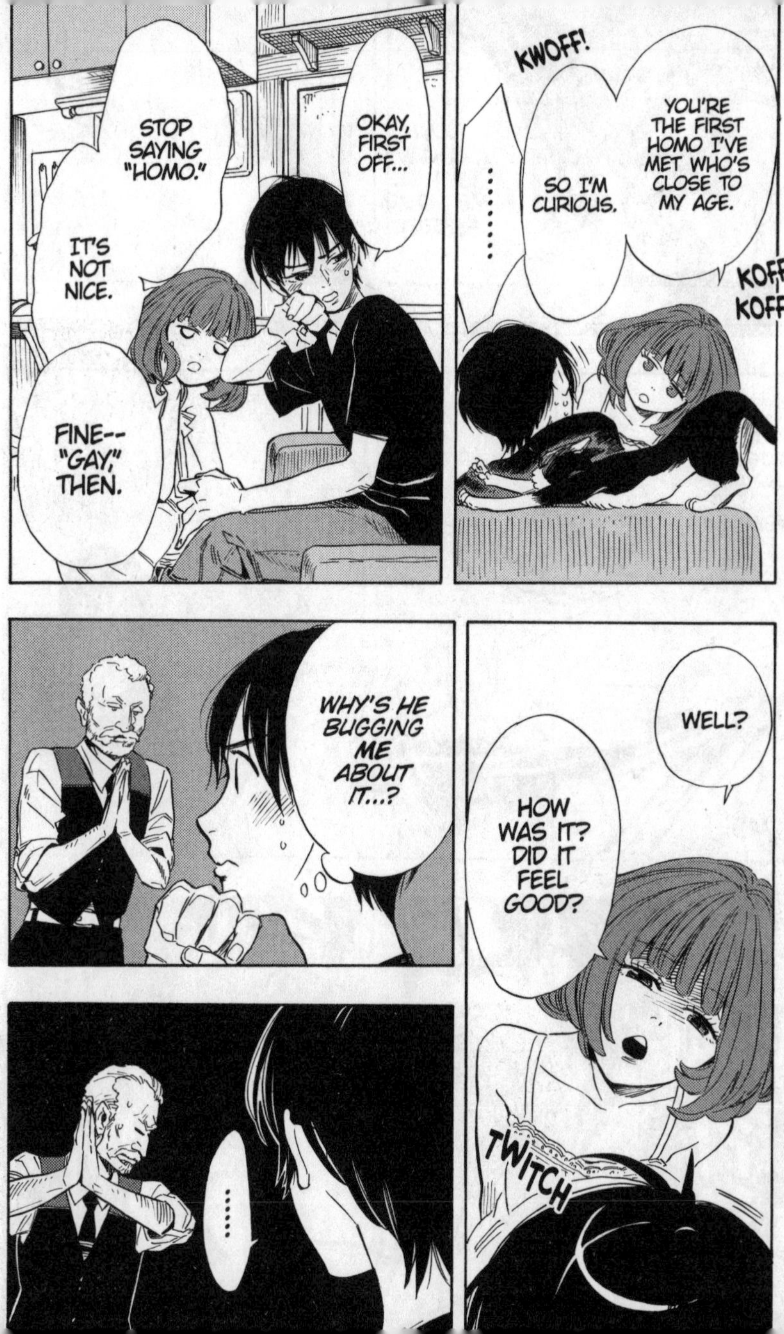
KWOFF!
YOU'RE THE FIRST HOMO I'VE MET WHO'S CLOSE TO MY AGE.
SO I'M CURIOUS.
......
KOFF! KOFF!
OKAY, FIRST OFF...
STOP SAYING "HOMO."
IT'S NOT NICE.
FINE-- "GAY," THEN.
WELL?
HOW WAS IT? DID IT FEEL GOOD?
TWITCH
WHY'S HE BUGGING ME ABOUT IT...?
......

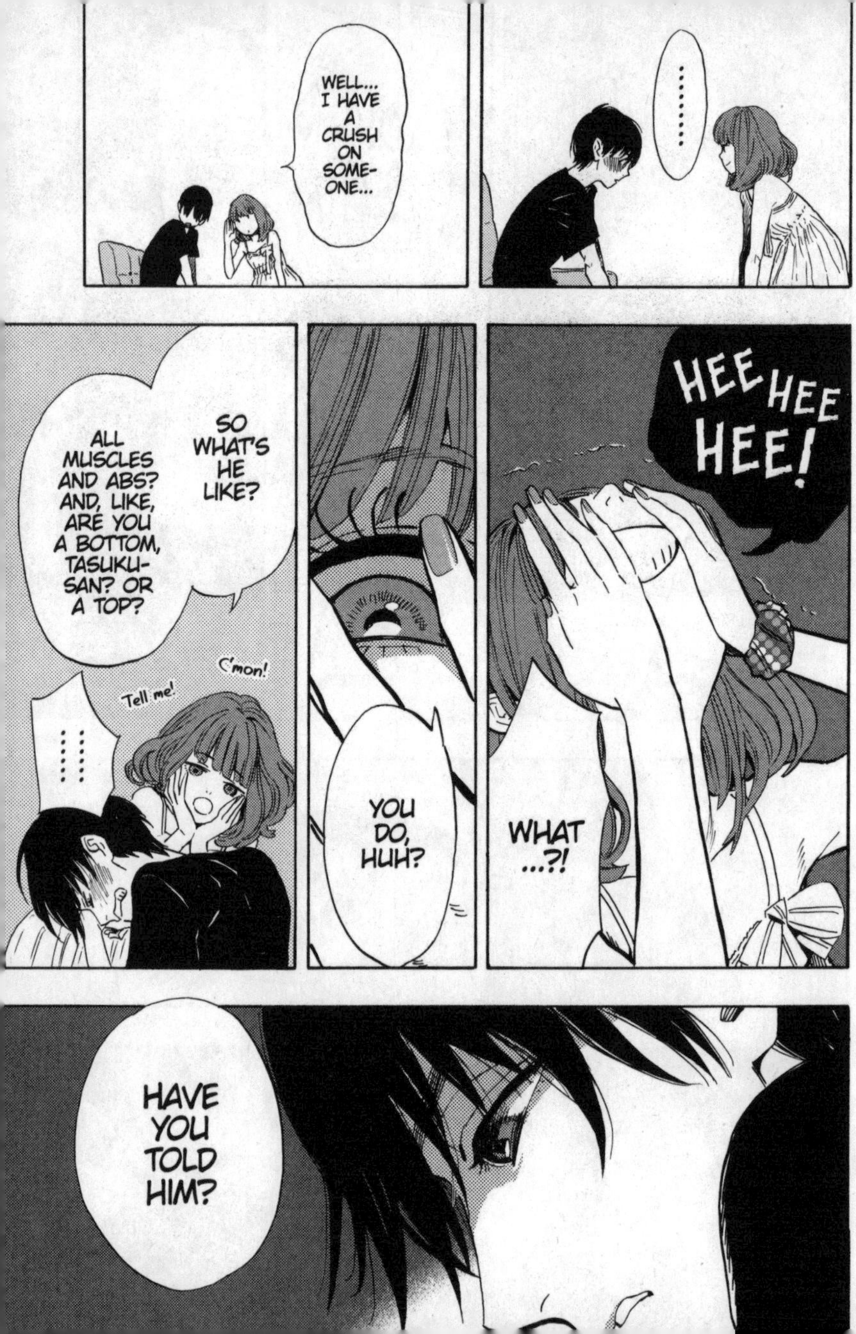
......
WELL... I HAVE A CRUSH ON SOME-ONE...
WHAT ...?!
HEE HEE HEE!
YOU DO, HUH?
SO WHAT'S HE LIKE?
ALL MUSCLES AND ABS? AND, LIKE, ARE YOU A BOTTOM, TASUKU-SAN? OR A TOP?
C'mon!
Tell me!
......
HAVE YOU TOLD HIM?

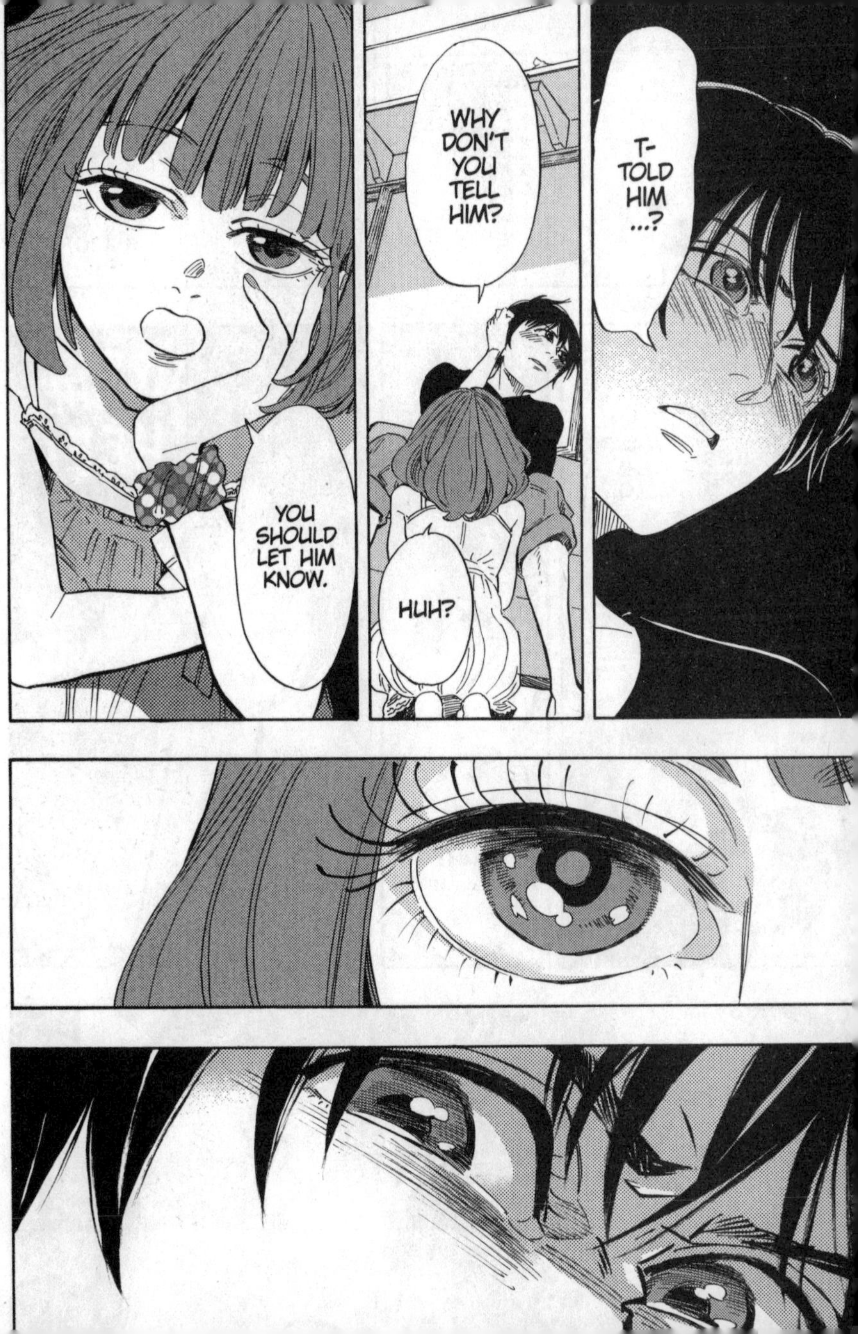
T-TOLD HIM ...?
WHY DON'T YOU TELL HIM?
HUH?
YOU SHOULD LET HIM KNOW.

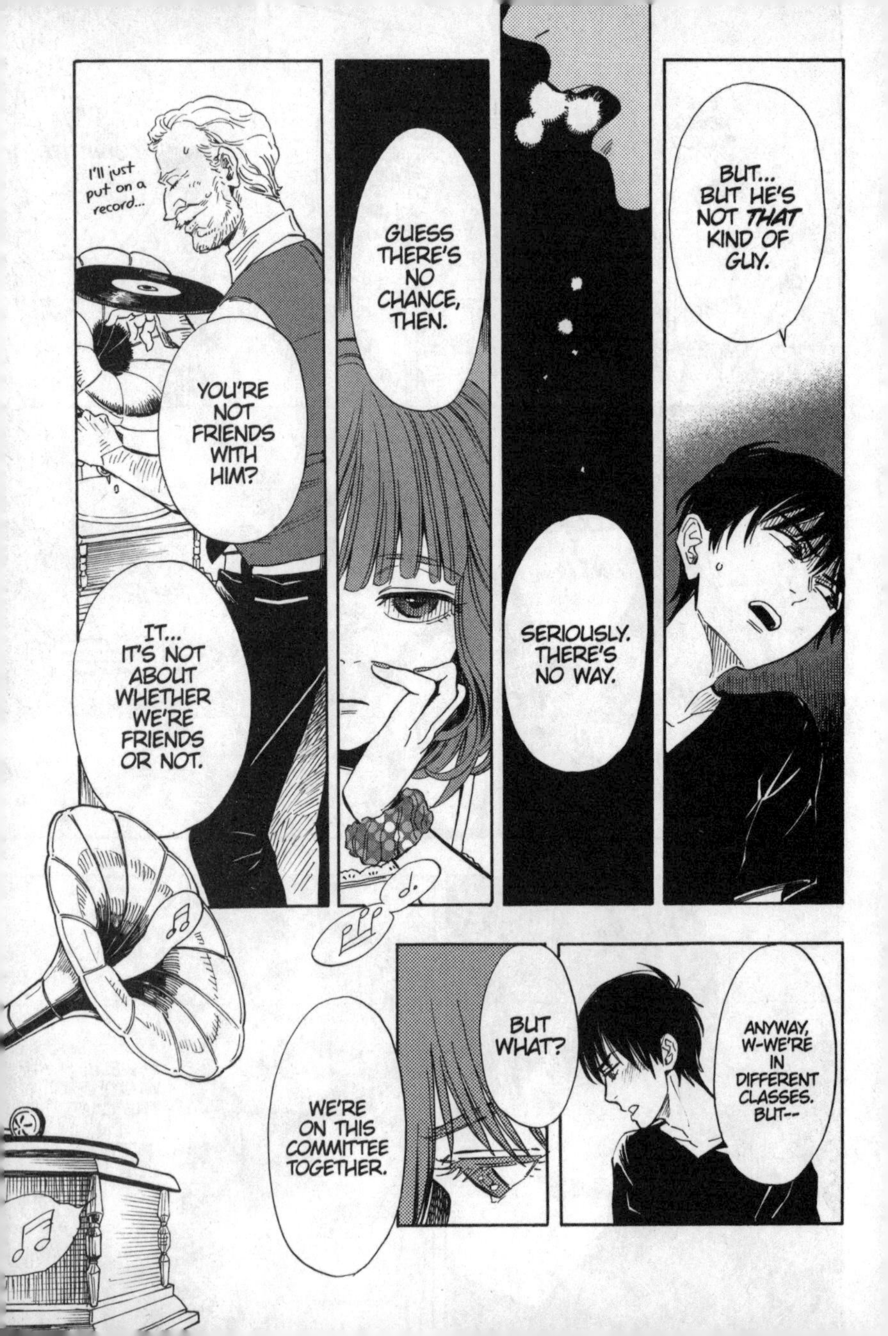
BUT... BUT HE'S NOT *THAT* KIND OF GUY.
SERIOUSLY. THERE'S NO WAY.
GUESS THERE'S NO CHANCE, THEN.
I'll just put on a record...
YOU'RE NOT FRIENDS WITH HIM?
IT... IT'S NOT ABOUT WHETHER WE'RE FRIENDS OR NOT.
ANYWAY, W-WE'RE IN DIFFERENT CLASSES. BUT--
BUT WHAT?
WE'RE ON THIS COMMITTEE TOGETHER.

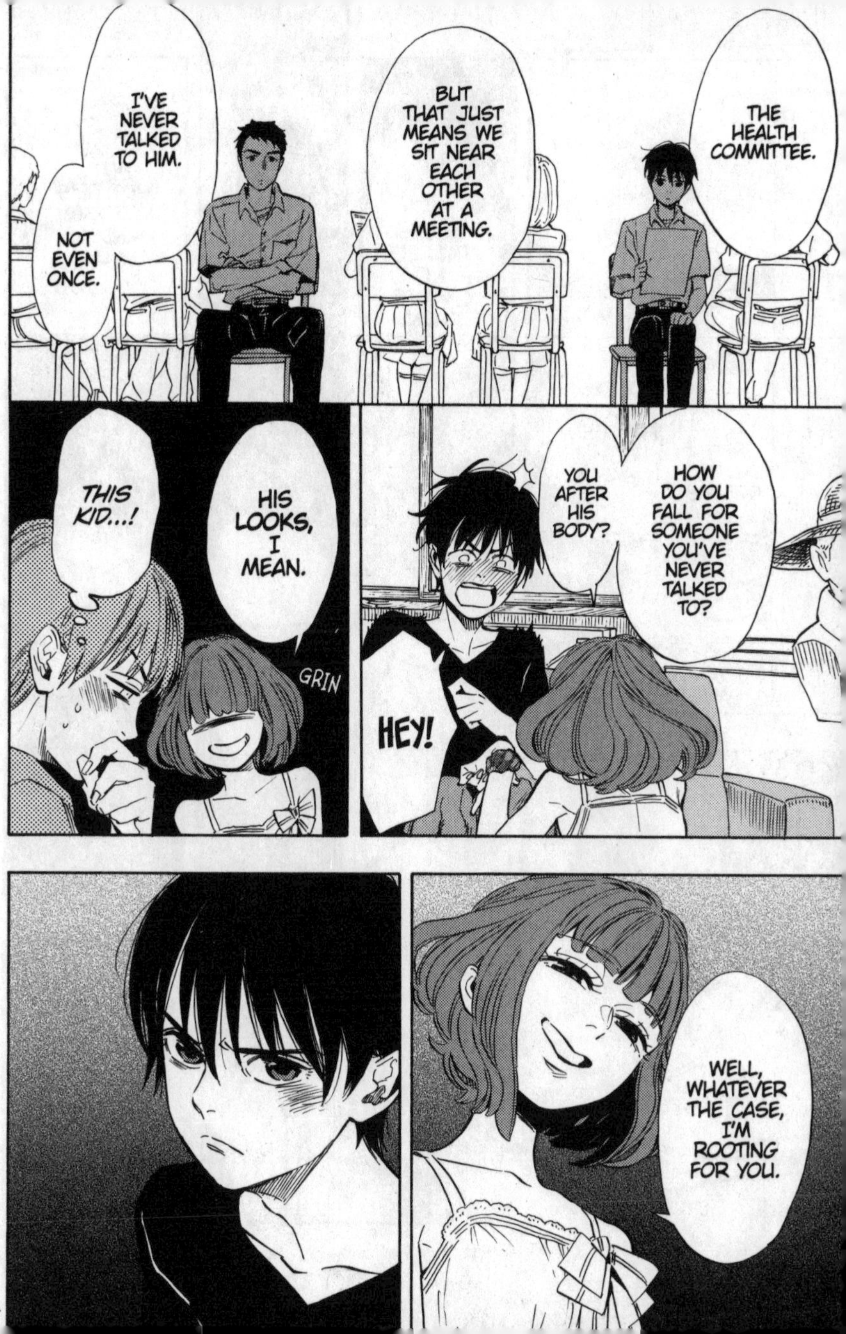
THE HEALTH COMMITTEE.
BUT THAT JUST MEANS WE SIT NEAR EACH OTHER AT A MEETING.
I'VE NEVER TALKED TO HIM.
NOT EVEN ONCE.
HOW DO YOU FALL FOR SOMEONE YOU'VE NEVER TALKED TO?
YOU AFTER HIS BODY?
HEY!
HIS LOOKS, I MEAN.
GRIN
THIS KID...!
WELL, WHATEVER THE CASE, I'M ROOTING FOR YOU.

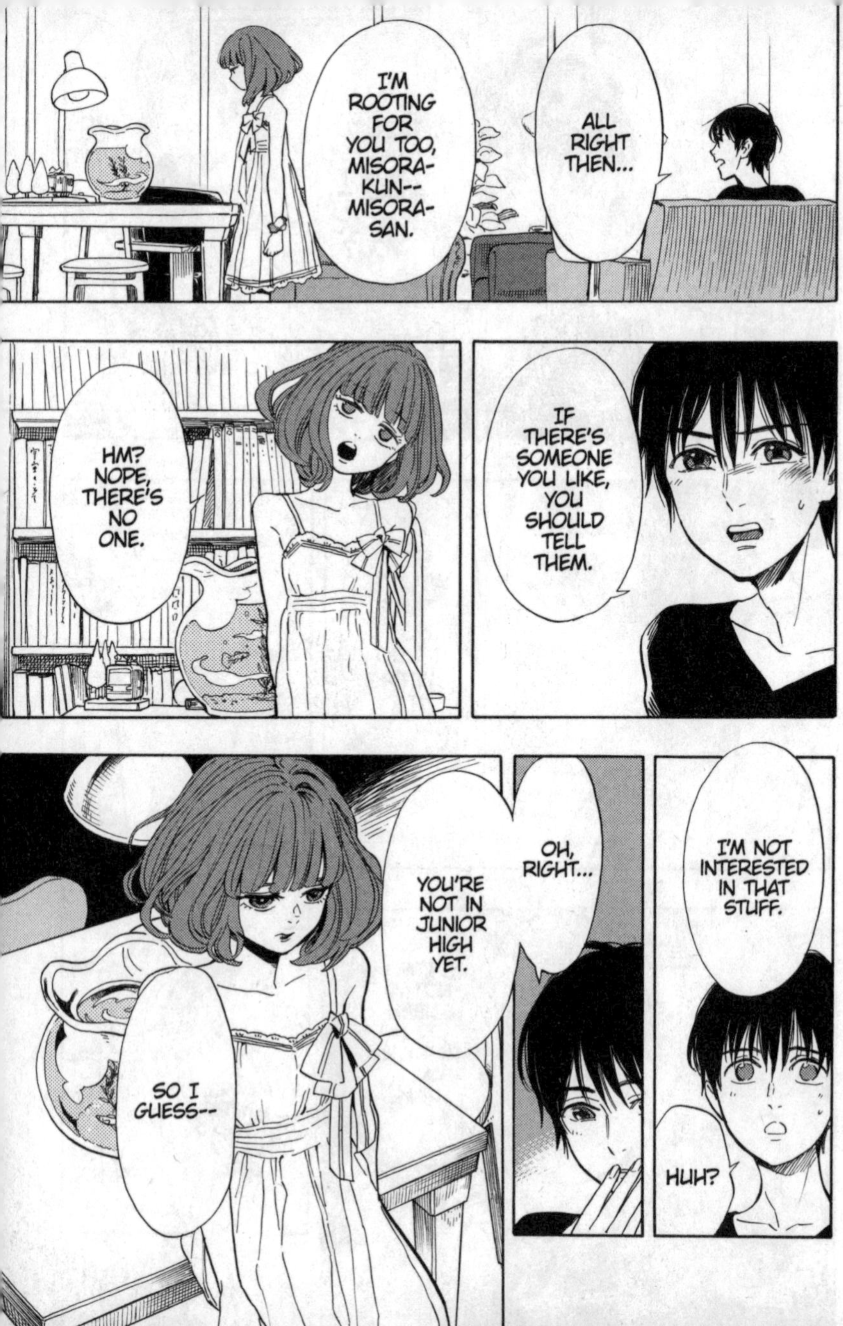
ALL RIGHT THEN...
I'M ROOTING FOR YOU TOO, MISORA-KUN-- MISORA-SAN.
IF THERE'S SOMEONE YOU LIKE, YOU SHOULD TELL THEM.
HM? NOPE, THERE'S NO ONE.
I'M NOT INTERESTED IN THAT STUFF.
HUH?
OH, RIGHT...
YOU'RE NOT IN JUNIOR HIGH YET.
SO I GUESS--

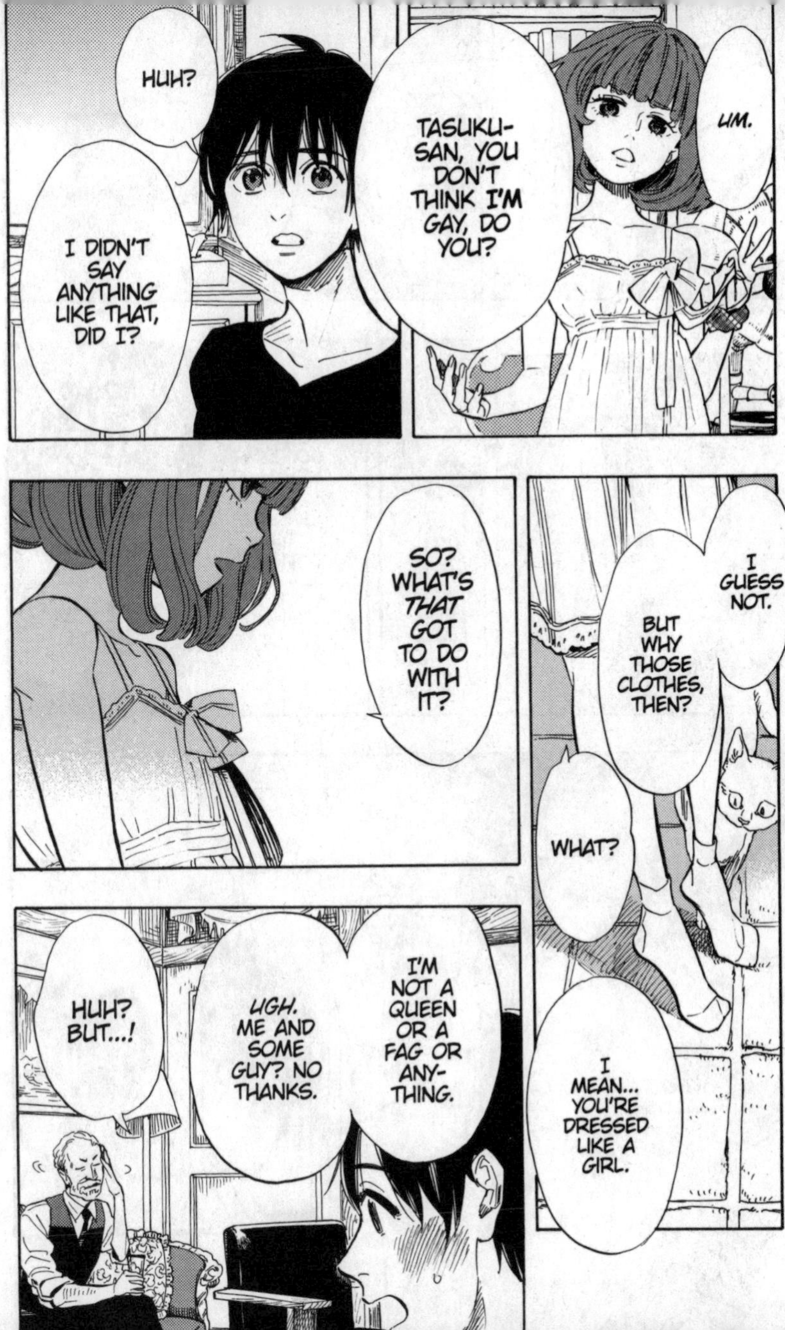
UM.
TASUKU-SAN, YOU DON'T THINK I'M GAY, DO YOU?
HUH?
I DIDN'T SAY ANYTHING LIKE THAT, DID I?
I GUESS NOT.
BUT WHY THOSE CLOTHES, THEN?
WHAT?
I MEAN... YOU'RE DRESSED LIKE A GIRL.
SO? WHAT'S *THAT* GOT TO DO WITH IT?
I'M NOT A QUEEN OR A FAG OR ANY-THING.
UGH. ME AND SOME GUY? NO THANKS.
HUH? BUT...!

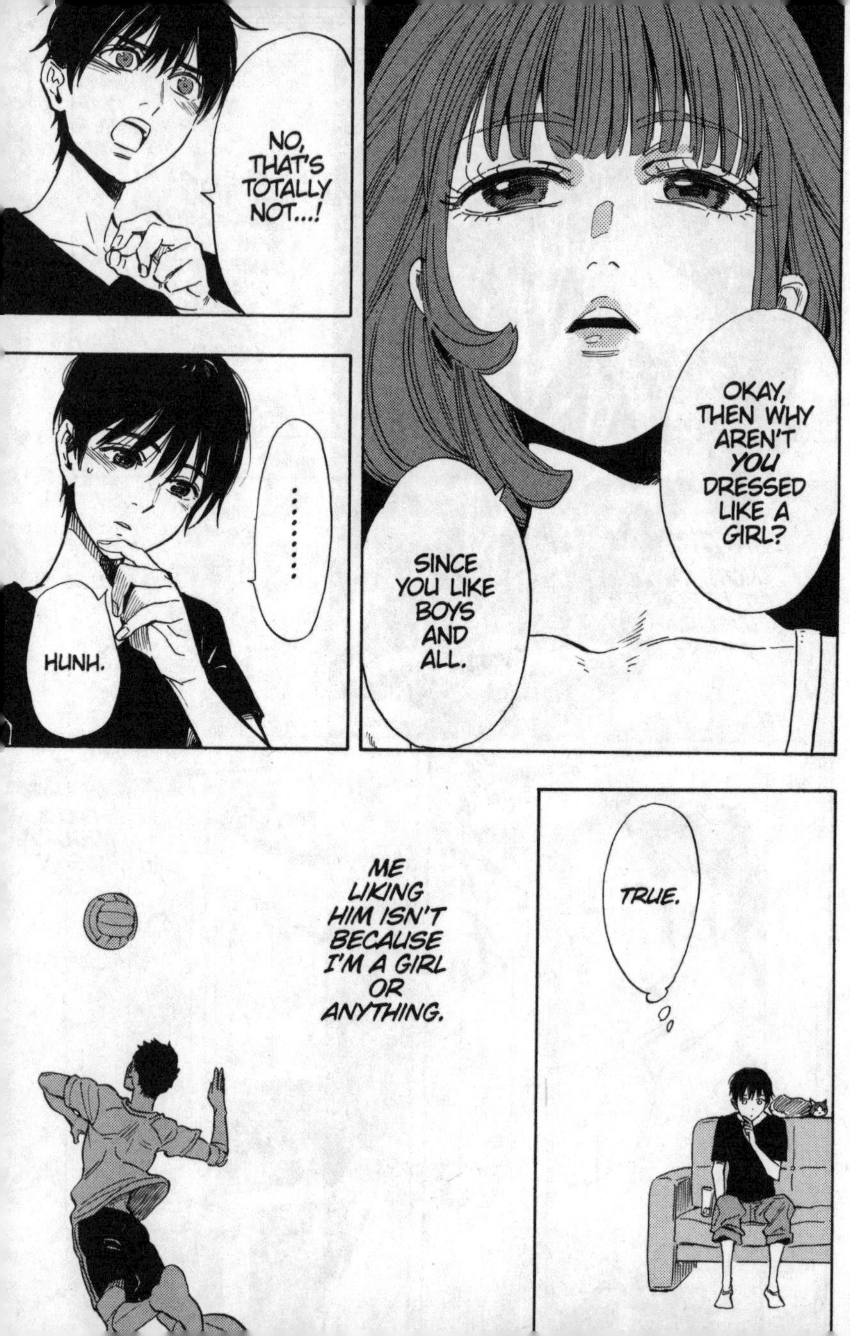
OKAY, THEN WHY AREN'T YOU DRESSED LIKE A GIRL?
SINCE YOU LIKE BOYS AND ALL.
NO, THAT'S TOTALLY NOT...!
......
HUNH.
TRUE.
ME LIKING HIM ISN'T BECAUSE I'M A GIRL OR ANYTHING.

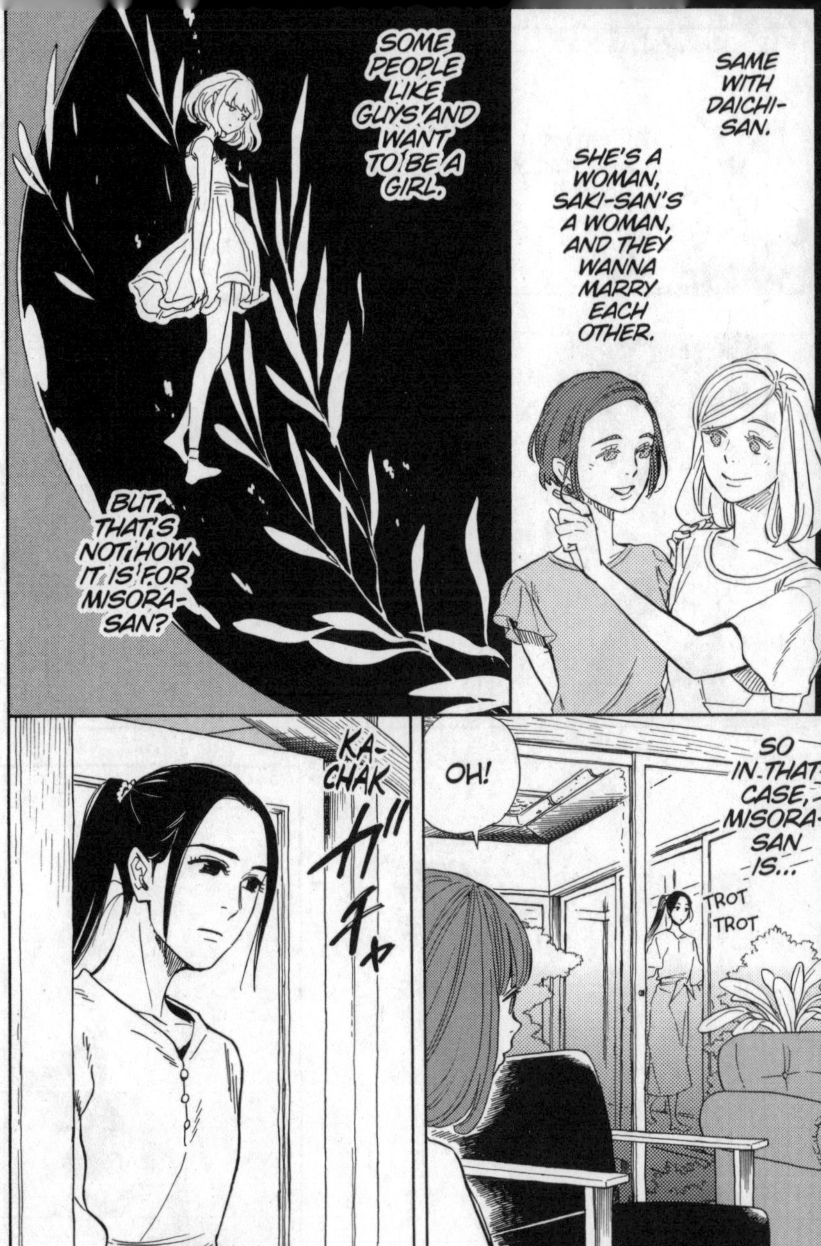
SAME WITH DAICHI-SAN.
SHE'S A WOMAN, SAKI-SAN'S A WOMAN, AND THEY WANNA MARRY EACH OTHER.
SOME PEOPLE LIKE GUYS AND WANT TO BE A GIRL.
BUT THAT'S NOT HOW IT IS FOR MISORA-SAN?
SO IN THAT CASE, MISORA-SAN IS...
TROT TROT
OH!
KA-CHAK

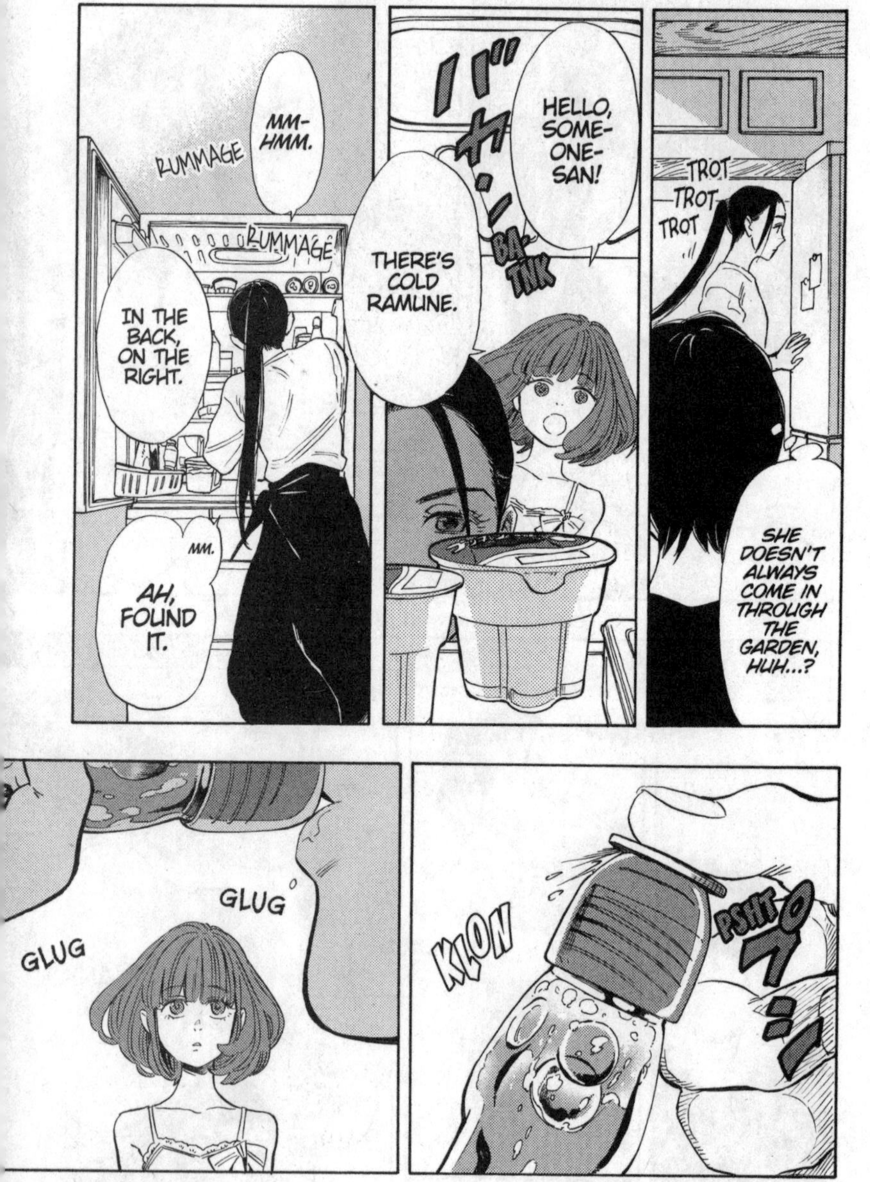
TROT
TROT
TROT
SHE DOESN'T ALWAYS COME IN THROUGH THE GARDEN, HUH...?
HELLO, SOME-ONE-SAN!
BA-TNK
THERE'S COLD RAMUNE.
MM-HMM.
RUMMAGE
RUMMAGE
IN THE BACK, ON THE RIGHT.
MM.
AH, FOUND IT.
PSHT
KLON
GLUG
GLUG

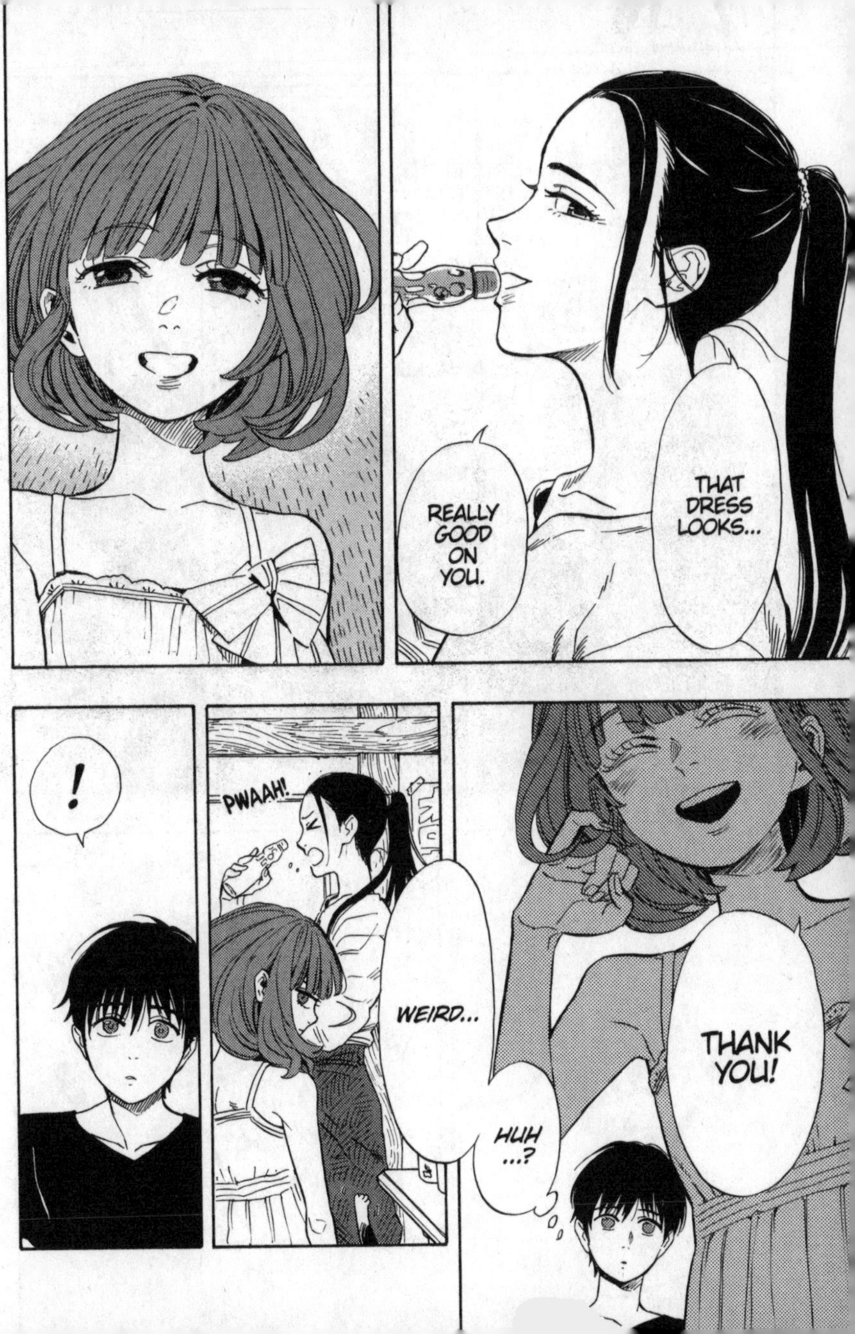
THAT DRESS LOOKS...
REALLY GOOD ON YOU.
THANK YOU!
HUH ...?
PWAAH!
WEIRD...
!

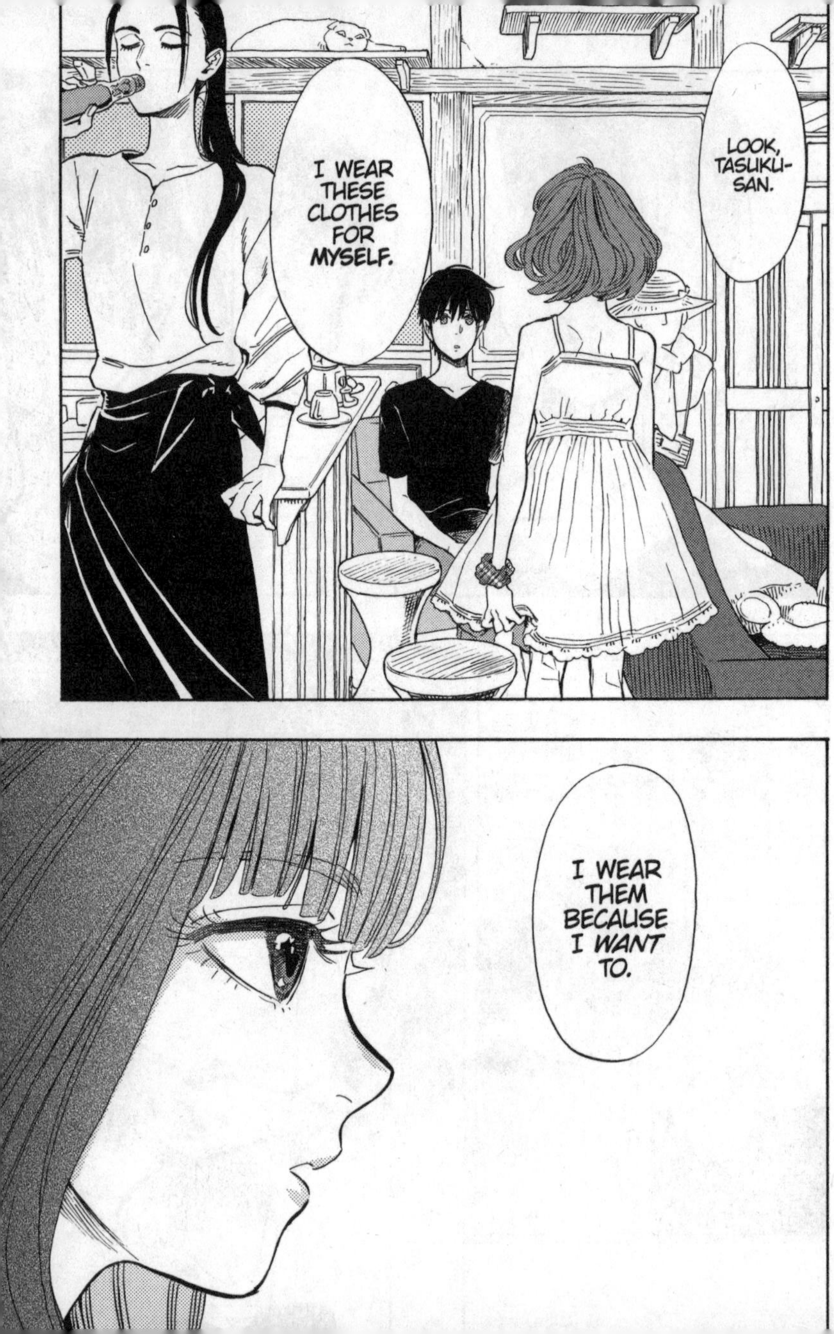
LOOK, TASUKU-SAN.
I WEAR THESE CLOTHES FOR MYSELF.
I WEAR THEM BECAUSE I *WANT* TO.

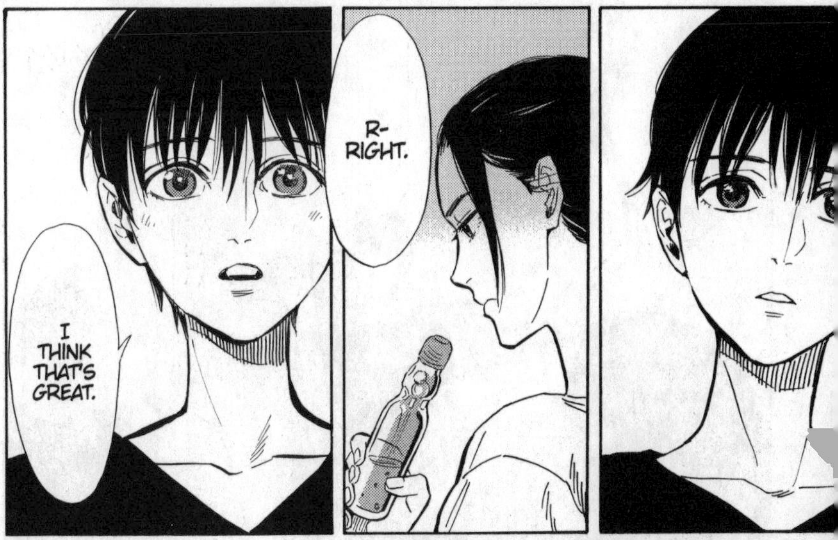
R-
RIGHT.
I THINK THAT'S GREAT.

Lantern: "Full House"

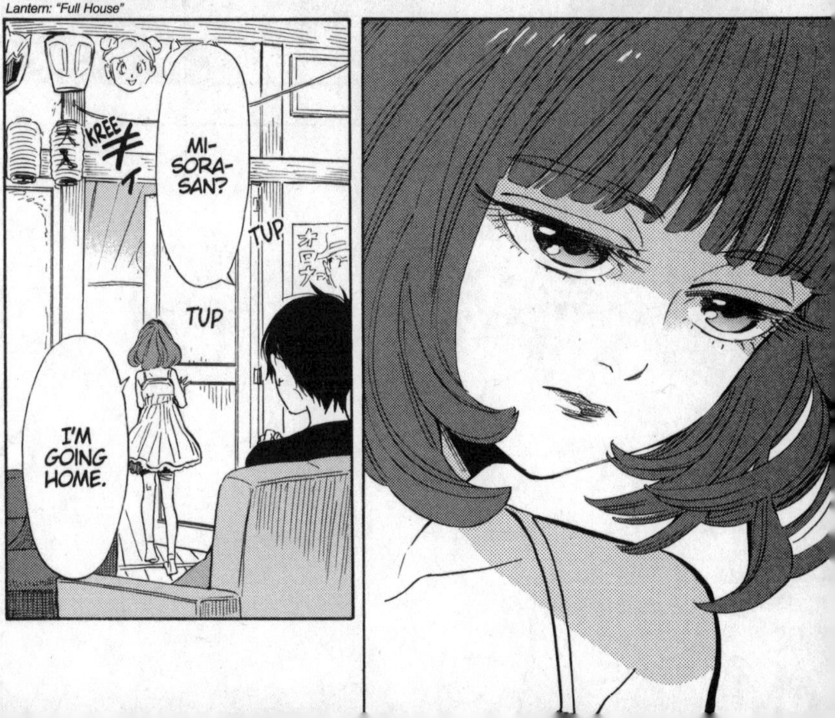
KREE
MI-SORA-SAN?
TUP
TUP
I'M GOING HOME.

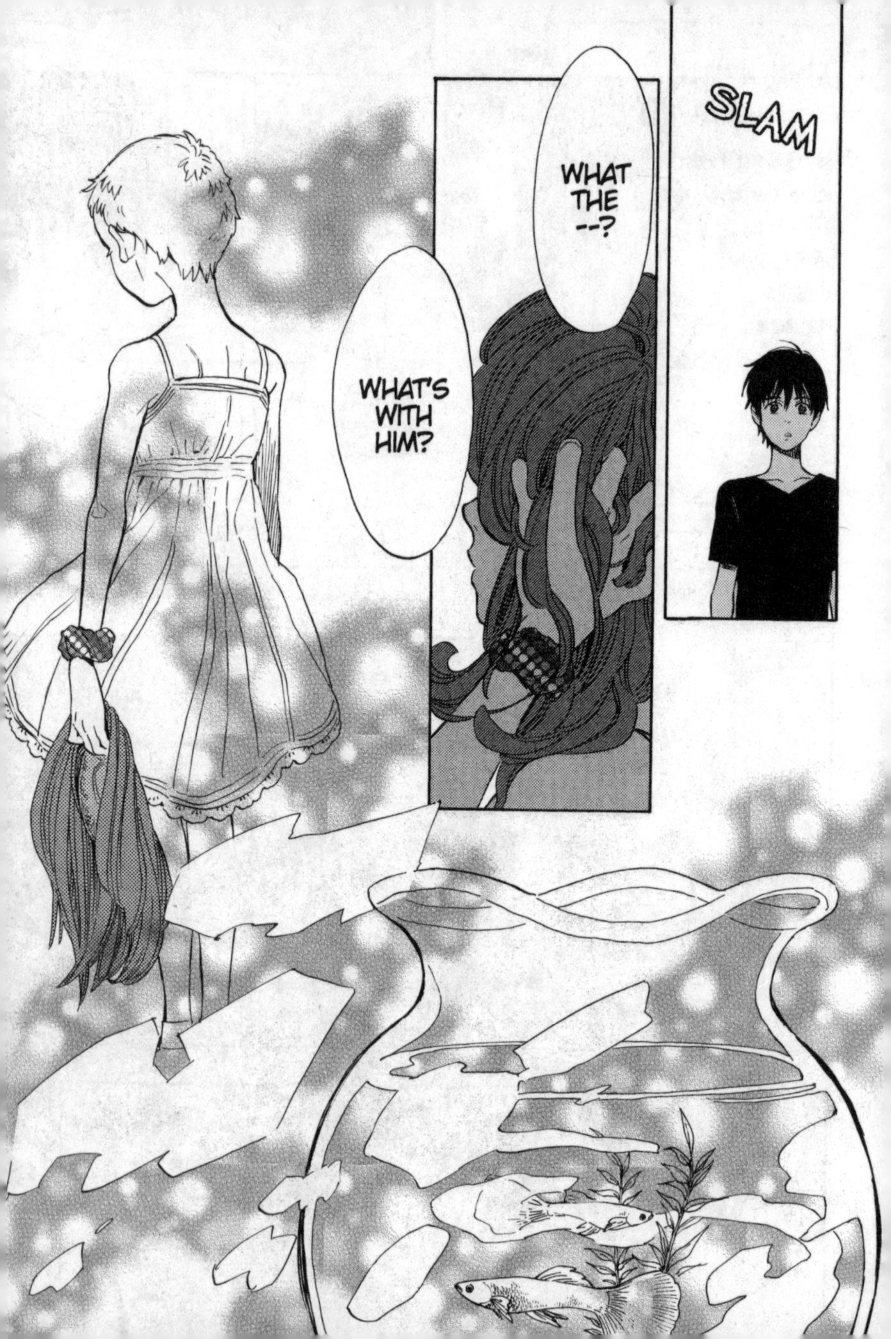
SLAM
WHAT THE --?
WHAT'S WITH HIM?

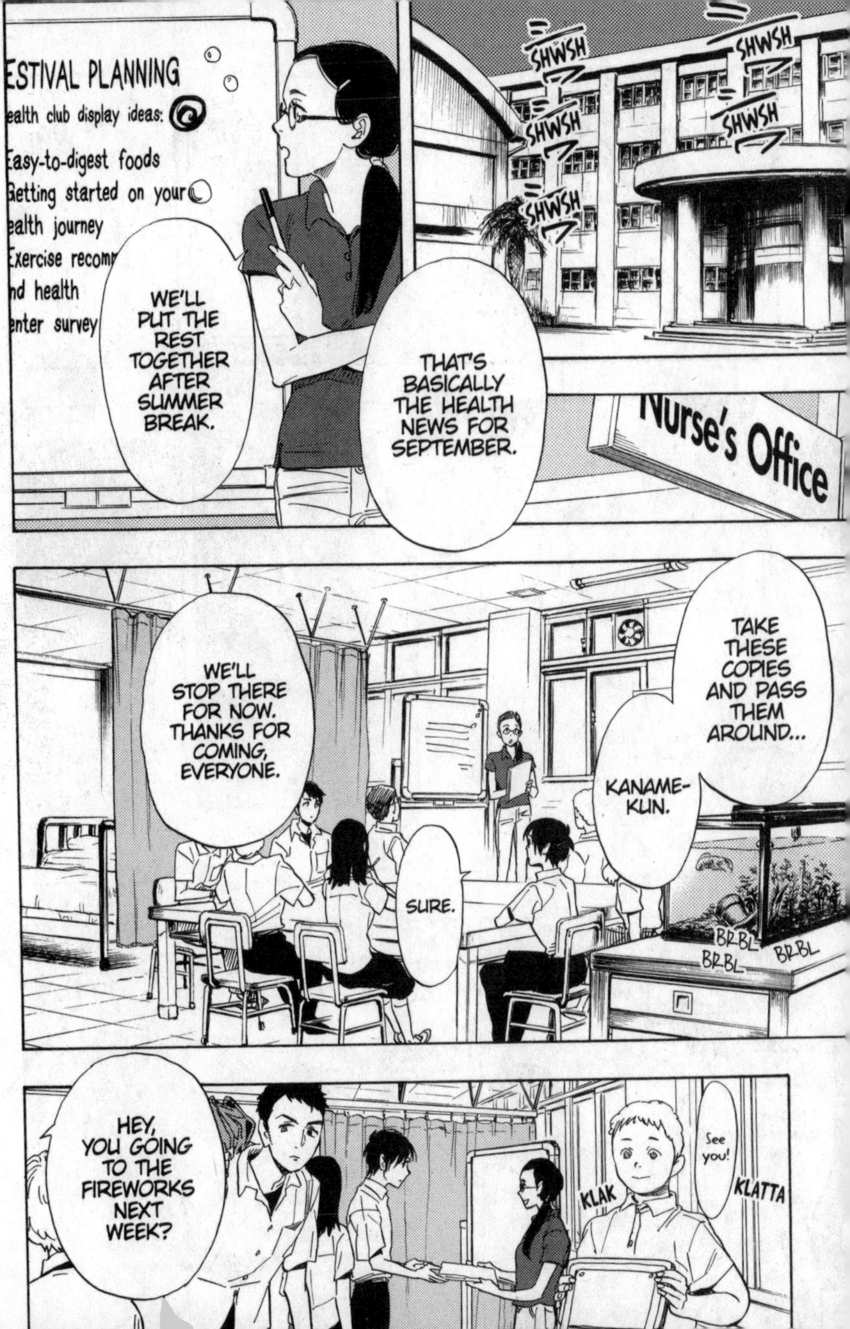

SHWSH
SHWSH
SHWSH
SHWSH
SHWSH
Nurse's Office
THAT'S BASICALLY THE HEALTH NEWS FOR SEPTEMBER.
ESTIVAL PLANNING
ealth club display ideas:
Easy-to-digest foods
Getting started on your ealth journey
Exercise recomm
nd health
enter survey
WE'LL PUT THE REST TOGETHER AFTER SUMMER BREAK.
WE'LL STOP THERE FOR NOW. THANKS FOR COMING, EVERYONE.
TAKE THESE COPIES AND PASS THEM AROUND...
KANAME-KUN.
SURE.
BRBL
BRBL
BRBL
See you!
KLATTA
KLAK
HEY, YOU GOING TO THE FIREWORKS NEXT WEEK?

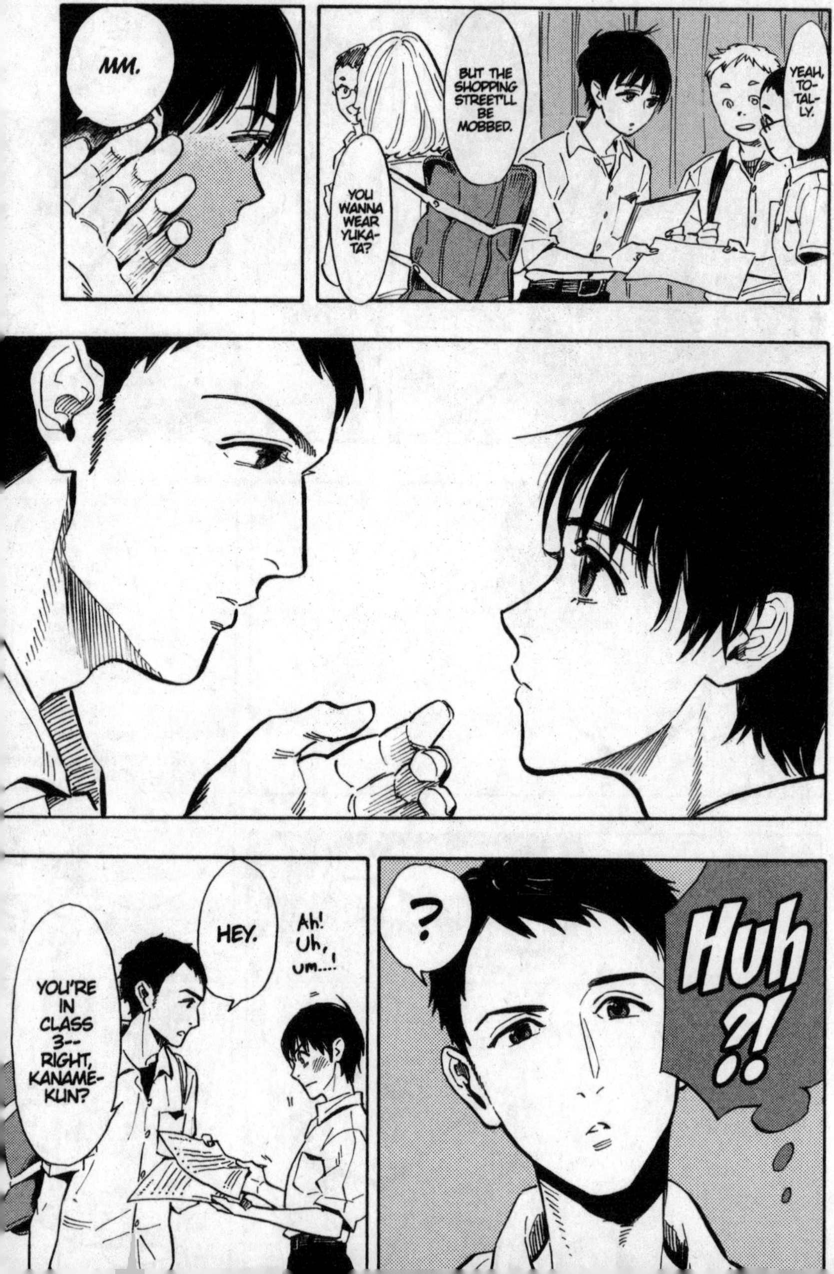
YOU WANNA WEAR YUKATA?
BUT THE SHOPPING STREET'LL BE MOBBED.
YEAH, TO-TAL-LY.
MM.
?
Huh?!
HEY.
YOU'RE IN CLASS 3-- RIGHT, KANAME-KUN?
Ah! Uh, um...!

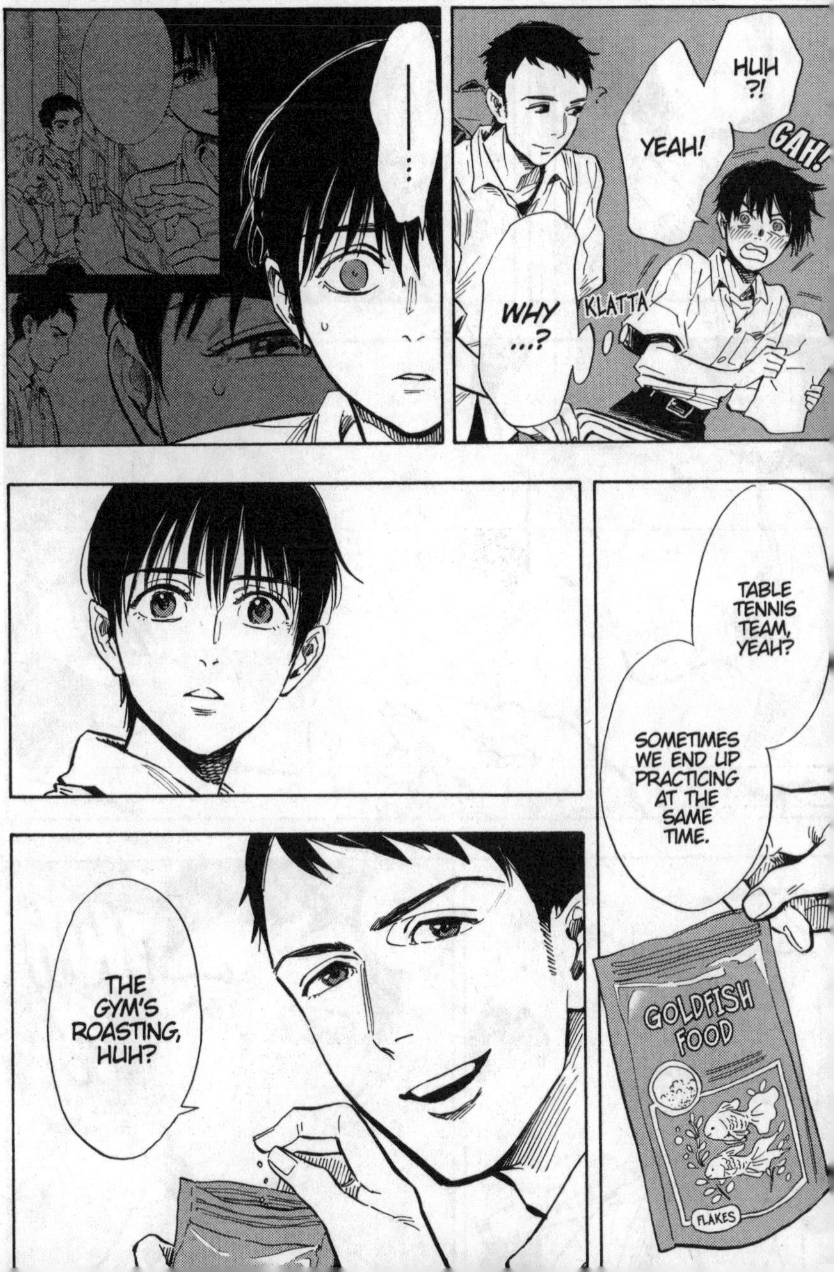

HUH ?!
YEAH!
GAH!
KLATTA
WHY ...?
......
TABLE TENNIS TEAM, YEAH?
SOMETIMES WE END UP PRACTICING AT THE SAME TIME.
GOLDFISH FOOD
FLAKES
THE GYM'S ROASTING, HUH?

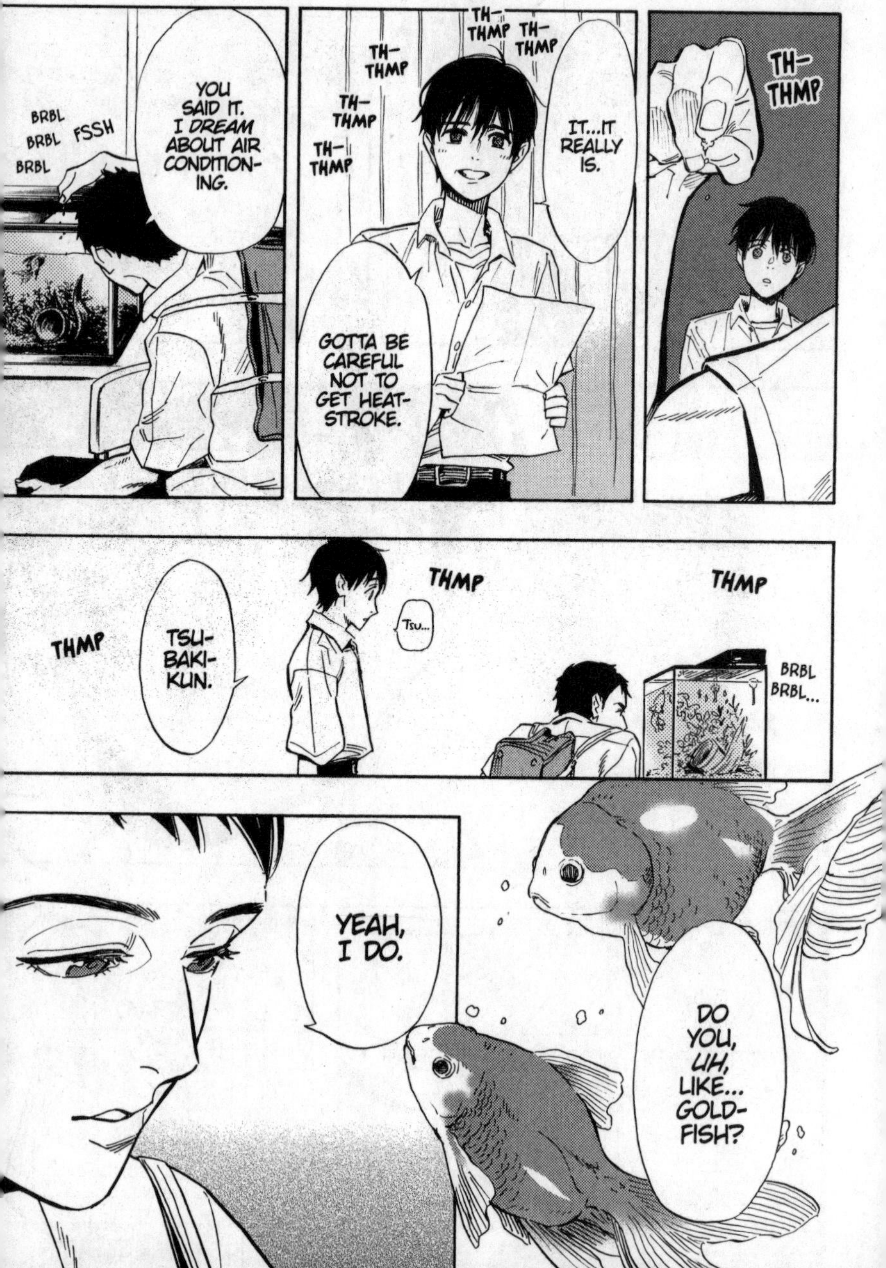
TH-THMP
TH-THMP TH-THMP
IT...IT REALLY IS.
TH-THMP
TH-THMP
TH-THMP
GOTTA BE CAREFUL NOT TO GET HEAT-STROKE.
YOU SAID IT. I DREAM ABOUT AIR CONDITIONING.
BRBL BRBL FSSH BRBL
BRBL BRBL...
THMP
THMP
Tsu...
TSU-BAKI-KUN.
THMP
DO YOU, UH, LIKE... GOLD-FISH?
YEAH, I DO.

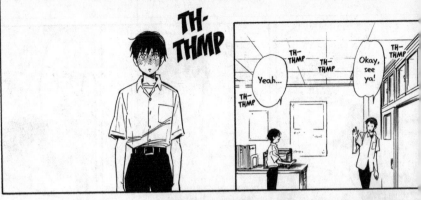

TH-THMP

TH-THMP

TH-THMP

TH-THMP

Yeah...

Okay, see ya!

TH-THMP

TH-THMP

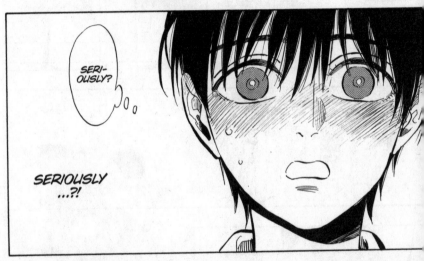

SERI-OUSLY?

SERIOUSLY...?!

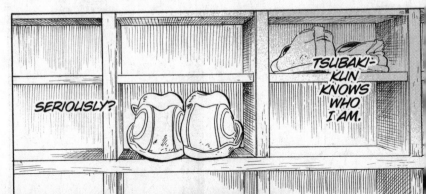

SERIOUSLY?

TSUBAKI-KUN KNOWS WHO I AM.

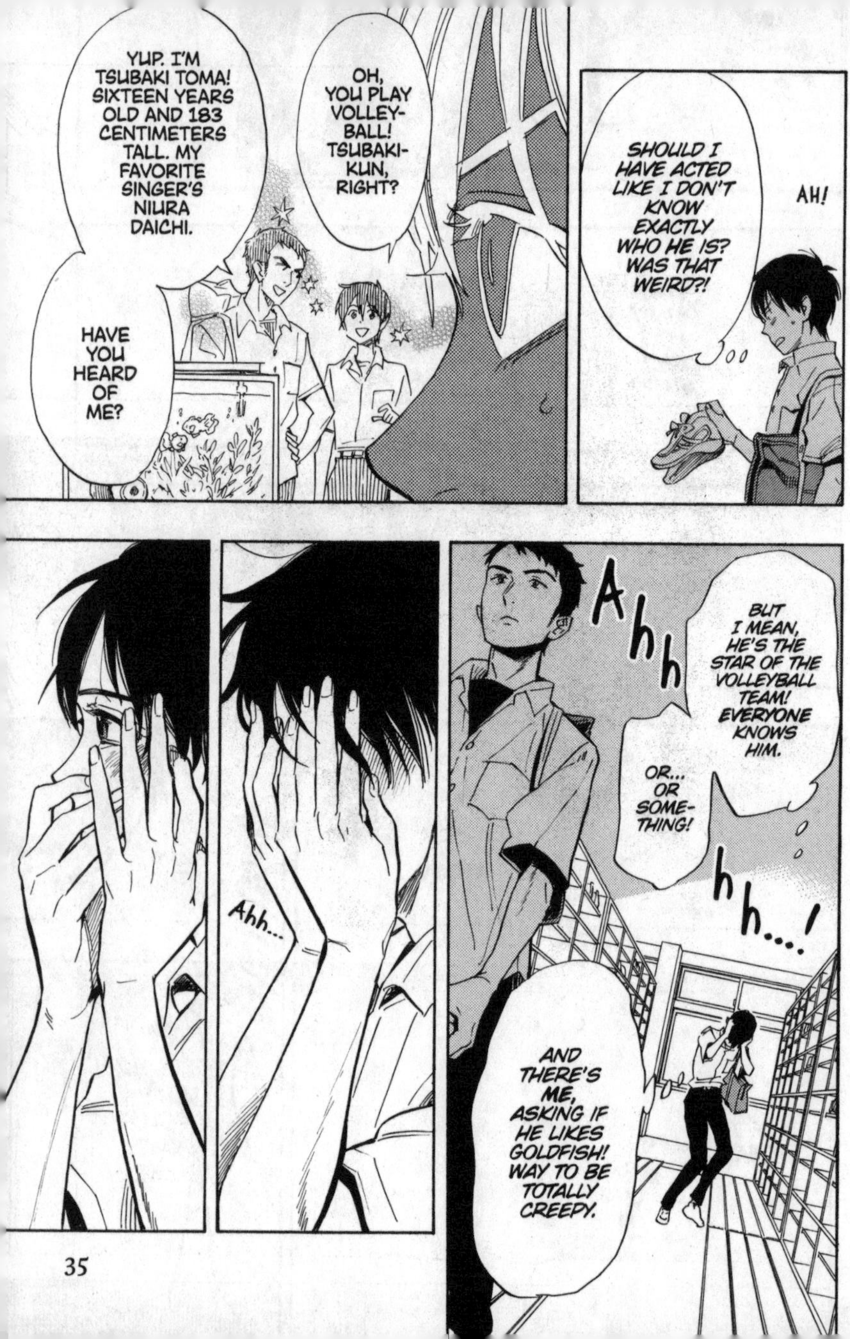
AH!
SHOULD I HAVE ACTED LIKE I DON'T KNOW EXACTLY WHO HE IS? WAS THAT WEIRD?!
OH, YOU PLAY VOLLEY-BALL! TSUBAKI-KUN, RIGHT?
YUP. I'M TSUBAKI TOMA! SIXTEEN YEARS OLD AND 183 CENTIMETERS TALL. MY FAVORITE SINGER'S NIURA DAICHI.
HAVE YOU HEARD OF ME?
Ahh
BUT I MEAN, HE'S THE STAR OF THE VOLLEYBALL TEAM! EVERYONE KNOWS HIM.
OR... OR SOME-THING!
hh...!
AND THERE'S ME, ASKING IF HE LIKES GOLDFISH! WAY TO BE TOTALLY CREEPY.
Ahh...

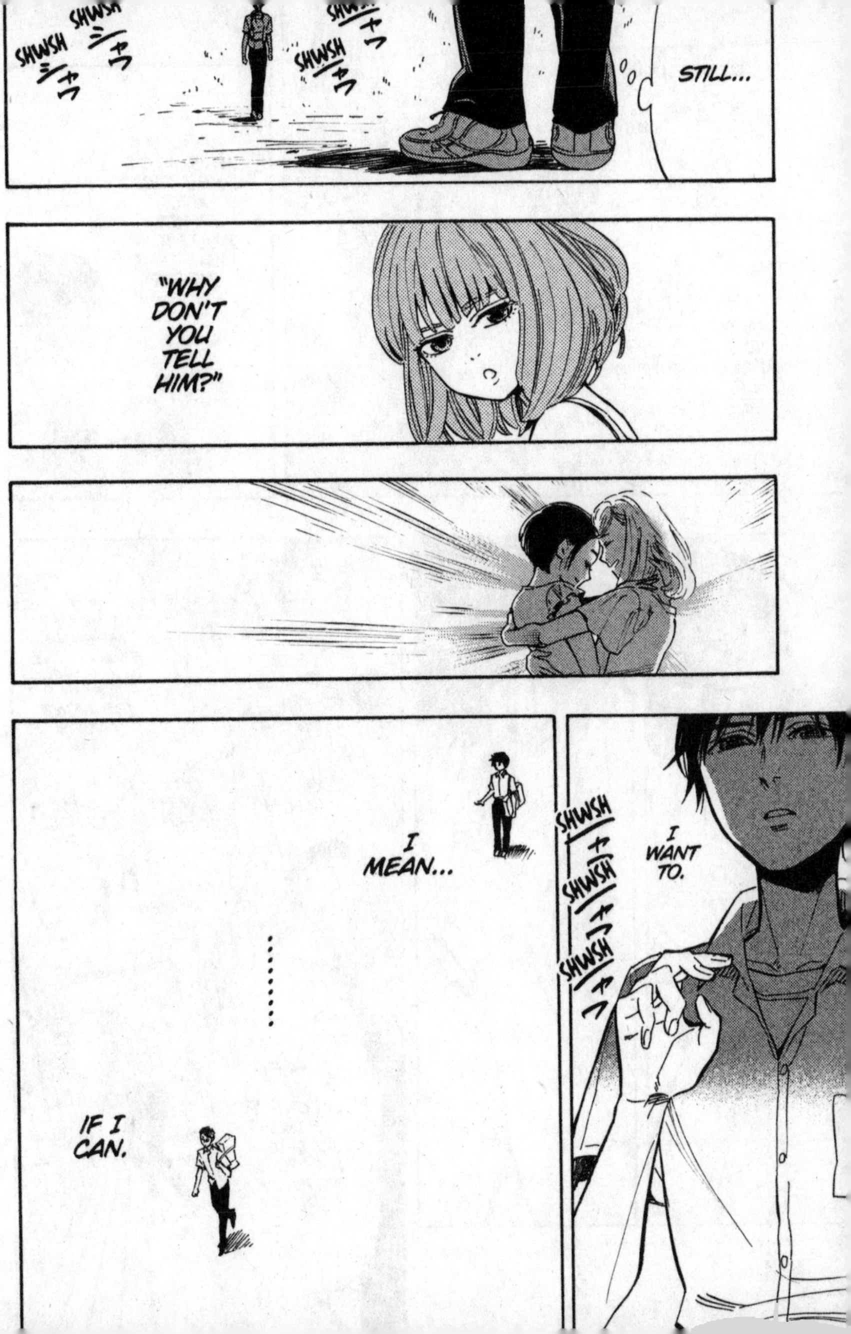
STILL...
SHWSH シャワ
SHWSH シャワ
SHWSH シャワ
SHWSH シャワ
"WHY DON'T YOU TELL HIM?"
I WANT TO.
SHWSH シャワ
SHWSH シャワ
SHWSH シャワ
I MEAN...
......
IF I CAN.

Our Dreams at Dusk

SHIMANAMI TASOGARE

Onomichi is also a town of shrines and temples. It's been an important trading post on the Inland Sea since the Middle Ages, and a huge number of temples were built at the behest of the wealthy merchants.

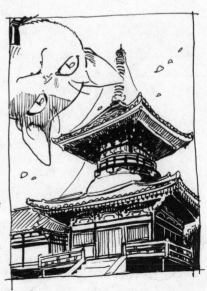

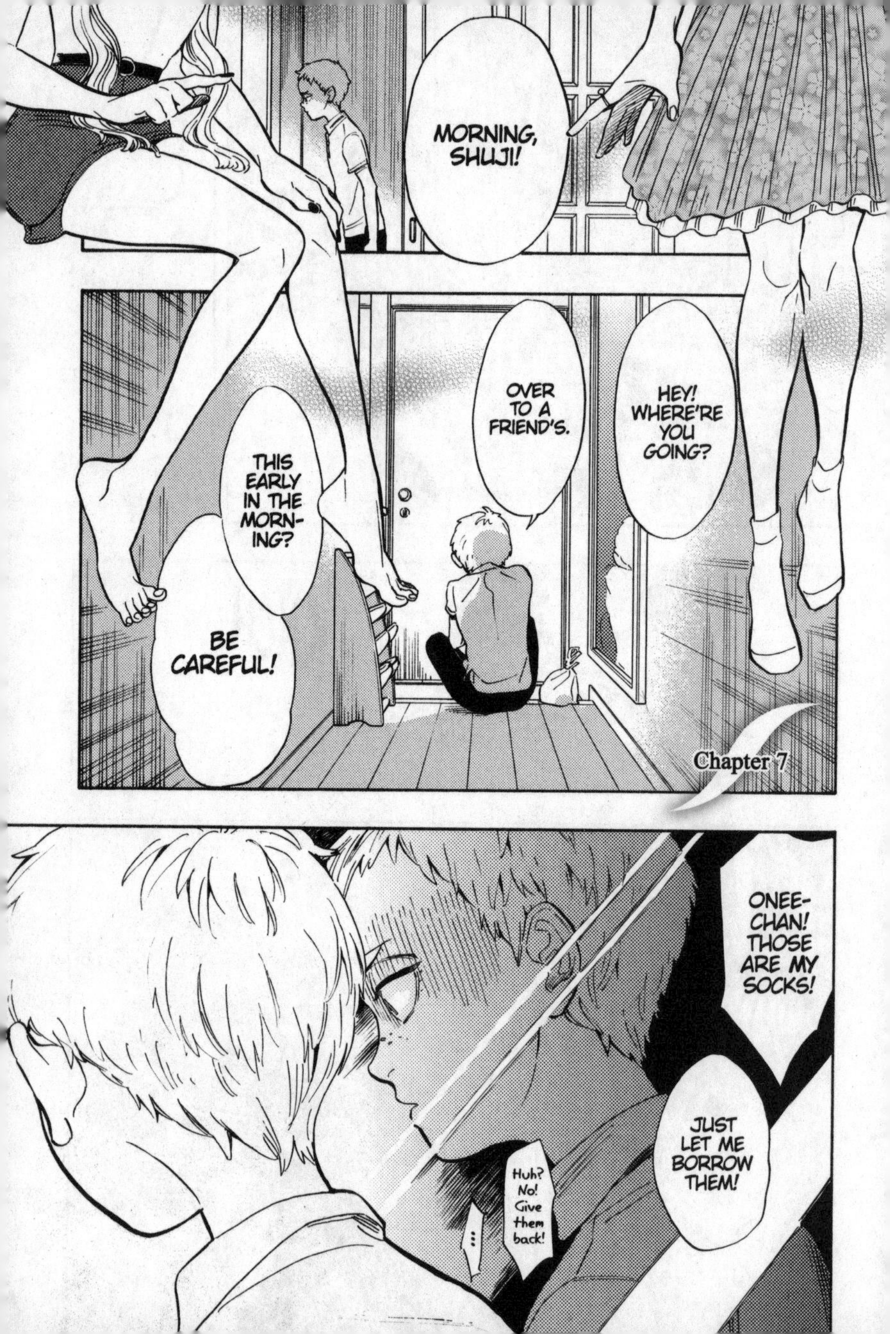
MORNING, SHUJI!
HEY! WHERE'RE YOU GOING?
OVER TO A FRIEND'S.
THIS EARLY IN THE MORN-ING?
BE CAREFUL!
Chapter 7
ONEE-CHAN! THOSE ARE MY SOCKS!
JUST LET ME BORROW THEM!
Huh? No! Give them back!
...

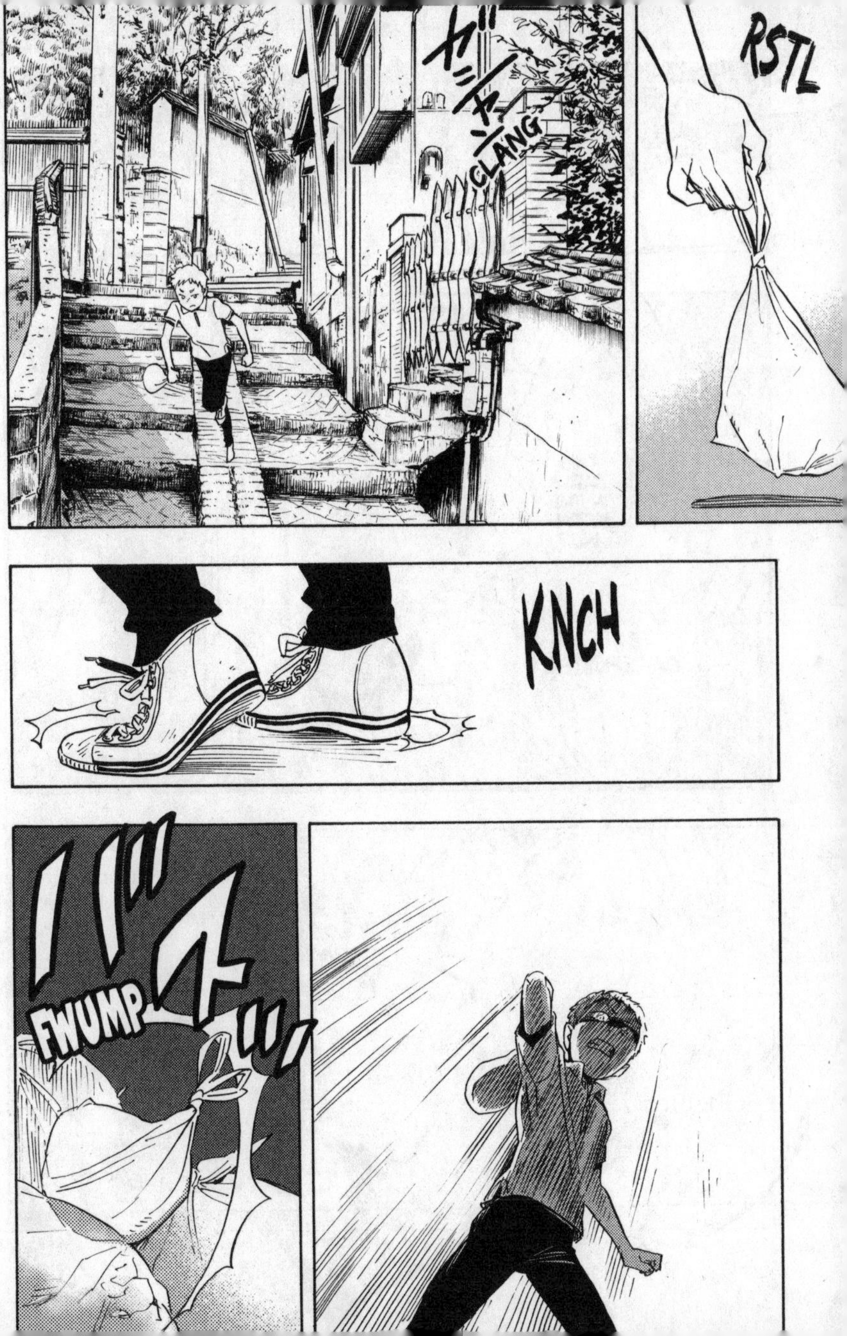
RSTL
CLANG
KNCH
FWUMP

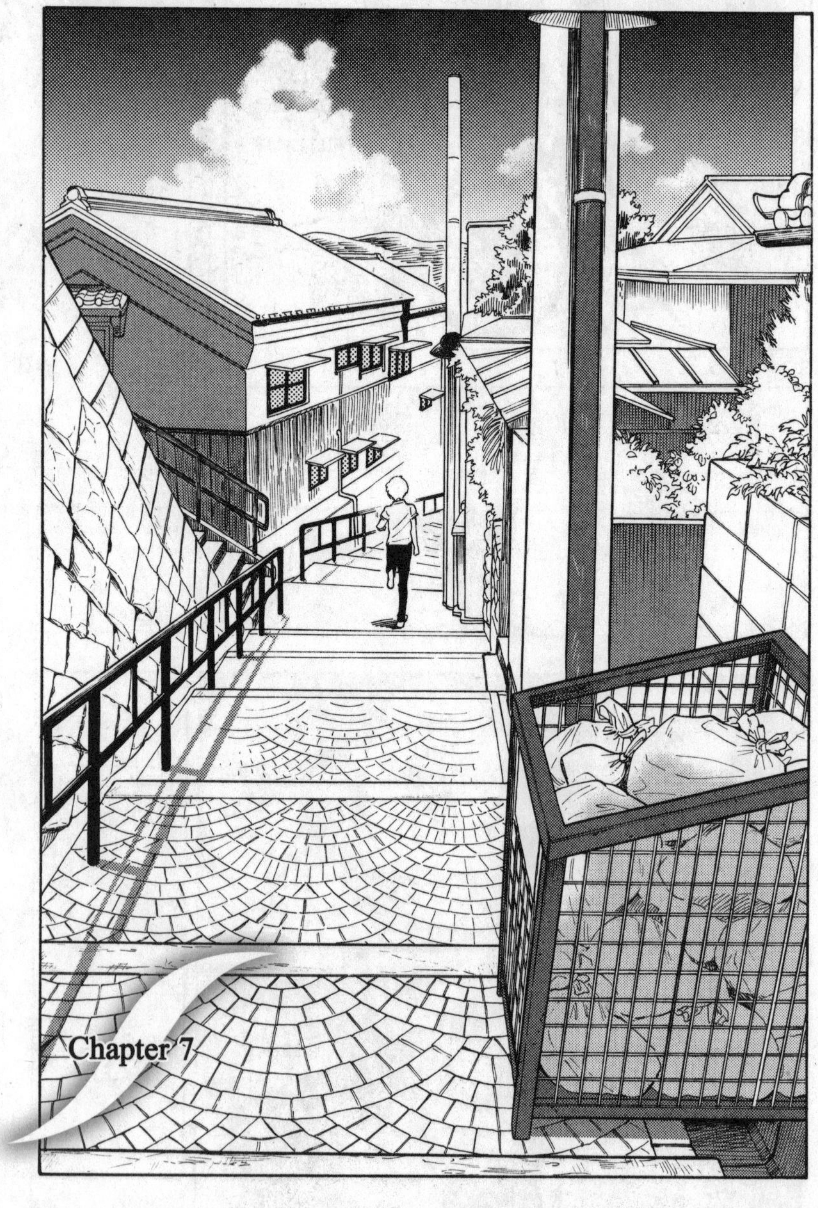
Chapter 7

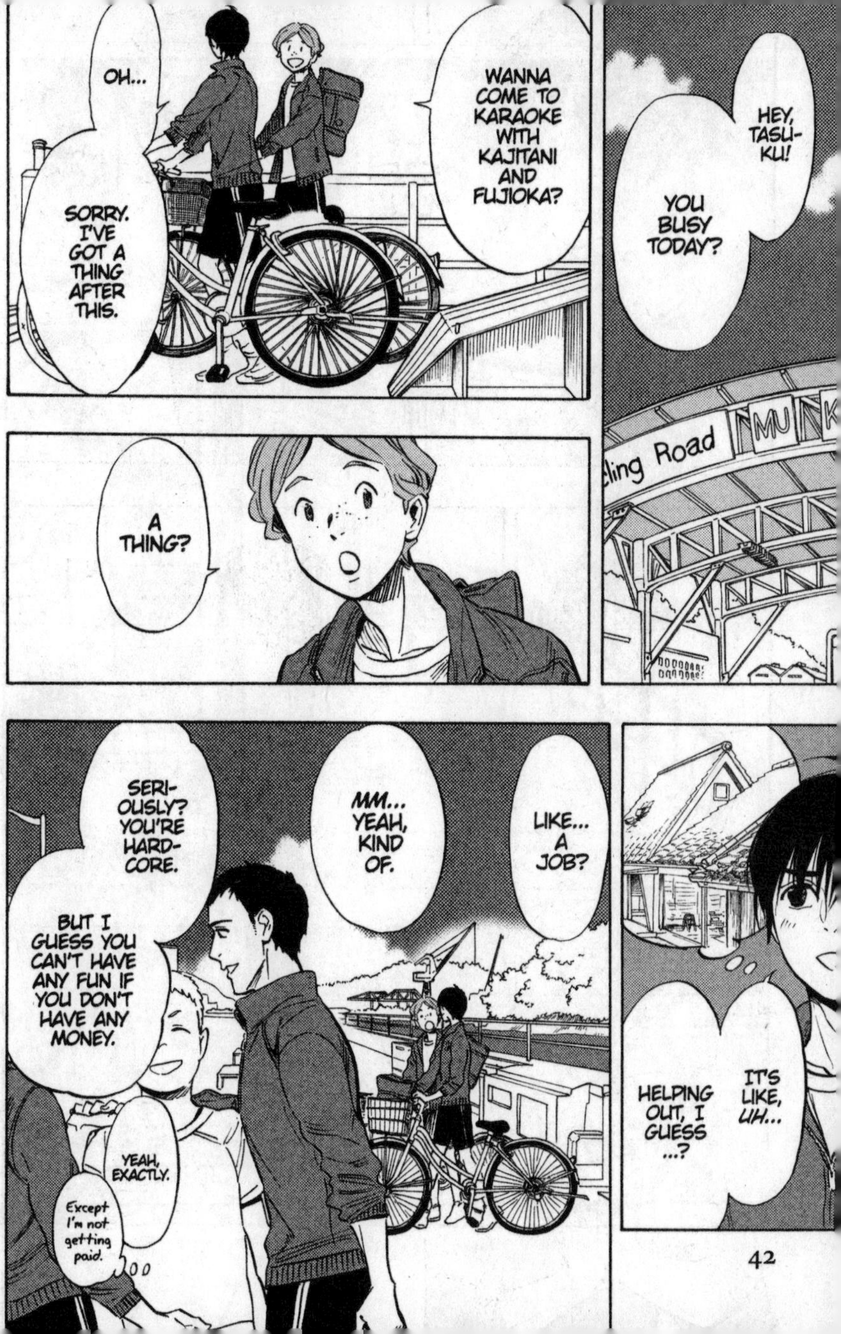
HEY, TASUKU!
YOU BUSY TODAY?
WANNA COME TO KARAOKE WITH KAJITANI AND FUJIOKA?
OH...
SORRY. I'VE GOT A THING AFTER THIS.
A THING?
IT'S LIKE, UH...
HELPING OUT, I GUESS ...?
LIKE... A JOB?
MM... YEAH, KIND OF.
SERIOUSLY? YOU'RE HARDCORE.
BUT I GUESS YOU CAN'T HAVE ANY FUN IF YOU DON'T HAVE ANY MONEY.
YEAH, EXACTLY.
Except I'm not getting paid.

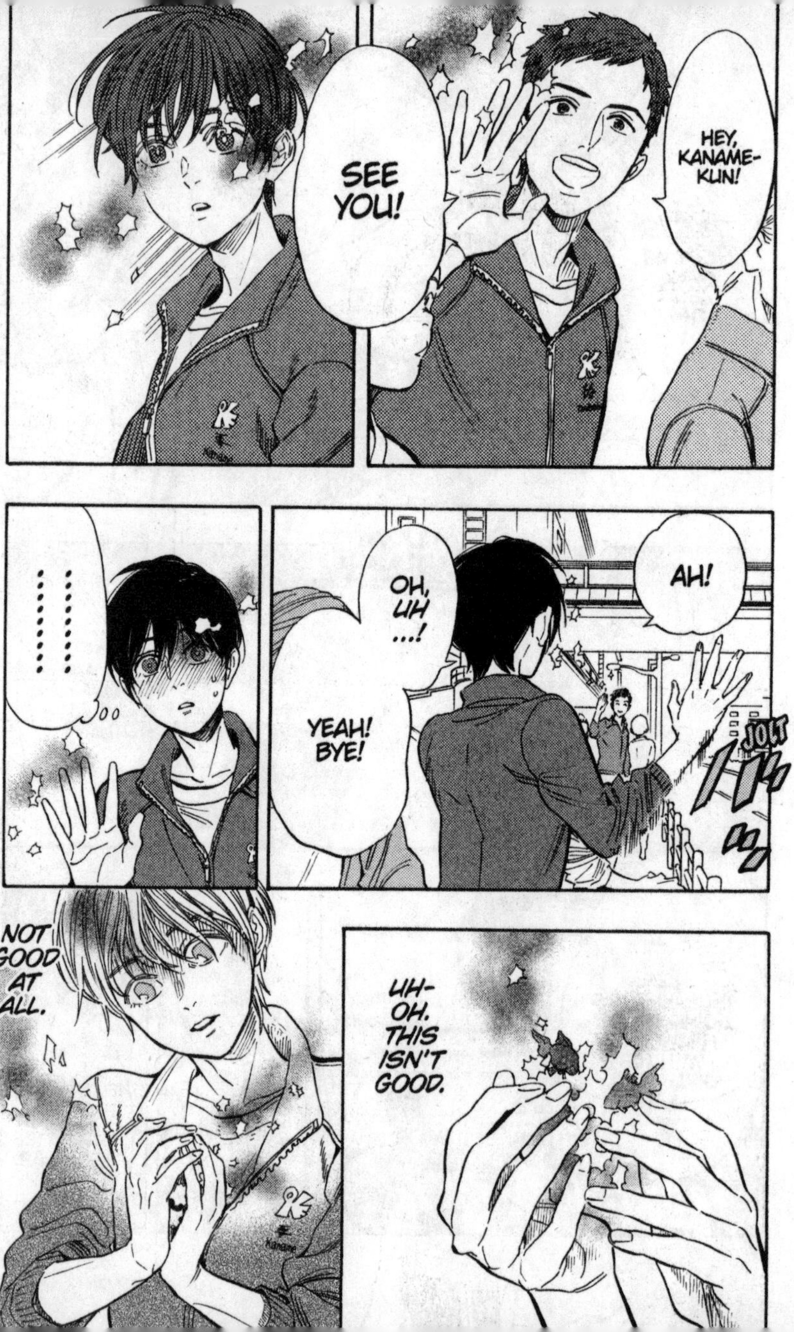
HEY, KANAME-KUN!
SEE YOU!
AH!
OH, UH ...!
YEAH! BYE!
JOLT
......
......
UH-OH. THIS ISN'T GOOD.
NOT GOOD AT ALL.

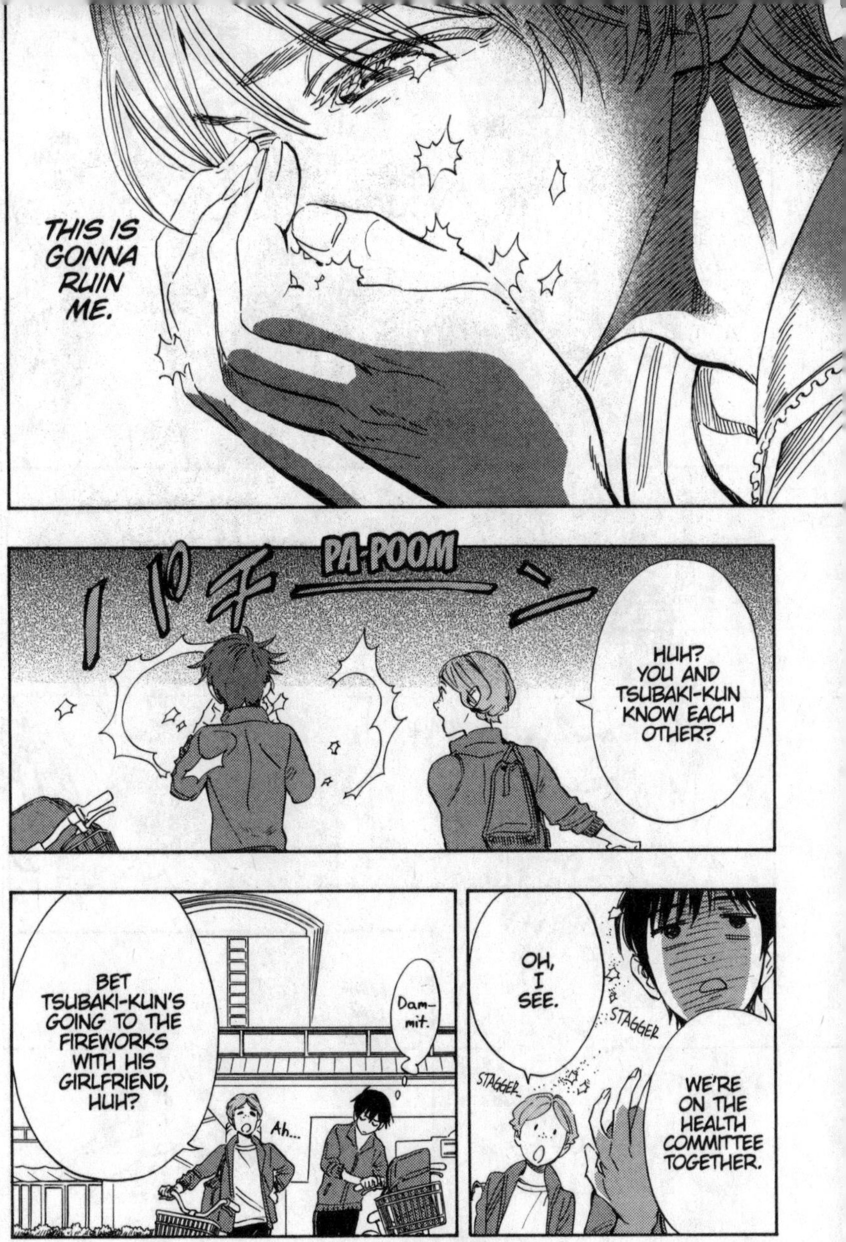
THIS IS GONNA RUIN ME.
PA-POOM
HUH? YOU AND TSUBAKI-KUN KNOW EACH OTHER?
STAGGER
WE'RE ON THE HEALTH COMMITTEE TOGETHER.
OH, I SEE.
STAGGER
BET TSUBAKI-KUN'S GOING TO THE FIREWORKS WITH HIS GIRLFRIEND, HUH?
Dam-mit.
Ah...

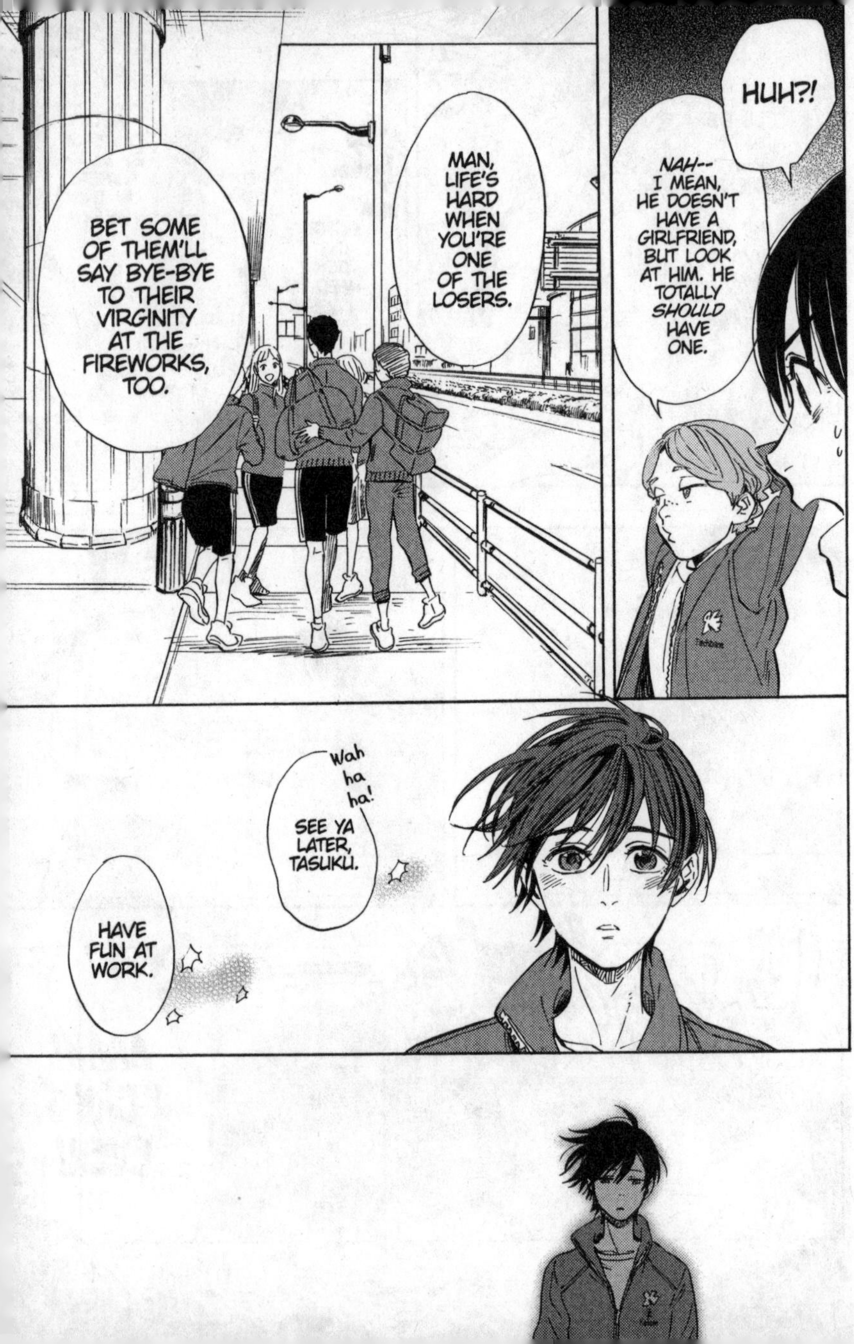
HUH?!
NAH-- I MEAN, HE DOESN'T HAVE A GIRLFRIEND, BUT LOOK AT HIM. HE TOTALLY *SHOULD* HAVE ONE.
MAN, LIFE'S HARD WHEN YOU'RE ONE OF THE LOSERS.
BET SOME OF THEM'LL SAY BYE-BYE TO THEIR VIRGINITY AT THE FIREWORKS, TOO.
Wah ha ha!
SEE YA LATER, TASUKU.
HAVE FUN AT WORK.

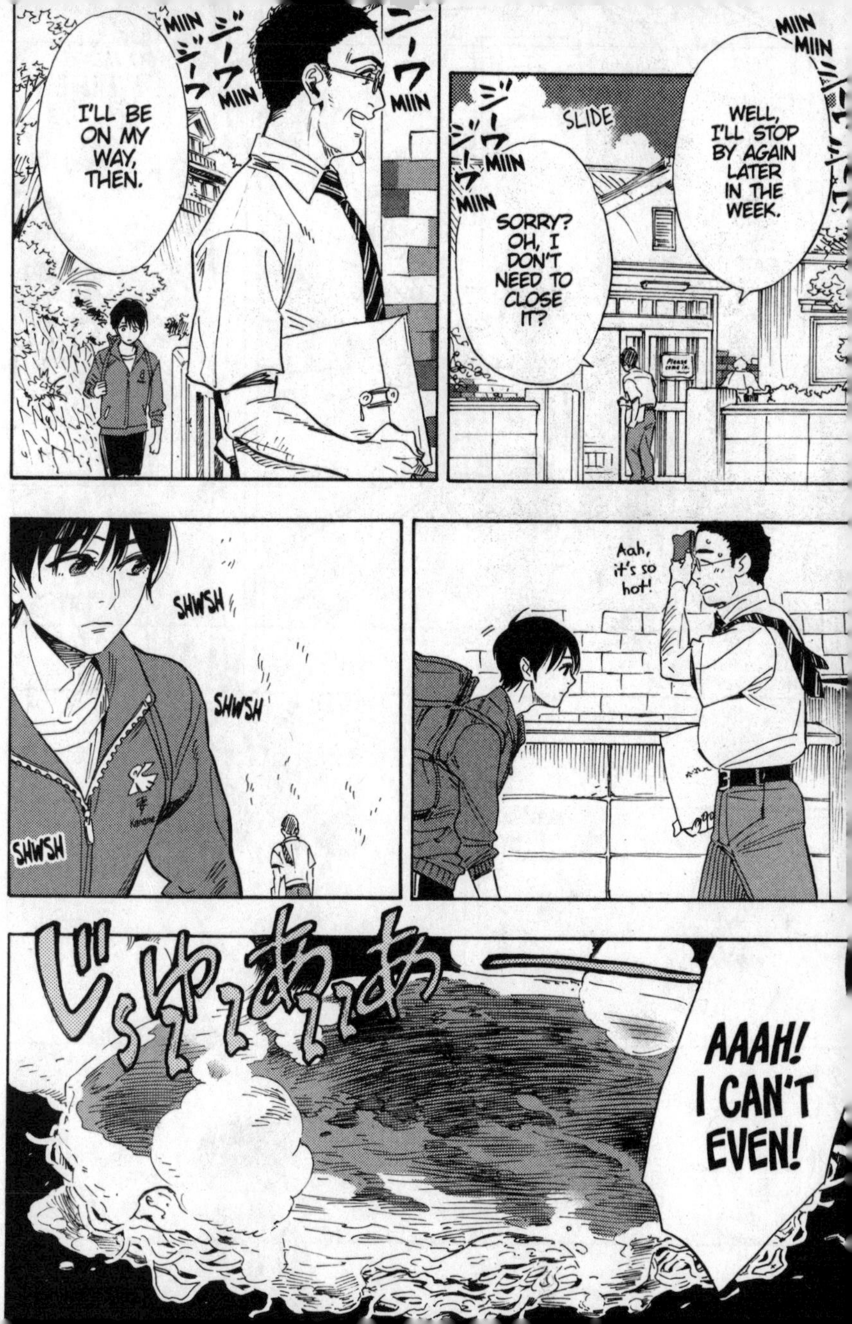
MIIN MIIN
WELL, I'LL STOP BY AGAIN LATER IN THE WEEK.
SLIDE
MIIN MIIN
SORRY? OH, I DON'T NEED TO CLOSE IT?
MIIN MIIN MIIN MIIN
I'LL BE ON MY WAY, THEN.
Aah, it's so hot!
SHWSH
SHWSH
SHWSH
じゅあああ
AAAH! I CAN'T EVEN!

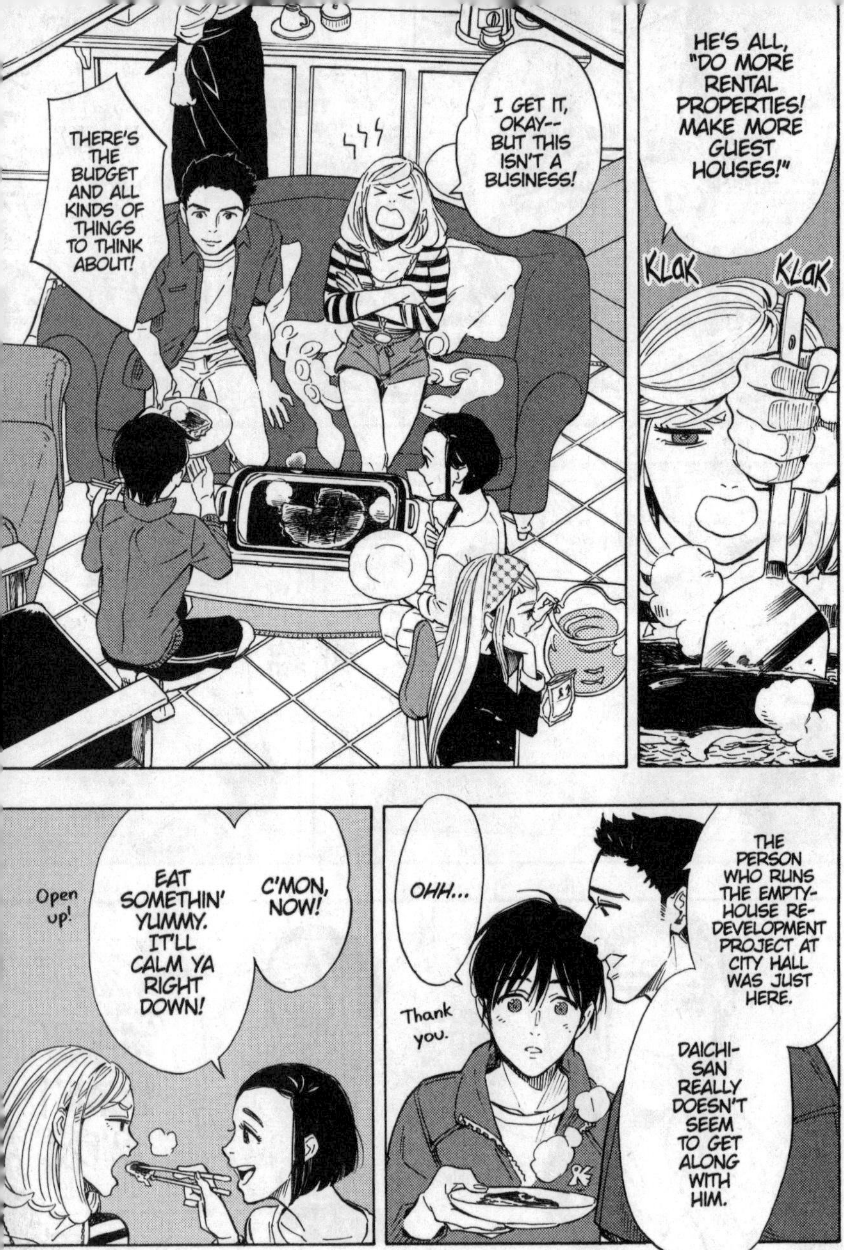
HE'S ALL, "DO MORE RENTAL PROPERTIES! MAKE MORE GUEST HOUSES!"
KLAK KLAK
THERE'S THE BUDGET AND ALL KINDS OF THINGS TO THINK ABOUT!
I GET IT, OKAY-- BUT THIS ISN'T A BUSINESS!
THE PERSON WHO RUNS THE EMPTY-HOUSE RE-DEVELOPMENT PROJECT AT CITY HALL WAS JUST HERE.
OHH...
Thank you.
DAICHI-SAN REALLY DOESN'T SEEM TO GET ALONG WITH HIM.
C'MON, NOW!
EAT SOMETHIN' YUMMY. IT'LL CALM YA RIGHT DOWN!
Open up!

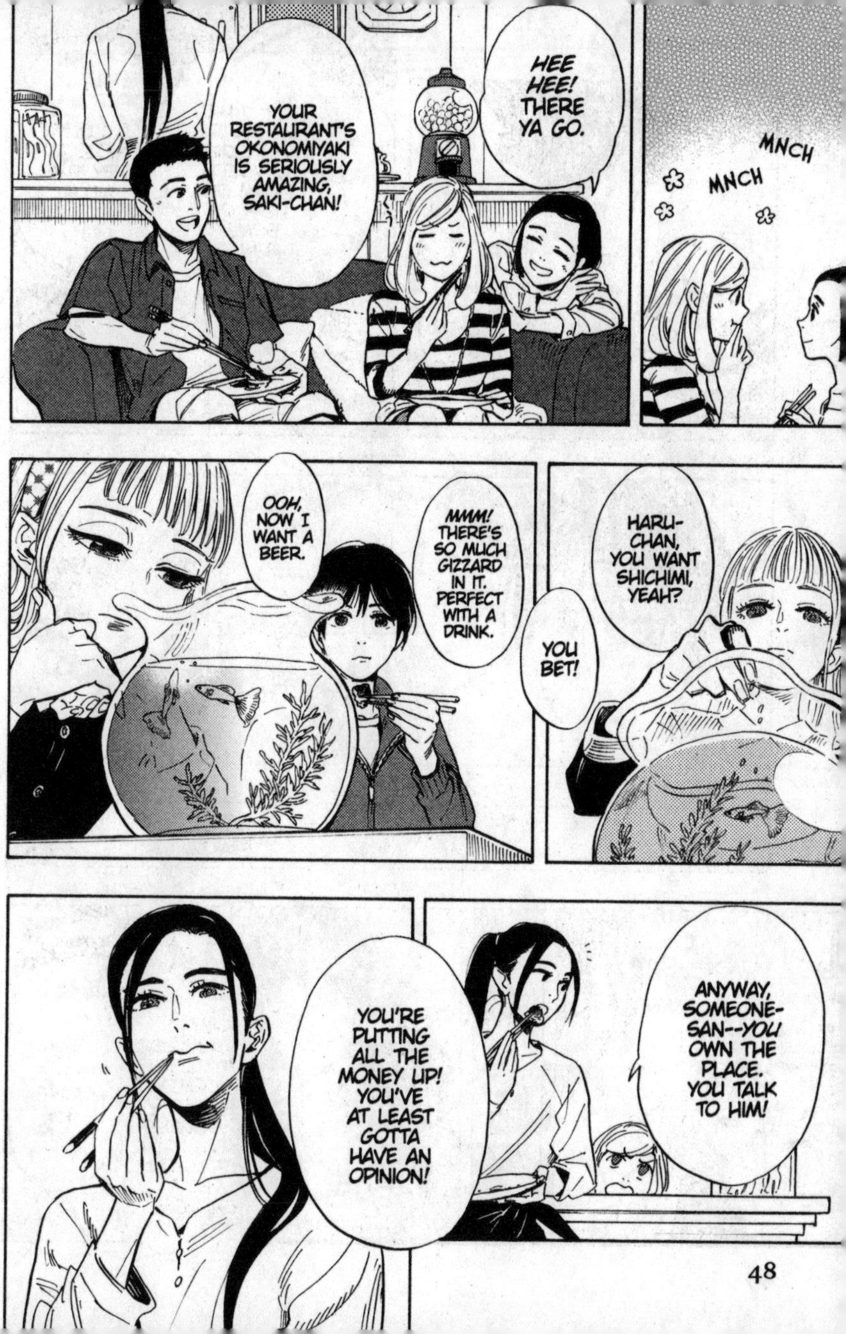
MNCH
MNCH
YOUR RESTAURANT'S OKONOMIYAKI IS SERIOUSLY AMAZING, SAKI-CHAN!
HEE HEE! THERE YA GO.
HARU-CHAN, YOU WANT SHICHIMI, YEAH?
YOU BET!
MMM! THERE'S SO MUCH GIZZARD IN IT. PERFECT WITH A DRINK.
OOH, NOW I WANT A BEER.
ANYWAY, SOMEONE-SAN--YOU OWN THE PLACE. YOU TALK TO HIM!
YOU'RE PUTTING ALL THE MONEY UP! YOU'VE AT LEAST GOTTA HAVE AN OPINION!

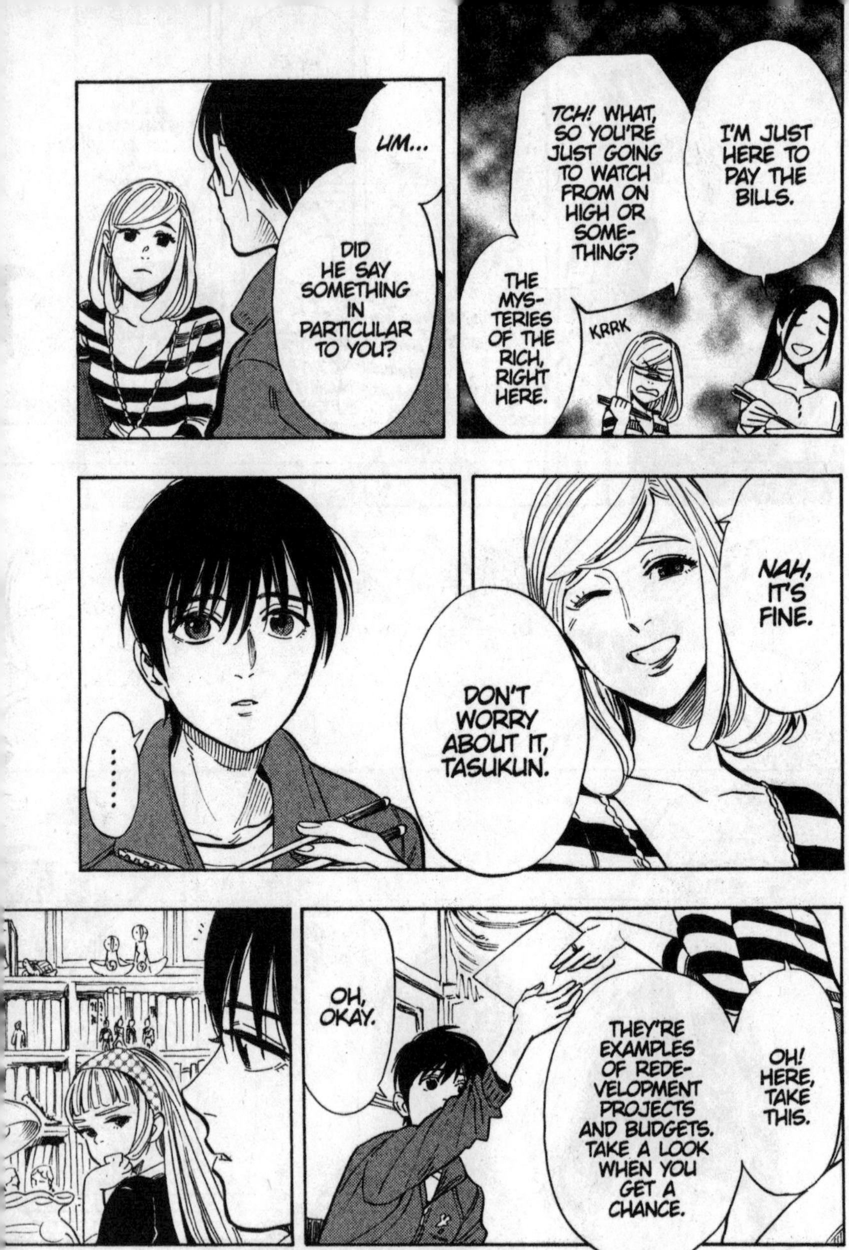
I'M JUST HERE TO PAY THE BILLS.
TCH! WHAT, SO YOU'RE JUST GOING TO WATCH FROM ON HIGH OR SOME-THING?
KRRK
THE MYS-TERIES OF THE RICH, RIGHT HERE.
UM...
DID HE SAY SOMETHING IN PARTICULAR TO YOU?
NAH, IT'S FINE.
DON'T WORRY ABOUT IT, TASUKUN.
......
OH! HERE, TAKE THIS.
THEY'RE EXAMPLES OF REDE-VELOPMENT PROJECTS AND BUDGETS. TAKE A LOOK WHEN YOU GET A CHANCE.
OH, OKAY.

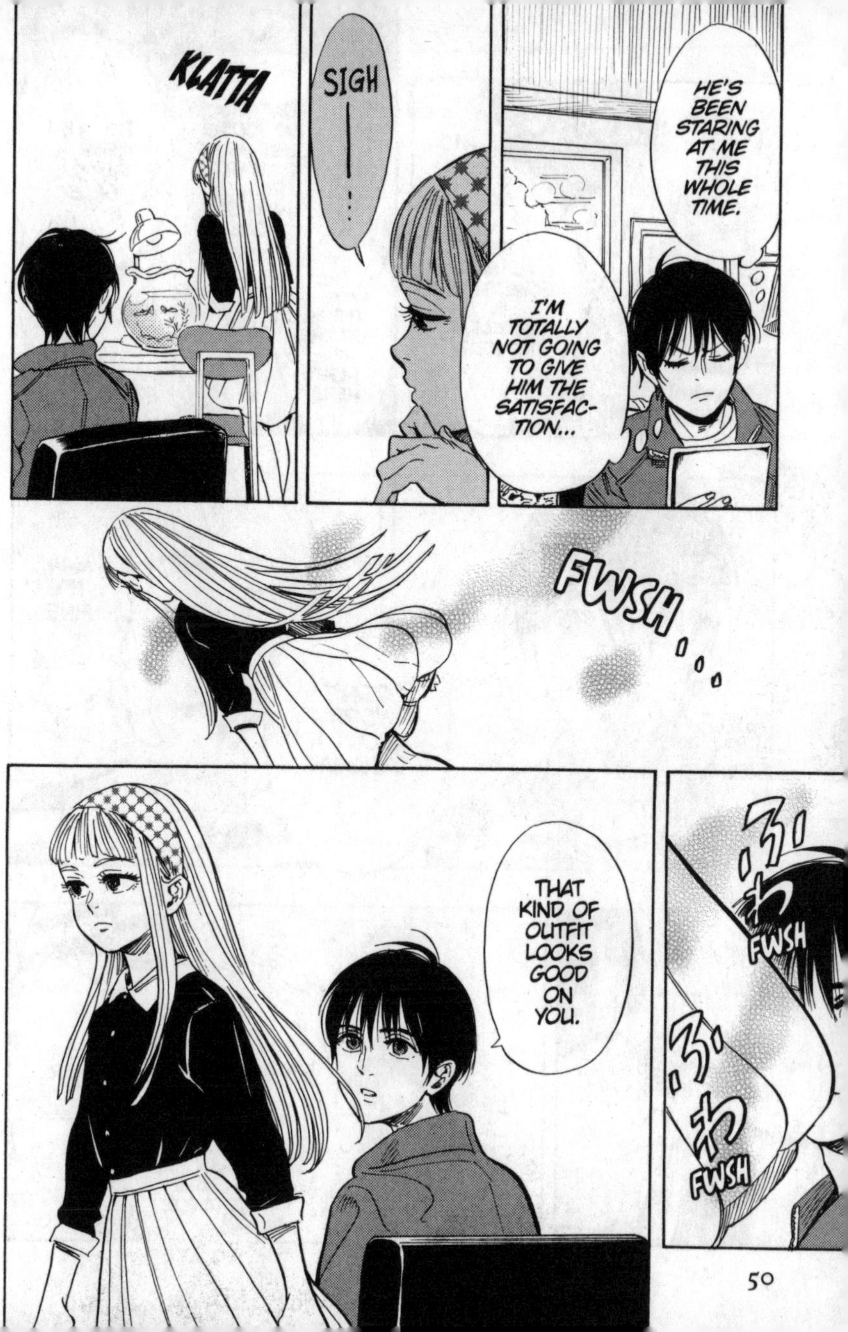
HE'S BEEN STARING AT ME THIS WHOLE TIME.
I'M TOTALLY NOT GOING TO GIVE HIM THE SATISFACTION...
SIGH
KLATTA
FWSH...
ふわ
FWSH
ふわ
FWSH
THAT KIND OF OUTFIT LOOKS GOOD ON YOU.

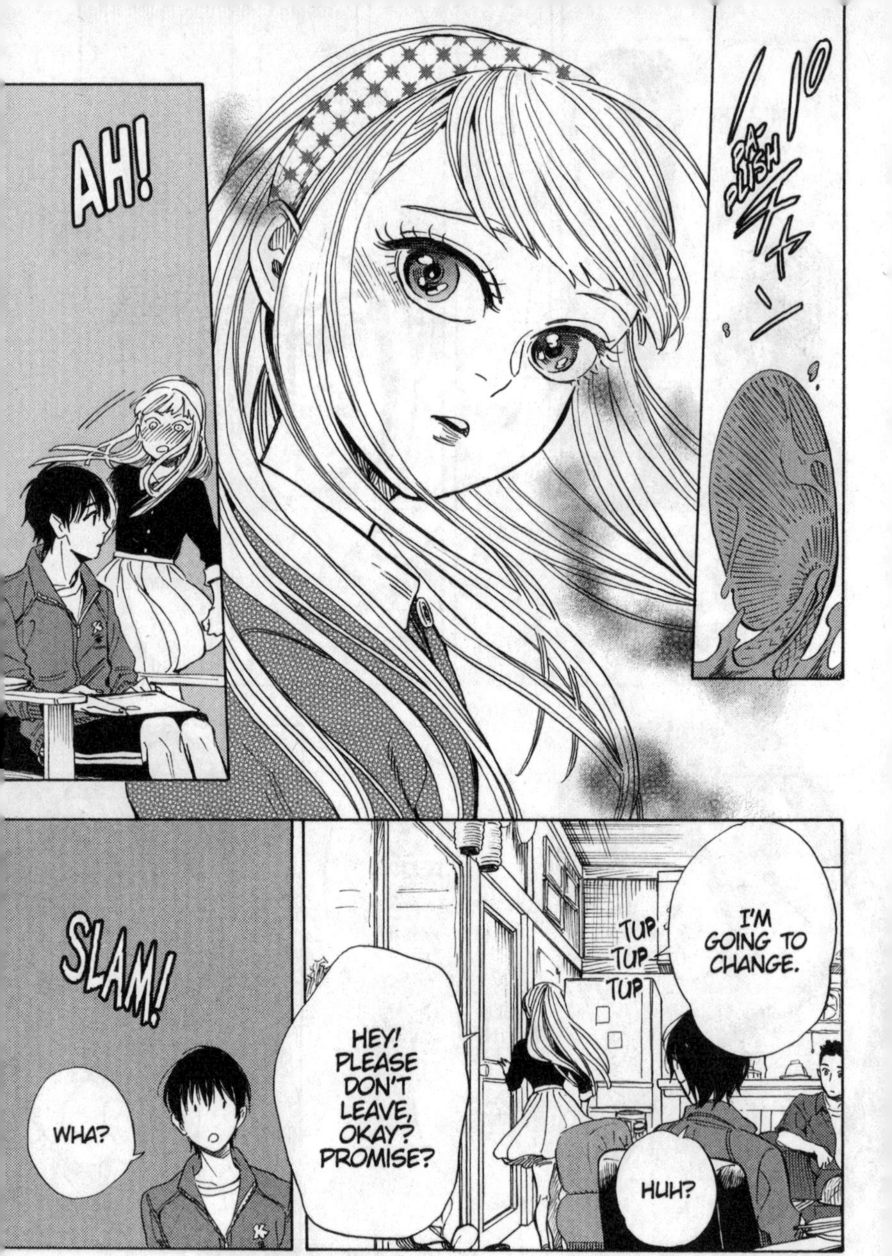
PA-PLISH
AH!
I'M GOING TO CHANGE.
TUP TUP TUP
HEY! PLEASE DON'T LEAVE, OKAY? PROMISE?
HUH?
SLAM!
WHA?

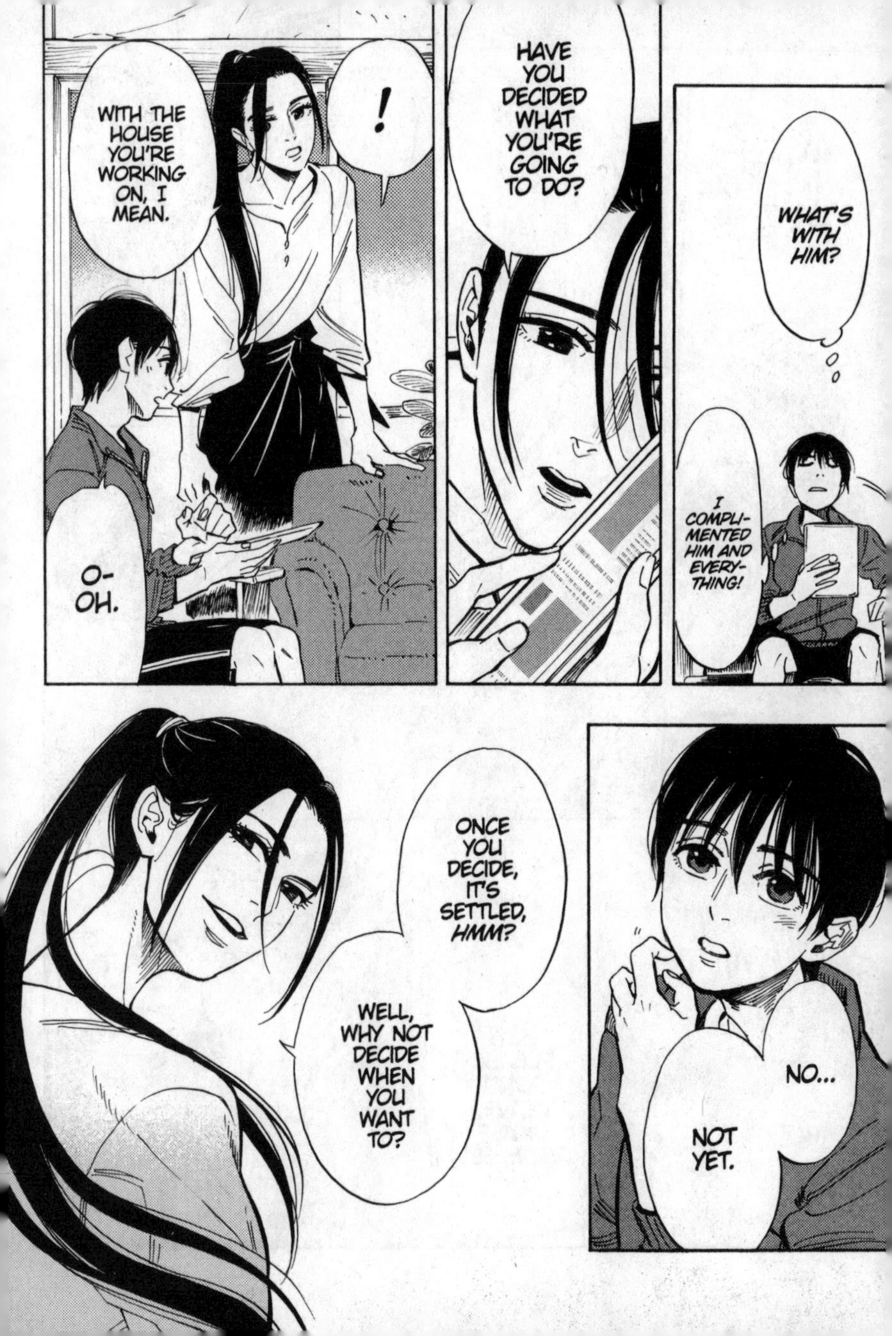
WHAT'S WITH HIM?
I COMPLIMENTED HIM AND EVERYTHING!
HAVE YOU DECIDED WHAT YOU'RE GOING TO DO?
!
WITH THE HOUSE YOU'RE WORKING ON, I MEAN.
O-OH.
NO... NOT YET.
ONCE YOU DECIDE, IT'S SETTLED, *HMM?*
WELL, WHY NOT DECIDE WHEN YOU WANT TO?

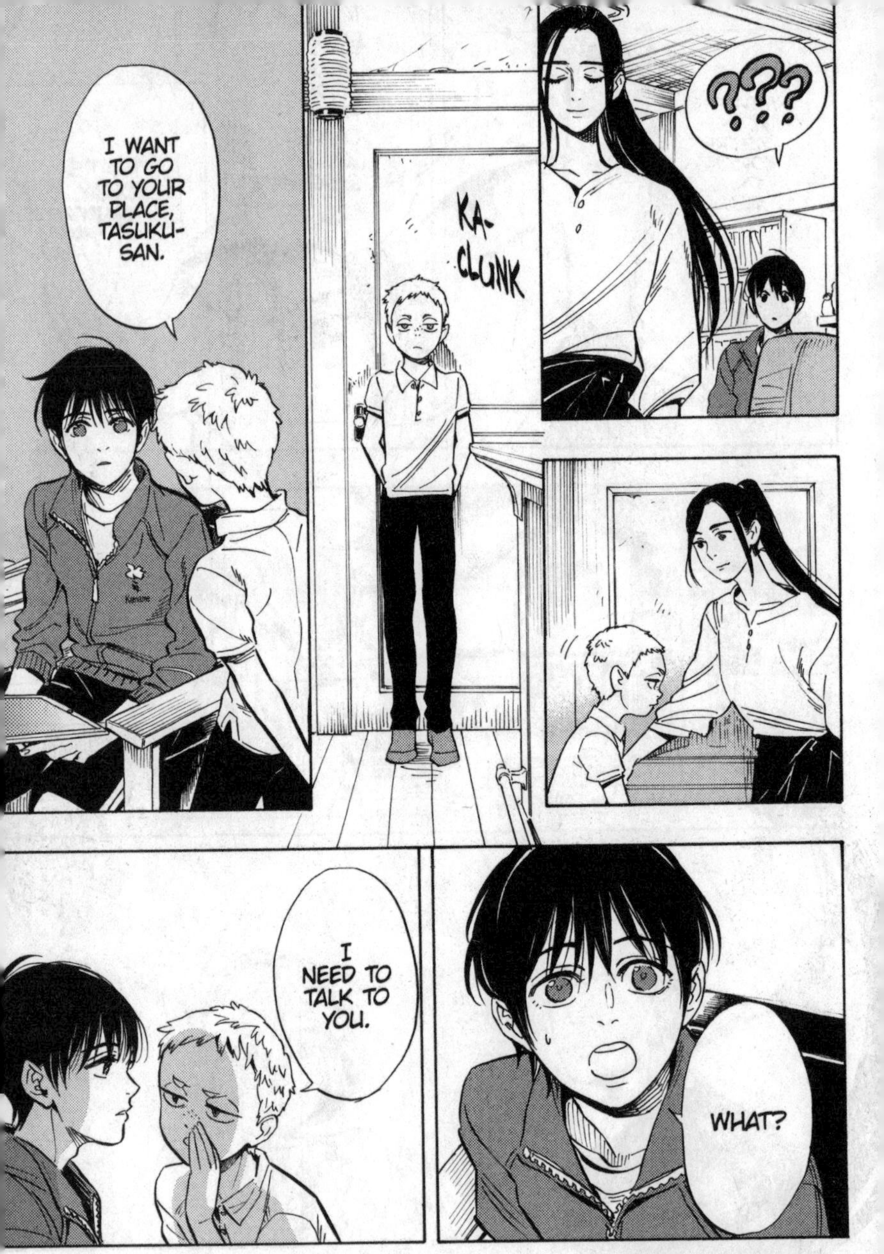
???
KA-CLUNK
I WANT TO GO TO YOUR PLACE, TASUKU-SAN.
WHAT?
I NEED TO TALK TO YOU.

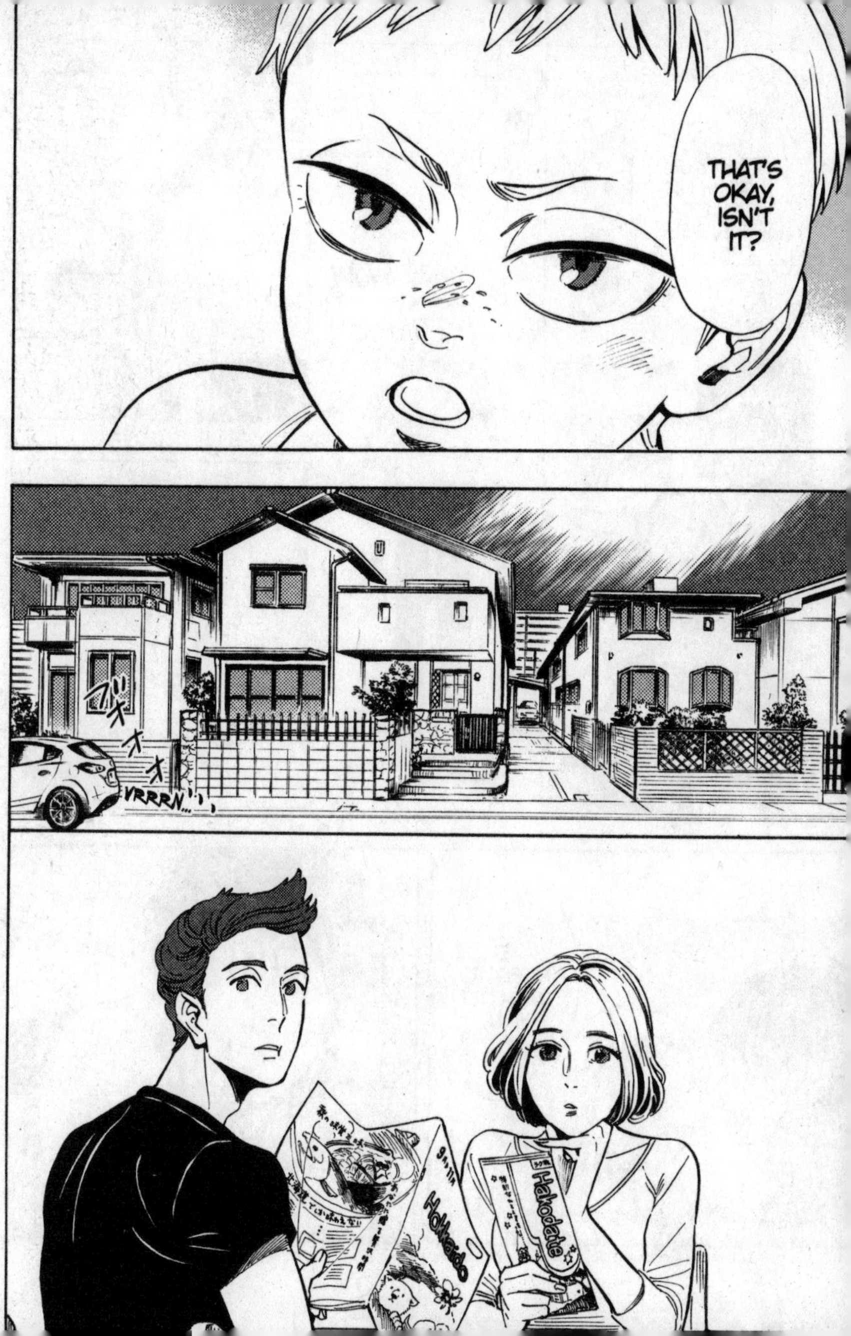
THAT'S OKAY, ISN'T IT?
VRRRN...
Hokkaido
Hakodate

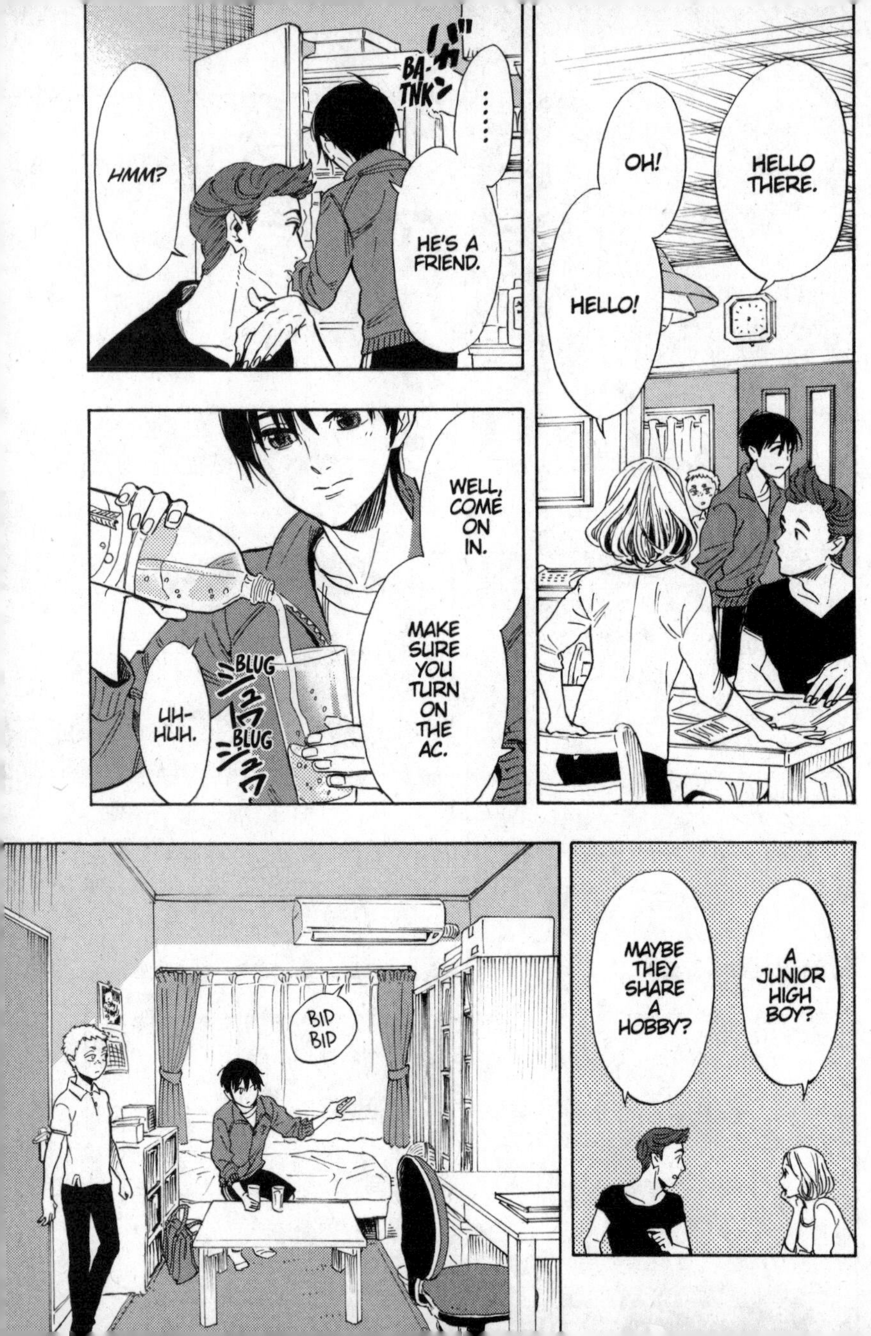
HELLO THERE.
OH!
HELLO!
BA-TNK
......
HE'S A FRIEND.
HMM?
WELL, COME ON IN.
MAKE SURE YOU TURN ON THE AC.
BLUG
BLUG
UH-HUH.
A JUNIOR HIGH BOY?
MAYBE THEY SHARE A HOBBY?
BIP BIP

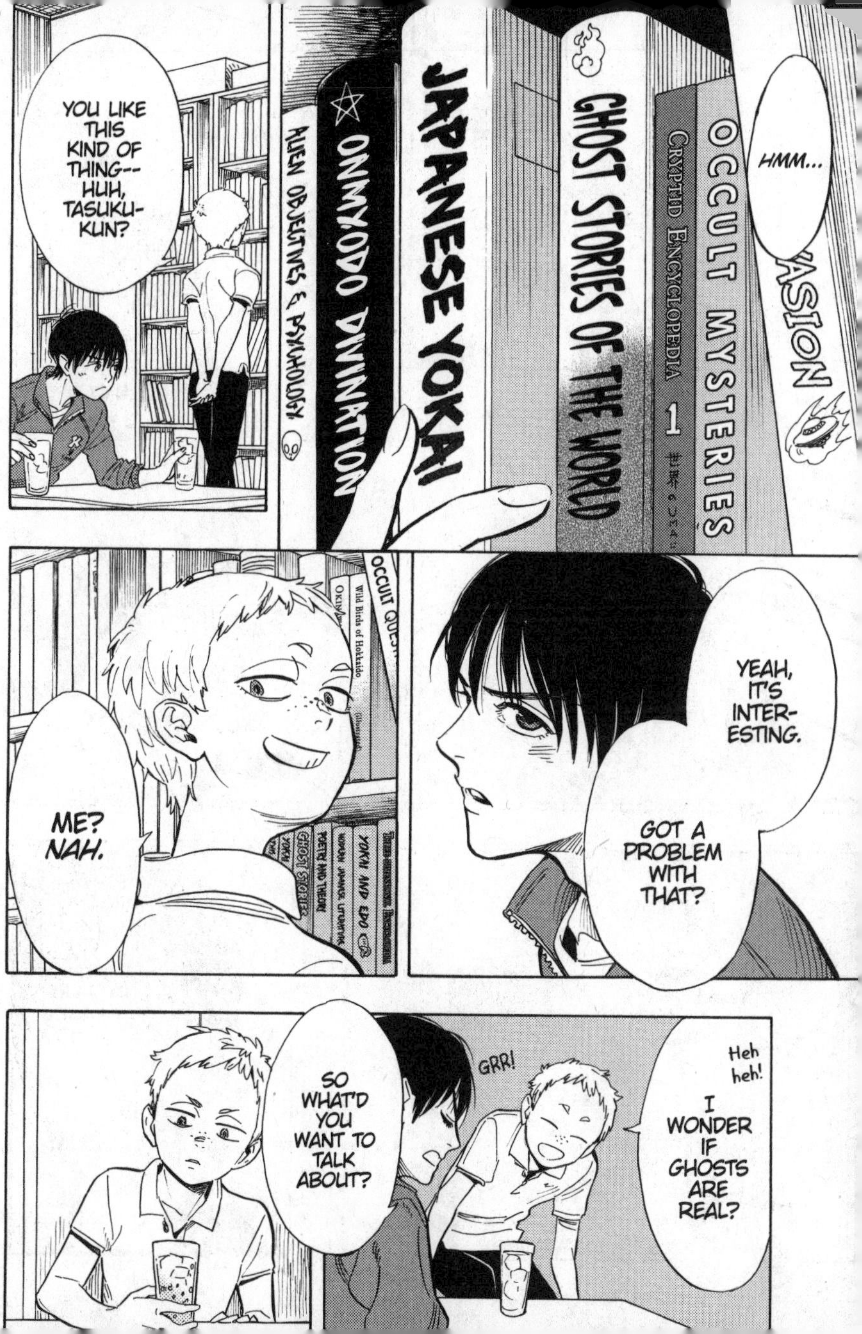
HMM...
OCCULT MYSTERIES
CRYPTID ENCYCLOPEDIA 1
GHOST STORIES OF THE WORLD
JAPANESE YOKAI
ONMYODO DIVINATION
ALIEN OBJECTIVES & PSYCHOLOGY
YOU LIKE THIS KIND OF THING-- HUH, TASUKU-KUN?
YEAH, IT'S INTER-ESTING.
GOT A PROBLEM WITH THAT?
Wild Birds of Hokkaido
ME? NAH.
Heh heh!
I WONDER IF GHOSTS ARE REAL?
GRR!
SO WHAT'D YOU WANT TO TALK ABOUT?

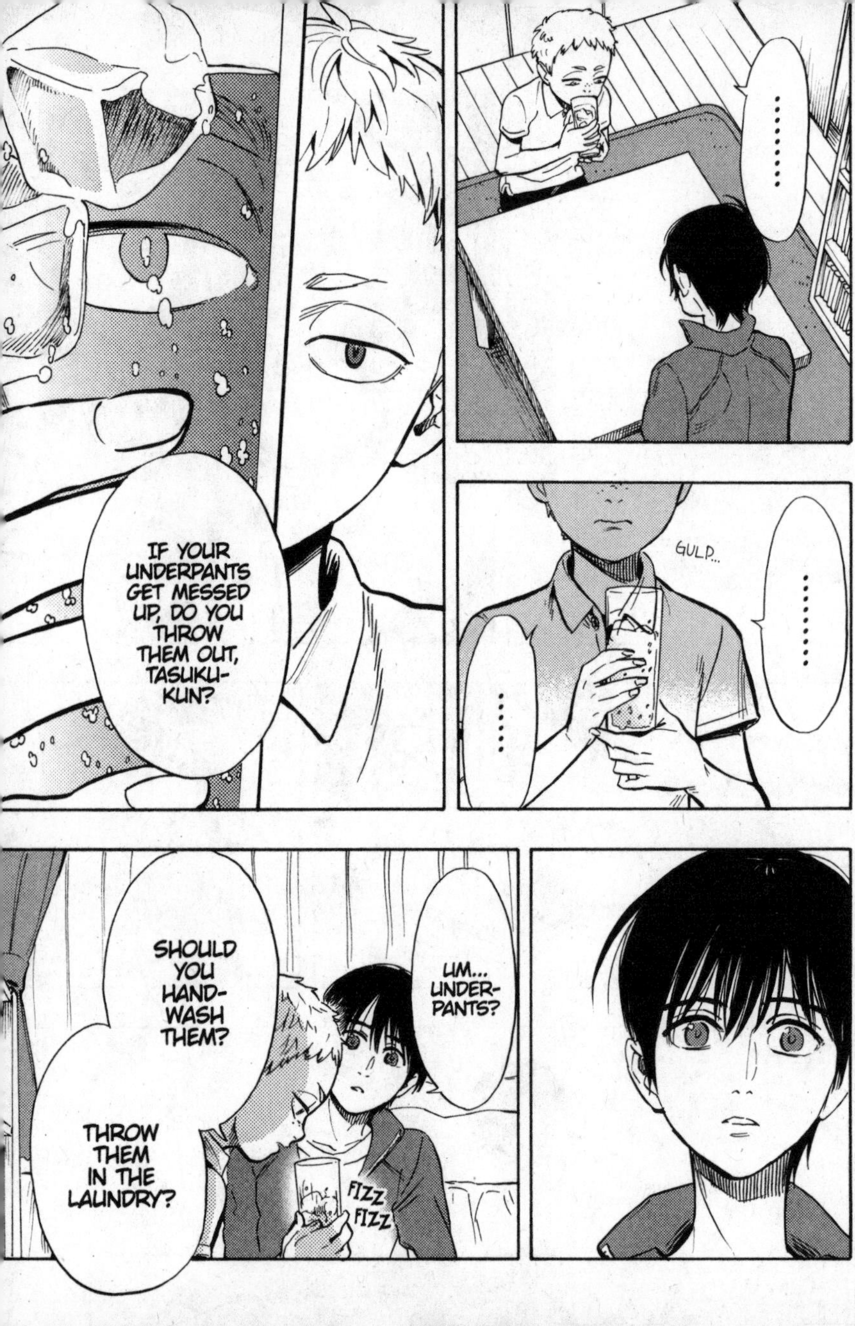
……
……
GULP…
……
IF YOUR UNDERPANTS GET MESSED UP, DO YOU THROW THEM OUT, TASUKU-KUN?
UM… UNDER-PANTS?
SHOULD YOU HAND-WASH THEM?
THROW THEM IN THE LAUNDRY?
FIZZ FIZZ

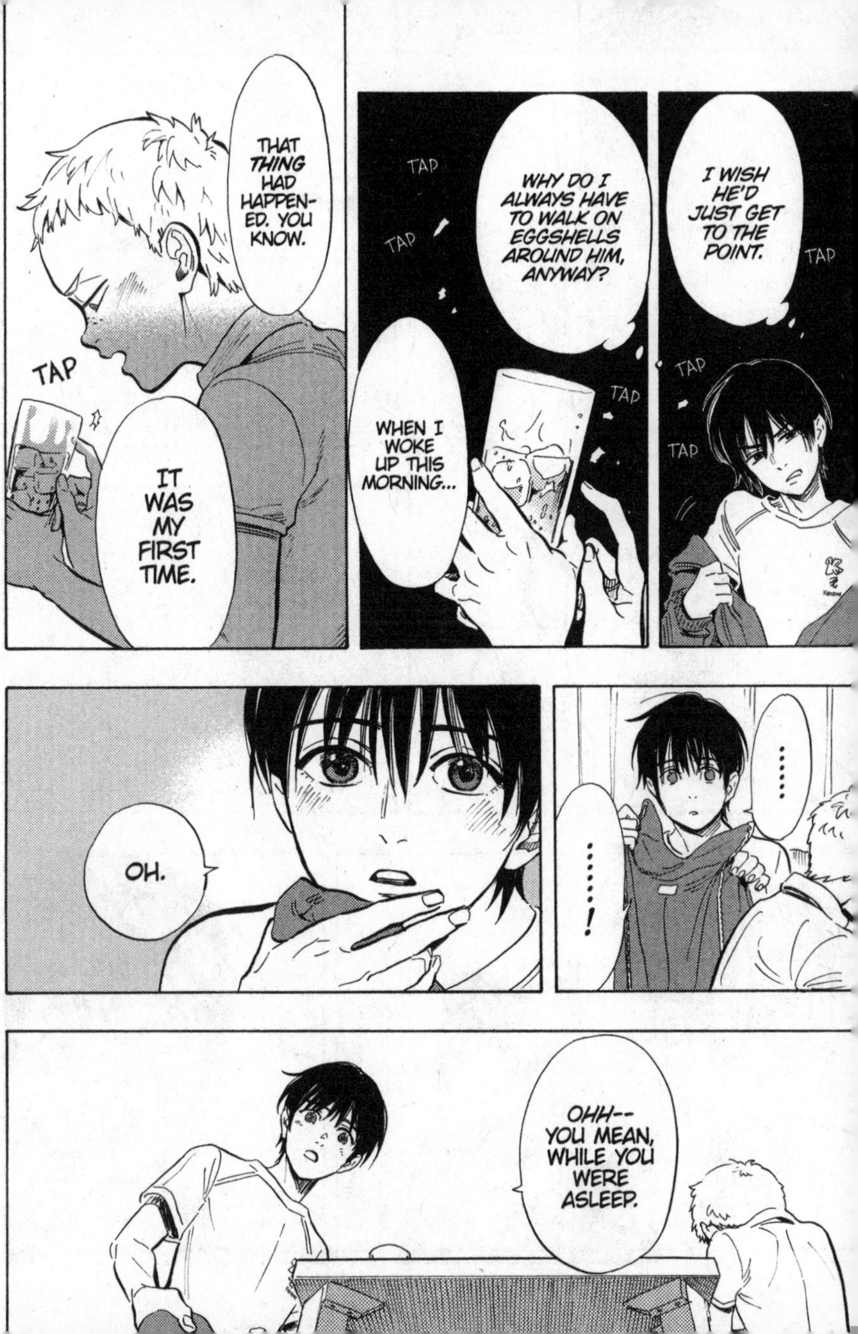
I WISH HE'D JUST GET TO THE POINT.
TAP
TAP
TAP
TAP
WHY DO I ALWAYS HAVE TO WALK ON EGGSHELLS AROUND HIM, ANYWAY?
TAP
TAP
WHEN I WOKE UP THIS MORNING...
THAT *THING* HAD HAPPEN-ED. YOU KNOW.
TAP
IT WAS MY FIRST TIME.
......
......!
OH.
OHH-- YOU MEAN, WHILE YOU WERE ASLEEP.

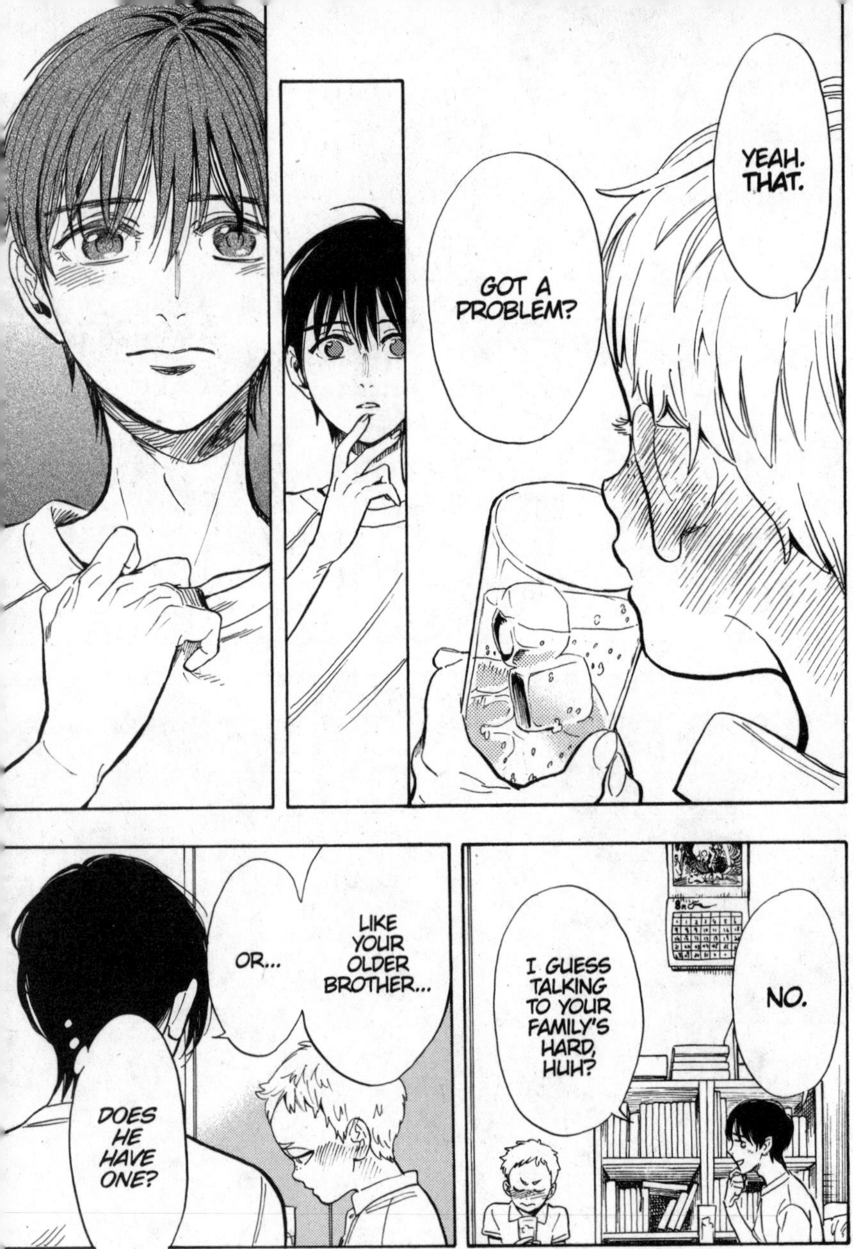
YEAH. THAT.
GOT A PROBLEM?
NO.
I GUESS TALKING TO YOUR FAMILY'S HARD, HUH?
LIKE YOUR OLDER BROTHER...
OR...
DOES HE HAVE ONE?

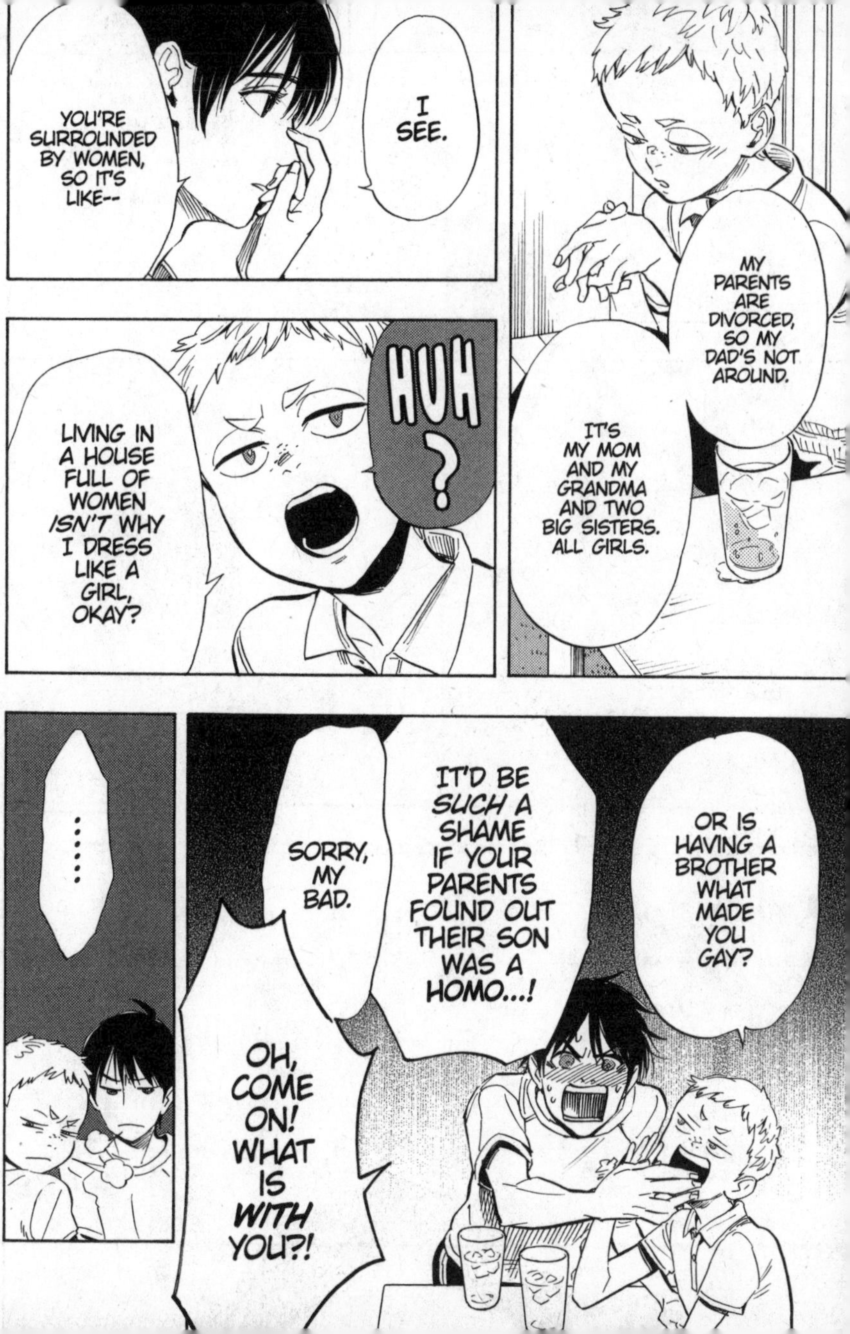
MY PARENTS ARE DIVORCED, SO MY DAD'S NOT AROUND.
IT'S MY MOM AND MY GRANDMA AND TWO BIG SISTERS. ALL GIRLS.
I SEE.
YOU'RE SURROUNDED BY WOMEN, SO IT'S LIKE--
HUH?
LIVING IN A HOUSE FULL OF WOMEN *ISN'T* WHY I DRESS LIKE A GIRL, OKAY?
OR IS HAVING A BROTHER WHAT MADE YOU GAY?
IT'D BE *SUCH* A SHAME IF YOUR PARENTS FOUND OUT THEIR SON WAS A HOMO...!
SORRY, MY BAD.
OH, COME ON! WHAT IS *WITH* YOU?!
......

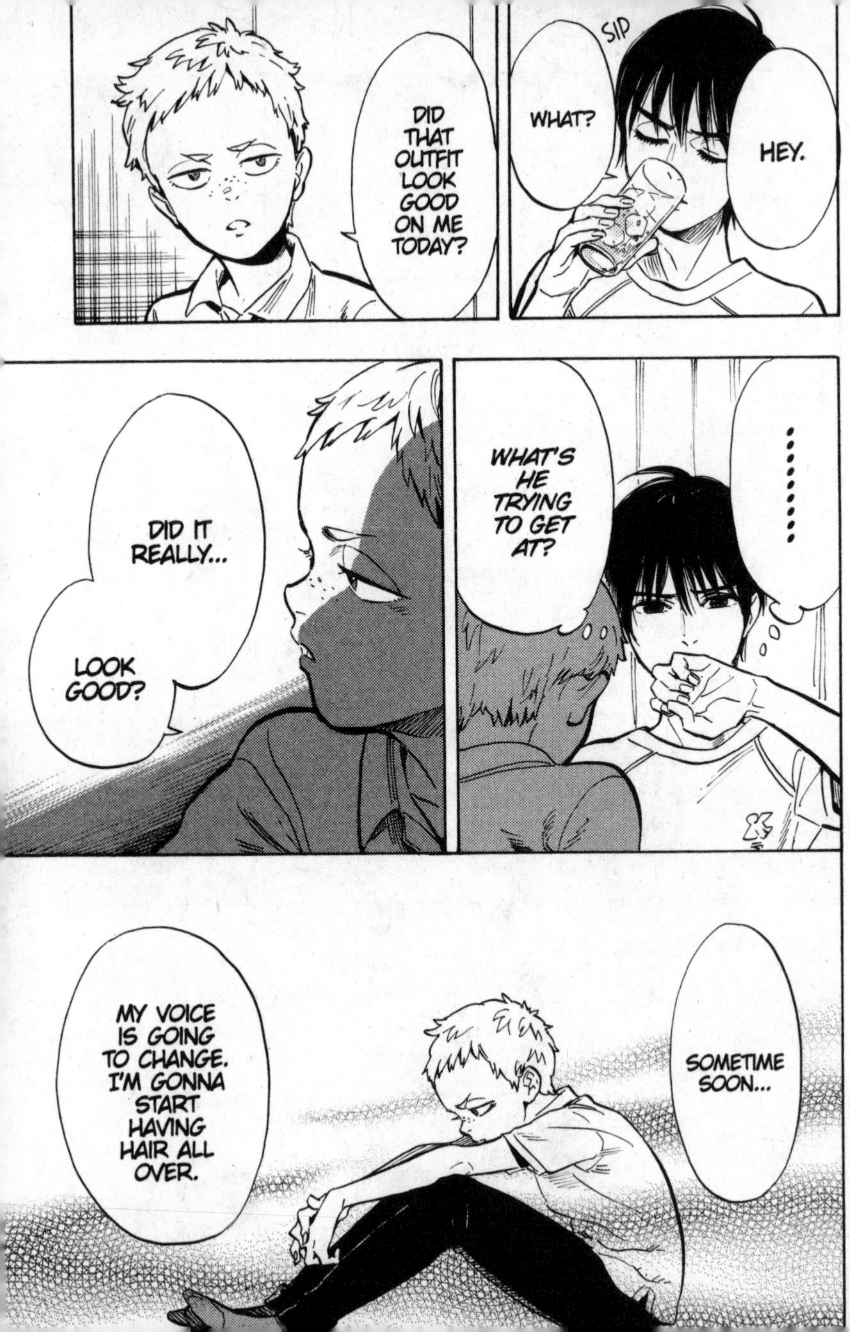
HEY.
SIP
WHAT?
DID THAT OUTFIT LOOK GOOD ON ME TODAY?
......
WHAT'S HE TRYING TO GET AT?
DID IT REALLY...
LOOK GOOD?
SOMETIME SOON...
MY VOICE IS GOING TO CHANGE. I'M GONNA START HAVING HAIR ALL OVER.

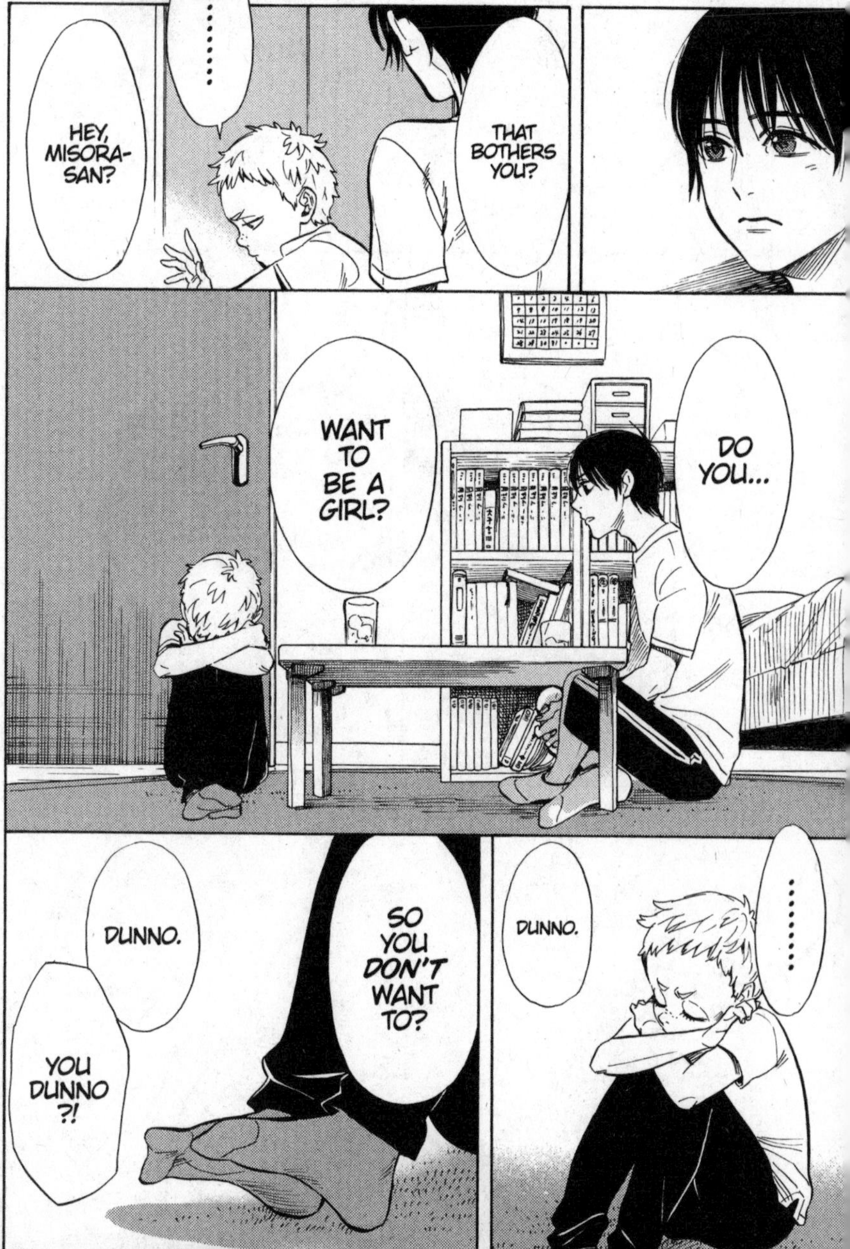
THAT BOTHERS YOU?
……
HEY, MISORA-SAN?
DO YOU...
WANT TO BE A GIRL?
……
DUNNO.
SO YOU *DON'T* WANT TO?
DUNNO.
YOU DUNNO ?!

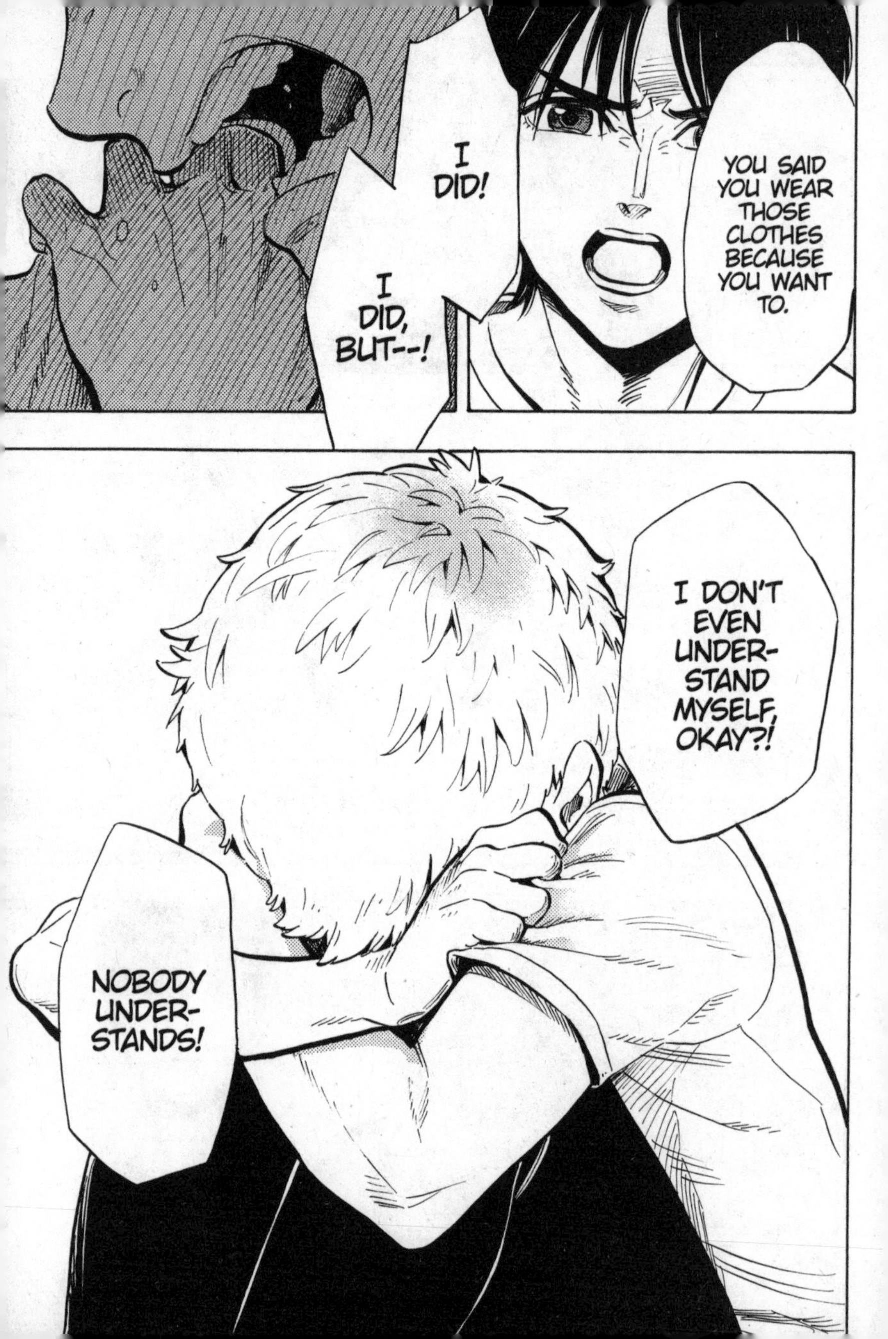
YOU SAID YOU WEAR THOSE CLOTHES BECAUSE YOU WANT TO.
I DID!
I DID, BUT--!
I DON'T EVEN UNDER-STAND MYSELF, OKAY?!
NOBODY UNDER-STANDS!

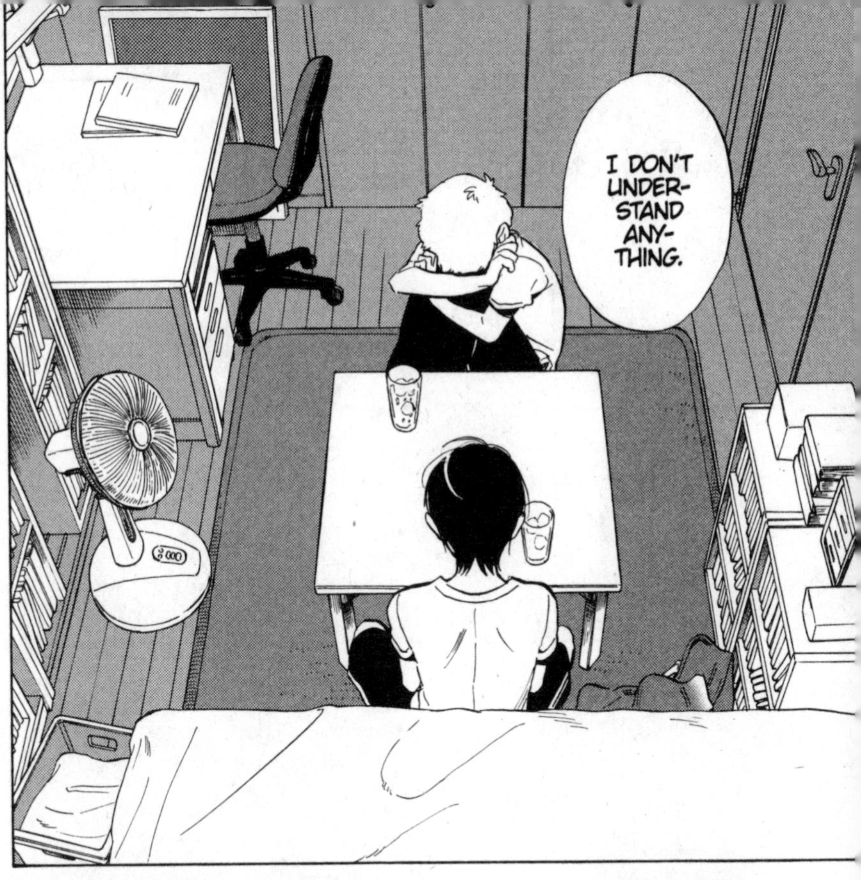
I DON'T UNDER-STAND ANY-THING.
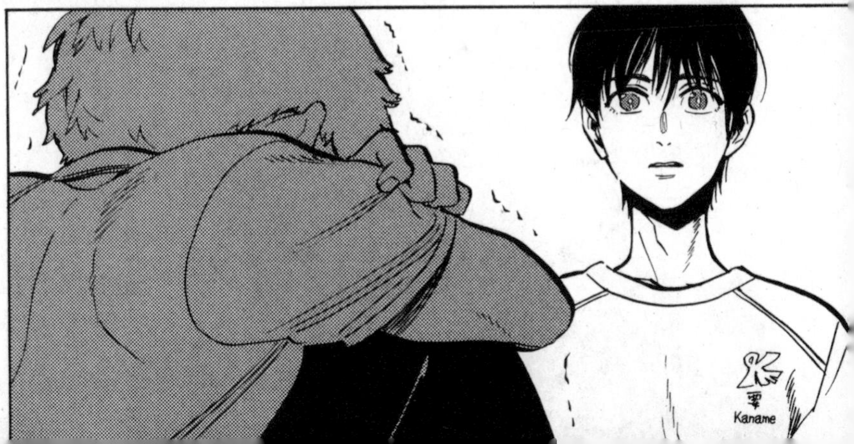
Kaname

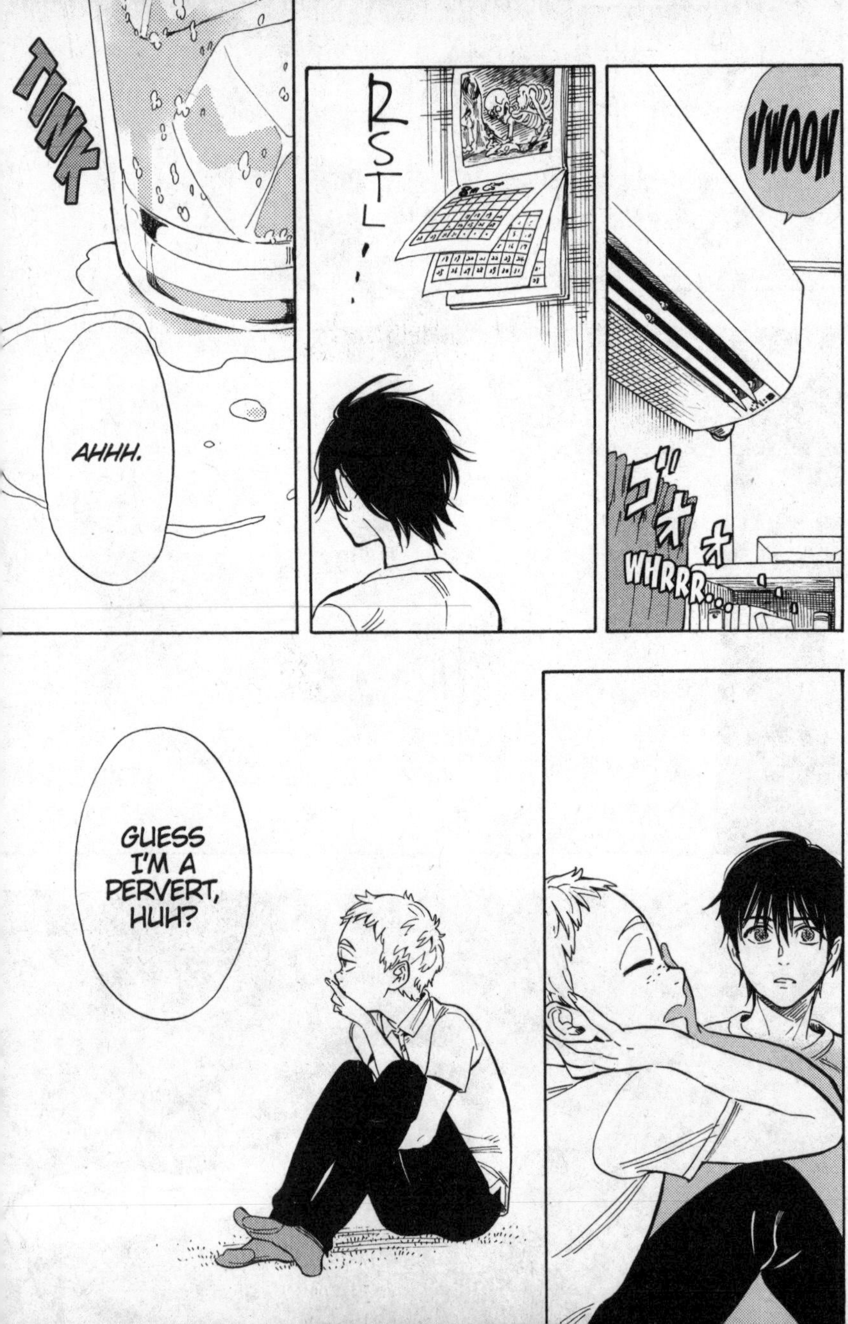
VWOON
ゴオオ
WHRRR...
RSTL
TINK
AHHH.
GUESS I'M A PERVERT, HUH?

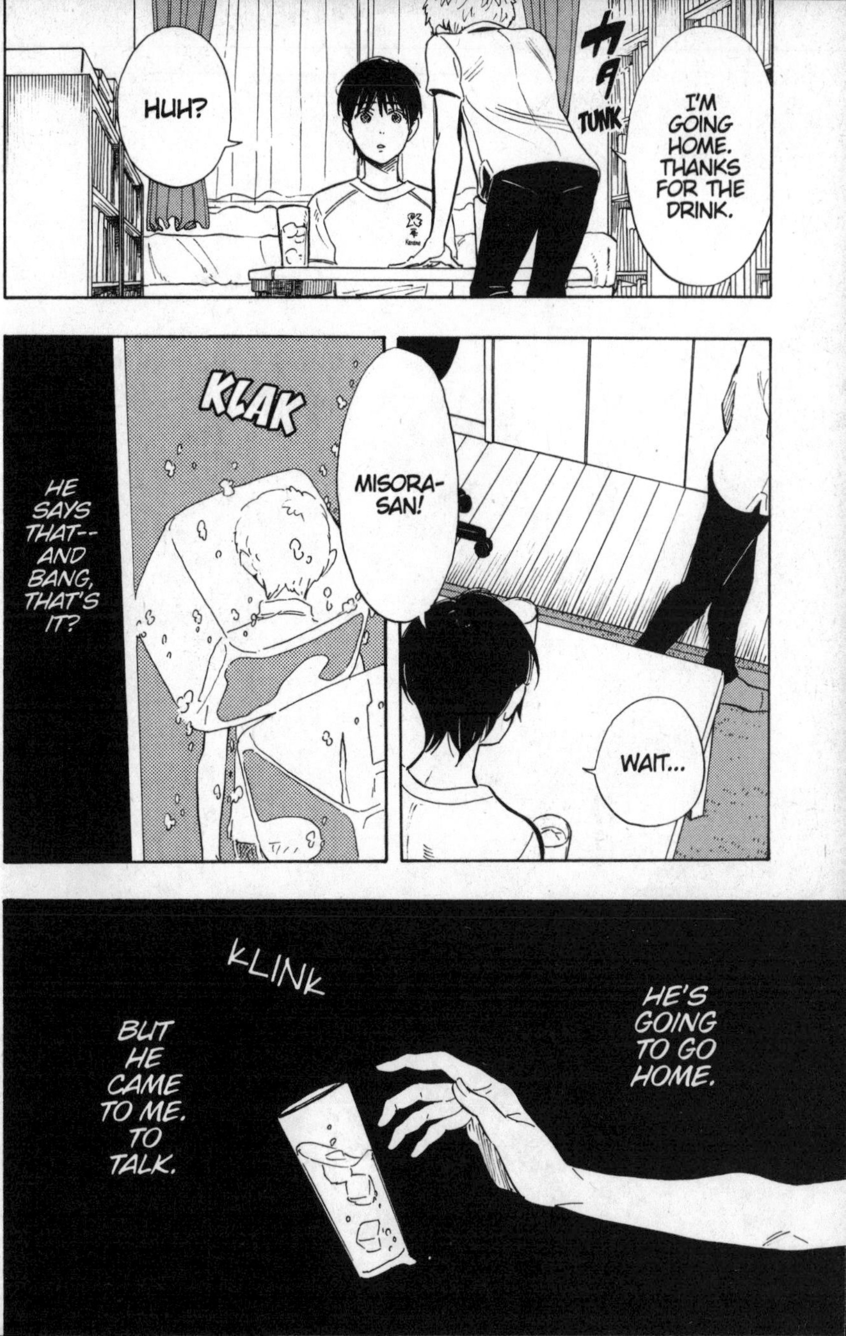
カタ
TUNK
I'M GOING HOME. THANKS FOR THE DRINK.
HUH?
MISORA-SAN!
WAIT...
KLAK
HE SAYS THAT-- AND BANG, THAT'S IT?
KLINK
HE'S GOING TO GO HOME.
BUT HE CAME TO ME. TO TALK.

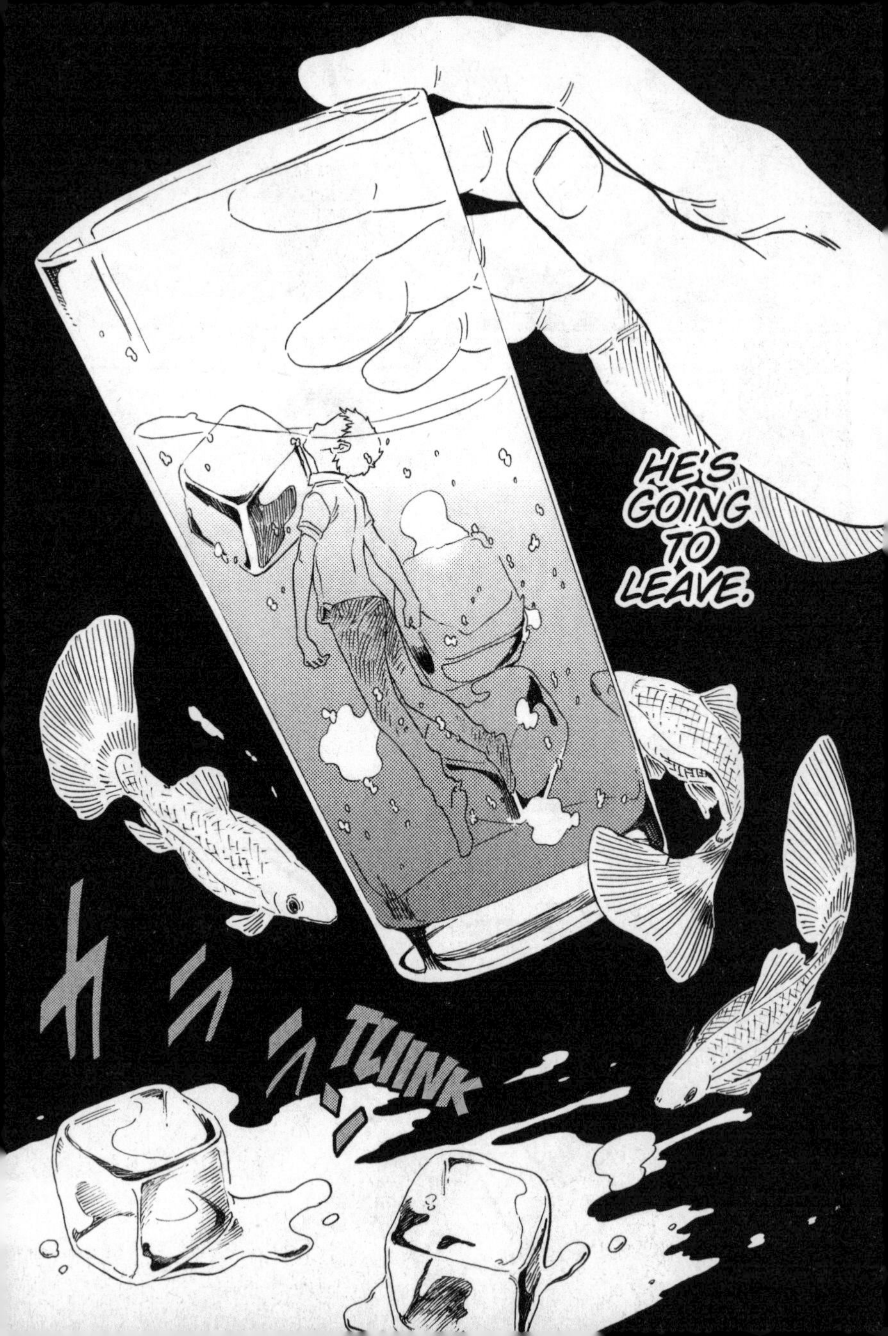
HE'S GOING TO LEAVE.
TLIINK

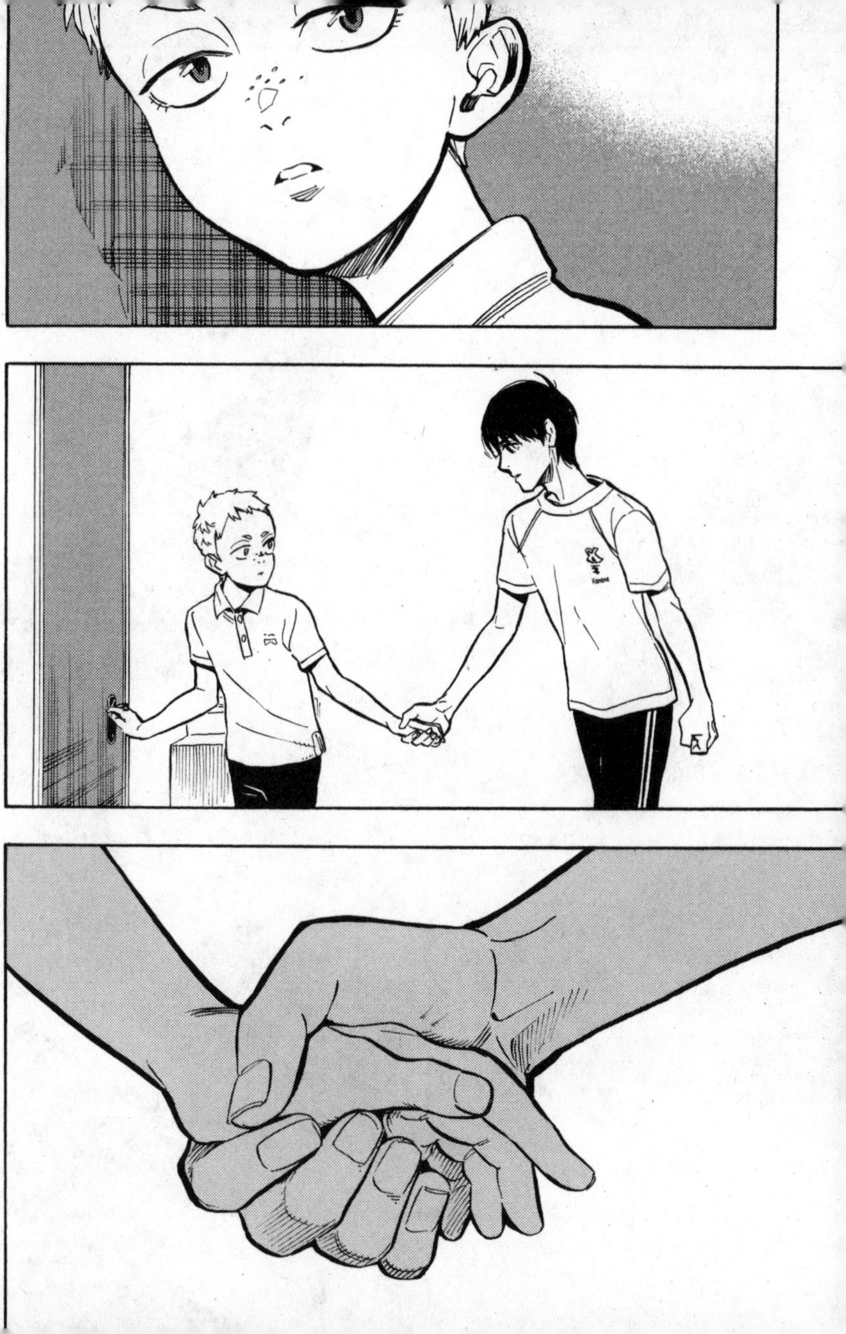

Our Dreams at Dusk

SHIMANAMI **TASOGARE**

Shimanami Kaido
This bridge road, which connects the islands from Onomichi to Imabari in Ehime prefecture, has recently gained international attention as a cycling road.

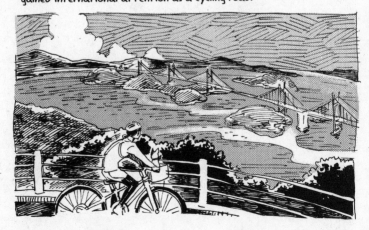

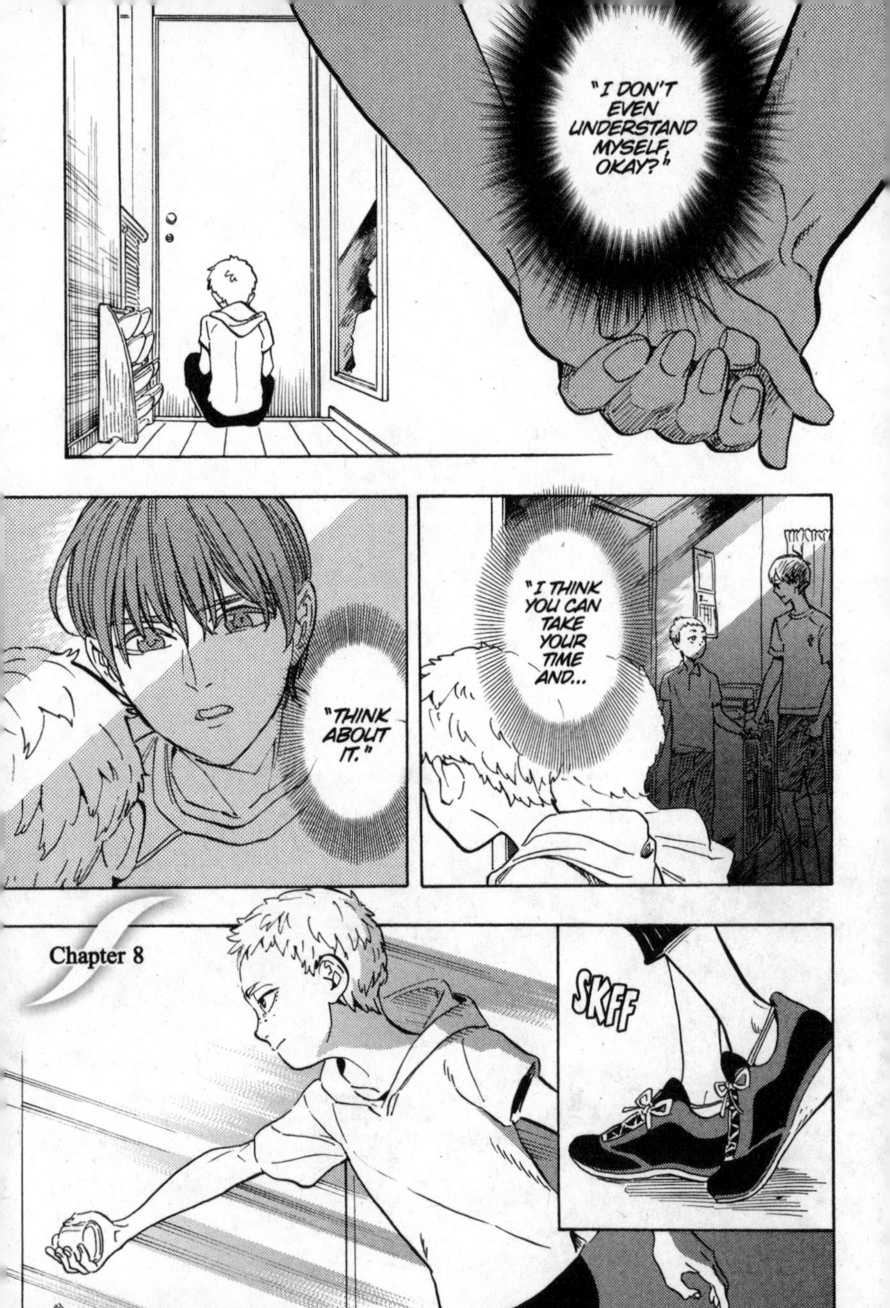
"I DON'T EVEN UNDERSTAND MYSELF, OKAY?"
"I THINK YOU CAN TAKE YOUR TIME AND...
"THINK ABOUT IT."
SKFF
Chapter 8

Chapter 8

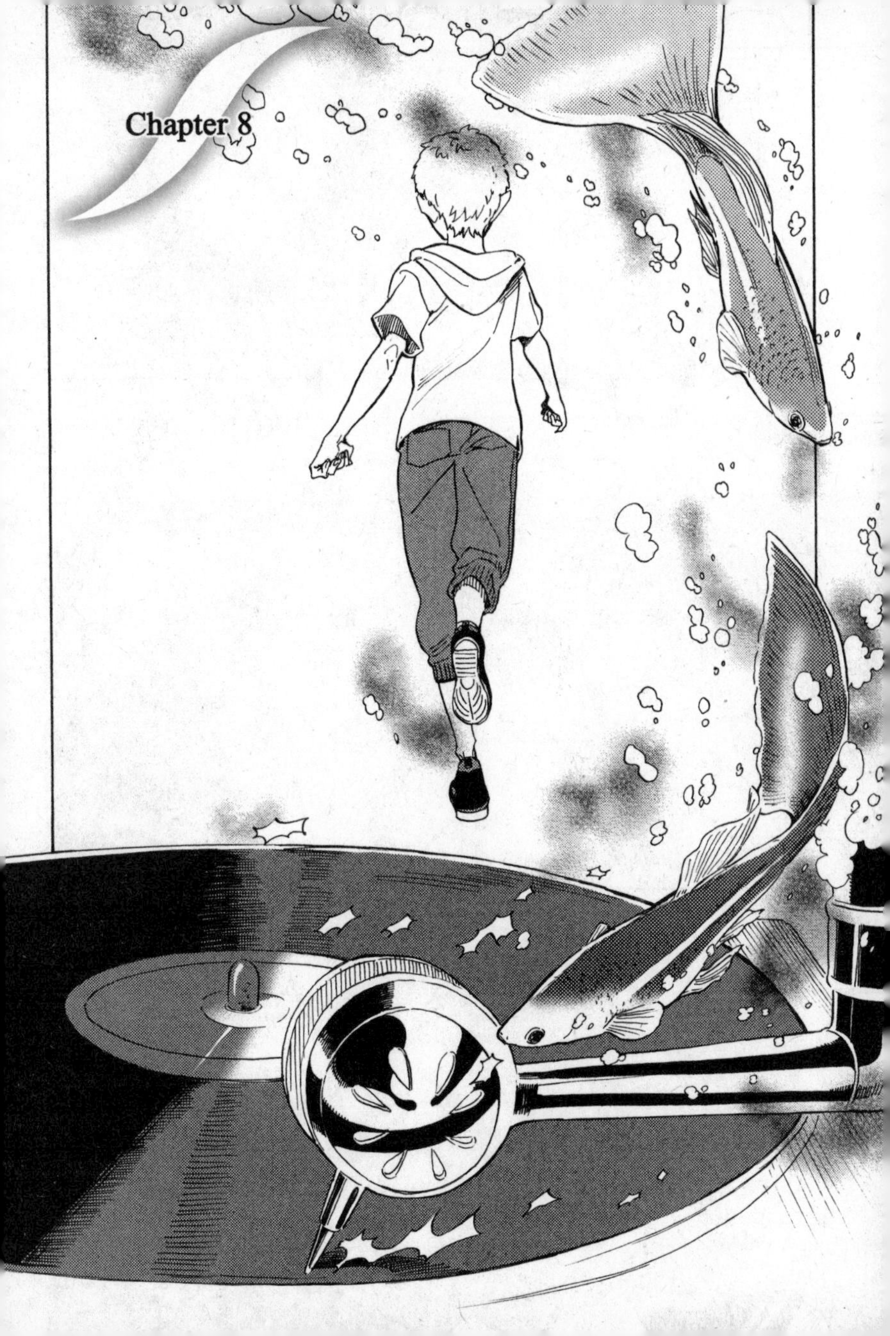

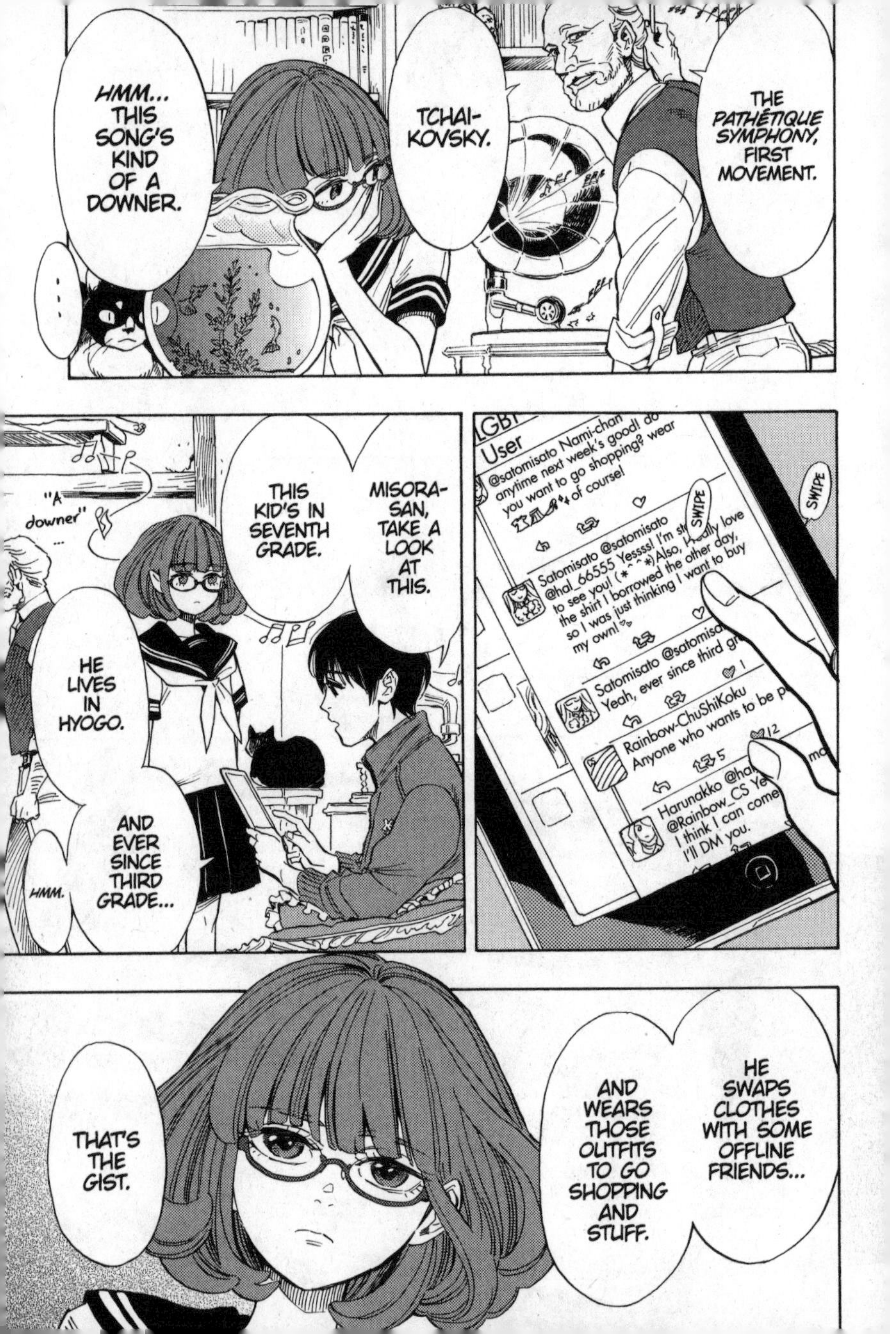
THE PATHÉTIQUE SYMPHONY, FIRST MOVEMENT.
TCHAI-KOVSKY.
HMM... THIS SONG'S KIND OF A DOWNER.
...
LGBT
User
@satomisato Nami-chan anytime next week's good! do you want to go shopping? wear
of course!
SWIPE
SWIPE
Satomisato @satomisato @hal_66555 Yessss! I'm st
to see you! (*^^*)Also,
really love the shirt I borrowed the other day, so I was just thinking I want to buy my own!♡
Satomisato @satomisato Yeah, ever since third gr
Rainbow-ChuShiKoku Anyone who wants to be p
5
12
Harunakko @ha
@Rainbow_CS Ye
I think I can come
I'll DM you.
MISORA-SAN, TAKE A LOOK AT THIS.
THIS KID'S IN SEVENTH GRADE.
"A downer" ...
HE LIVES IN HYOGO.
AND EVER SINCE THIRD GRADE...
HMM.
HE SWAPS CLOTHES WITH SOME OFFLINE FRIENDS...
AND WEARS THOSE OUTFITS TO GO SHOPPING AND STUFF.
THAT'S THE GIST.

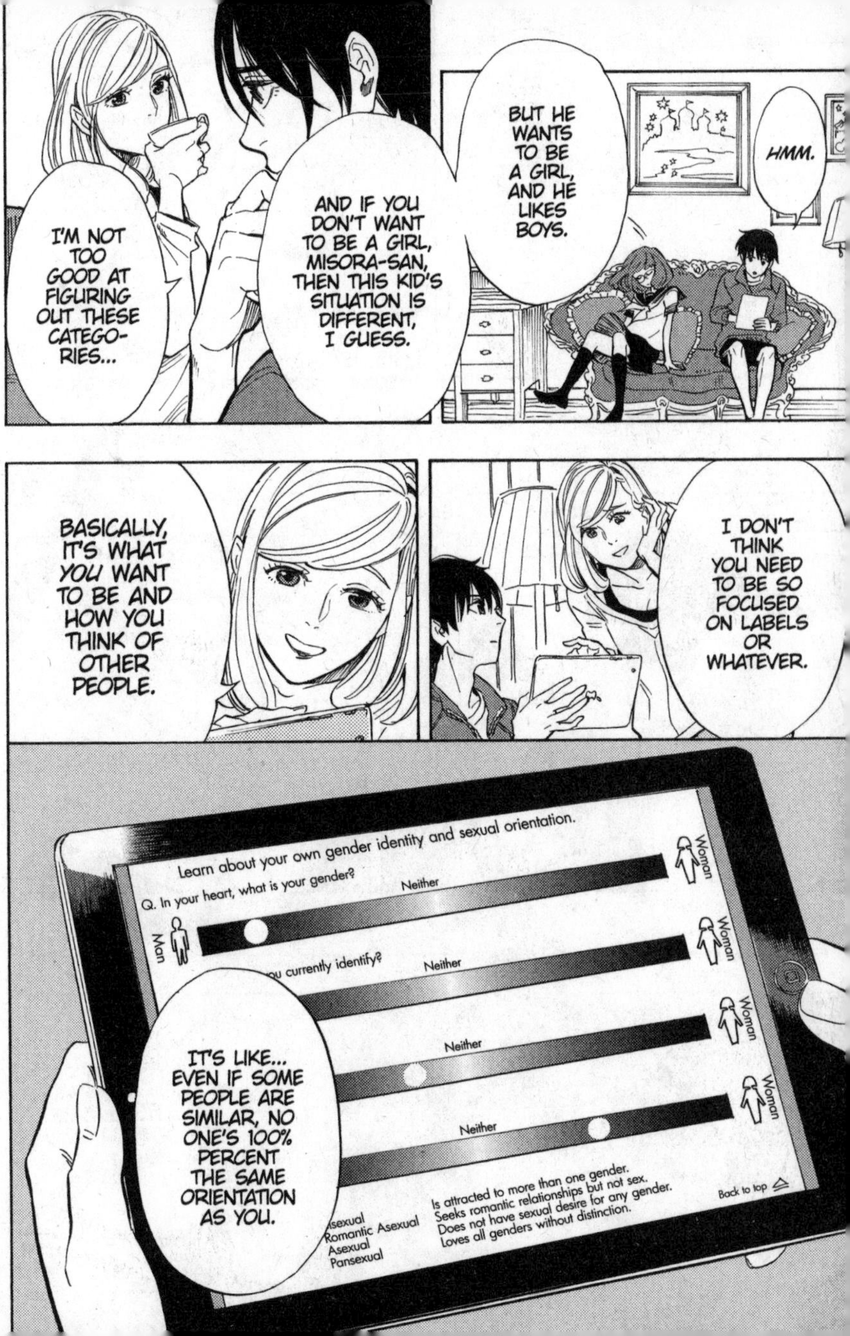
HMM.
BUT HE WANTS TO BE A GIRL, AND HE LIKES BOYS.
AND IF YOU DON'T WANT TO BE A GIRL, MISORA-SAN, THEN THIS KID'S SITUATION IS DIFFERENT, I GUESS.
I'M NOT TOO GOOD AT FIGURING OUT THESE CATEGO-RIES...
I DON'T THINK YOU NEED TO BE SO FOCUSED ON LABELS OR WHATEVER.
BASICALLY, IT'S WHAT *YOU* WANT TO BE AND HOW YOU THINK OF OTHER PEOPLE.
Learn about your own gender identity and sexual orientation.
Q. In your heart, what is your gender?
Man
Neither
Woman
ou currently identify?
Neither
Woman
Neither
Woman
Neither
Woman
IT'S LIKE... EVEN IF SOME PEOPLE ARE SIMILAR, NO ONE'S 100% PERCENT THE SAME ORIENTATION AS YOU.
sexual
Romantic Asexual
Asexual
Pansexual
Is attracted to more than one gender.
Seeks romantic relationships but not sex.
Does not have sexual desire for any gender.
Loves all genders without distinction.
Back to top

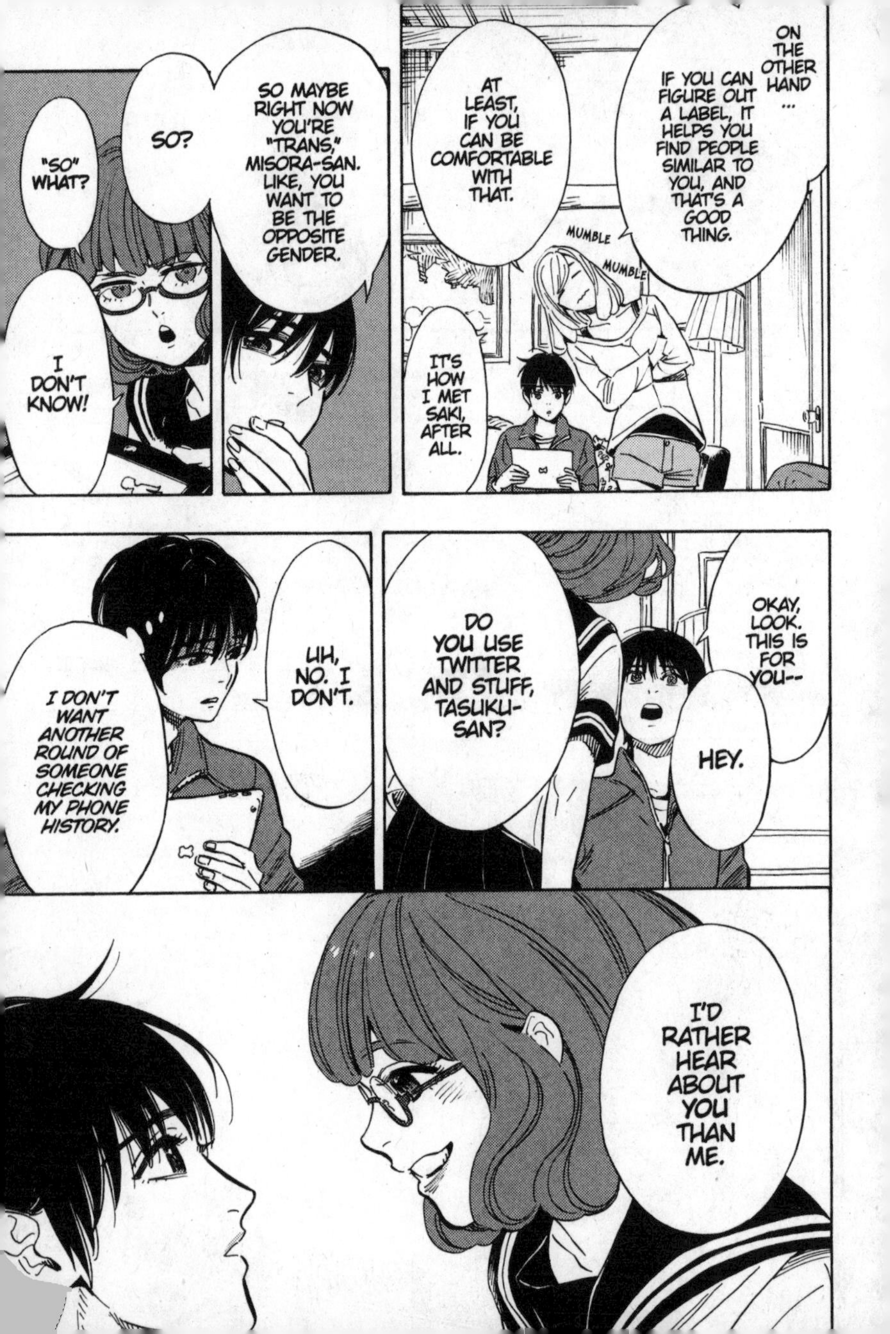
ON THE OTHER HAND ...
IF YOU CAN FIGURE OUT A LABEL, IT HELPS YOU FIND PEOPLE SIMILAR TO YOU, AND THAT'S A GOOD THING.
AT LEAST, IF YOU CAN BE COMFORTABLE WITH THAT.
MUMBLE
MUMBLE
IT'S HOW I MET SAKI, AFTER ALL.
SO MAYBE RIGHT NOW YOU'RE "TRANS," MISORA-SAN. LIKE, YOU WANT TO BE THE OPPOSITE GENDER.
SO?
"SO" WHAT?
I DON'T KNOW!
OKAY, LOOK. THIS IS FOR YOU--
HEY.
DO YOU USE TWITTER AND STUFF, TASUKU-SAN?
UH, NO. I DON'T.
I DON'T WANT ANOTHER ROUND OF SOMEONE CHECKING MY PHONE HISTORY.
I'D RATHER HEAR ABOUT YOU THAN ME.

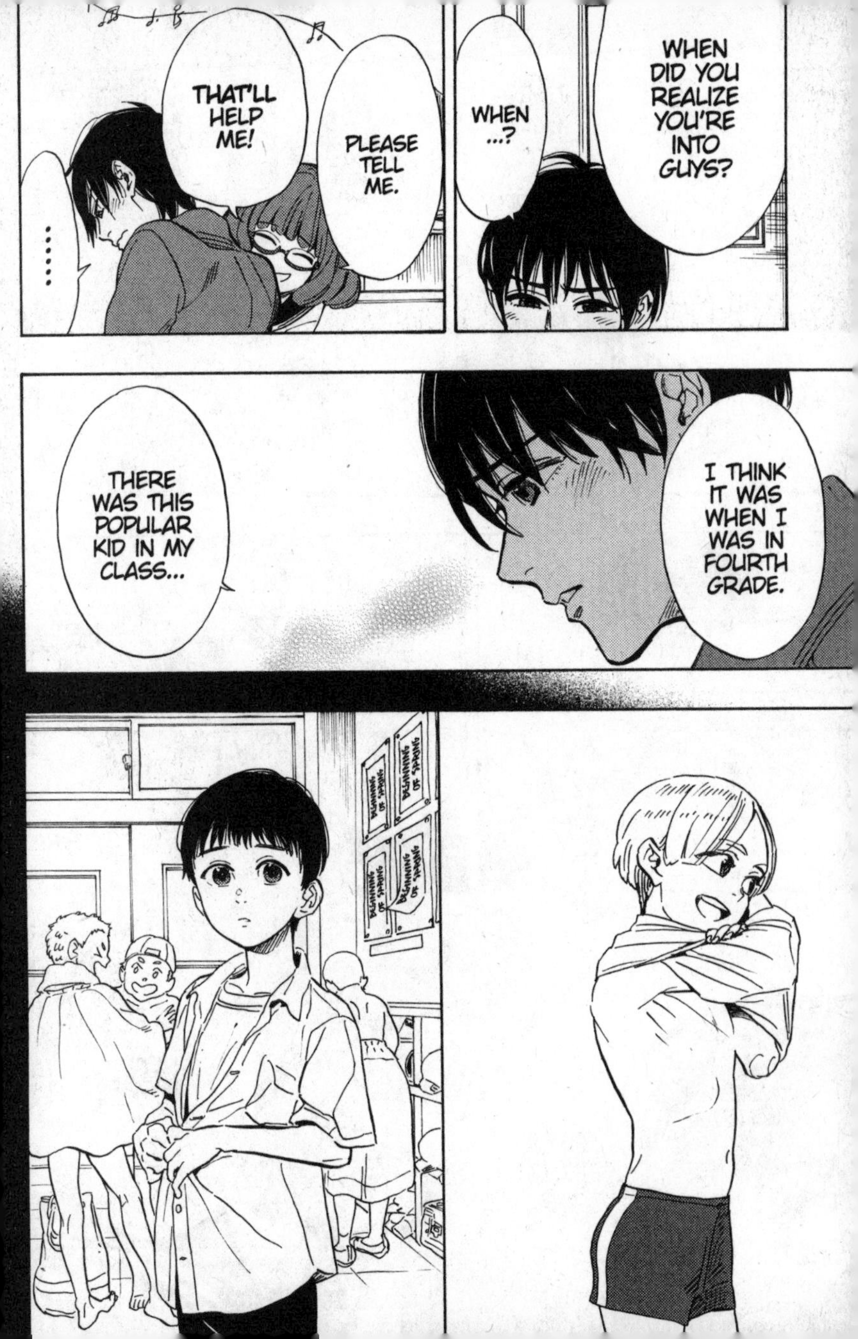
WHEN DID YOU REALIZE YOU'RE INTO GUYS?
WHEN ...?
PLEASE TELL ME.
THAT'LL HELP ME!
......
I THINK IT WAS WHEN I WAS IN FOURTH GRADE.
THERE WAS THIS POPULAR KID IN MY CLASS...
BEGINNING OF SPRING
BEGINNING OF SPRING
BEGINNING OF SPRING
BEGINNING OF SPRING

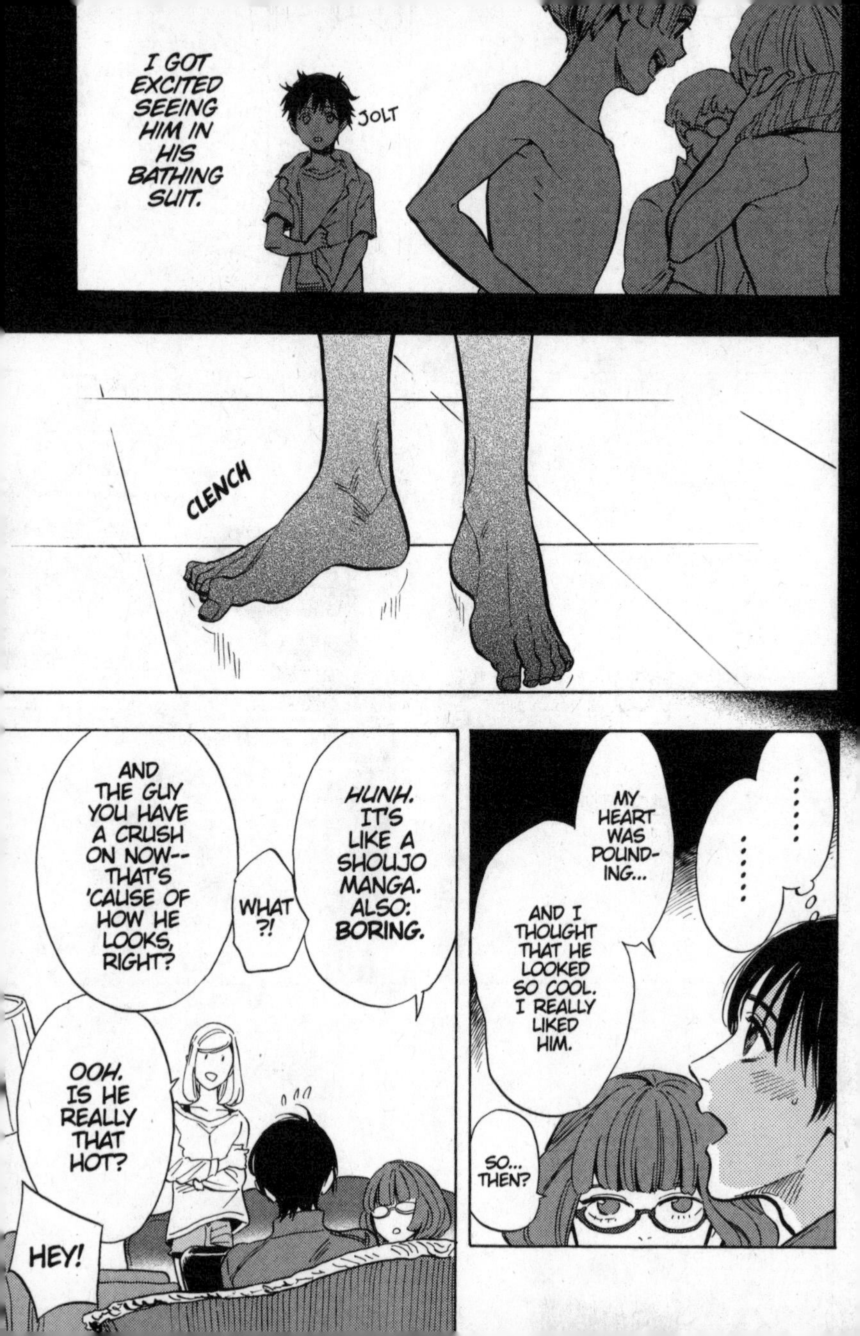
I GOT EXCITED SEEING HIM IN HIS BATHING SUIT.
JOLT
CLENCH
......
......
MY HEART WAS POUNDING...
AND I THOUGHT THAT HE LOOKED SO COOL. I REALLY LIKED HIM.
SO... THEN?
HUNH. IT'S LIKE A SHOUJO MANGA. ALSO: BORING.
WHAT?!
AND THE GUY YOU HAVE A CRUSH ON NOW--THAT'S 'CAUSE OF HOW HE LOOKS, RIGHT?
OOH. IS HE REALLY THAT HOT?
HEY!

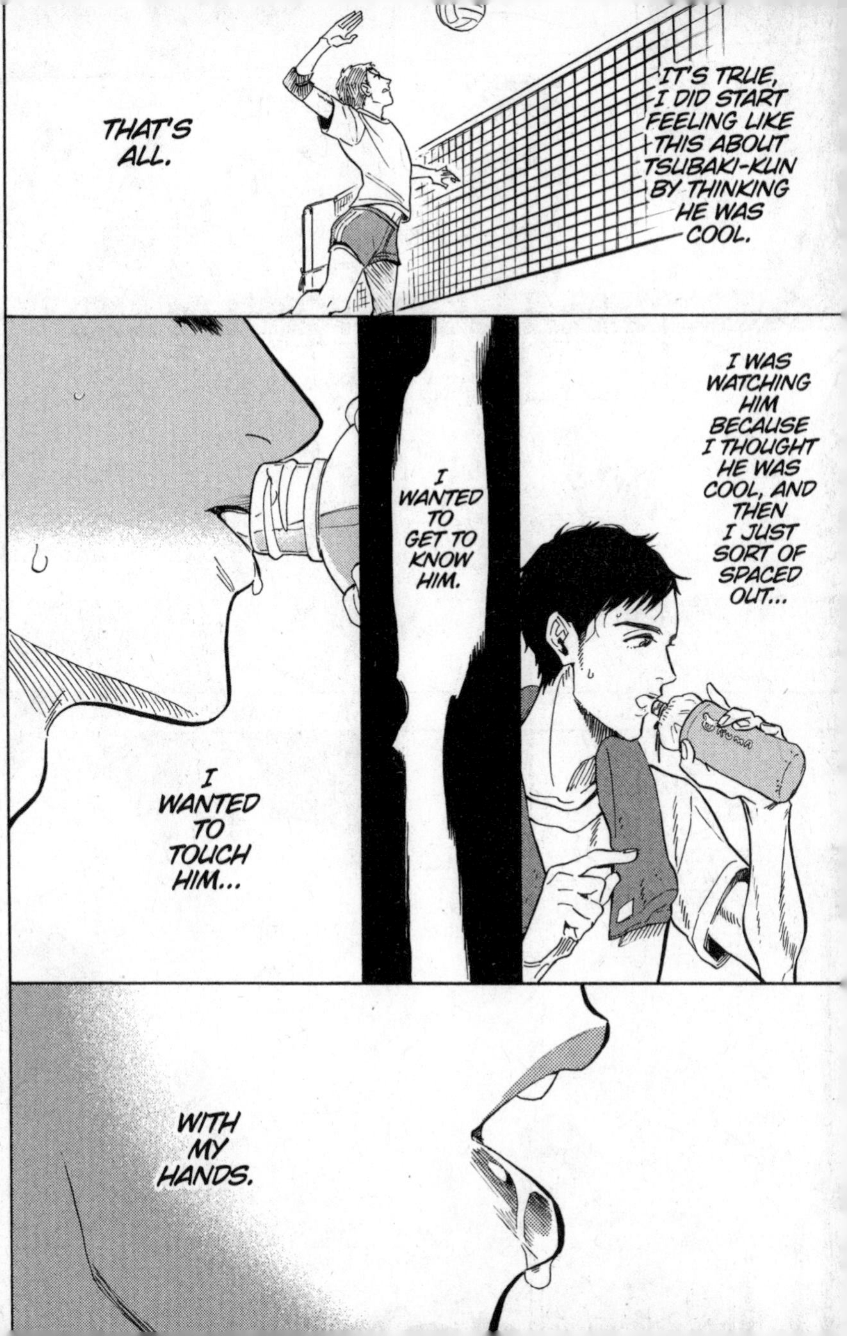
IT'S TRUE, I DID START FEELING LIKE THIS ABOUT TSUBAKI-KUN BY THINKING HE WAS COOL.
THAT'S ALL.
I WAS WATCHING HIM BECAUSE I THOUGHT HE WAS COOL, AND THEN I JUST SORT OF SPACED OUT...
I WANTED TO GET TO KNOW HIM.
I WANTED TO TOUCH HIM...
WITH MY HANDS.

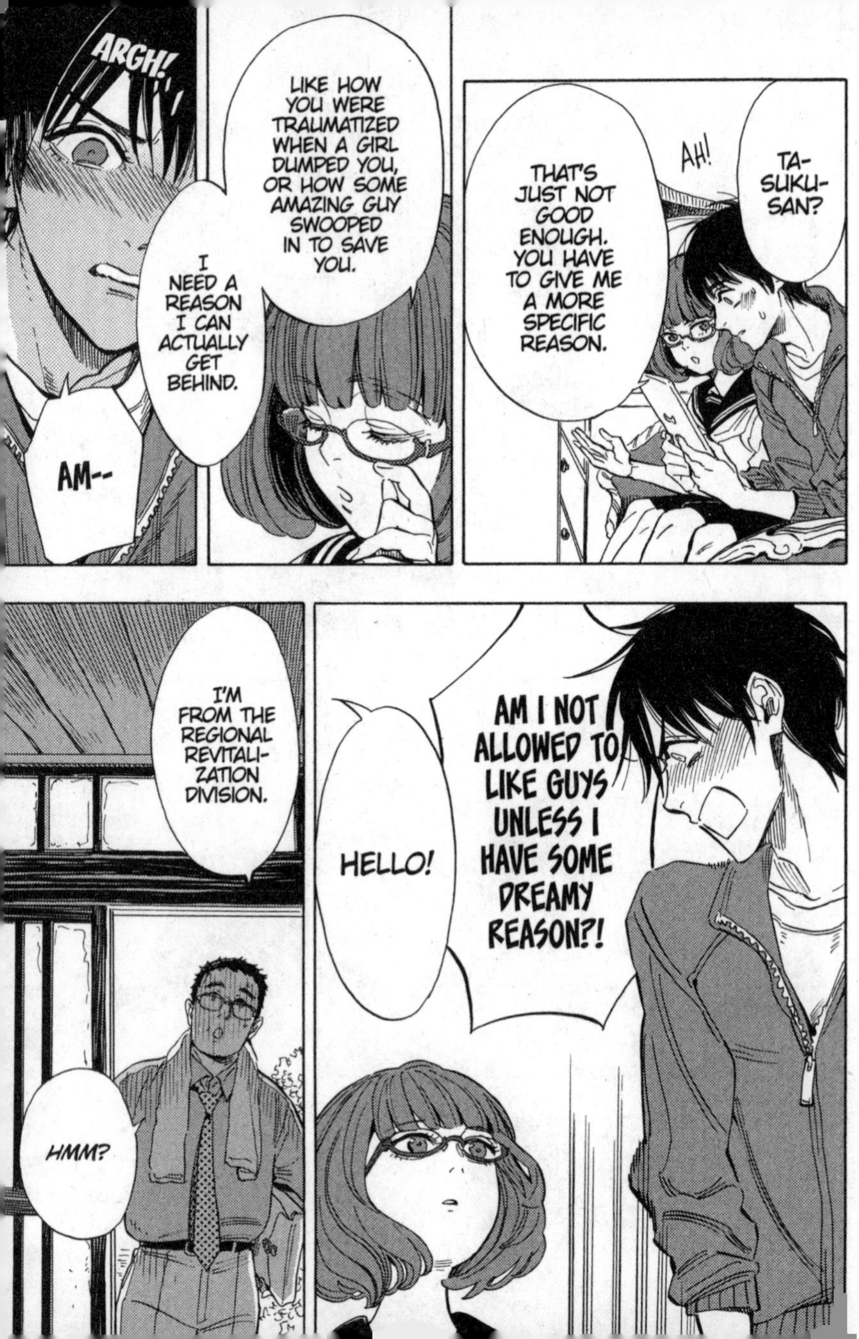
TA-SUKU-SAN?
AH!
THAT'S JUST NOT GOOD ENOUGH. YOU HAVE TO GIVE ME A MORE SPECIFIC REASON.
LIKE HOW YOU WERE TRAUMATIZED WHEN A GIRL DUMPED YOU, OR HOW SOME AMAZING GUY SWOOPED IN TO SAVE YOU.
I NEED A REASON I CAN ACTUALLY GET BEHIND.
ARGH!
AM--
AM I NOT ALLOWED TO LIKE GUYS UNLESS I HAVE SOME DREAMY REASON?!
HELLO!
I'M FROM THE REGIONAL REVITALI-ZATION DIVISION.
HMM?

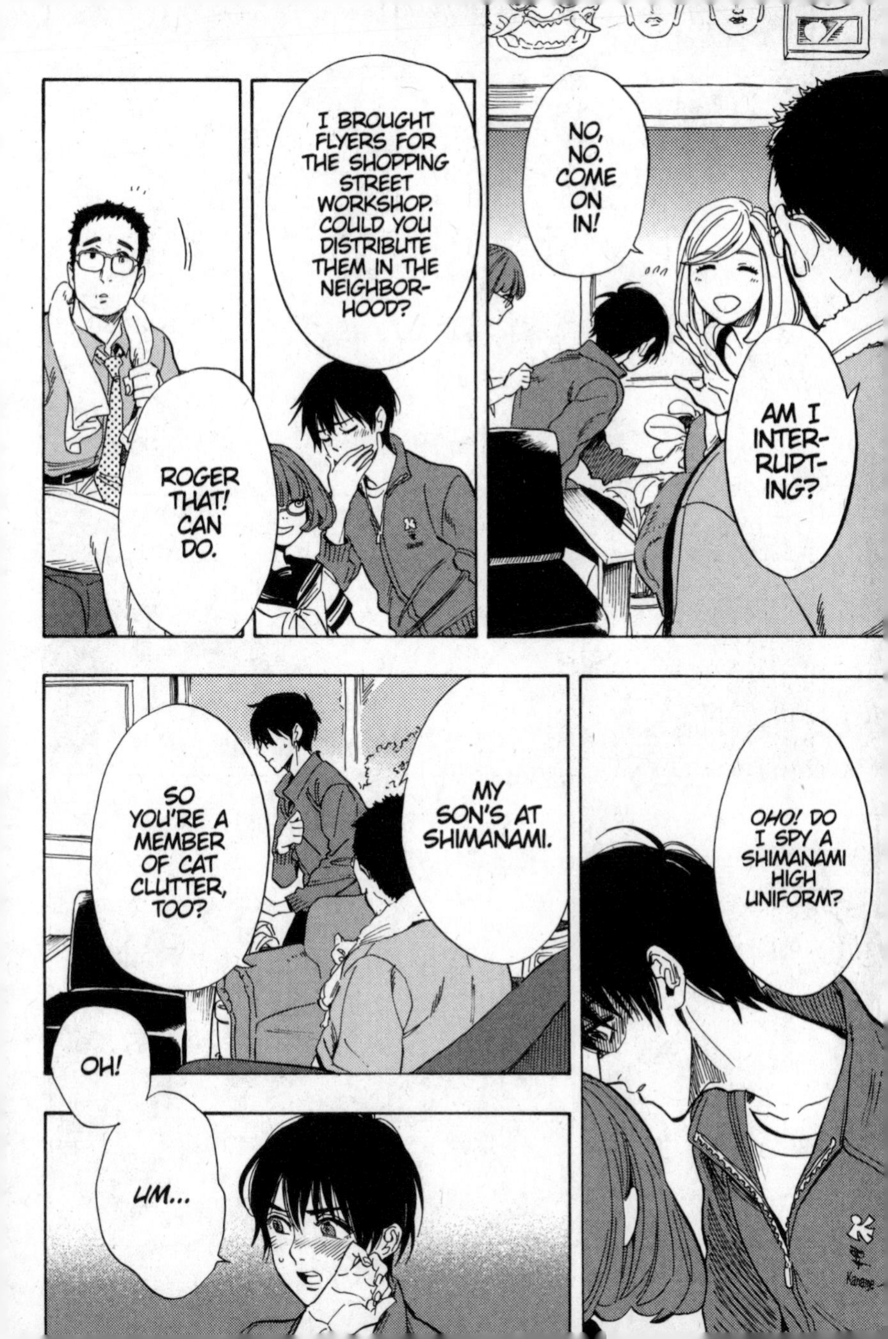
AM I INTERRUPTING?
NO, NO. COME ON IN!
I BROUGHT FLYERS FOR THE SHOPPING STREET WORKSHOP. COULD YOU DISTRIBUTE THEM IN THE NEIGHBORHOOD?
ROGER THAT! CAN DO.
OHO! DO I SPY A SHIMANAMI HIGH UNIFORM?
MY SON'S AT SHIMANAMI.
SO YOU'RE A MEMBER OF CAT CLUTTER, TOO?
OH!
UM...

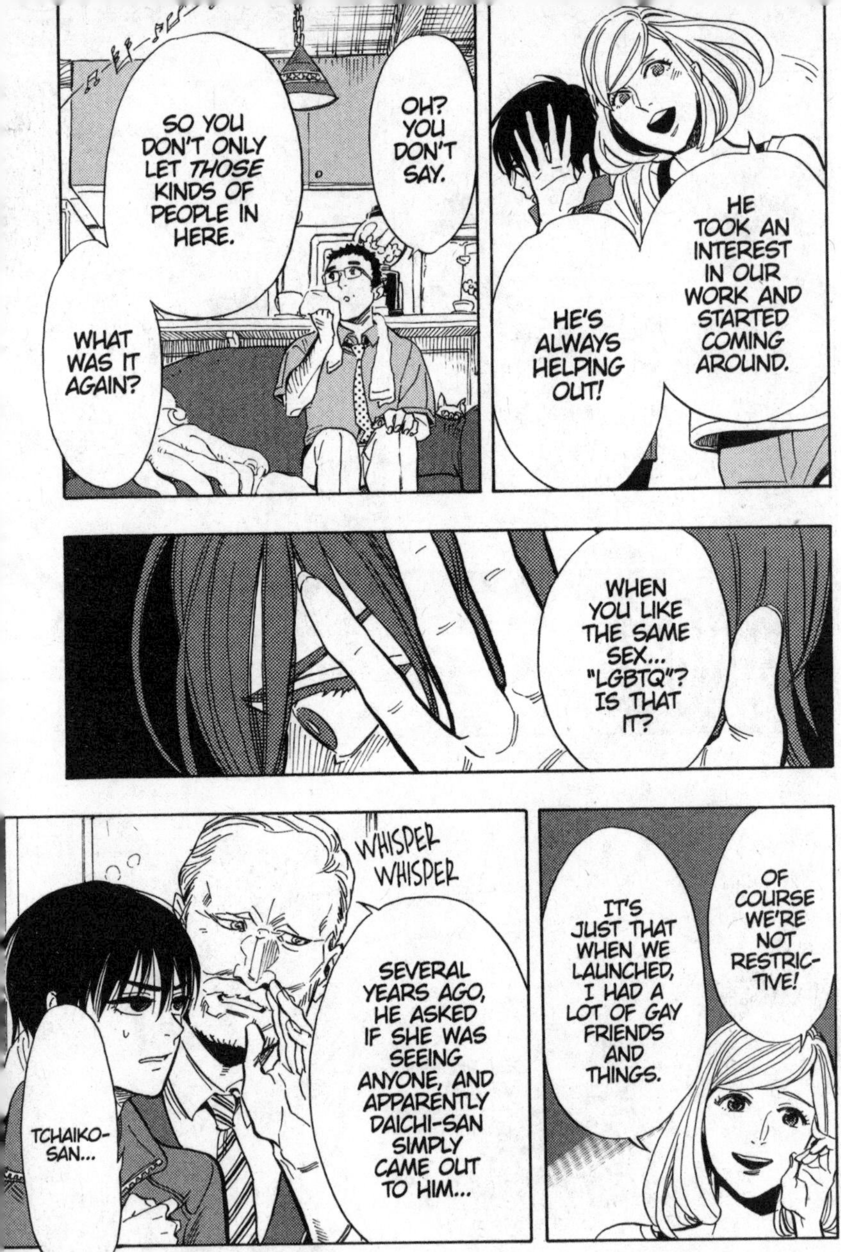
HE TOOK AN INTEREST IN OUR WORK AND STARTED COMING AROUND.
HE'S ALWAYS HELPING OUT!
OH? YOU DON'T SAY.
SO YOU DON'T ONLY LET *THOSE* KINDS OF PEOPLE IN HERE.
WHAT WAS IT AGAIN?
WHEN YOU LIKE THE SAME SEX... "LGBTQ"? IS THAT IT?
OF COURSE WE'RE NOT RESTRIC-TIVE!
IT'S JUST THAT WHEN WE LAUNCHED, I HAD A LOT OF GAY FRIENDS AND THINGS.
WHISPER WHISPER
SEVERAL YEARS AGO, HE ASKED IF SHE WAS SEEING ANYONE, AND APPARENTLY DAICHI-SAN SIMPLY CAME OUT TO HIM...
TCHAIKO-SAN...

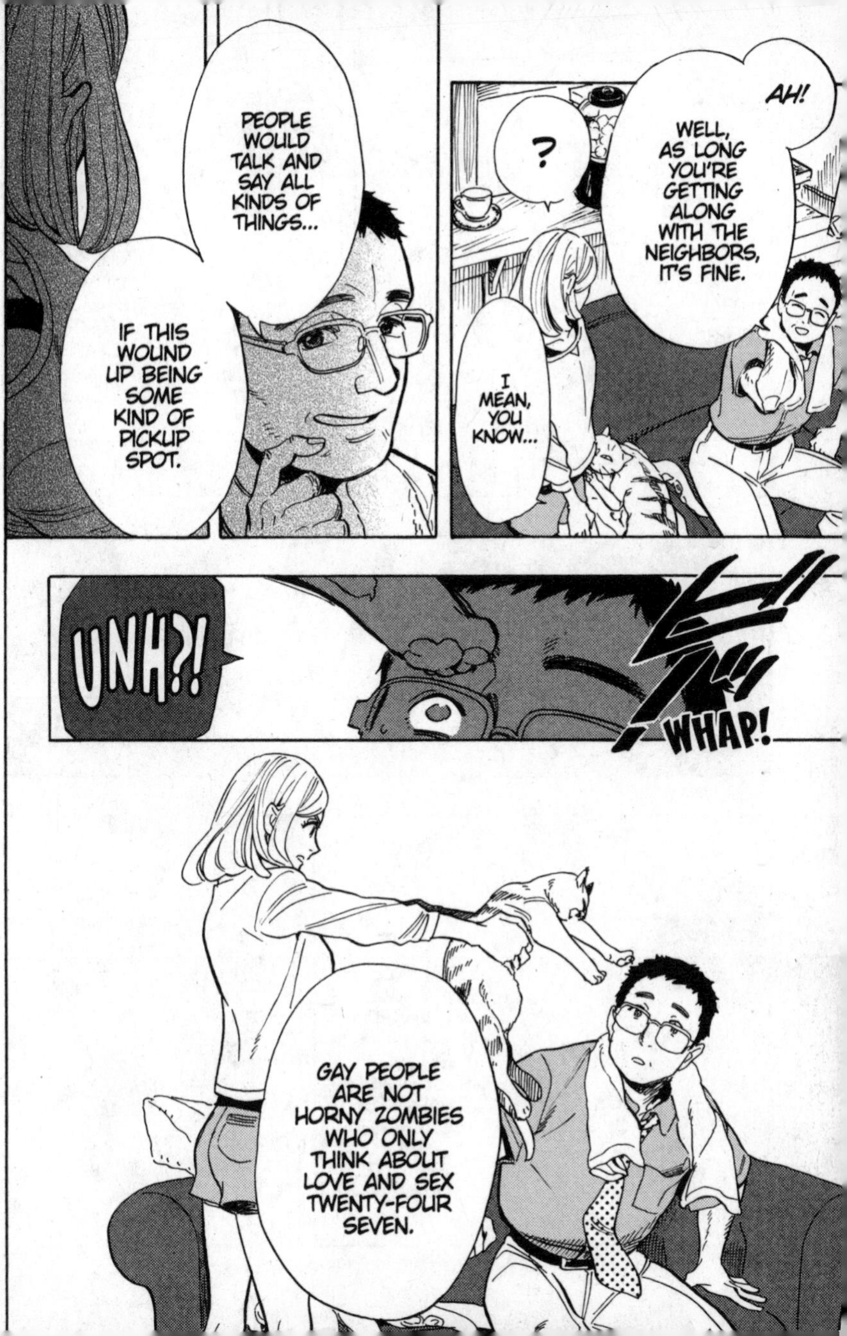
AH!
WELL, AS LONG YOU'RE GETTING ALONG WITH THE NEIGHBORS, IT'S FINE.
?
I MEAN, YOU KNOW...
PEOPLE WOULD TALK AND SAY ALL KINDS OF THINGS...
IF THIS WOUND UP BEING SOME KIND OF PICKUP SPOT.
UNH?!
WHAP!
GAY PEOPLE ARE NOT HORNY ZOMBIES WHO ONLY THINK ABOUT LOVE AND SEX TWENTY-FOUR SEVEN.

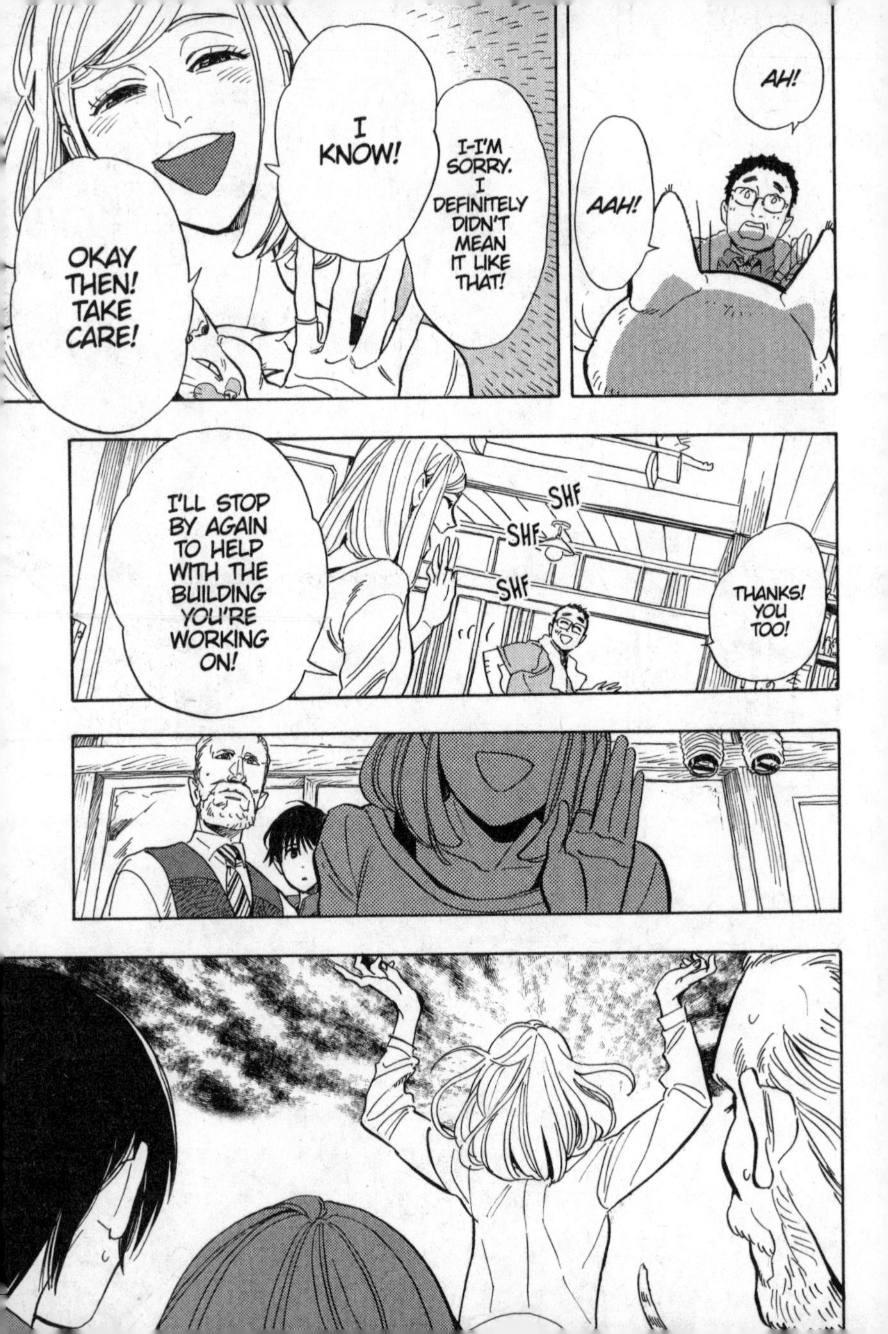
AH!
AAH!
I-I'M SORRY. I DEFINITELY DIDN'T MEAN IT LIKE THAT!
I KNOW!
OKAY THEN! TAKE CARE!
THANKS! YOU TOO!
SHF
SHF
SHF
I'LL STOP BY AGAIN TO HELP WITH THE BUILDING YOU'RE WORKING ON!

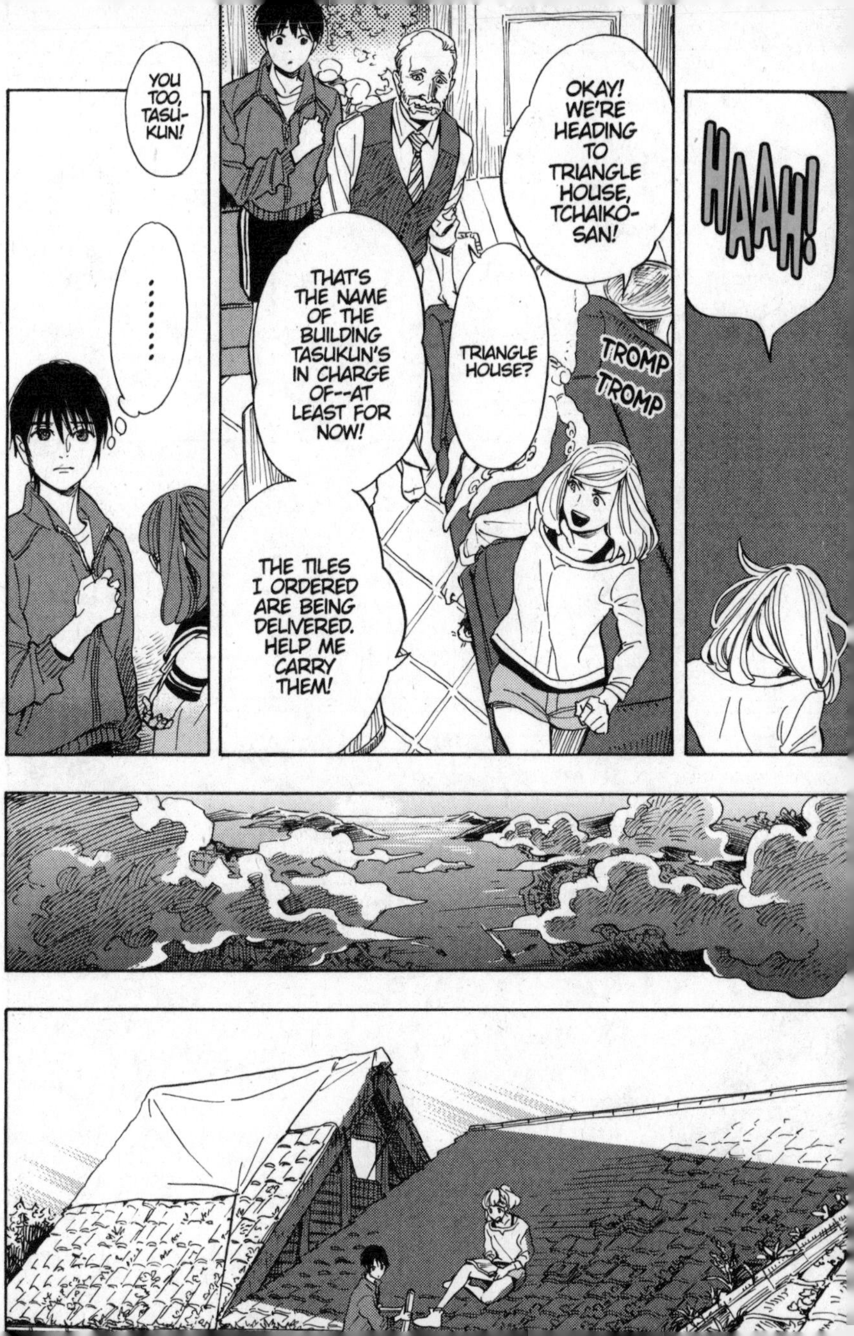
HAAH!
OKAY! WE'RE HEADING TO TRIANGLE HOUSE, TCHAIKO-SAN!
TROMP TROMP
TRIANGLE HOUSE?
THAT'S THE NAME OF THE BUILDING TASUKUN'S IN CHARGE OF--AT LEAST FOR NOW!
THE TILES I ORDERED ARE BEING DELIVERED. HELP ME CARRY THEM!
YOU TOO, TASU-KUN!
......

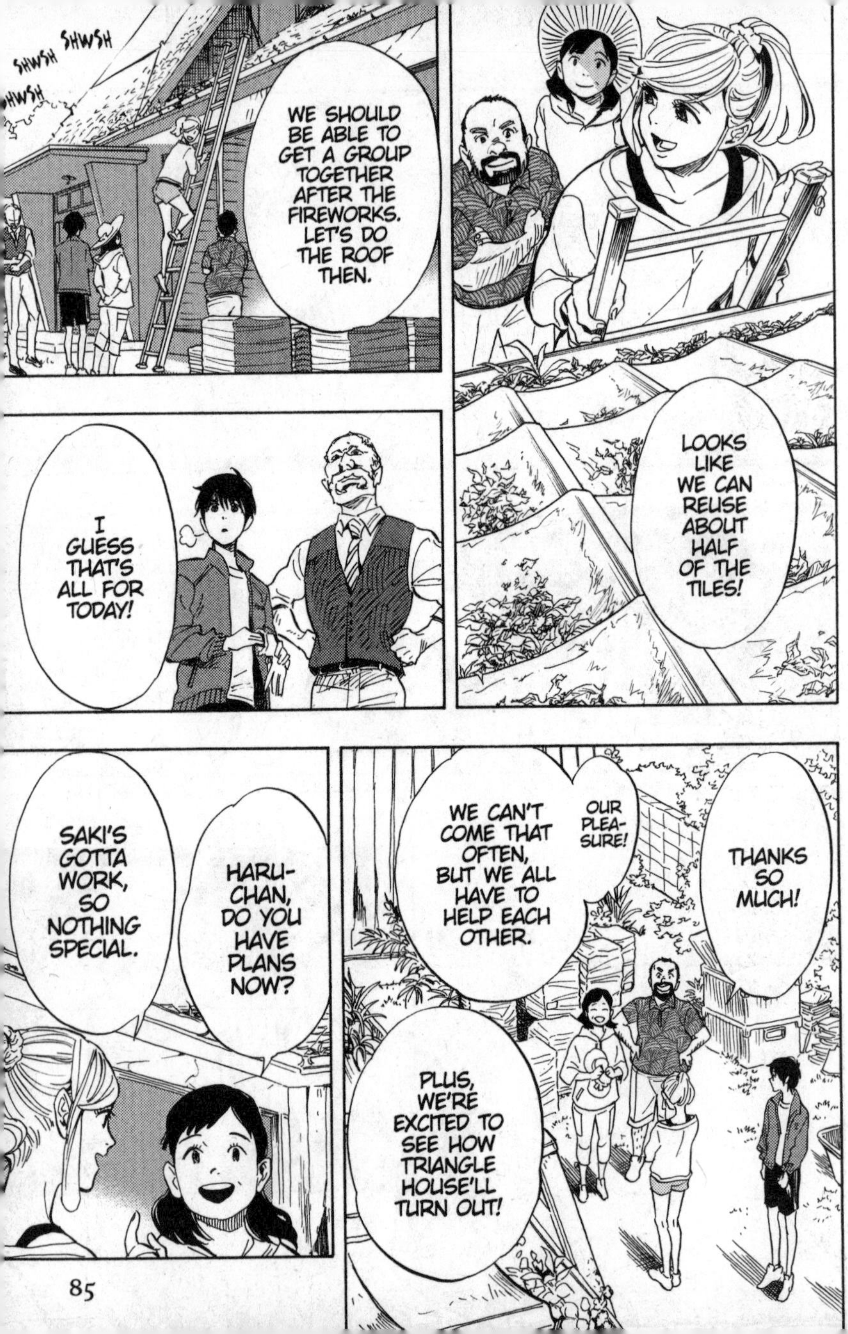
LOOKS LIKE WE CAN REUSE ABOUT HALF OF THE TILES!
SHWSH SHWSH
SHWSH
WE SHOULD BE ABLE TO GET A GROUP TOGETHER AFTER THE FIREWORKS. LET'S DO THE ROOF THEN.
I GUESS THAT'S ALL FOR TODAY!
THANKS SO MUCH!
OUR PLEASURE!
WE CAN'T COME THAT OFTEN, BUT WE ALL HAVE TO HELP EACH OTHER.
PLUS, WE'RE EXCITED TO SEE HOW TRIANGLE HOUSE'LL TURN OUT!
HARU-CHAN, DO YOU HAVE PLANS NOW?
SAKI'S GOTTA WORK, SO NOTHING SPECIAL.

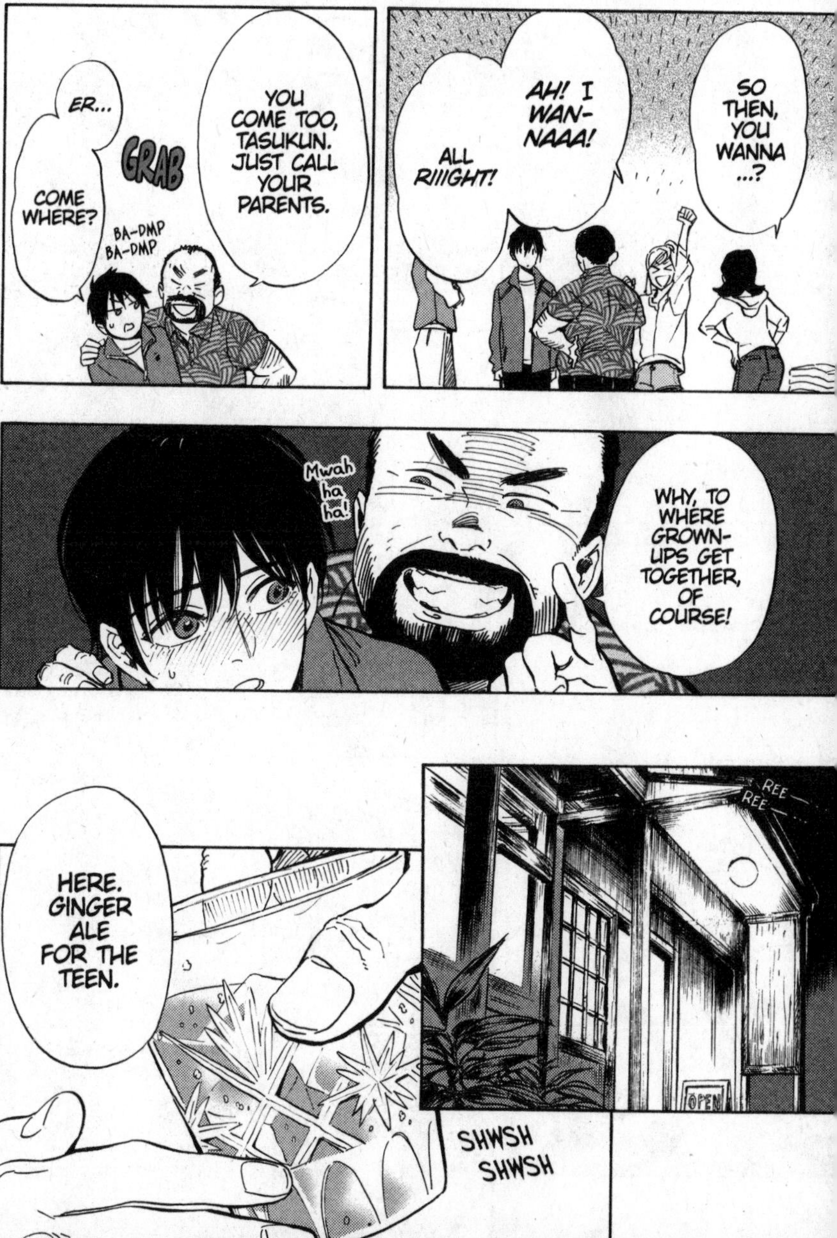
SO THEN, YOU WANNA ...?
AH! I WAN-NAAA!
ALL RIIIGHT!
YOU COME TOO, TASUKUN. JUST CALL YOUR PARENTS.
GRAB
ER...
COME WHERE?
BA-DMP BA-DMP
WHY, TO WHERE GROWN-UPS GET TOGETHER, OF COURSE!
Mwah ha ha!
REE REE
OPEN
HERE. GINGER ALE FOR THE TEEN.
SHWSH SHWSH

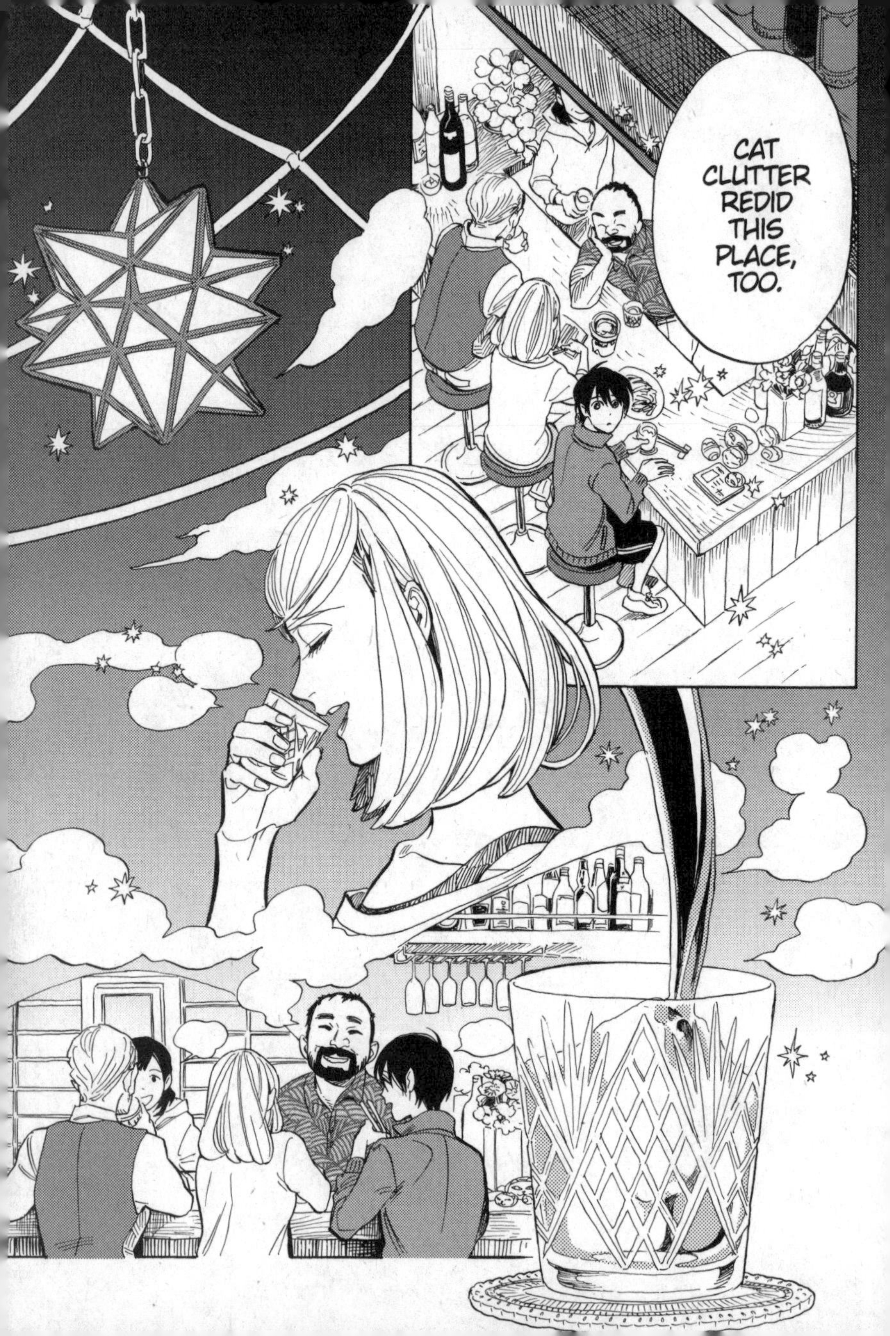
CAT CLUTTER REDID THIS PLACE, TOO.

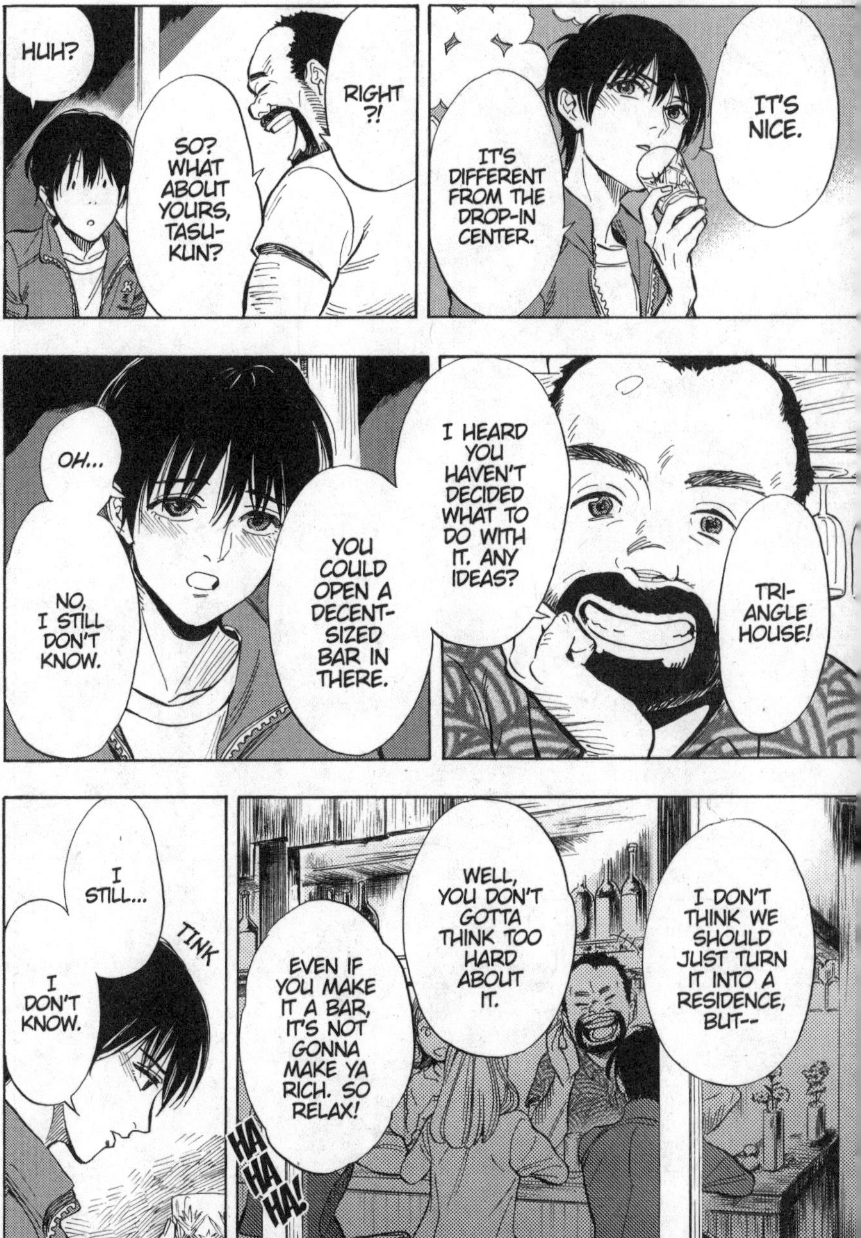
IT'S NICE.
IT'S DIFFERENT FROM THE DROP-IN CENTER.
RIGHT ?!
SO? WHAT ABOUT YOURS, TASU-KUN?
HUH?
TRI-ANGLE HOUSE!
I HEARD YOU HAVEN'T DECIDED WHAT TO DO WITH IT. ANY IDEAS?
YOU COULD OPEN A DECENT-SIZED BAR IN THERE.
OH...
NO, I STILL DON'T KNOW.
I DON'T THINK WE SHOULD JUST TURN IT INTO A RESIDENCE, BUT--
WELL, YOU DON'T GOTTA THINK TOO HARD ABOUT IT.
EVEN IF YOU MAKE IT A BAR, IT'S NOT GONNA MAKE YA RICH. SO RELAX!
HA HA HA!
I STILL...
TINK
I DON'T KNOW.

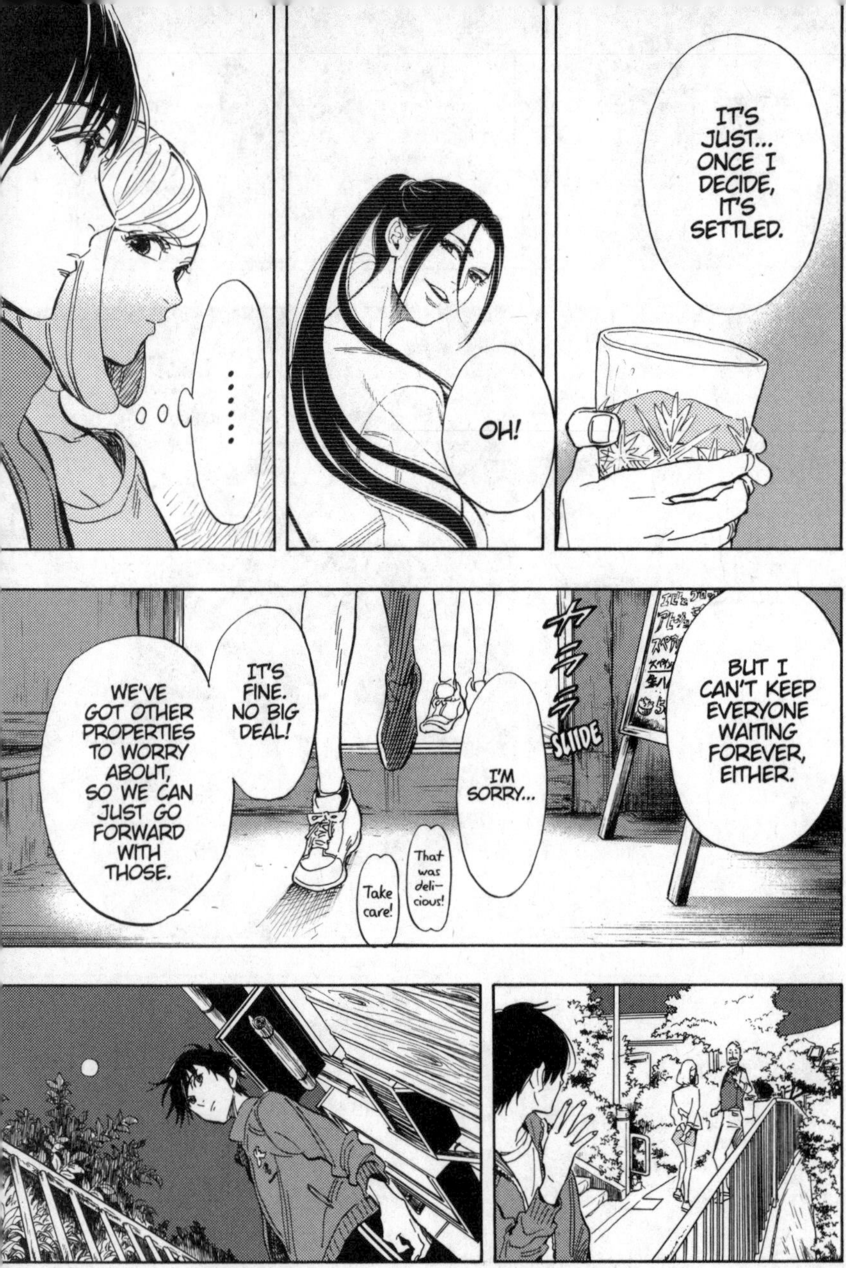
IT'S JUST... ONCE I DECIDE, IT'S SETTLED.
OH!
......
BUT I CAN'T KEEP EVERYONE WAITING FOREVER, EITHER.
SLIIDE
I'M SORRY...
That was deli-cious!
Take care!
IT'S FINE. NO BIG DEAL!
WE'VE GOT OTHER PROPERTIES TO WORRY ABOUT, SO WE CAN JUST GO FORWARD WITH THOSE.

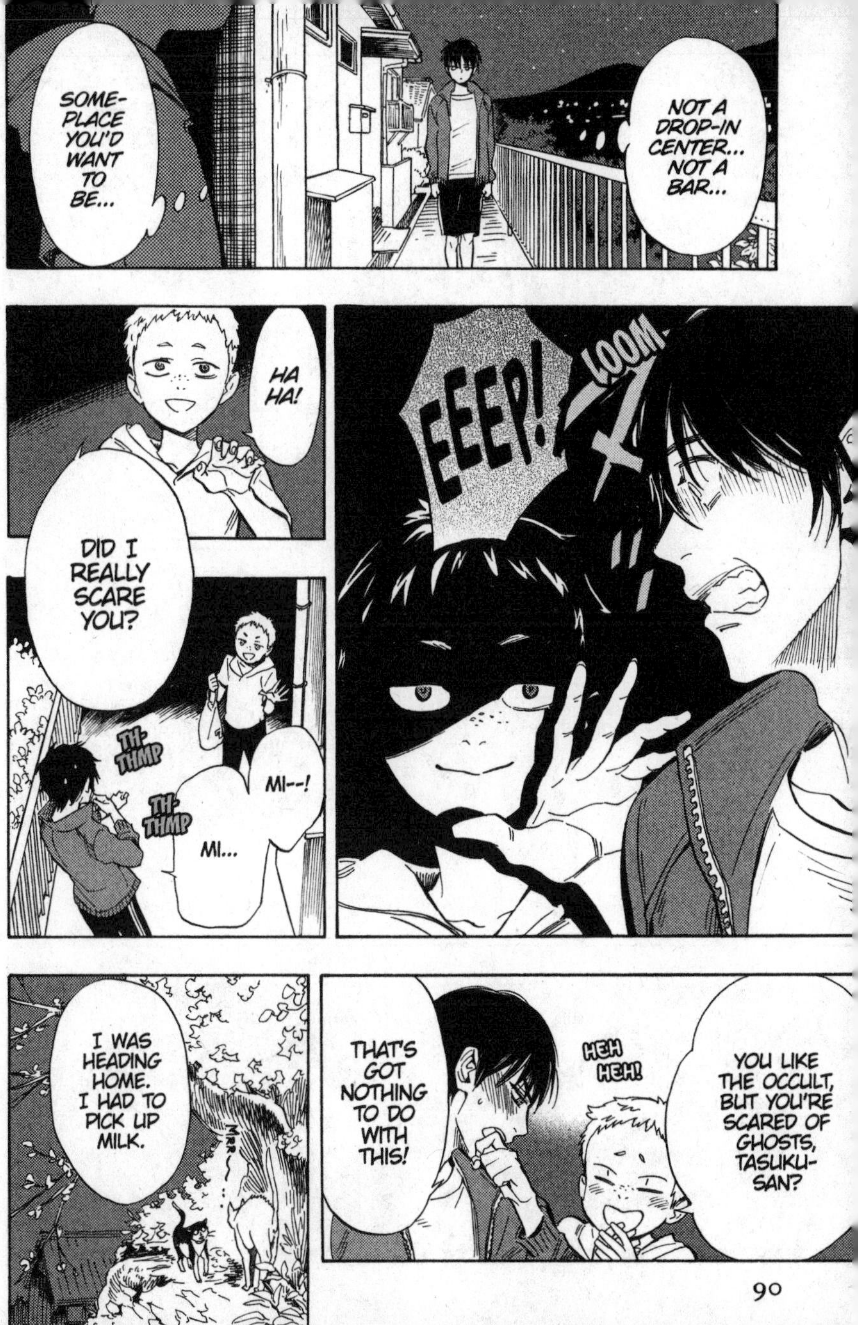
NOT A DROP-IN CENTER... NOT A BAR...
SOME-PLACE YOU'D WANT TO BE...
LOOM
EEEP!
HA HA!
DID I REALLY SCARE YOU?
MI--!
TH-THMP
TH-THMP
MI...
YOU LIKE THE OCCULT, BUT YOU'RE SCARED OF GHOSTS, TASUKU-SAN?
HEH HEH!
THAT'S GOT NOTHING TO DO WITH THIS!
I WAS HEADING HOME. I HAD TO PICK UP MILK.
MRR~

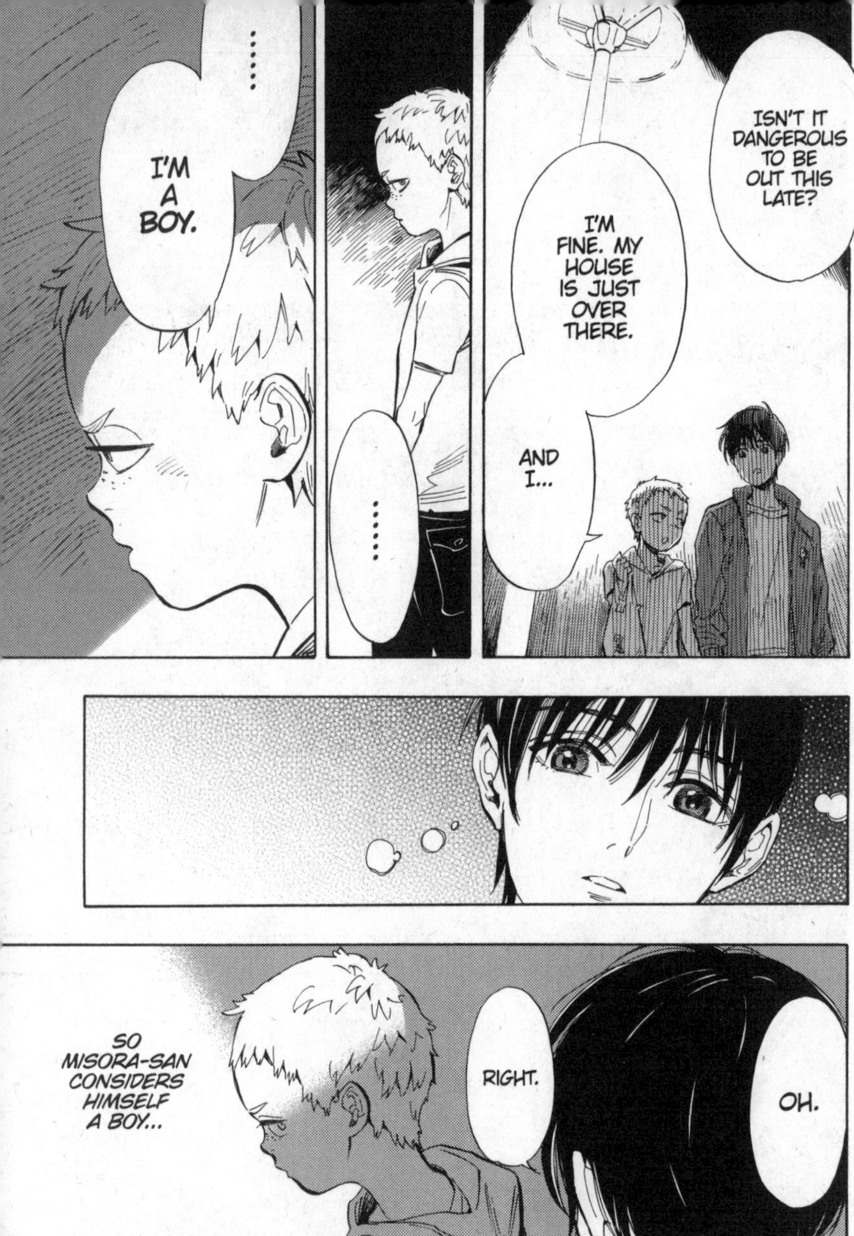
ISN'T IT DANGEROUS TO BE OUT THIS LATE?
I'M FINE. MY HOUSE IS JUST OVER THERE.
AND I...
......
......
I'M A BOY.
OH.
RIGHT.
SO MISORA-SAN CONSIDERS HIMSELF A BOY...

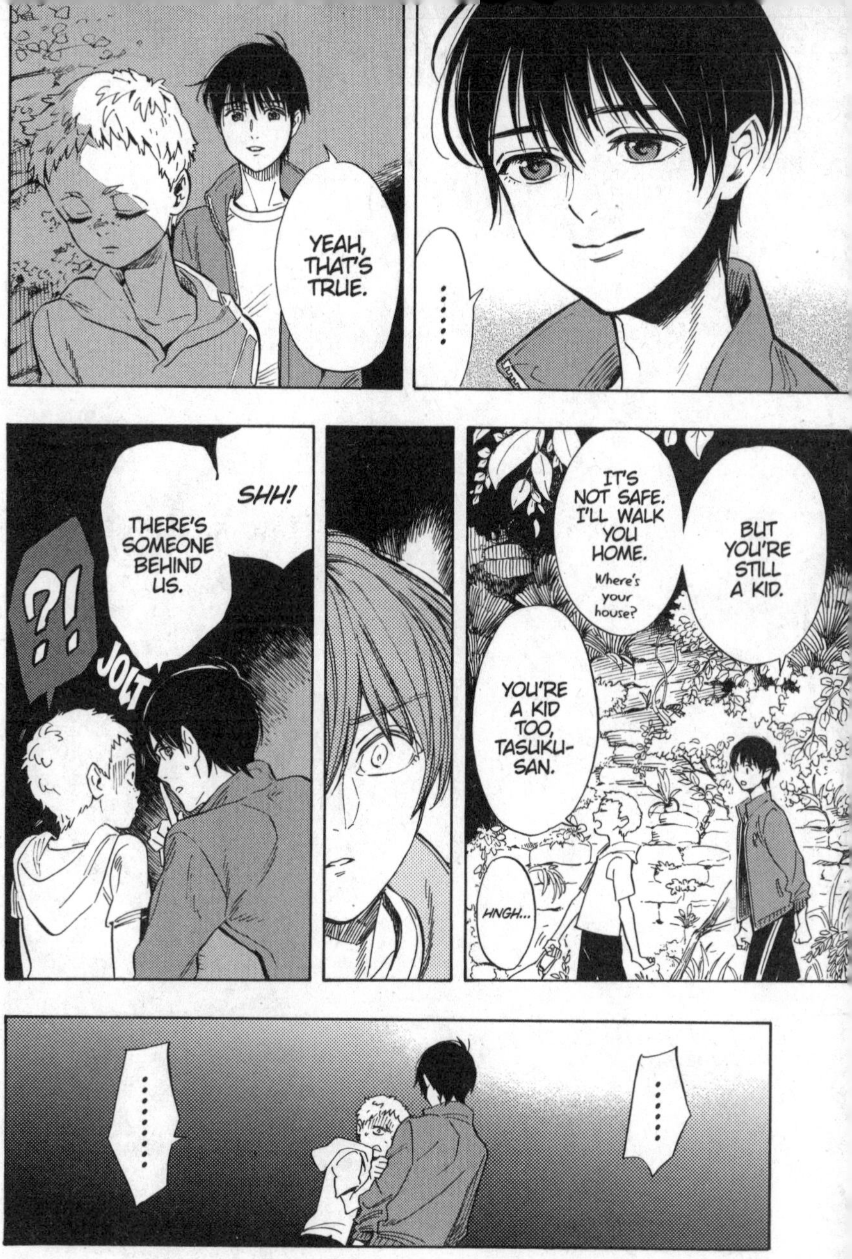
......
YEAH, THAT'S TRUE.
BUT YOU'RE STILL A KID.
IT'S NOT SAFE. I'LL WALK YOU HOME. Where's your house?
YOU'RE A KID TOO, TASUKU-SAN.
HNGH...
SHH! THERE'S SOMEONE BEHIND US.
?!
JOLT
......
......

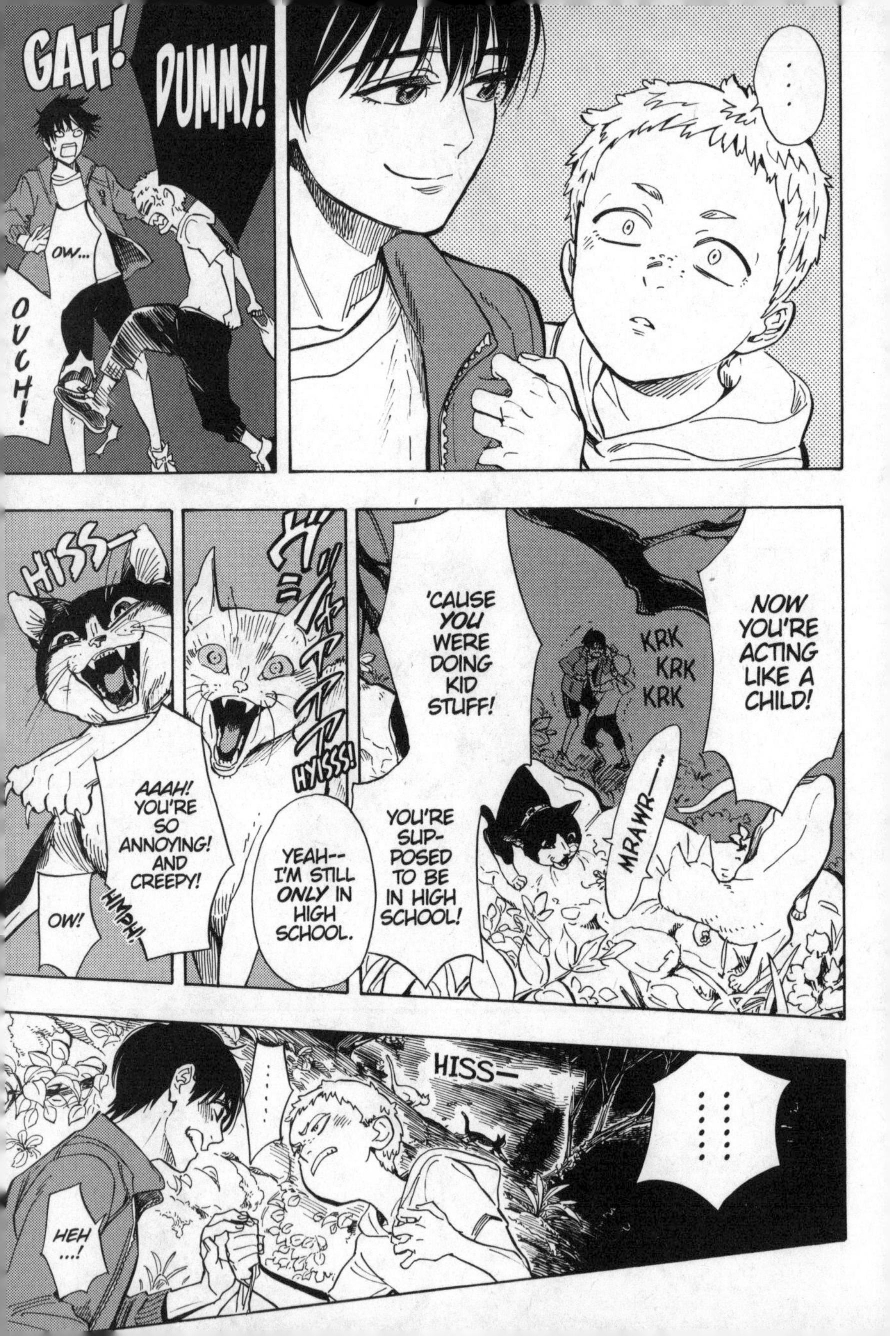
...
DUMMY!
GAH!
OW...
OUCH!
NOW YOU'RE ACTING LIKE A CHILD!
KRK KRK KRK
'CAUSE *YOU* WERE DOING KID STUFF!
MRAWR——
YOU'RE SUP-POSED TO BE IN HIGH SCHOOL!
YEAH-- I'M STILL *ONLY* IN HIGH SCHOOL.
HYISSS!
HISS—
AAAH! YOU'RE SO ANNOYING! AND CREEPY!
HMPH!
OW!
......
HISS—
...
HEH ...!

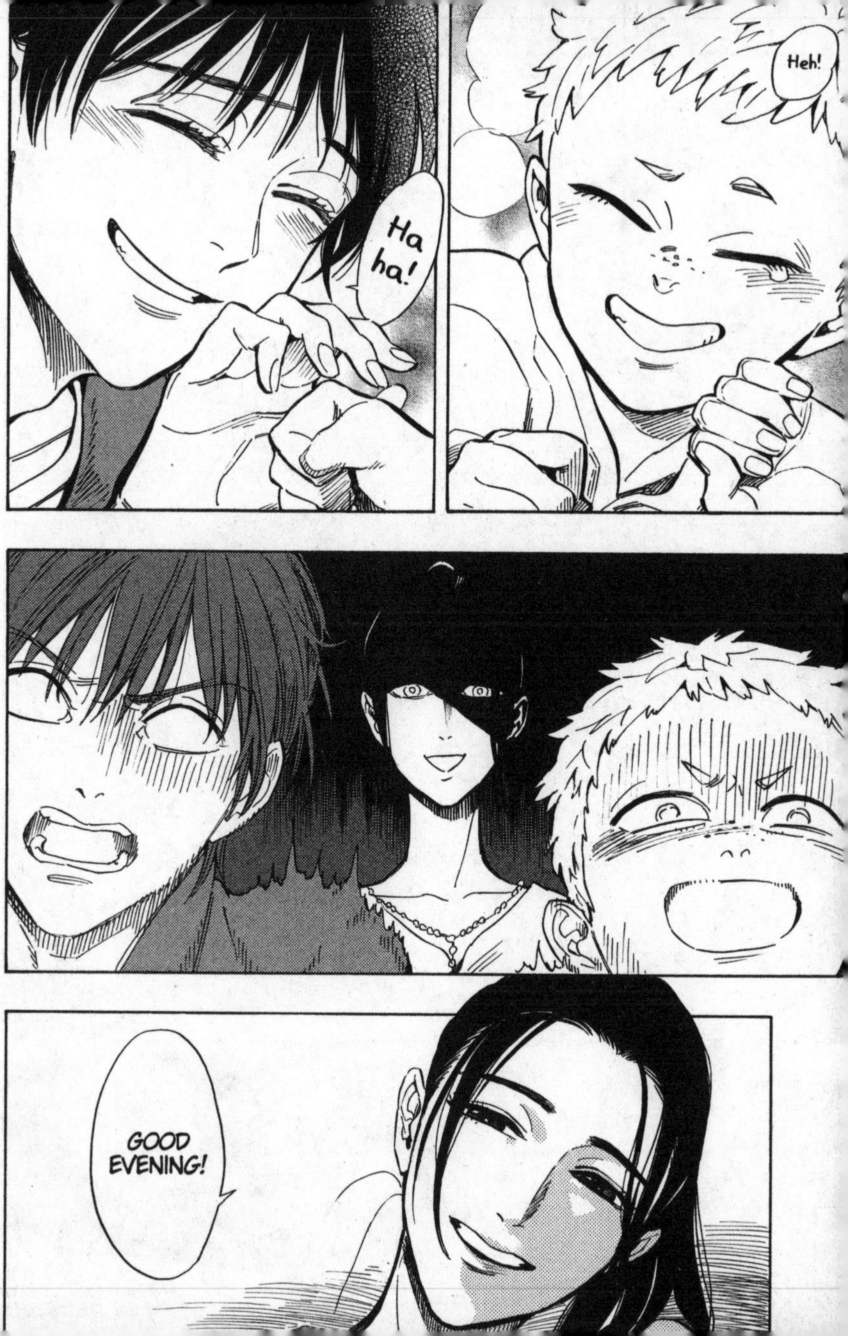
Heh!
Ha ha!
GOOD EVENING!

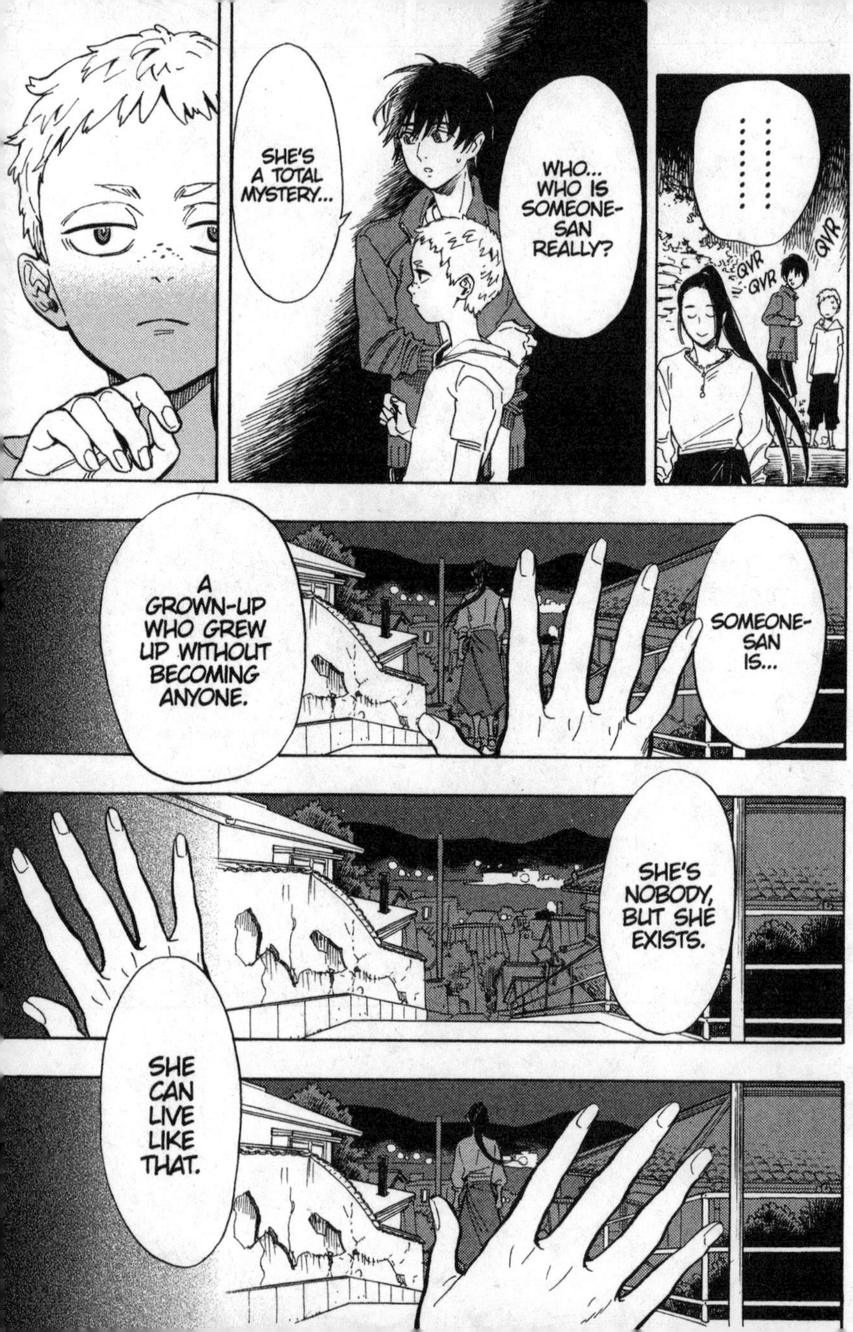
......
QVR
QVR
QVR
WHO... WHO IS SOMEONE-SAN REALLY?
SHE'S A TOTAL MYSTERY...
SOMEONE-SAN IS...
A GROWN-UP WHO GREW UP WITHOUT BECOMING ANYONE.
SHE'S NOBODY, BUT SHE EXISTS.
SHE CAN LIVE LIKE THAT.

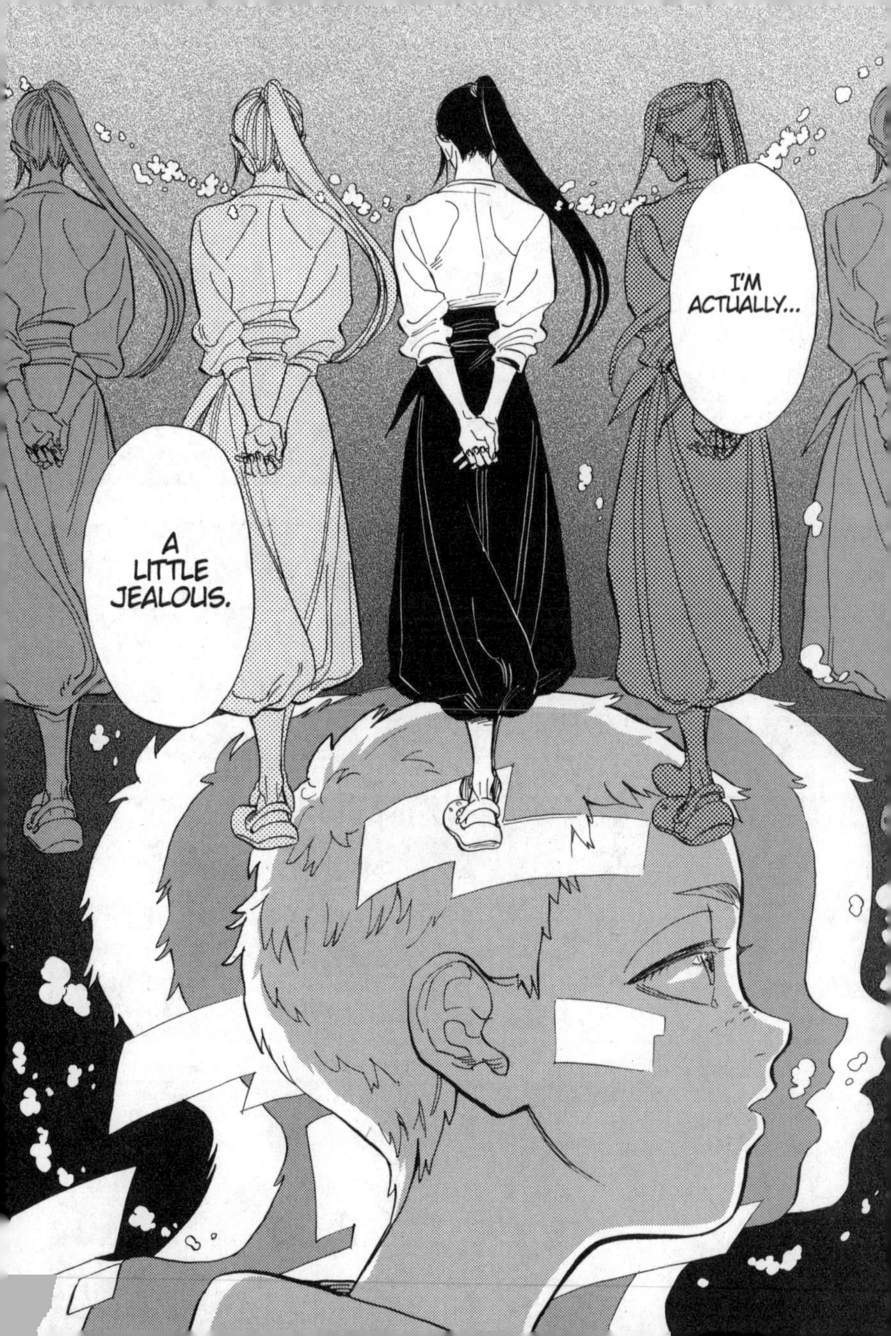
I'M ACTUALLY...
A LITTLE JEALOUS.

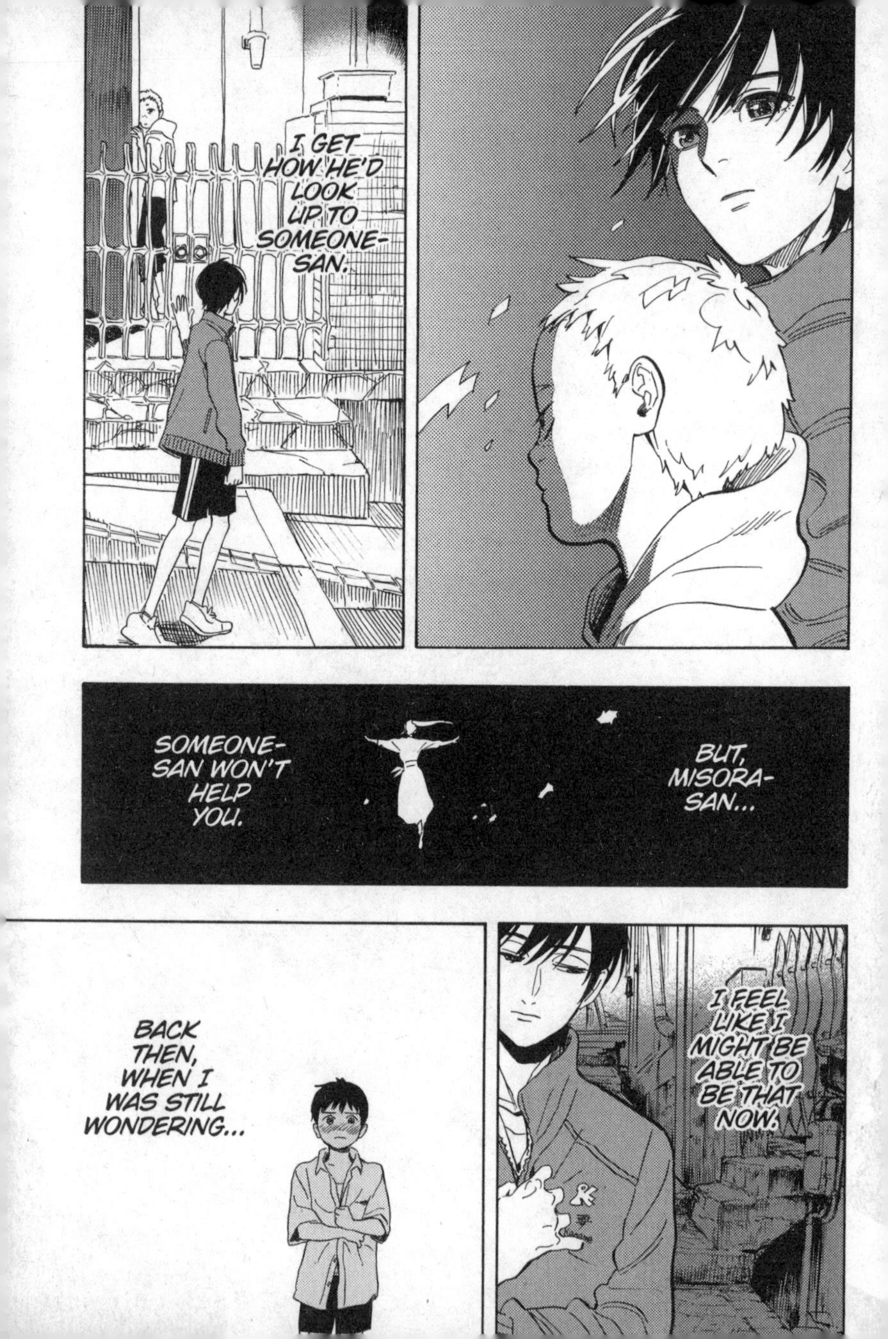
I GET HOW HE'D LOOK UP TO SOMEONE-SAN.
BUT, MISORA-SAN...
SOMEONE-SAN WON'T HELP YOU.
I FEEL LIKE I MIGHT BE ABLE TO BE THAT NOW.
BACK THEN, WHEN I WAS STILL WONDERING...

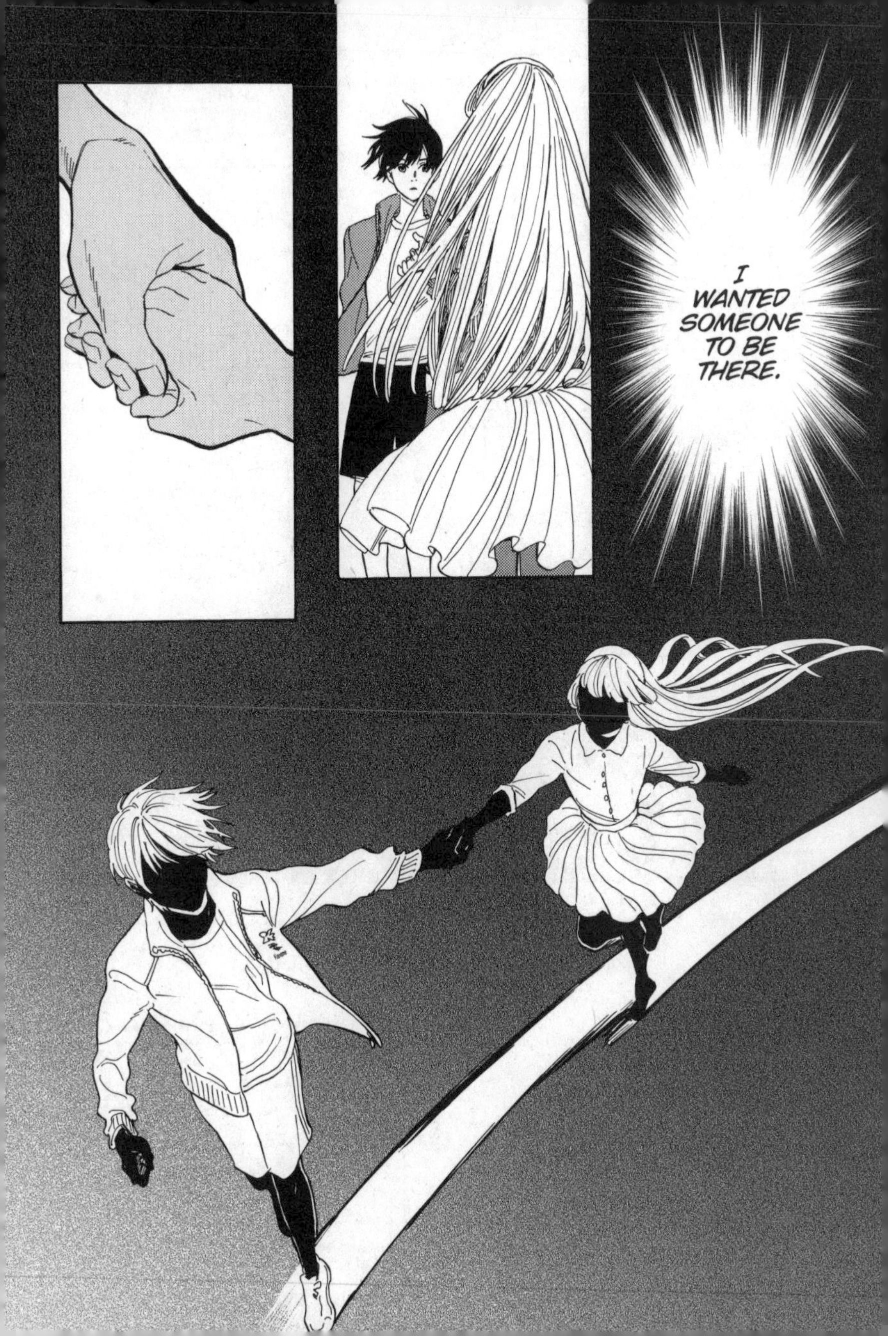
I WANTED SOMEONE TO BE THERE.

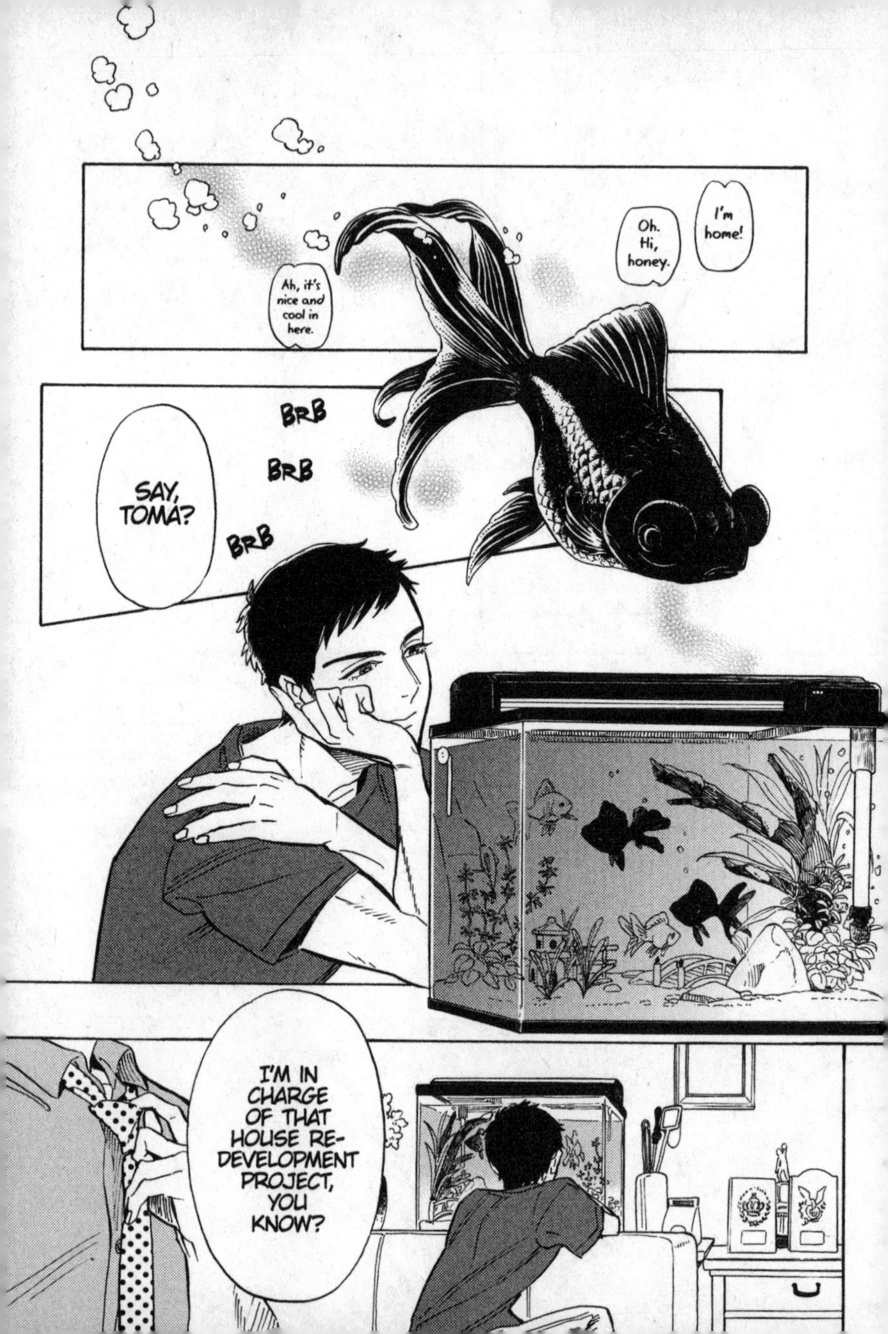
I'm home!
Oh. Hi, honey.
Ah, it's nice and cool in here.
BRB
BRB
BRB
SAY, TOMA?
I'M IN CHARGE OF THAT HOUSE RE-DEVELOPMENT PROJECT, YOU KNOW?

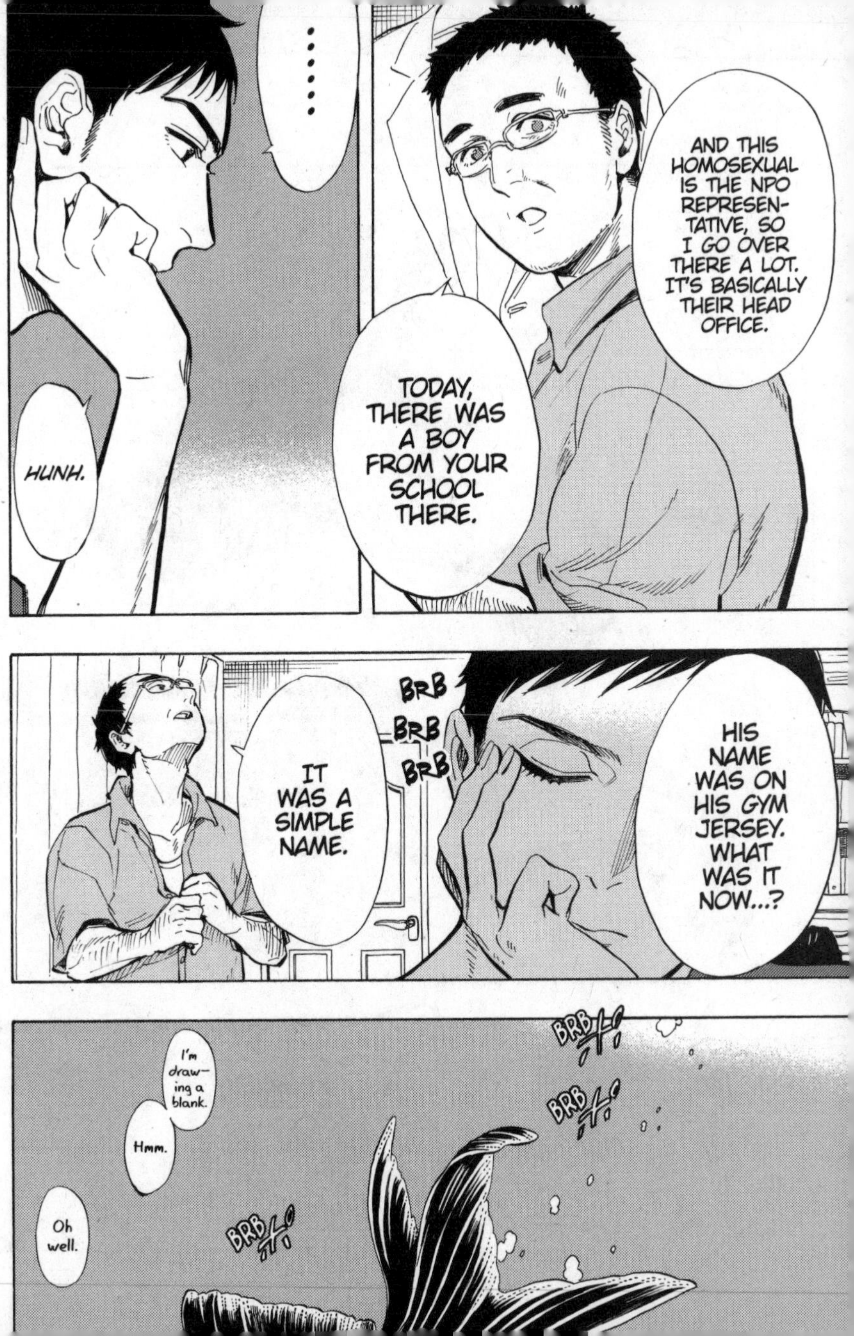
AND THIS HOMOSEXUAL IS THE NPO REPRESEN-TATIVE, SO I GO OVER THERE A LOT. IT'S BASICALLY THEIR HEAD OFFICE.
TODAY, THERE WAS A BOY FROM YOUR SCHOOL THERE.
......
HUNH.
HIS NAME WAS ON HIS GYM JERSEY. WHAT WAS IT NOW...?
BRB BRB BRB
IT WAS A SIMPLE NAME.
BRB
BRB
I'm draw-ing a blank.
Hmm.
Oh well.
BRB

Our Dreams at Dusk

SHIMANAMI TASOGARE

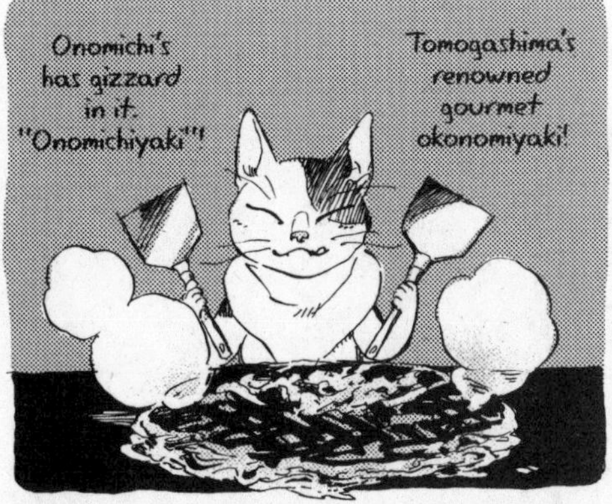
Tomogashima's renowned gourmet okonomiyaki!
Onomichi's has gizzard in it. "Onomichiyaki"!

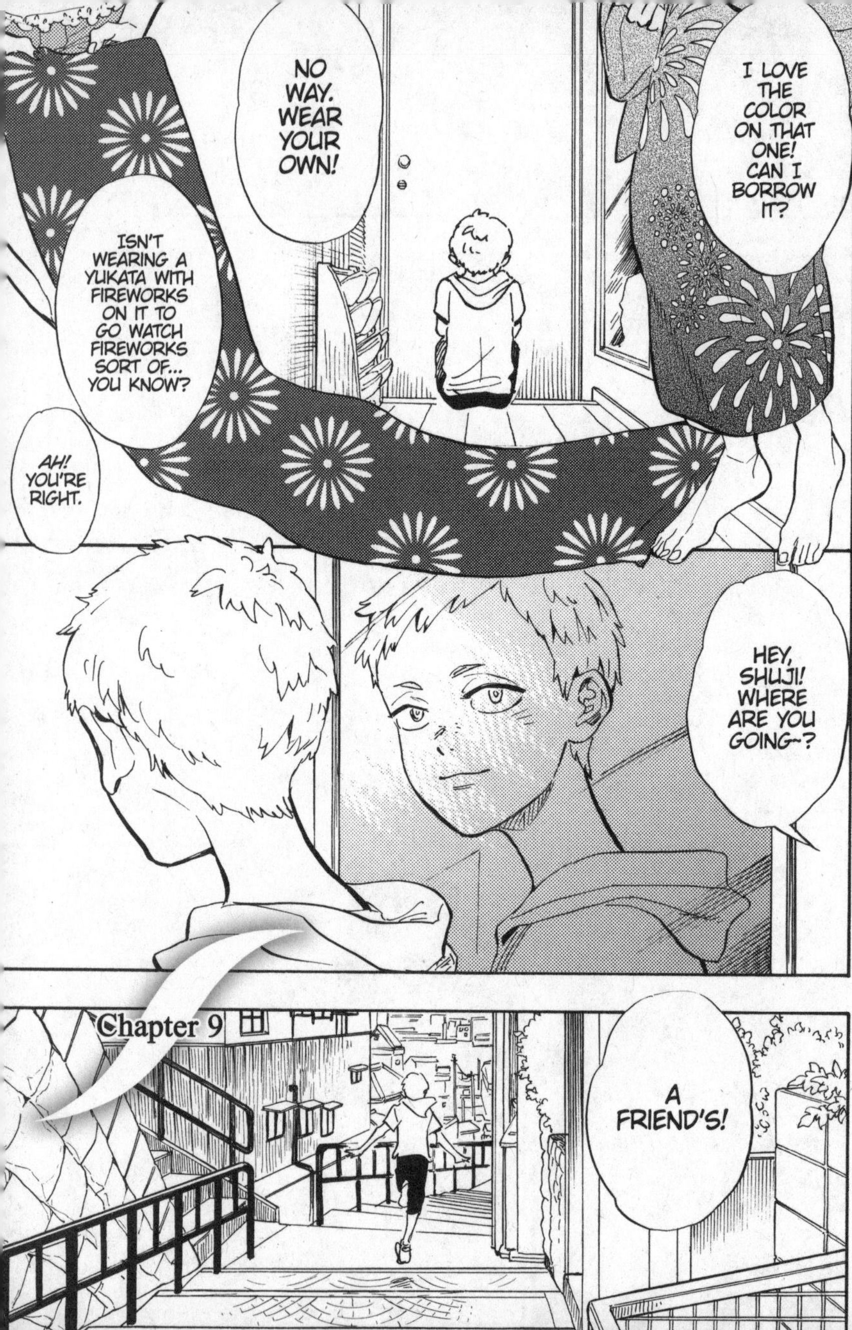
I LOVE THE COLOR ON THAT ONE! CAN I BORROW IT?
NO WAY. WEAR YOUR OWN!
ISN'T WEARING A YUKATA WITH FIREWORKS ON IT TO GO WATCH FIREWORKS SORT OF... YOU KNOW?
AH! YOU'RE RIGHT.
HEY, SHUJI! WHERE ARE YOU GOING~?
A FRIEND'S!
Chapter 9

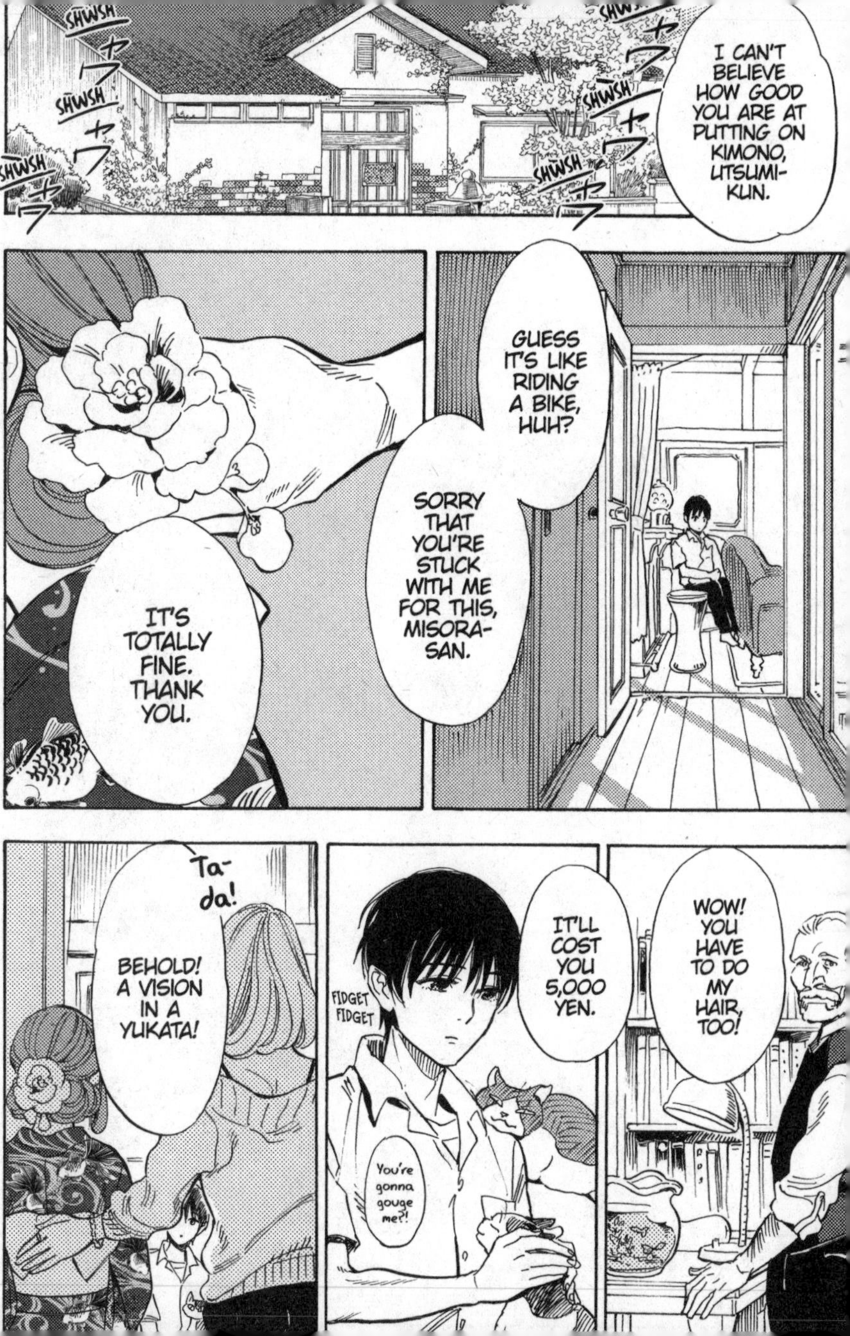
SHWSH
SHWSH
SHWSH
SHWSH
SHWSH
SHWSH
I CAN'T BELIEVE HOW GOOD YOU ARE AT PUTTING ON KIMONO, UTSUMI-KUN.
GUESS IT'S LIKE RIDING A BIKE, HUH?
SORRY THAT YOU'RE STUCK WITH ME FOR THIS, MISORA-SAN.
IT'S TOTALLY FINE. THANK YOU.
WOW! YOU HAVE TO DO MY HAIR, TOO!
IT'LL COST YOU 5,000 YEN.
FIDGET FIDGET
You're gonna gouge me?!
Ta-da!
BEHOLD! A VISION IN A YUKATA!

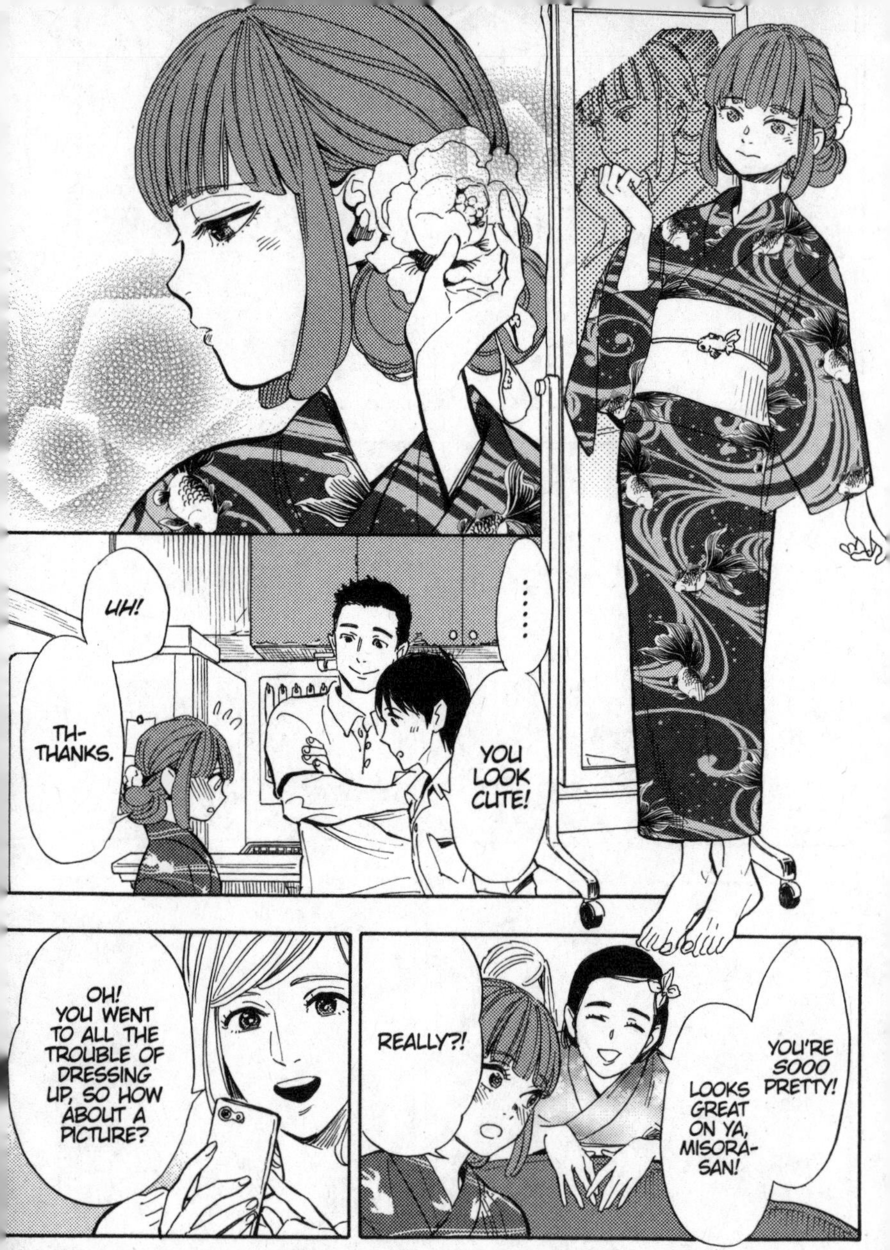
......
YOU LOOK CUTE!
UH!
TH-THANKS.
YOU'RE SOOO PRETTY!
LOOKS GREAT ON YA, MISORA-SAN!
REALLY?!
OH! YOU WENT TO ALL THE TROUBLE OF DRESSING UP, SO HOW ABOUT A PICTURE?

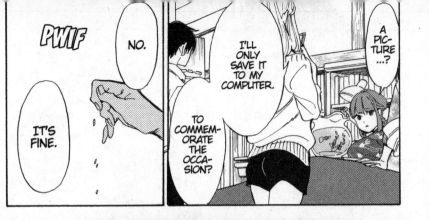

PWIF

NO.

IT'S FINE.

I'LL ONLY SAVE IT TO MY COMPUTER.

TO COMMEMORATE THE OCCASION?

A PICTURE...?

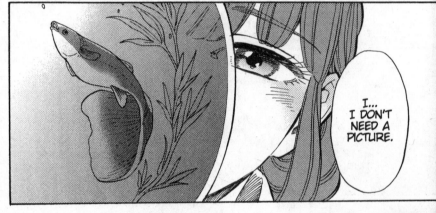

I... I DON'T NEED A PICTURE.

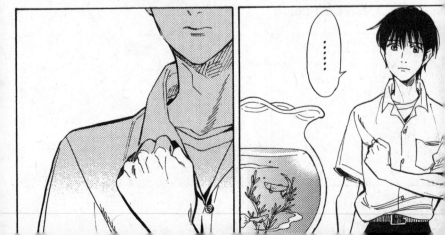

......

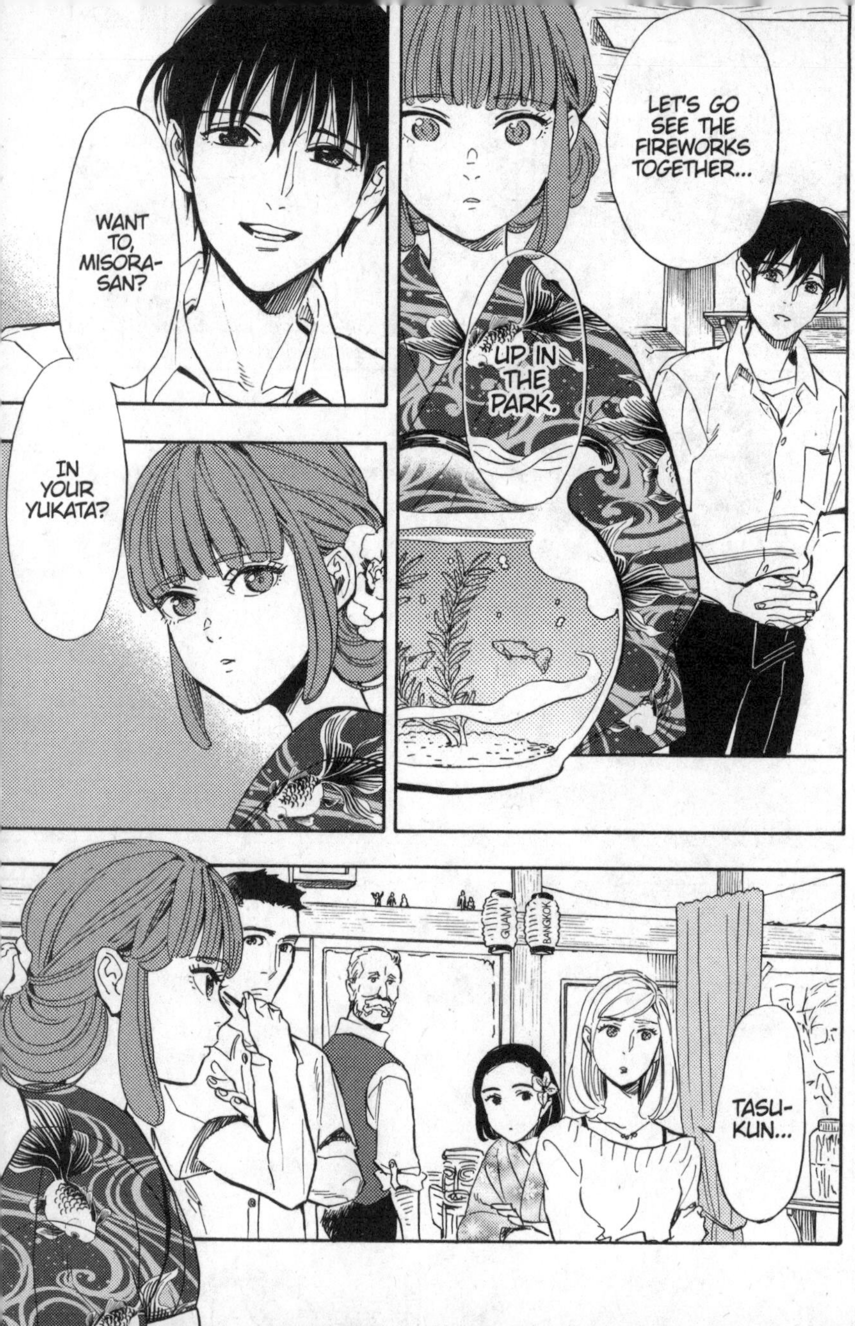
LET'S GO SEE THE FIREWORKS TOGETHER...
UP IN THE PARK.
WANT TO, MISORA-SAN?
IN YOUR YUKATA?
GUAM
BANGKOK
TASU-KUN...

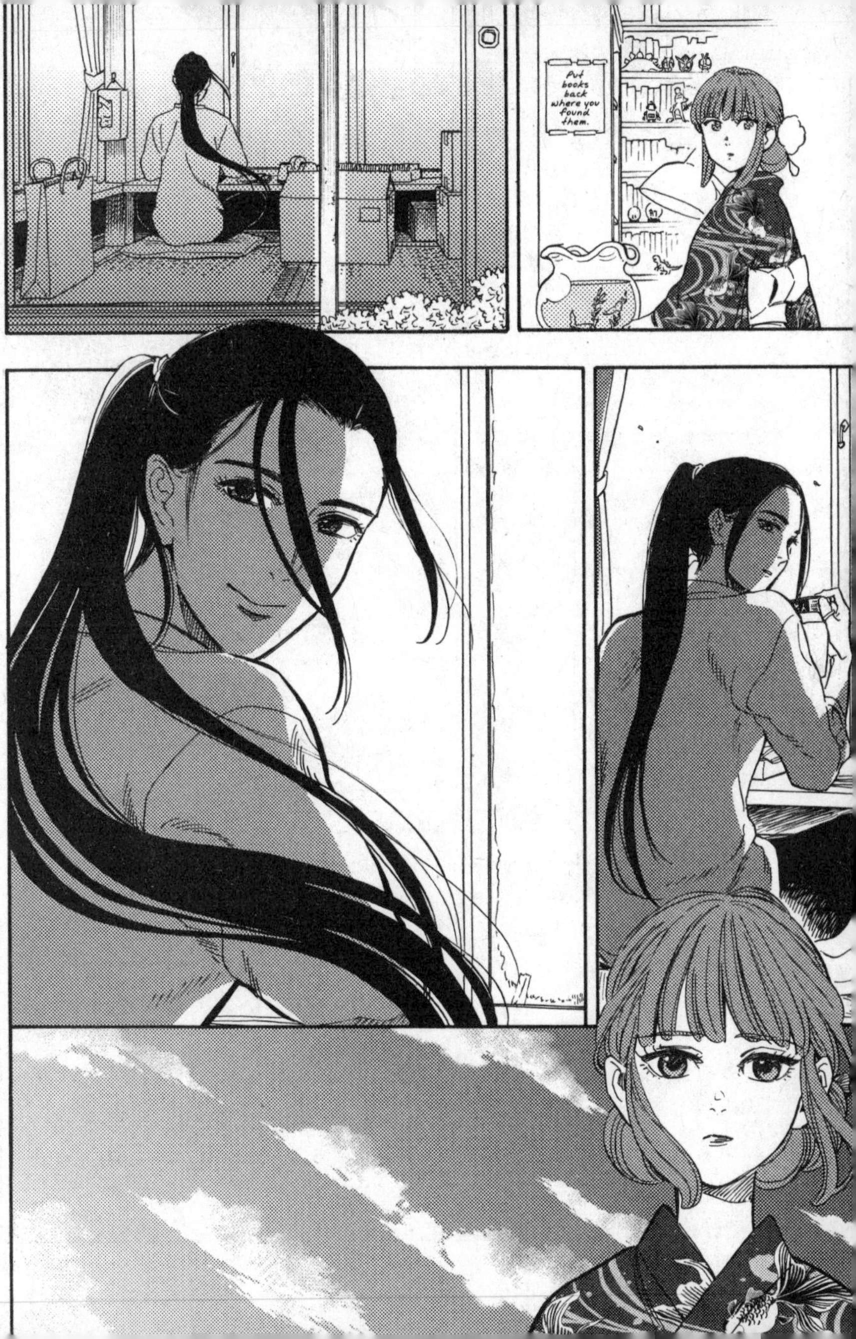
Put books back where you found them.

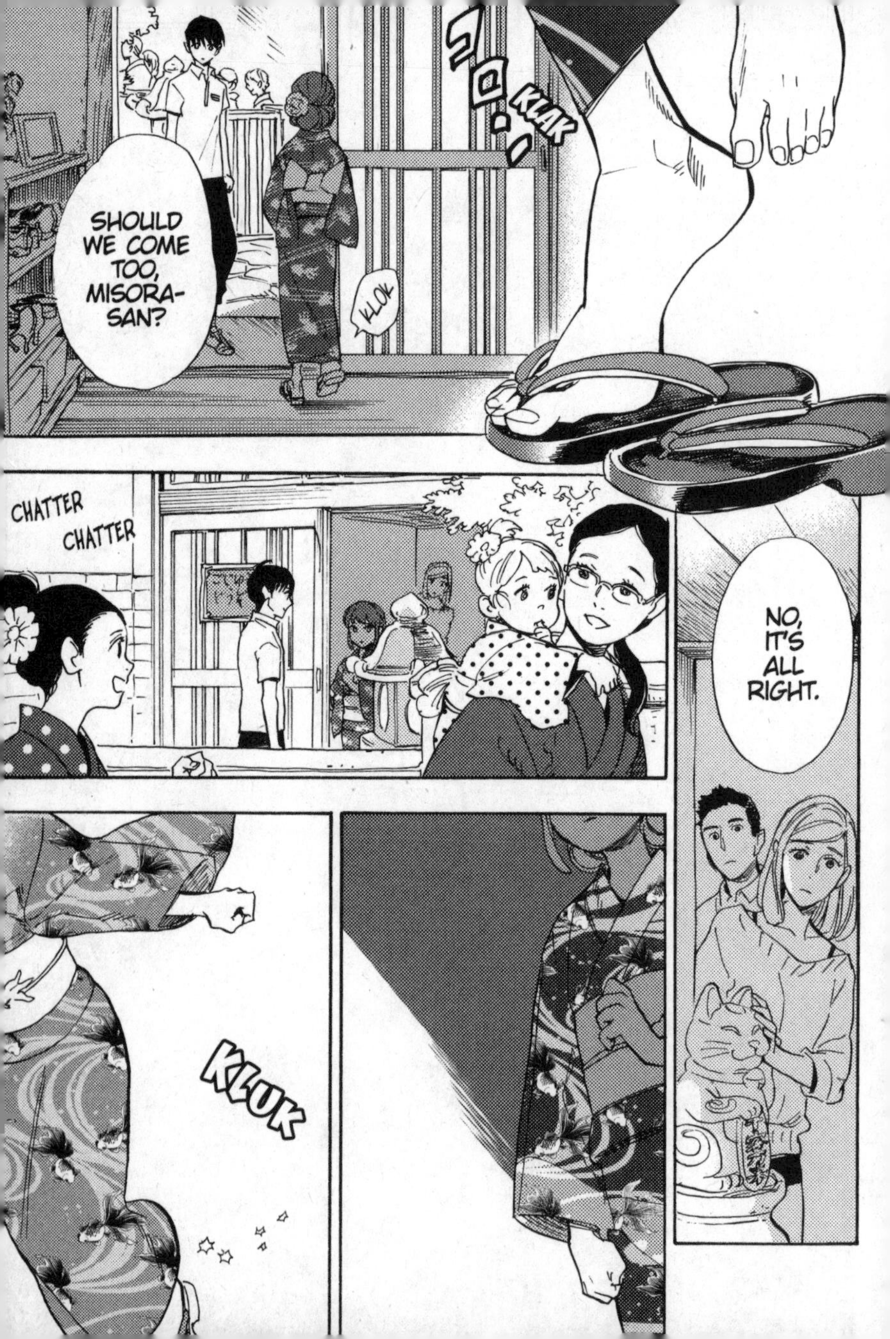

コロ
KLAK
SHOULD WE COME TOO, MISORA-SAN?
KLOK
NO, IT'S ALL RIGHT.
CHATTER CHATTER
KLUK

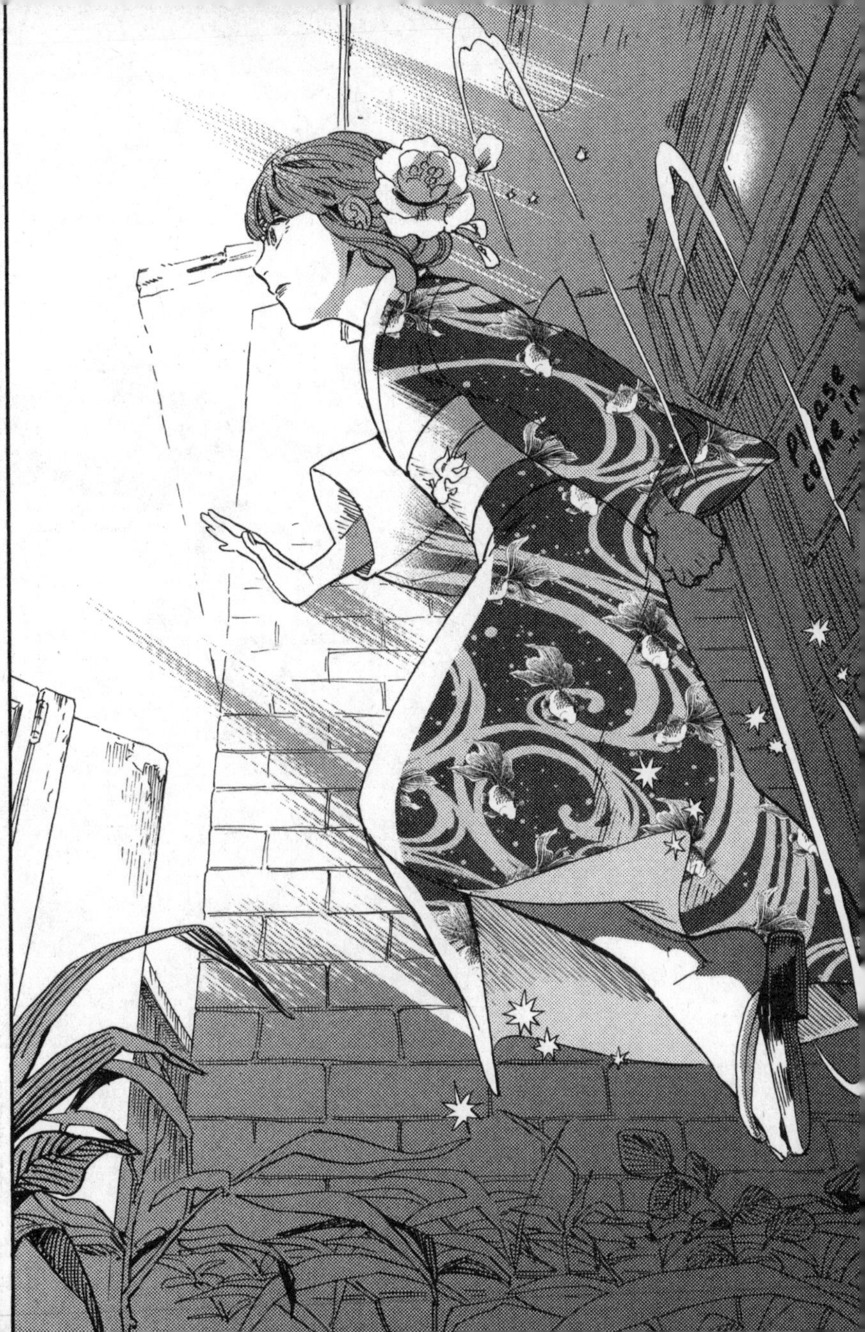
Please come in

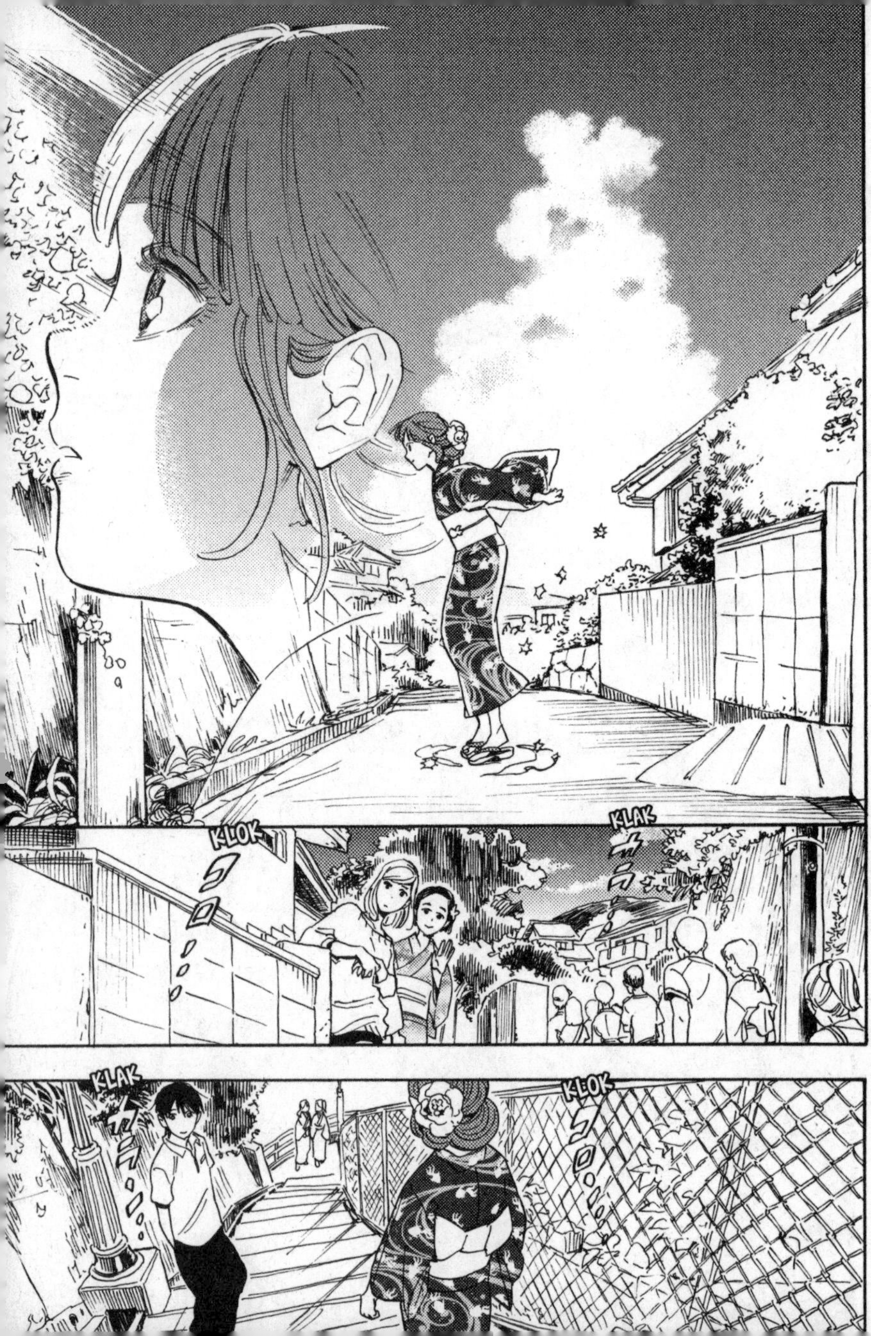
KLAK
KLOK
KLOK
KLAK

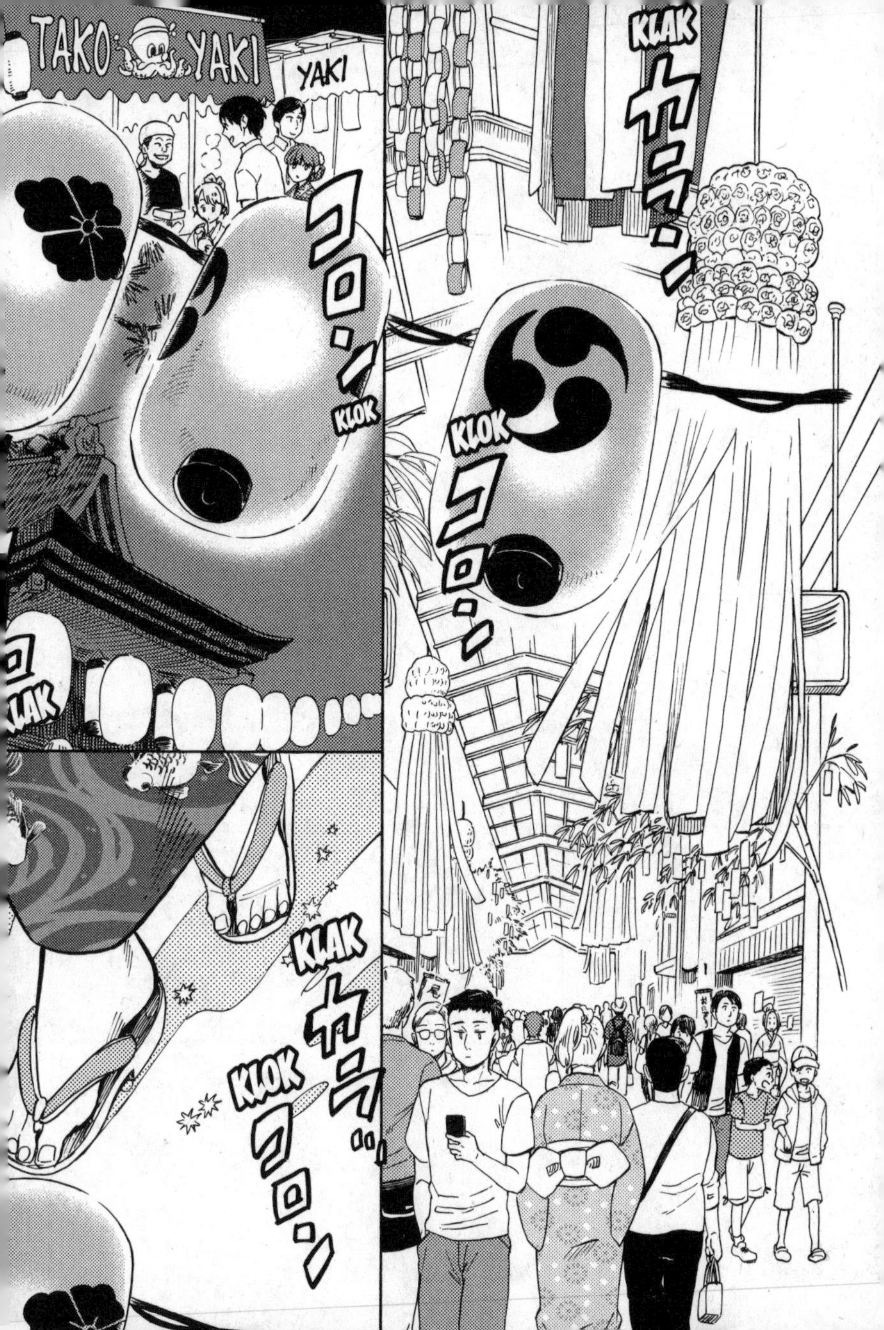
KLAK
カラ
KLOK
コロ
TAKO YAKI
YAKI
コロン
KLOK
KLAK
KLAK
カラ
KLOK
コロン

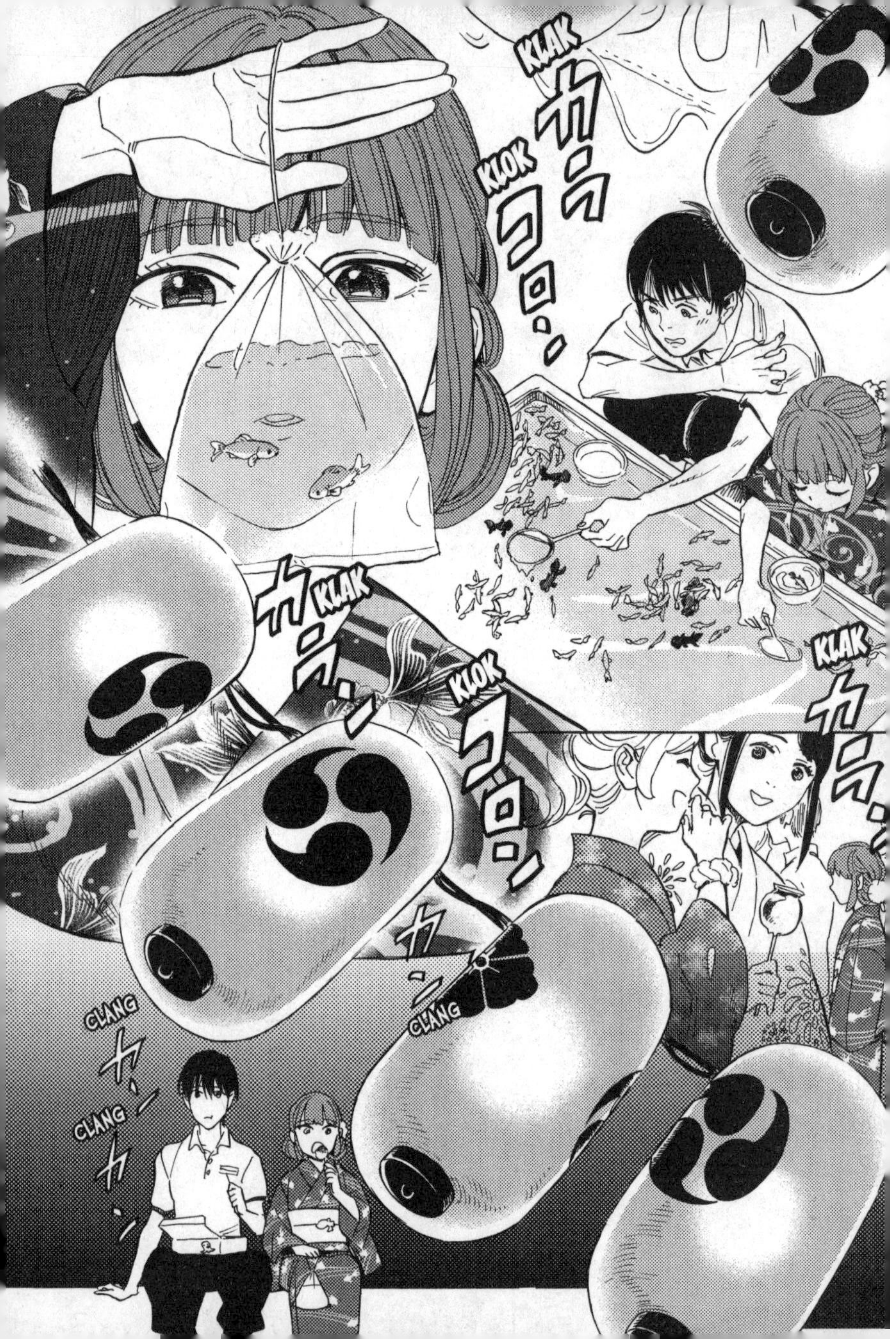
KLAK
KLOK
KLAK
KLOK
KLAK
CLANG
CLANG
CLANG

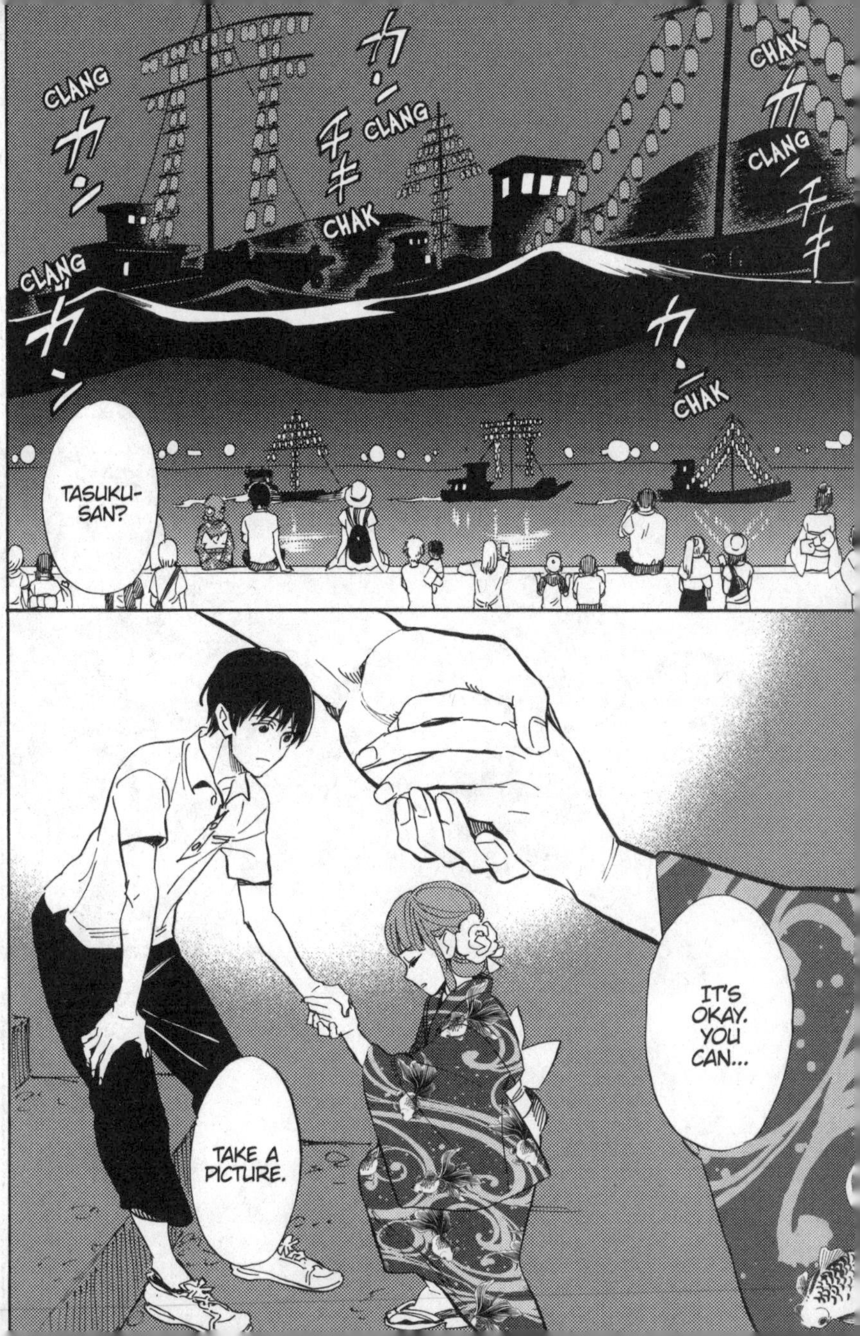
CHAK
カ
CLANG
チキ
CLANG
カン
チキ
CLANG
CHAK
CLANG
カン
カ
CHAK
TASUKU-SAN?
IT'S OKAY. YOU CAN...
TAKE A PICTURE.

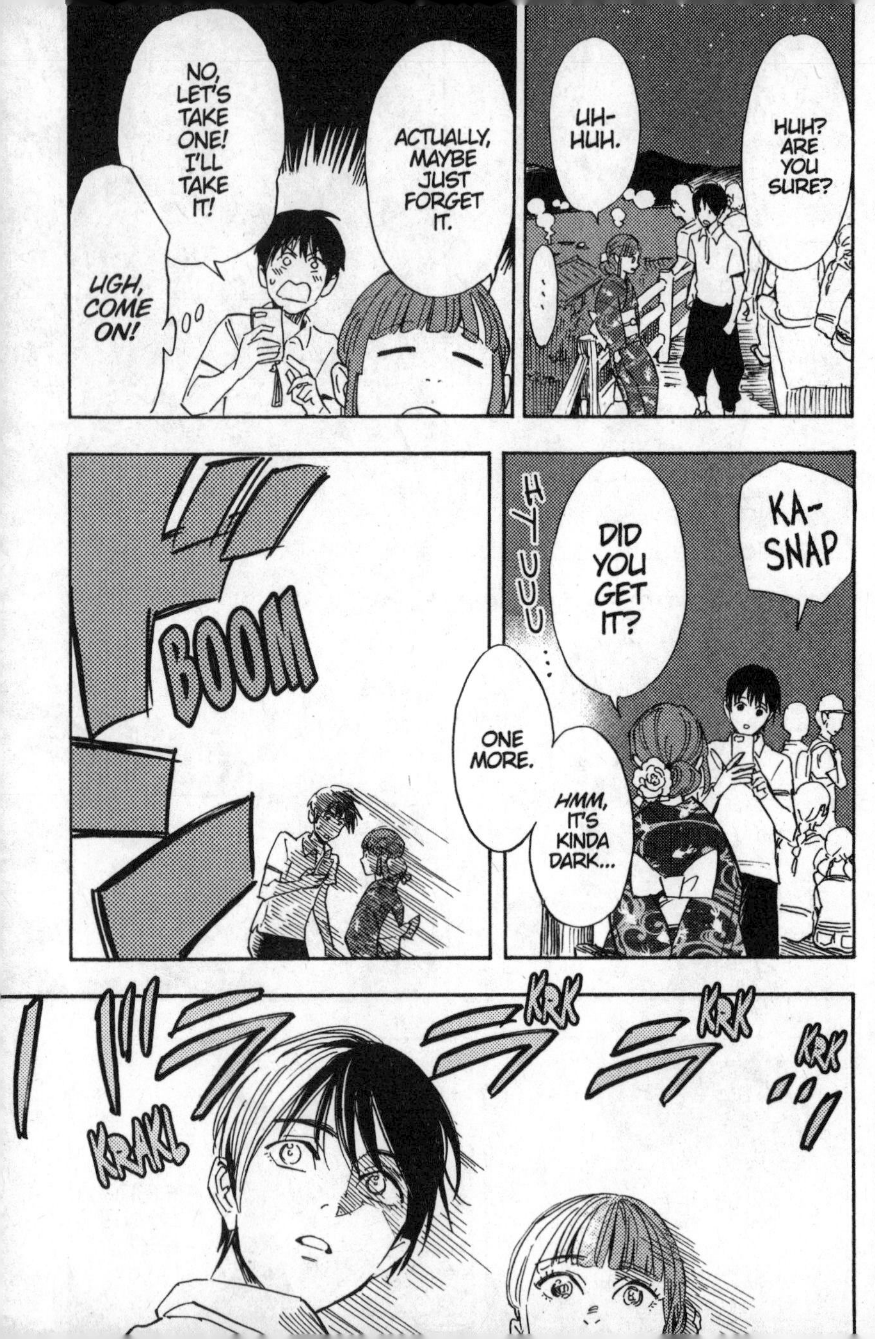
HUH? ARE YOU SURE?
UH-HUH.
...
ACTUALLY, MAYBE JUST FORGET IT.
NO, LET'S TAKE ONE! I'LL TAKE IT!
UGH, COME ON!
KA-SNAP
DID YOU GET IT?
ONE MORE.
HMM, IT'S KINDA DARK...
BOOM
KRK
KRK
KRK
KRAKL

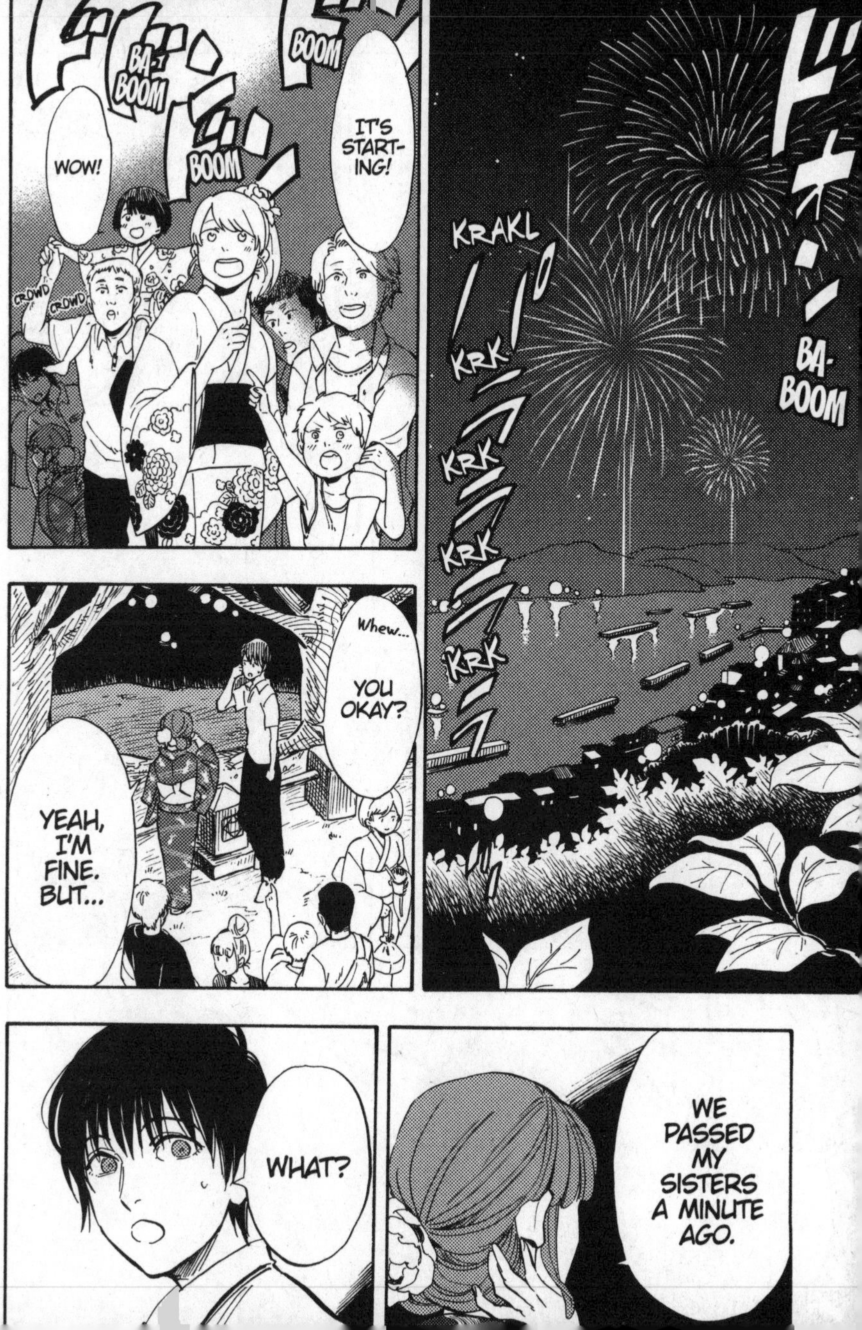
BA-BOOM
KRAKL
KRK
KRK
KRK
KRK
BOOM
IT'S STARTING!
BA-BOOM
BOOM
WOW!
CROWD
CROWD
Whew...
YOU OKAY?
YEAH, I'M FINE. BUT...
WE PASSED MY SISTERS A MINUTE AGO.
WHAT?

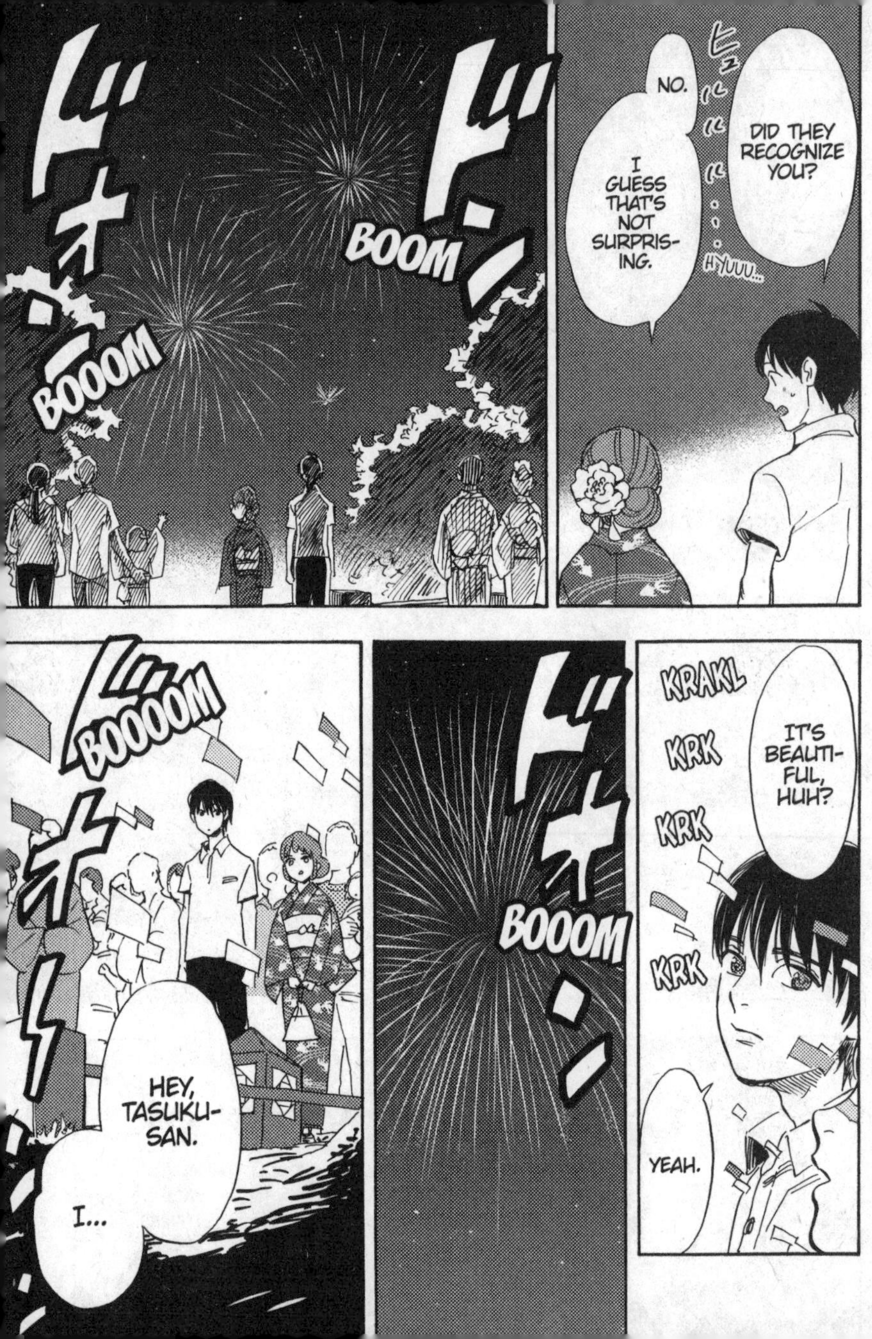
DID THEY RECOGNIZE YOU?
HYUUU...
NO.
I GUESS THAT'S NOT SURPRISING.
BOOM
BOOOM
KRAKL
KRK
KRK
KRK
IT'S BEAUTIFUL, HUH?
YEAH.
BOOOM
BOOOOM
HEY, TASUKU-SAN.
I...

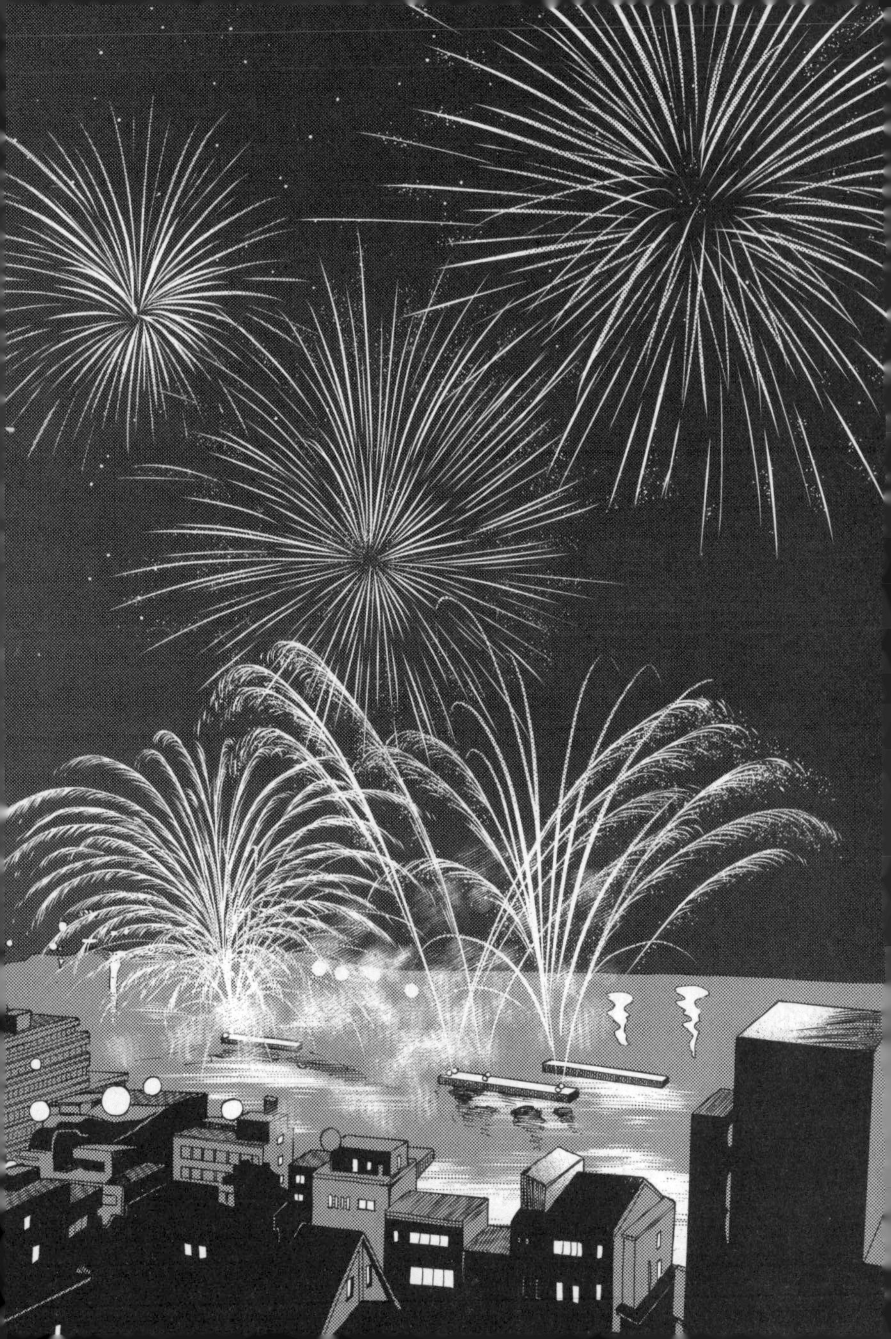

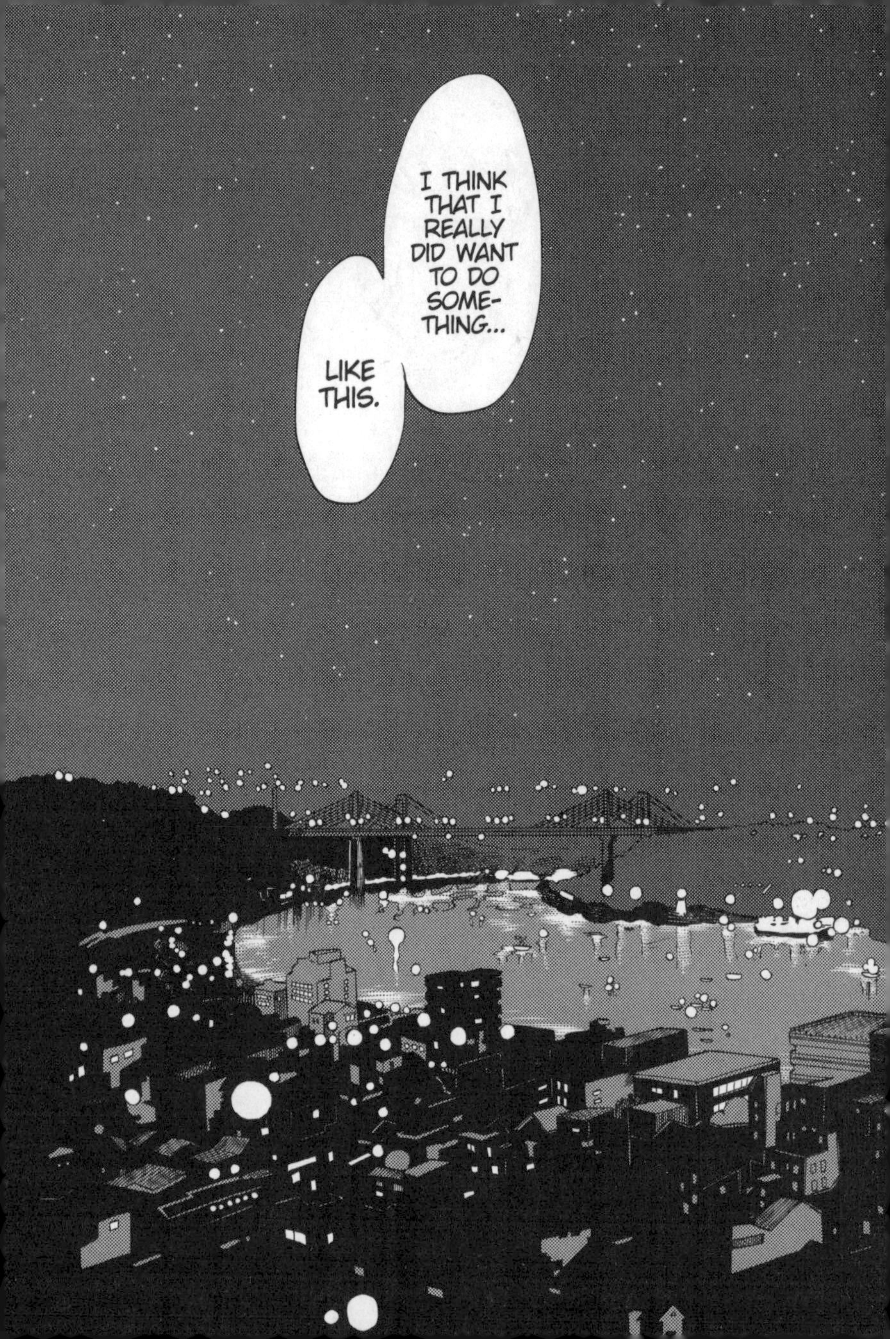
I THINK THAT I REALLY DID WANT TO DO SOME-THING...
LIKE THIS.

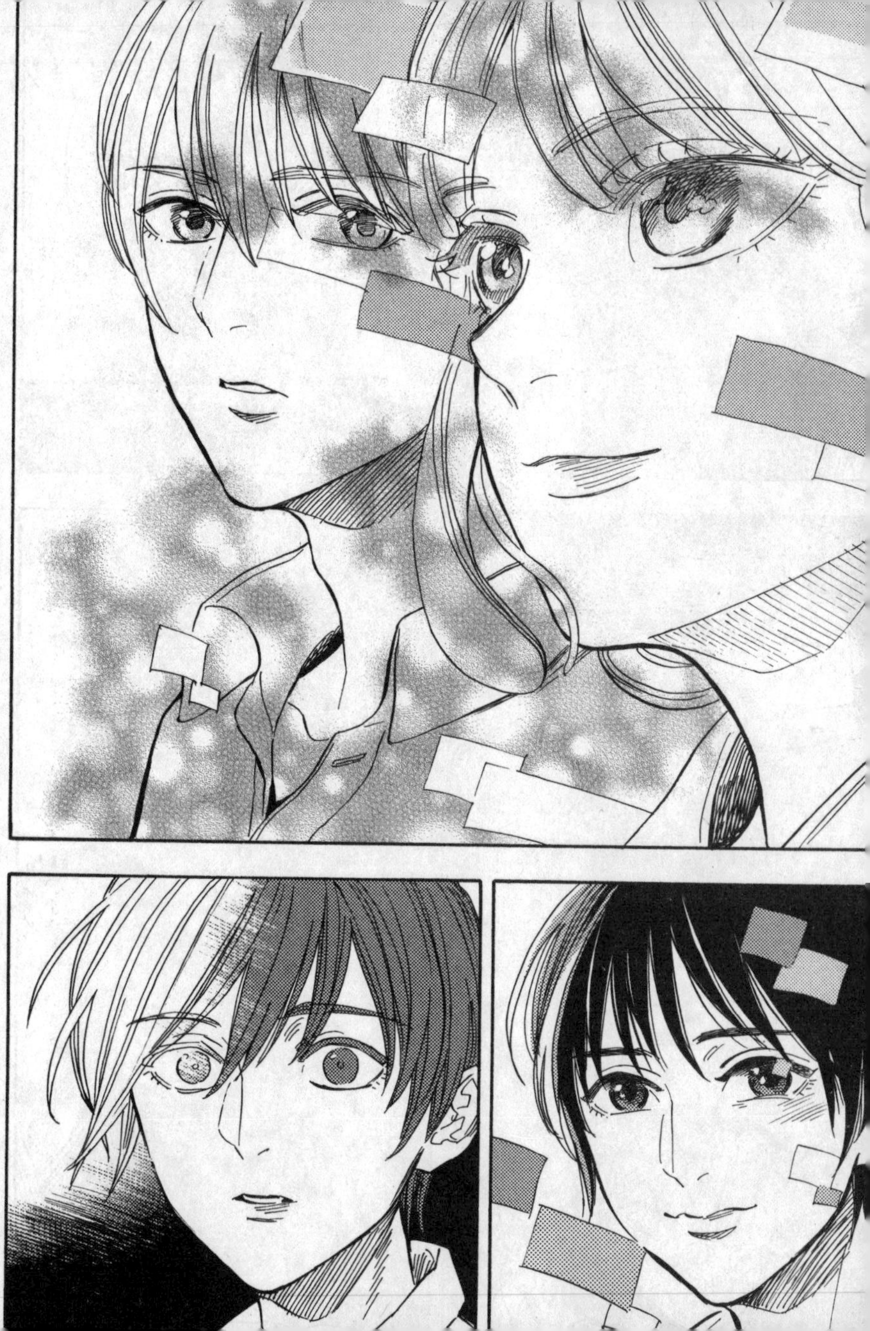

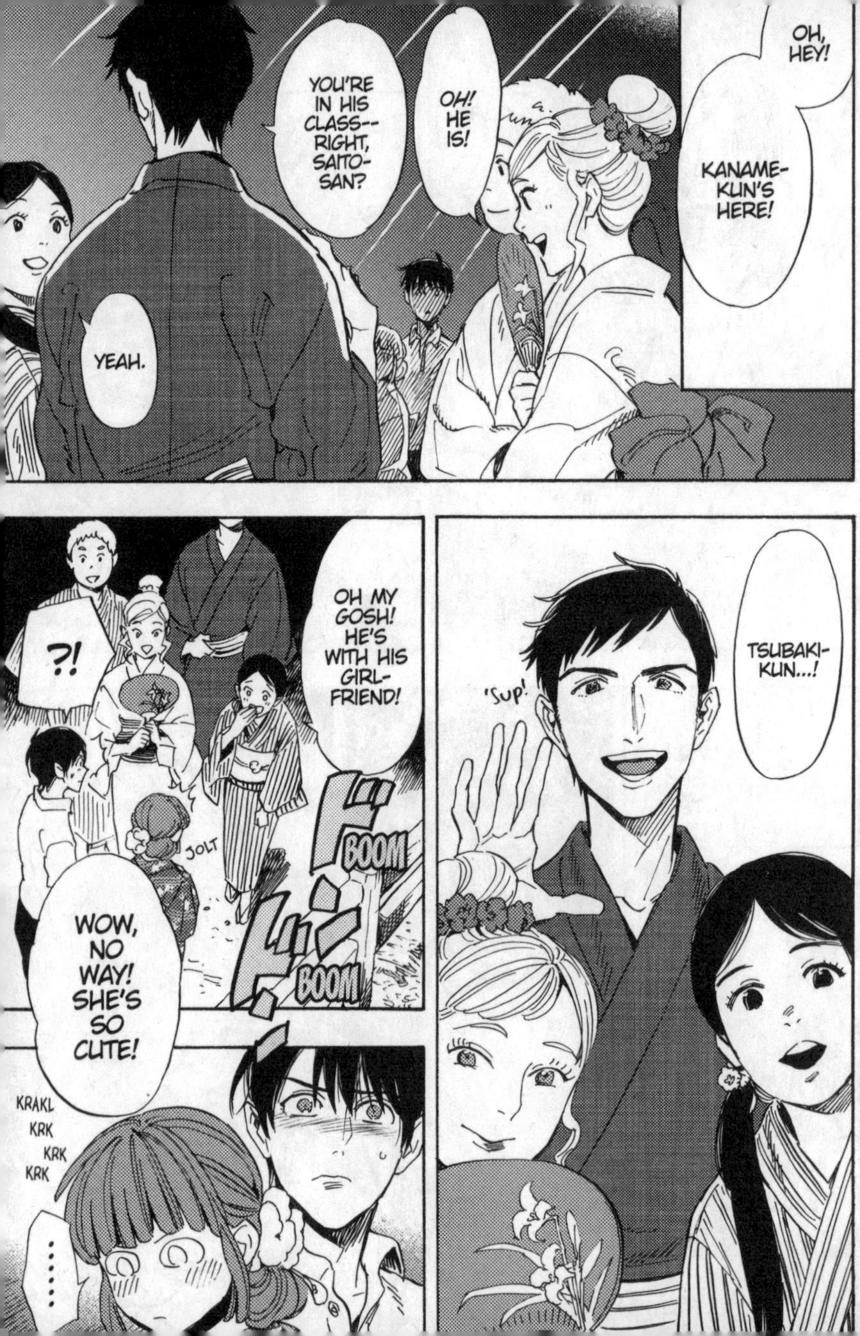
OH, HEY!
KANAME-KUN'S HERE!
OH! HE IS!
YOU'RE IN HIS CLASS-- RIGHT, SAITO-SAN?
YEAH.
TSUBAKI-KUN...!
'Sup!
OH MY GOSH! HE'S WITH HIS GIRL-FRIEND!
?!
BOOM
JOLT
BOOM
WOW, NO WAY! SHE'S SO CUTE!
KRAKL
KRK
KRK
KRK
......

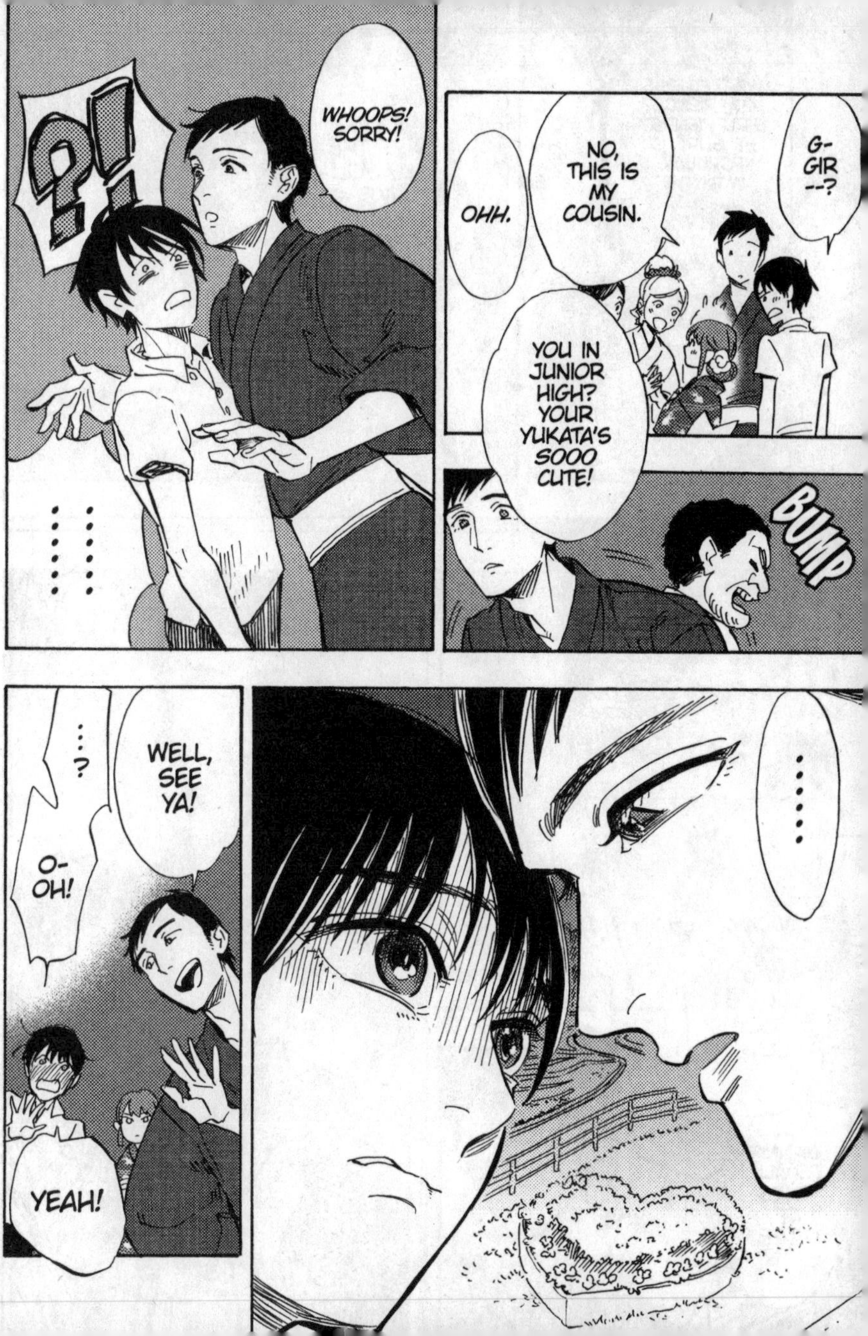
G-GIR--?
NO, THIS IS MY COUSIN.
OHH.
YOU IN JUNIOR HIGH? YOUR YUKATA'S SOOO CUTE!
BUMP
WHOOPS! SORRY!
?!
......
......
WELL, SEE YA!
...?
O-OH!
YEAH!

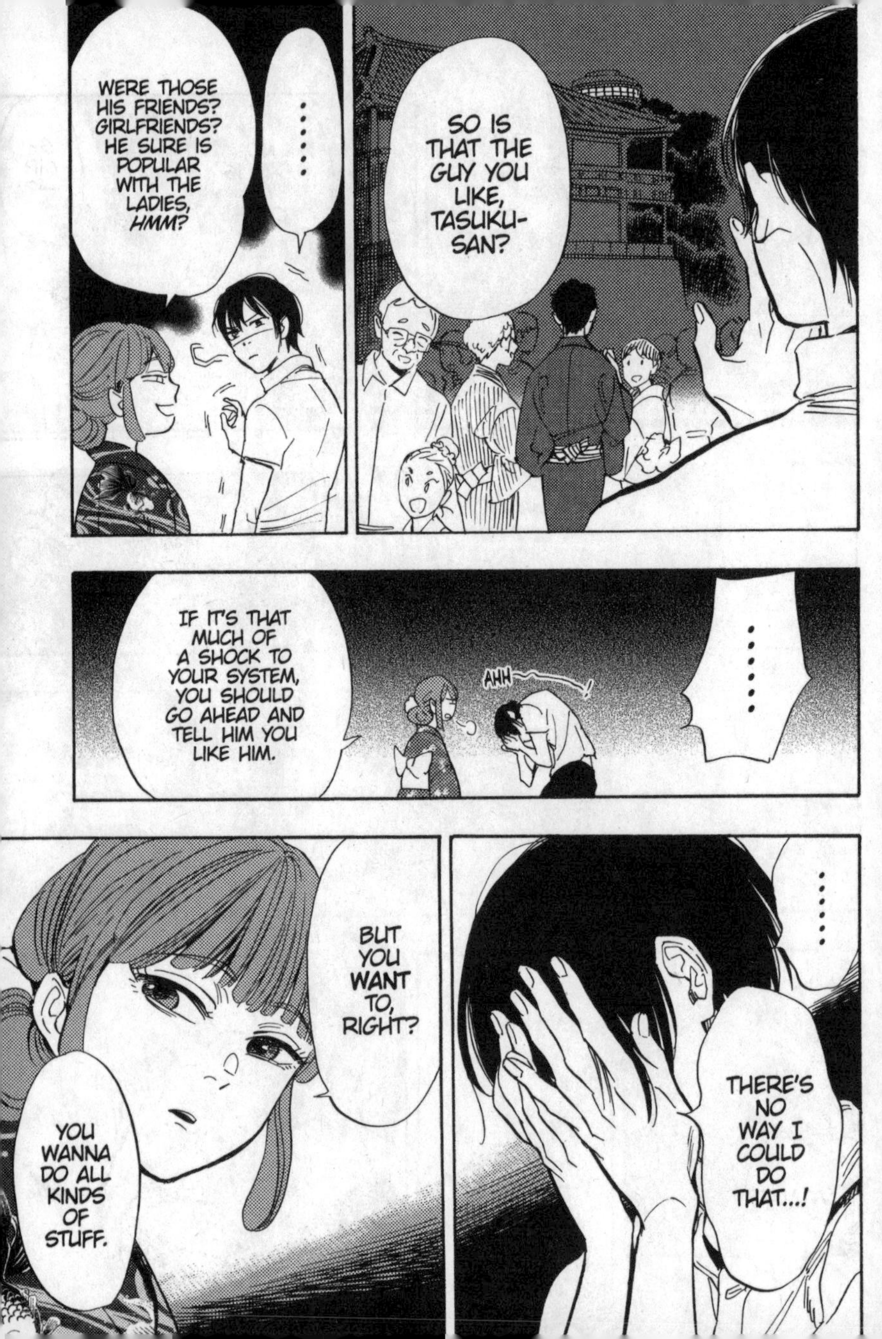
SO IS THAT THE GUY YOU LIKE, TASUKU-SAN?
......
WERE THOSE HIS FRIENDS? GIRLFRIENDS? HE SURE IS POPULAR WITH THE LADIES, *HMM?*
......
AHH~!
IF IT'S THAT MUCH OF A SHOCK TO YOUR SYSTEM, YOU SHOULD GO AHEAD AND TELL HIM YOU LIKE HIM.
......
THERE'S NO WAY I COULD DO THAT...!
BUT YOU WANT TO, RIGHT?
YOU WANNA DO ALL KINDS OF STUFF.

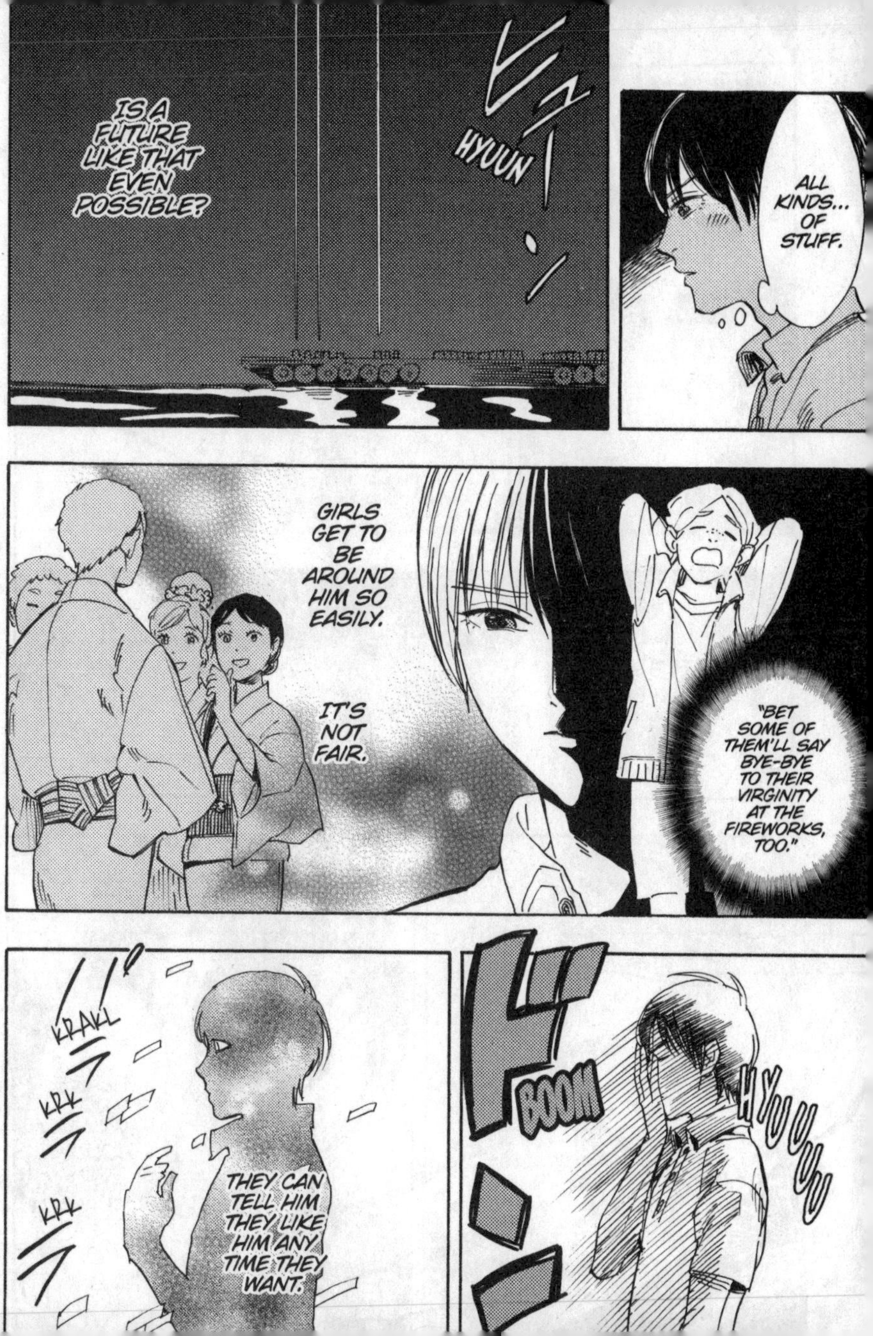
ALL KINDS... OF STUFF.
HYUUN
IS A FUTURE LIKE THAT EVEN POSSIBLE?
"BET SOME OF THEM'LL SAY BYE-BYE TO THEIR VIRGINITY AT THE FIREWORKS, TOO."
GIRLS GET TO BE AROUND HIM SO EASILY.
IT'S NOT FAIR.
BOOM
HYUUUUU
KRAKL
KRK
KRK
THEY CAN TELL HIM THEY LIKE HIM ANY TIME THEY WANT.

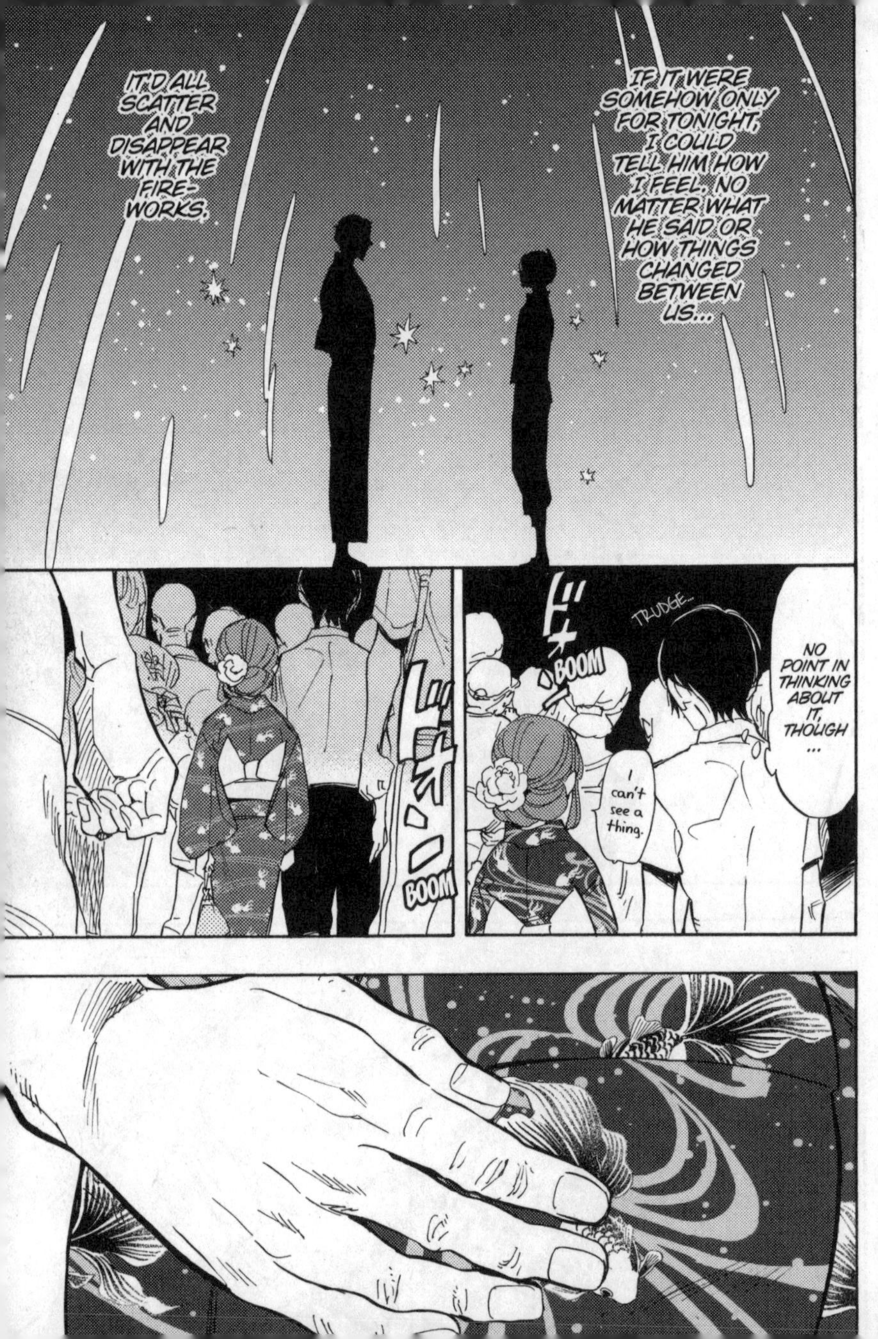
IF IT WERE SOMEHOW ONLY FOR TONIGHT, I COULD TELL HIM HOW I FEEL. NO MATTER WHAT HE SAID OR HOW THINGS CHANGED BETWEEN US...
IT'D ALL SCATTER AND DISAPPEAR WITH THE FIRE-WORKS.
NO POINT IN THINKING ABOUT IT, THOUGH...
TRUDGE...
BOOM
I can't see a thing.
BOOM

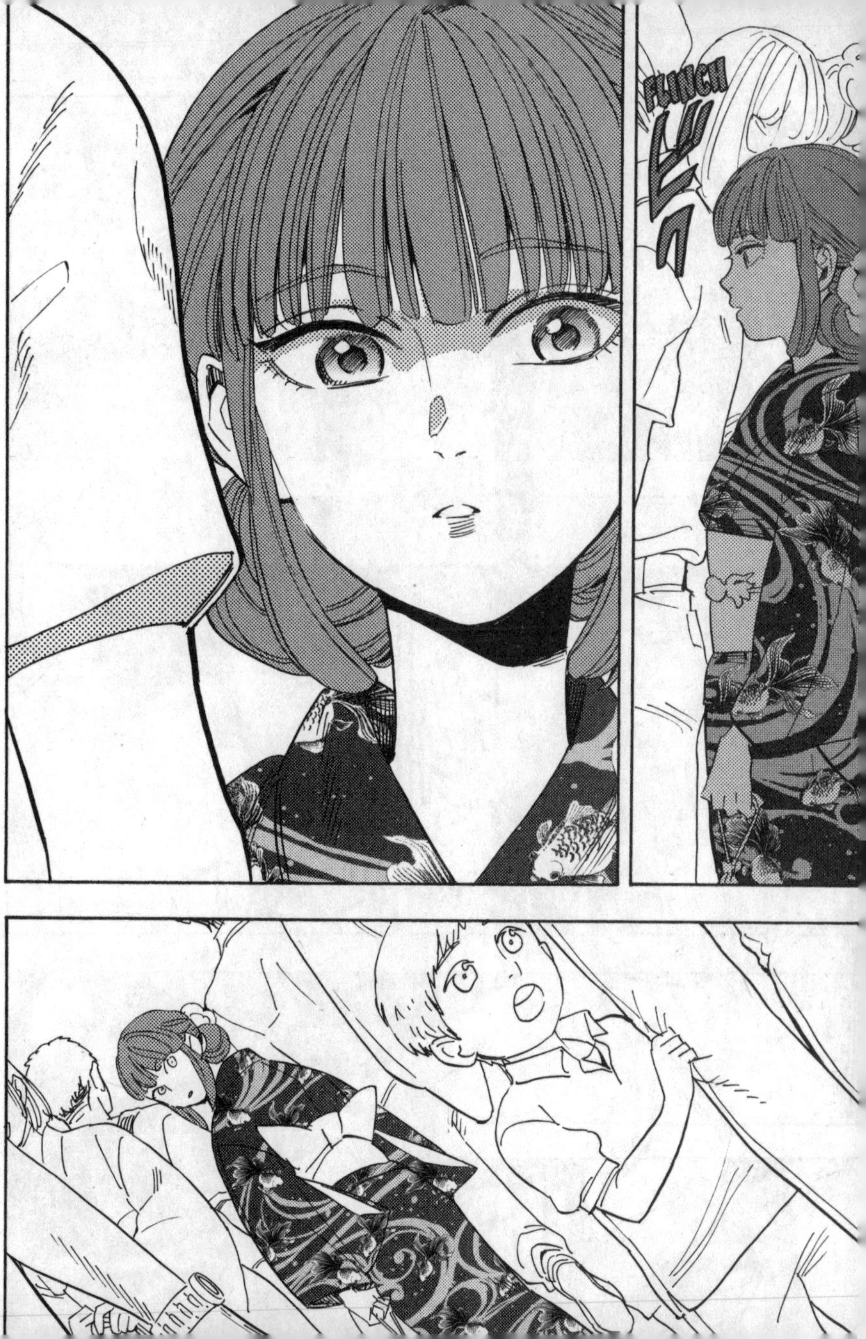
FLINCH

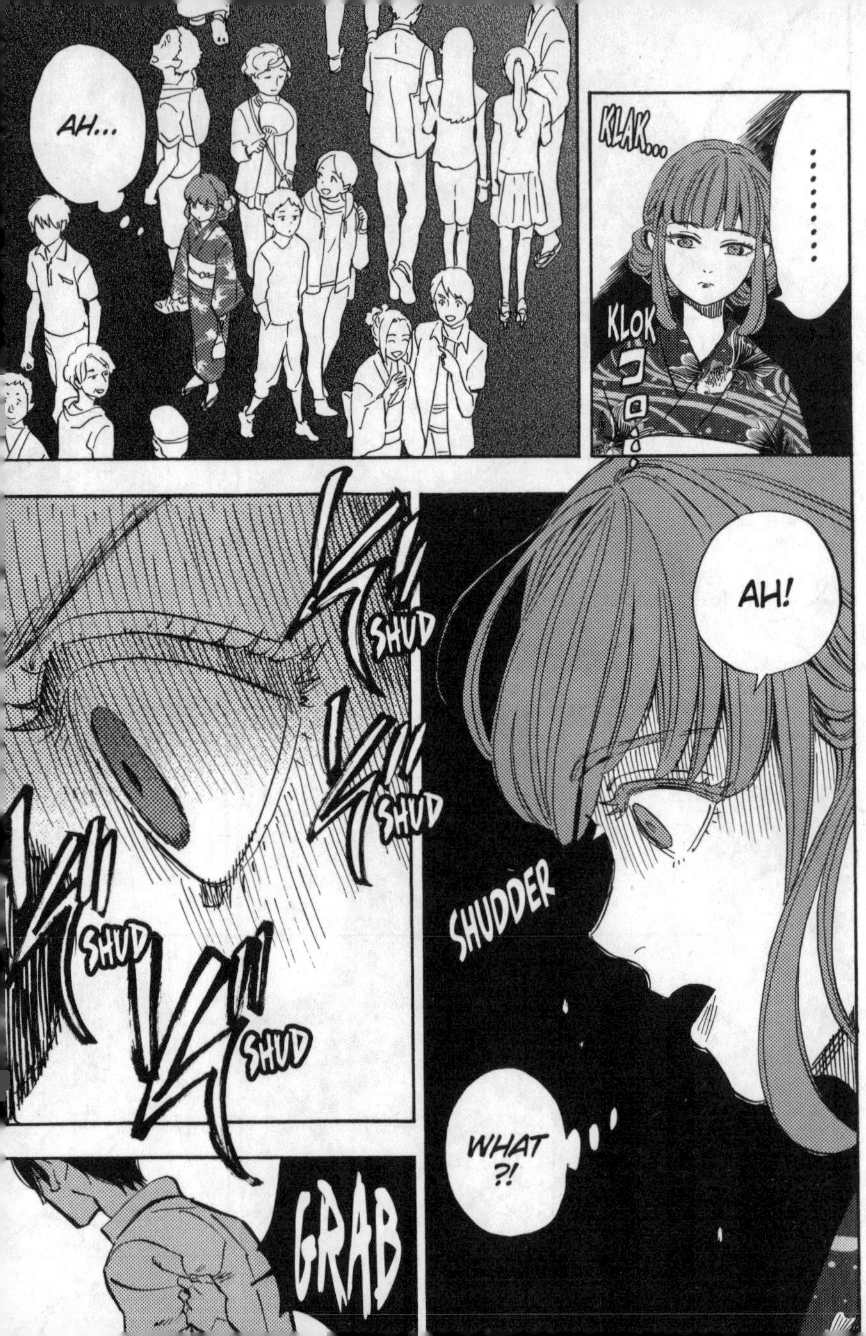
KLAK...
......
KLOK
コロ
AH...
AH!
SHUDDER
WHAT ?!
SHUD
SHUD
SHUD
SHUD
GRAB

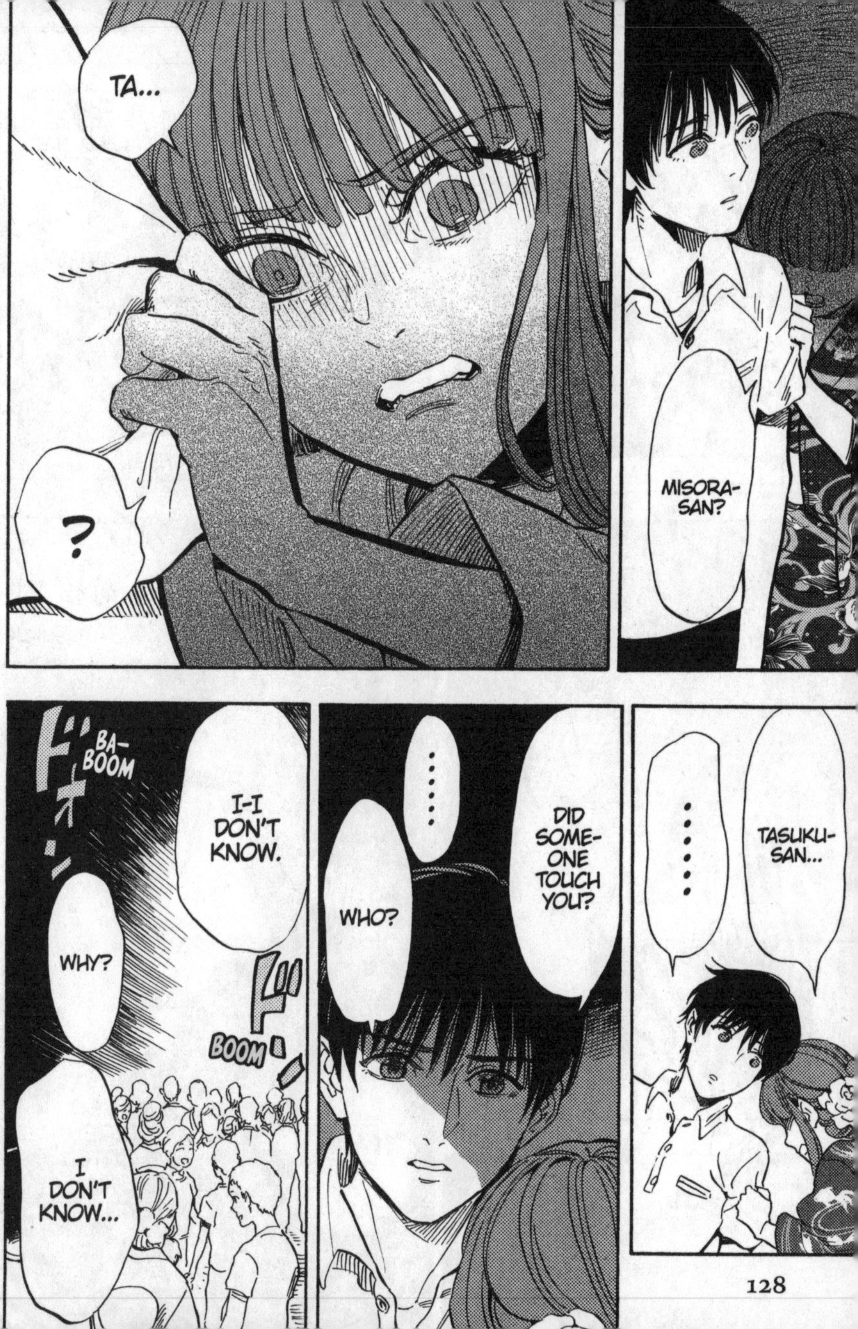
MISORA-SAN?
TA...
?
TASUKU-SAN...
......
DID SOME-ONE TOUCH YOU?
......
WHO?
BOOM
BA-BOOM
I-I DON'T KNOW.
WHY?
I DON'T KNOW...

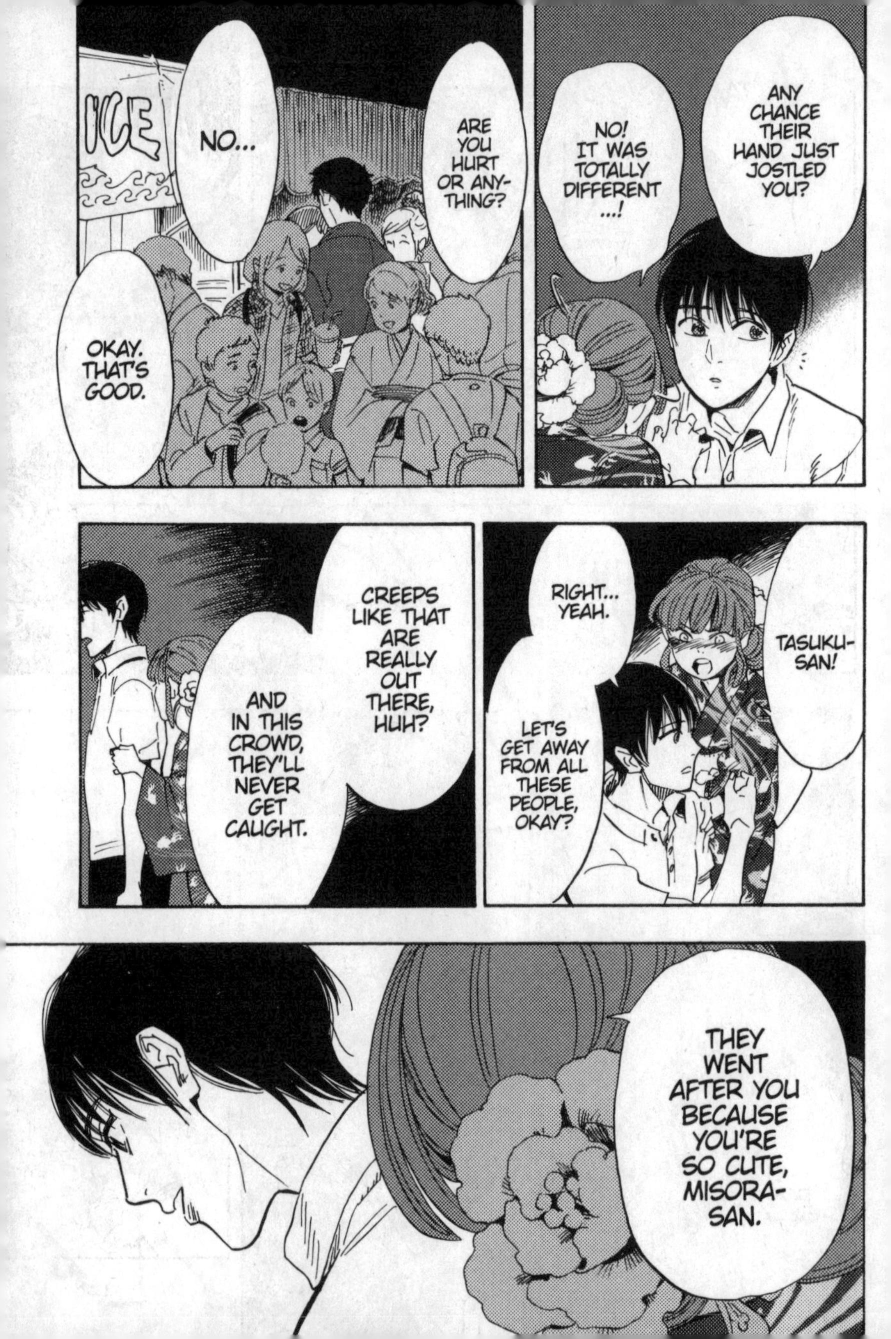
ANY CHANCE THEIR HAND JUST JOSTLED YOU?
NO! IT WAS TOTALLY DIFFERENT ...!
ICE
ARE YOU HURT OR ANY-THING?
NO...
OKAY. THAT'S GOOD.
TASUKU-SAN!
RIGHT... YEAH.
LET'S GET AWAY FROM ALL THESE PEOPLE, OKAY?
CREEPS LIKE THAT ARE REALLY OUT THERE, HUH?
AND IN THIS CROWD, THEY'LL NEVER GET CAUGHT.
THEY WENT AFTER YOU BECAUSE YOU'RE SO CUTE, MISORA-SAN.

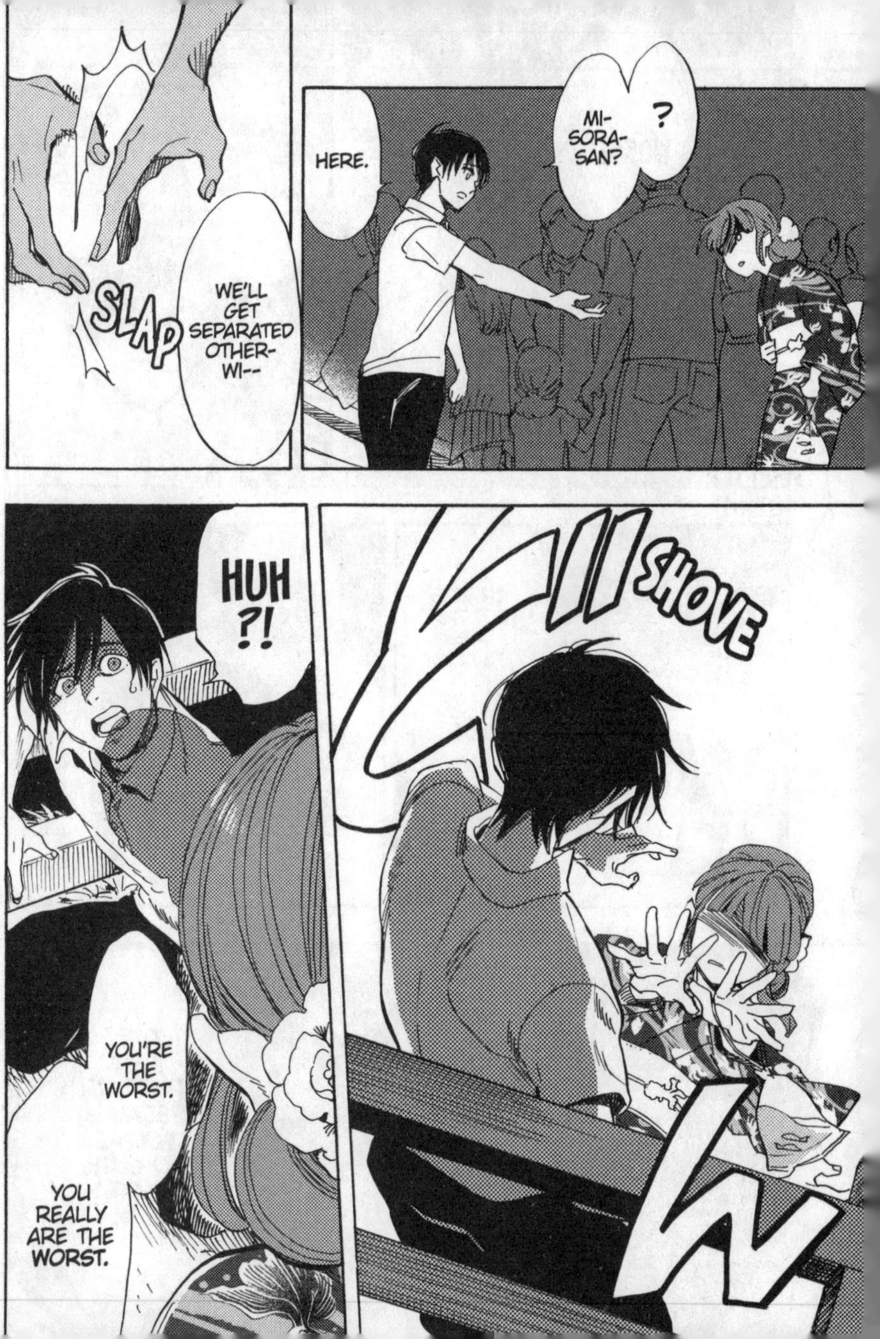
MI-SORA-SAN?
?
HERE.
SLAP
WE'LL GET SEPARATED OTHER-WI--
SHOVE
HUH?!
YOU'RE THE WORST.
YOU REALLY ARE THE WORST.

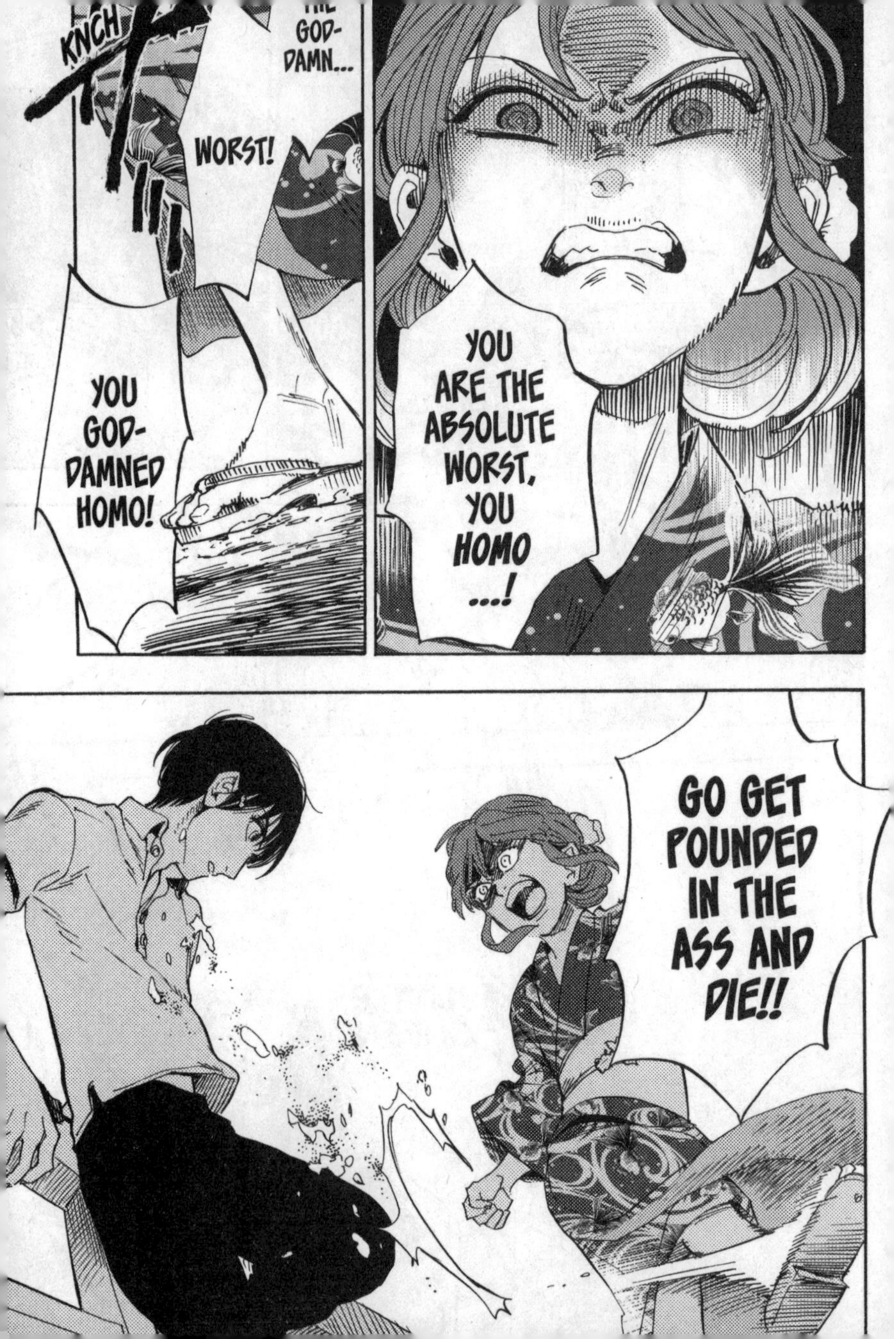
YOU ARE THE ABSOLUTE WORST, YOU HOMO ...!
GOD-DAMN...
KNCH
WORST!
YOU GOD-DAMNED HOMO!
GO GET POUNDED IN THE ASS AND DIE!!

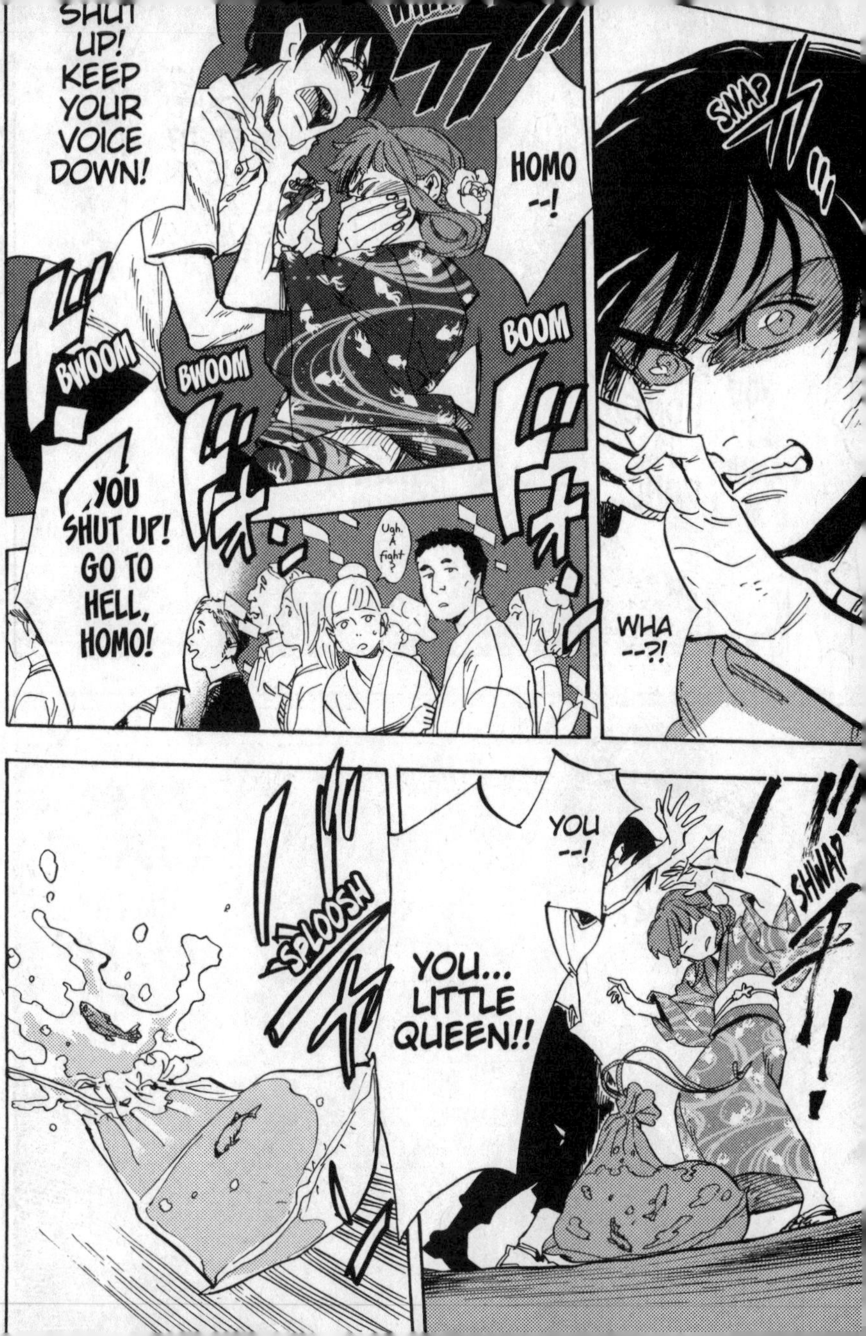
SNAP
WHA --?!
SHUT UP! KEEP YOUR VOICE DOWN!
HOMO --!
BOOM
BWOOM
BWOOM
Ugh. A fight?
YOU SHUT UP! GO TO HELL, HOMO!
YOU --!
SHWAP
YOU... LITTLE QUEEN!!
SPLOOSH

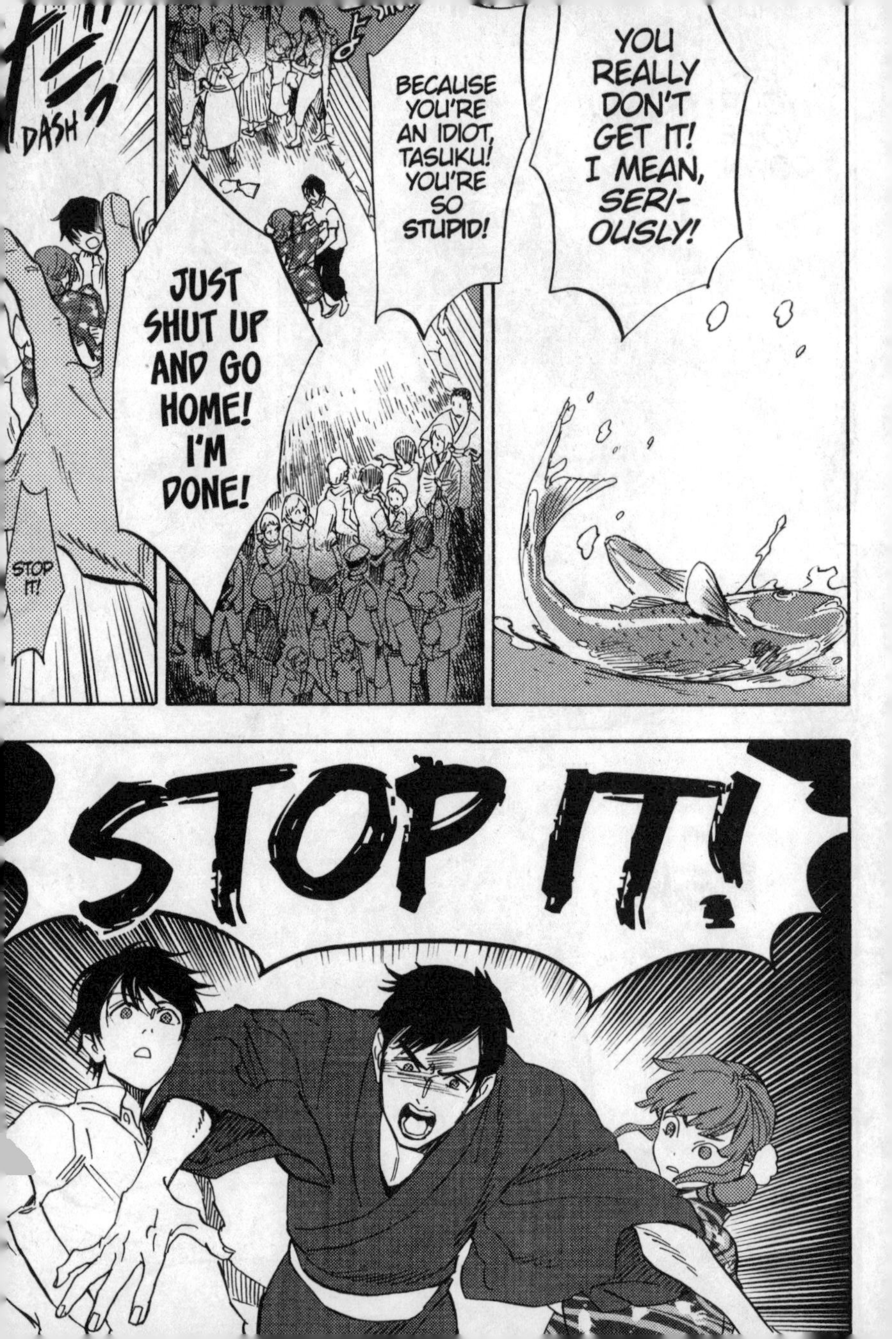
YOU REALLY DON'T GET IT! I MEAN, SERI-OUSLY!
BECAUSE YOU'RE AN IDIOT, TASUKU! YOU'RE SO STUPID!
JUST SHUT UP AND GO HOME! I'M DONE!
DASH
STOP IT!
STOP IT!

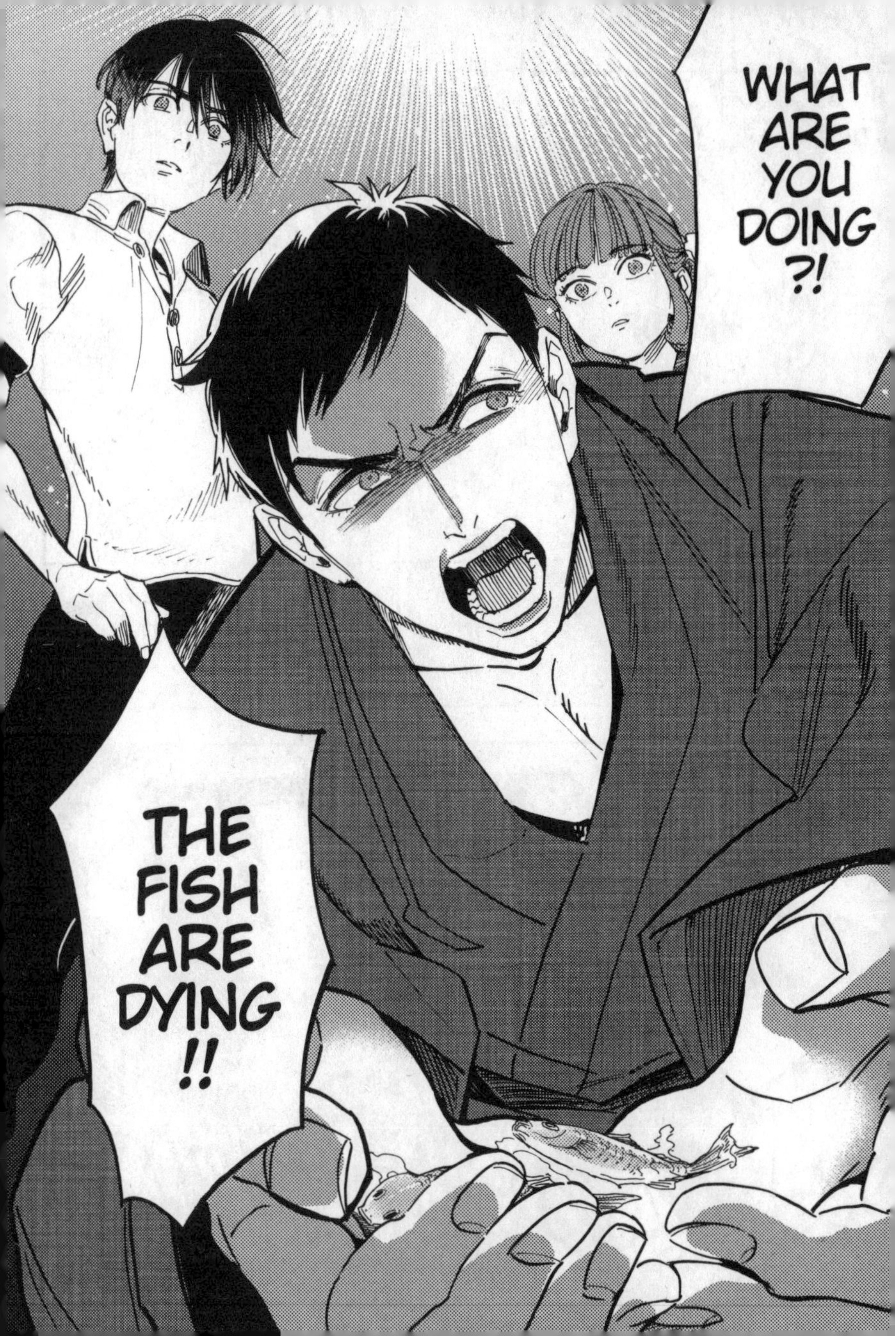
WHAT ARE YOU DOING ?!
THE FISH ARE DYING !!

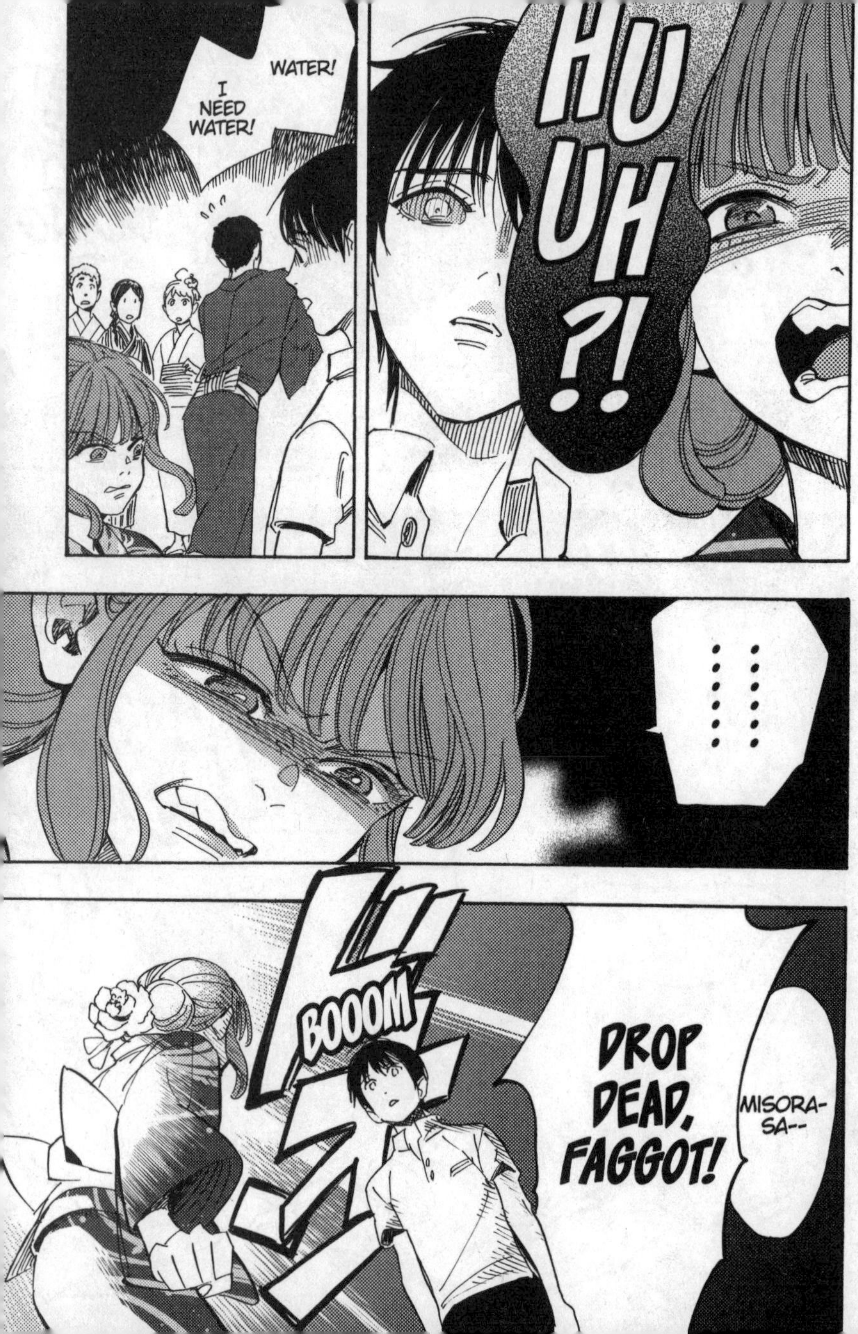
HUUH?!
WATER!
I NEED WATER!
......
MISORA-SA--
DROP DEAD, FAGGOT!
BOOOM

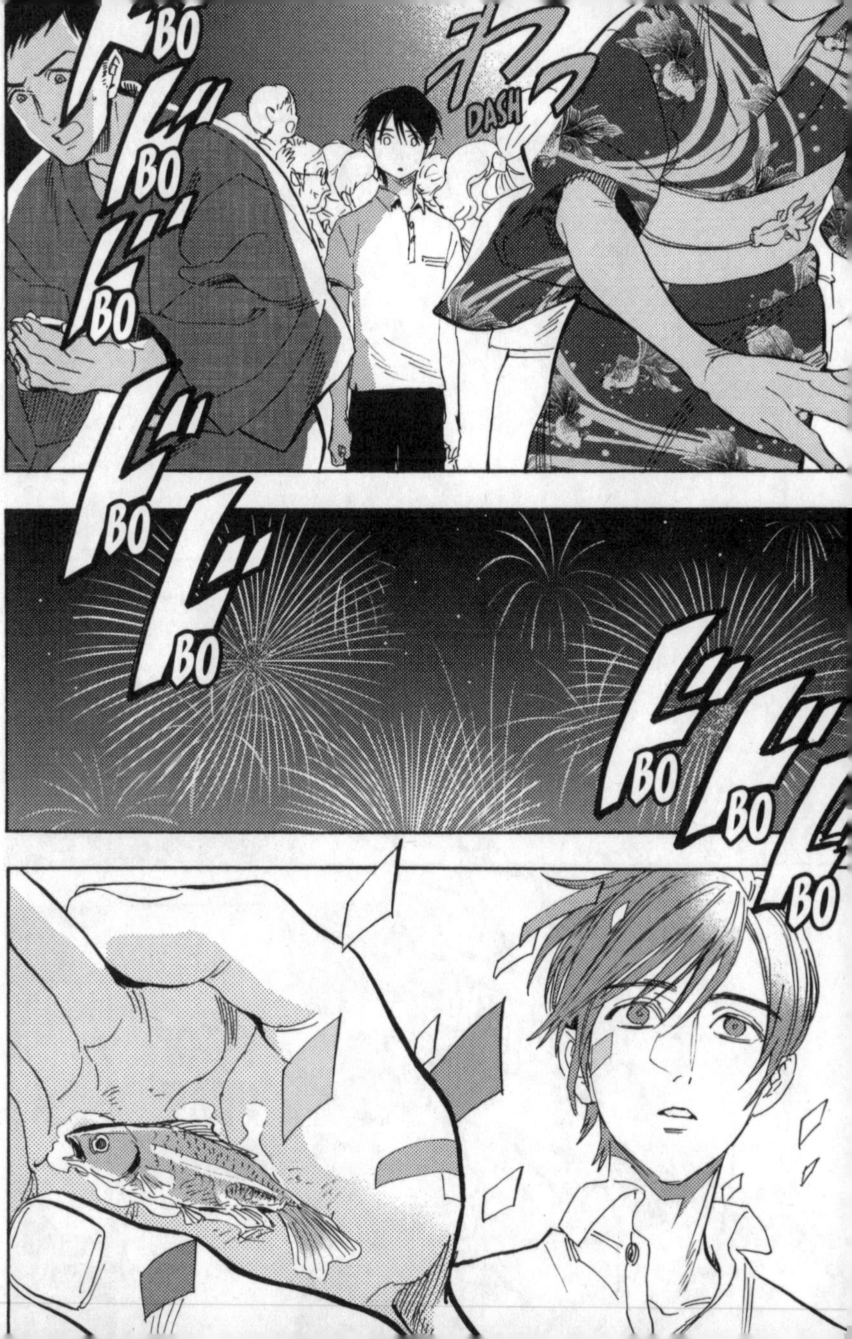
DASH
BO
BO
BO
BO
BO
BO
BO
BO

Our Dreams at Dusk

SHIMANAMI TASOGARE

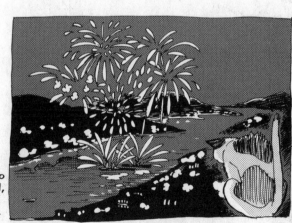

Sumiyoshi
Fireworks
Festival
Prayers for
prosperous
business
and
marine-
traffic
safety.

They're so
powerful,
it's
thrilling.

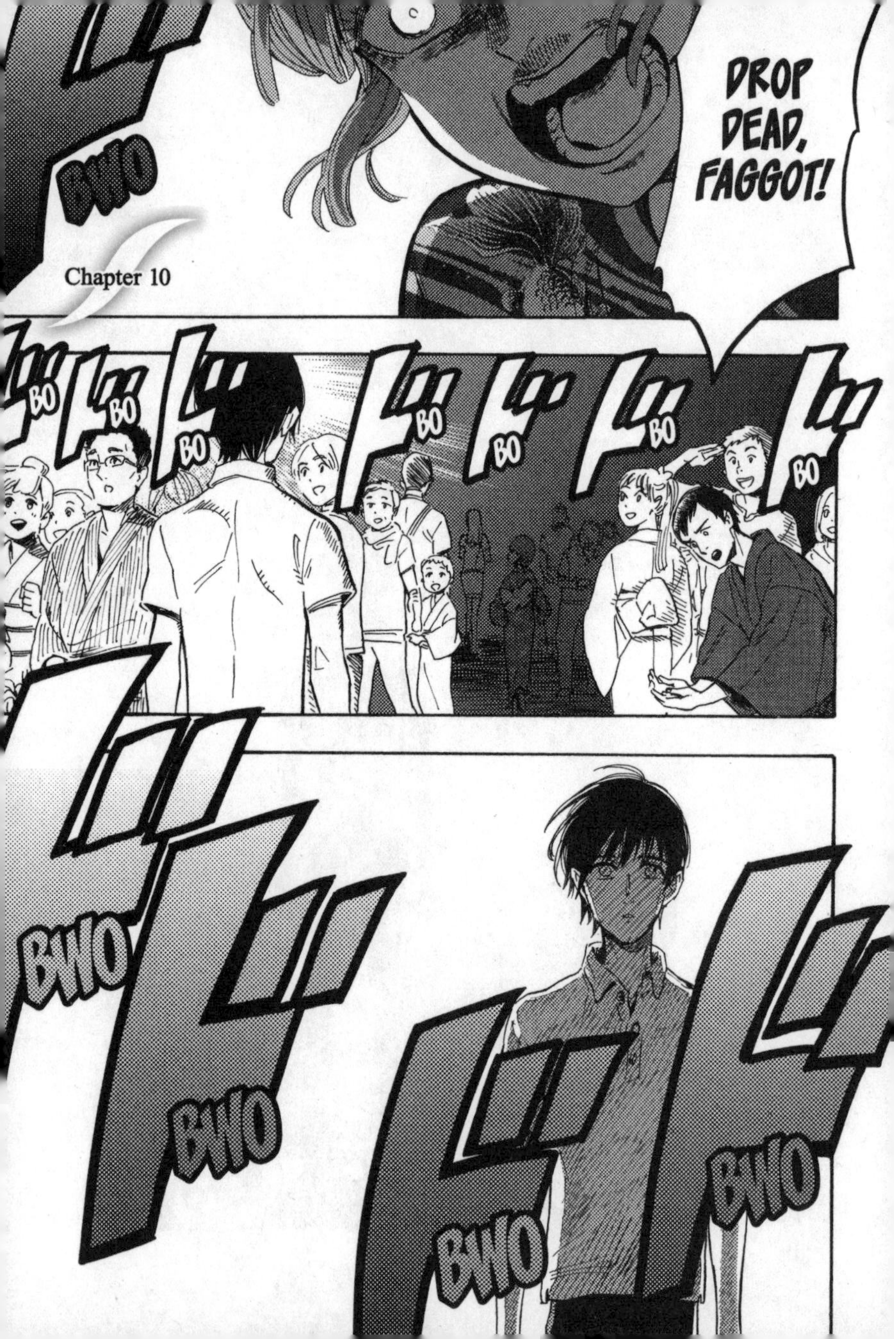
DROP DEAD, FAGGOT!
BWO
Chapter 10
BO
BO
BO
BO
BO
BO
BO
BWO
BWO
BWO
BWO

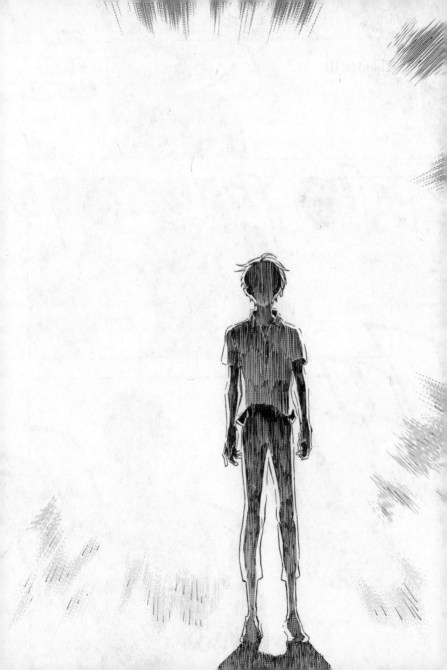

Chapter 10

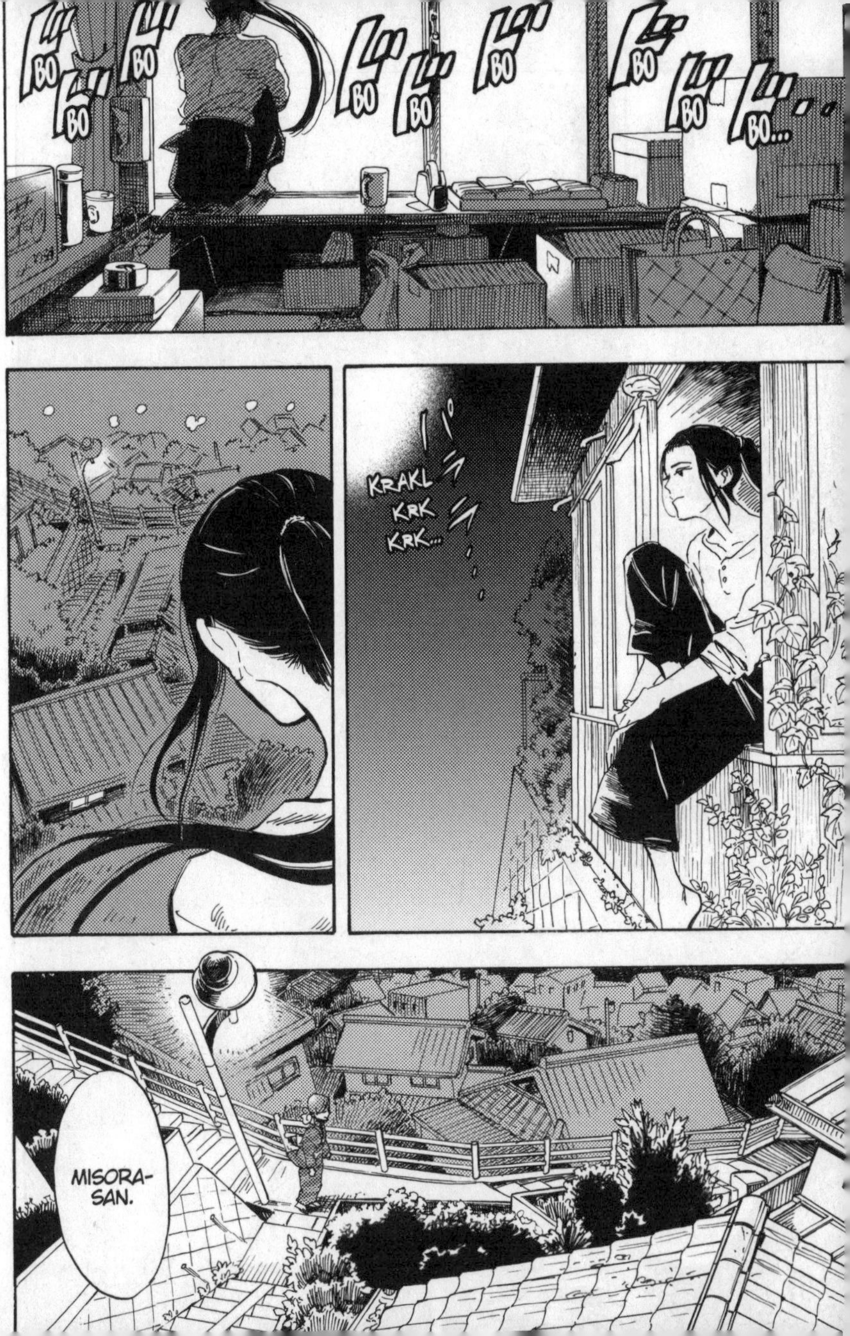

BO BO BO BO BO BO BO BO BO...
KRAKL KRK KRK...
MISORA-SAN.

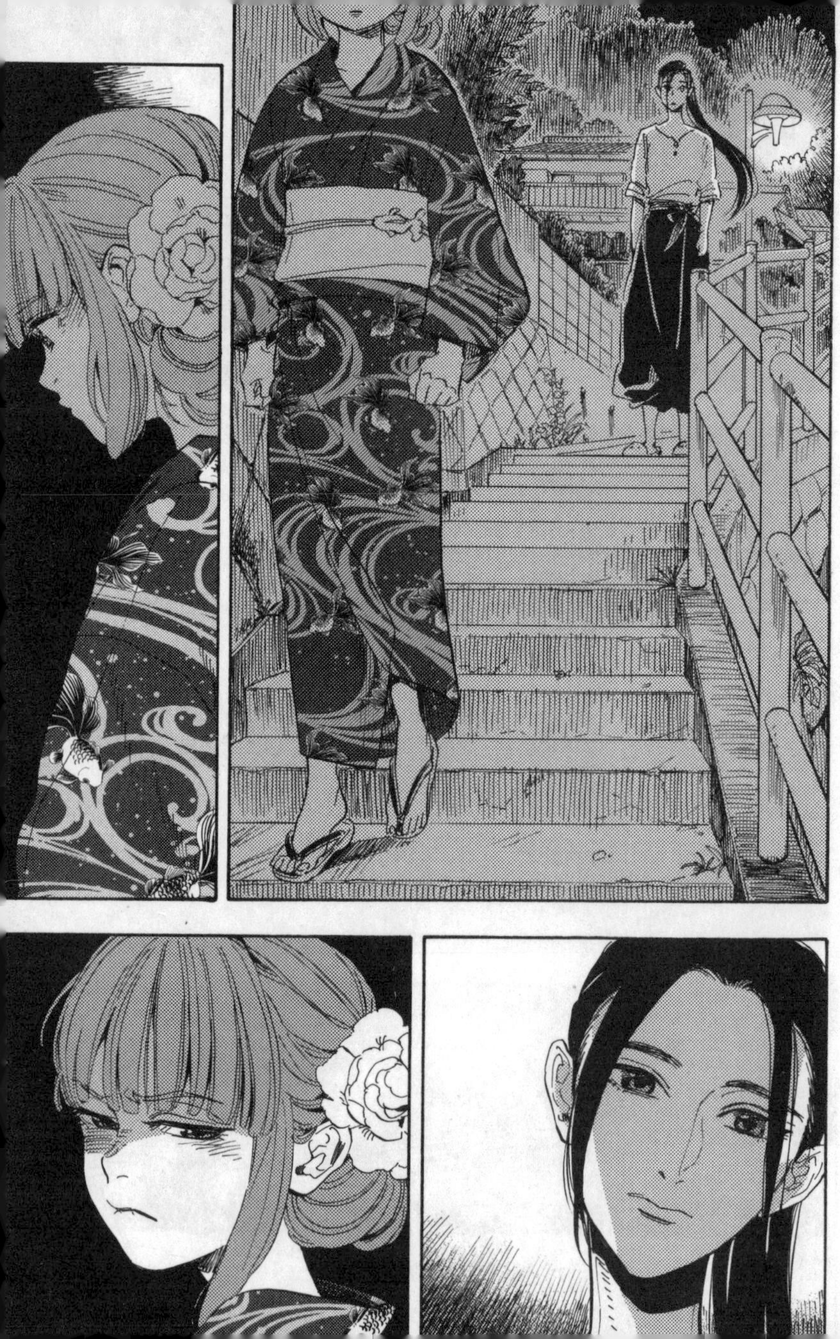

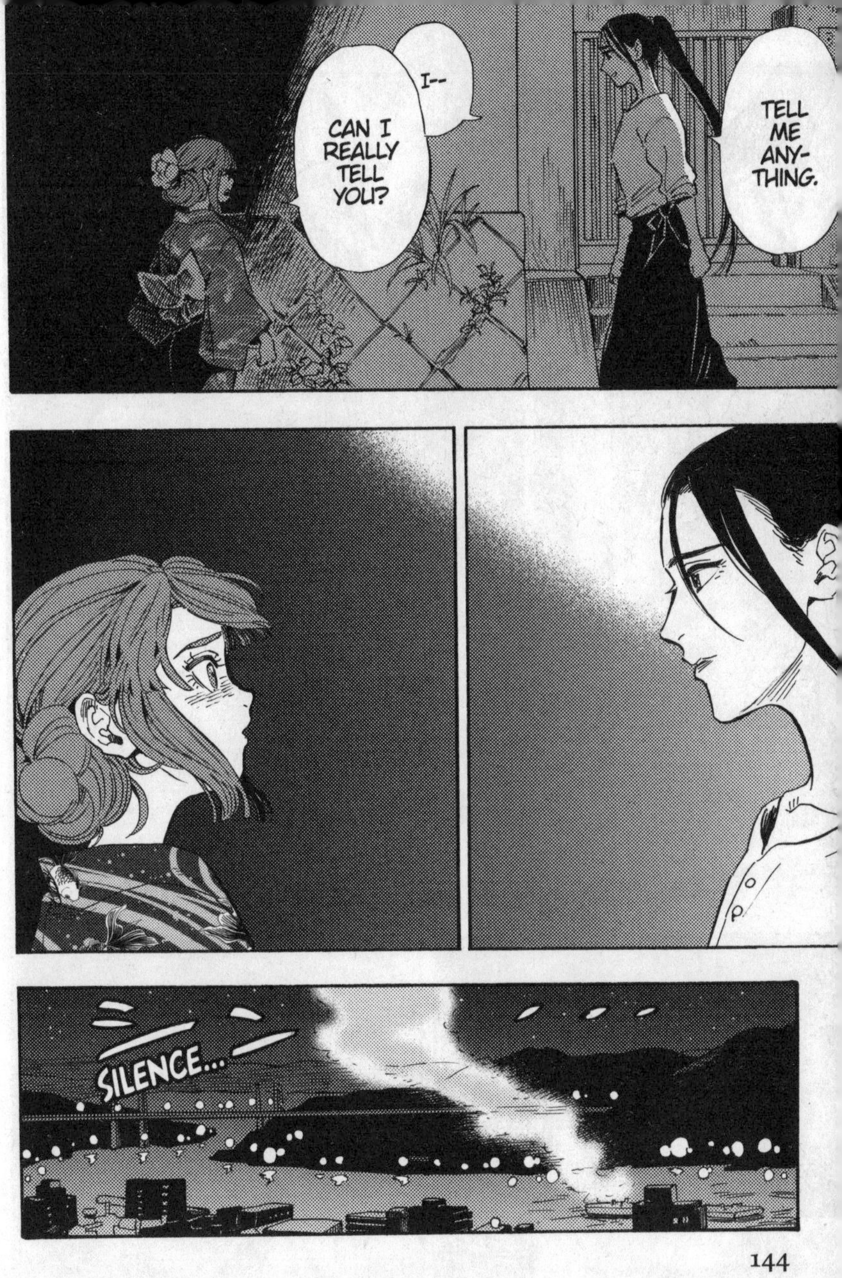
TELL ME ANY-THING.
I--
CAN I REALLY TELL YOU?
SILENCE...

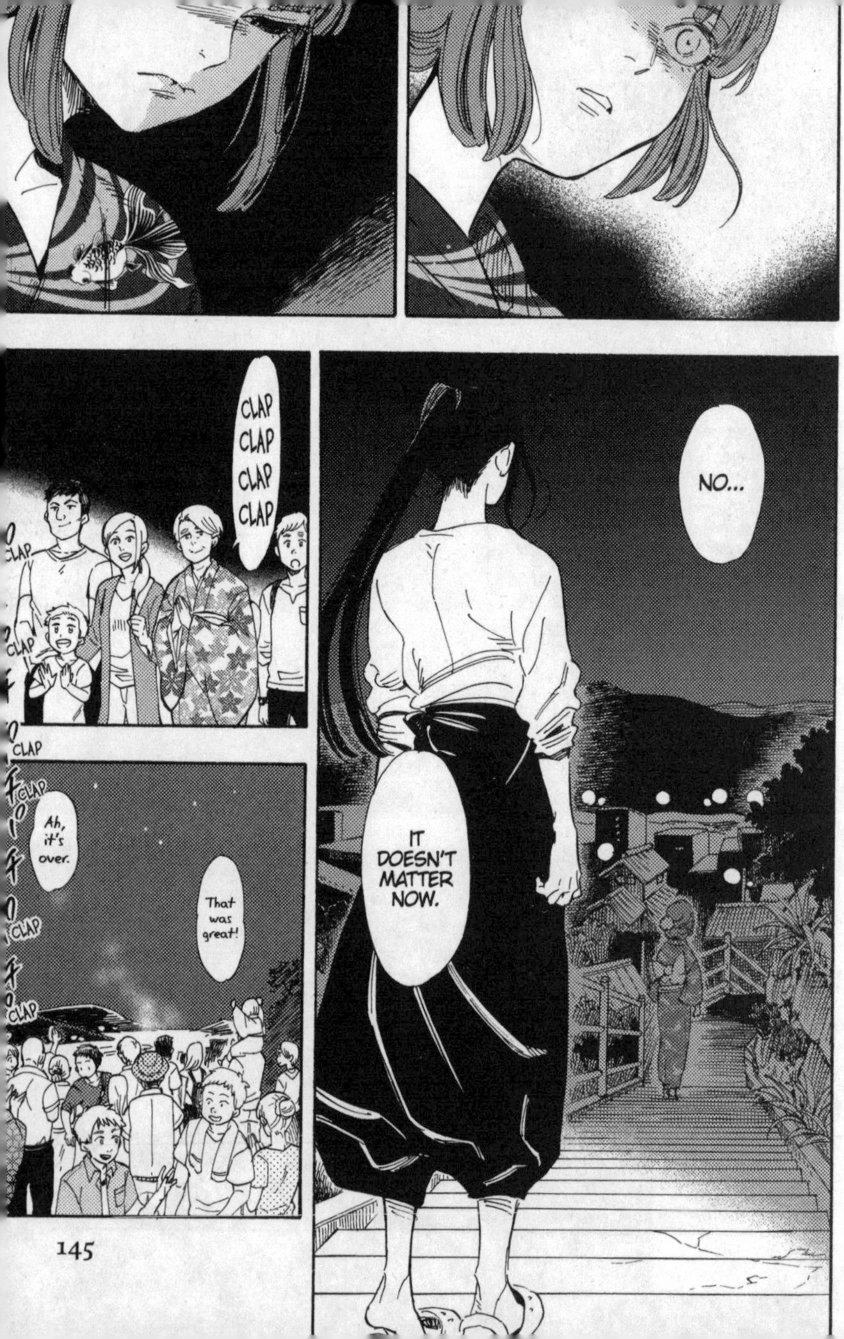
NO...
IT DOESN'T MATTER NOW.
CLAP CLAP CLAP CLAP
CLAP
CLAP
CLAP
CLAP
CLAP
CLAP
Ah, it's over.
That was great!

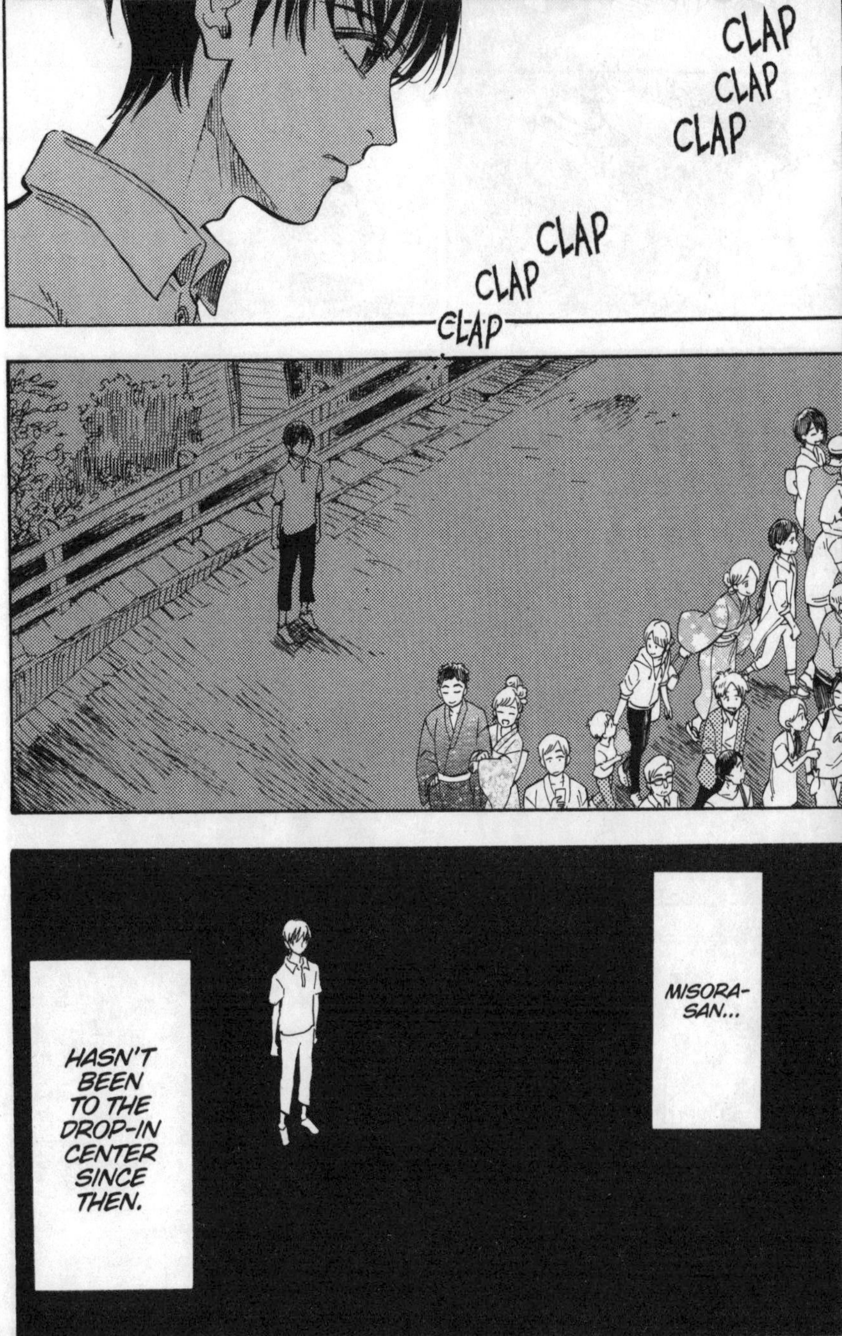
CLAP
CLAP
CLAP
CLAP
CLAP
CLAP
MISORA-SAN...
HASN'T BEEN TO THE DROP-IN CENTER SINCE THEN.

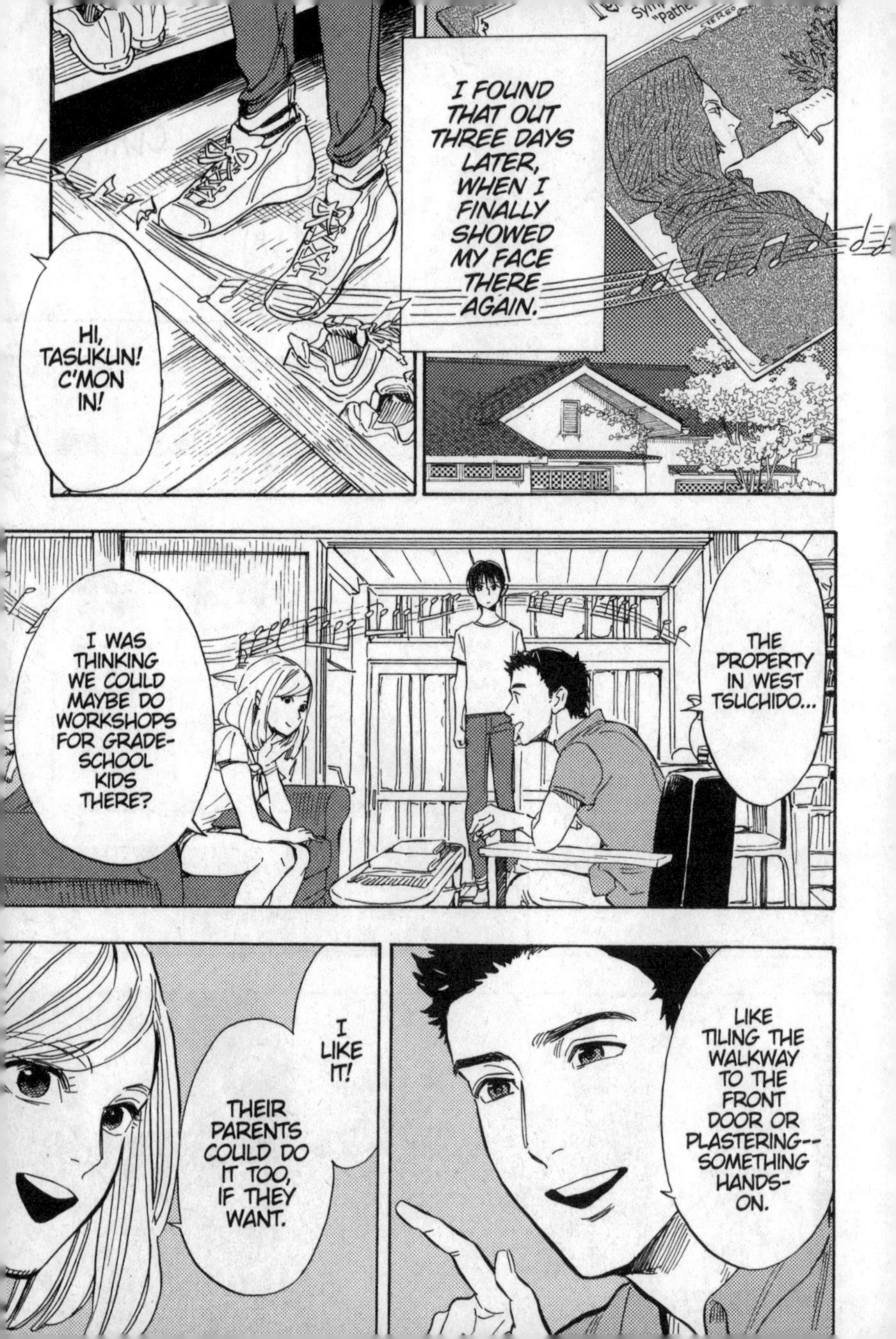
I FOUND THAT OUT THREE DAYS LATER, WHEN I FINALLY SHOWED MY FACE THERE AGAIN.
HI, TASUKUN! C'MON IN!
THE PROPERTY IN WEST TSUCHIDO...
I WAS THINKING WE COULD MAYBE DO WORKSHOPS FOR GRADE-SCHOOL KIDS THERE?
LIKE TILING THE WALKWAY TO THE FRONT DOOR OR PLASTERING--SOMETHING HANDS-ON.
I LIKE IT!
THEIR PARENTS COULD DO IT TOO, IF THEY WANT.

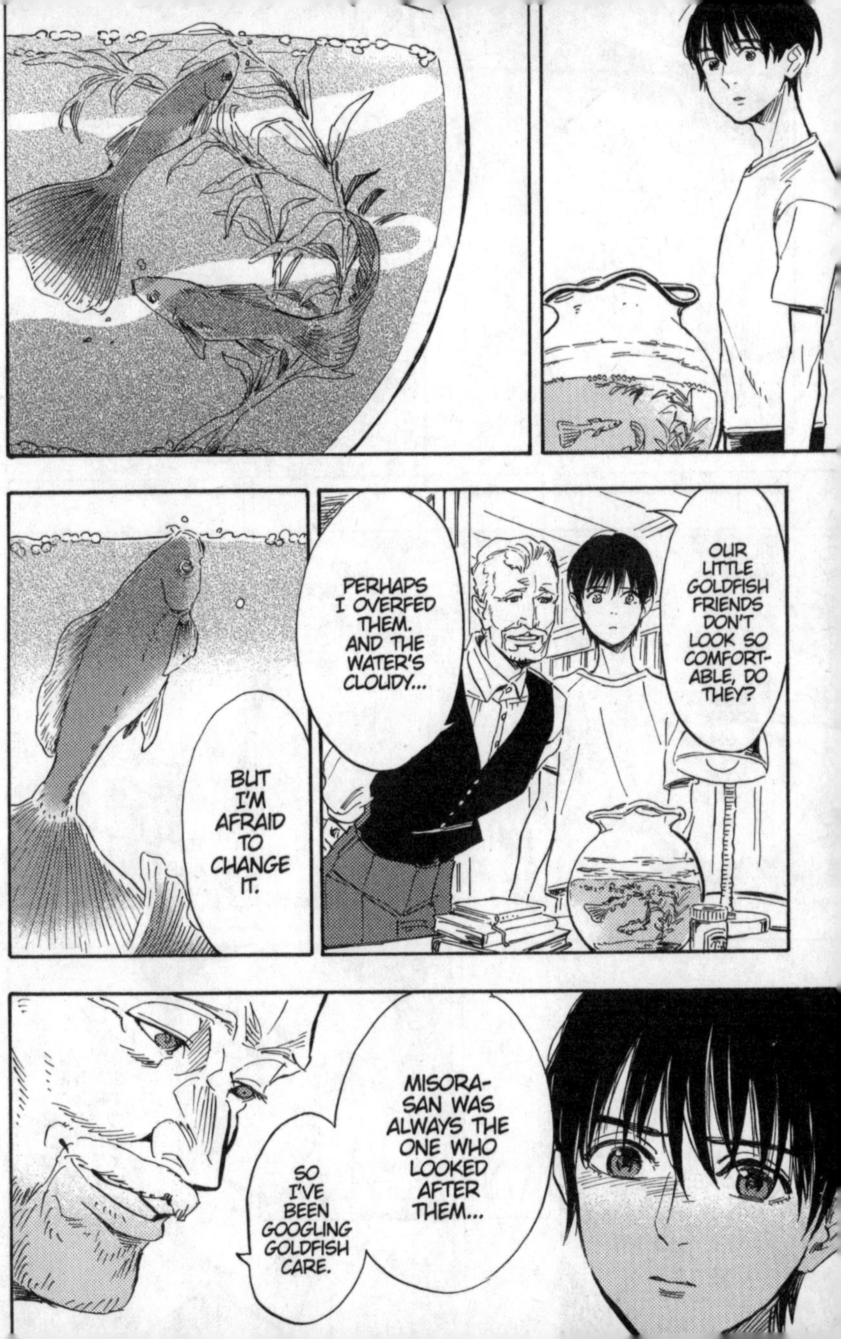
OUR LITTLE GOLDFISH FRIENDS DON'T LOOK SO COMFORT-ABLE, DO THEY?
PERHAPS I OVERFED THEM. AND THE WATER'S CLOUDY...
BUT I'M AFRAID TO CHANGE IT.
MISORA-SAN WAS ALWAYS THE ONE WHO LOOKED AFTER THEM...
SO I'VE BEEN GOOGLING GOLDFISH CARE.

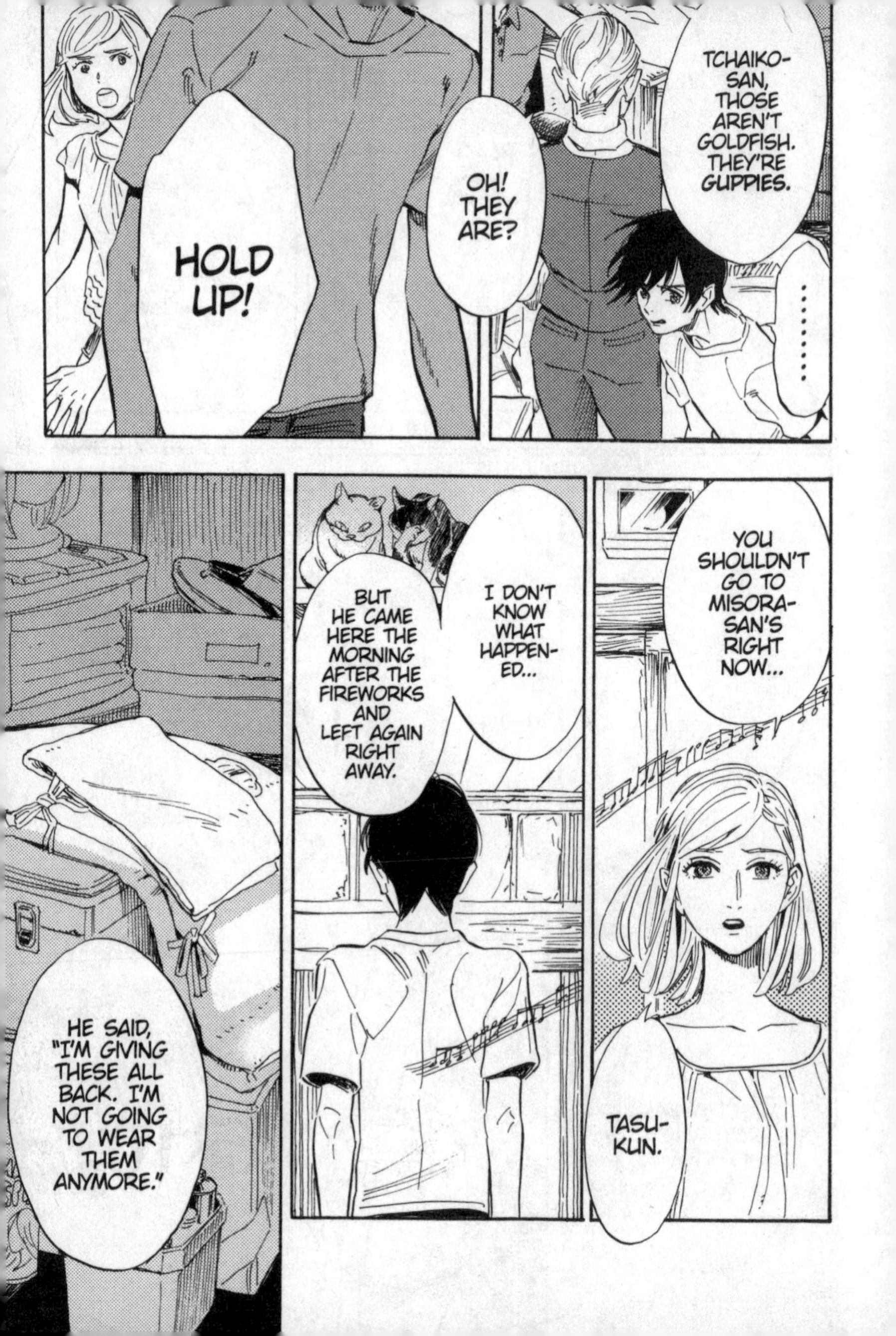
TCHAIKO-SAN, THOSE AREN'T GOLDFISH. THEY'RE GUPPIES.
OH! THEY ARE?
......
HOLD UP!
YOU SHOULDN'T GO TO MISORA-SAN'S RIGHT NOW...
TASU-KUN.
I DON'T KNOW WHAT HAPPEN-ED...
BUT HE CAME HERE THE MORNING AFTER THE FIREWORKS AND LEFT AGAIN RIGHT AWAY.
HE SAID, "I'M GIVING THESE ALL BACK. I'M NOT GOING TO WEAR THEM ANYMORE."

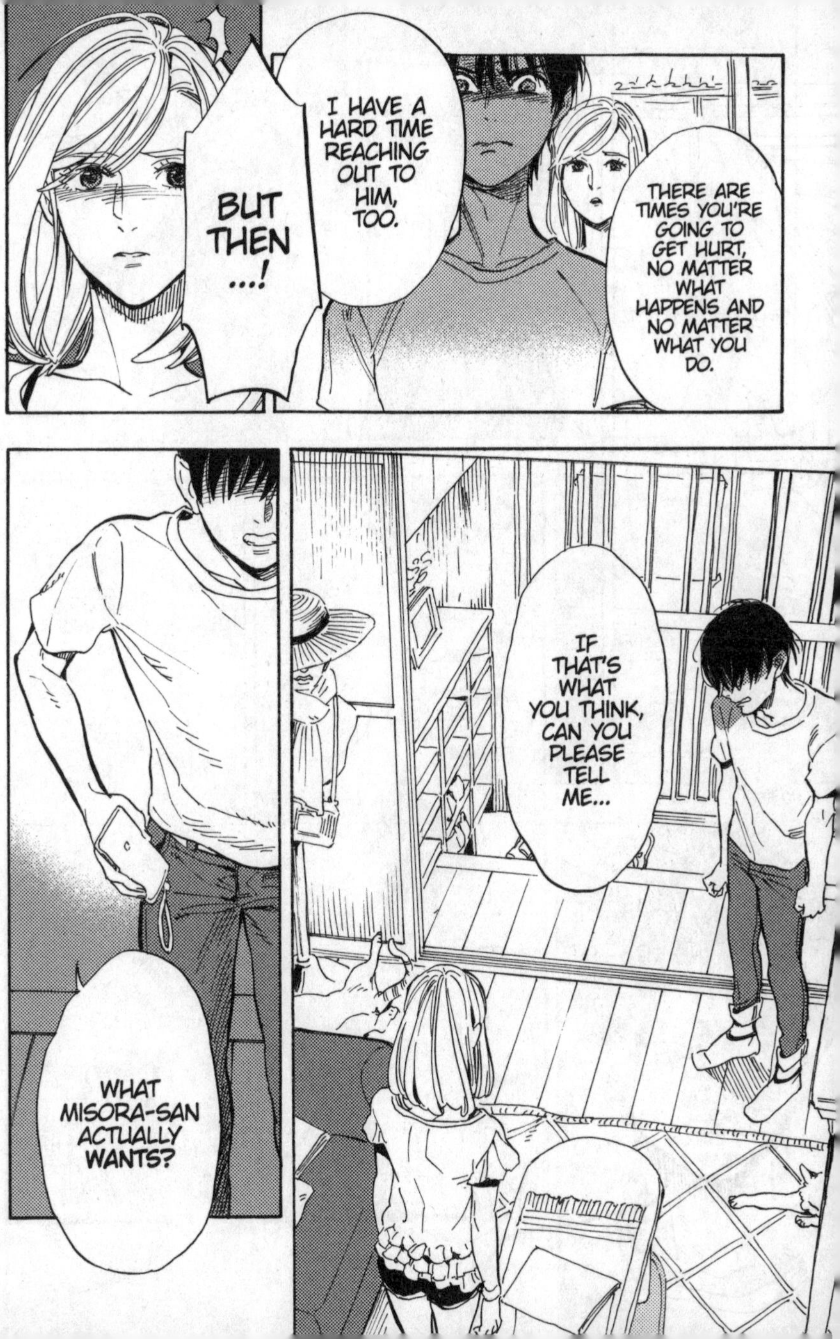
THERE ARE TIMES YOU'RE GOING TO GET HURT, NO MATTER WHAT HAPPENS AND NO MATTER WHAT YOU DO.
I HAVE A HARD TIME REACHING OUT TO HIM, TOO.
BUT THEN ...!
IF THAT'S WHAT YOU THINK, CAN YOU PLEASE TELL ME...
WHAT MISORA-SAN ACTUALLY WANTS?

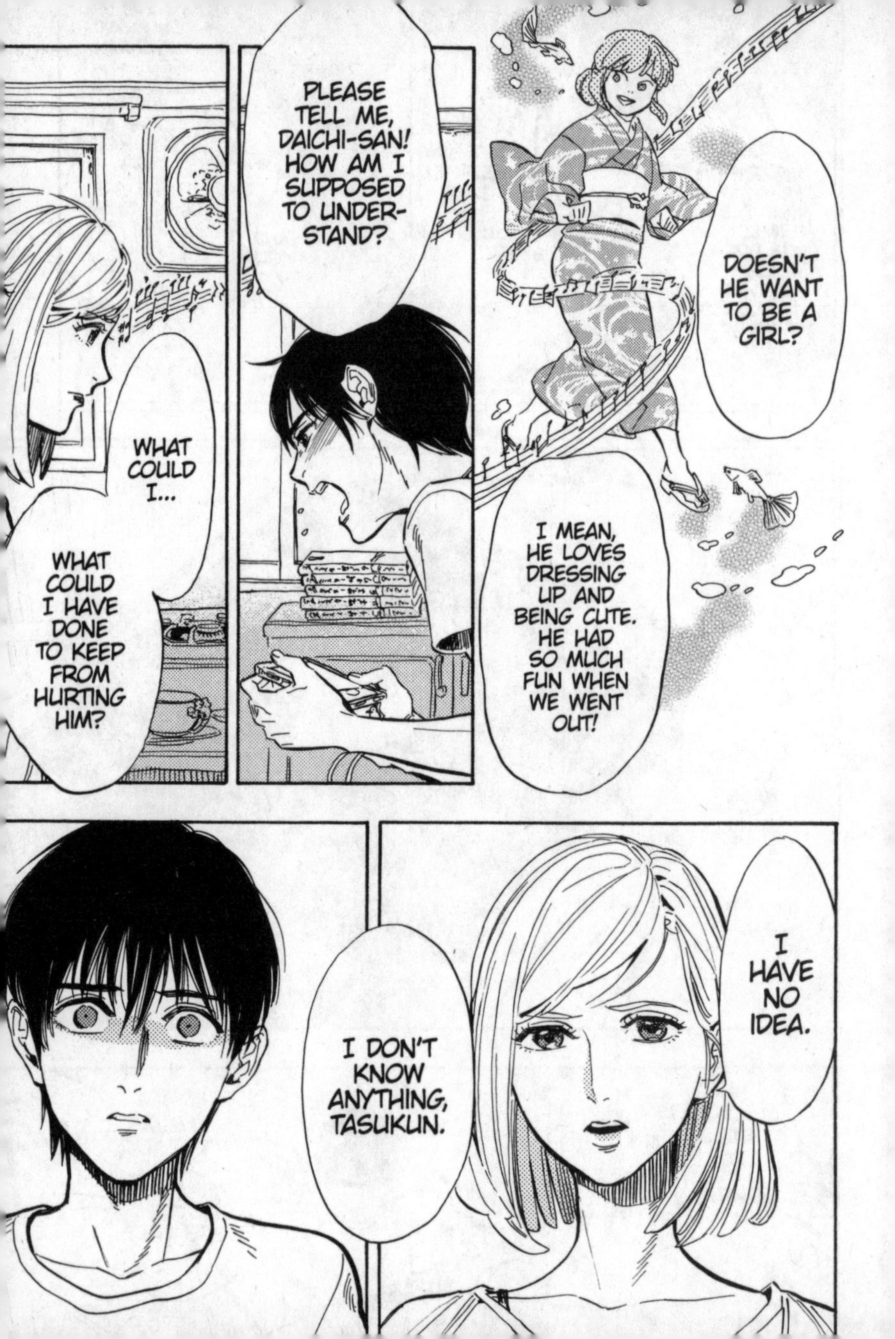
DOESN'T HE WANT TO BE A GIRL?
I MEAN, HE LOVES DRESSING UP AND BEING CUTE. HE HAD SO MUCH FUN WHEN WE WENT OUT!
PLEASE TELL ME, DAICHI-SAN! HOW AM I SUPPOSED TO UNDER-STAND?
WHAT COULD I...
WHAT COULD I HAVE DONE TO KEEP FROM HURTING HIM?
I HAVE NO IDEA.
I DON'T KNOW ANYTHING, TASUKUN.

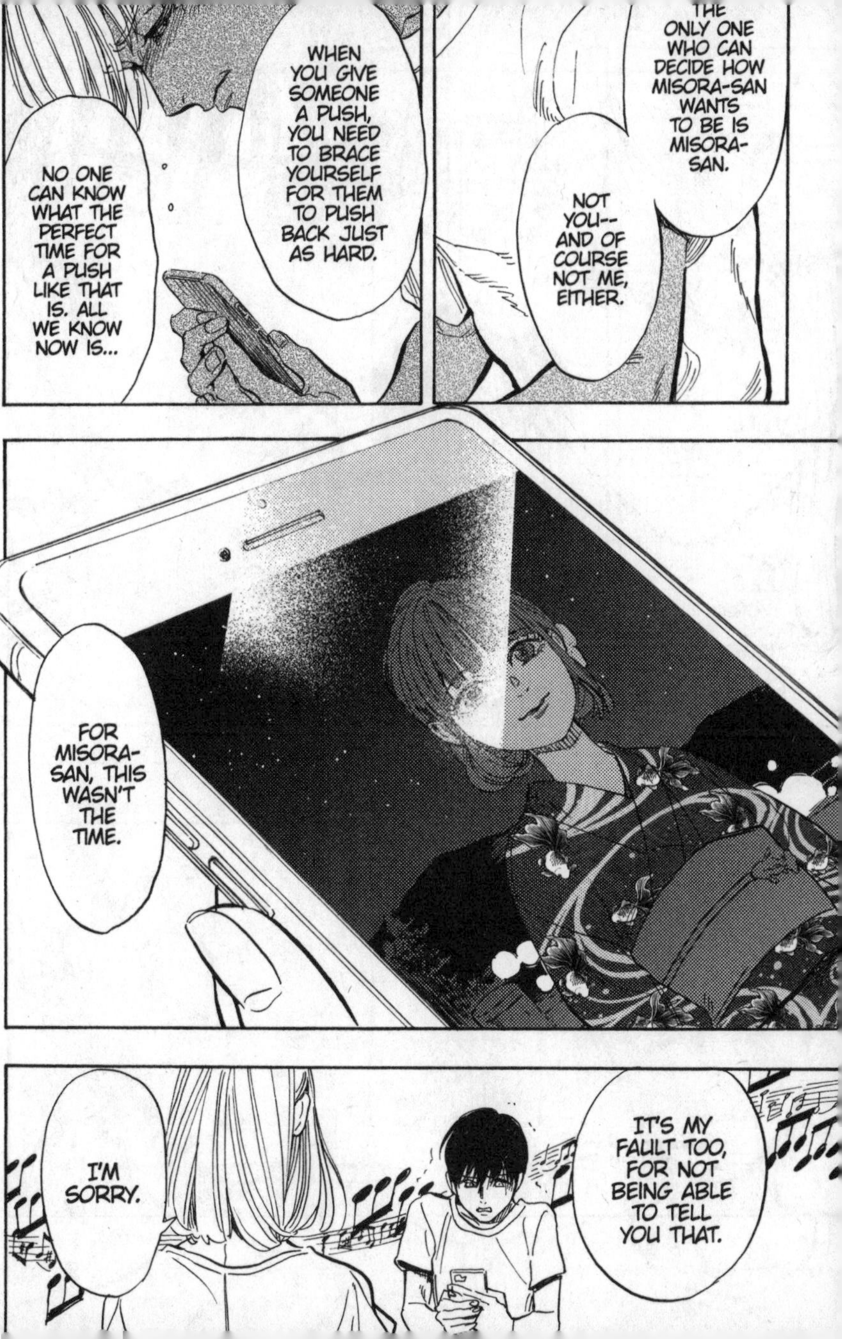
THE ONLY ONE WHO CAN DECIDE HOW MISORA-SAN WANTS TO BE IS MISORA-SAN.
NOT YOU-- AND OF COURSE NOT ME, EITHER.
WHEN YOU GIVE SOMEONE A PUSH, YOU NEED TO BRACE YOURSELF FOR THEM TO PUSH BACK JUST AS HARD.
NO ONE CAN KNOW WHAT THE PERFECT TIME FOR A PUSH LIKE THAT IS. ALL WE KNOW NOW IS...
FOR MISORA-SAN, THIS WASN'T THE TIME.
IT'S MY FAULT TOO, FOR NOT BEING ABLE TO TELL YOU THAT.
I'M SORRY.

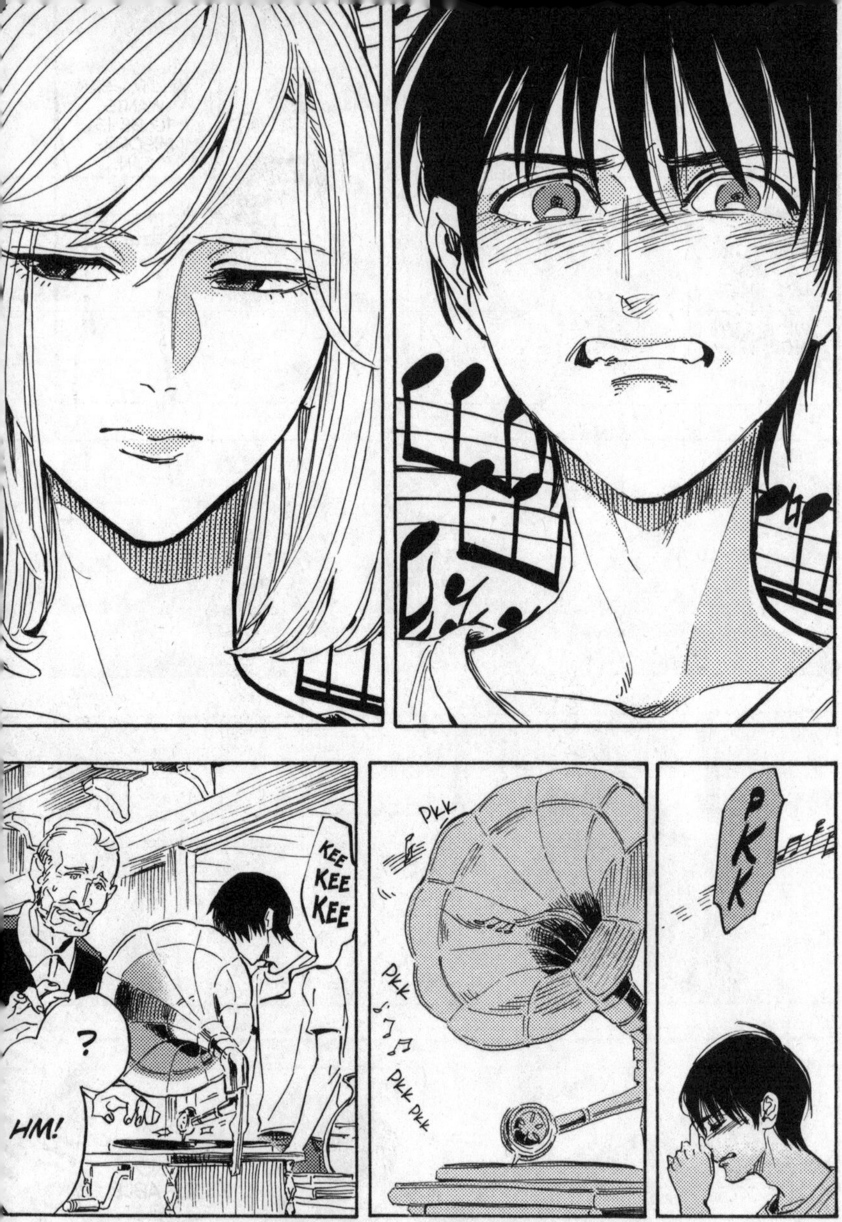
PKK
PKK
PKK
PKK PKK PKK
KEE KEE KEE
?
HM!

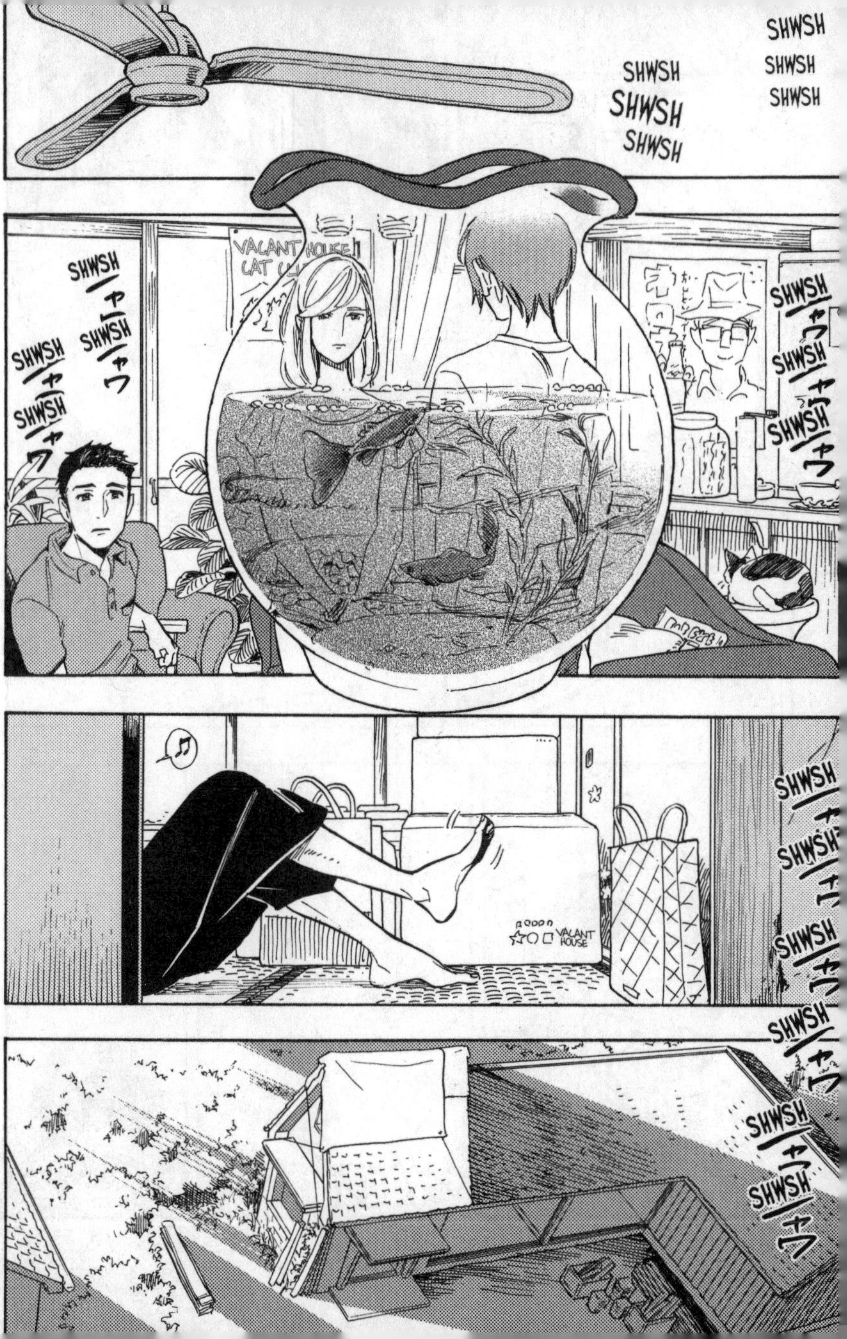
SHWSH
SHWSH
SHWSH
SHWSH
SHWSH
SHWSH
SHWSH
SHWSH
SHWSH
VACANT HOUSE
CAT
SHWSH
SHWSH
SHWSH
SHWSH
SHWSH
SHWSH
SHWSH
VACANT HOUSE
SHWSH
SHWSH
SHWSH

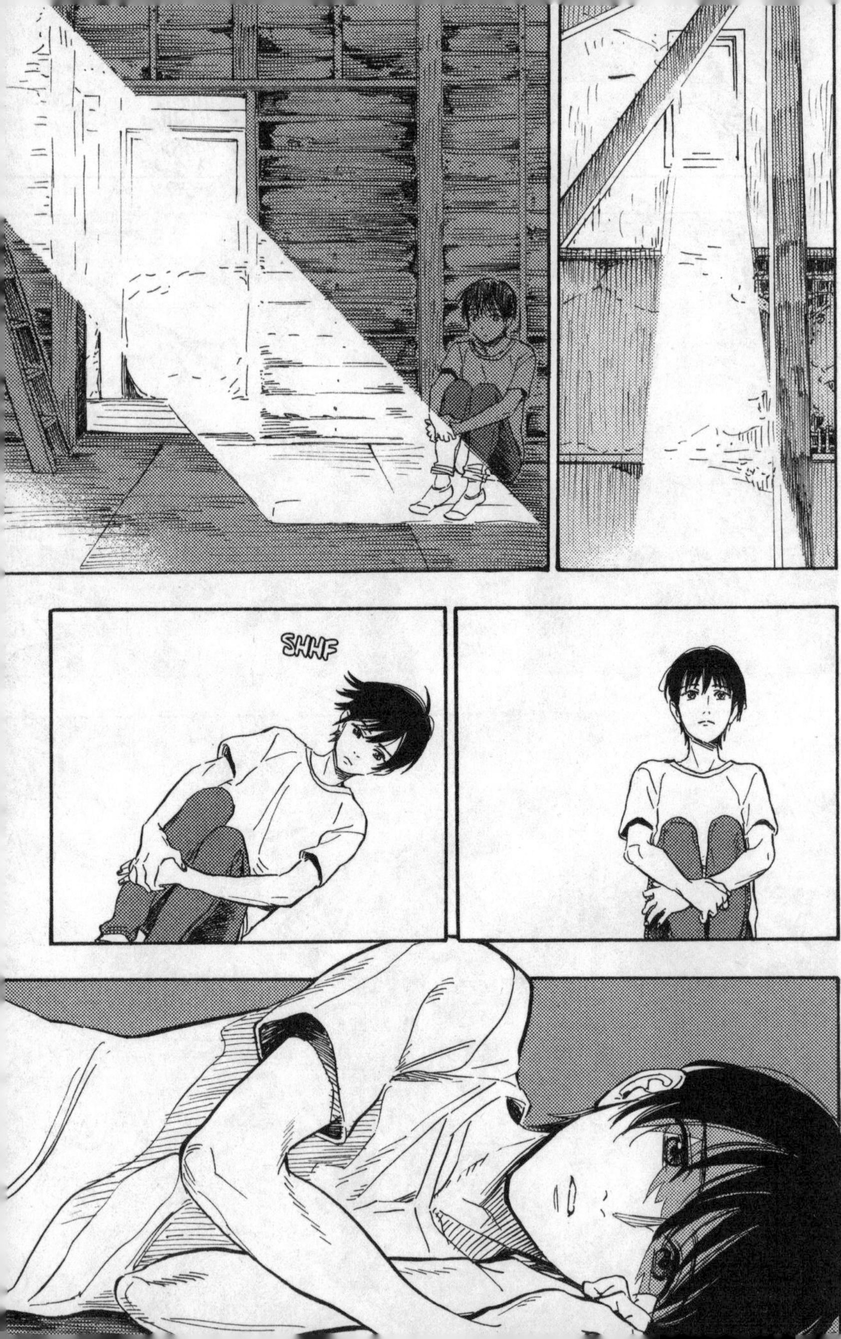
SHHF

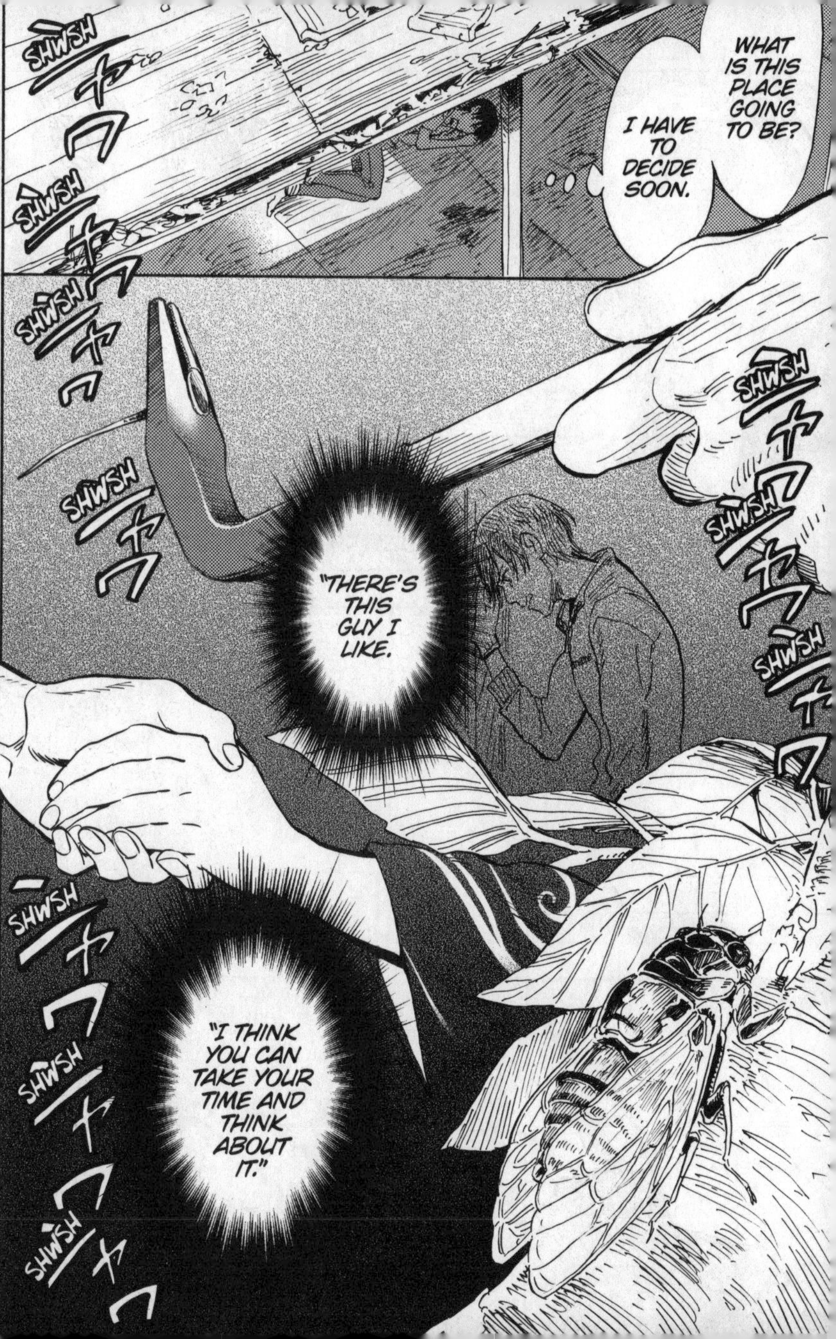
WHAT IS THIS PLACE GOING TO BE?
I HAVE TO DECIDE SOON.
SHWSH
SHWSH
SHWSH
SHWSH
SHWSH
SHWSH
"THERE'S THIS GUY I LIKE.
SHWSH
SHWSH
SHWSH
"I THINK YOU CAN TAKE YOUR TIME AND THINK ABOUT IT."
SHWSH

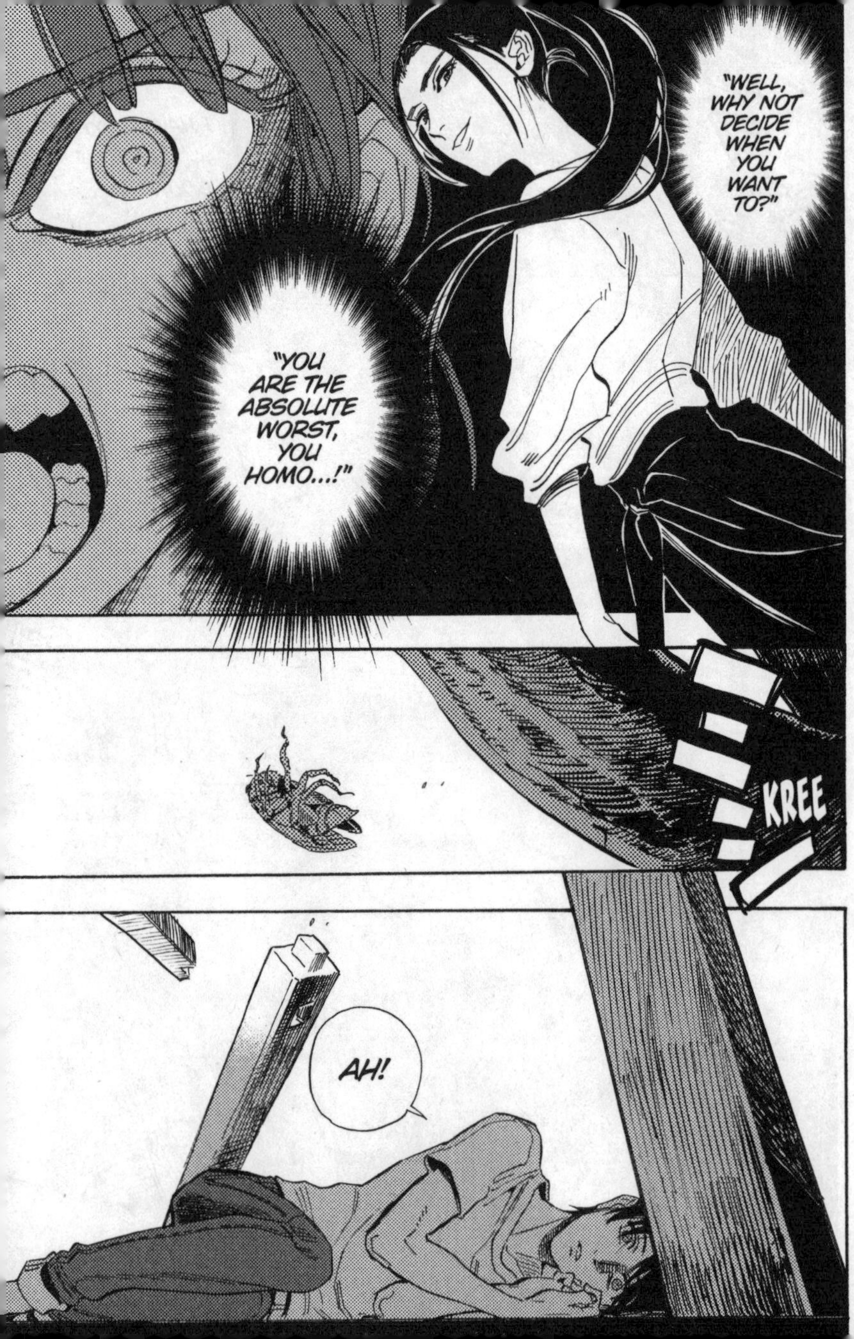
"WELL, WHY NOT DECIDE WHEN YOU WANT TO?"
"YOU ARE THE ABSOLUTE WORST, YOU HOMO...!"
KREE
AH!

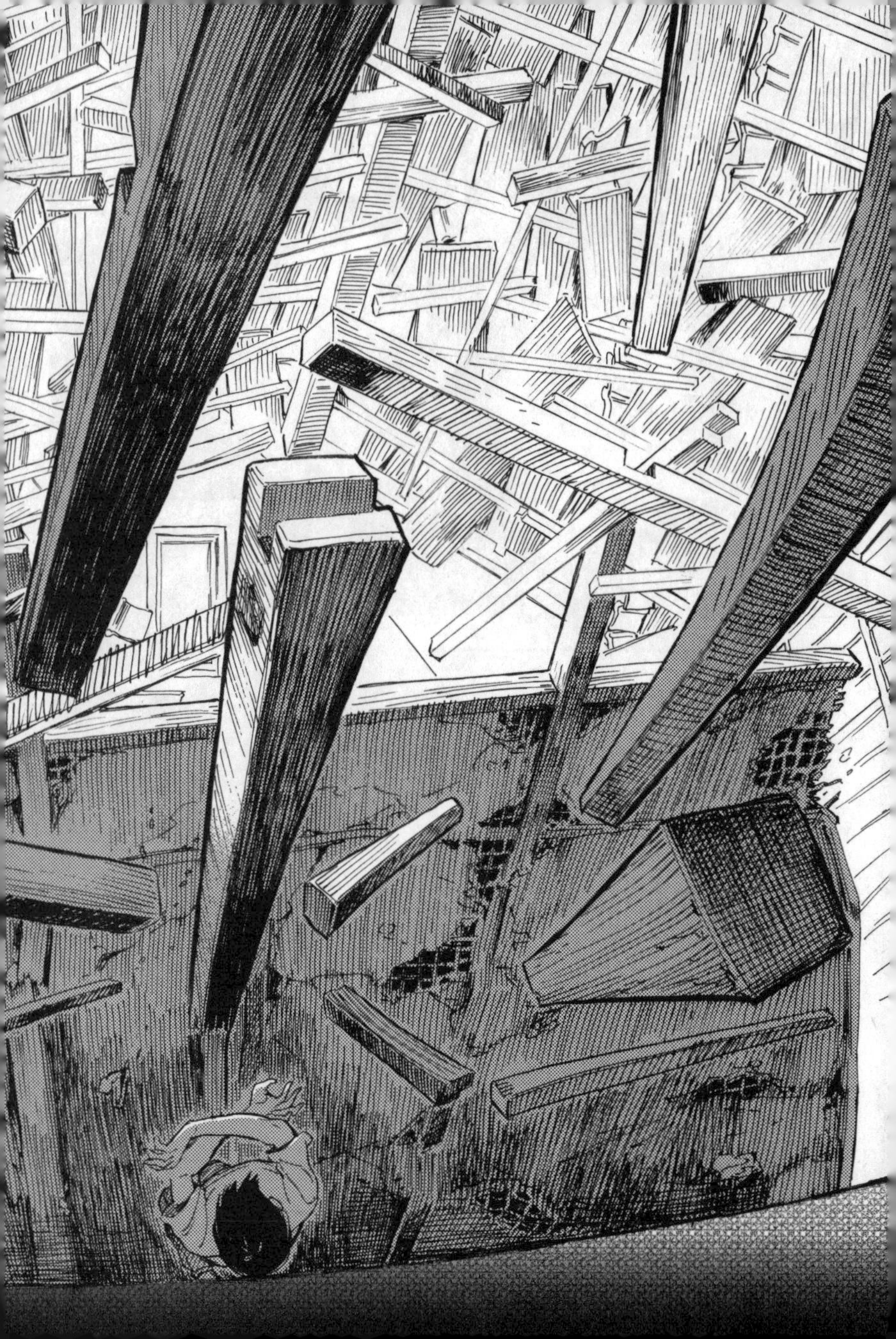

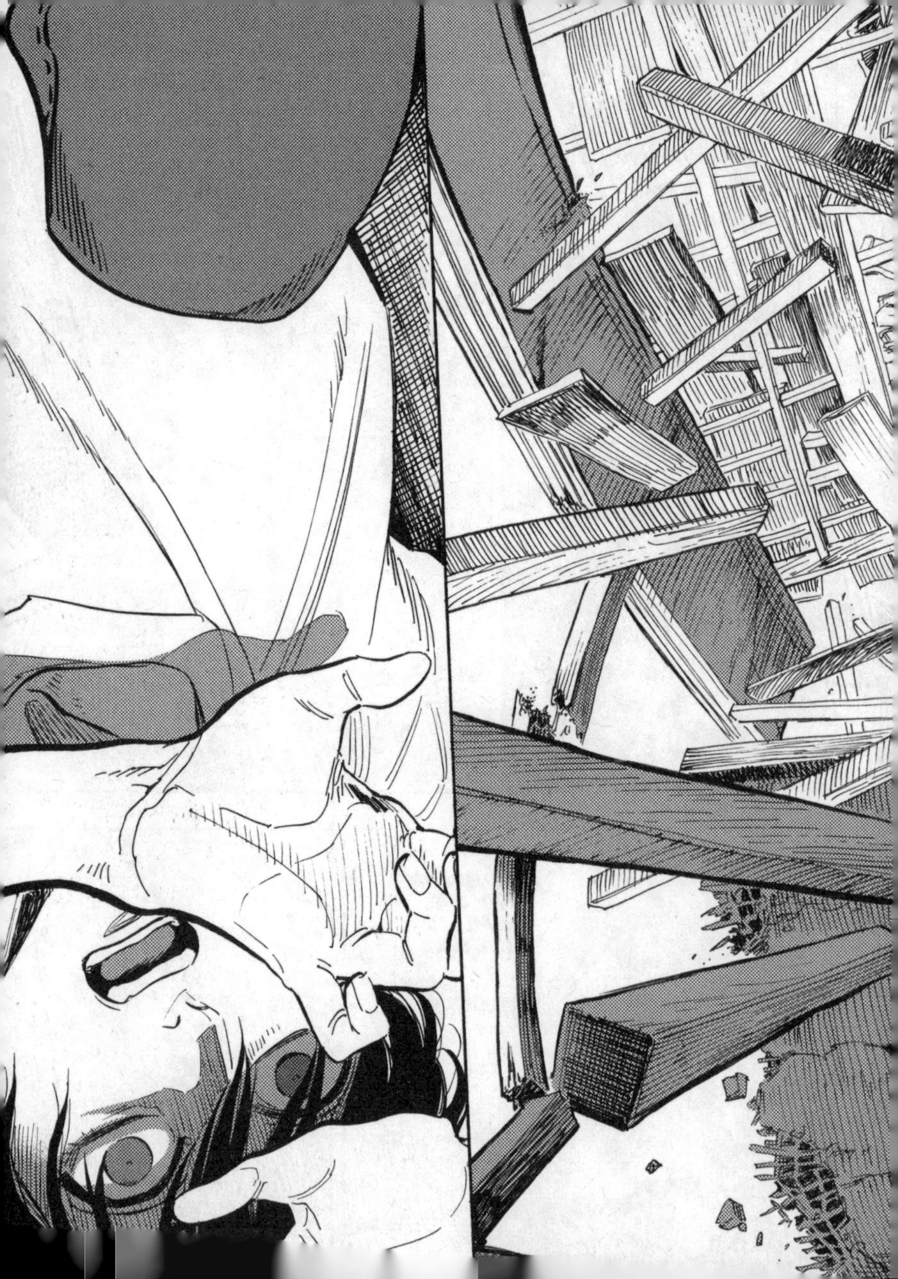

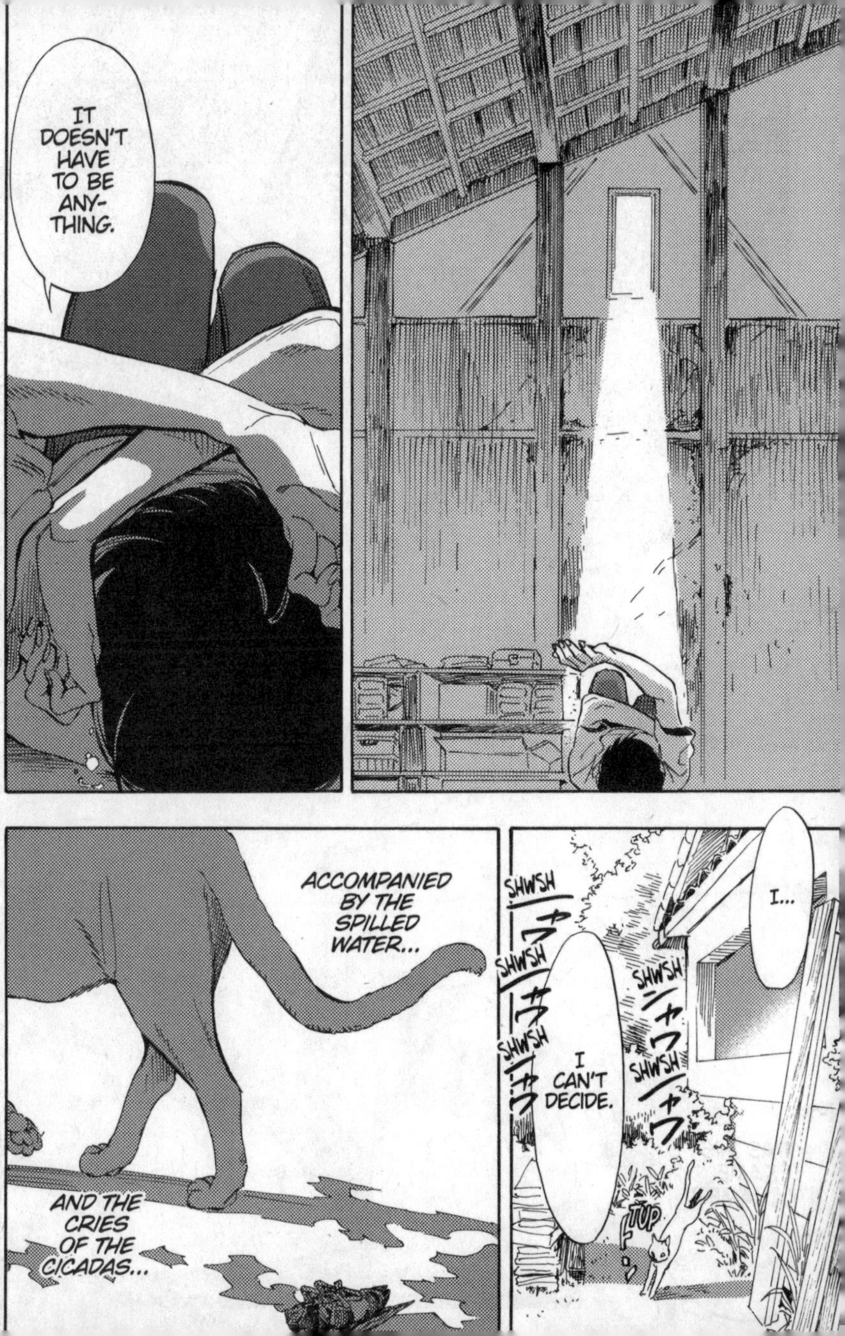
IT DOESN'T HAVE TO BE ANY-THING.
I...
SHWSH
SHWSH
SHWSH
SHWSH
SHWSH
I CAN'T DECIDE.
TUP
ACCOMPANIED BY THE SPILLED WATER...
AND THE CRIES OF THE CICADAS...

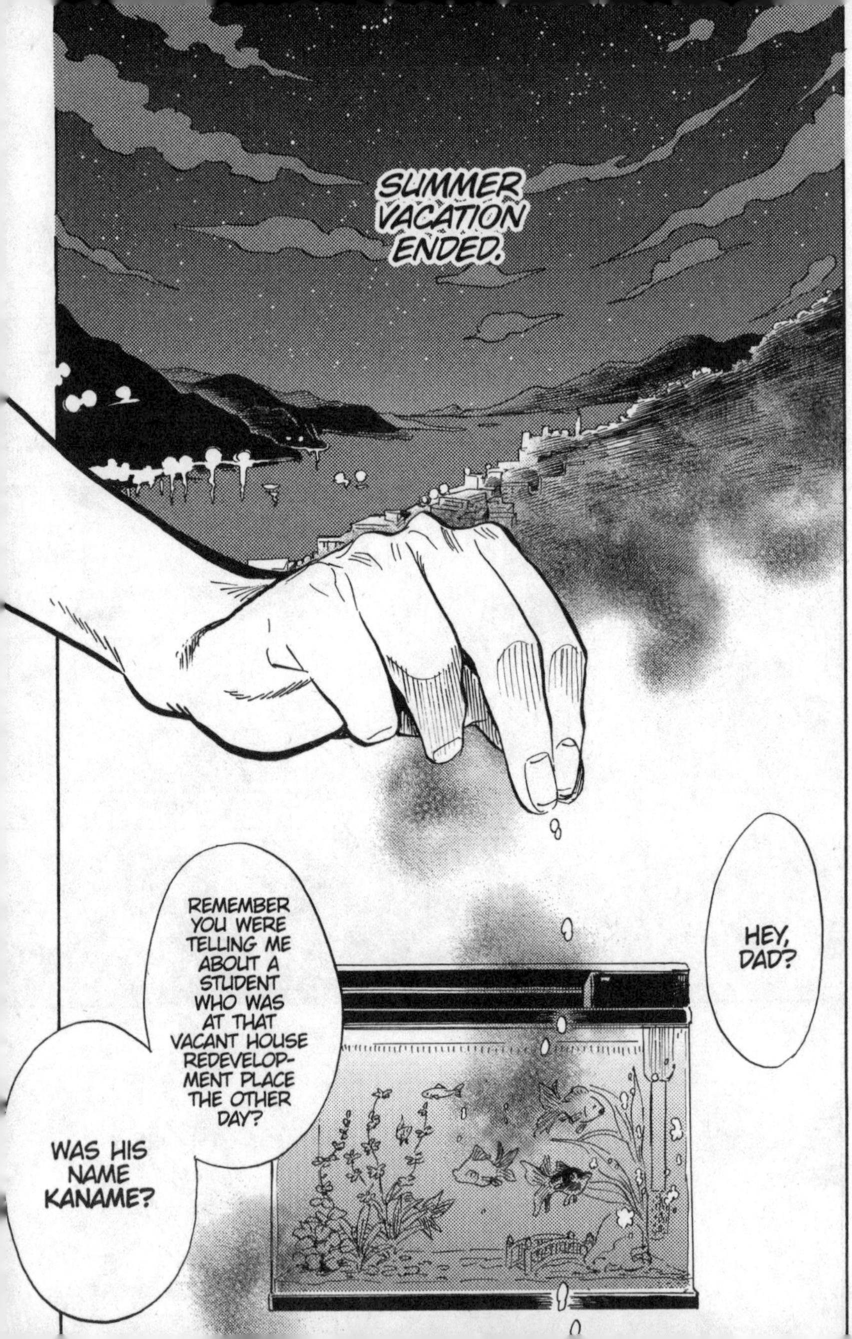
SUMMER VACATION ENDED.
HEY, DAD?
REMEMBER YOU WERE TELLING ME ABOUT A STUDENT WHO WAS AT THAT VACANT HOUSE REDEVELOPMENT PLACE THE OTHER DAY?
WAS HIS NAME KANAME?

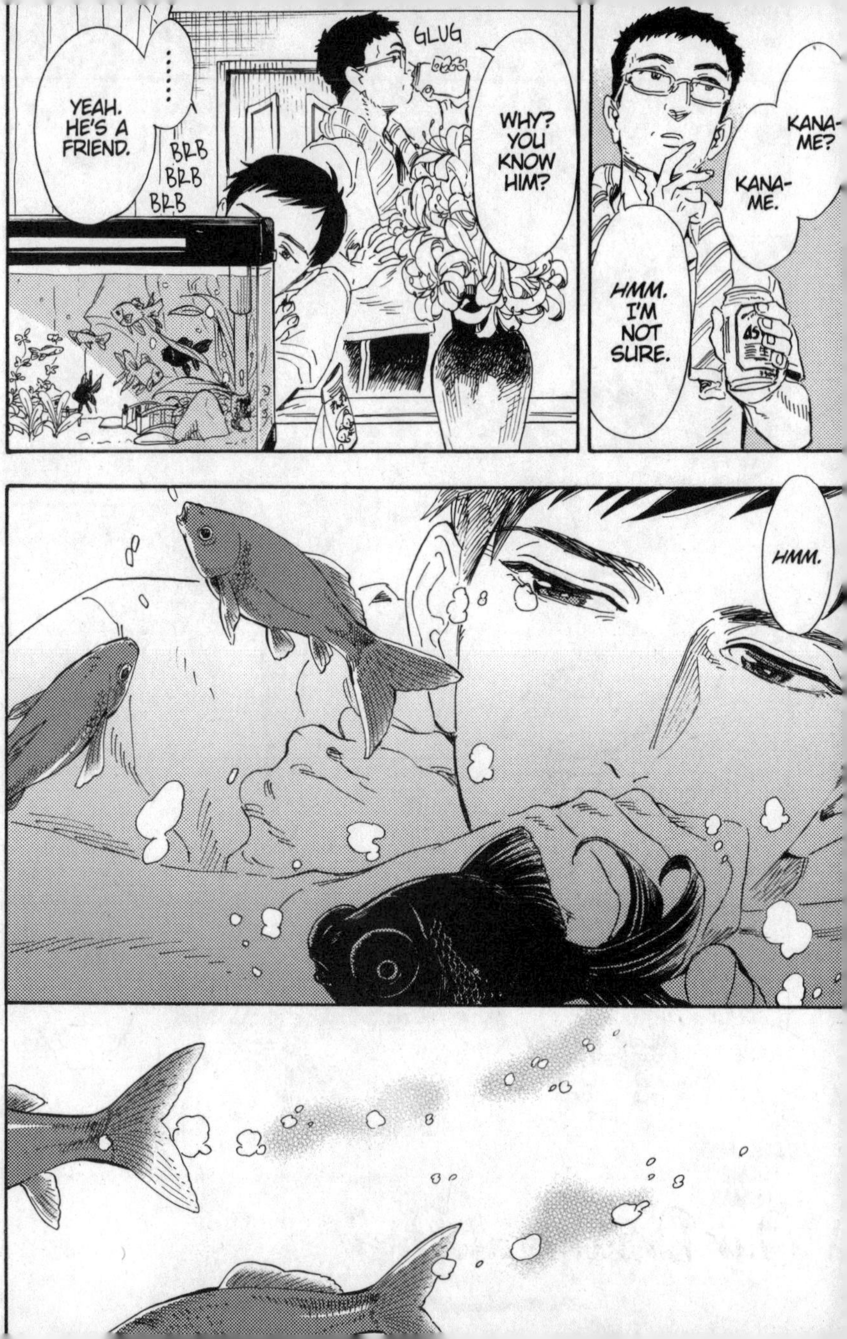
KANA-ME?
KANA-ME.
HMM. I'M NOT SURE.
GLUG
WHY? YOU KNOW HIM?
......
YEAH. HE'S A FRIEND.
BRB BRB BRB
HMM.

[Research Assistance]

NPO Onomichi Akiya Saisei Project
Masako Toyota

Trois Couleurs Co., Ltd.
Hiroko Masahara
Koyuki Higashi

Kentaro Tsuru
Mizuki Kunigi

Onomichi Municipal Tourism Department

SHIMANAMI **TASOGARE**

Our Dreams at Dusk (2) end

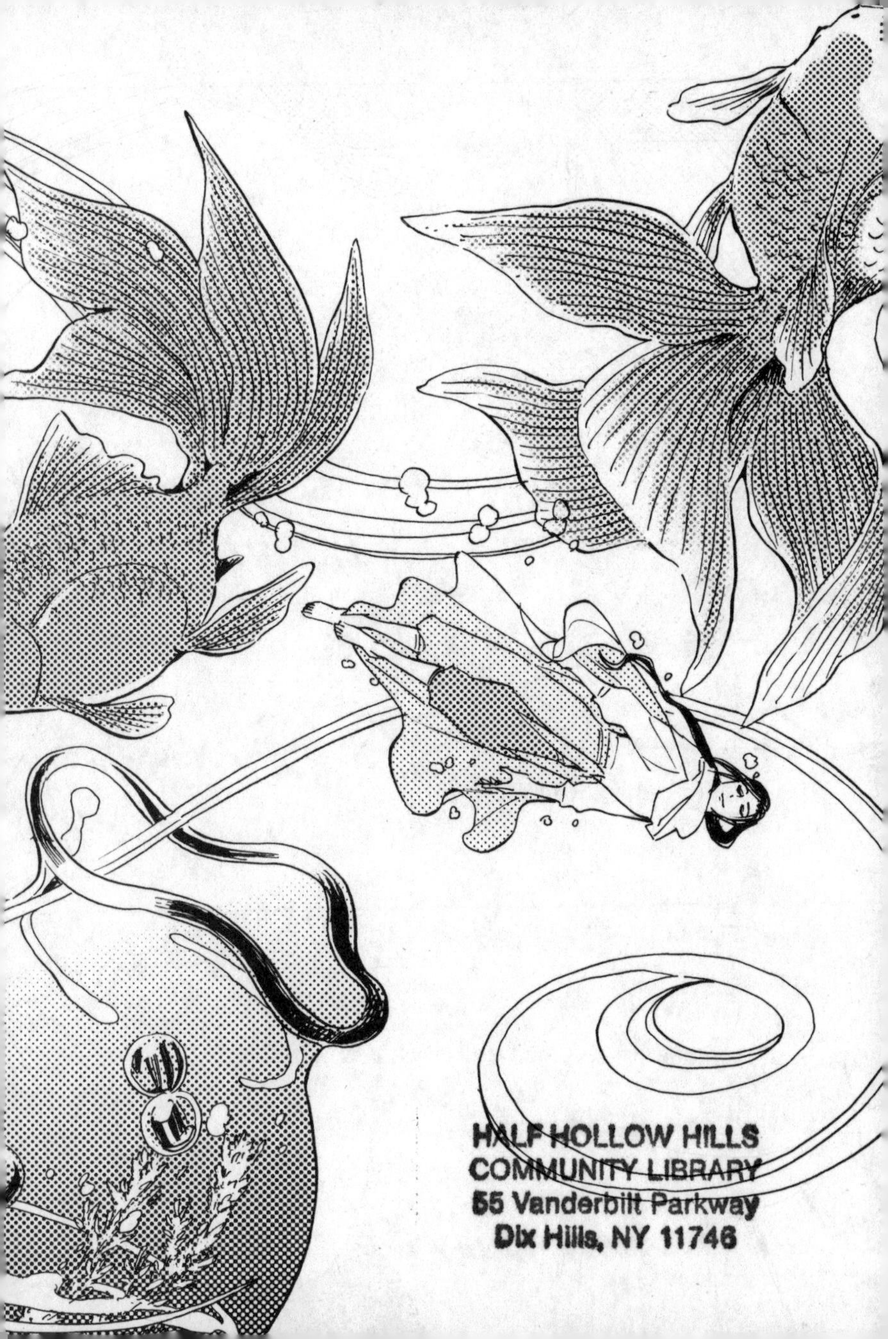

SEVEN SEAS ENTERTAIN[MENT]

P9-DIG-675

Our Dreams at Dusk

SHIMANAMI **TASOGARE** story and art by YUHKI KAMATANI VOL. 2

TRANSLATION
Jocelyne Allen

ADAPTATION
Ysabet MacFarlane

LETTERING AND RETOUCH
Kaitlyn Wiley

COVER DESIGN
KC Fabellon

ORIGINAL EDITION DESIGNER
Hiroshi NIIGAMI (NARTI ; S)

PROOFREADER
Kurestin Armada
Danielle King

EDITOR
Jenn Grunigen

PRODUCTION MANAGER
Lissa Pattillo

EDITOR-IN-CHIEF
Adam Arnold

PUBLISHER
Jason DeAngelis

SHIMANAMI TASOGARE Vol. 2 by Yuhki KAMATANI
© 2015 Yuhki KAMATANI
All rights reserved.
Original Japanese edition published by SHOGAKUKAN.
English translation rights in the United States of America, Canada, and the
United Kingdom arranged with SHOGAKUKAN through Tuttle-Mori Agency

Seven Seas press and purchase enquiries can be sent to Marketing [Manager]
Lianne Sentar at press@gomanga.com. Information regarding the d[istribution]
and purchase of digital editions is available from Digital Manager C[K Russell]
at digital@gomanga.com.

Seven Seas and the Seven Seas logo are trademarks of
Seven Seas Entertainment. All rights reserved.

ISBN: 978-1-64275-061-4

Printed in Canada

First Printing: July 2019

10 9 8 7 6 5 4 3 2 1

FOLLOW US ONLINE: www.sevenseasentertainmen[t.com]

READING DIRECTIONS

This book reads from *right to left*, Japanese style.
If this is your first time reading manga, you start
reading from the top right panel on each page and
take it from there. If you get lost, just follow the
numbered diagram here. It may seem backwards at
first, but you'll get the hang of it! Have fun!!

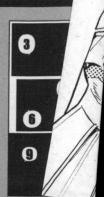

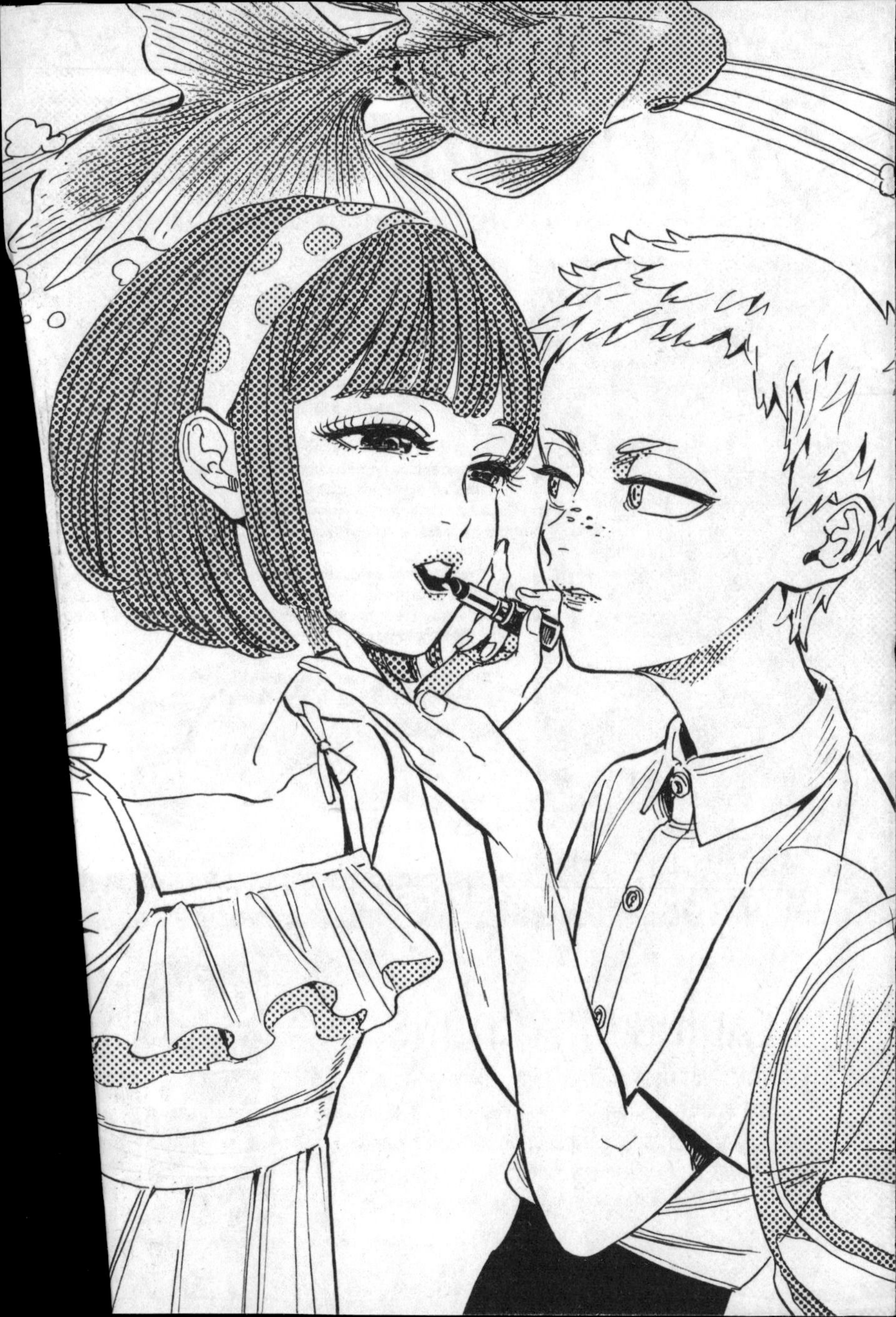

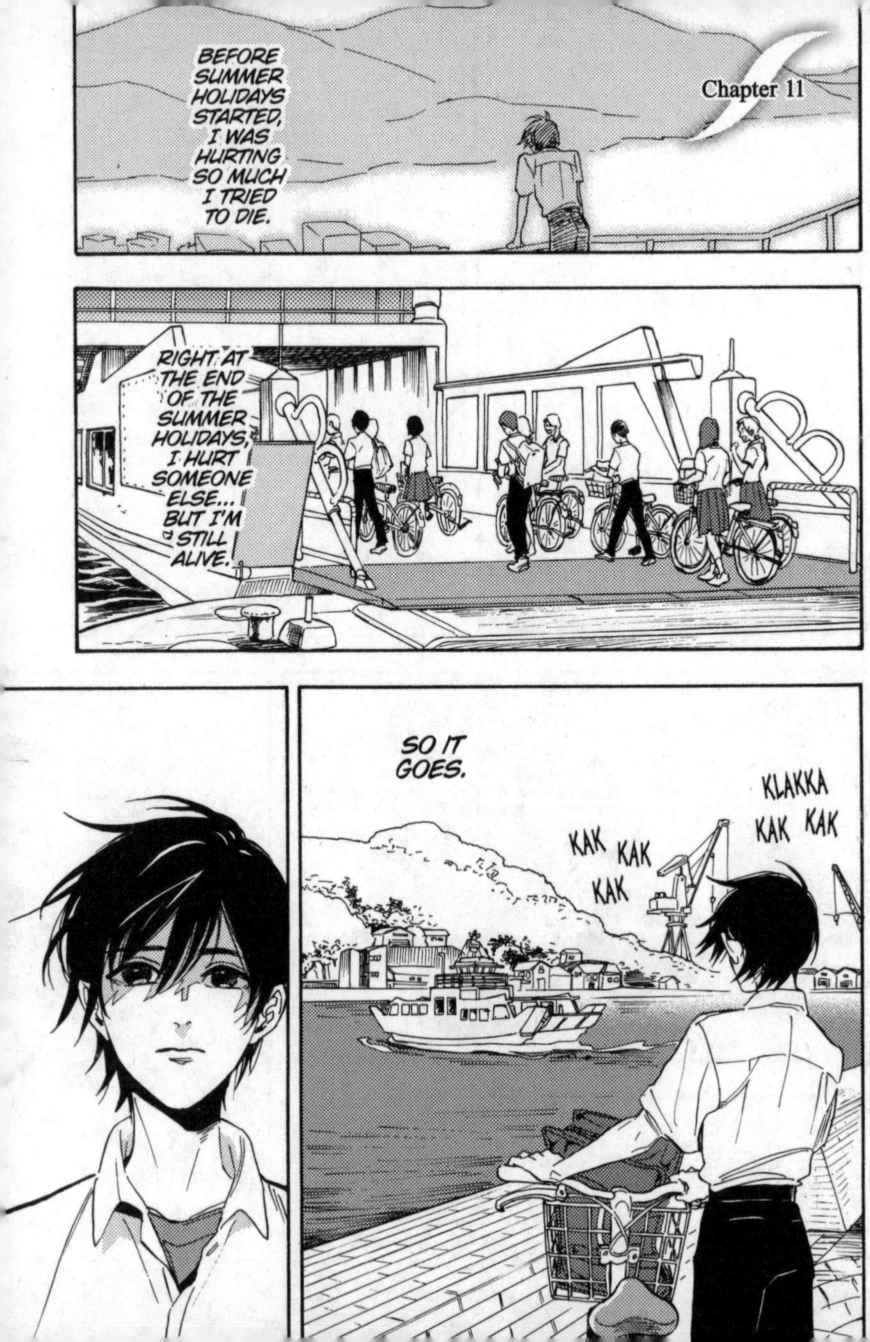
Chapter 11
BEFORE SUMMER HOLIDAYS STARTED, I WAS HURTING SO MUCH I TRIED TO DIE.
RIGHT AT THE END OF THE SUMMER HOLIDAYS, I HURT SOMEONE ELSE... BUT I'M STILL ALIVE.
SO IT GOES.
KLAKKA
KAK KAK
KAK KAK
KAK

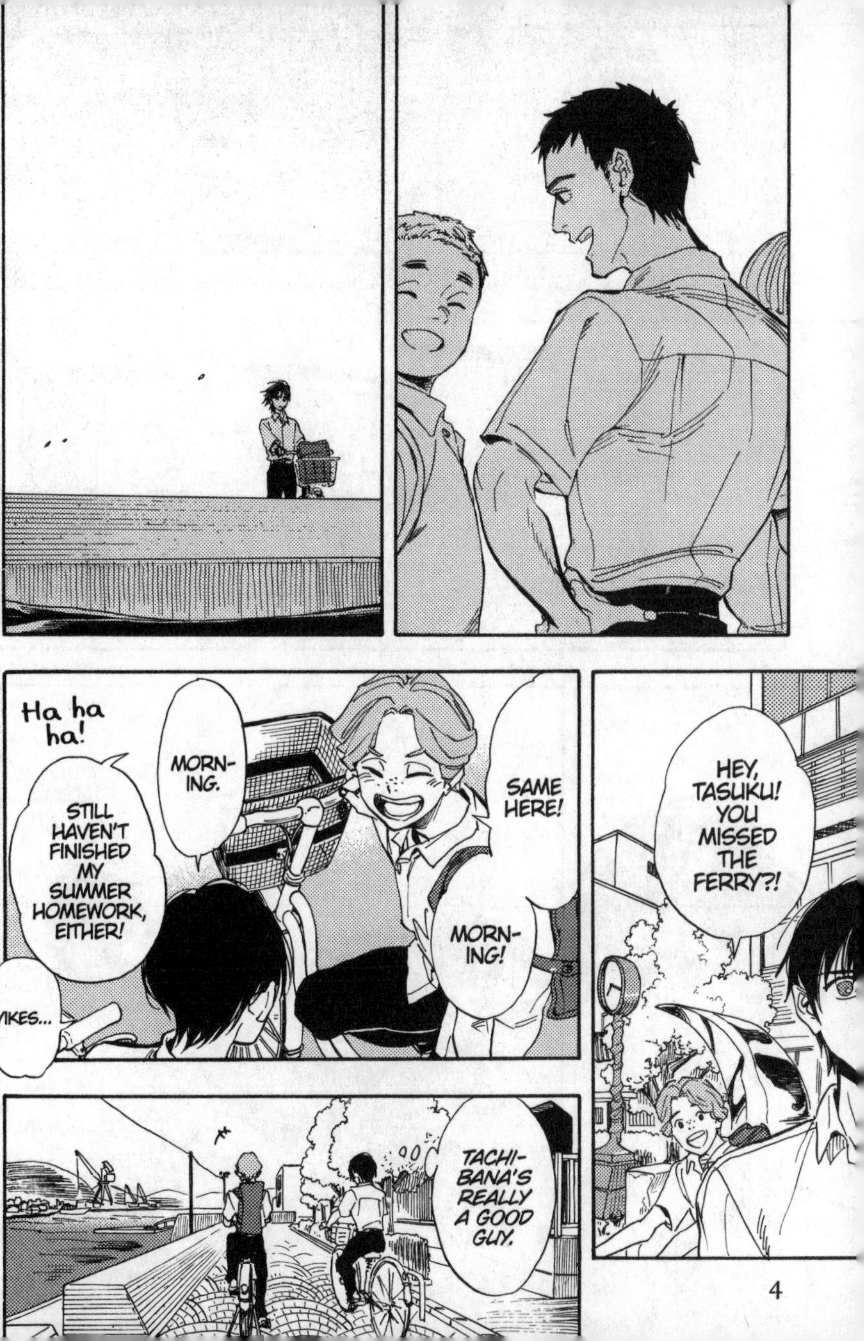
HEY, TASUKU! YOU MISSED THE FERRY?!
SAME HERE!
MORN-ING!
MORN-ING.
STILL HAVEN'T FINISHED MY SUMMER HOMEWORK, EITHER!
Ha ha ha!
YIKES...
TACHI-BANA'S REALLY A GOOD GUY.

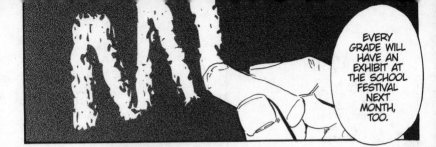

EVERY GRADE WILL HAVE AN EXHIBIT AT THE SCHOOL FESTIVAL NEXT MONTH, TOO.

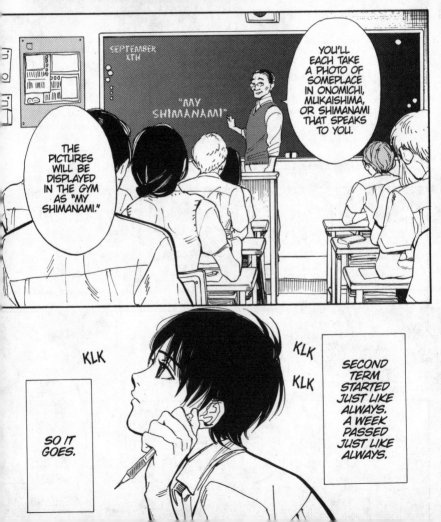

YOU'LL EACH TAKE A PHOTO OF SOMEPLACE IN ONOMICHI, MUKAISHIMA, OR SHIMANAMI THAT SPEAKS TO YOU.

SEPTEMBER XTH

"MY SHIMANAMI"

THE PICTURES WILL BE DISPLAYED IN THE GYM AS "MY SHIMANAMI."

KLK

KLK

KLK

SECOND TERM STARTED JUST LIKE ALWAYS. A WEEK PASSED JUST LIKE ALWAYS.

SO IT GOES.

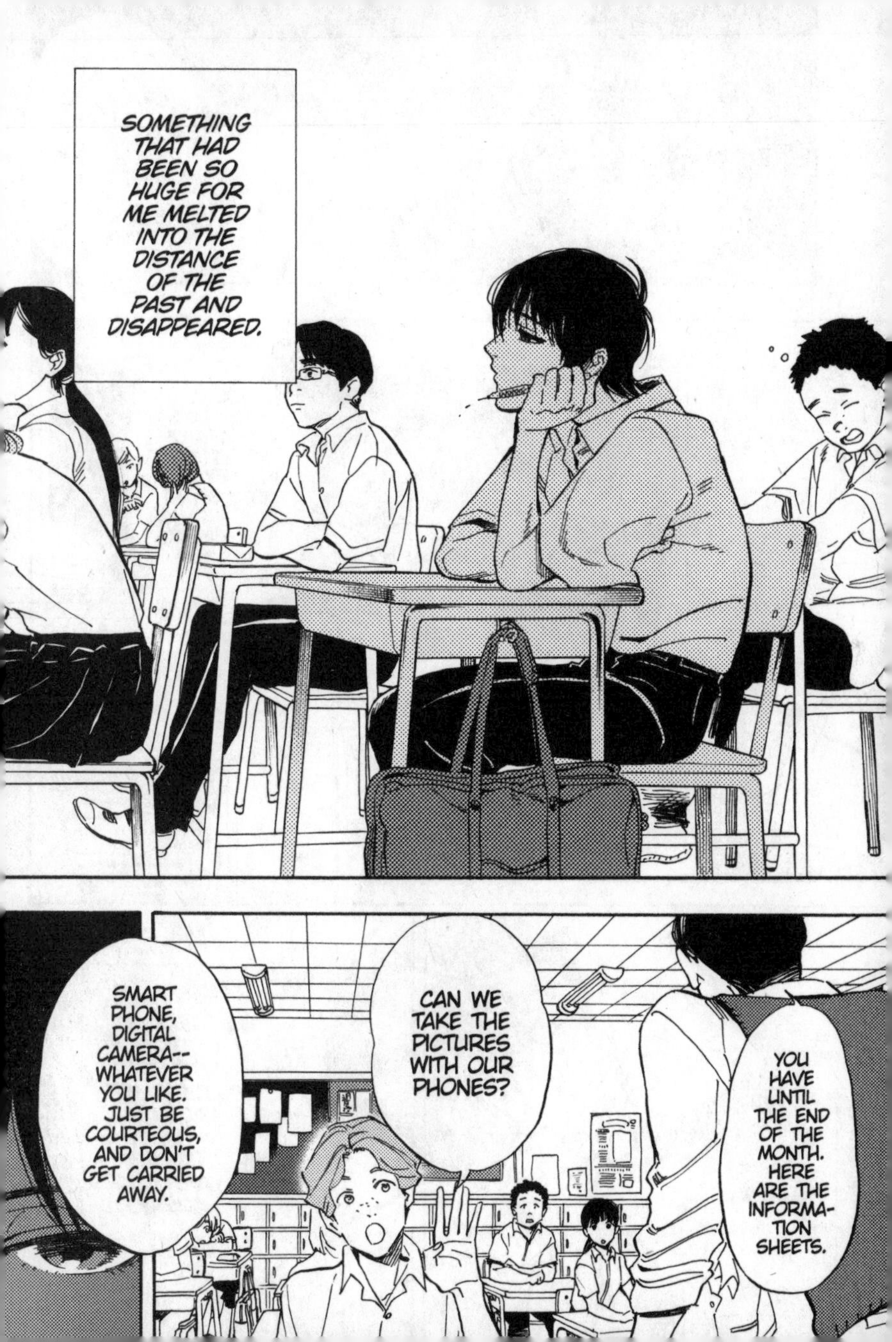
SOMETHING THAT HAD BEEN SO HUGE FOR ME MELTED INTO THE DISTANCE OF THE PAST AND DISAPPEARED.
YOU HAVE UNTIL THE END OF THE MONTH. HERE ARE THE INFORMATION SHEETS.
CAN WE TAKE THE PICTURES WITH OUR PHONES?
SMART PHONE, DIGITAL CAMERA-- WHATEVER YOU LIKE. JUST BE COURTEOUS, AND DON'T GET CARRIED AWAY.

Chapter 11

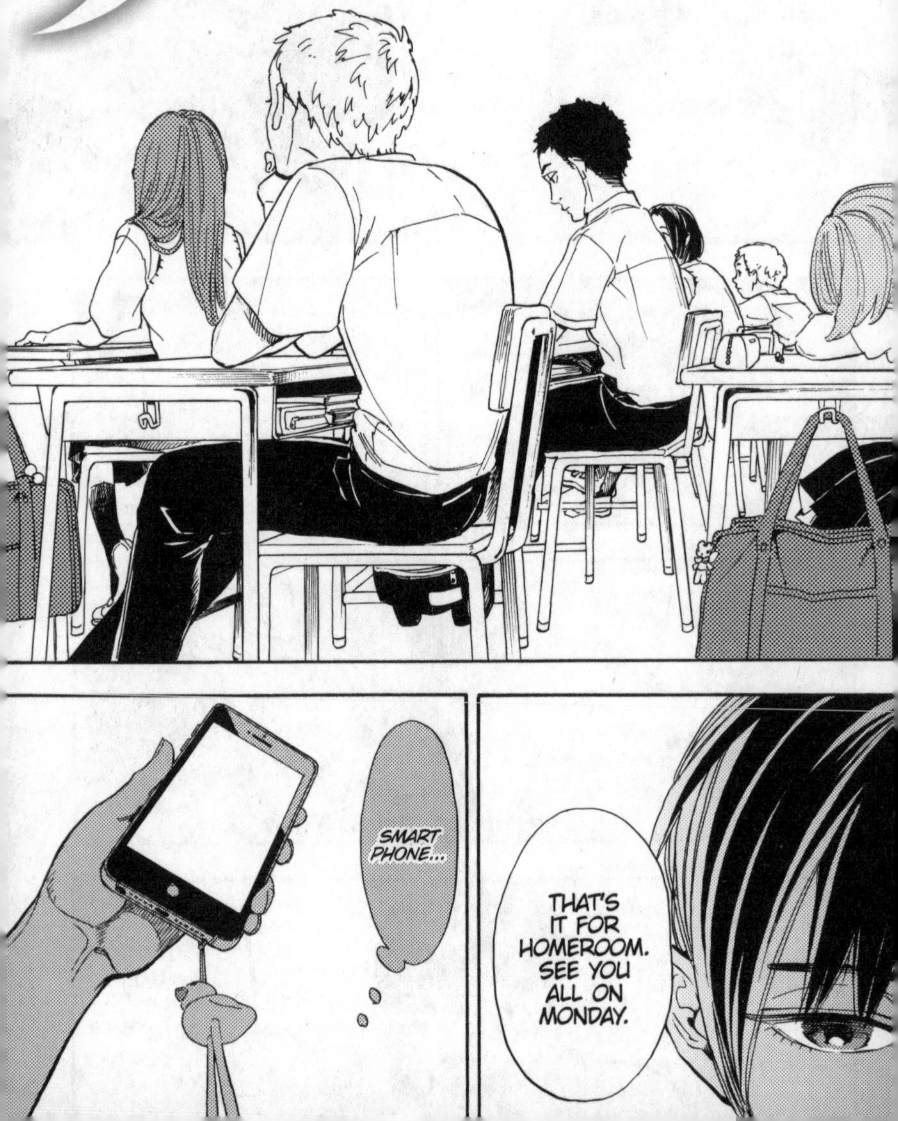
THAT'S IT FOR HOMEROOM. SEE YOU ALL ON MONDAY.
SMART PHONE...

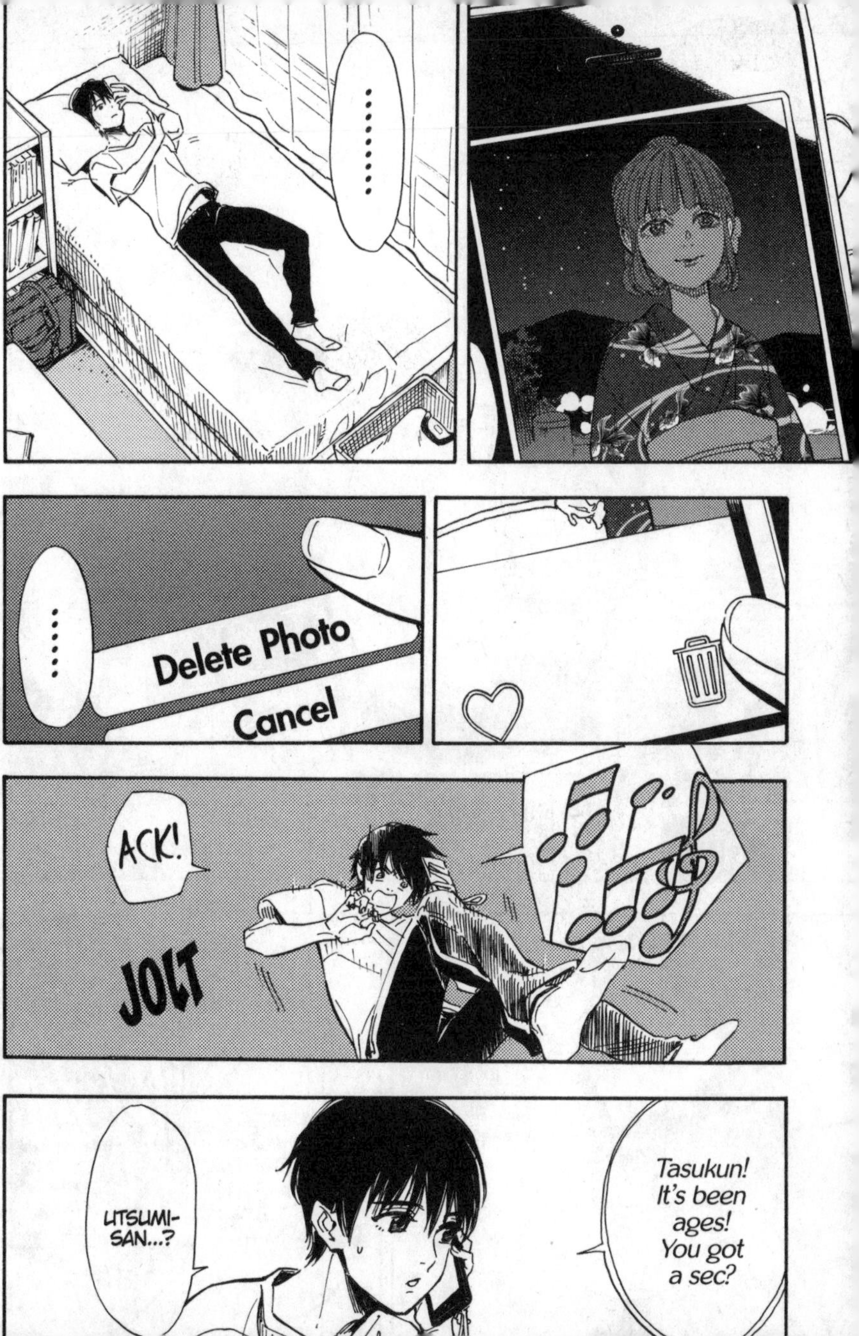
....
......
Delete Photo
Cancel
ACK!
JOLT
Tasukun! It's been ages! You got a sec?
UTSUMI-SAN...?

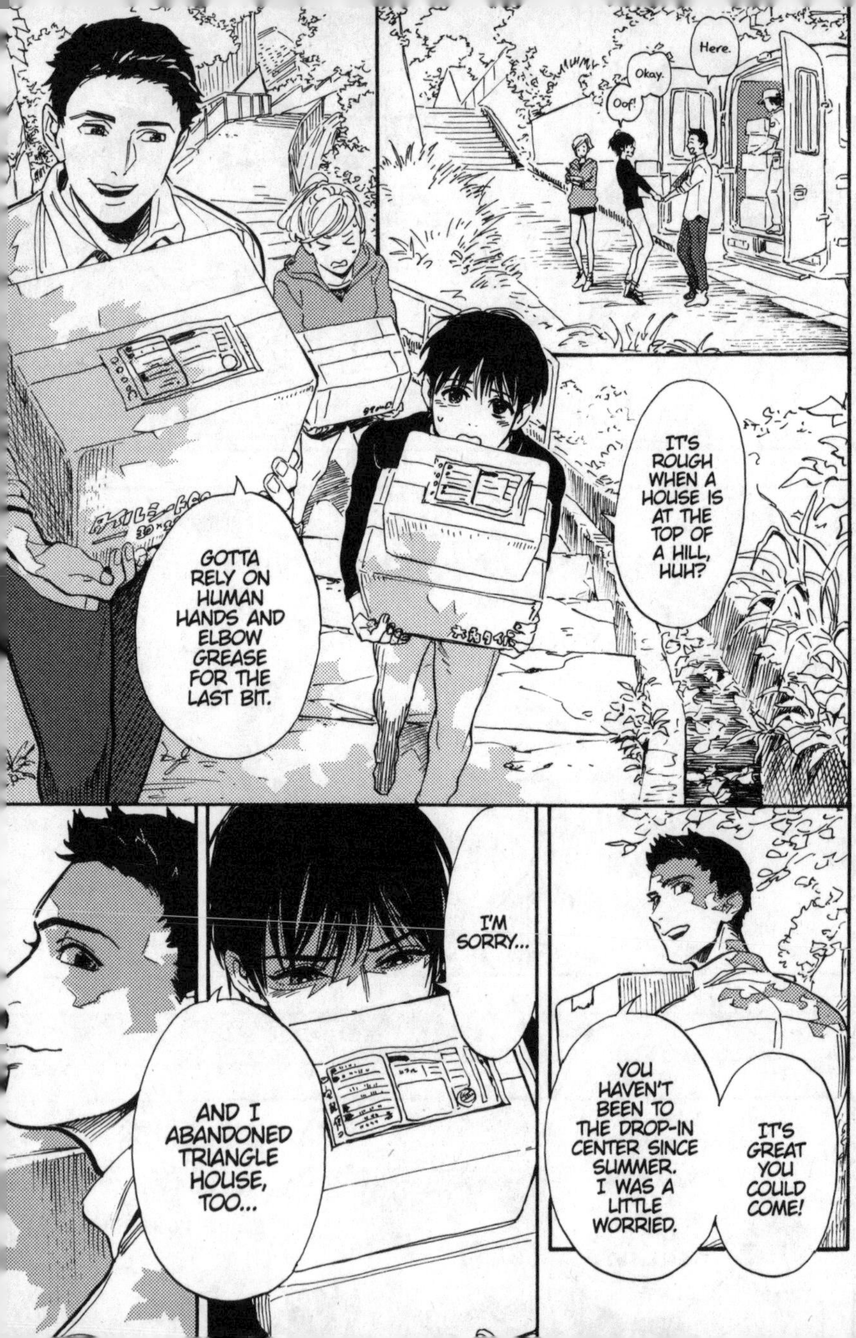
Here.
Okay.
Oof!
IT'S ROUGH WHEN A HOUSE IS AT THE TOP OF A HILL, HUH?
GOTTA RELY ON HUMAN HANDS AND ELBOW GREASE FOR THE LAST BIT.
YOU HAVEN'T BEEN TO THE DROP-IN CENTER SINCE SUMMER. I WAS A LITTLE WORRIED.
IT'S GREAT YOU COULD COME!
I'M SORRY...
AND I ABANDONED TRIANGLE HOUSE, TOO...

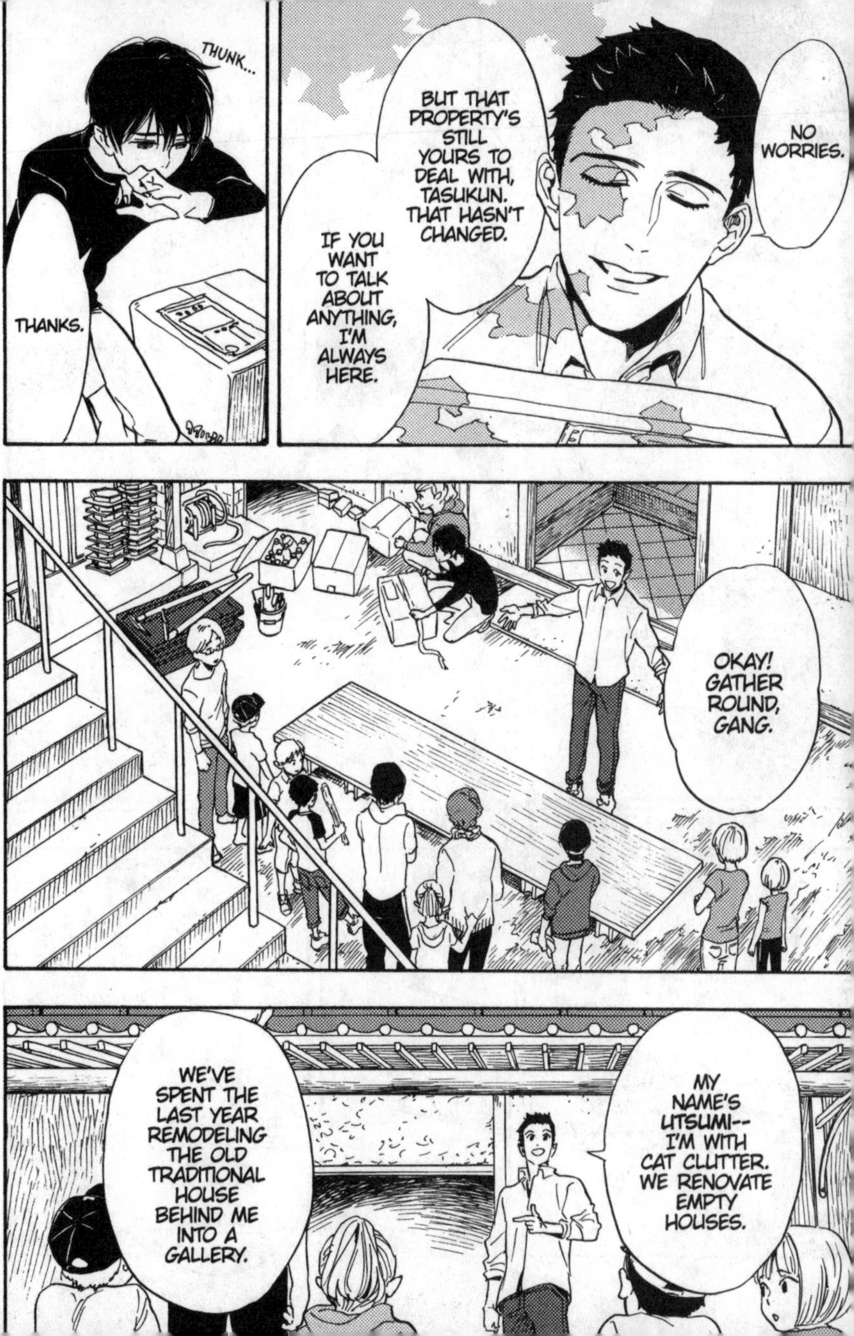
NO WORRIES.
BUT THAT PROPERTY'S STILL YOURS TO DEAL WITH, TASUKUN. THAT HASN'T CHANGED.
IF YOU WANT TO TALK ABOUT ANYTHING, I'M ALWAYS HERE.
THUNK...
THANKS.
OKAY! GATHER ROUND, GANG.
MY NAME'S UTSUMI-- I'M WITH CAT CLUTTER. WE RENOVATE EMPTY HOUSES.
WE'VE SPENT THE LAST YEAR REMODELING THE OLD TRADITIONAL HOUSE BEHIND ME INTO A GALLERY.

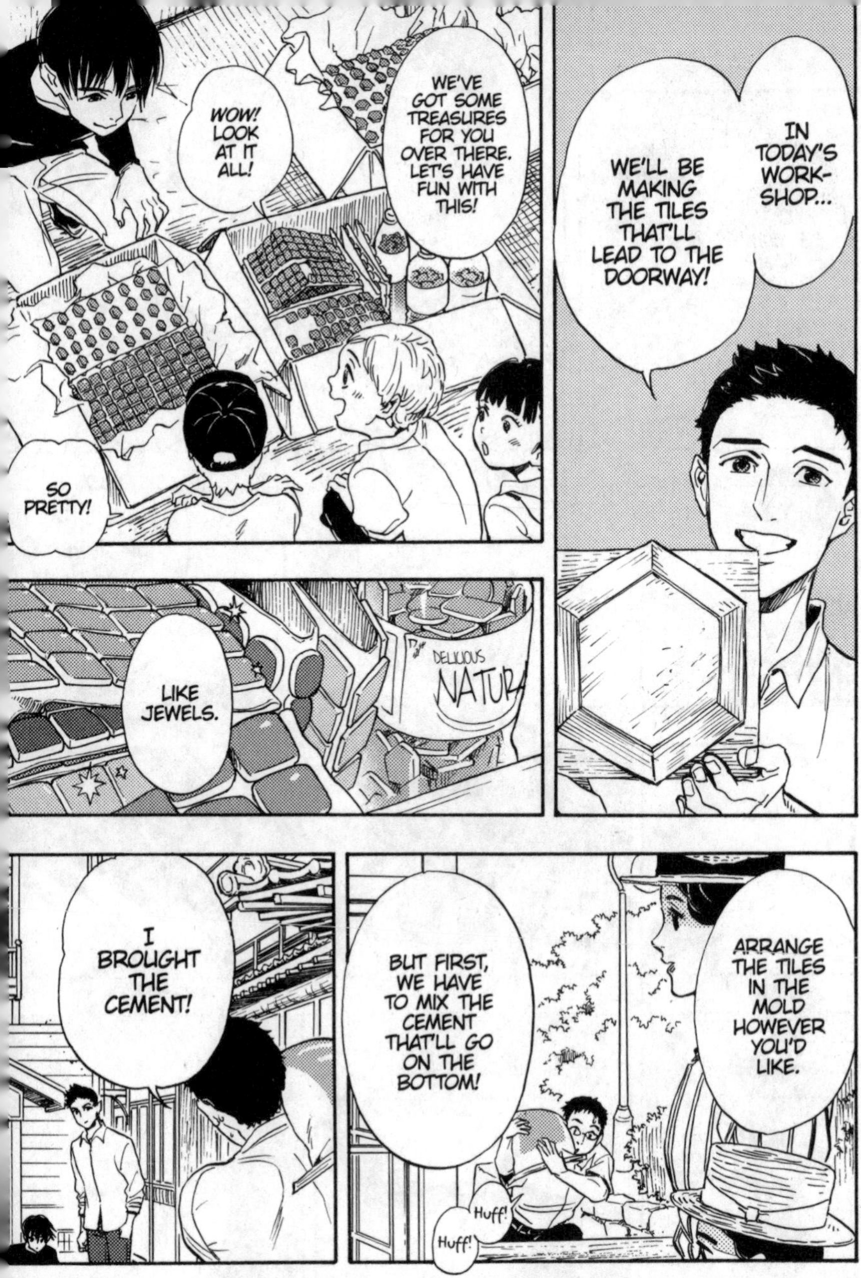
IN TODAY'S WORK-SHOP...
WE'LL BE MAKING THE TILES THAT'LL LEAD TO THE DOORWAY!
WE'VE GOT SOME TREASURES FOR YOU OVER THERE. LET'S HAVE FUN WITH THIS!
WOW! LOOK AT IT ALL!
SO PRETTY!
LIKE JEWELS.
DELICIOUS
NATUR
ARRANGE THE TILES IN THE MOLD HOWEVER YOU'D LIKE.
BUT FIRST, WE HAVE TO MIX THE CEMENT THAT'LL GO ON THE BOTTOM!
Huff!
Huff!
I BROUGHT THE CEMENT!

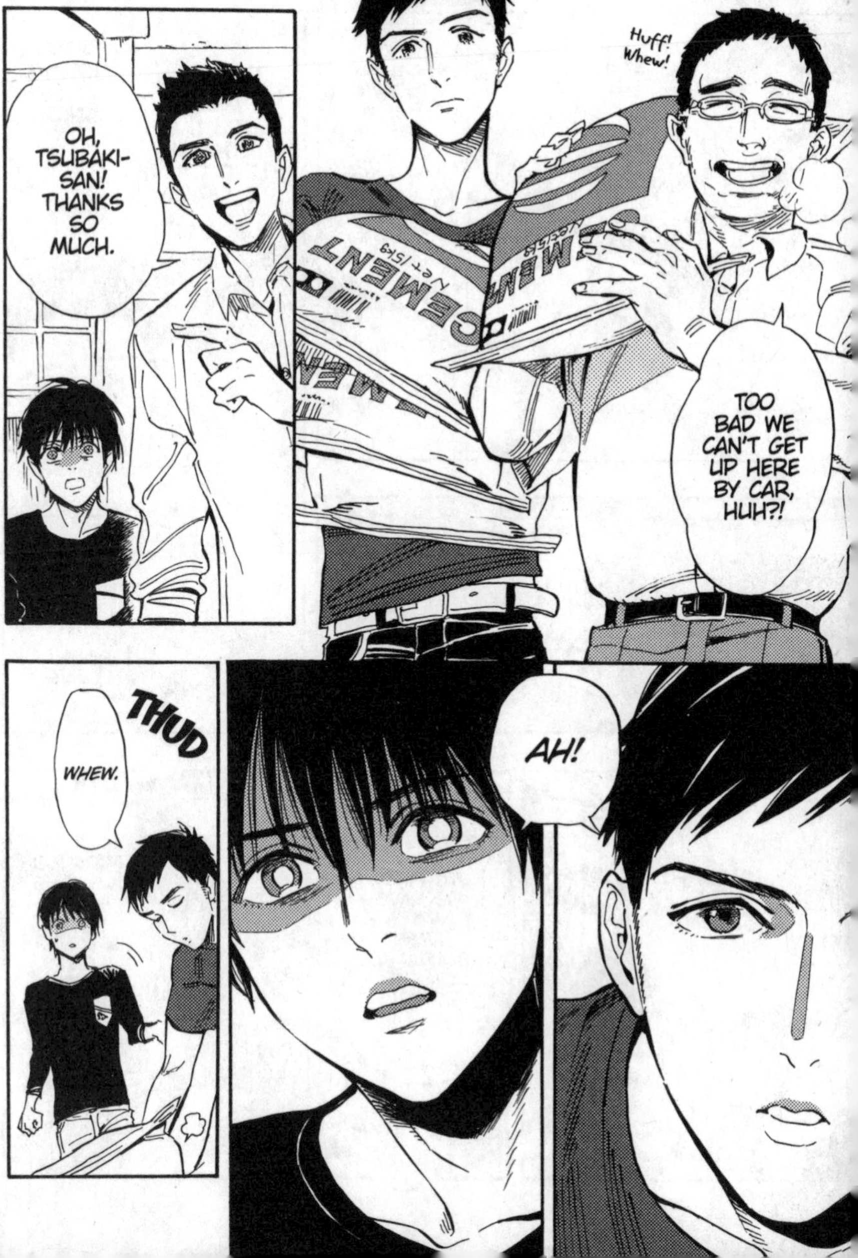
Huff! Whew!
TOO BAD WE CAN'T GET UP HERE BY CAR, HUH?!
OH, TSUBAKI-SAN! THANKS SO MUCH.
AH!
THUD
WHEW.

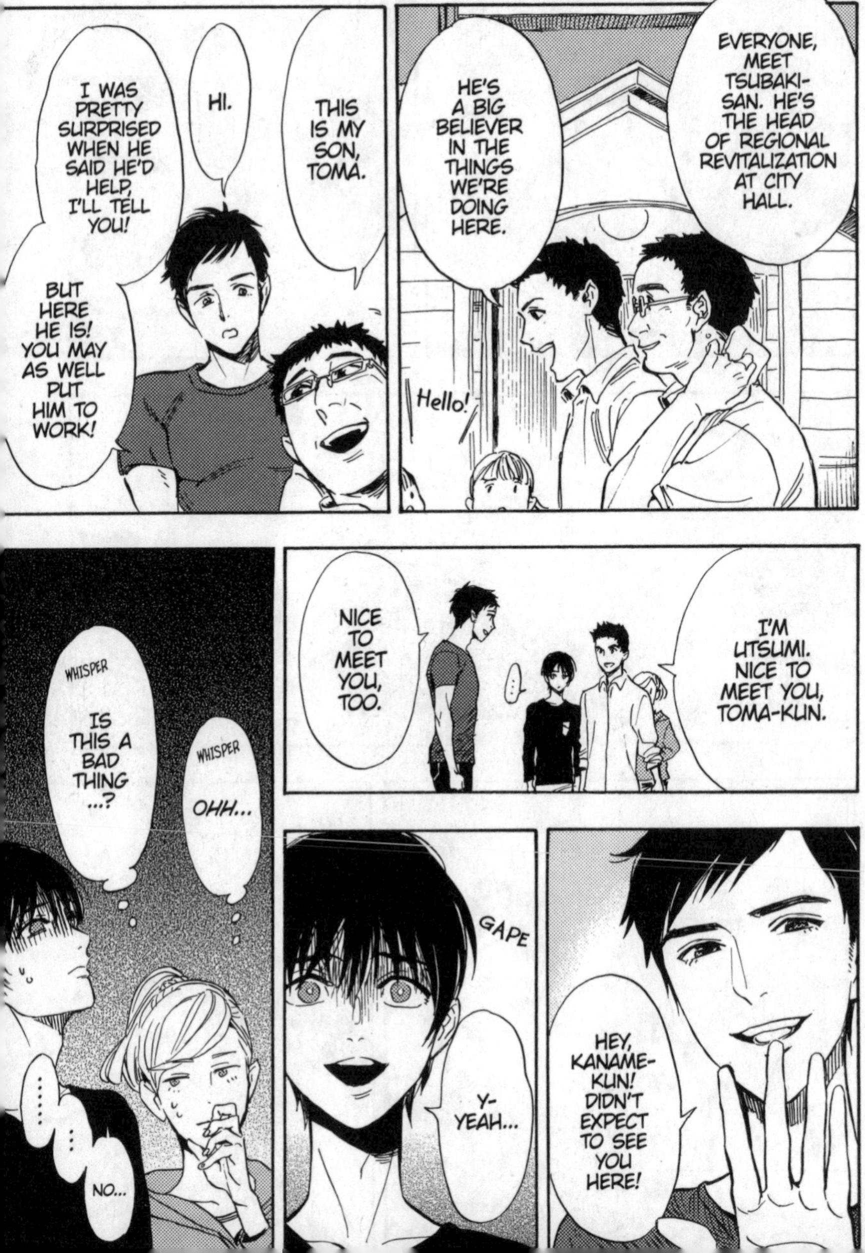
EVERYONE, MEET TSUBAKI-SAN. HE'S THE HEAD OF REGIONAL REVITALIZATION AT CITY HALL.
HE'S A BIG BELIEVER IN THE THINGS WE'RE DOING HERE.
Hello!
THIS IS MY SON, TOMA.
HI.
I WAS PRETTY SURPRISED WHEN HE SAID HE'D HELP, I'LL TELL YOU!
BUT HERE HE IS! YOU MAY AS WELL PUT HIM TO WORK!
I'M UTSUMI. NICE TO MEET YOU, TOMA-KUN.
...
NICE TO MEET YOU, TOO.
HEY, KANAME-KUN! DIDN'T EXPECT TO SEE YOU HERE!
GAPE
Y-YEAH...
WHISPER
OHH...
WHISPER
IS THIS A BAD THING ...?
......
... NO...

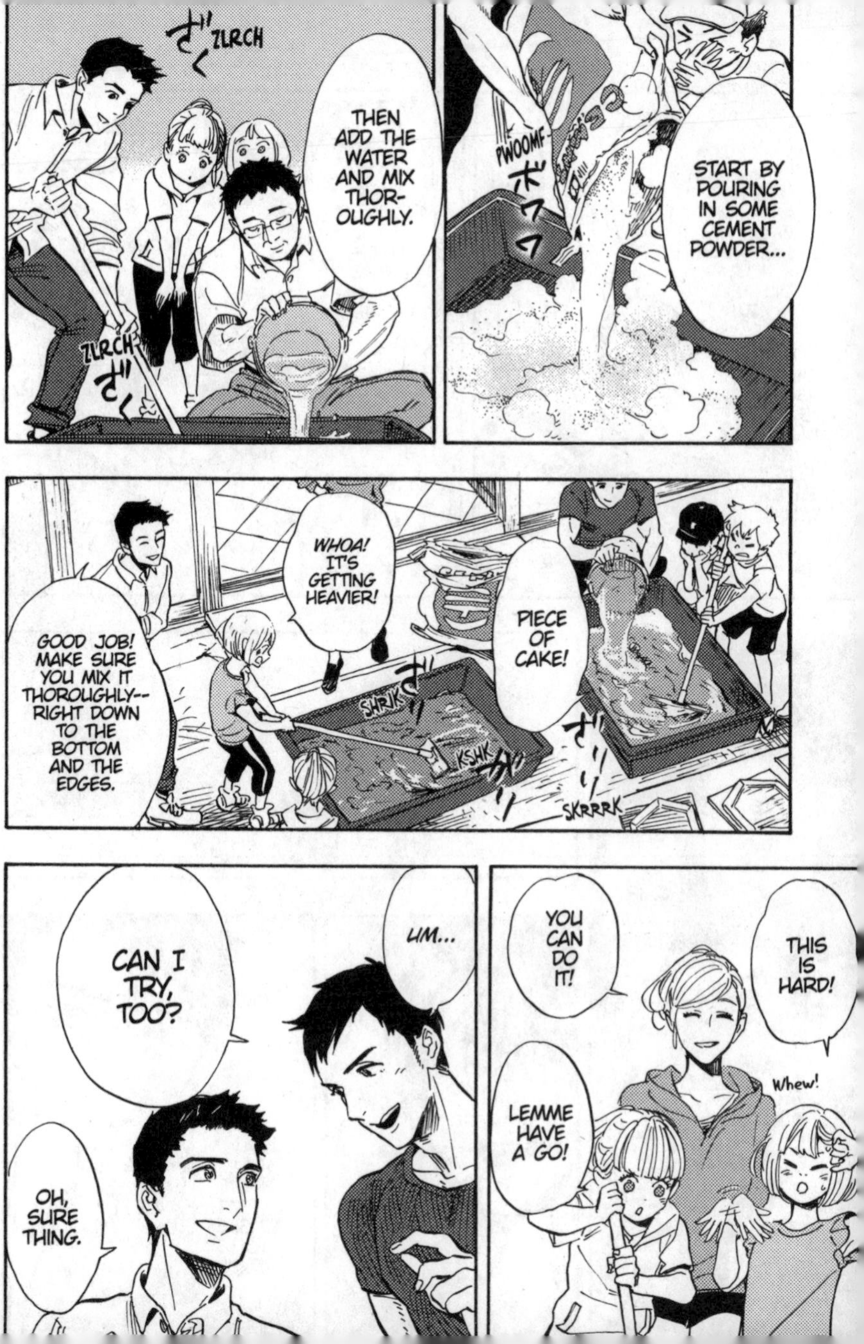
START BY POURING IN SOME CEMENT POWDER...
PWOOMF
ボフ
THEN ADD THE WATER AND MIX THOR-OUGHLY.
ざく ZLRCH
ZLRCH ざく
PIECE OF CAKE!
ざりり SKRRRK
WHOA! IT'S GETTING HEAVIER!
SHRIK
KSHK
GOOD JOB! MAKE SURE YOU MIX IT THOROUGHLY-- RIGHT DOWN TO THE BOTTOM AND THE EDGES.
THIS IS HARD!
YOU CAN DO IT!
Whew!
LEMME HAVE A GO!
UM...
CAN I TRY, TOO?
OH, SURE THING.

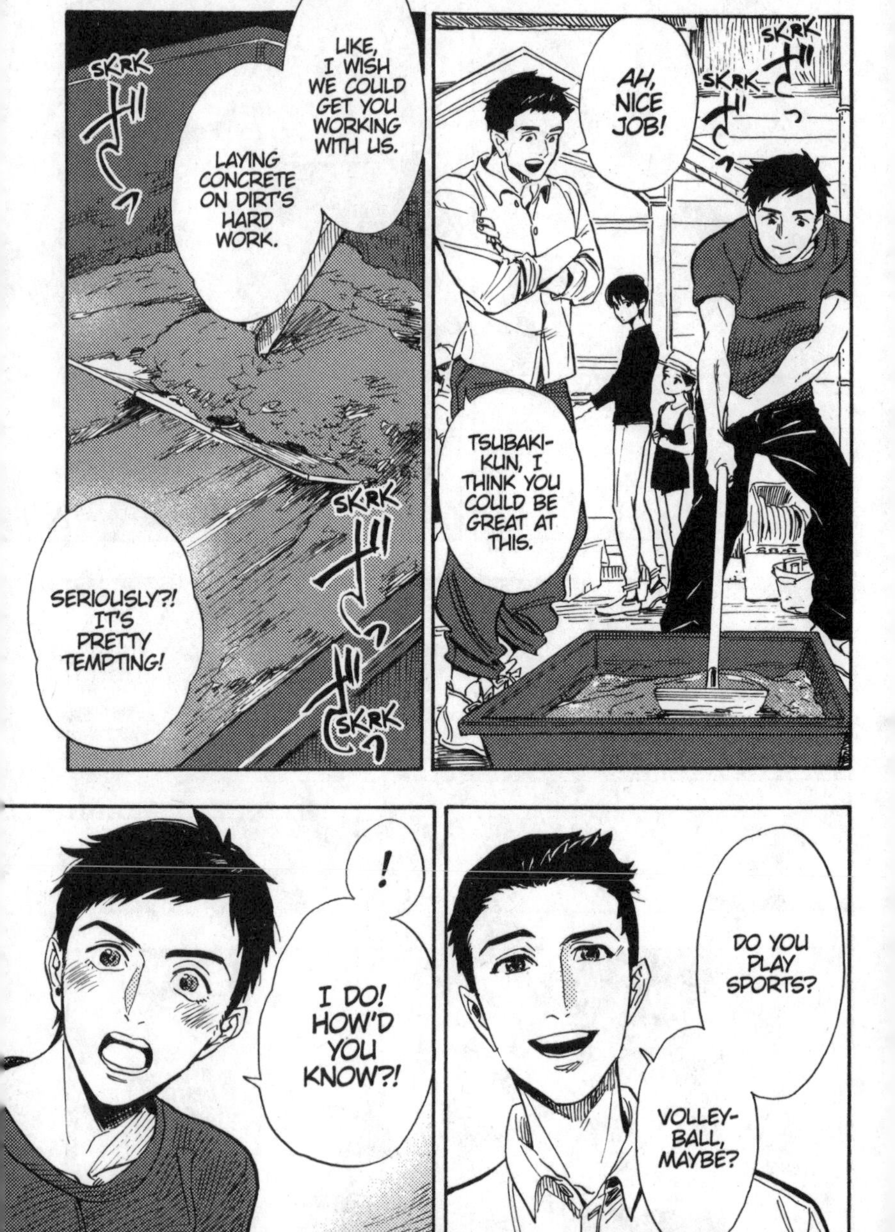
SKRK
SKRK
AH, NICE JOB!
TSUBAKI-KUN, I THINK YOU COULD BE GREAT AT THIS.
LIKE, I WISH WE COULD GET YOU WORKING WITH US.
LAYING CONCRETE ON DIRT'S HARD WORK.
SKRK
SKRK
SKRK
SERIOUSLY?! IT'S PRETTY TEMPTING!
DO YOU PLAY SPORTS?
VOLLEY-BALL, MAYBE?
!
I DO! HOW'D YOU KNOW?!

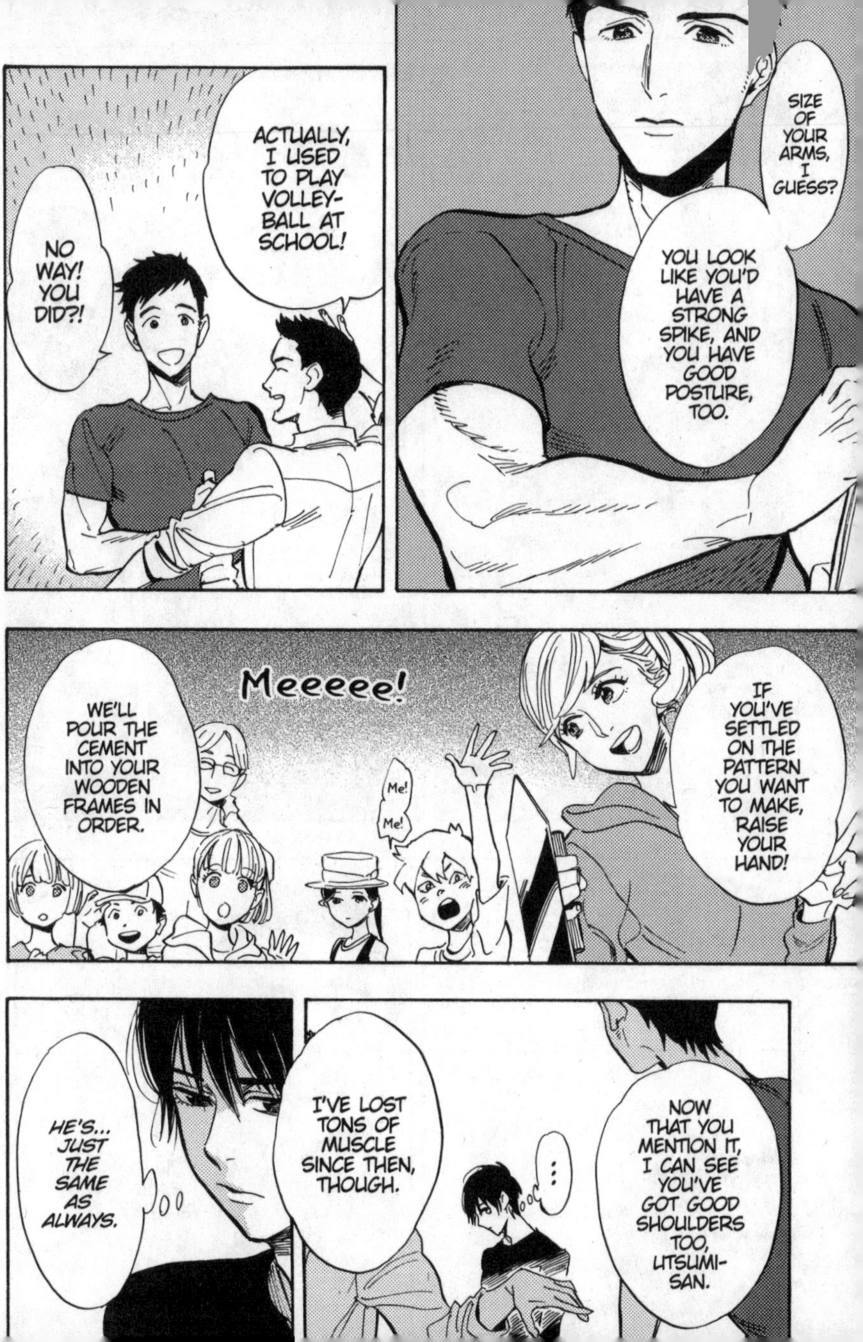
SIZE OF YOUR ARMS, I GUESS?
YOU LOOK LIKE YOU'D HAVE A STRONG SPIKE, AND YOU HAVE GOOD POSTURE, TOO.
ACTUALLY, I USED TO PLAY VOLLEY-BALL AT SCHOOL!
NO WAY! YOU DID?!
IF YOU'VE SETTLED ON THE PATTERN YOU WANT TO MAKE, RAISE YOUR HAND!
Me!
Me!
Meeeee!
WE'LL POUR THE CEMENT INTO YOUR WOODEN FRAMES IN ORDER.
NOW THAT YOU MENTION IT, I CAN SEE YOU'VE GOT GOOD SHOULDERS TOO, UTSUMI-SAN.
...
I'VE LOST TONS OF MUSCLE SINCE THEN, THOUGH.
HE'S... JUST THE SAME AS ALWAYS.

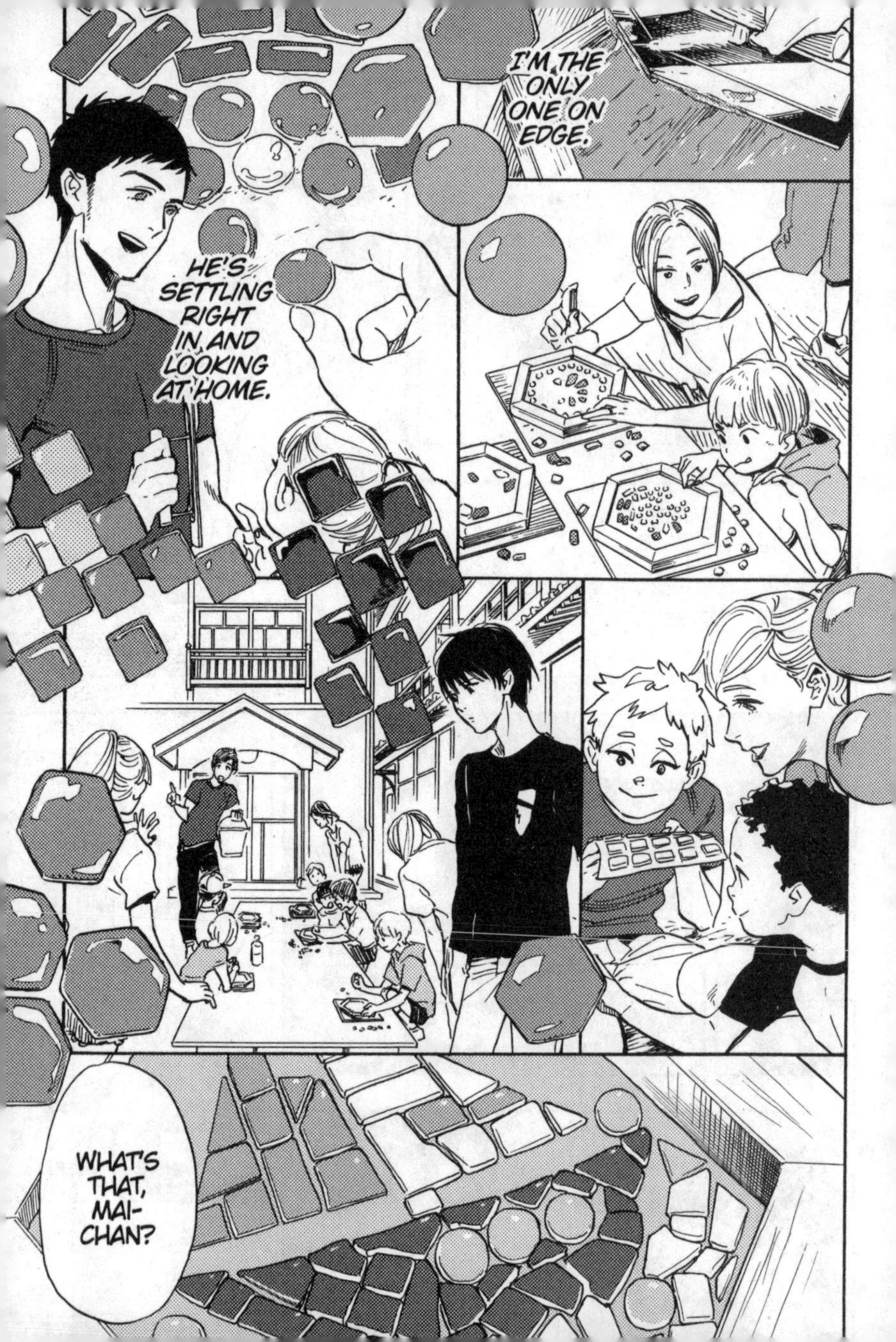
I'M THE ONLY ONE ON EDGE.
HE'S SETTLING RIGHT IN AND LOOKING AT HOME.
WHAT'S THAT, MAI-CHAN?

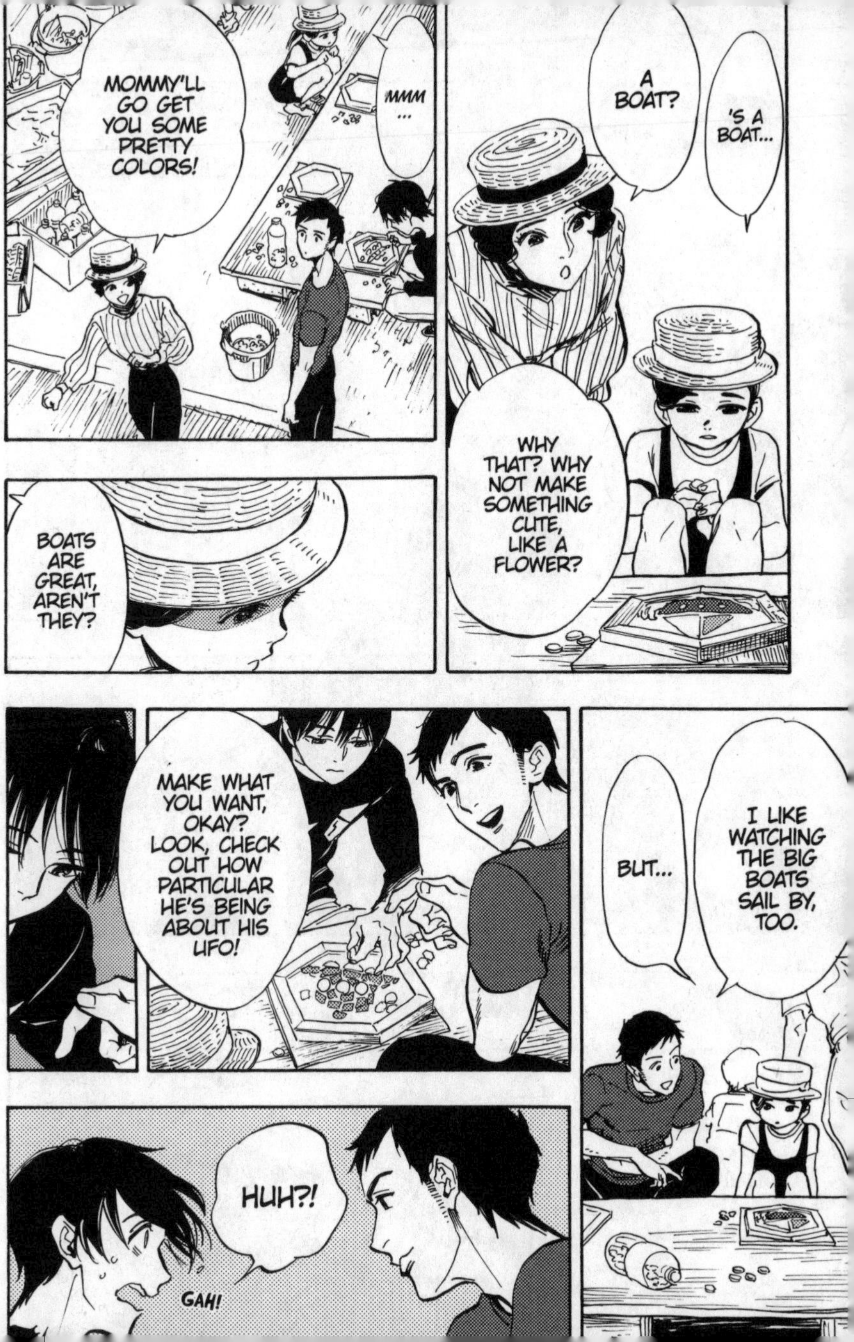
'S A BOAT...
A BOAT?
WHY THAT? WHY NOT MAKE SOMETHING CUTE, LIKE A FLOWER?
MMM ...
MOMMY'LL GO GET YOU SOME PRETTY COLORS!
BOATS ARE GREAT, AREN'T THEY?
I LIKE WATCHING THE BIG BOATS SAIL BY, TOO.
BUT...
MAKE WHAT YOU WANT, OKAY? LOOK, CHECK OUT HOW PARTICULAR HE'S BEING ABOUT HIS UFO!
HUH?!
GAH!

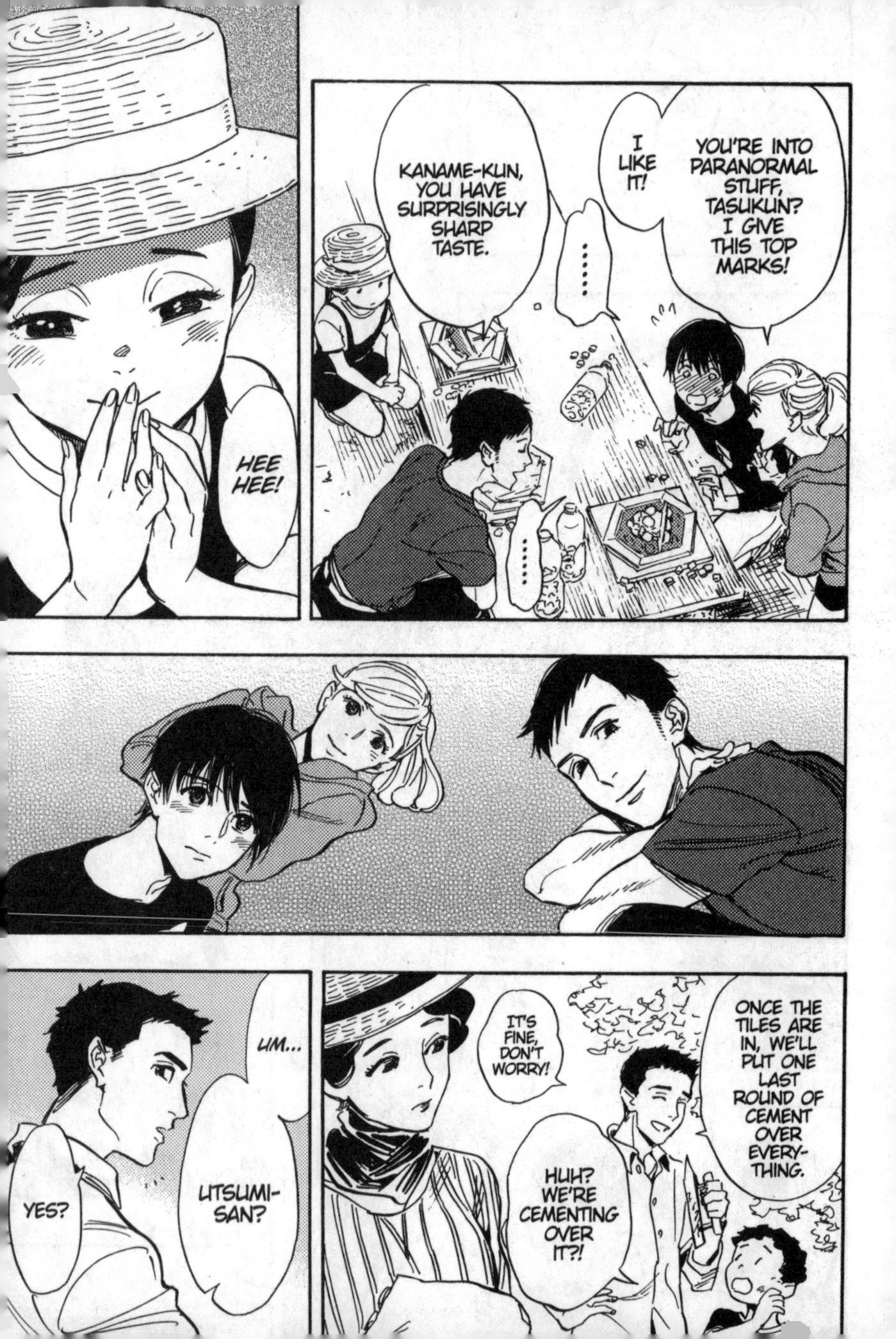
YOU'RE INTO PARANORMAL STUFF, TASUKUN? I GIVE THIS TOP MARKS!
I LIKE IT!
......
KANAME-KUN, YOU HAVE SURPRISINGLY SHARP TASTE.
......
HEE HEE!
ONCE THE TILES ARE IN, WE'LL PUT ONE LAST ROUND OF CEMENT OVER EVERYTHING.
HUH? WE'RE CEMENTING OVER IT?!
IT'S FINE, DON'T WORRY!
UM...
UTSUMI-SAN?
YES?

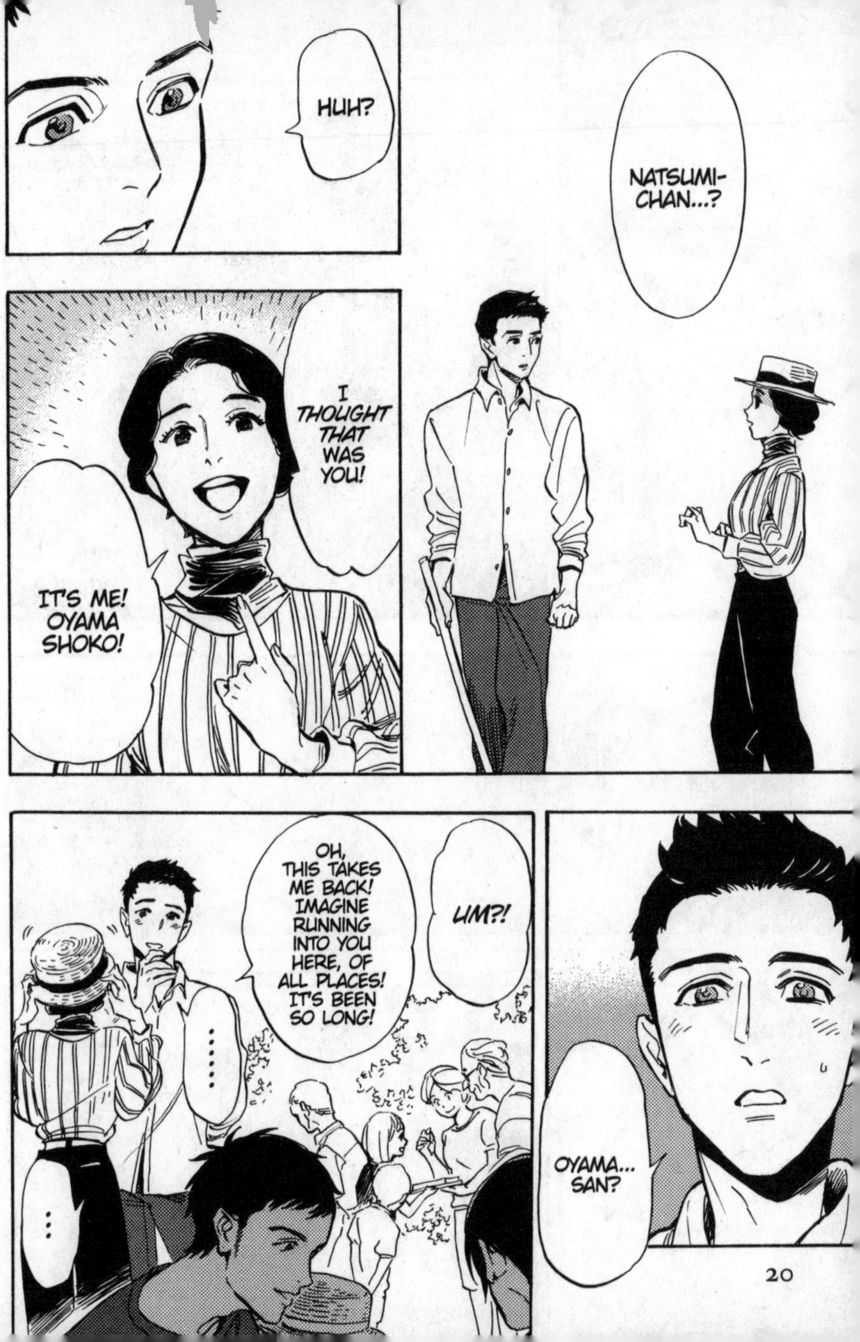
NATSUMI-CHAN...?
HUH?
I THOUGHT THAT WAS YOU!
IT'S ME! OYAMA SHOKO!
OYAMA... SAN?
UM?!
OH, THIS TAKES ME BACK! IMAGINE RUNNING INTO YOU HERE, OF ALL PLACES! IT'S BEEN SO LONG!
......
...

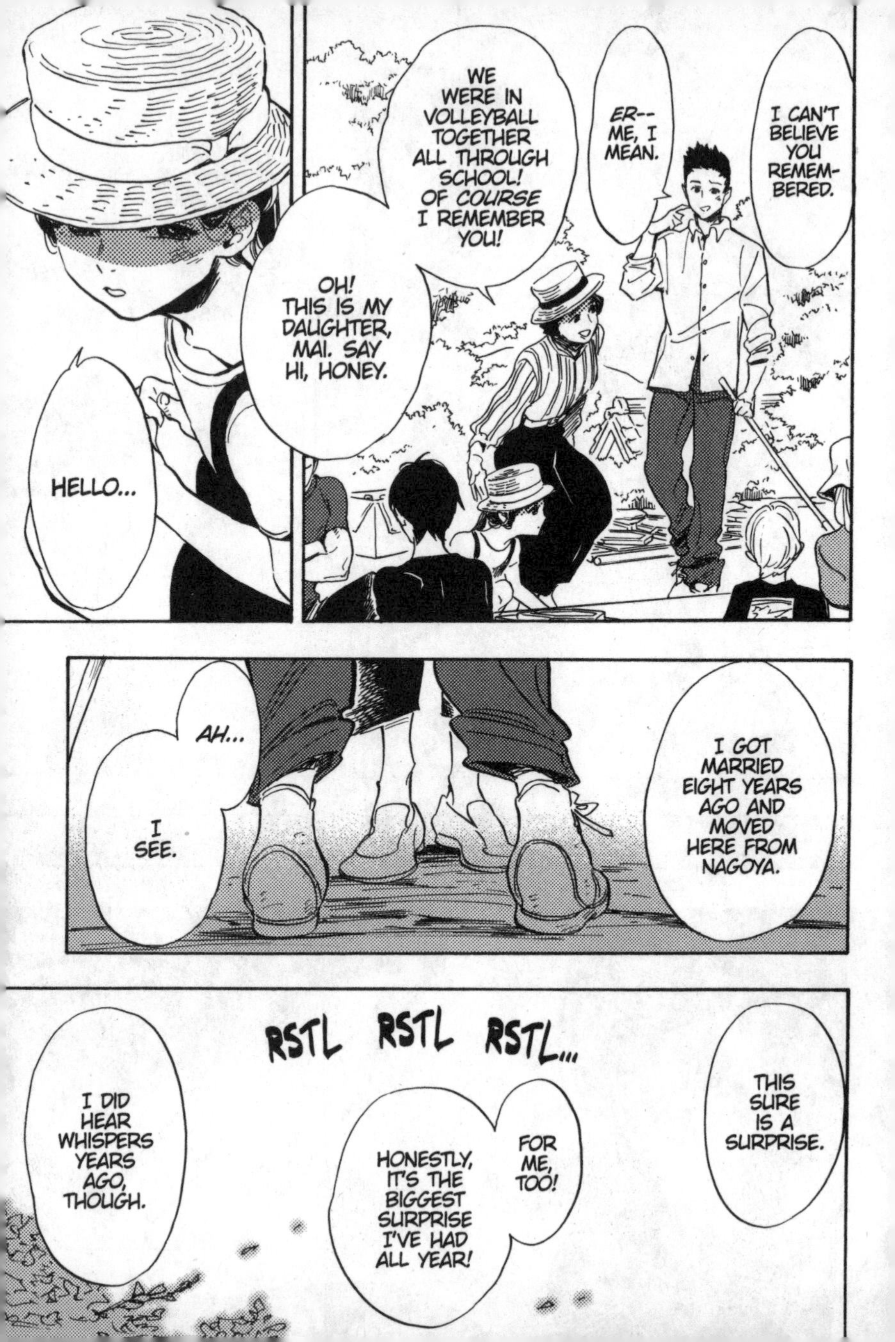

I CAN'T BELIEVE YOU REMEMBERED.
ER-- ME, I MEAN.
WE WERE IN VOLLEYBALL TOGETHER ALL THROUGH SCHOOL! OF COURSE I REMEMBER YOU!
OH! THIS IS MY DAUGHTER, MAI. SAY HI, HONEY.
HELLO...
I GOT MARRIED EIGHT YEARS AGO AND MOVED HERE FROM NAGOYA.
AH... I SEE.
THIS SURE IS A SURPRISE.
RSTL RSTL RSTL...
FOR ME, TOO!
HONESTLY, IT'S THE BIGGEST SURPRISE I'VE HAD ALL YEAR!
I DID HEAR WHISPERS YEARS AGO, THOUGH.

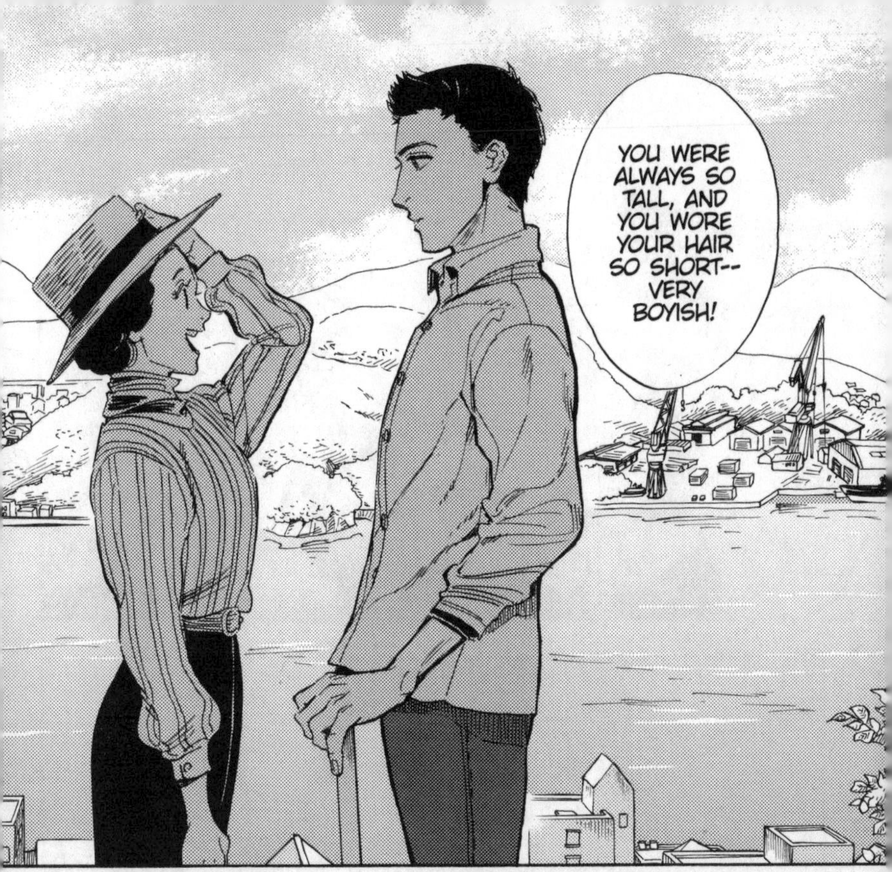
YOU WERE ALWAYS SO TALL, AND YOU WORE YOUR HAIR SO SHORT-- VERY BOYISH!
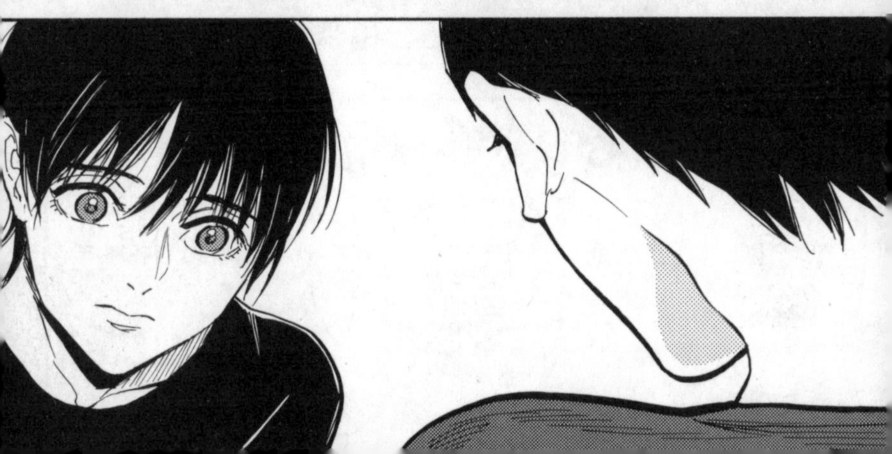

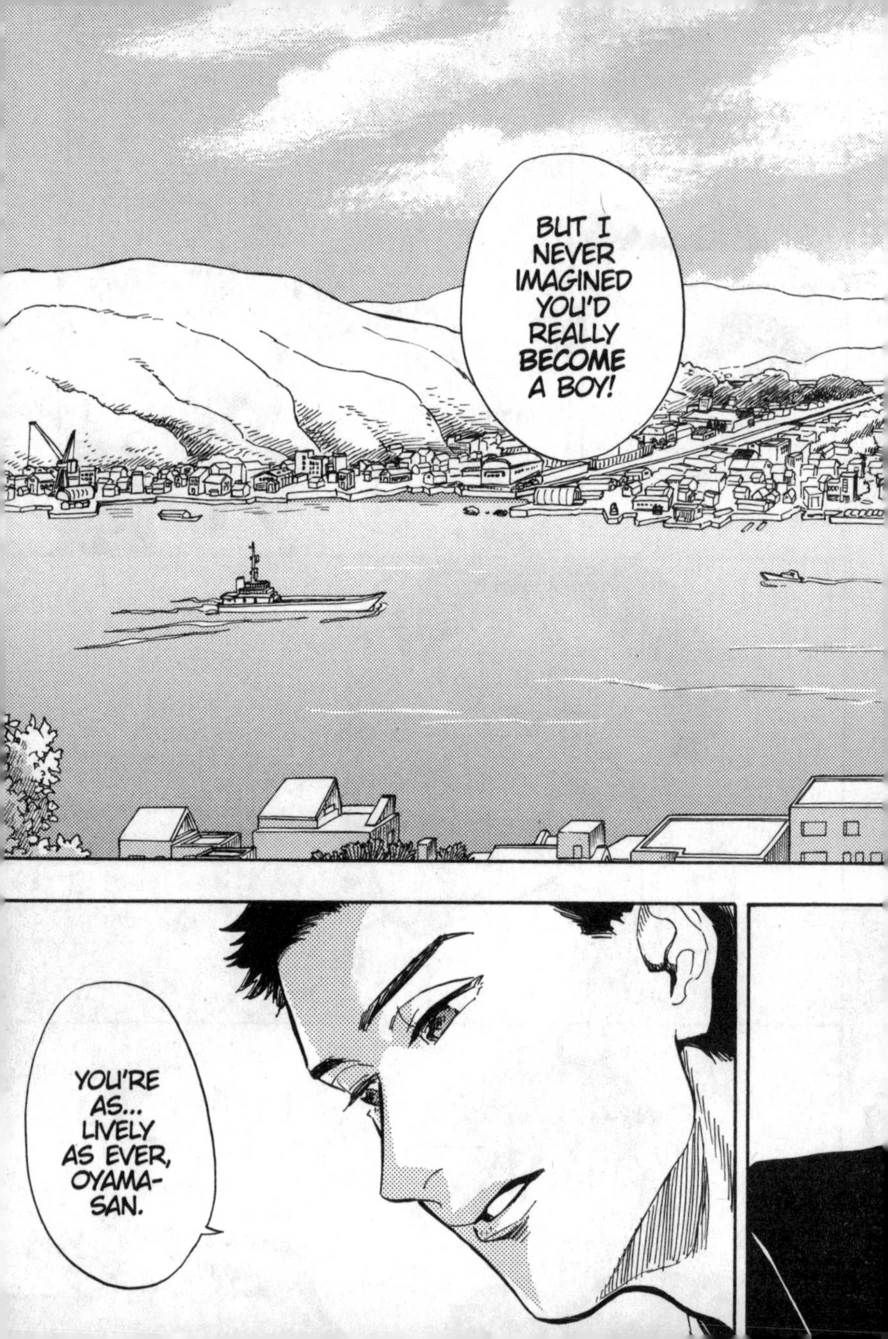
BUT I NEVER IMAGINED YOU'D REALLY BECOME A BOY!
YOU'RE AS... LIVELY AS EVER, OYAMA-SAN.

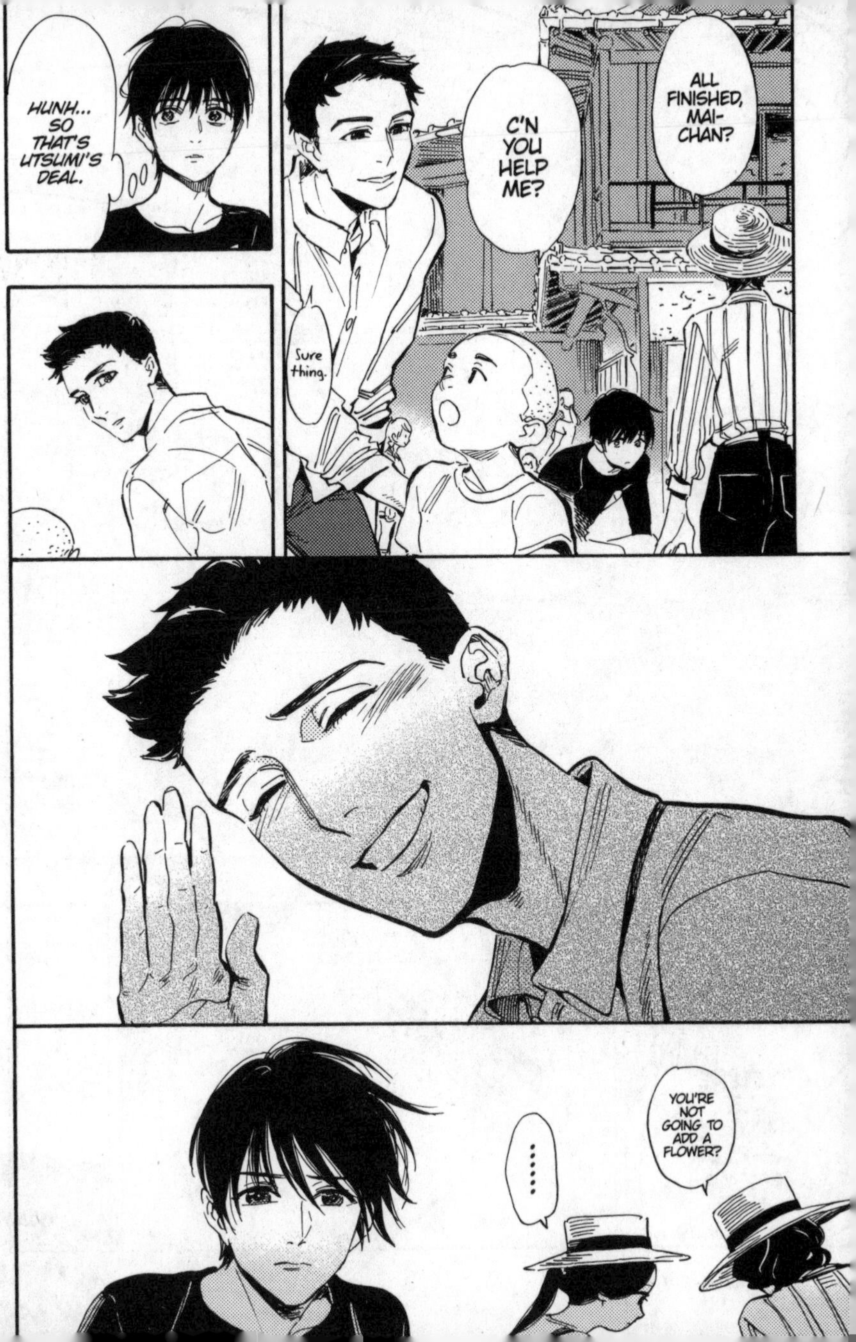
ALL FINISHED, MAI-CHAN?
C'N YOU HELP ME?
Sure thing.
HUNH... SO THAT'S UTSUMI'S DEAL.
YOU'RE NOT GOING TO ADD A FLOWER?
......

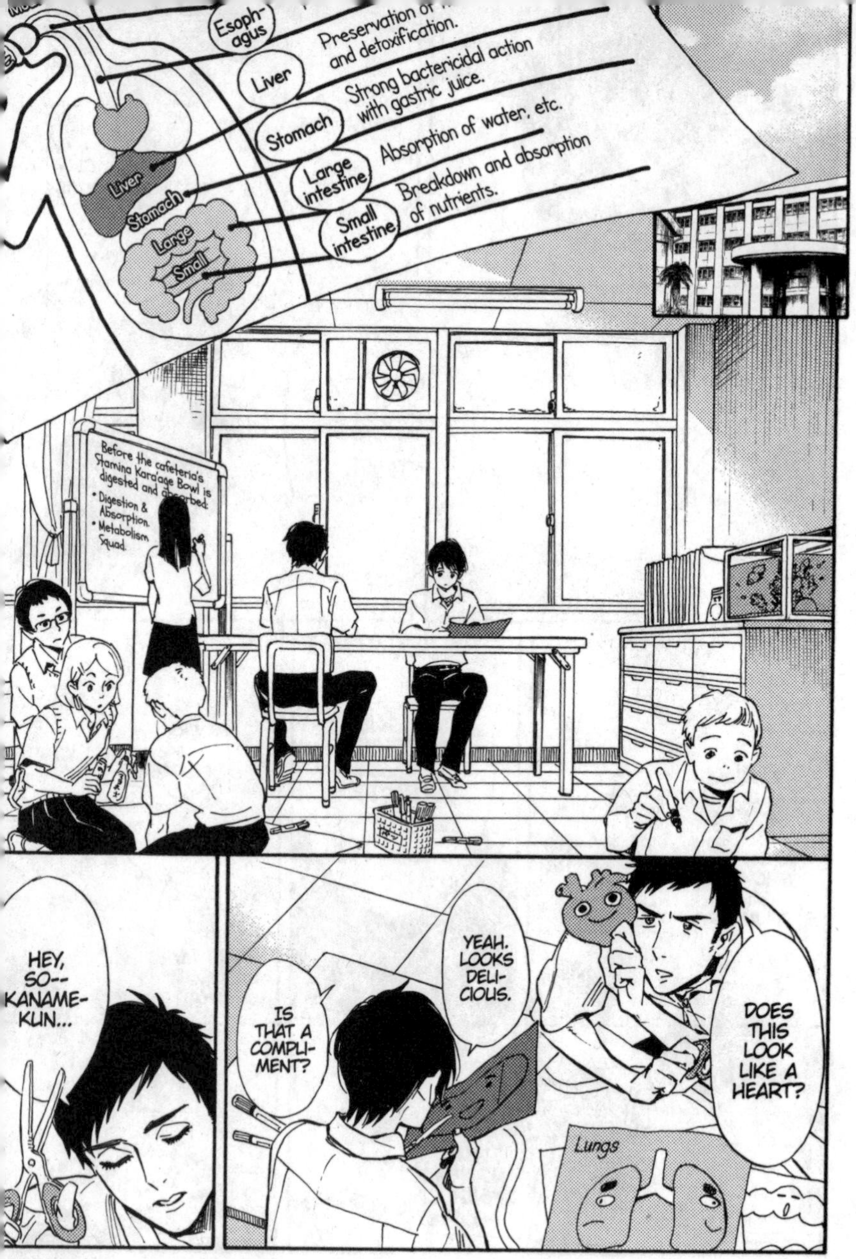

Esoph-agus
Preservation of
and detoxification.
Liver
Strong bactericidal action with gastric juice.
Stomach
Absorption of water, etc.
Large intestine
Breakdown and absorption of nutrients.
Small intestine
Liver
Stomach
Large
Small
Before the cafeteria's Stamina Kara'age Bowl is digested and absorbed:
• Digestion & Absorption.
• Metabolism Squad.
DOES THIS LOOK LIKE A HEART?
YEAH. LOOKS DELICIOUS.
IS THAT A COMPLIMENT?
Lungs
HEY, SO-- KANAME-KUN...

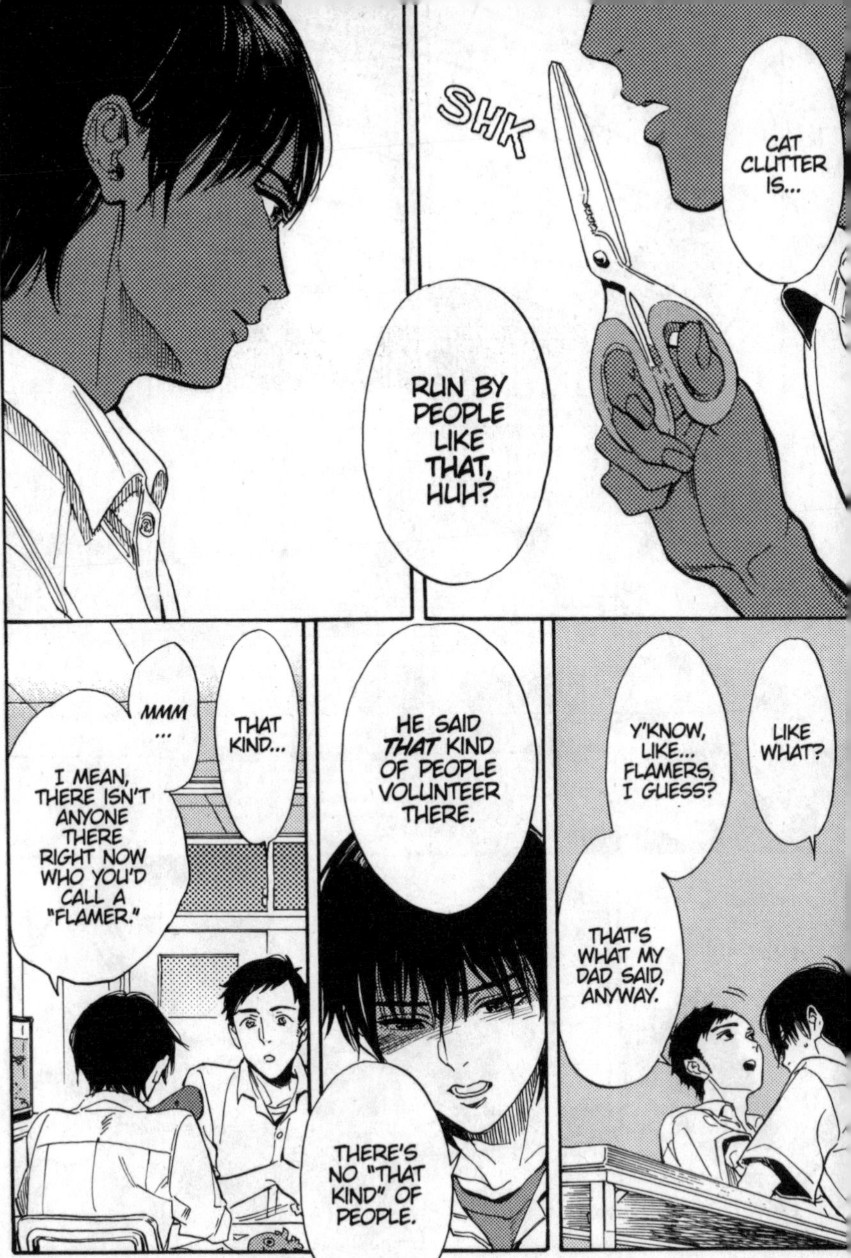
CAT CLUTTER IS...
SHK
RUN BY PEOPLE LIKE THAT, HUH?
LIKE WHAT?
Y'KNOW, LIKE... FLAMERS, I GUESS?
THAT'S WHAT MY DAD SAID, ANYWAY.
HE SAID *THAT* KIND OF PEOPLE VOLUNTEER THERE.
THERE'S NO "THAT KIND" OF PEOPLE.
THAT KIND...
MMM...
I MEAN, THERE ISN'T ANYONE THERE RIGHT NOW WHO YOU'D CALL A "FLAMER."

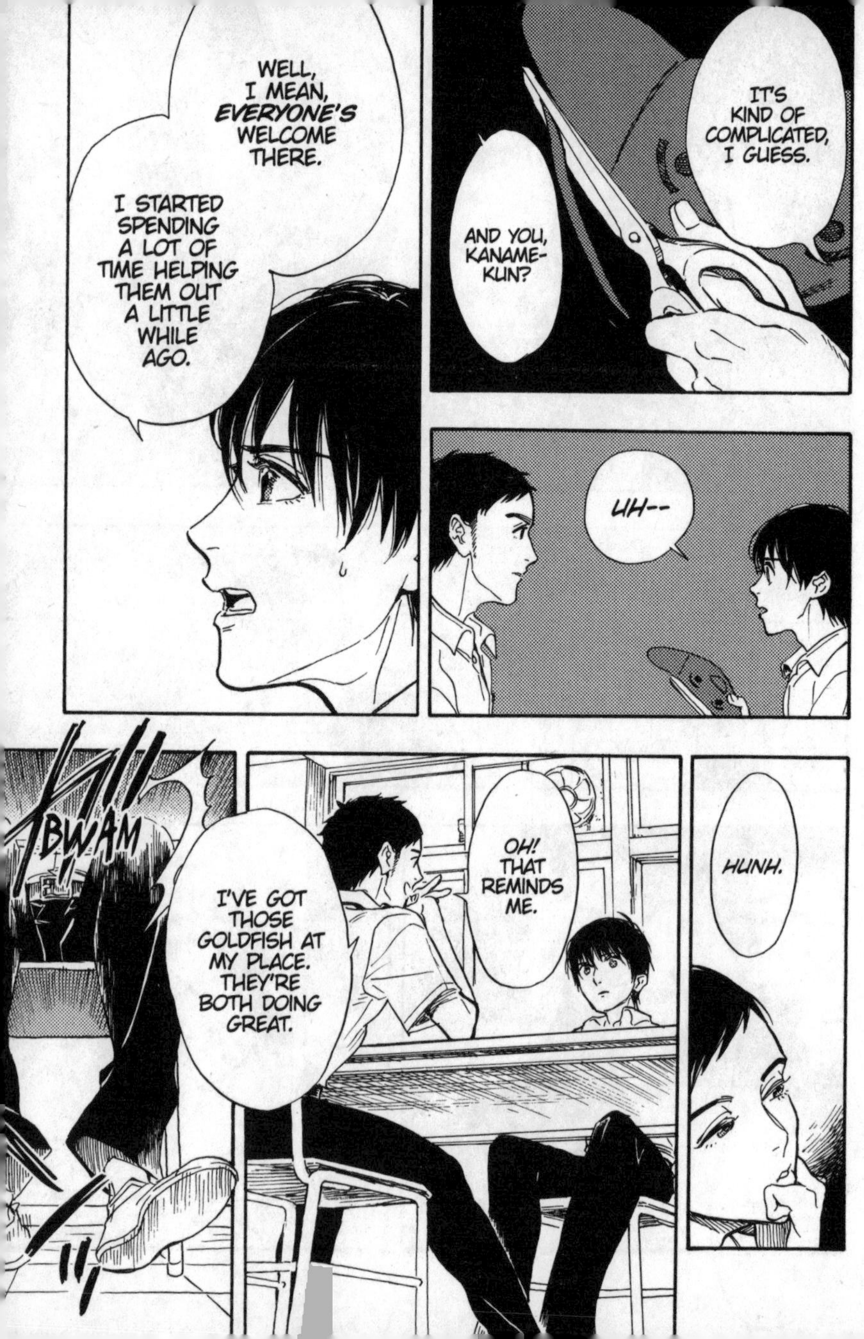
IT'S KIND OF COMPLICATED, I GUESS.
AND YOU, KANAME-KUN?
UH--
WELL, I MEAN, EVERYONE'S WELCOME THERE.
I STARTED SPENDING A LOT OF TIME HELPING THEM OUT A LITTLE WHILE AGO.
HUNH.
OH! THAT REMINDS ME.
I'VE GOT THOSE GOLDFISH AT MY PLACE. THEY'RE BOTH DOING GREAT.
BWAM

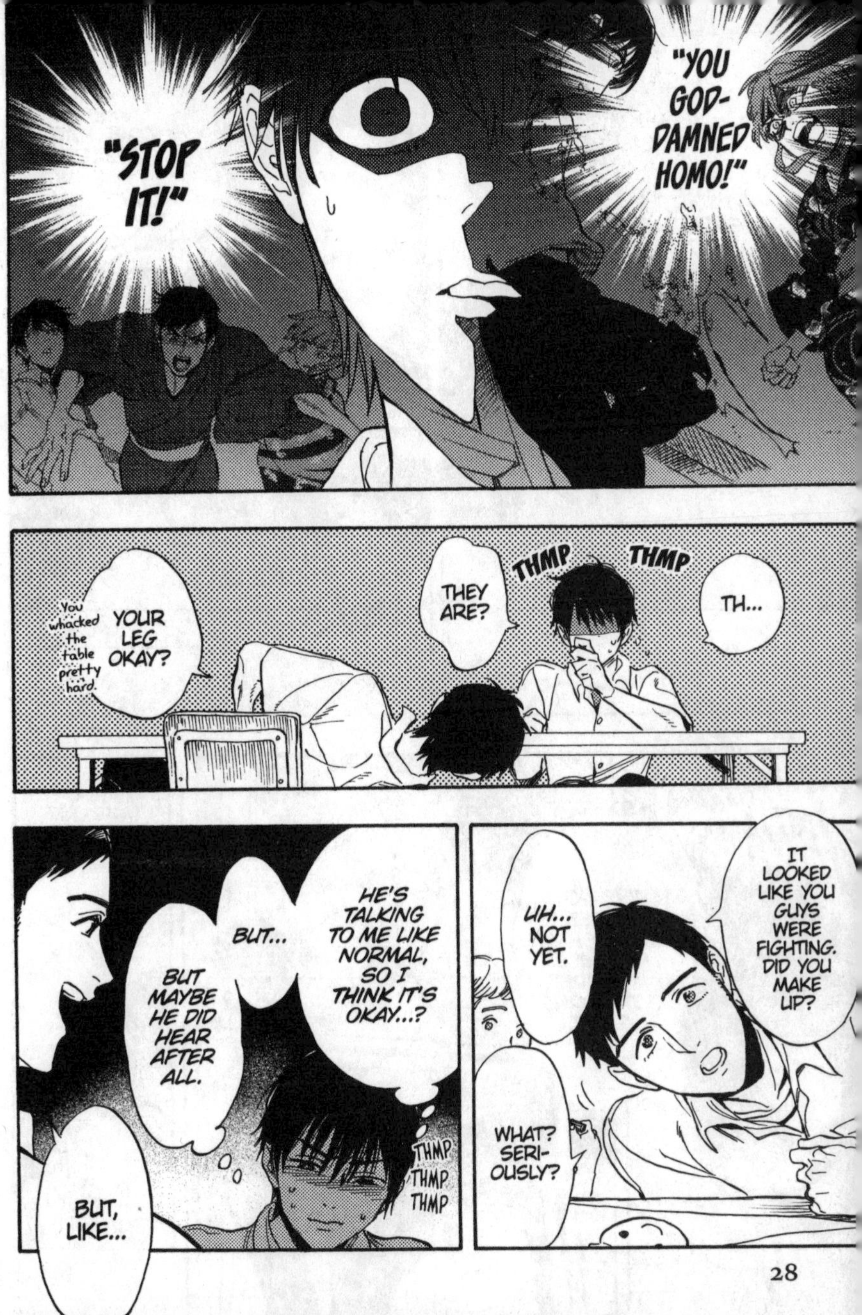
"YOU GOD-DAMNED HOMO!"
"STOP IT!"
TH...
THMP THMP
THEY ARE?
YOUR LEG OKAY?
You whacked the table pretty hard.
IT LOOKED LIKE YOU GUYS WERE FIGHTING. DID YOU MAKE UP?
UH... NOT YET.
WHAT? SERI-OUSLY?
HE'S TALKING TO ME LIKE NORMAL, SO I THINK IT'S OKAY...?
BUT...
BUT MAYBE HE DID HEAR AFTER ALL.
THMP THMP THMP
BUT, LIKE...

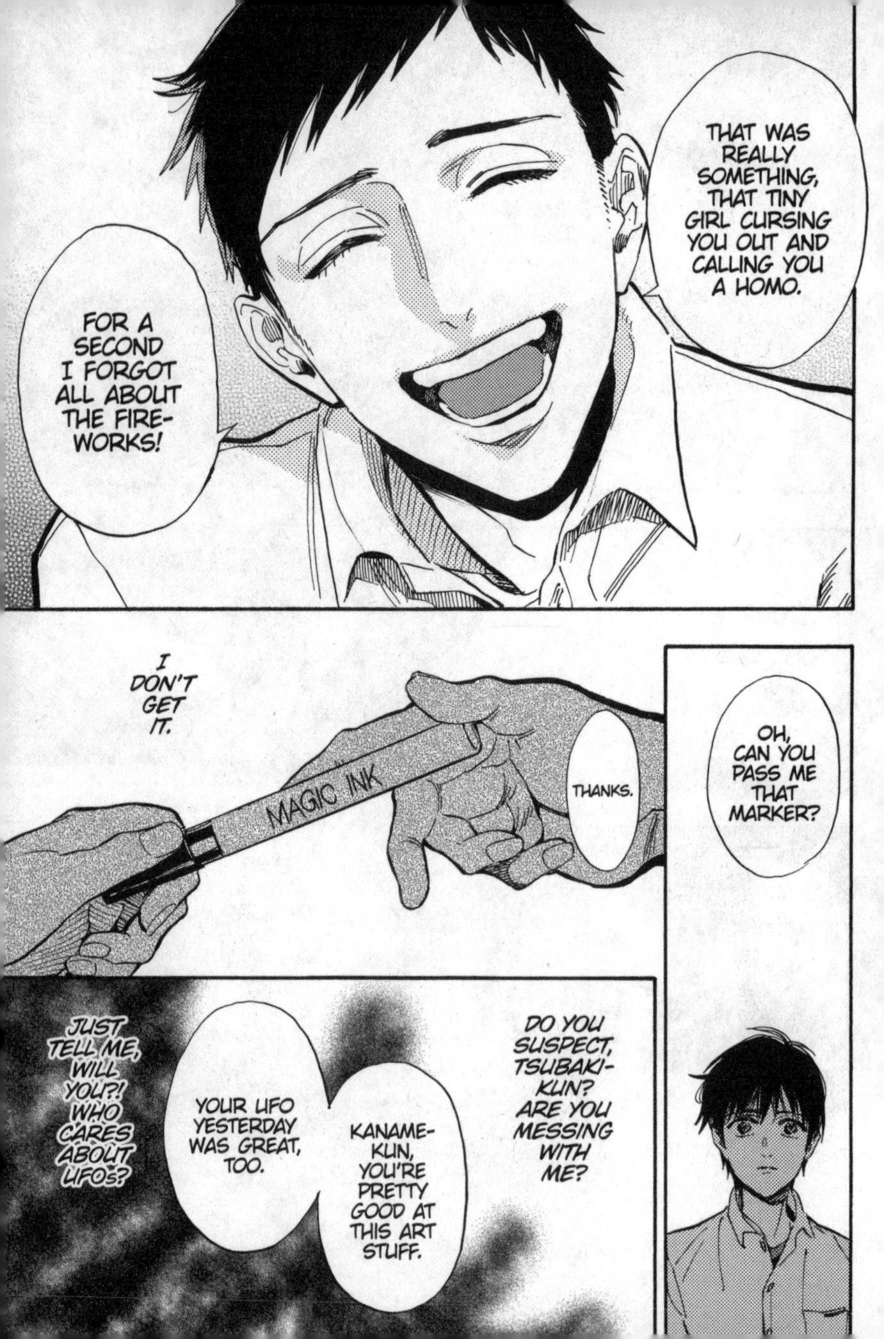
THAT WAS REALLY SOMETHING, THAT TINY GIRL CURSING YOU OUT AND CALLING YOU A HOMO.
FOR A SECOND I FORGOT ALL ABOUT THE FIRE-WORKS!
OH, CAN YOU PASS ME THAT MARKER?
THANKS.
MAGIC INK
I DON'T GET IT.
DO YOU SUSPECT, TSUBAKI-KUN? ARE YOU MESSING WITH ME?
KANAME-KUN, YOU'RE PRETTY GOOD AT THIS ART STUFF.
YOUR UFO YESTERDAY WAS GREAT, TOO.
JUST TELL ME, WILL YOU?! WHO CARES ABOUT UFOs?

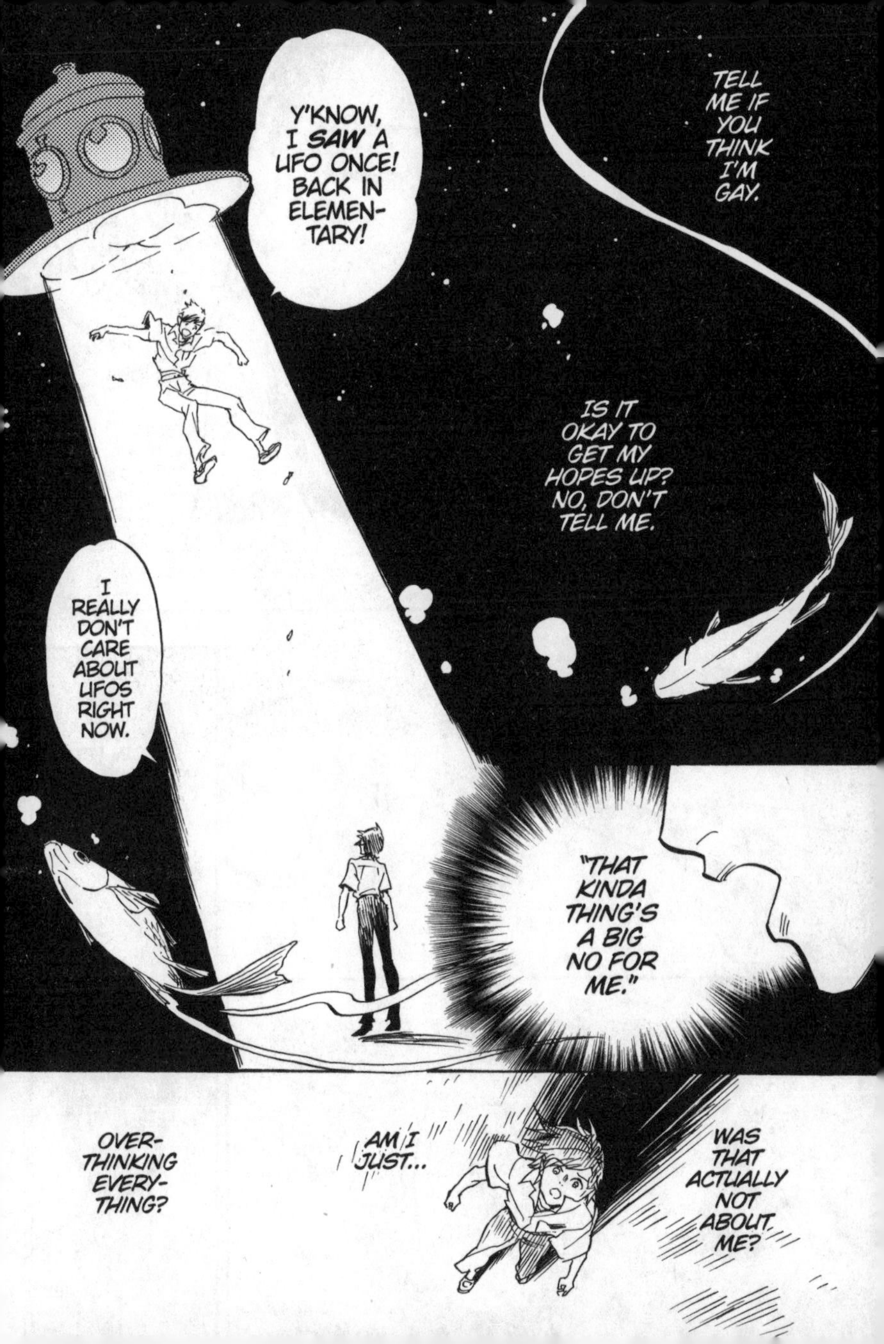
TELL ME IF YOU THINK I'M GAY.
Y'KNOW, I SAW A UFO ONCE! BACK IN ELEMEN-TARY!
IS IT OKAY TO GET MY HOPES UP? NO, DON'T TELL ME.
I REALLY DON'T CARE ABOUT UFOS RIGHT NOW.
"THAT KINDA THING'S A BIG NO FOR ME."
WAS THAT ACTUALLY NOT ABOUT ME?
AM I JUST...
OVER-THINKING EVERY-THING?

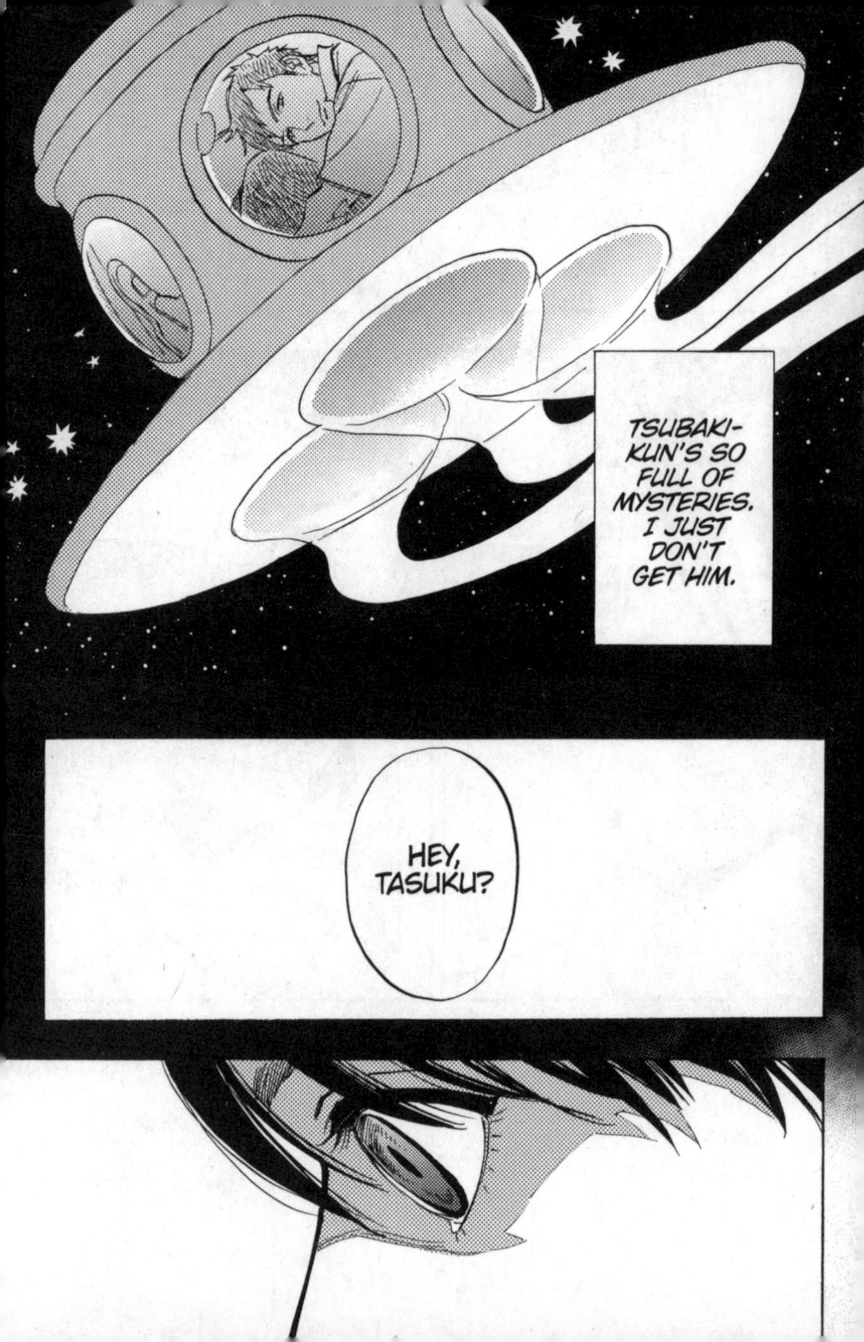
TSUBAKI-KUN'S SO FULL OF MYSTERIES. I JUST DON'T GET HIM.
HEY, TASUKU?

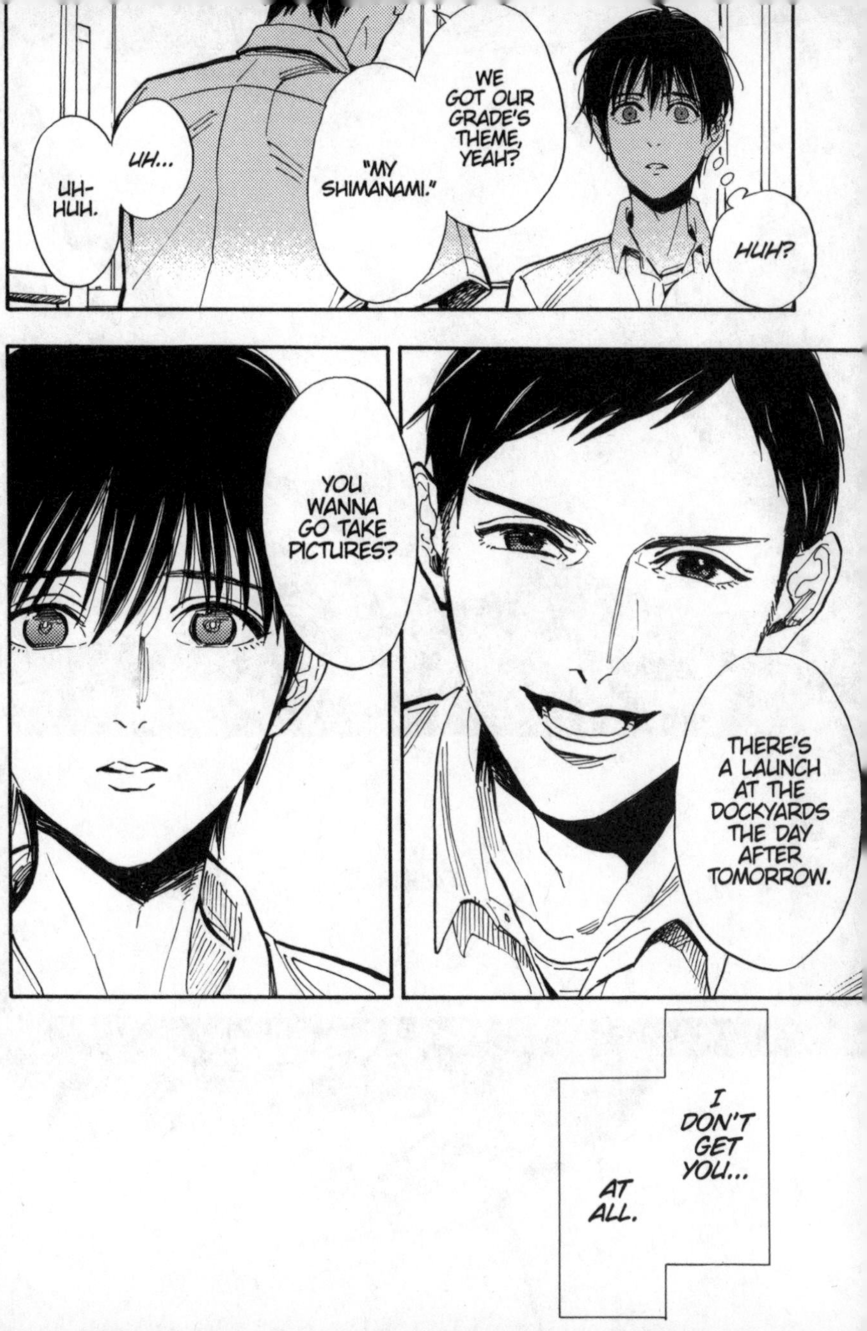
HUH?
WE GOT OUR GRADE'S THEME, YEAH?
"MY SHIMANAMI."
UH...
UH-HUH.
THERE'S A LAUNCH AT THE DOCKYARDS THE DAY AFTER TOMORROW.
YOU WANNA GO TAKE PICTURES?
I DON'T GET YOU...
AT ALL.

Our Dreams at Dusk

SHIMANAMI TASOGARE

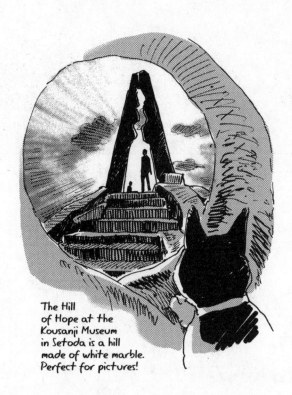

The Hill
of Hope at the
Kousanji Museum
in Setoda is a hill
made of white marble.
Perfect for pictures!

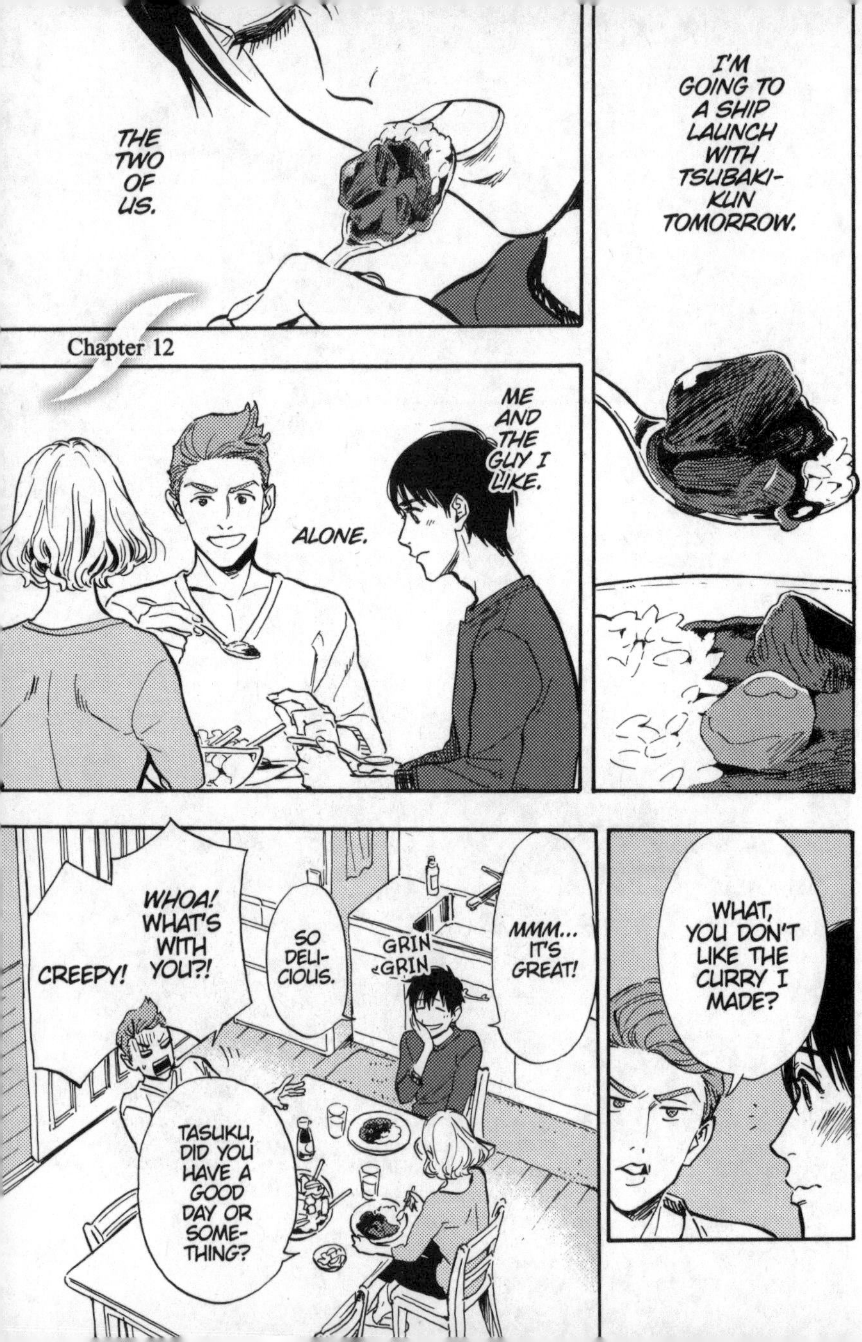
I'M GOING TO A SHIP LAUNCH WITH TSUBAKI-KUN TOMORROW.
THE TWO OF US.
Chapter 12
ME AND THE GUY I LIKE.
ALONE.
WHAT, YOU DON'T LIKE THE CURRY I MADE?
MMM... IT'S GREAT!
GRIN GRIN
SO DELI-CIOUS.
WHOA! WHAT'S WITH YOU?!
CREEPY!
TASUKU, DID YOU HAVE A GOOD DAY OR SOME-THING?

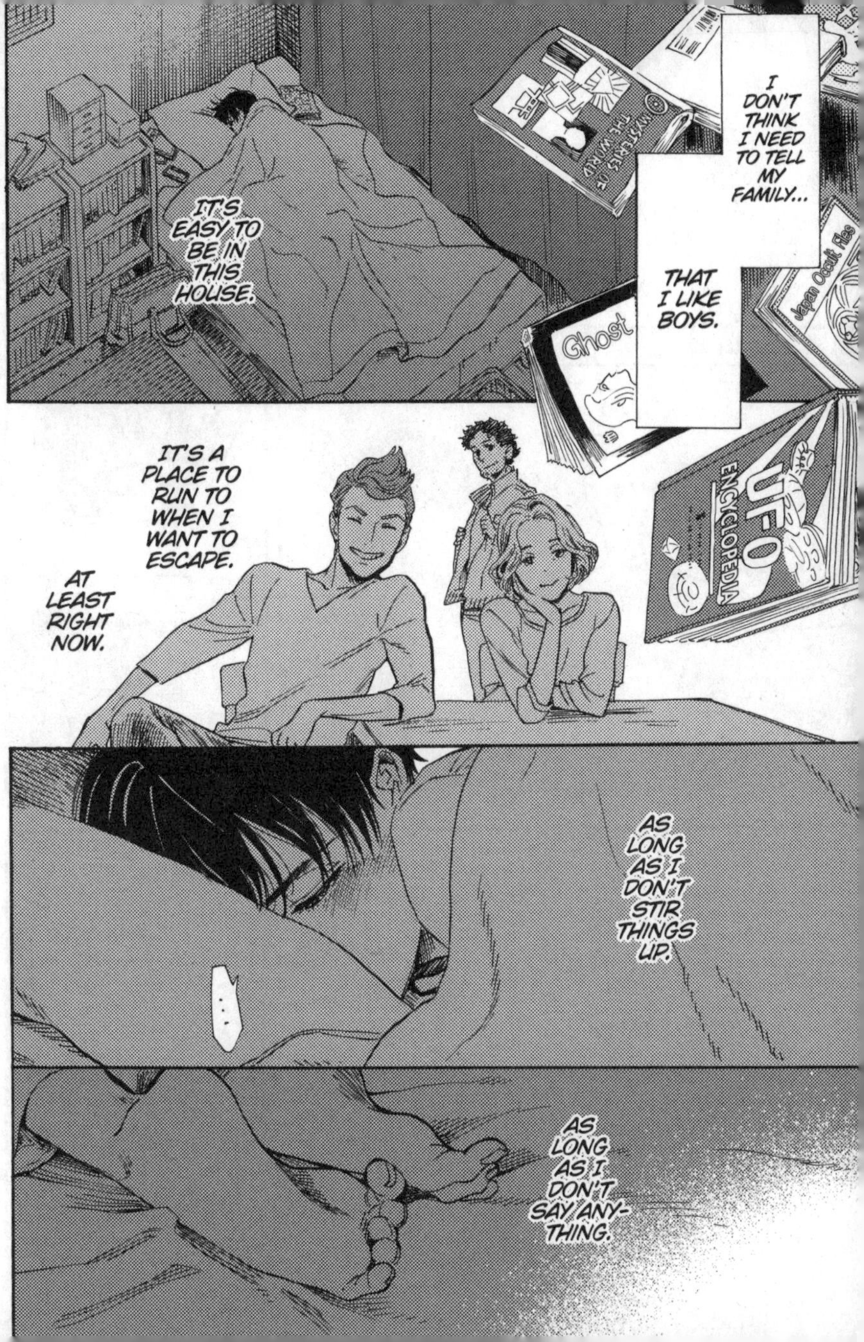
I DON'T THINK I NEED TO TELL MY FAMILY...
THAT I LIKE BOYS.
Japan Occult Files
Ghost
IT'S EASY TO BE IN THIS HOUSE.
UFO ENCYCLOPEDIA
IT'S A PLACE TO RUN TO WHEN I WANT TO ESCAPE.
AT LEAST RIGHT NOW.
AS LONG AS I DON'T STIR THINGS UP.
...
AS LONG AS I DON'T SAY ANY-THING.

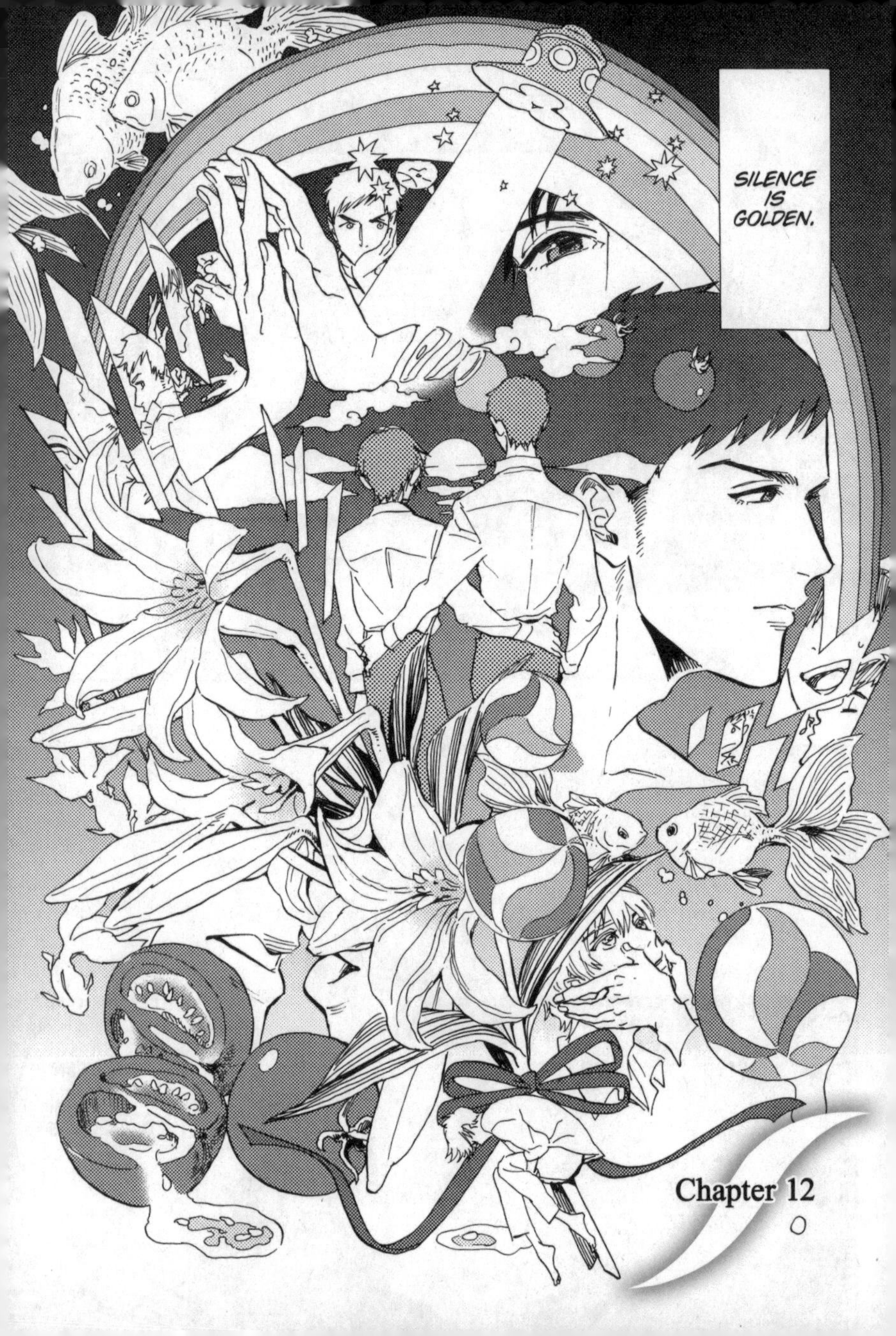
SILENCE IS GOLDEN.

Chapter 12

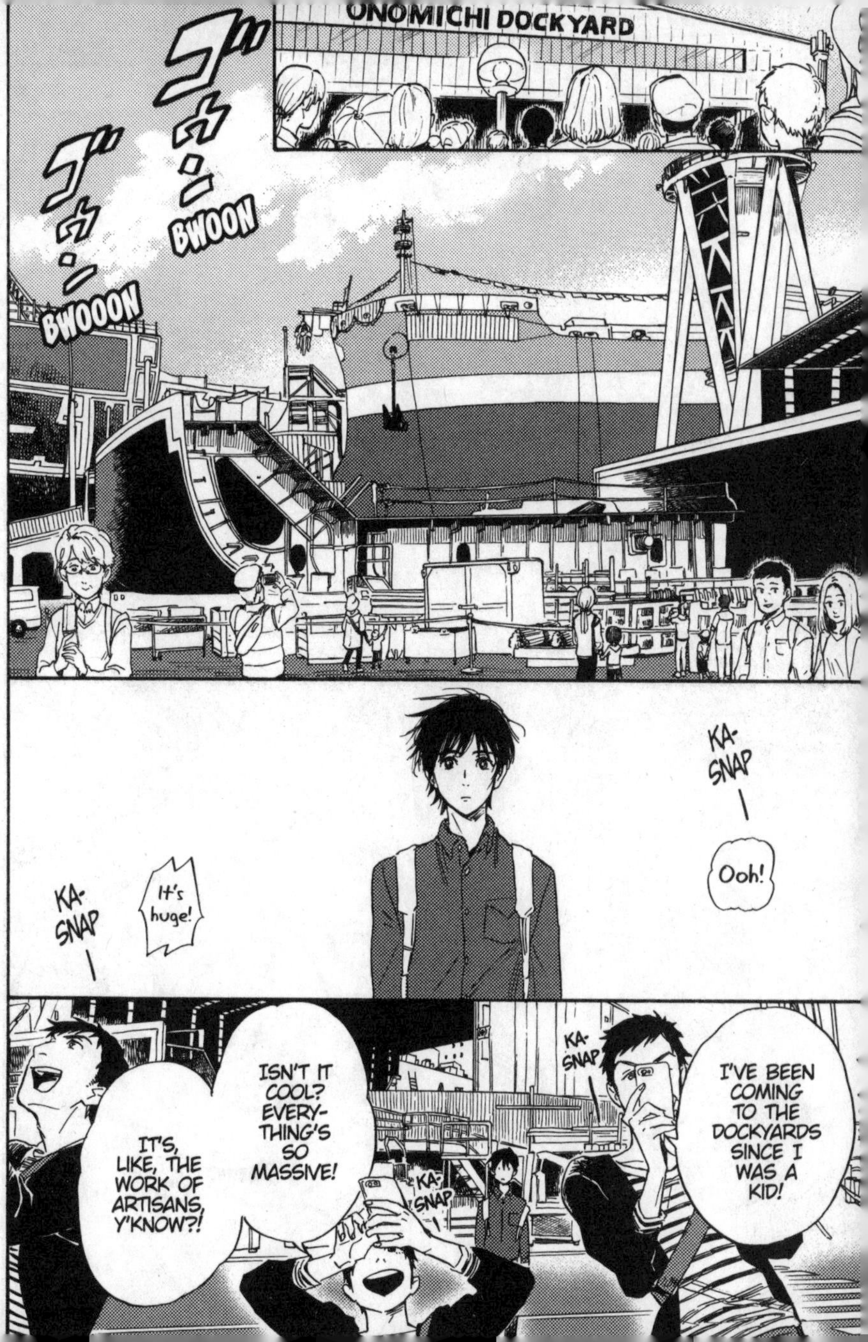
ONOMICHI DOCKYARD
BWOON
BWOOON
KA-SNAP
Ooh!
It's huge!
KA-SNAP
I'VE BEEN COMING TO THE DOCKYARDS SINCE I WAS A KID!
KA-SNAP
ISN'T IT COOL? EVERY-THING'S SO MASSIVE!
KA-SNAP
IT'S, LIKE, THE WORK OF ARTISANS, Y'KNOW?!

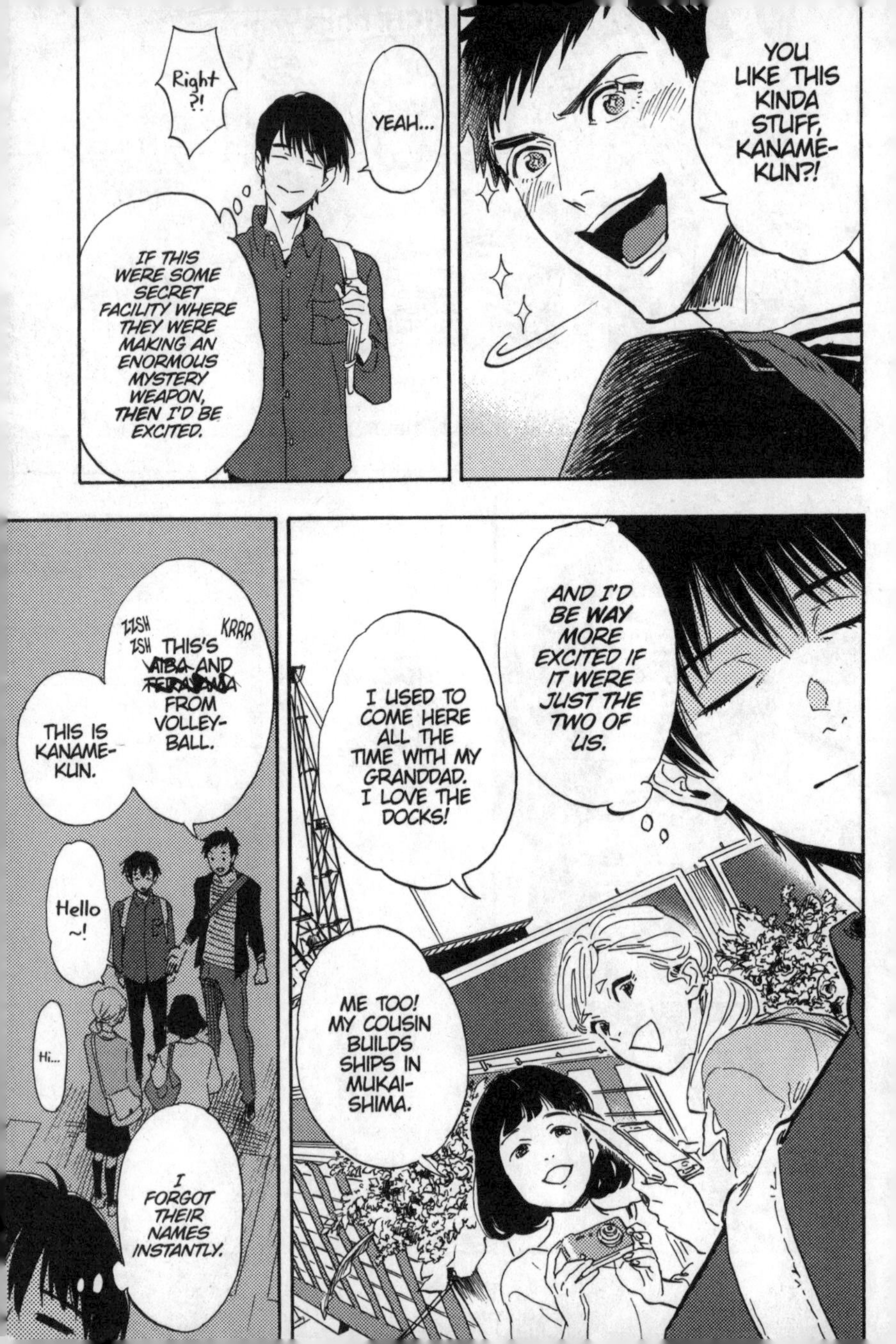
YOU LIKE THIS KINDA STUFF, KANAME-KUN?!
YEAH...
Right?!
IF THIS WERE SOME SECRET FACILITY WHERE THEY WERE MAKING AN ENORMOUS MYSTERY WEAPON, THEN I'D BE EXCITED.
AND I'D BE WAY MORE EXCITED IF IT WERE JUST THE TWO OF US.
I USED TO COME HERE ALL THE TIME WITH MY GRANDDAD. I LOVE THE DOCKS!
ME TOO! MY COUSIN BUILDS SHIPS IN MUKAI-SHIMA.
KRRR
ZZSH ZSH
THIS'S ~~AIBA~~ AND ~~TERASAWA~~ FROM VOLLEY-BALL.
THIS IS KANAME-KUN.
Hello~!
Hi...
I FORGOT THEIR NAMES INSTANTLY.

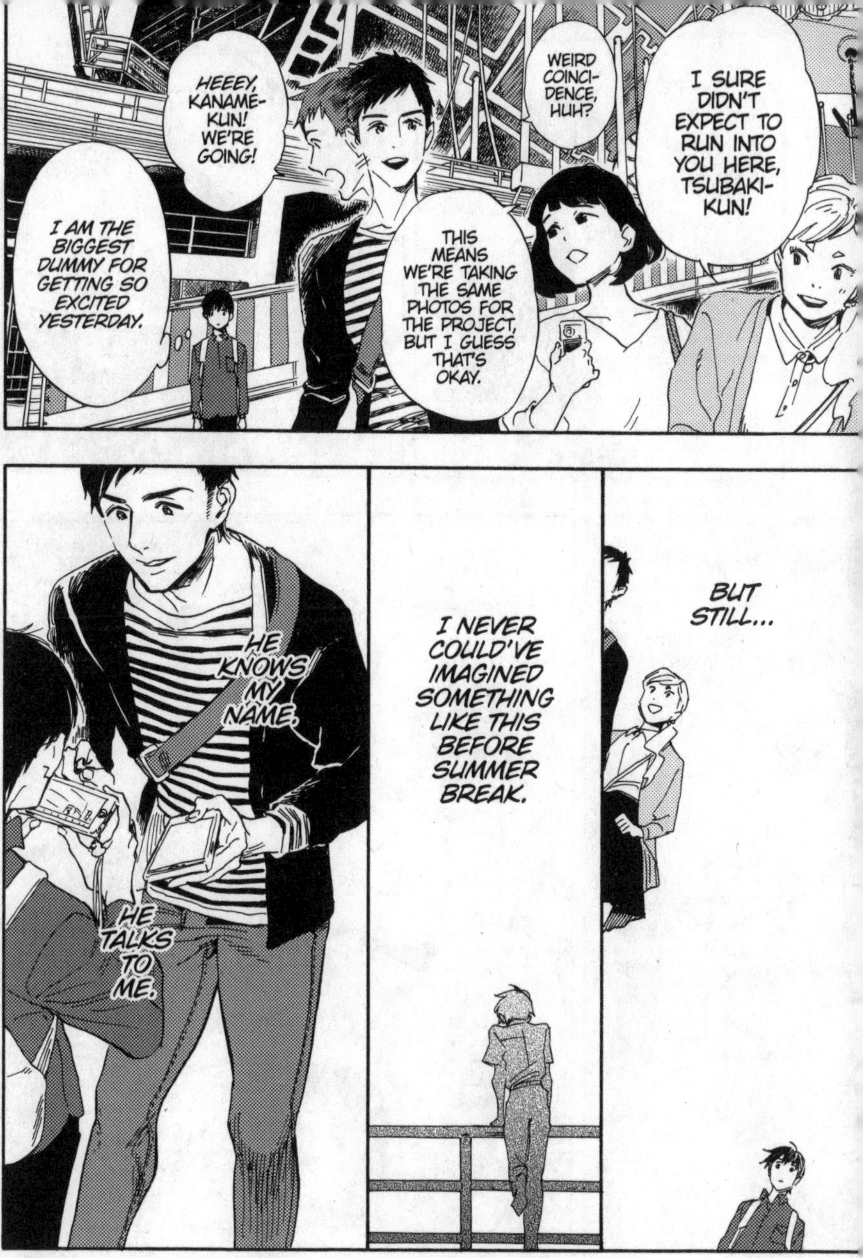
I SURE DIDN'T EXPECT TO RUN INTO YOU HERE, TSUBAKI-KUN!
WEIRD COINCIDENCE, HUH?
THIS MEANS WE'RE TAKING THE SAME PHOTOS FOR THE PROJECT, BUT I GUESS THAT'S OKAY.
HEEEY, KANAME-KUN! WE'RE GOING!
I AM THE BIGGEST DUMMY FOR GETTING SO EXCITED YESTERDAY.
BUT STILL...
I NEVER COULD'VE IMAGINED SOMETHING LIKE THIS BEFORE SUMMER BREAK.
HE KNOWS MY NAME.
HE TALKS TO ME.

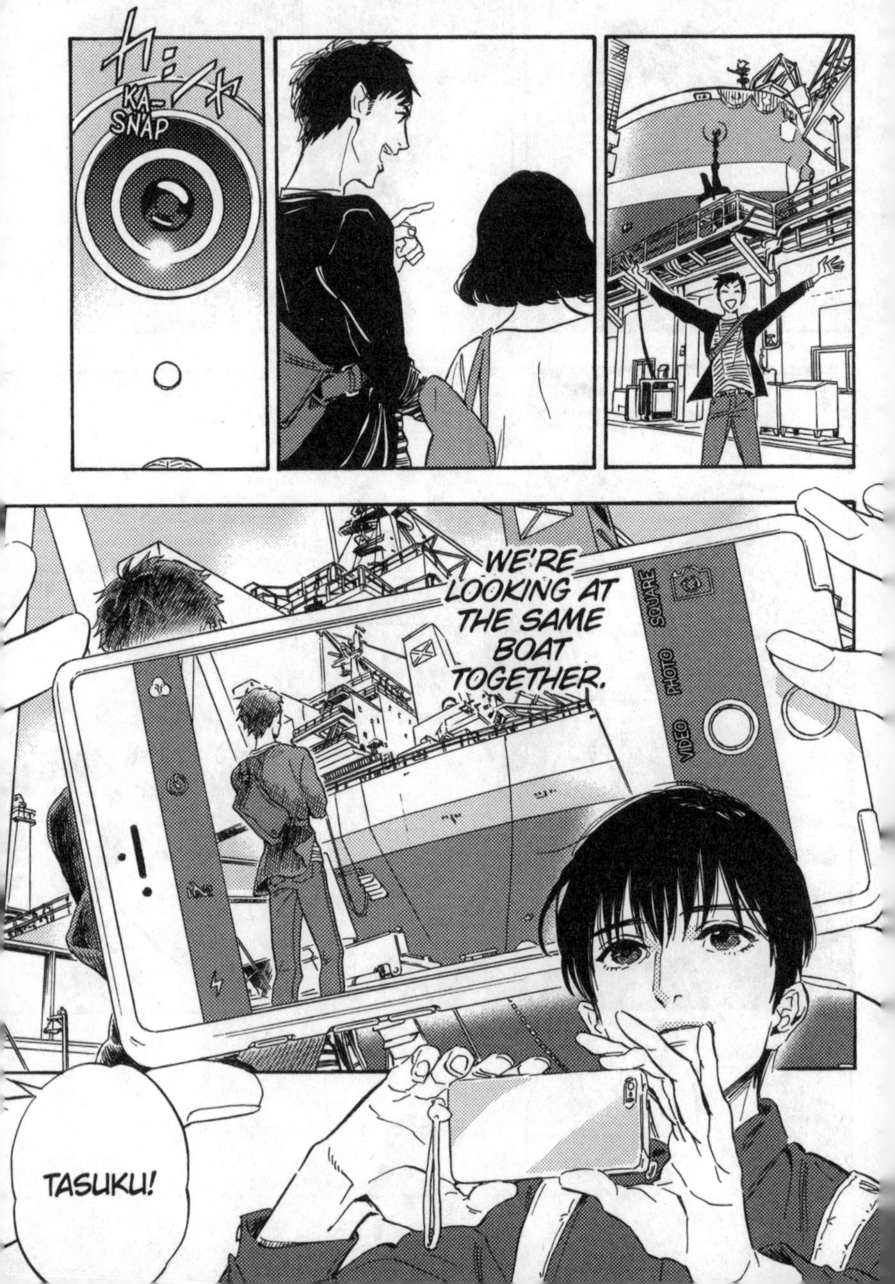
カシャ
KA-SNAP
SQUARE
PHOTO
VIDEO
WE'RE LOOKING AT THE SAME BOAT TOGETHER.
TASUKU!

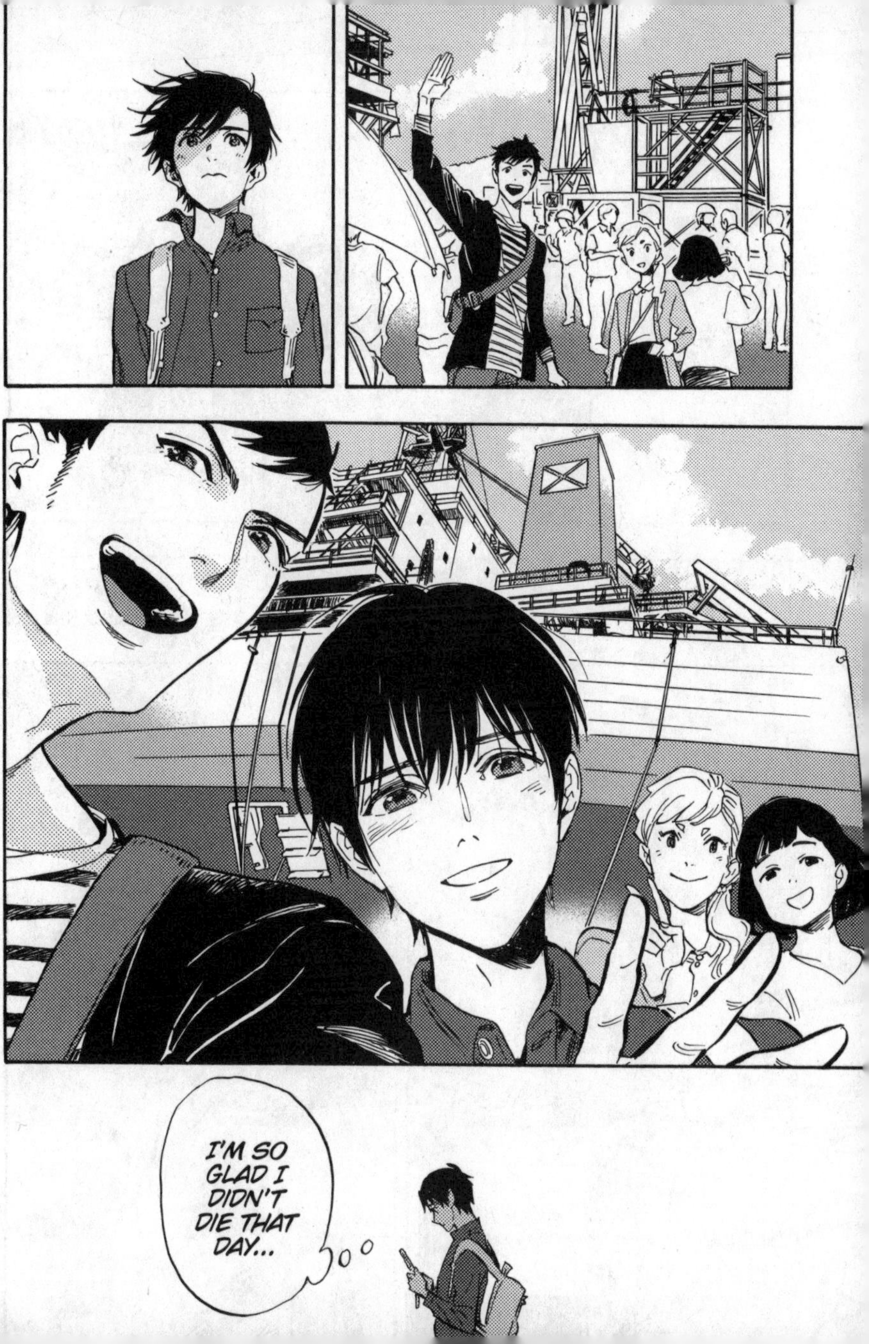
I'M SO GLAD I DIDN'T DIE THAT DAY...

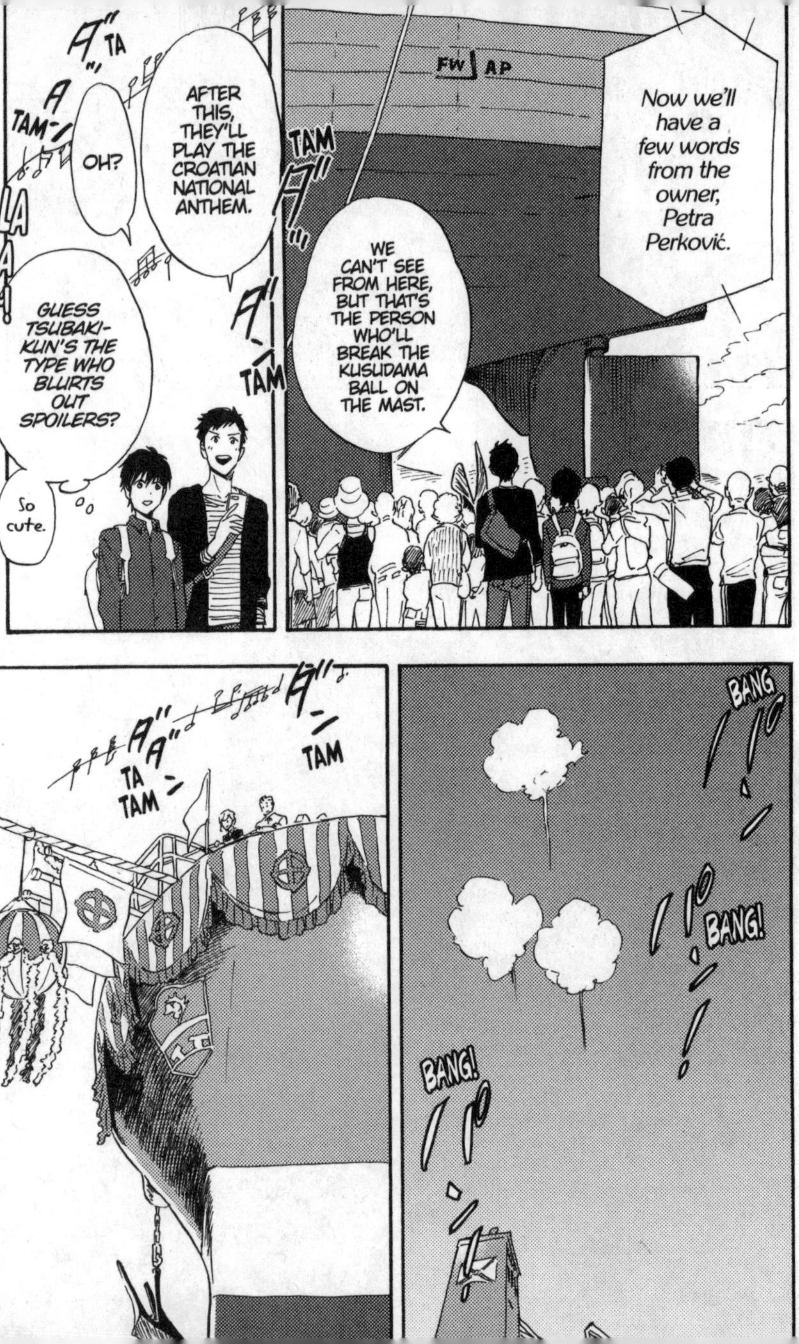
Now we'll have a few words from the owner, Petra Perković.
WE CAN'T SEE FROM HERE, BUT THAT'S THE PERSON WHO'LL BREAK THE KUSUDAMA BALL ON THE MAST.
TAM
TAM
AFTER THIS, THEY'LL PLAY THE CROATIAN NATIONAL ANTHEM.
OH?
TA
TAM
LA LA LA~!
GUESS TSUBAKI-KUN'S THE TYPE WHO BLURTS OUT SPOILERS?
So cute.
BANG
BANG!
BANG!
TAM
TA TAM

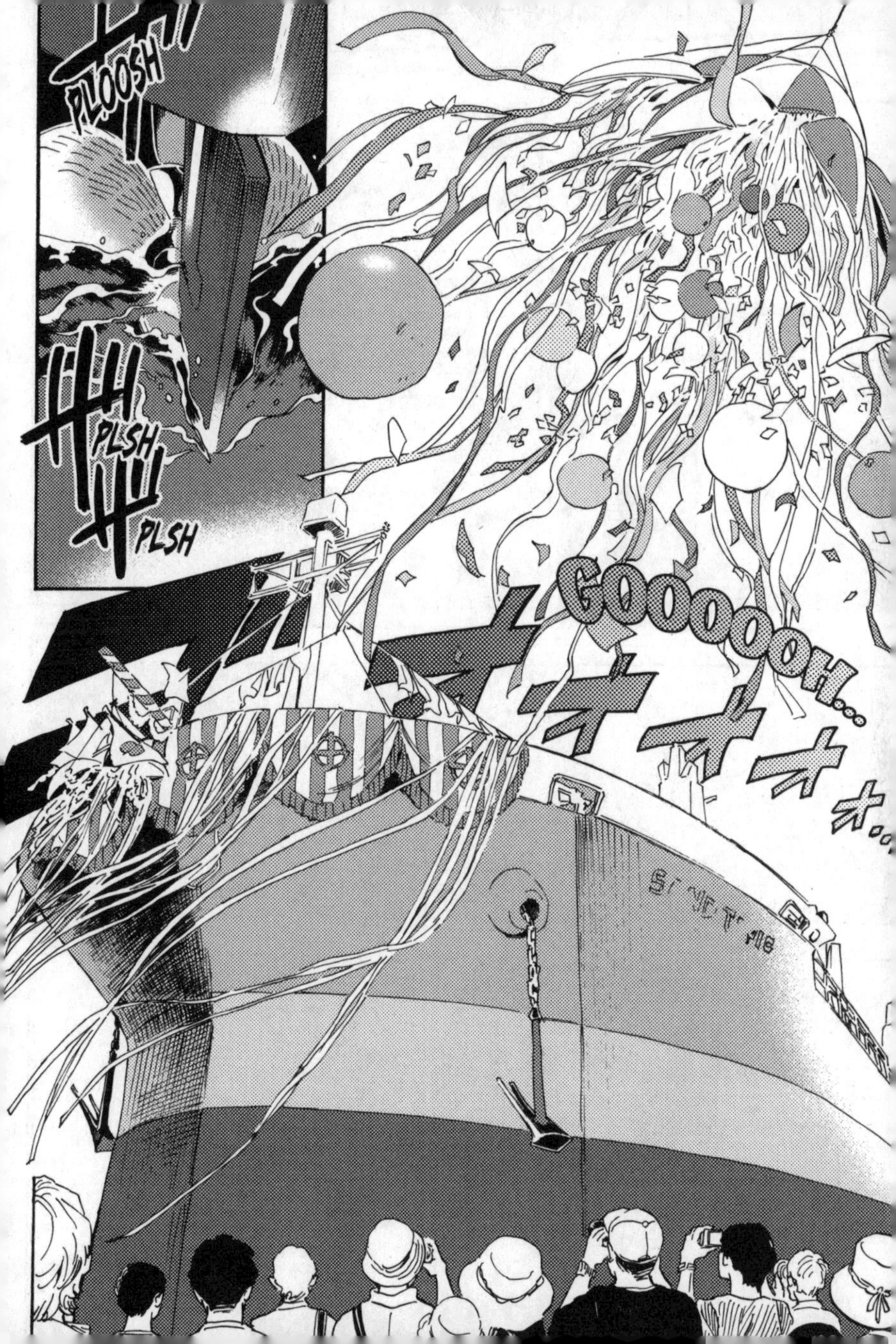
GOOOOOOH...
PLOOSH
PLSH
PLSH

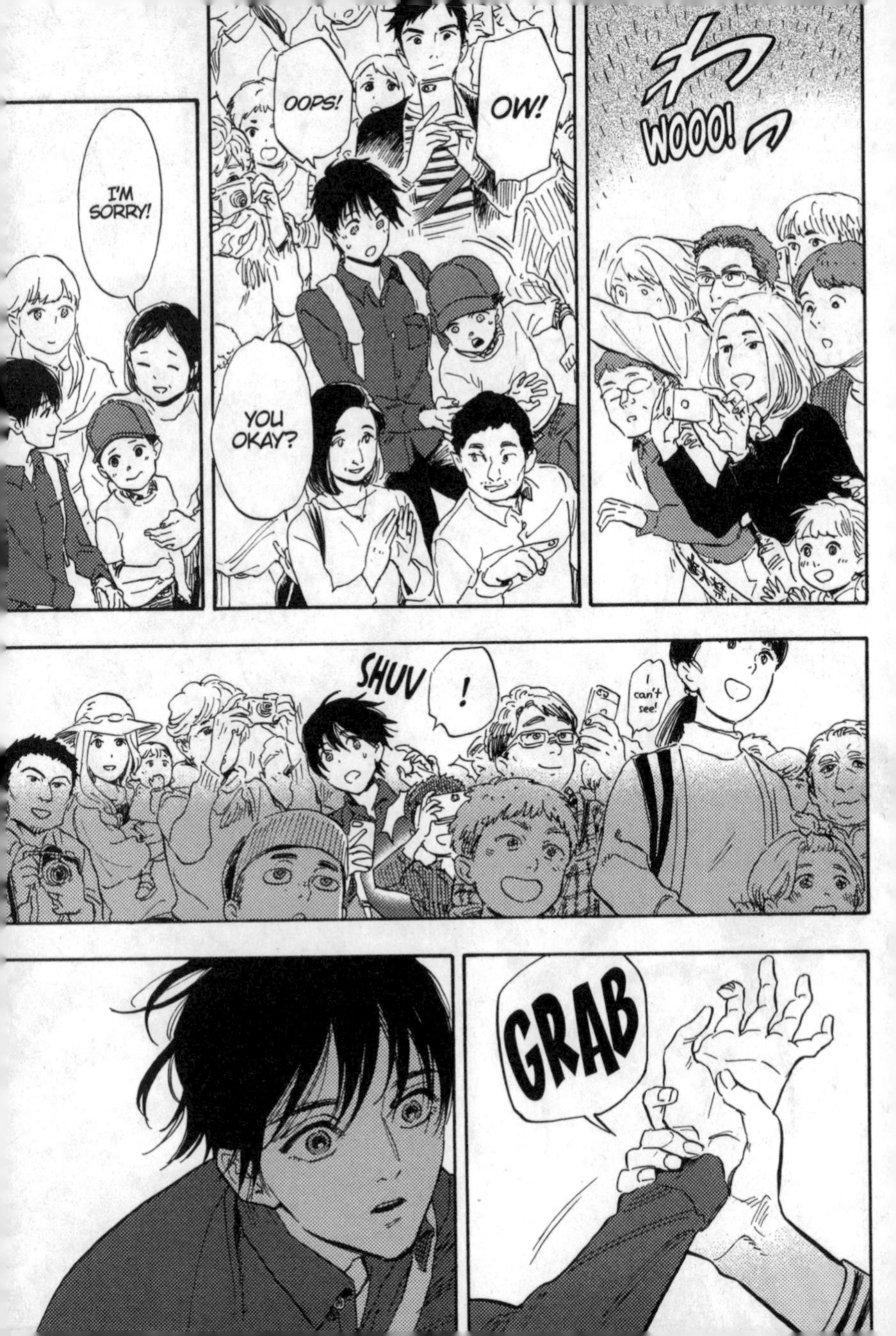
WOOO!
OW!
OOPS!
YOU OKAY?
I'M SORRY!
I can't see!
!
SHUV
GRAB

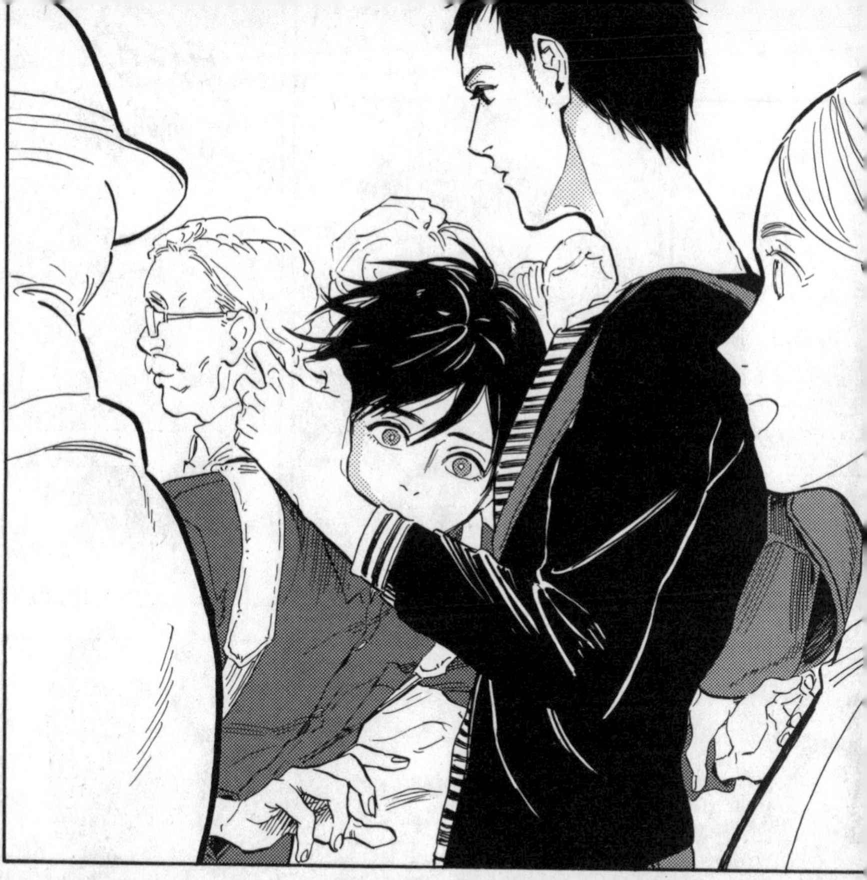
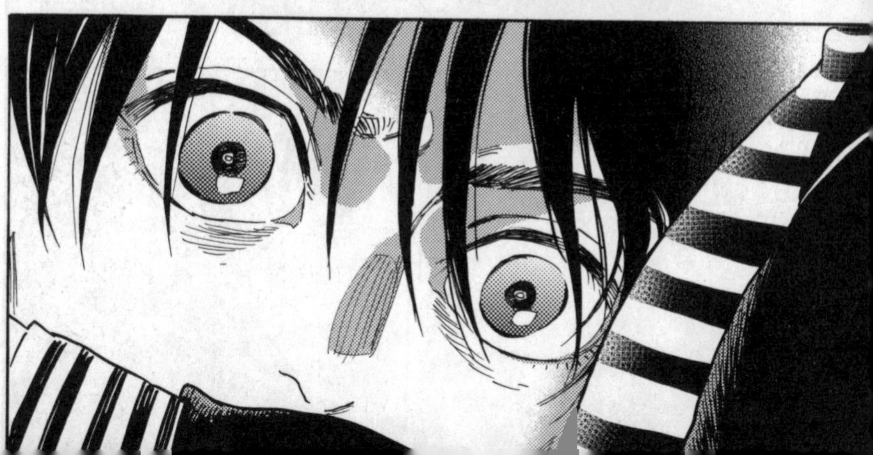

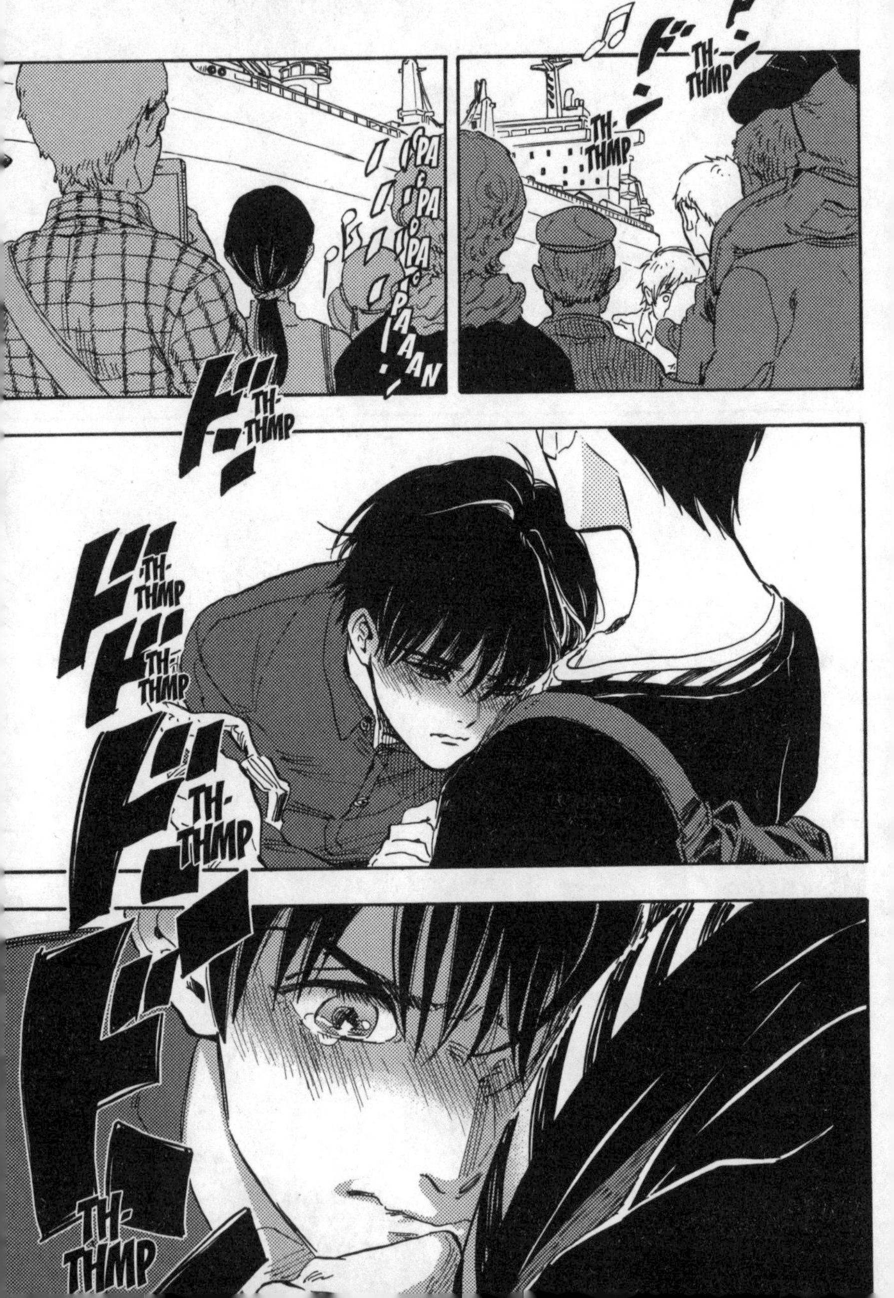
TH-THMP
TH-THMP
PA PA PA PAAAAN
TH-THMP
TH-THMP
TH-THMP
TH-THMP
TH-THMP

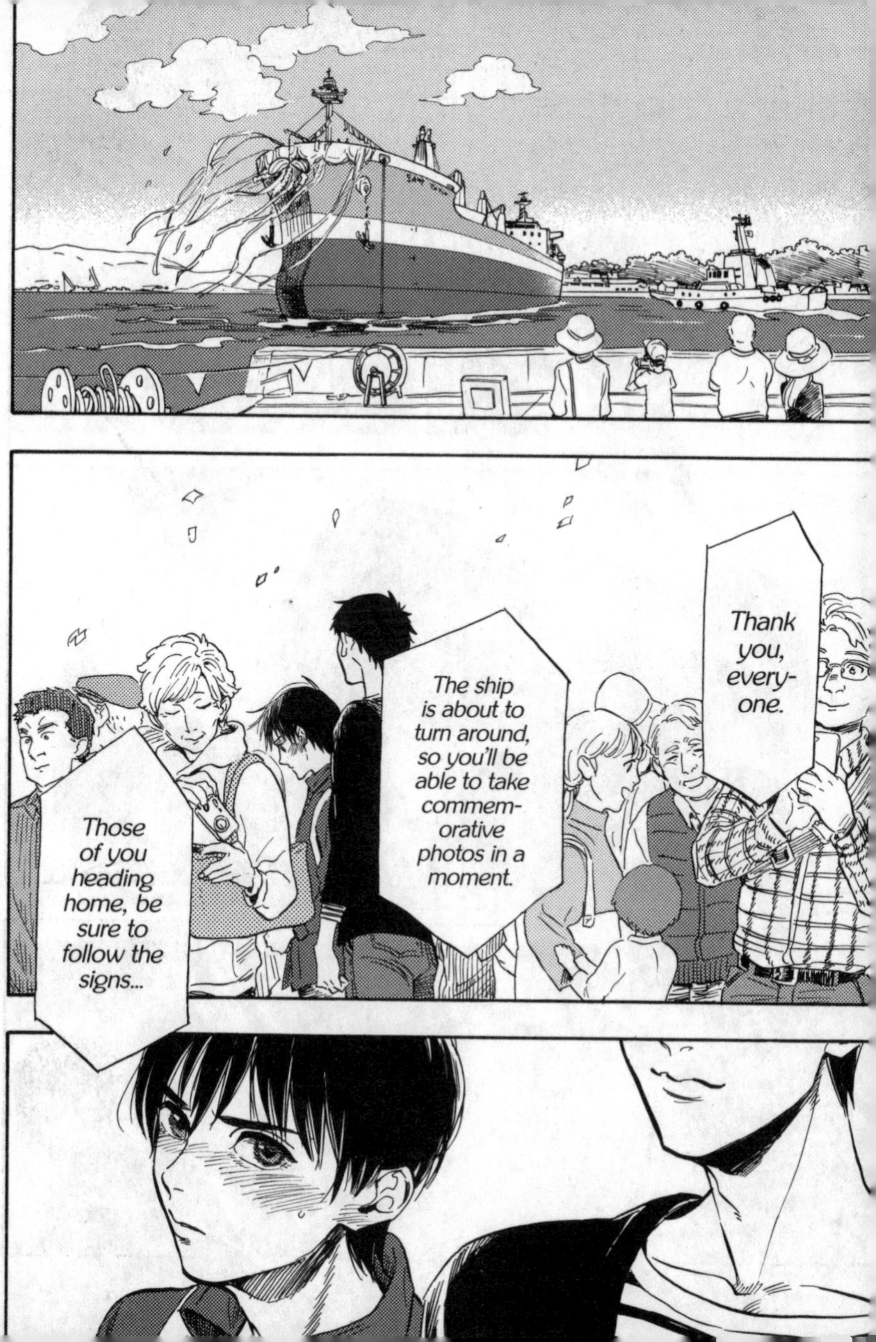
Thank you, everyone.
The ship is about to turn around, so you'll be able to take commemorative photos in a moment.
Those of you heading home, be sure to follow the signs...

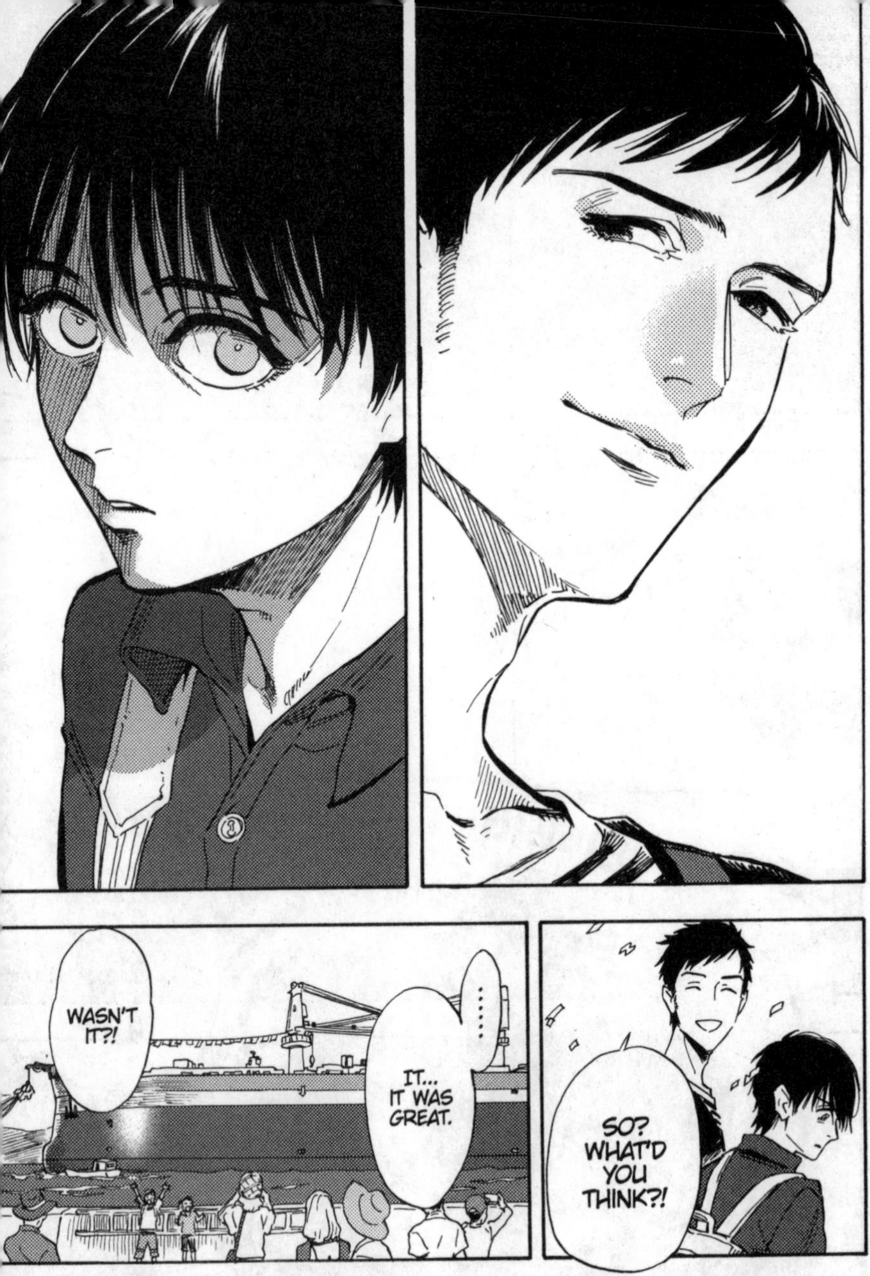
SO? WHAT'D YOU THINK?!
......
IT... IT WAS GREAT.
WASN'T IT?!

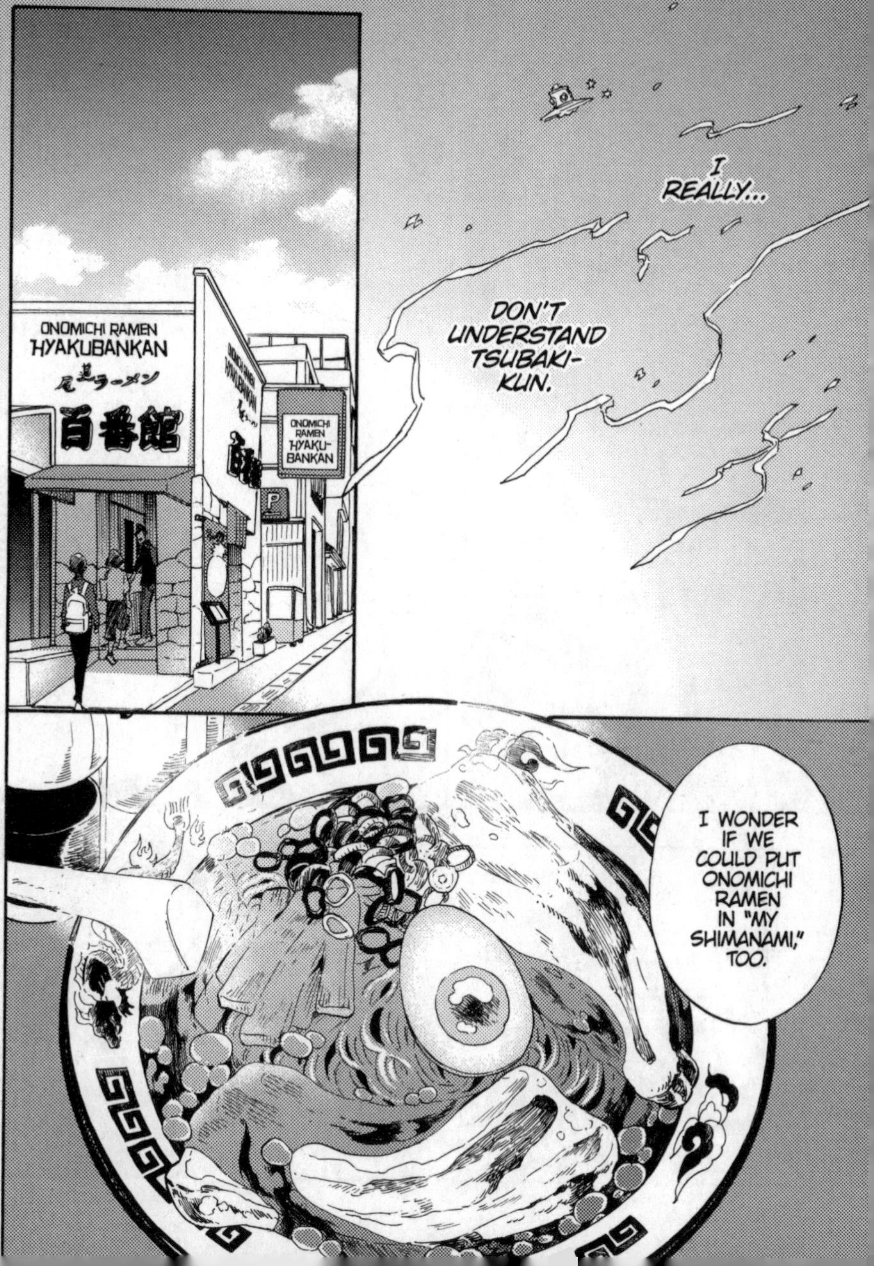
I REALLY... DON'T UNDERSTAND TSUBAKI-KUN.
ONOMICHI RAMEN HYAKU-BANKAN
ONOMICHI RAMEN HYAKUBANKAN
尾道ラーメン
百番館
I WONDER IF WE COULD PUT ONOMICHI RAMEN IN "MY SHIMANAMI," TOO.

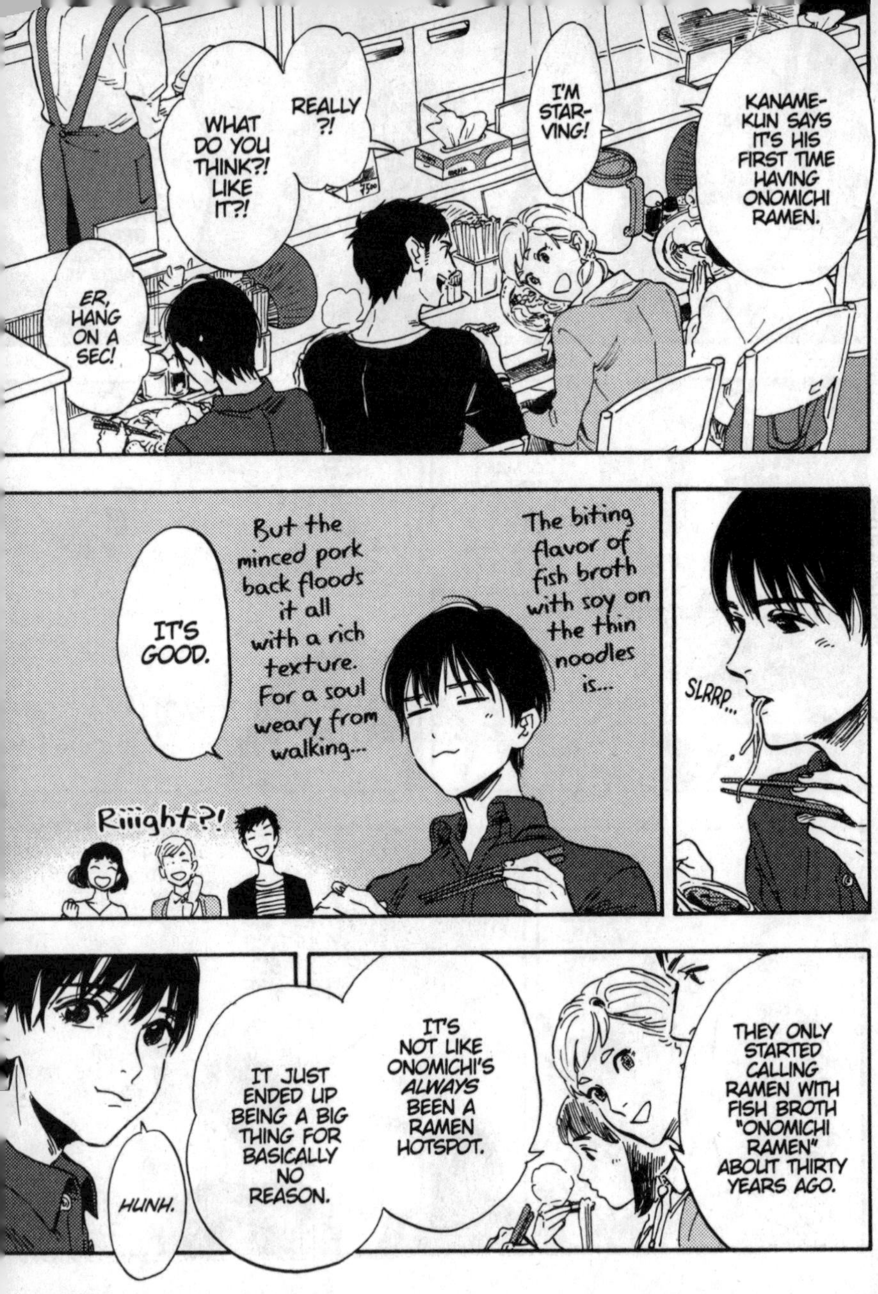
KANAME-KUN SAYS IT'S HIS FIRST TIME HAVING ONOMICHI RAMEN.
I'M STAR-VING!
REALLY?!
WHAT DO YOU THINK?! LIKE IT?!
ER, HANG ON A SEC!
SLRRP...
The biting flavor of fish broth with soy on the thin noodles is...
But the minced pork back floods it all with a rich texture. For a soul weary from walking...
IT'S GOOD.
Riiight?!
THEY ONLY STARTED CALLING RAMEN WITH FISH BROTH "ONOMICHI RAMEN" ABOUT THIRTY YEARS AGO.
IT'S NOT LIKE ONOMICHI'S *ALWAYS* BEEN A RAMEN HOTSPOT.
IT JUST ENDED UP BEING A BIG THING FOR BASICALLY NO REASON.
HUNH.

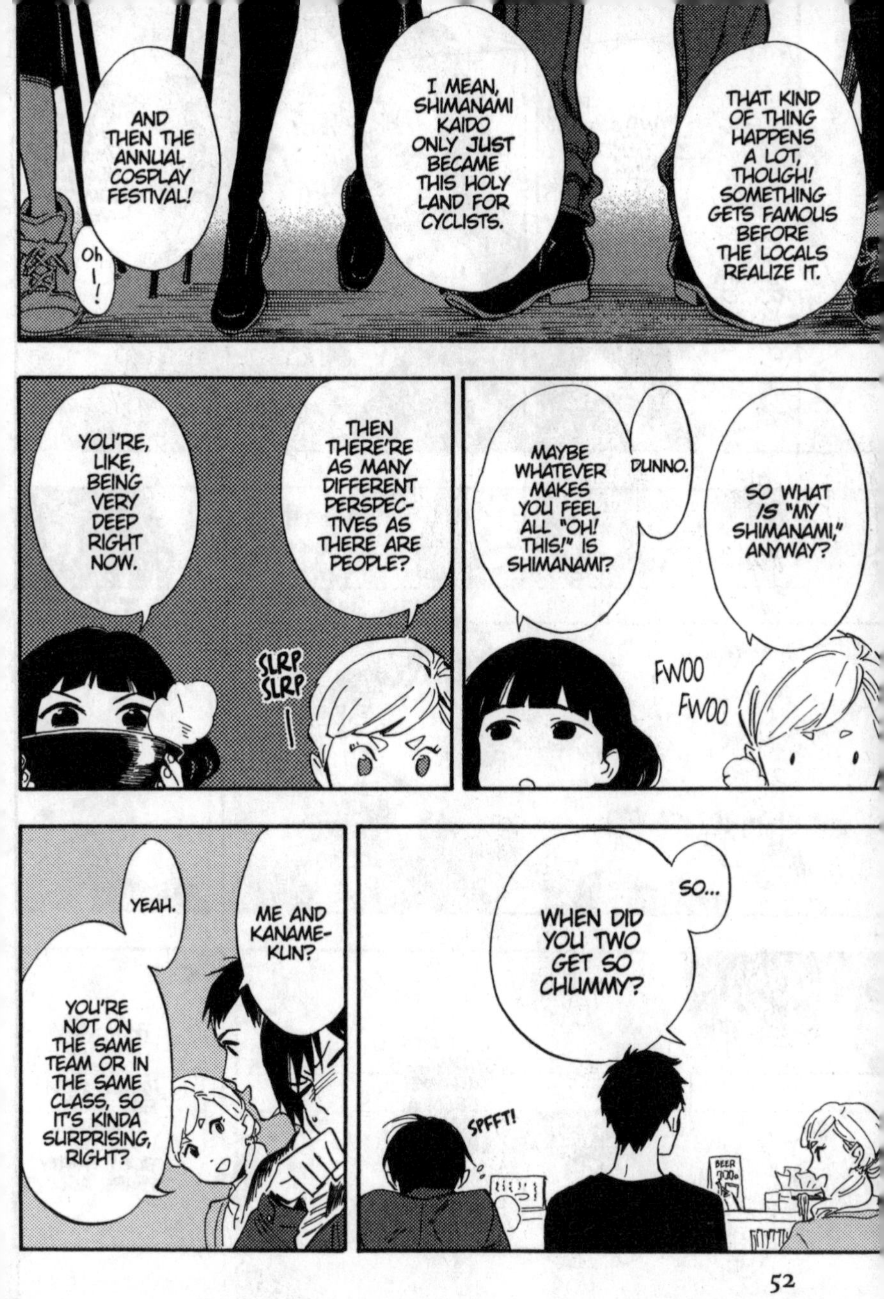
THAT KIND OF THING HAPPENS A LOT, THOUGH! SOMETHING GETS FAMOUS BEFORE THE LOCALS REALIZE IT.
I MEAN, SHIMANAMI KAIDO ONLY JUST BECAME THIS HOLY LAND FOR CYCLISTS.
AND THEN THE ANNUAL COSPLAY FESTIVAL!
Oh!
SO WHAT IS "MY SHIMANAMI," ANYWAY?
DUNNO.
MAYBE WHATEVER MAKES YOU FEEL ALL "OH! THIS!" IS SHIMANAMI?
FWOO FWOO
THEN THERE'RE AS MANY DIFFERENT PERSPEC-TIVES AS THERE ARE PEOPLE?
SLRP SLRP
YOU'RE, LIKE, BEING VERY DEEP RIGHT NOW.
SO...
WHEN DID YOU TWO GET SO CHUMMY?
SPFFT!
BEER
ME AND KANAME-KUN?
YEAH.
YOU'RE NOT ON THE SAME TEAM OR IN THE SAME CLASS, SO IT'S KINDA SURPRISING, RIGHT?

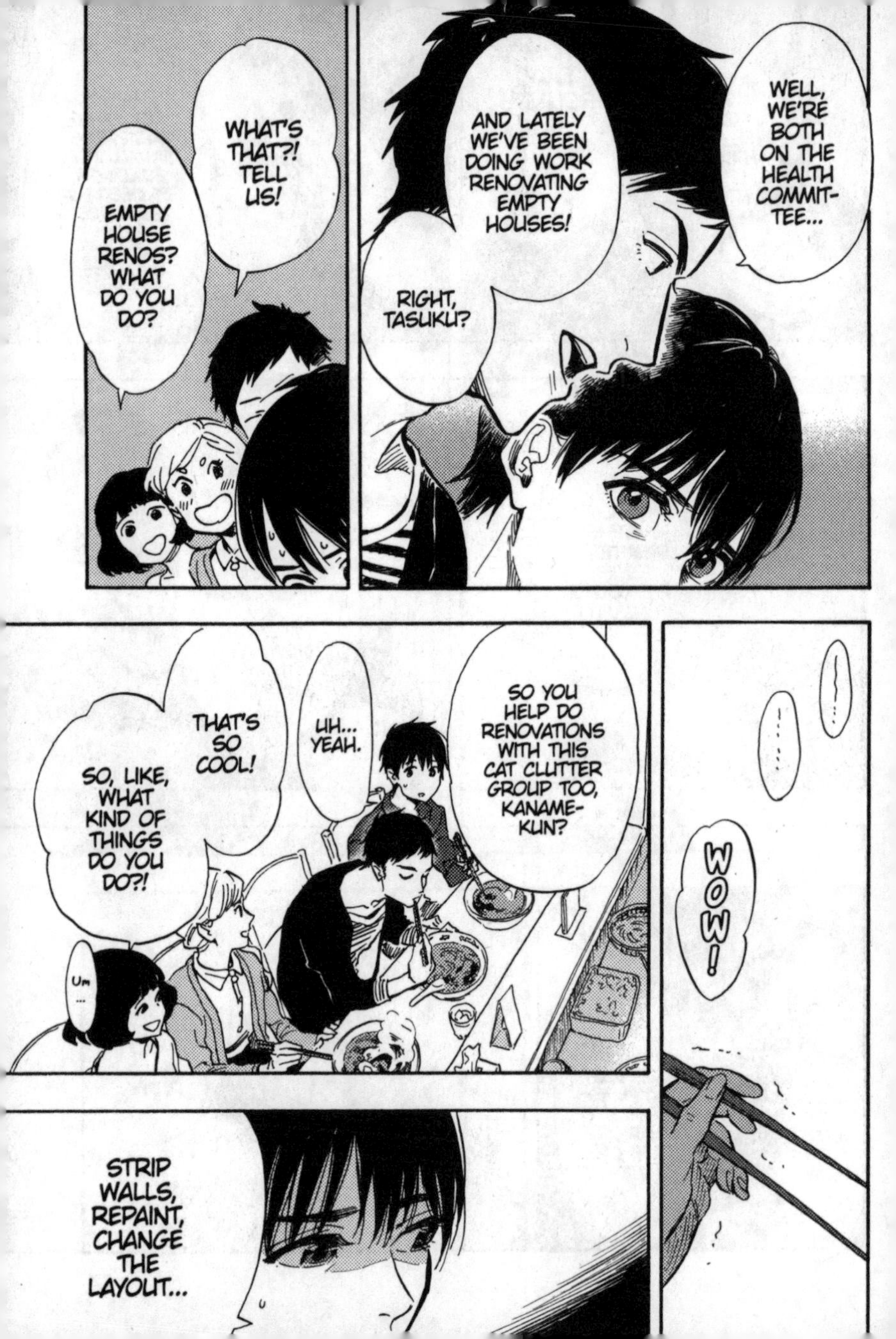

WELL, WE'RE BOTH ON THE HEALTH COMMIT-TEE...
AND LATELY WE'VE BEEN DOING WORK RENOVATING EMPTY HOUSES!
RIGHT, TASUKU?
WHAT'S THAT?! TELL US!
EMPTY HOUSE RENOS? WHAT DO YOU DO?
SO YOU HELP DO RENOVATIONS WITH THIS CAT CLUTTER GROUP TOO, KANAME-KUN?
UH... YEAH.
THAT'S SO COOL!
SO, LIKE, WHAT KIND OF THINGS DO YOU DO?!
Um ...
STRIP WALLS, REPAINT, CHANGE THE LAYOUT...
...
...
WOW!

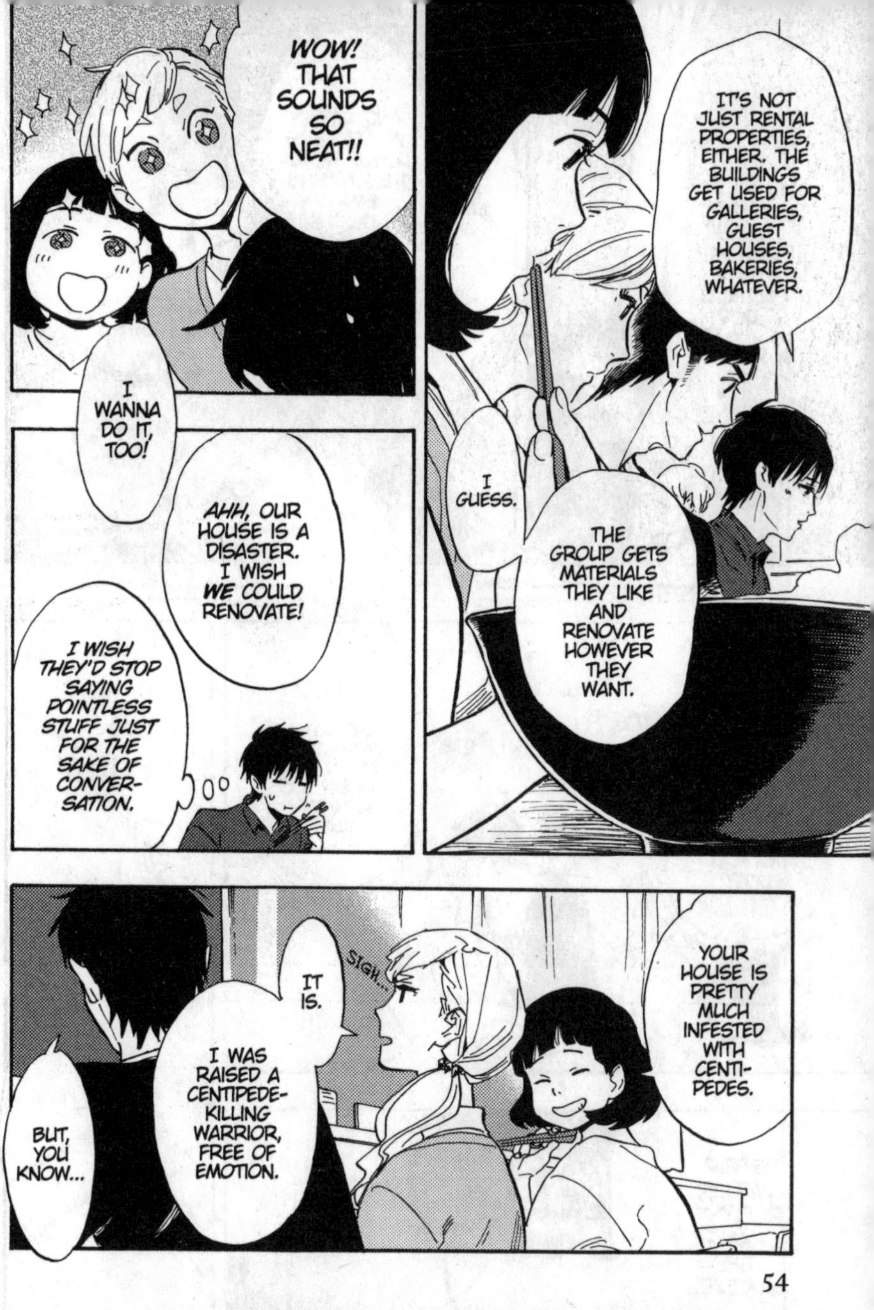
IT'S NOT JUST RENTAL PROPERTIES, EITHER. THE BUILDINGS GET USED FOR GALLERIES, GUEST HOUSES, BAKERIES, WHATEVER.
THE GROUP GETS MATERIALS THEY LIKE AND RENOVATE HOWEVER THEY WANT.
I GUESS.
WOW! THAT SOUNDS SO NEAT!!
I WANNA DO IT, TOO!
AHH, OUR HOUSE IS A DISASTER. I WISH *WE* COULD RENOVATE!
I WISH THEY'D STOP SAYING POINTLESS STUFF JUST FOR THE SAKE OF CONVERSATION.
YOUR HOUSE IS PRETTY MUCH INFESTED WITH CENTIPEDES.
SIGH...
IT IS.
I WAS RAISED A CENTIPEDE-KILLING WARRIOR, FREE OF EMOTION.
BUT, YOU KNOW...

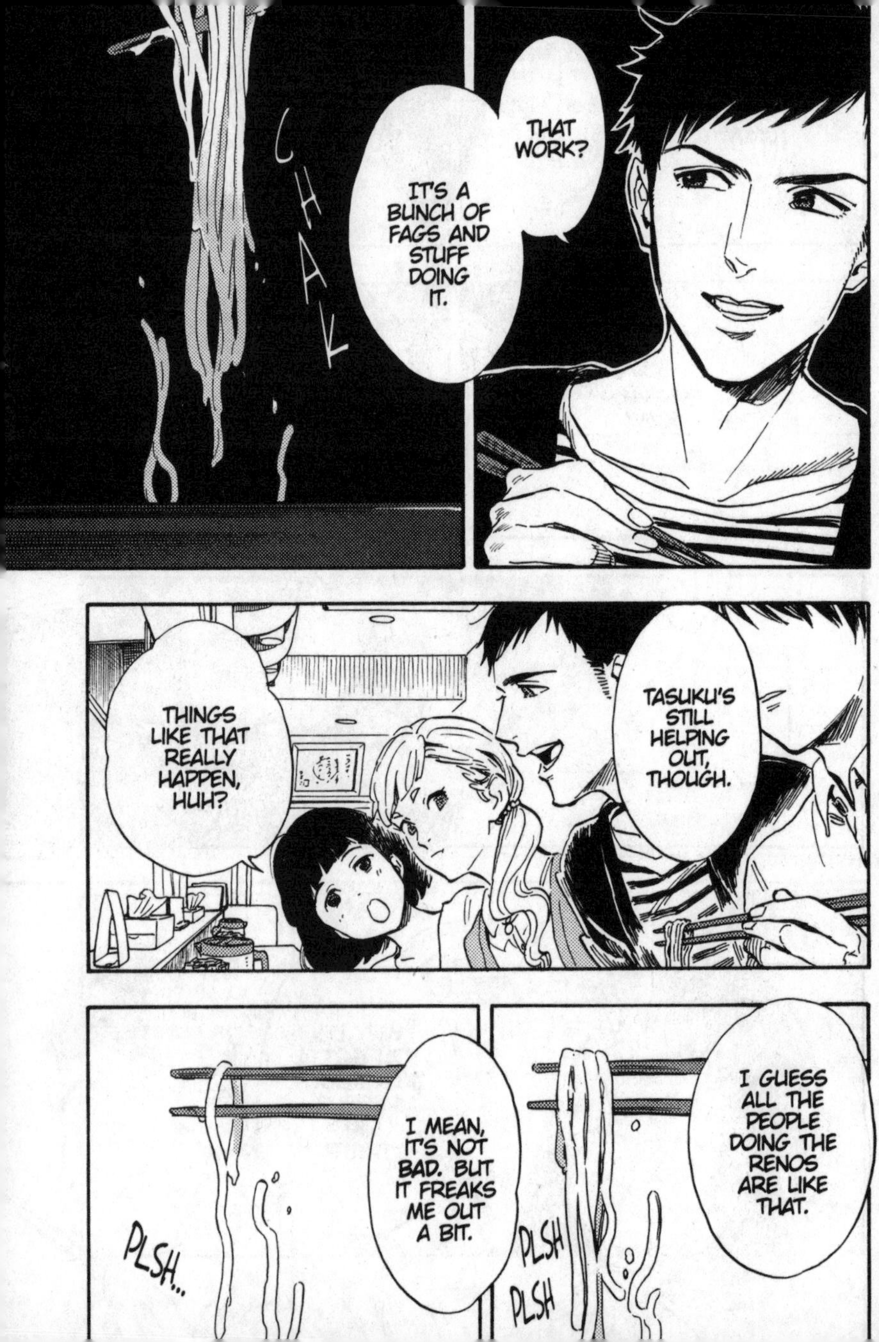
THAT WORK?
IT'S A BUNCH OF FAGS AND STUFF DOING IT.
CHAK
TASUKU'S STILL HELPING OUT, THOUGH.
THINGS LIKE THAT REALLY HAPPEN, HUH?
I GUESS ALL THE PEOPLE DOING THE RENOS ARE LIKE THAT.
PLSH
PLSH
I MEAN, IT'S NOT BAD. BUT IT FREAKS ME OUT A BIT.
PLSH...

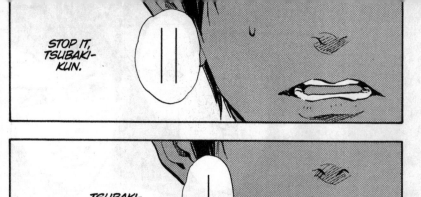

STOP IT, TSUBAKI-KUN.
TSUBAKI-KUN!
BETTER NOT TO GET DRAGGED INTO THAT KIND OF--
WHY DO YOU GOTTA TALK ABOUT PEOPLE LIKE THAT?

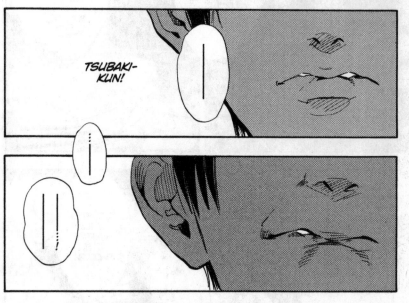

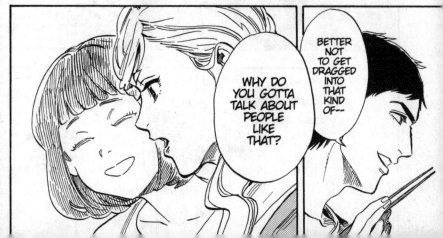

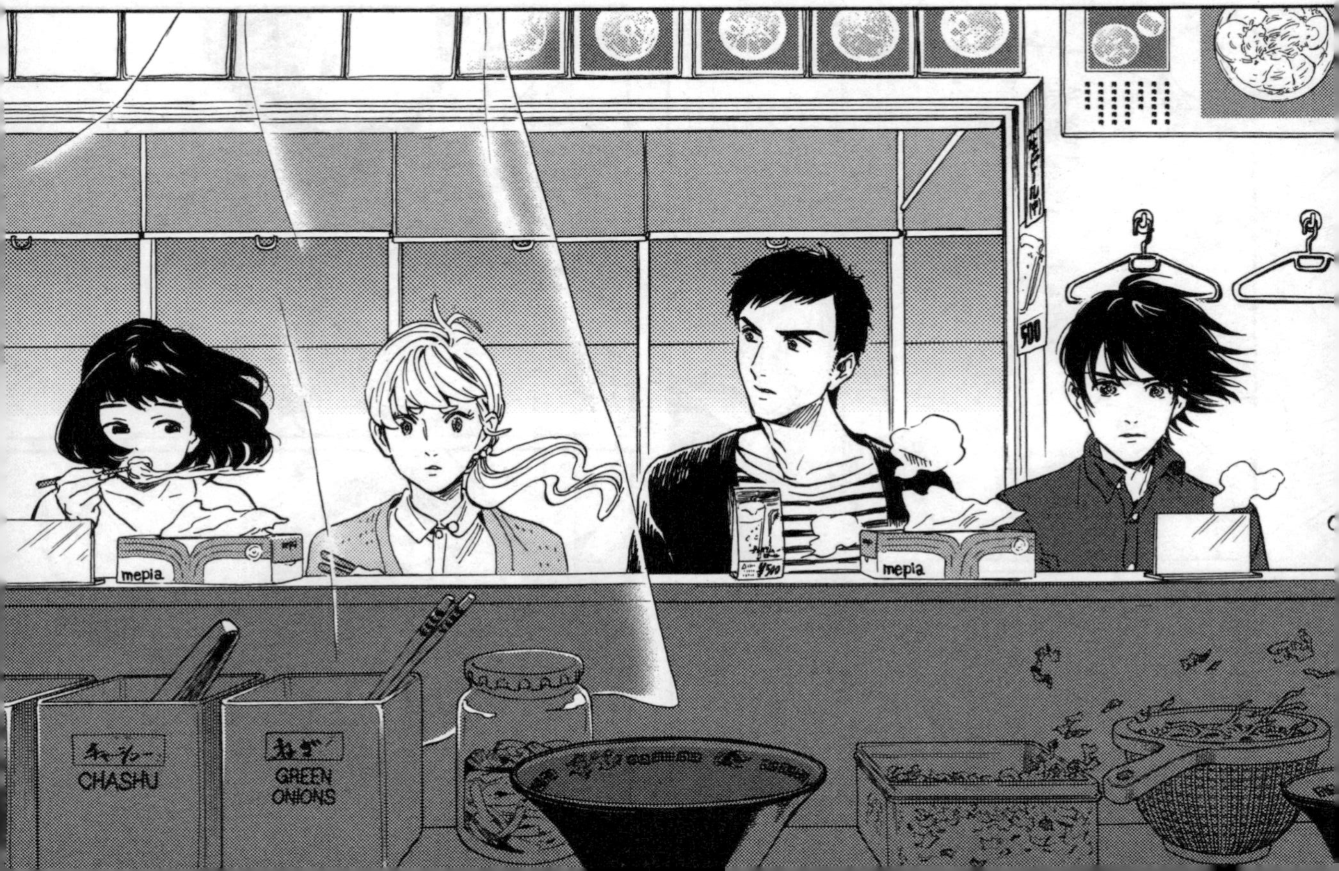
500
mepia
¥500
mepia
ねぎ
GREEN ONIONS
チャーシュー
CHASHU

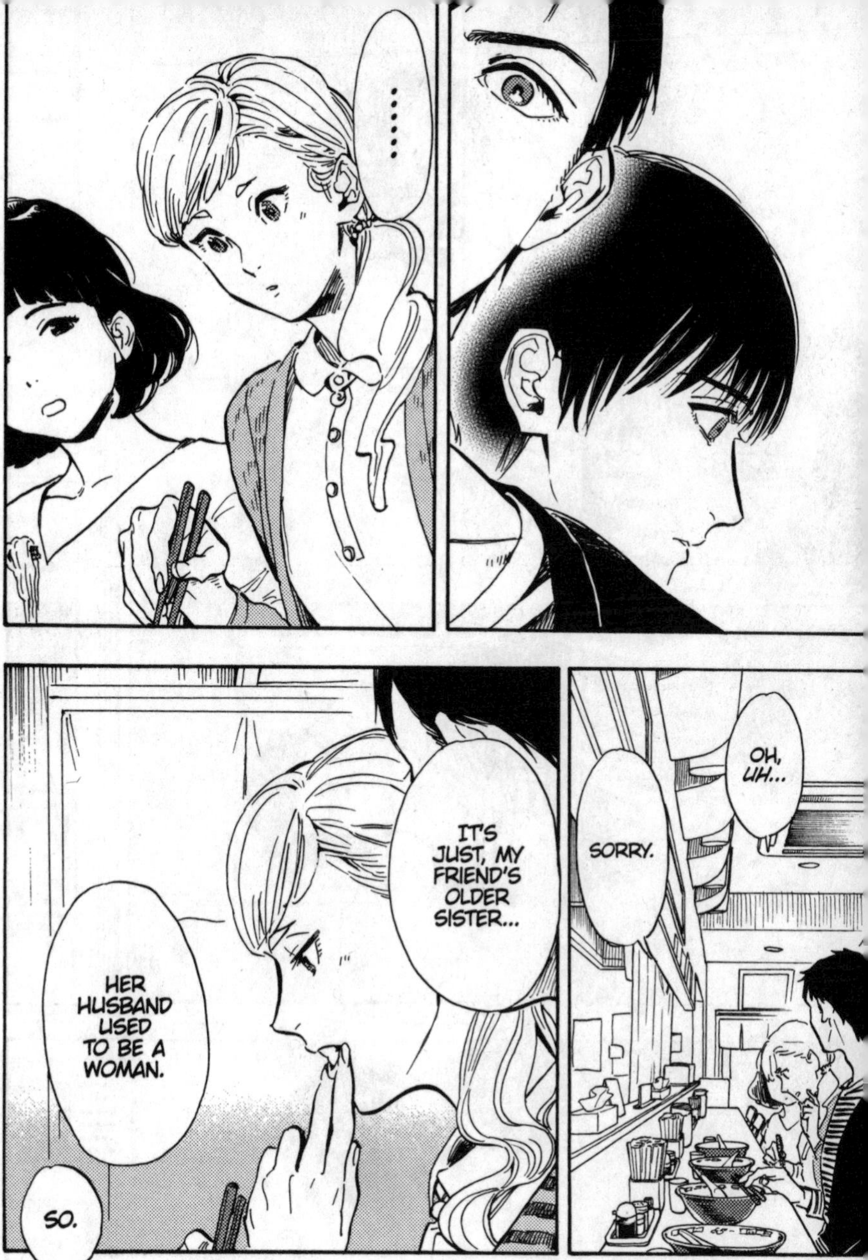
......
OH, UH...
SORRY.
IT'S JUST, MY FRIEND'S OLDER SISTER...
HER HUSBAND USED TO BE A WOMAN.
SO.

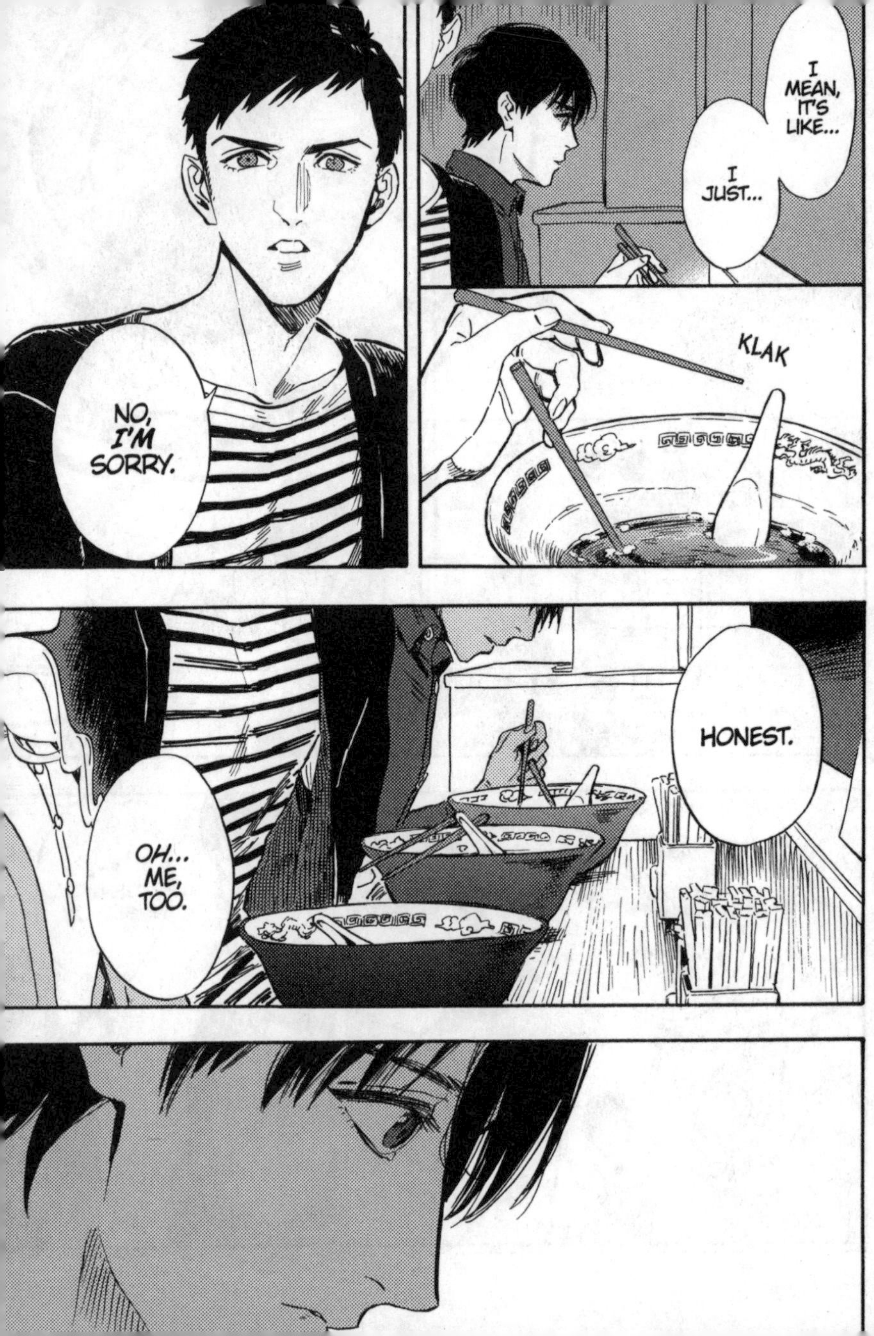
I MEAN, IT'S LIKE...
I JUST...
KLAK
NO, I'M SORRY.
HONEST.
OH... ME, TOO.

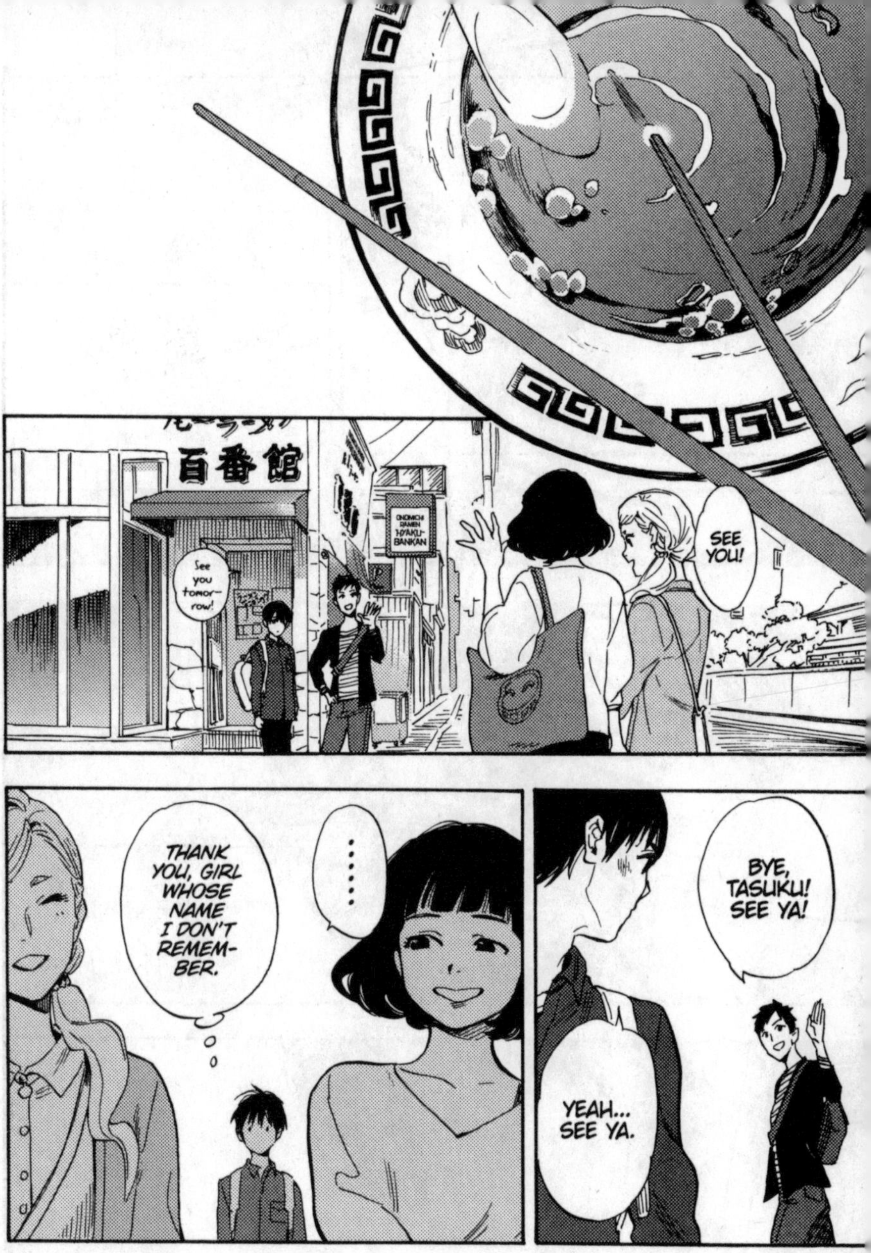
SEE YOU!
ONOMICHI RAMEN HYAKU-BANKAN
百番館
See you tomorrow!
BYE, TASUKU! SEE YA!
YEAH... SEE YA.
......
THANK YOU, GIRL WHOSE NAME I DON'T REMEMBER.

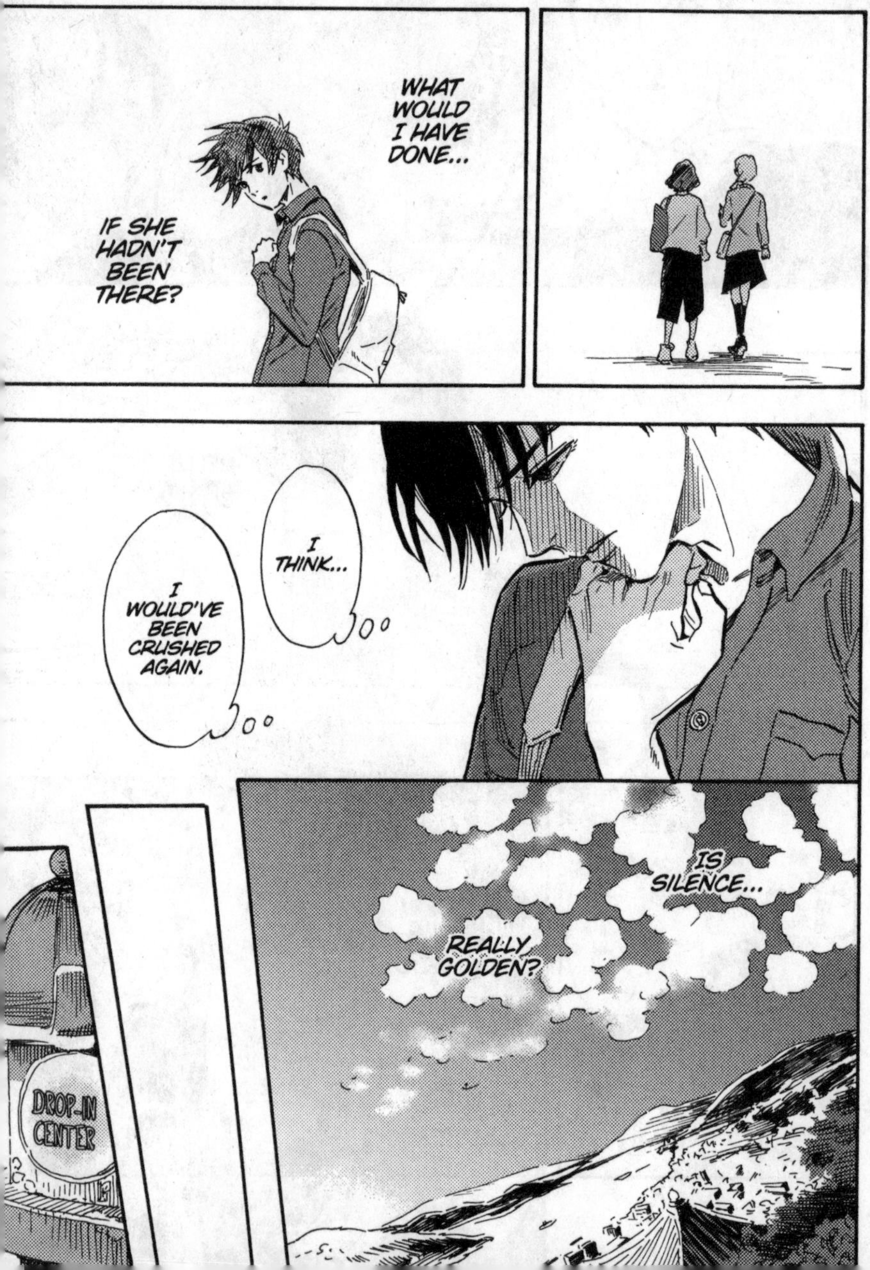
WHAT WOULD I HAVE DONE...
IF SHE HADN'T BEEN THERE?
I THINK...
I WOULD'VE BEEN CRUSHED AGAIN.
IS SILENCE...
REALLY GOLDEN?
DROP-IN CENTER

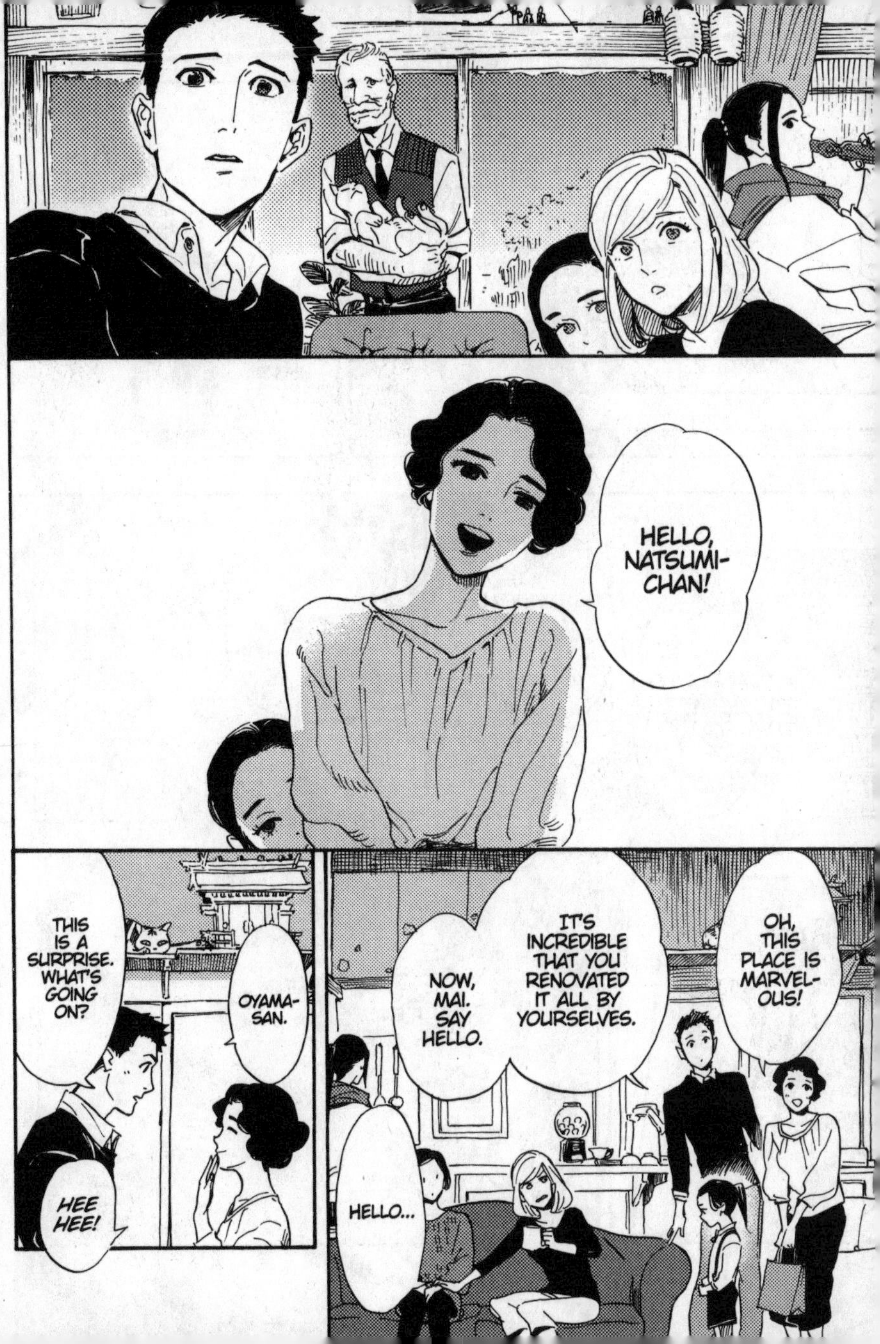
HELLO, NATSUMI-CHAN!
OH, THIS PLACE IS MARVEL-OUS!
IT'S INCREDIBLE THAT YOU RENOVATED IT ALL BY YOURSELVES.
NOW, MAI. SAY HELLO.
HELLO...
OYAMA-SAN.
THIS IS A SURPRISE. WHAT'S GOING ON?
HEE HEE!

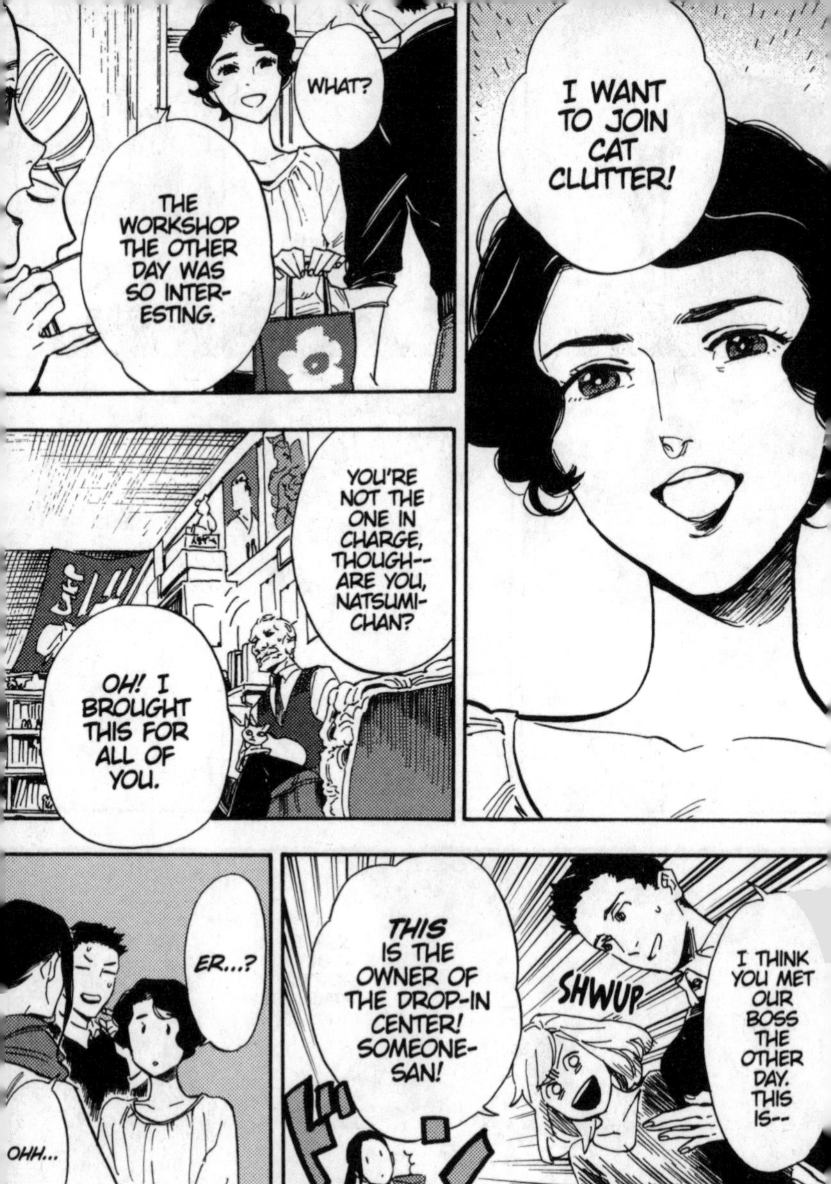
I WANT TO JOIN CAT CLUTTER!
WHAT?
THE WORKSHOP THE OTHER DAY WAS SO INTER-ESTING.
YOU'RE NOT THE ONE IN CHARGE, THOUGH--ARE YOU, NATSUMI-CHAN?
OH! I BROUGHT THIS FOR ALL OF YOU.
I THINK YOU MET OUR BOSS THE OTHER DAY. THIS IS--
SHWUP
THIS IS THE OWNER OF THE DROP-IN CENTER! SOMEONE-SAN!
VOILA!
ER...?
OHH...

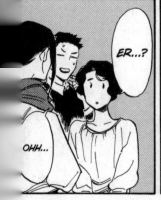

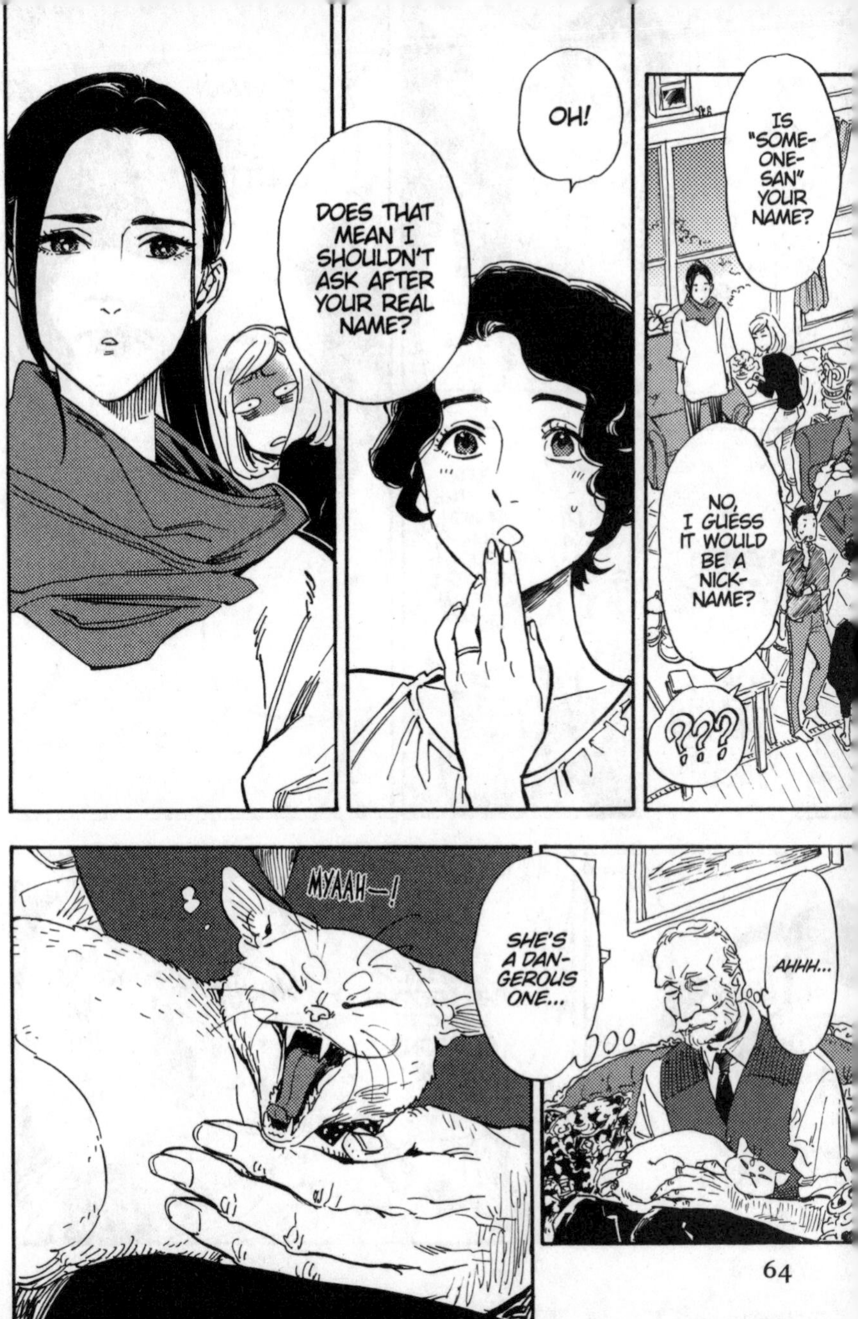
IS "SOME-ONE-SAN" YOUR NAME?
NO, I GUESS IT WOULD BE A NICK-NAME?
???
OH!
DOES THAT MEAN I SHOULDN'T ASK AFTER YOUR REAL NAME?
AHHH...
SHE'S A DAN-GEROUS ONE...
MYAAH—!

Our Dreams at Dusk
SHIMANAMI TASOGARE

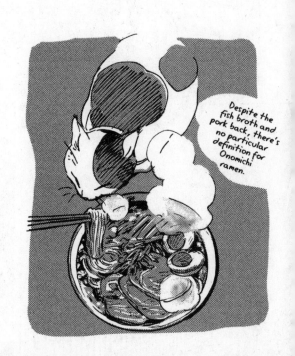

Despite the fish broth and pork back, there's no particular definition for Onomichi ramen.

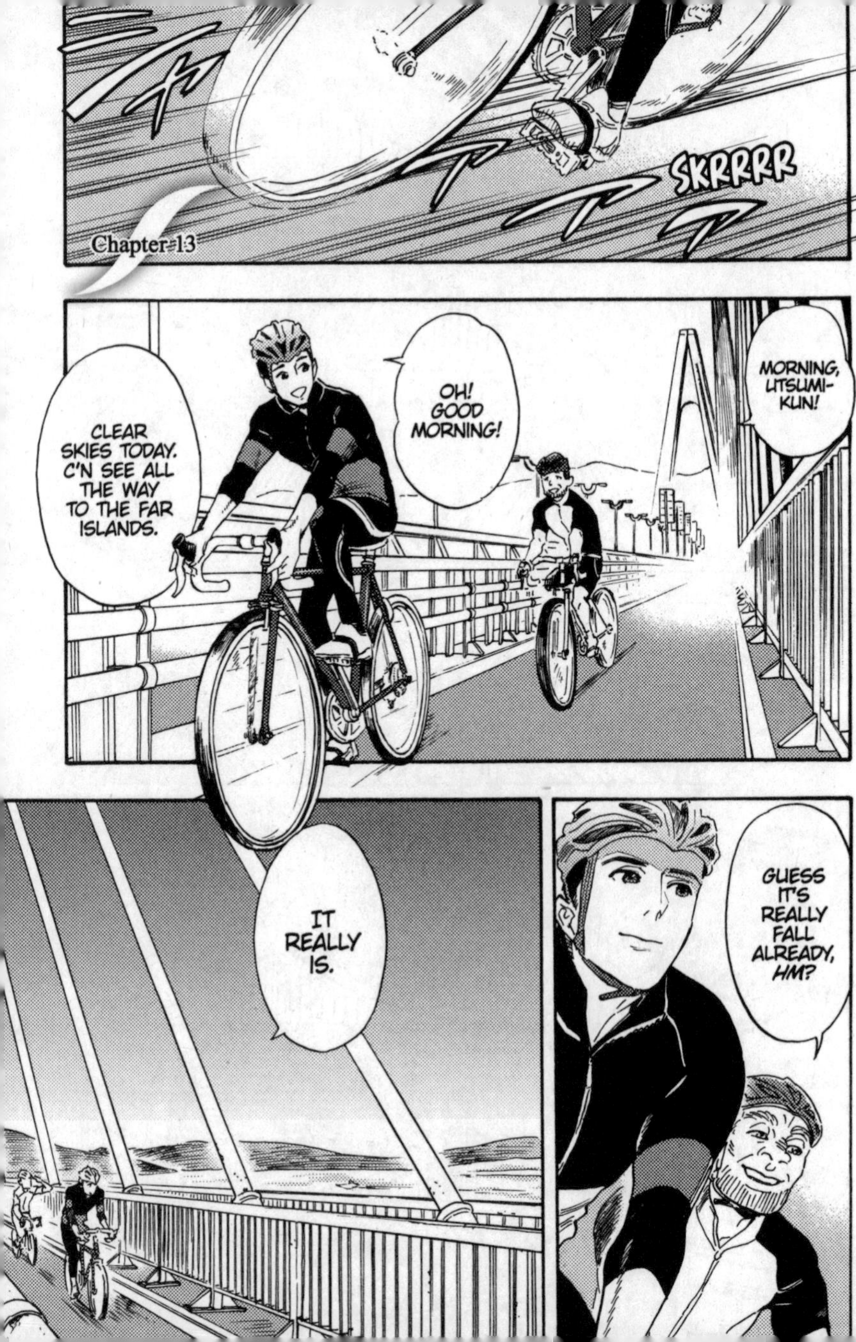
SKRRRR
Chapter 13
MORNING, UTSUMI-KUN!
OH! GOOD MORNING!
CLEAR SKIES TODAY. C'N SEE ALL THE WAY TO THE FAR ISLANDS.
GUESS IT'S REALLY FALL ALREADY, HM?
IT REALLY IS.

Chapter 13

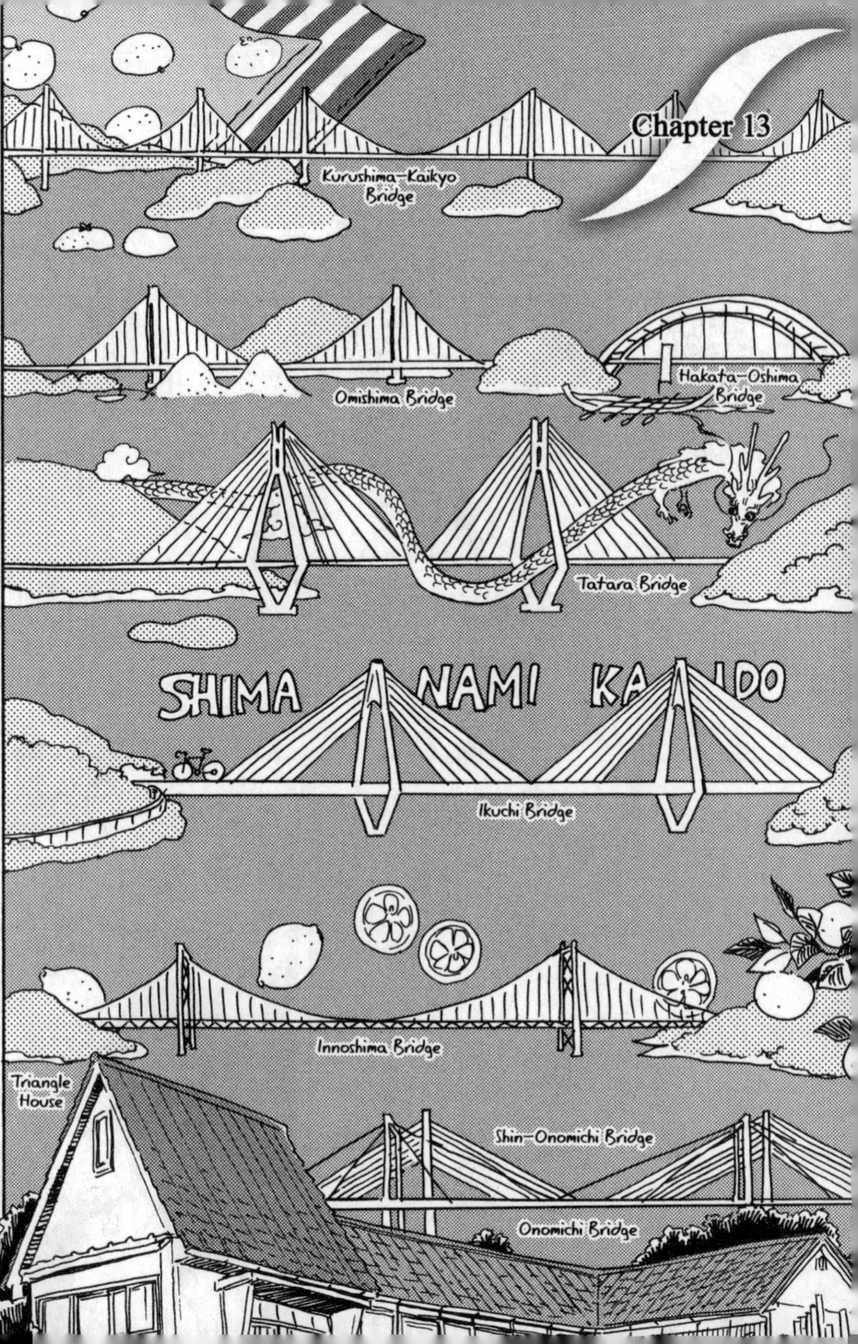
Kurushima-Kaikyo Bridge
Omishima Bridge
Hakata-Oshima Bridge
Tatara Bridge
SHIMA NAMI KAIDO
Ikuchi Bridge
Innoshima Bridge
Triangle House
Shin-Onomichi Bridge
Onomichi Bridge

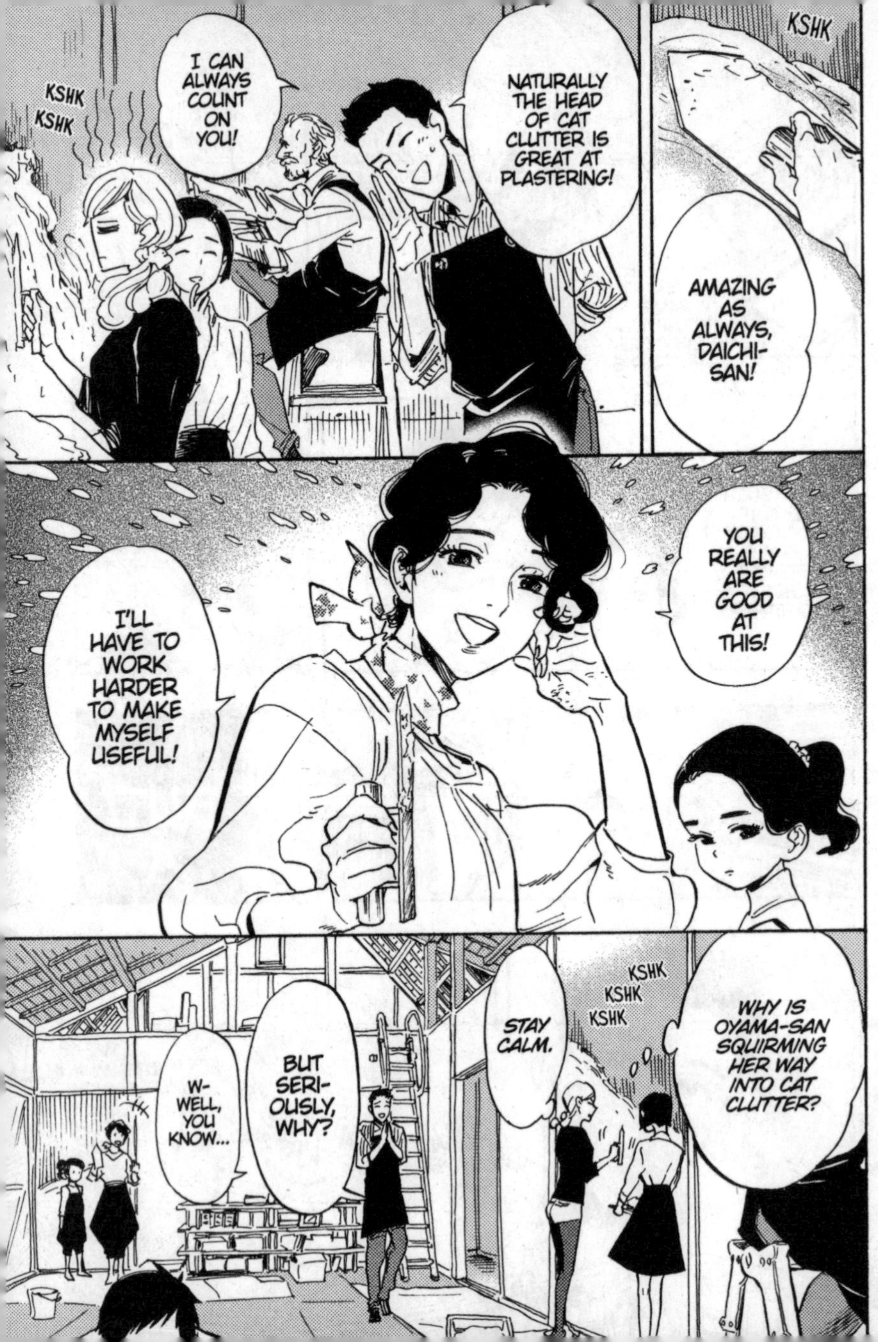
KSHK
AMAZING AS ALWAYS, DAICHI-SAN!
NATURALLY THE HEAD OF CAT CLUTTER IS GREAT AT PLASTERING!
I CAN ALWAYS COUNT ON YOU!
KSHK KSHK
YOU REALLY ARE GOOD AT THIS!
I'LL HAVE TO WORK HARDER TO MAKE MYSELF USEFUL!
WHY IS OYAMA-SAN SQUIRMING HER WAY INTO CAT CLUTTER?
KSHK KSHK KSHK
STAY CALM.
BUT SERIOUSLY, WHY?
W-WELL, YOU KNOW...

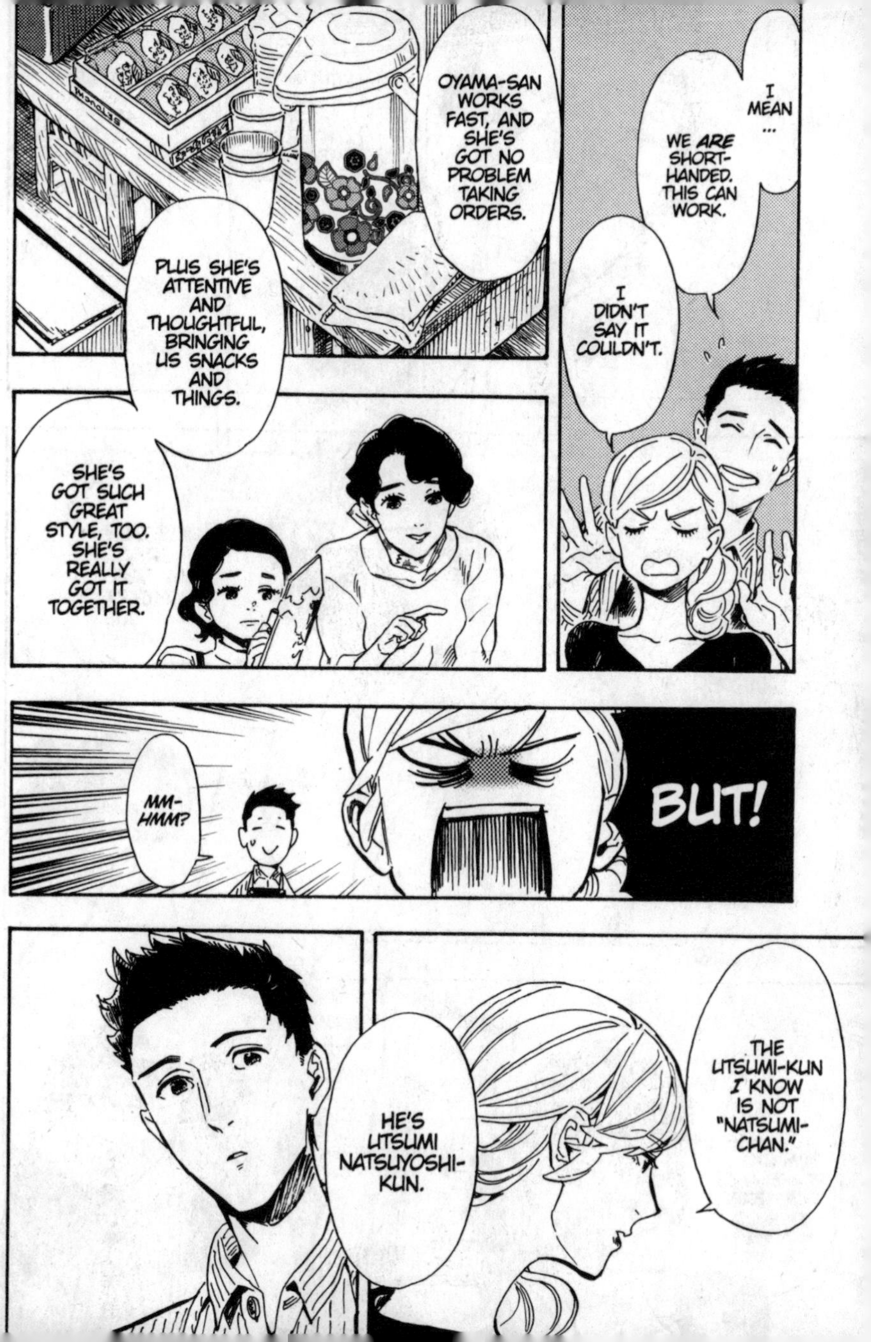
I MEAN ...
WE *ARE* SHORT-HANDED. THIS CAN WORK.
I DIDN'T SAY IT COULDN'T.
OYAMA-SAN WORKS FAST, AND SHE'S GOT NO PROBLEM TAKING ORDERS.
PLUS SHE'S ATTENTIVE AND THOUGHTFUL, BRINGING US SNACKS AND THINGS.
SHE'S GOT SUCH GREAT STYLE, TOO. SHE'S REALLY GOT IT TOGETHER.
BUT!
MM-HMM?
THE UTSUMI-KUN *I* KNOW IS NOT "NATSUMI-CHAN."
HE'S UTSUMI NATSUYOSHI-KUN.

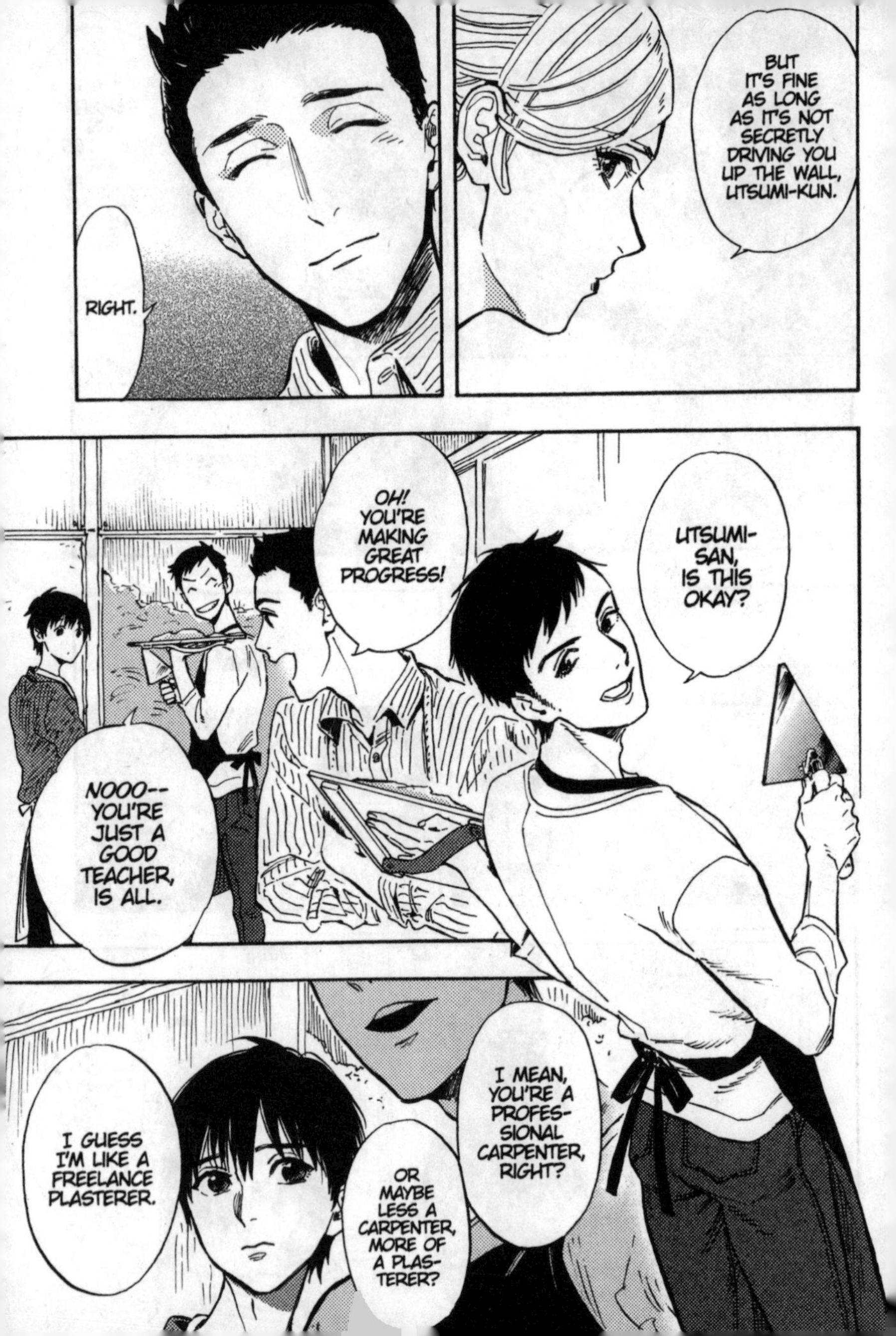
BUT IT'S FINE AS LONG AS IT'S NOT SECRETLY DRIVING YOU UP THE WALL, UTSUMI-KUN.
RIGHT.
UTSUMI-SAN, IS THIS OKAY?
OH! YOU'RE MAKING GREAT PROGRESS!
NOOO-- YOU'RE JUST A GOOD TEACHER, IS ALL.
I MEAN, YOU'RE A PROFES-SIONAL CARPENTER, RIGHT?
OR MAYBE LESS A CARPENTER, MORE OF A PLAS-TERER?
I GUESS I'M LIKE A FREELANCE PLASTERER.

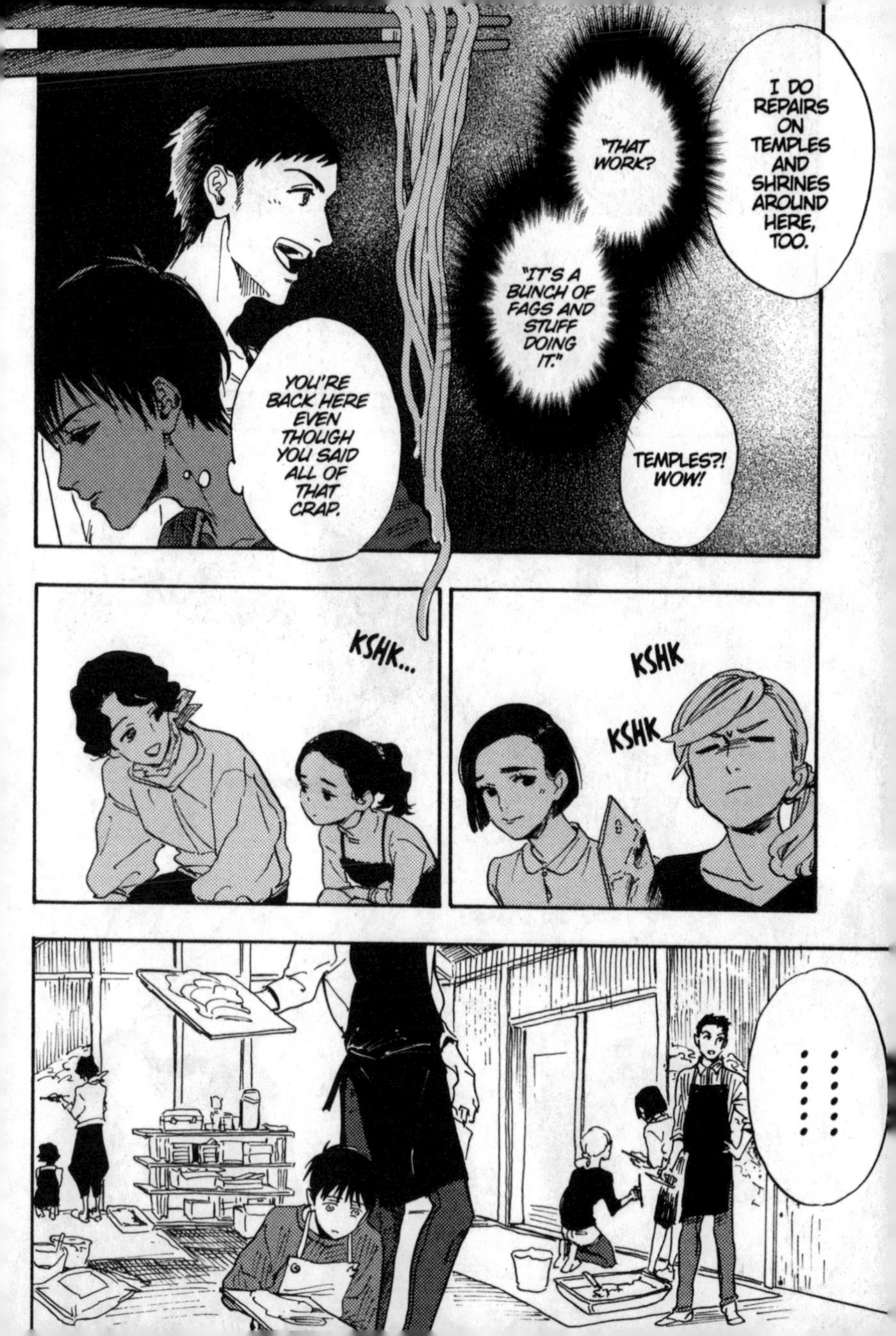
I DO REPAIRS ON TEMPLES AND SHRINES AROUND HERE, TOO.
TEMPLES?! WOW!
"THAT WORK?
"IT'S A BUNCH OF FAGS AND STUFF DOING IT."
YOU'RE BACK HERE EVEN THOUGH YOU SAID ALL OF THAT CRAP.
KSHK
KSHK
KSHK...
......

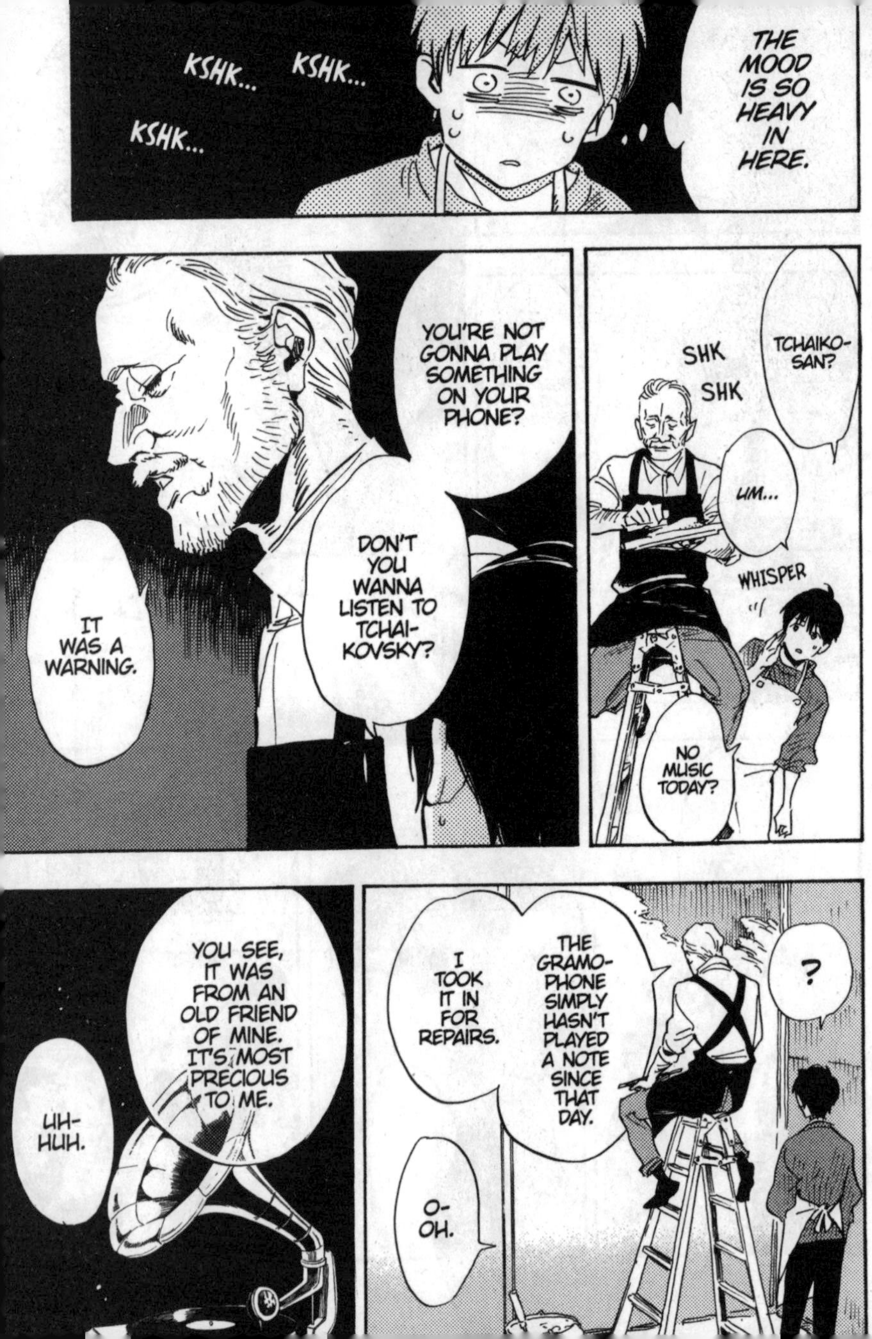
THE MOOD IS SO HEAVY IN HERE.
KSHK...
KSHK...
KSHK...
TCHAIKO-SAN?
SHK
SHK
UM...
WHISPER
NO MUSIC TODAY?
YOU'RE NOT GONNA PLAY SOMETHING ON YOUR PHONE?
DON'T YOU WANNA LISTEN TO TCHAI-KOVSKY?
IT WAS A WARNING.
?
THE GRAMO-PHONE SIMPLY HASN'T PLAYED A NOTE SINCE THAT DAY.
I TOOK IT IN FOR REPAIRS.
O-OH.
YOU SEE, IT WAS FROM AN OLD FRIEND OF MINE. IT'S MOST PRECIOUS TO ME.
UH-HUH.

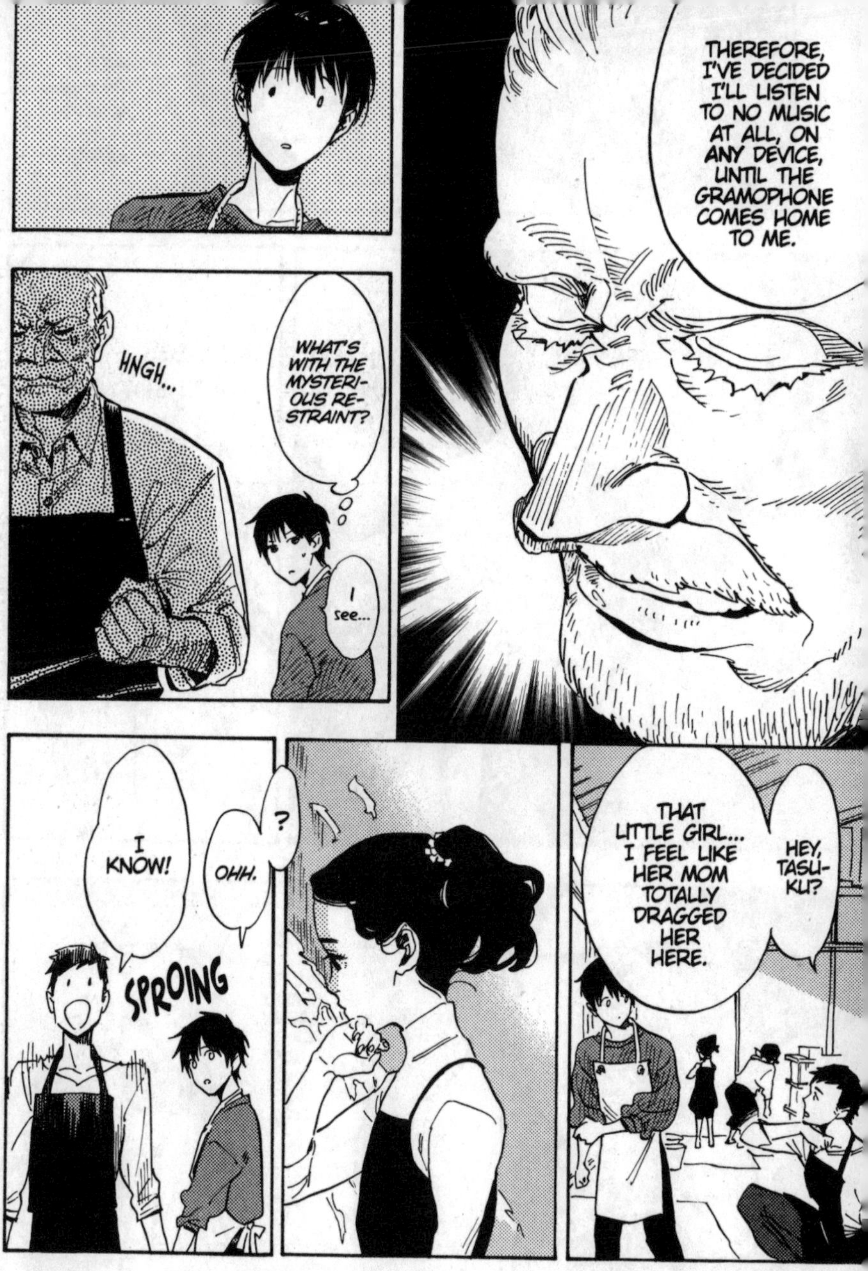
THEREFORE, I'VE DECIDED I'LL LISTEN TO NO MUSIC AT ALL, ON ANY DEVICE, UNTIL THE GRAMOPHONE COMES HOME TO ME.
WHAT'S WITH THE MYSTERIOUS RESTRAINT?
HNGH...
I see...
HEY, TASUKU?
THAT LITTLE GIRL... I FEEL LIKE HER MOM TOTALLY DRAGGED HER HERE.
?
OHH.
I KNOW!
SPROING

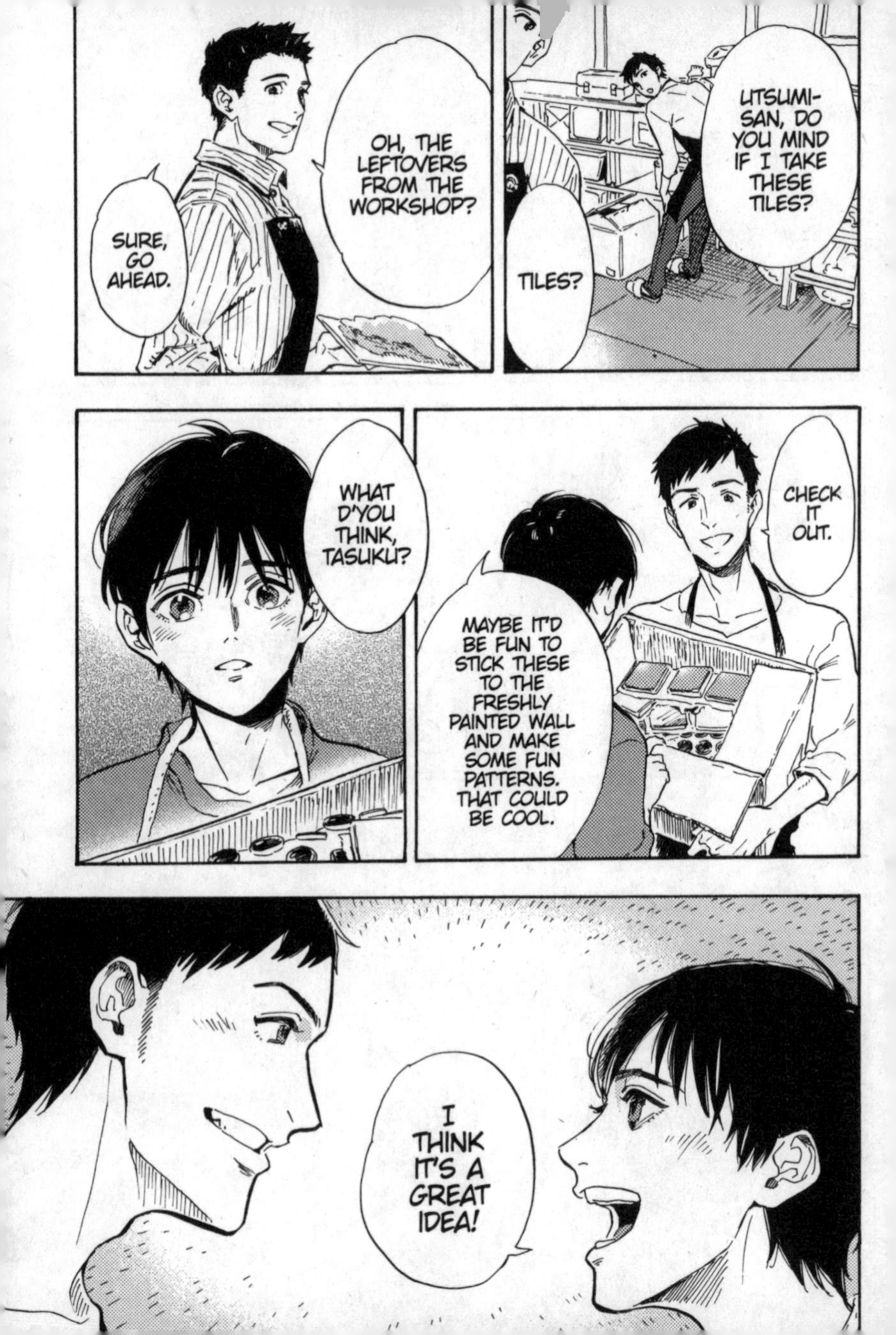
UTSUMI-SAN, DO YOU MIND IF I TAKE THESE TILES?
TILES?
OH, THE LEFTOVERS FROM THE WORKSHOP?
SURE, GO AHEAD.
CHECK IT OUT.
MAYBE IT'D BE FUN TO STICK THESE TO THE FRESHLY PAINTED WALL AND MAKE SOME FUN PATTERNS. THAT COULD BE COOL.
WHAT D'YOU THINK, TASUKU?
I THINK IT'S A GREAT IDEA!

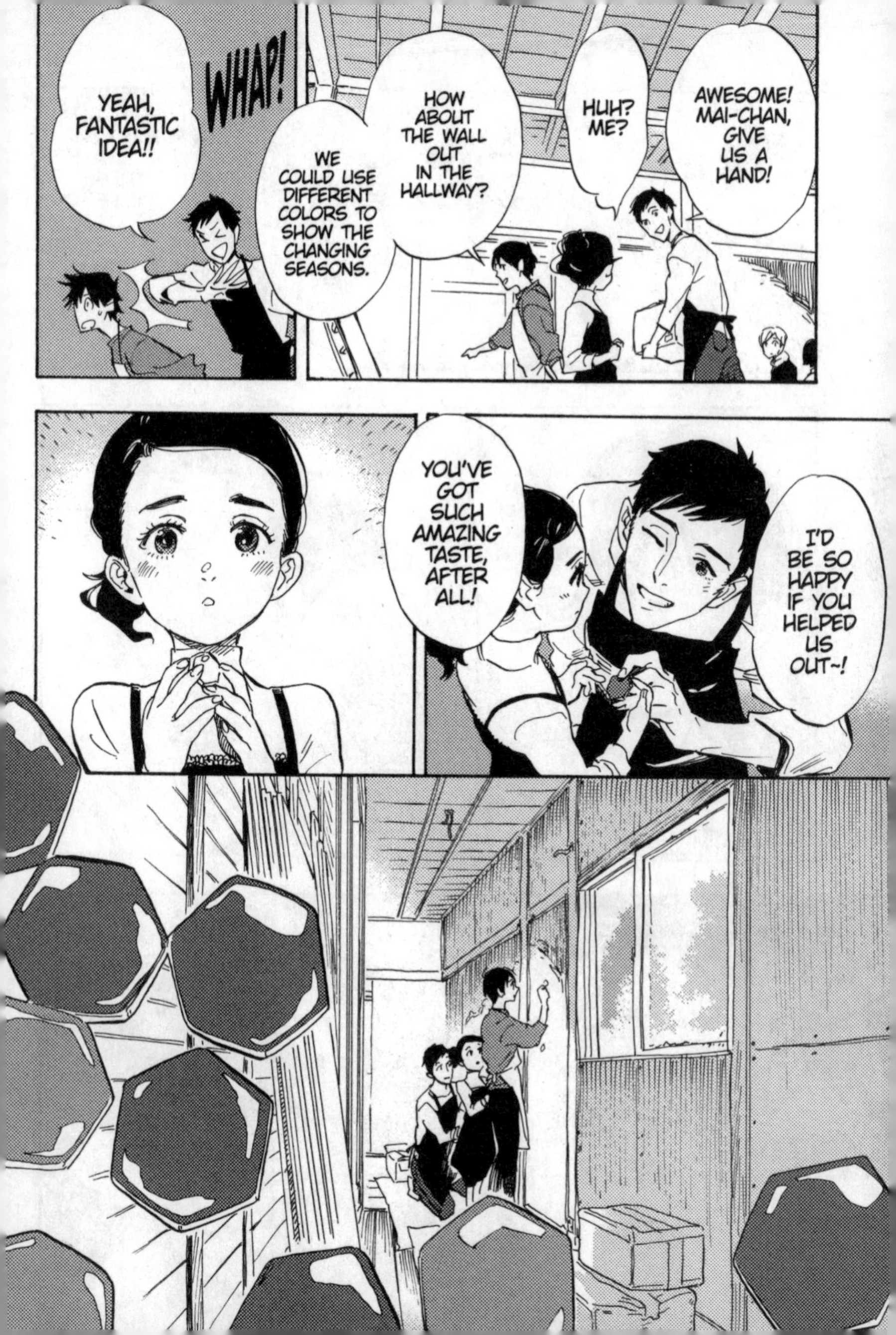
AWESOME! MAI-CHAN, GIVE US A HAND!
HUH? ME?
HOW ABOUT THE WALL OUT IN THE HALLWAY?
WE COULD USE DIFFERENT COLORS TO SHOW THE CHANGING SEASONS.
WHAP!
YEAH, FANTASTIC IDEA!!
YOU'VE GOT SUCH AMAZING TASTE, AFTER ALL!
I'D BE SO HAPPY IF YOU HELPED US OUT~!

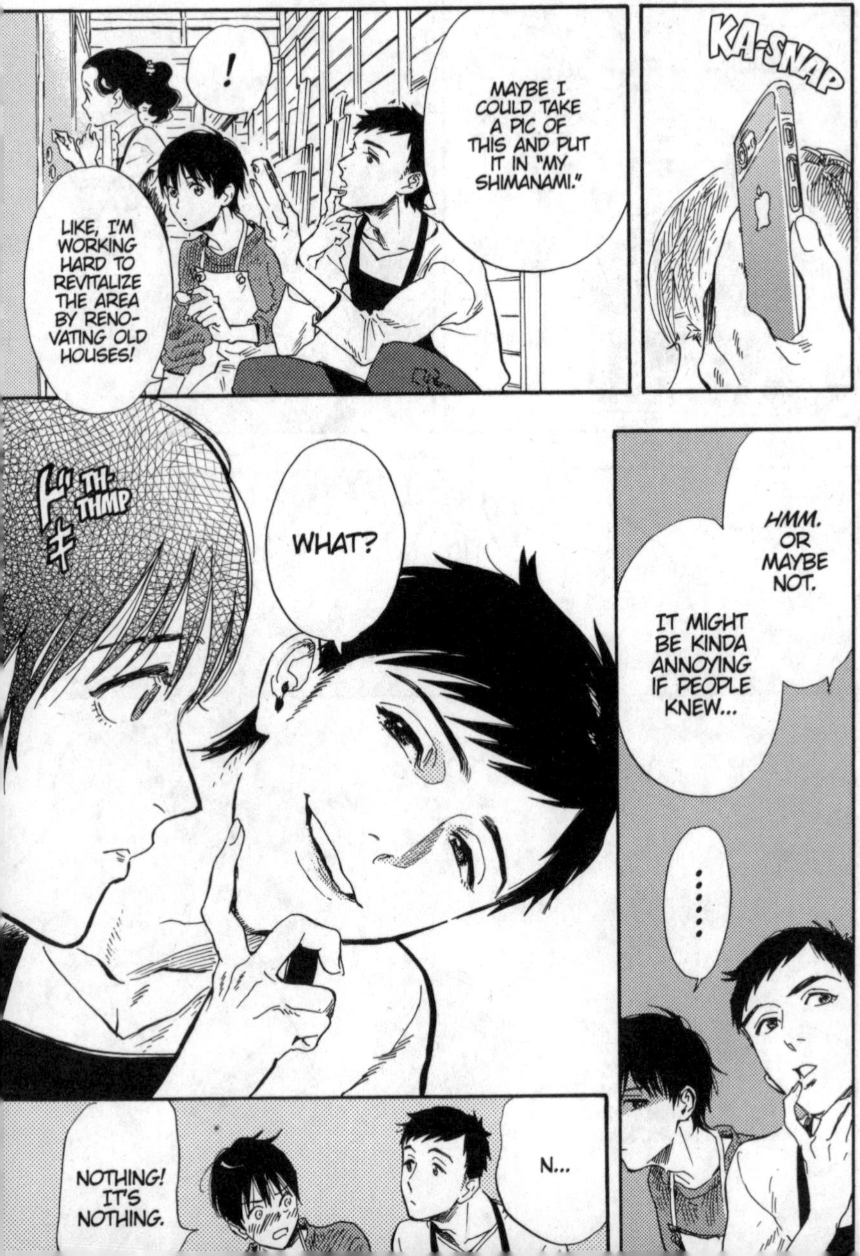
KA-SNAP
MAYBE I COULD TAKE A PIC OF THIS AND PUT IT IN "MY SHIMANAMI."
!
LIKE, I'M WORKING HARD TO REVITALIZE THE AREA BY RENO-VATING OLD HOUSES!
HMM. OR MAYBE NOT.
IT MIGHT BE KINDA ANNOYING IF PEOPLE KNEW...
......
WHAT?
ドキ TH-THMP
N...
NOTHING! IT'S NOTHING.

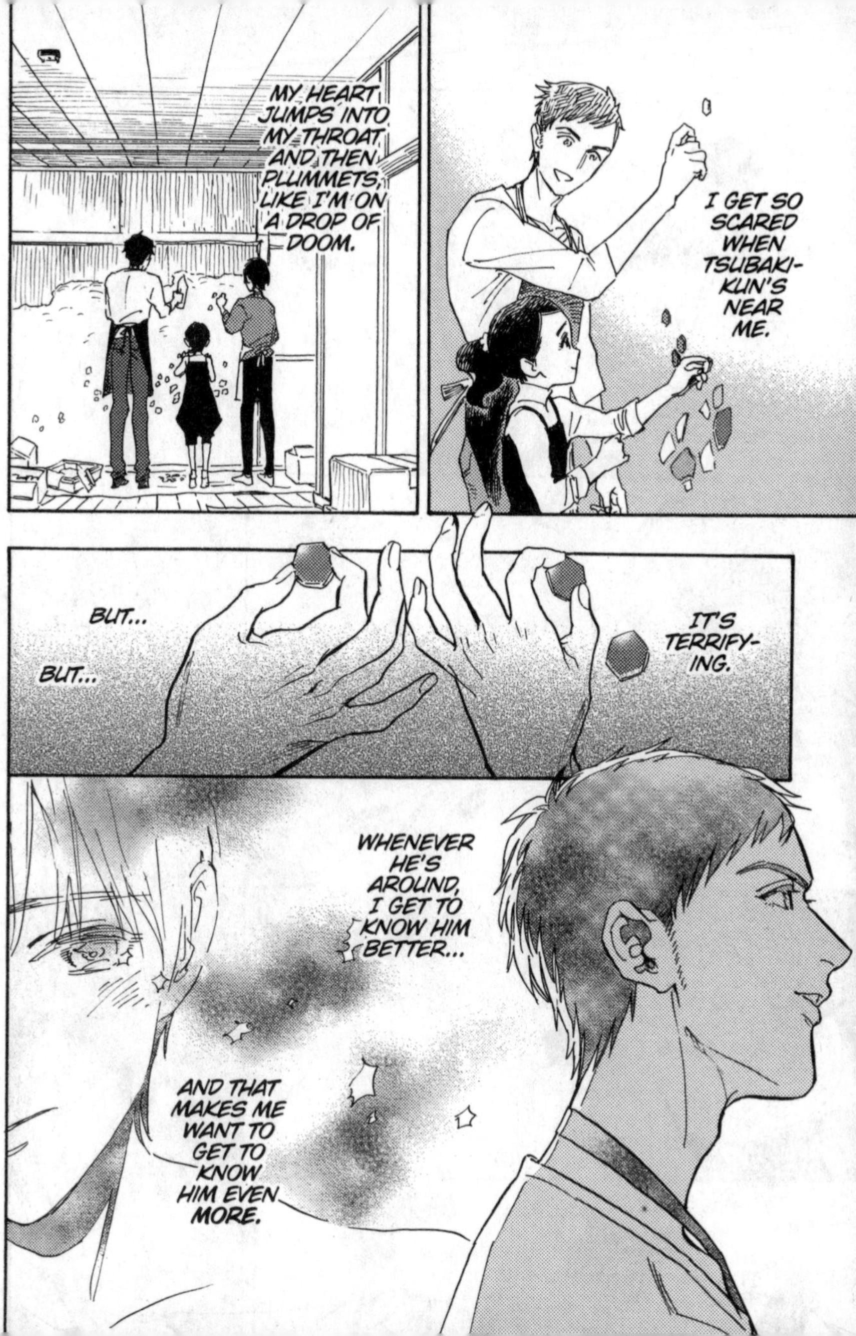
I GET SO SCARED WHEN TSUBAKI-KUN'S NEAR ME.
MY HEART JUMPS INTO MY THROAT AND THEN PLUMMETS, LIKE I'M ON A DROP OF DOOM.
IT'S TERRIFY-ING.
BUT...
BUT...
WHENEVER HE'S AROUND, I GET TO KNOW HIM BETTER...
AND THAT MAKES ME WANT TO GET TO KNOW HIM EVEN MORE.

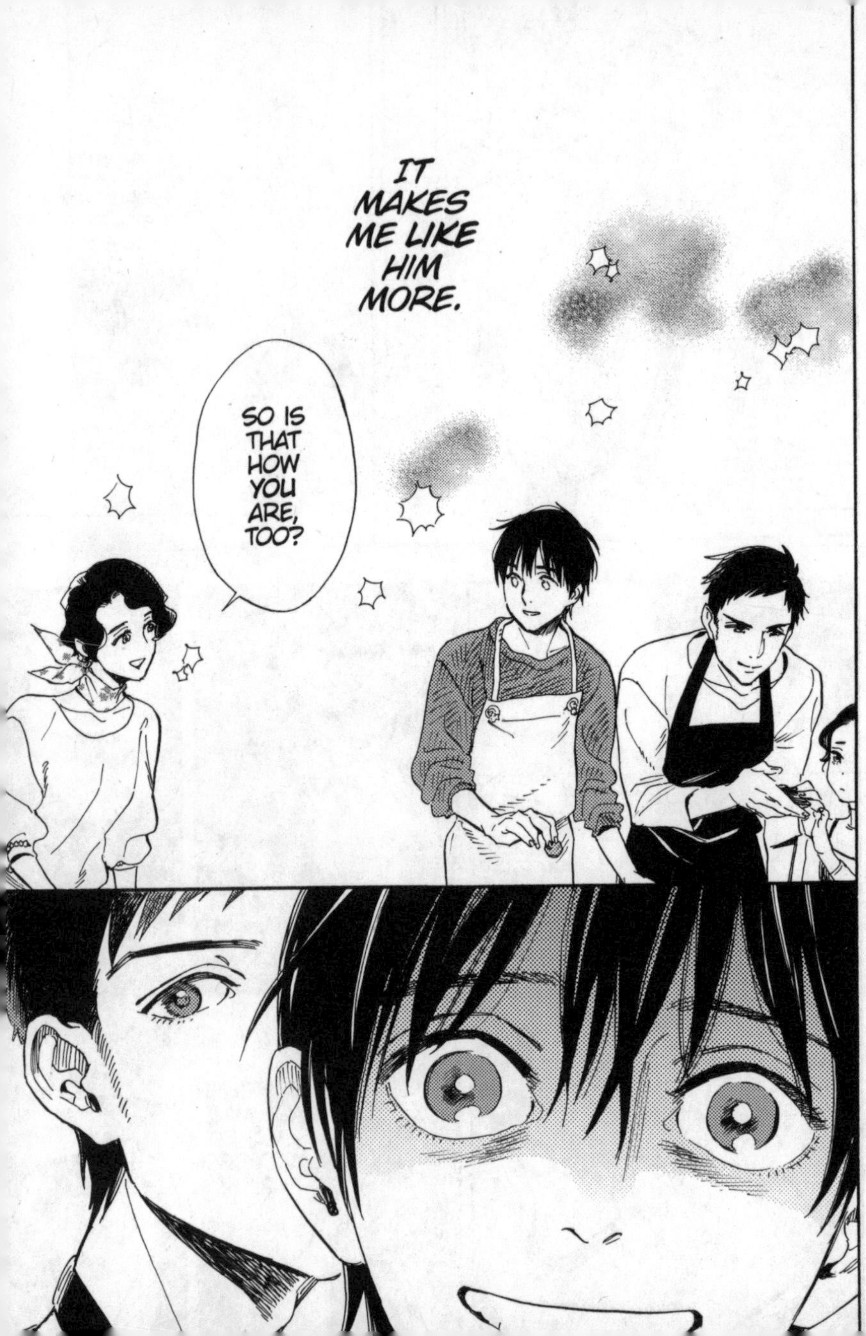
IT MAKES ME LIKE HIM MORE.
SO IS THAT HOW YOU ARE, TOO?

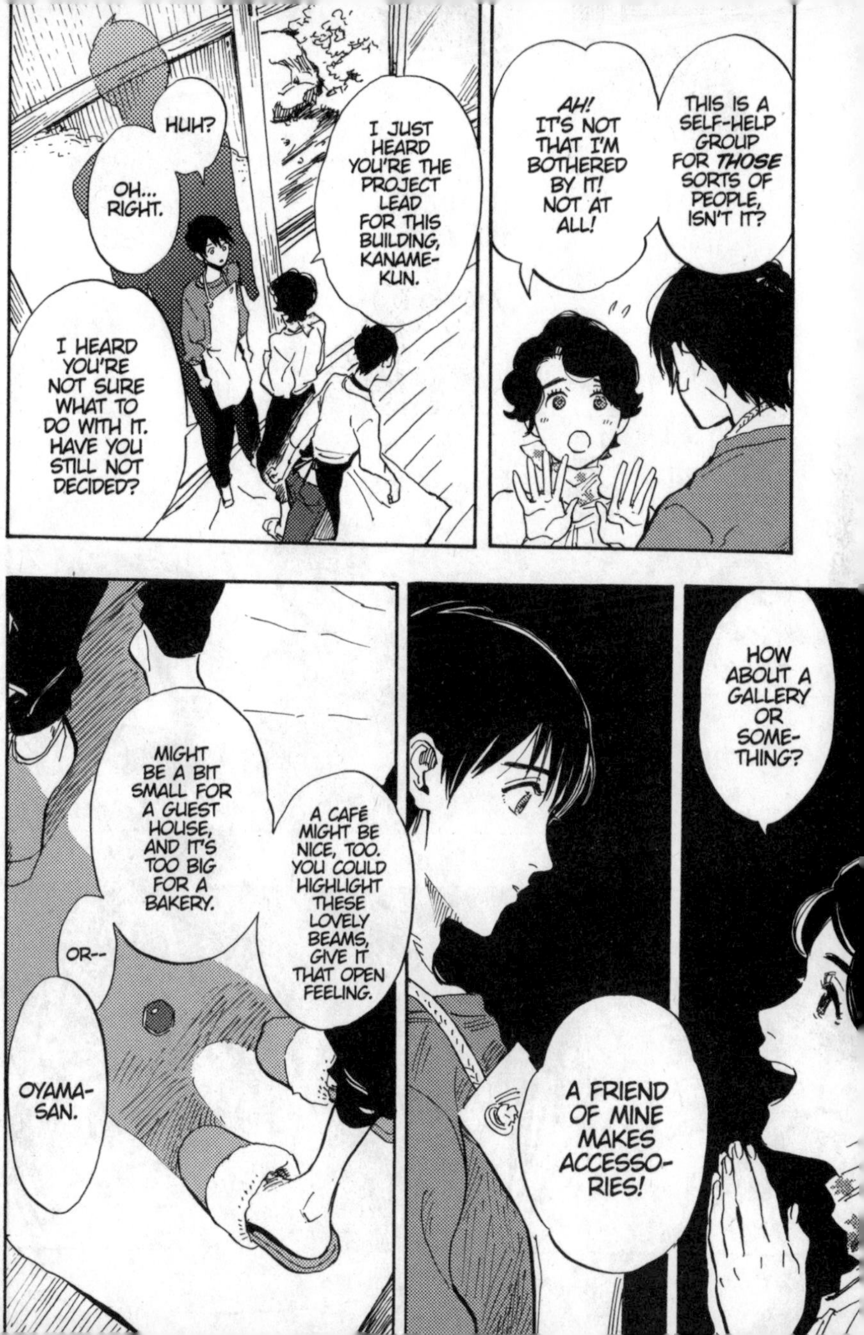
THIS IS A SELF-HELP GROUP FOR *THOSE* SORTS OF PEOPLE, ISN'T IT?
AH! IT'S NOT THAT I'M BOTHERED BY IT! NOT AT ALL!
I JUST HEARD YOU'RE THE PROJECT LEAD FOR THIS BUILDING, KANAME-KUN.
HUH?
OH... RIGHT.
I HEARD YOU'RE NOT SURE WHAT TO DO WITH IT. HAVE YOU STILL NOT DECIDED?
HOW ABOUT A GALLERY OR SOME-THING?
A FRIEND OF MINE MAKES ACCESSO-RIES!
A CAFÉ MIGHT BE NICE, TOO. YOU COULD HIGHLIGHT THESE LOVELY BEAMS, GIVE IT THAT OPEN FEELING.
MIGHT BE A BIT SMALL FOR A GUEST HOUSE, AND IT'S TOO BIG FOR A BAKERY.
OR--
OYAMA-SAN.

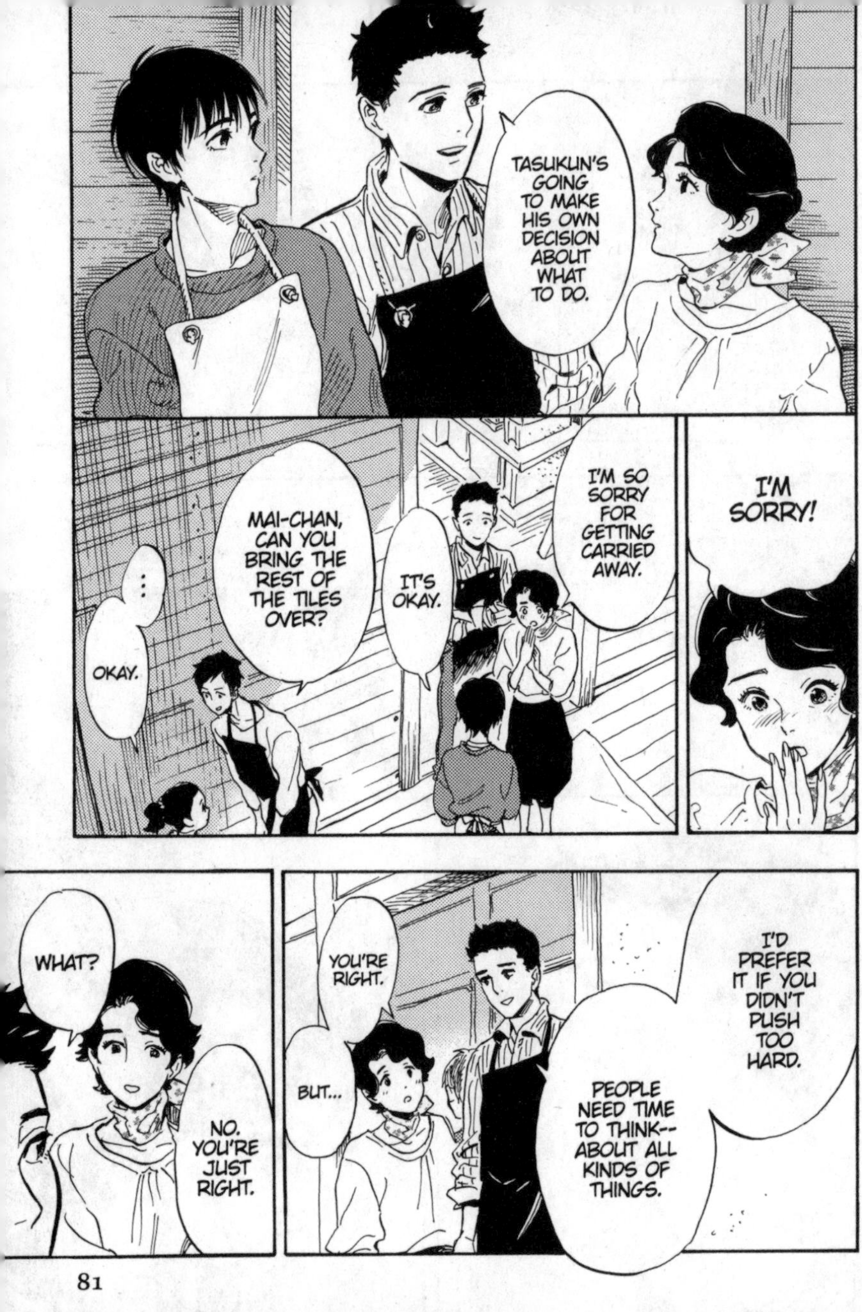
TASUKUN'S GOING TO MAKE HIS OWN DECISION ABOUT WHAT TO DO.
I'M SORRY!
I'M SO SORRY FOR GETTING CARRIED AWAY.
IT'S OKAY.
MAI-CHAN, CAN YOU BRING THE REST OF THE TILES OVER?
...
OKAY.
I'D PREFER IT IF YOU DIDN'T PUSH TOO HARD.
YOU'RE RIGHT.
PEOPLE NEED TIME TO THINK--ABOUT ALL KINDS OF THINGS.
BUT...
WHAT?
NO. YOU'RE JUST RIGHT.

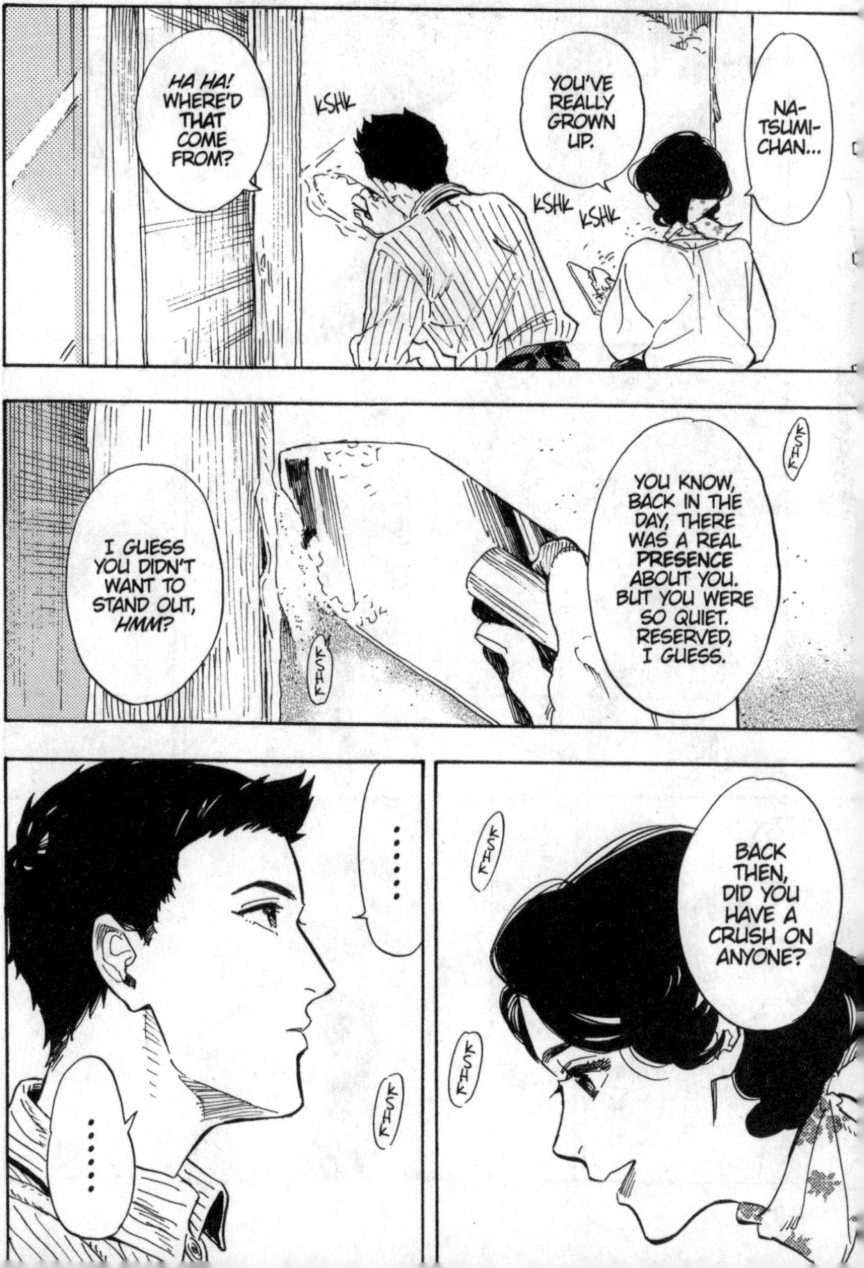
NA-TSUMI-CHAN...
YOU'VE REALLY GROWN UP.
KSHK
KSHK
KSHK
HA HA! WHERE'D THAT COME FROM?
KSHK
YOU KNOW, BACK IN THE DAY, THERE WAS A REAL PRESENCE ABOUT YOU. BUT YOU WERE SO QUIET. RESERVED, I GUESS.
KSHK
I GUESS YOU DIDN'T WANT TO STAND OUT, HMM?
BACK THEN, DID YOU HAVE A CRUSH ON ANYONE?
KSHK
KSHK
......
KSHK
......

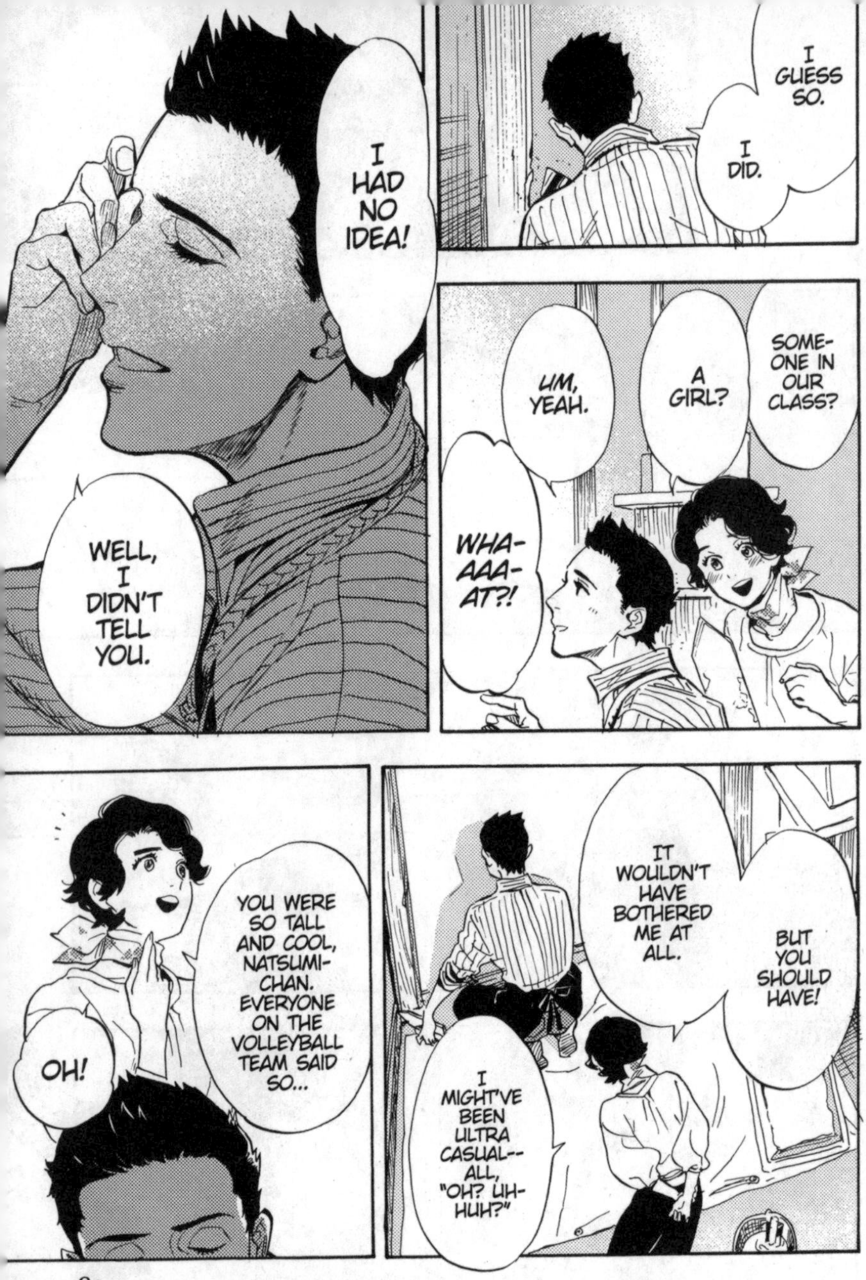
I GUESS SO.
I DID.
SOME-ONE IN OUR CLASS?
A GIRL?
UM, YEAH.
WHA-AAA-AT?!
I HAD NO IDEA!
WELL, I DIDN'T TELL YOU.
BUT YOU SHOULD HAVE!
IT WOULDN'T HAVE BOTHERED ME AT ALL.
I MIGHT'VE BEEN ULTRA CASUAL--ALL, "OH? UH-HUH?"
YOU WERE SO TALL AND COOL, NATSUMI-CHAN. EVERYONE ON THE VOLLEYBALL TEAM SAID SO...
OH!

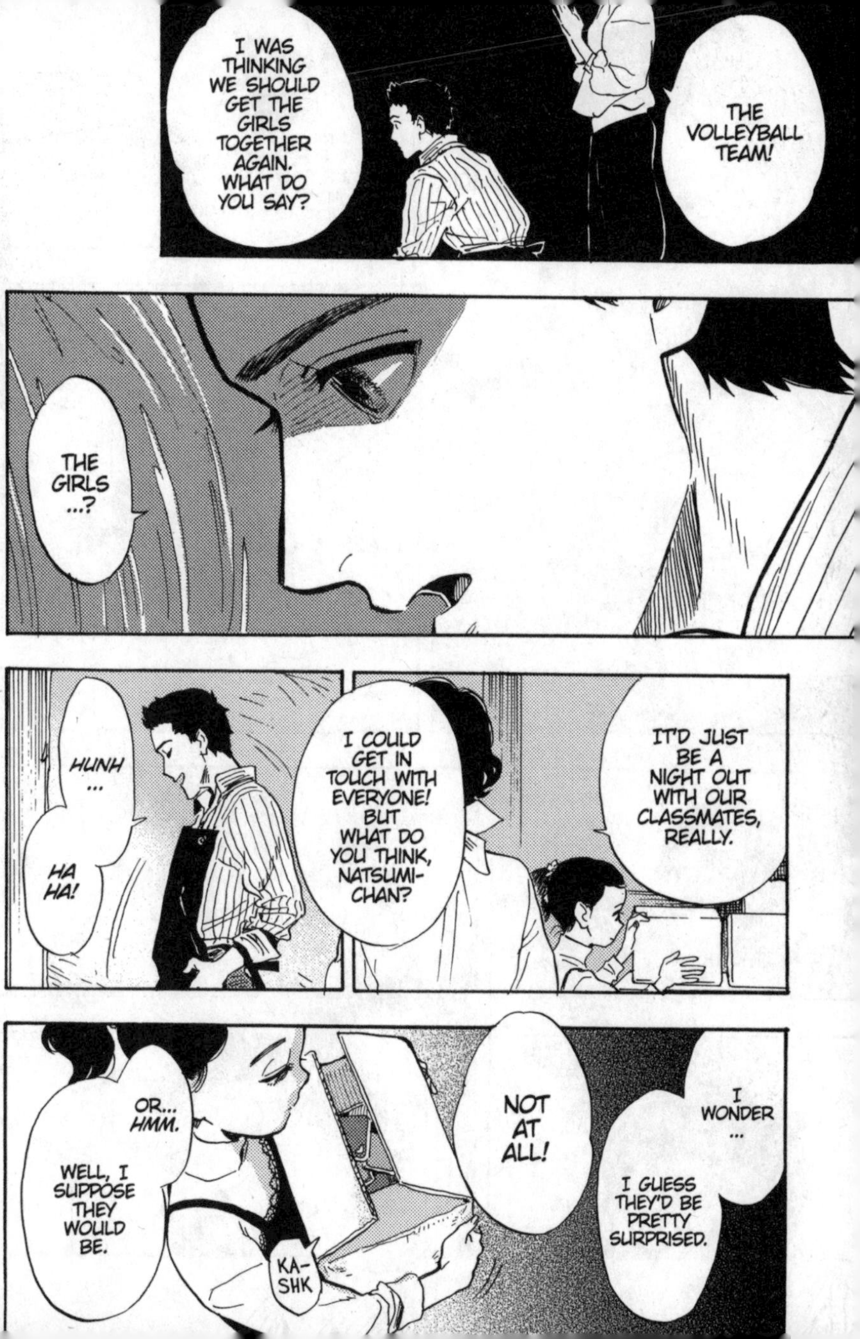
THE VOLLEYBALL TEAM!
I WAS THINKING WE SHOULD GET THE GIRLS TOGETHER AGAIN. WHAT DO YOU SAY?
THE GIRLS ...?
IT'D JUST BE A NIGHT OUT WITH OUR CLASSMATES, REALLY.
I COULD GET IN TOUCH WITH EVERYONE! BUT WHAT DO YOU THINK, NATSUMI-CHAN?
HUNH ...
HA HA!
I WONDER ...
I GUESS THEY'D BE PRETTY SURPRISED.
NOT AT ALL!
KA-SHK
OR... HMM.
WELL, I SUPPOSE THEY WOULD BE.

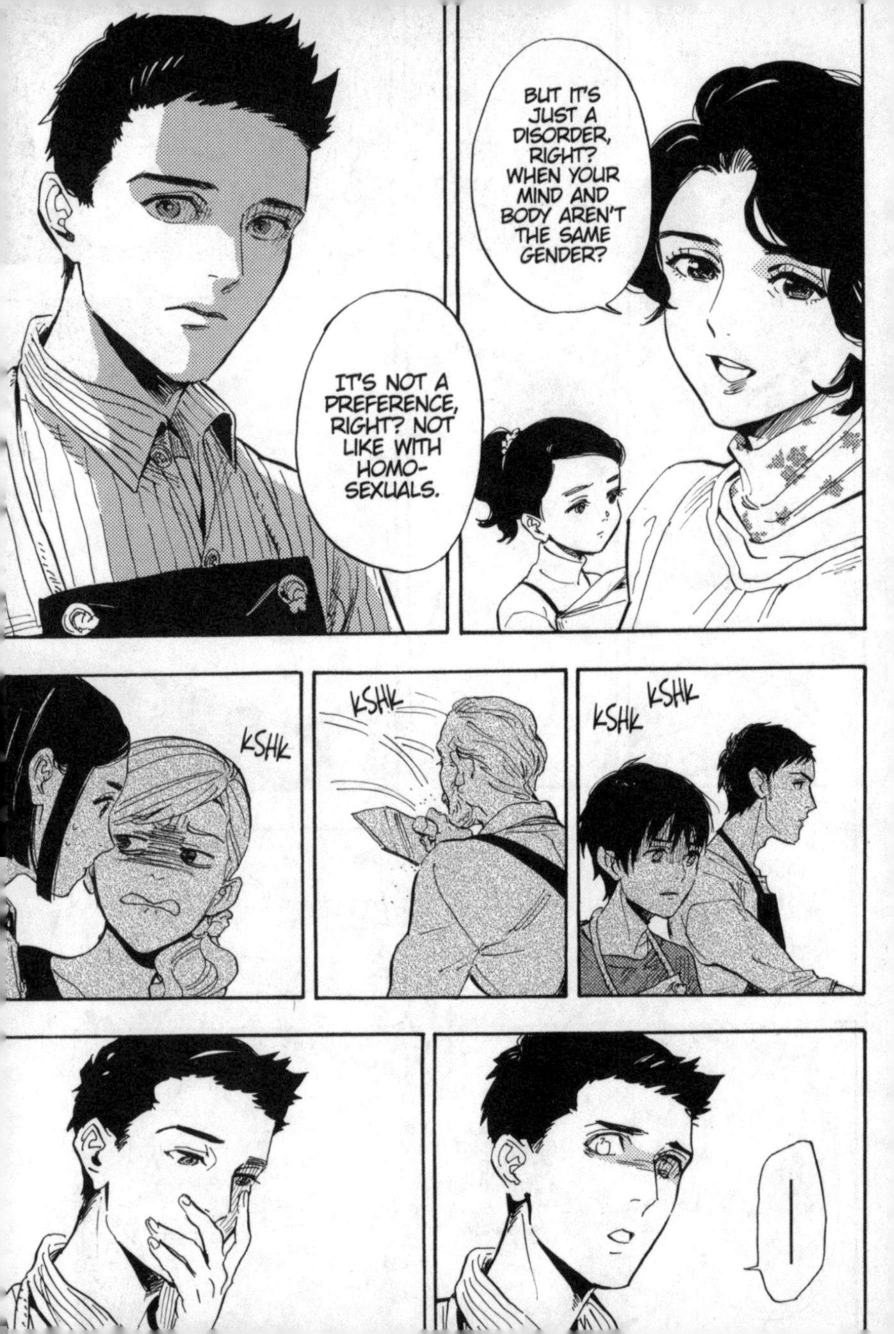
BUT IT'S JUST A DISORDER, RIGHT? WHEN YOUR MIND AND BODY AREN'T THE SAME GENDER?
IT'S NOT A PREFERENCE, RIGHT? NOT LIKE WITH HOMO-SEXUALS.
KSHK
KSHK
KSHK
KSHK

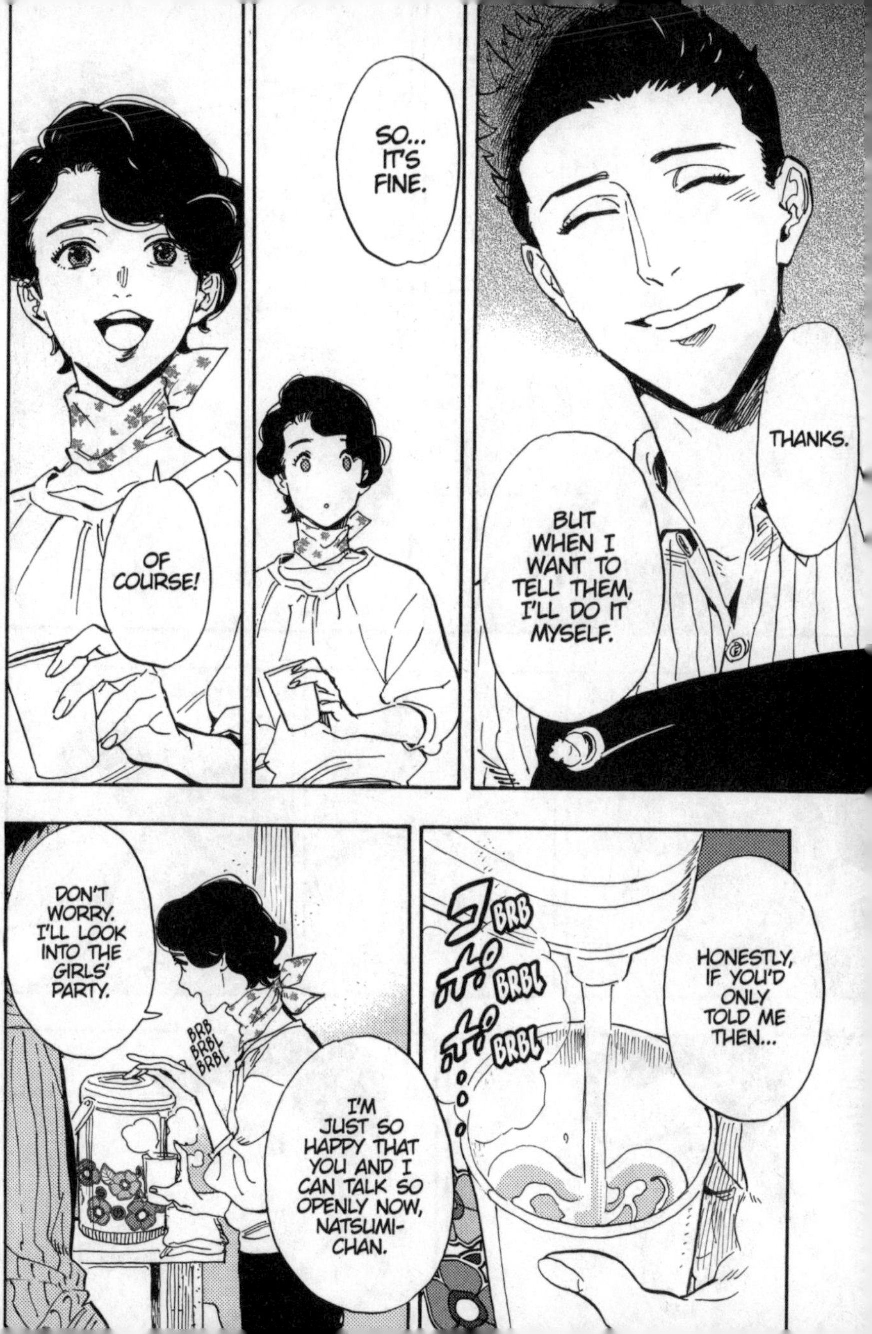
THANKS.
BUT WHEN I WANT TO TELL THEM, I'LL DO IT MYSELF.
SO... IT'S FINE.
OF COURSE!
BRB
BRBL
BRBL
HONESTLY, IF YOU'D ONLY TOLD ME THEN...
I'M JUST SO HAPPY THAT YOU AND I CAN TALK SO OPENLY NOW, NATSUMI-CHAN.
BRB BRBL BRBL
DON'T WORRY. I'LL LOOK INTO THE GIRLS' PARTY.

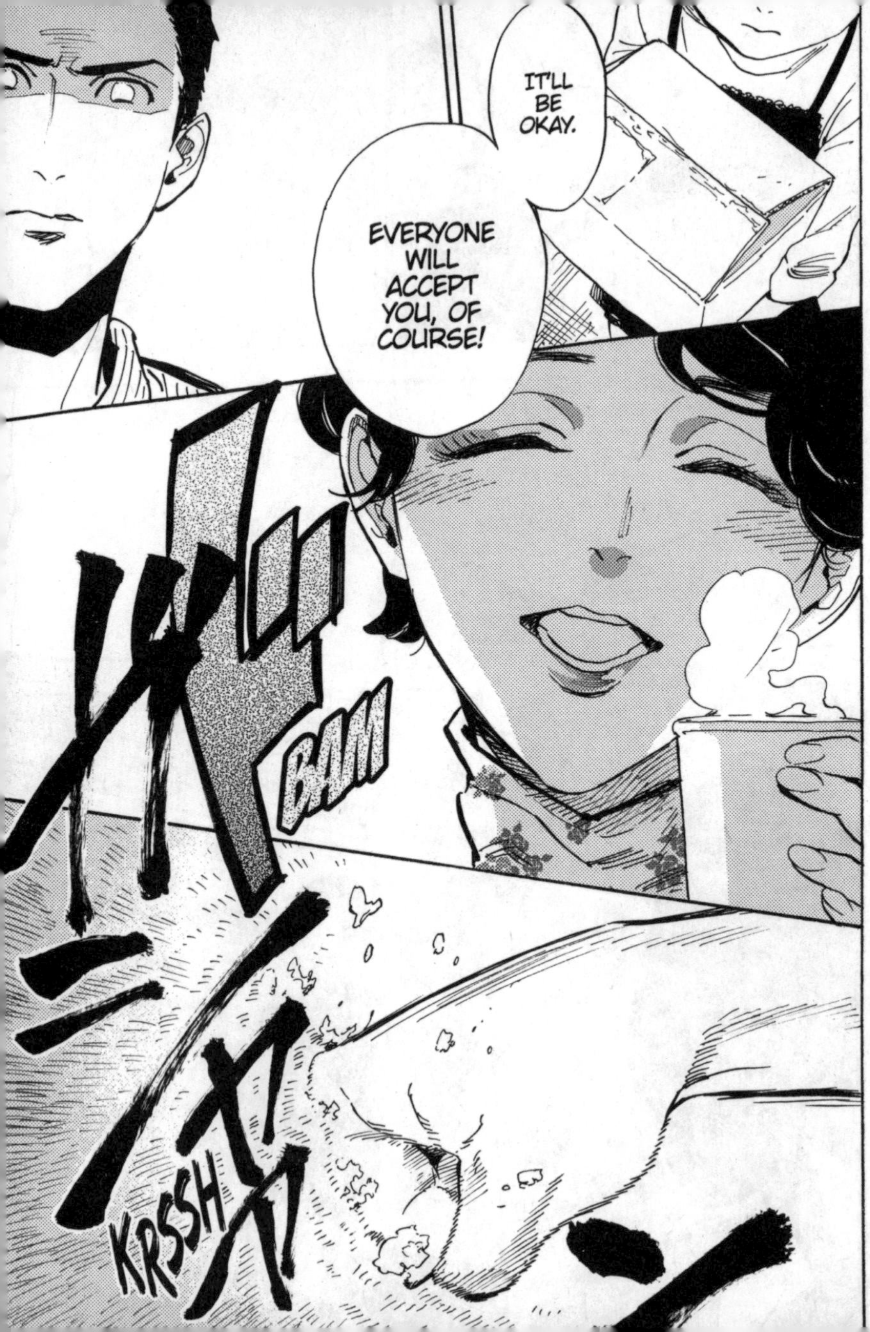
IT'LL BE OKAY.
EVERYONE WILL ACCEPT YOU, OF COURSE!
BAM
KRSSH

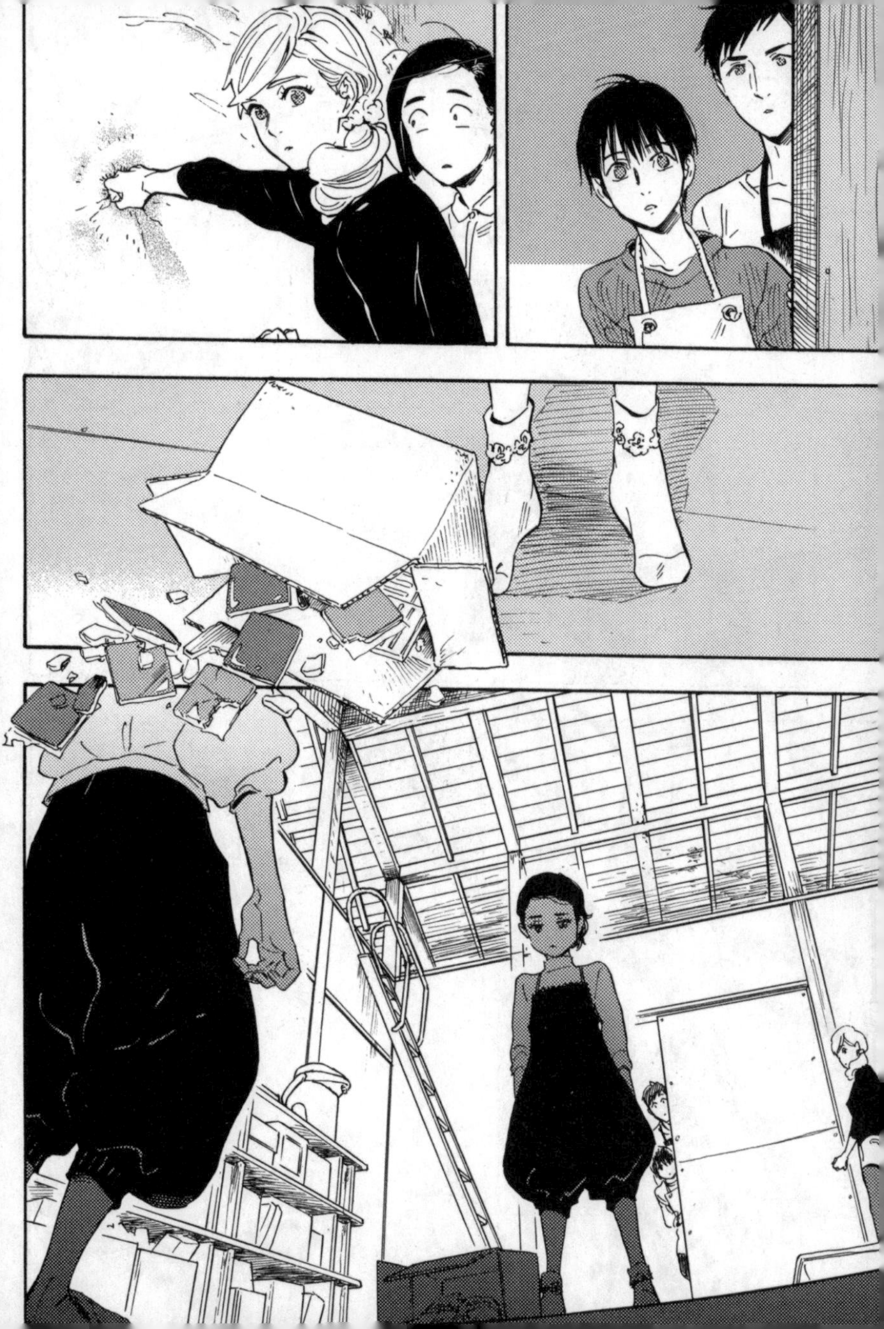

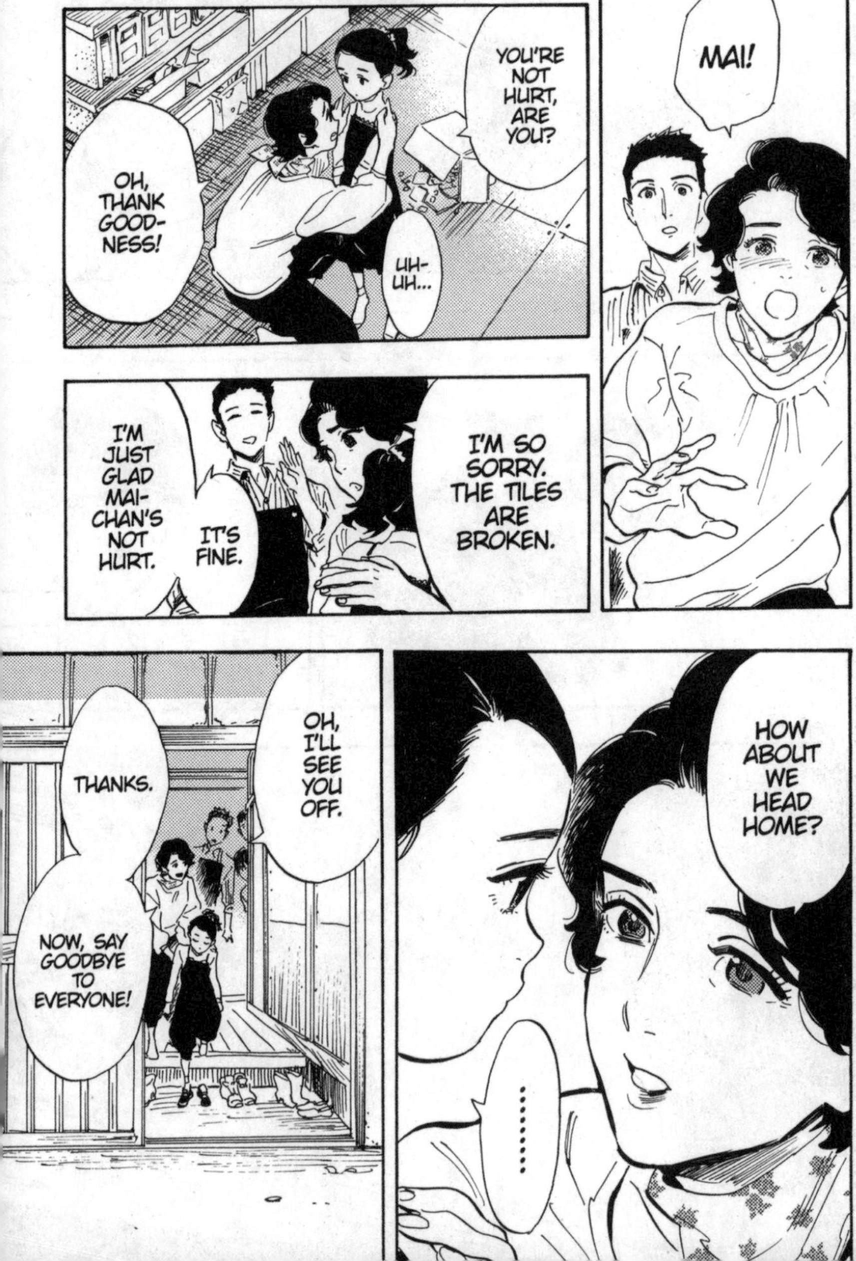
MAI!
YOU'RE NOT HURT, ARE YOU?
UH-UH...
OH, THANK GOOD-NESS!
I'M SO SORRY. THE TILES ARE BROKEN.
IT'S FINE.
I'M JUST GLAD MAI-CHAN'S NOT HURT.
HOW ABOUT WE HEAD HOME?
......
OH, I'LL SEE YOU OFF.
THANKS.
NOW, SAY GOODBYE TO EVERYONE!

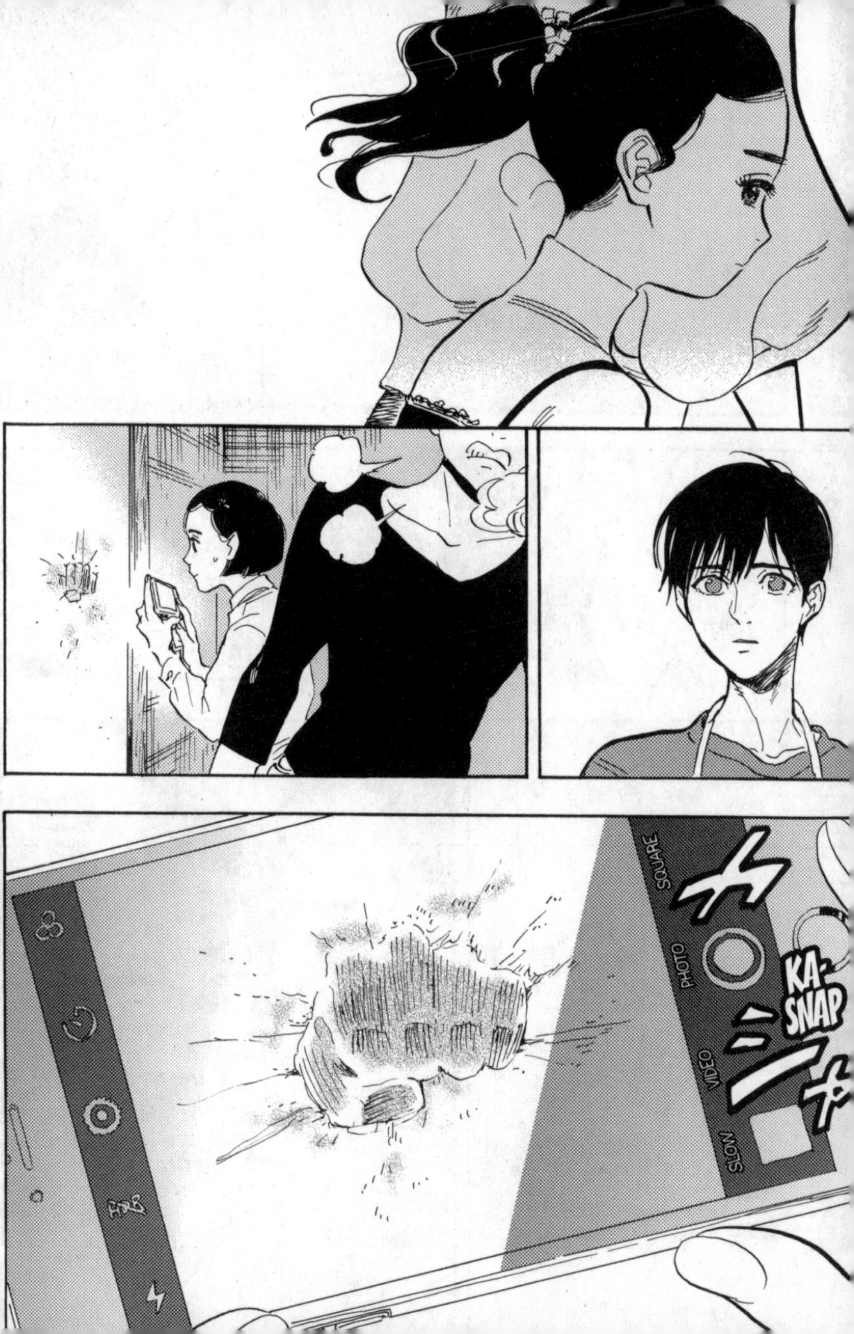
SQUARE
PHOTO
VIDEO
SLOW
KA-SNAP

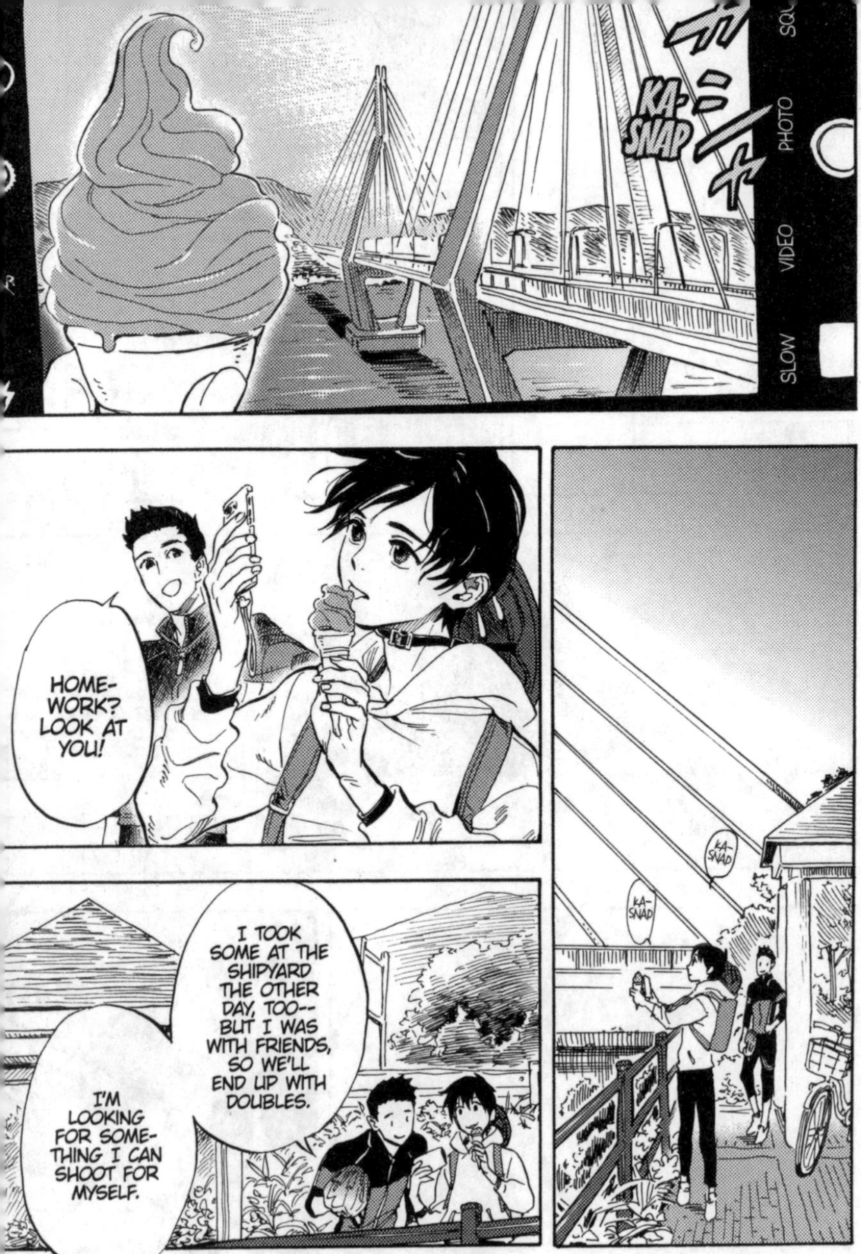
KA-SNAP
SQ
PHOTO
VIDEO
SLOW
KA-SNAP
KA-SNAP
HOME-WORK? LOOK AT YOU!
I TOOK SOME AT THE SHIPYARD THE OTHER DAY, TOO-- BUT I WAS WITH FRIENDS, SO WE'LL END UP WITH DOUBLES.
I'M LOOKING FOR SOME-THING I CAN SHOOT FOR MYSELF.

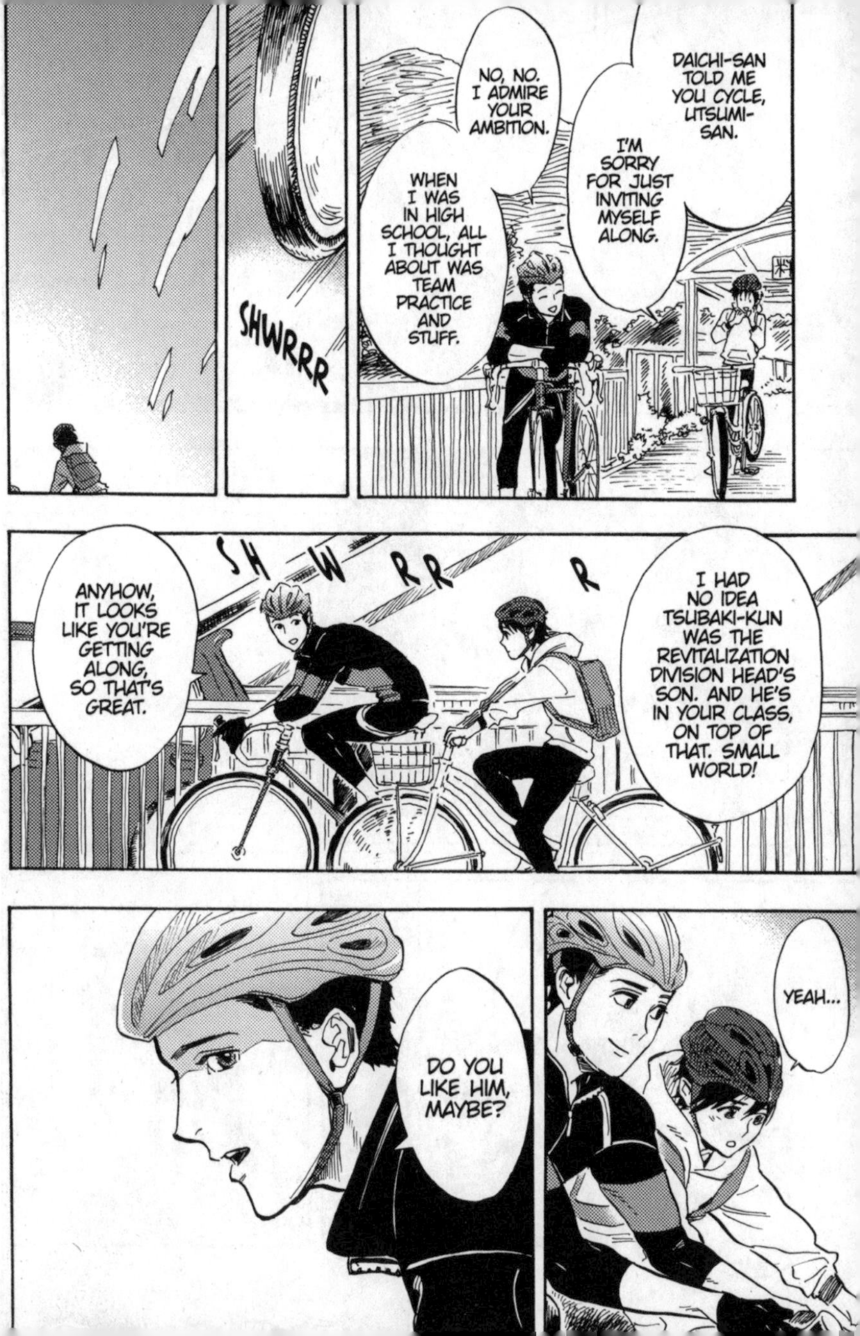
DAICHI-SAN TOLD ME YOU CYCLE, UTSUMI-SAN.
I'M SORRY FOR JUST INVITING MYSELF ALONG.
NO, NO. I ADMIRE YOUR AMBITION.
WHEN I WAS IN HIGH SCHOOL, ALL I THOUGHT ABOUT WAS TEAM PRACTICE AND STUFF.
SHWRRR
I HAD NO IDEA TSUBAKI-KUN WAS THE REVITALIZATION DIVISION HEAD'S SON. AND HE'S IN YOUR CLASS, ON TOP OF THAT. SMALL WORLD!
SHWRRR
ANYHOW, IT LOOKS LIKE YOU'RE GETTING ALONG, SO THAT'S GREAT.
YEAH...
DO YOU LIKE HIM, MAYBE?

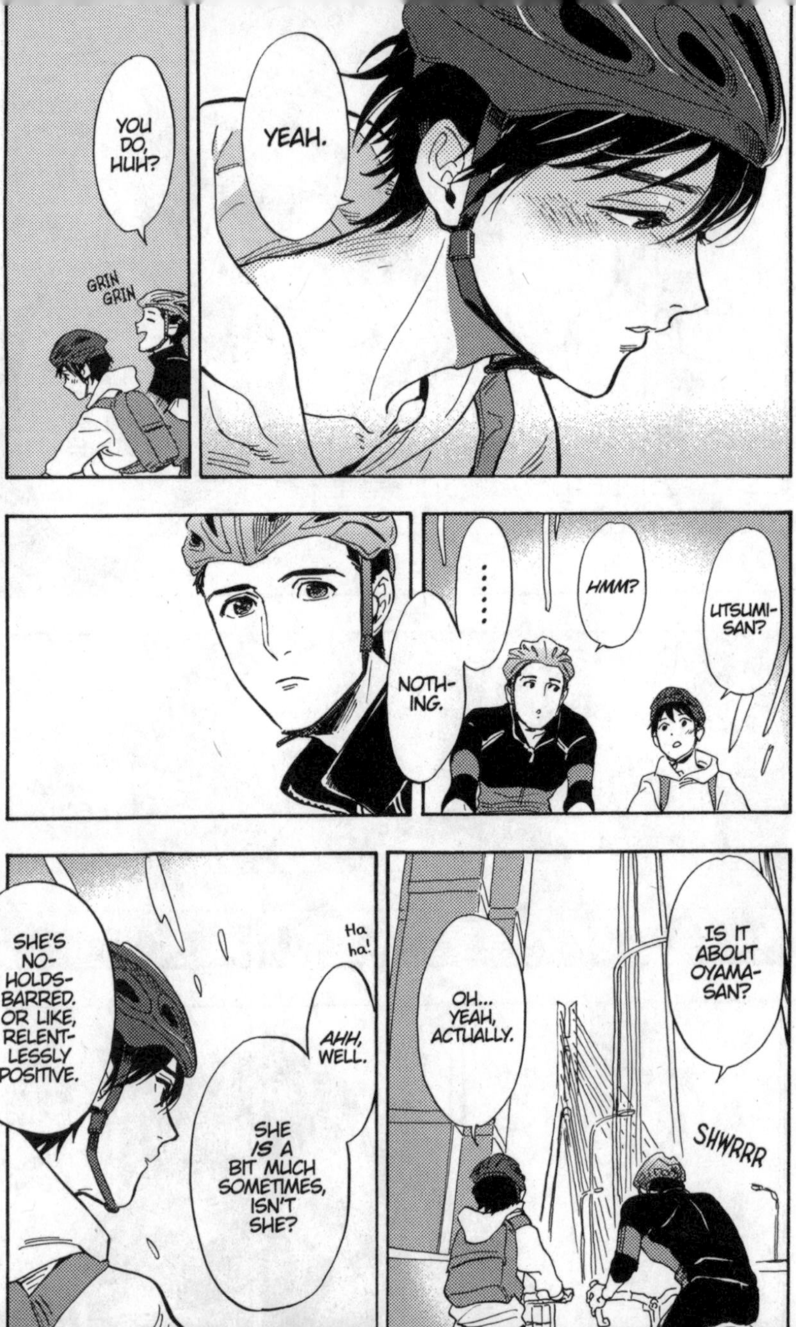
YEAH.
YOU DO, HUH?
GRIN GRIN
UTSUMI-SAN?
HMM?
......
NOTHING.
IS IT ABOUT OYAMA-SAN?
OH... YEAH, ACTUALLY.
SHWRRR
Ha ha!
AHH, WELL.
SHE *IS* A BIT MUCH SOMETIMES, ISN'T SHE?
SHE'S NO-HOLDS-BARRED. OR LIKE, RELENTLESSLY POSITIVE.

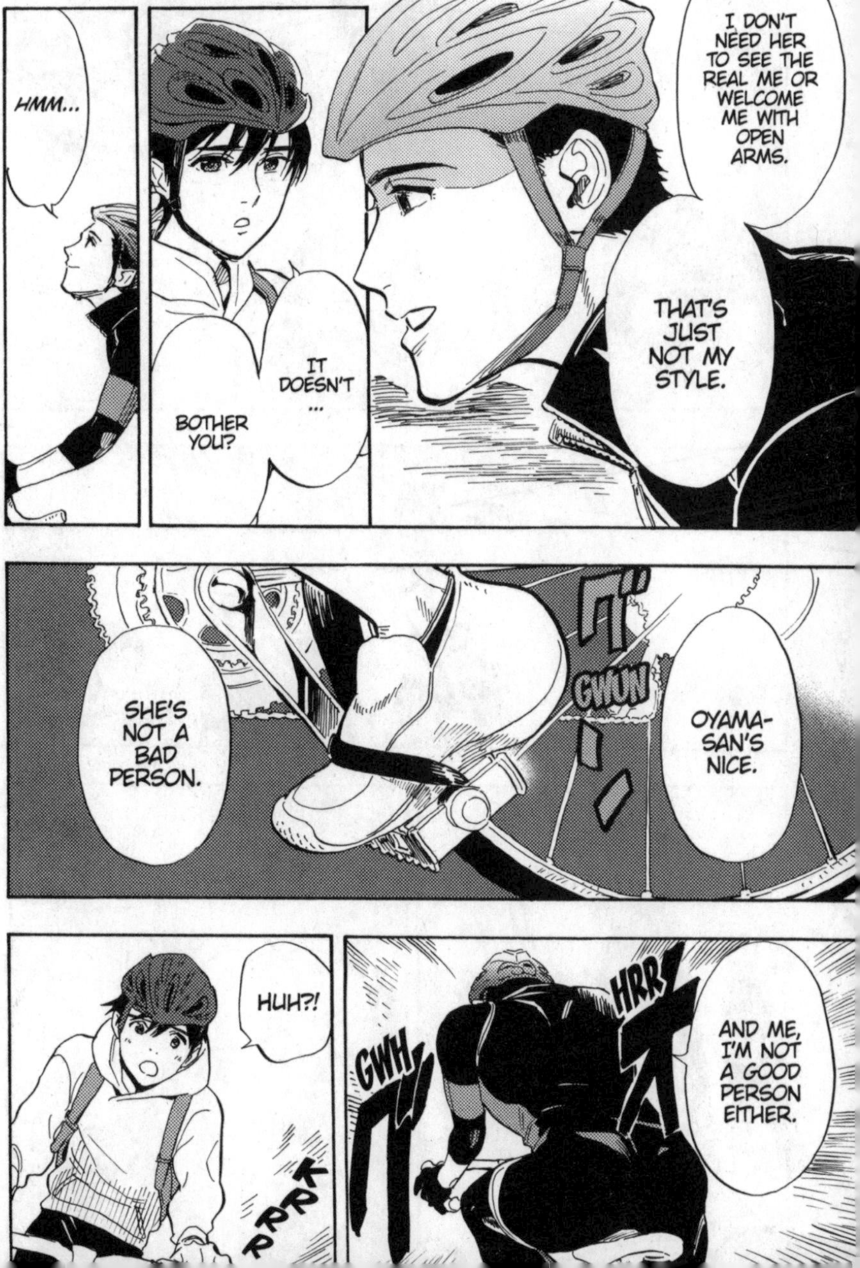
I DON'T NEED HER TO SEE THE REAL ME OR WELCOME ME WITH OPEN ARMS.
THAT'S JUST NOT MY STYLE.
IT DOESN'T ...
BOTHER YOU?
HMM...
OYAMA-SAN'S NICE.
GWUN
SHE'S NOT A BAD PERSON.
AND ME, I'M NOT A GOOD PERSON EITHER.
HRR
GWH
HUH?!
KRRR

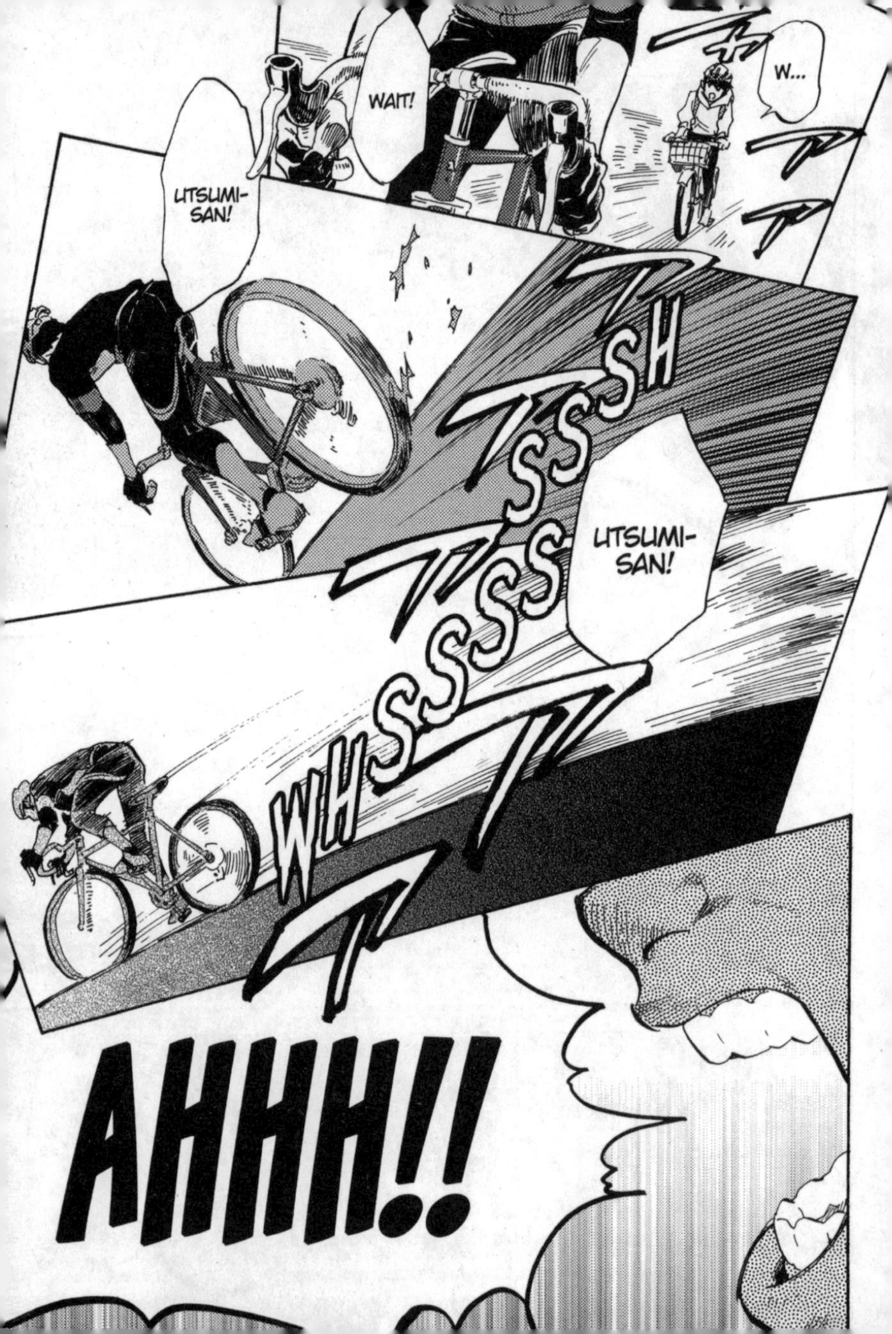
W...
WAIT!
UTSUMI-SAN!
UTSUMI-SAN!
WHSSSSSSSSH
AHHHH!!

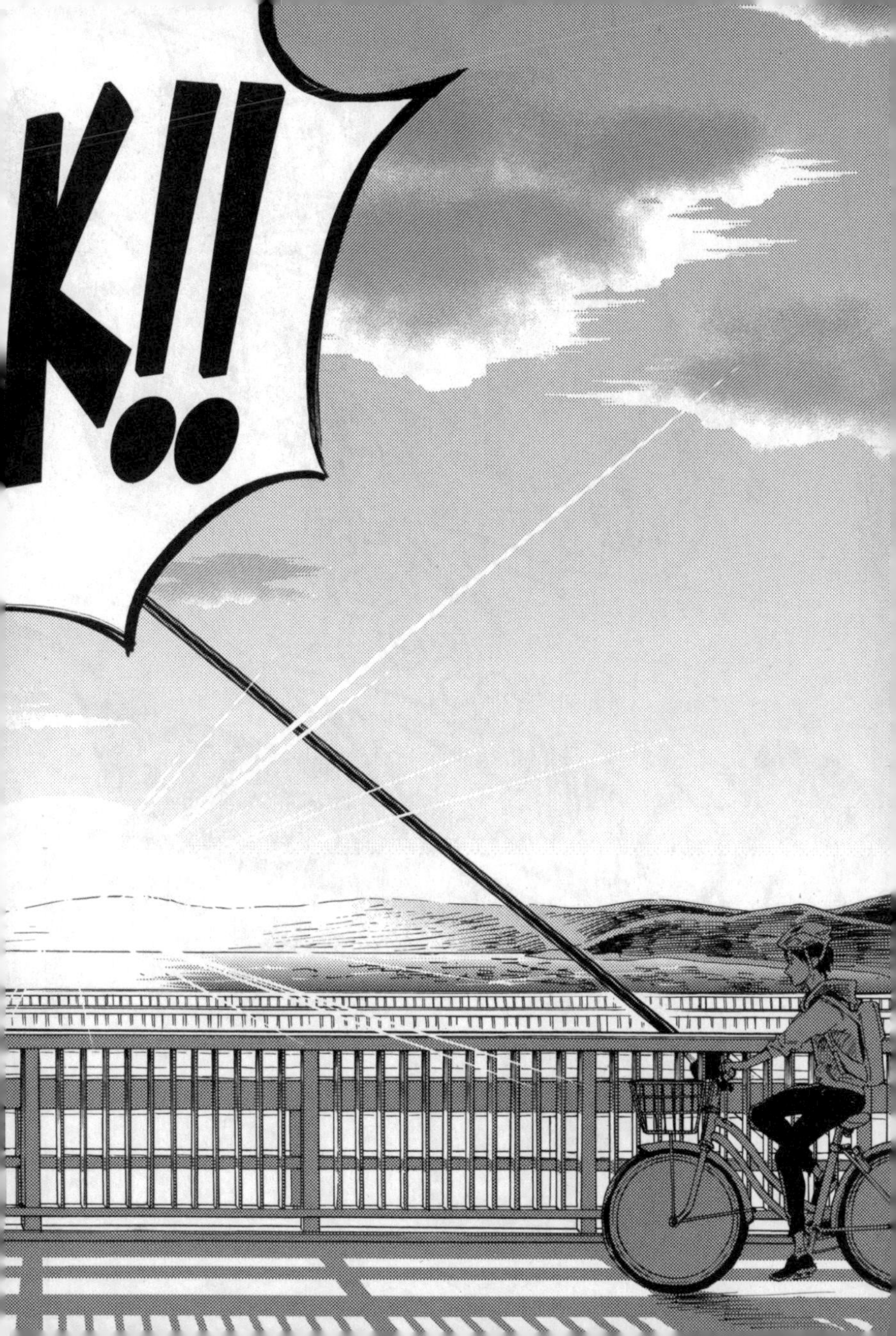
K!!

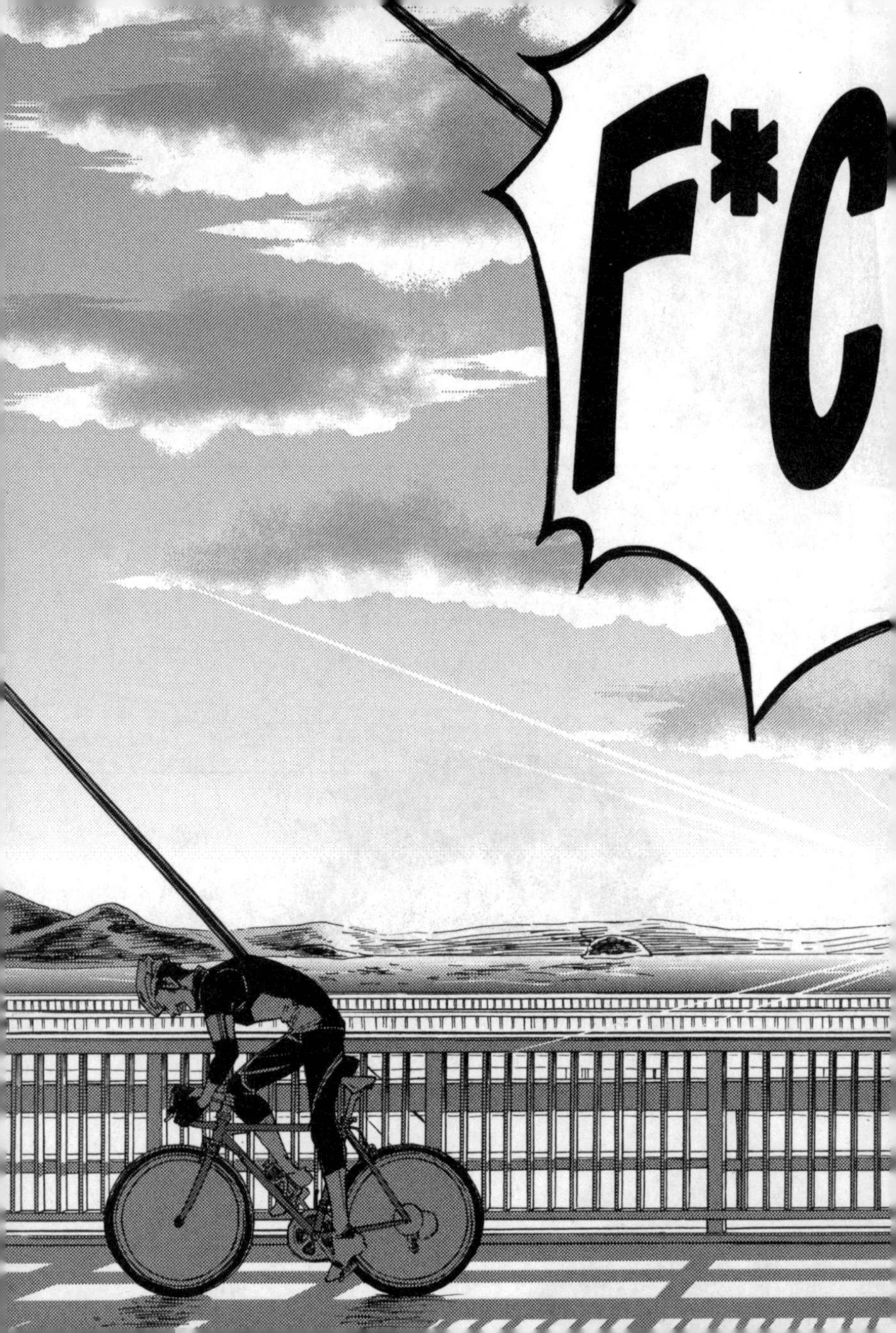
F*C

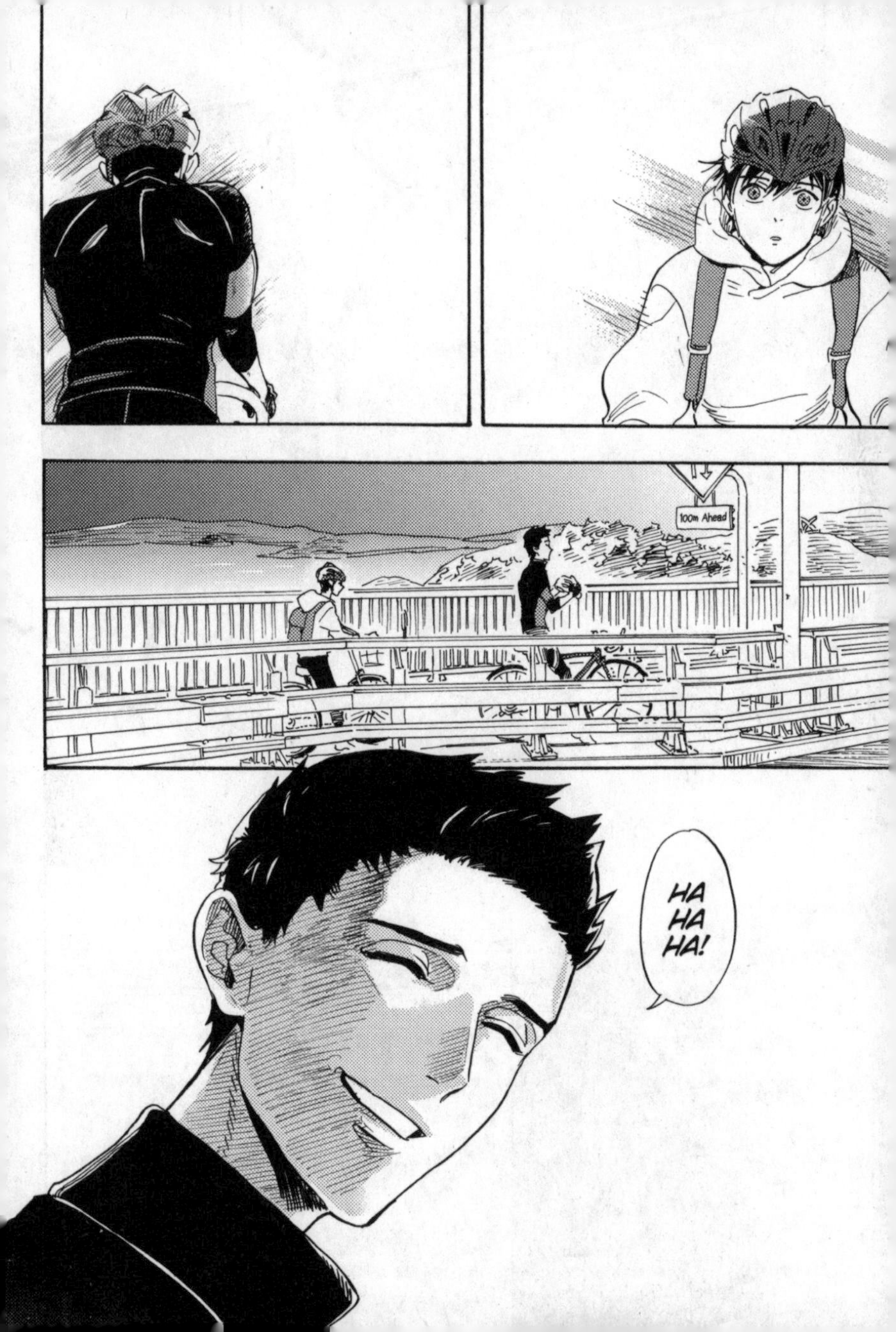
100m Ahead
HA HA HA!

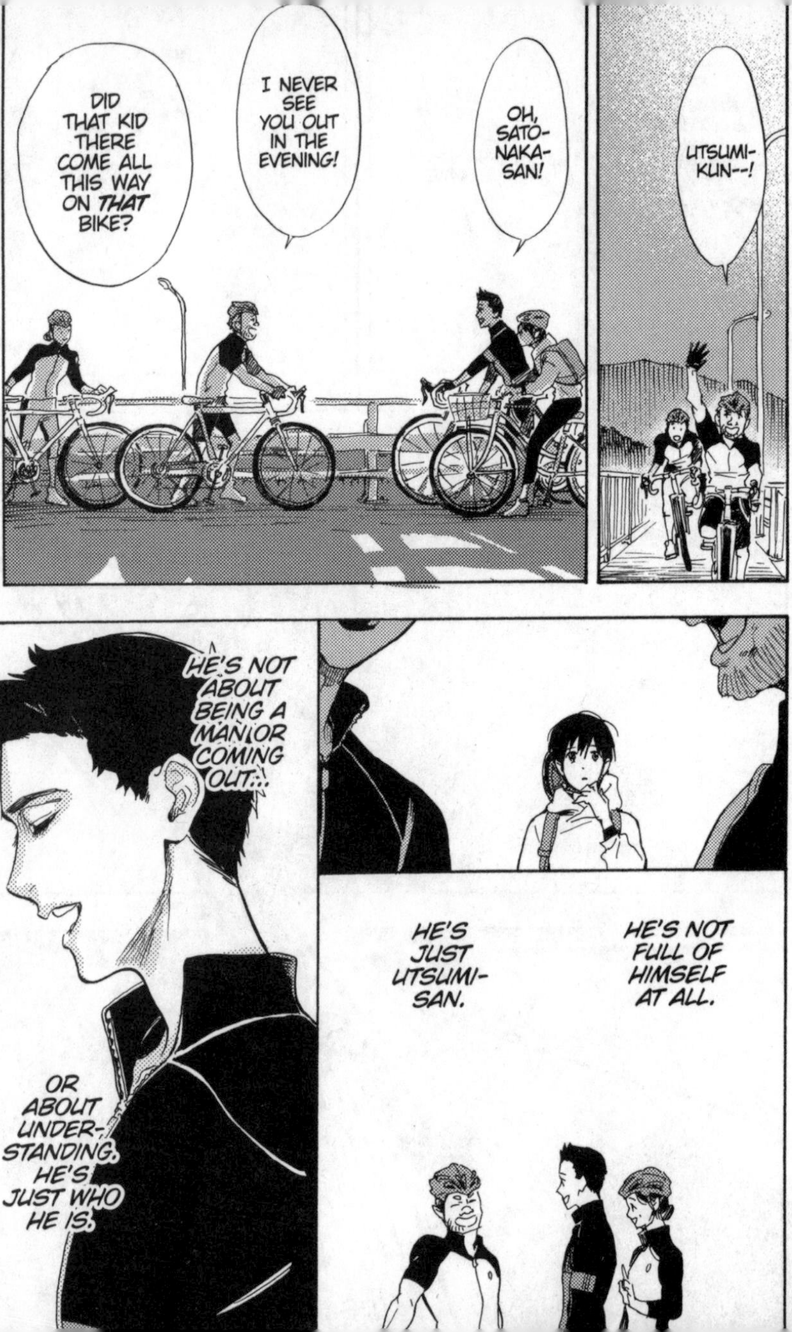
UTSUMI-KUN--!
OH, SATO-NAKA-SAN!
I NEVER SEE YOU OUT IN THE EVENING!
DID THAT KID THERE COME ALL THIS WAY ON *THAT* BIKE?
HE'S NOT FULL OF HIMSELF AT ALL.
HE'S JUST UTSUMI-SAN.
HE'S NOT ABOUT BEING A MAN OR COMING OUT...
OR ABOUT UNDER-STANDING. HE'S JUST WHO HE IS.

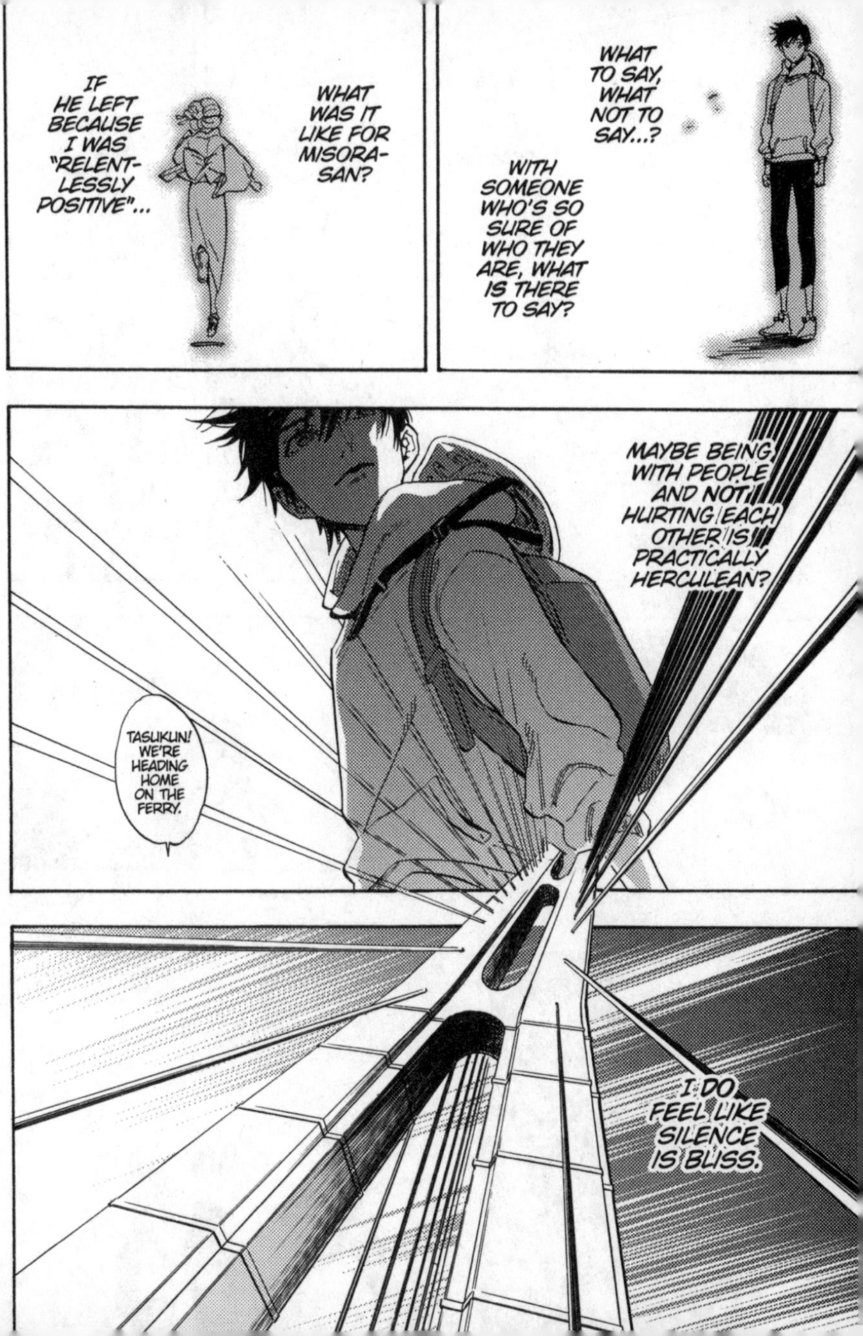
WHAT TO SAY, WHAT NOT TO SAY...?
WITH SOMEONE WHO'S SO SURE OF WHO THEY ARE, WHAT IS THERE TO SAY?
WHAT WAS IT LIKE FOR MISORA-SAN?
IF HE LEFT BECAUSE I WAS "RELENTLESSLY POSITIVE"...
MAYBE BEING WITH PEOPLE AND NOT HURTING EACH OTHER IS PRACTICALLY HERCULEAN?
TASUKUN! WE'RE HEADING HOME ON THE FERRY.
I DO FEEL LIKE SILENCE IS BLISS.

Our Dreams at Dusk

SHIMANAMI TASOGARE

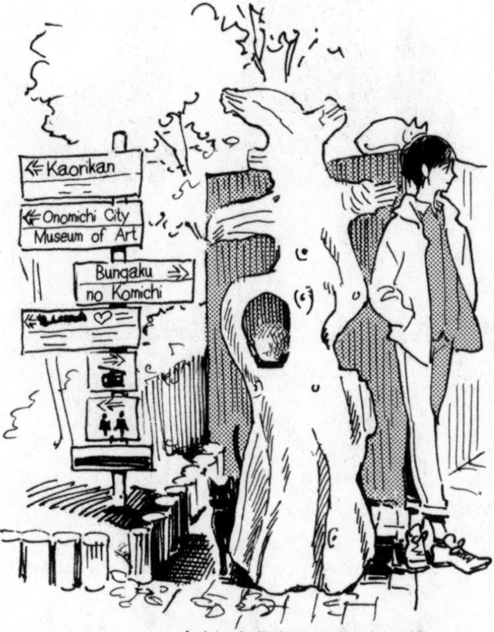
Kaorikan
Onomichi City
Museum of Art
Bungaku
no Komichi

Art installation in front of the Senko Temple park observatory.

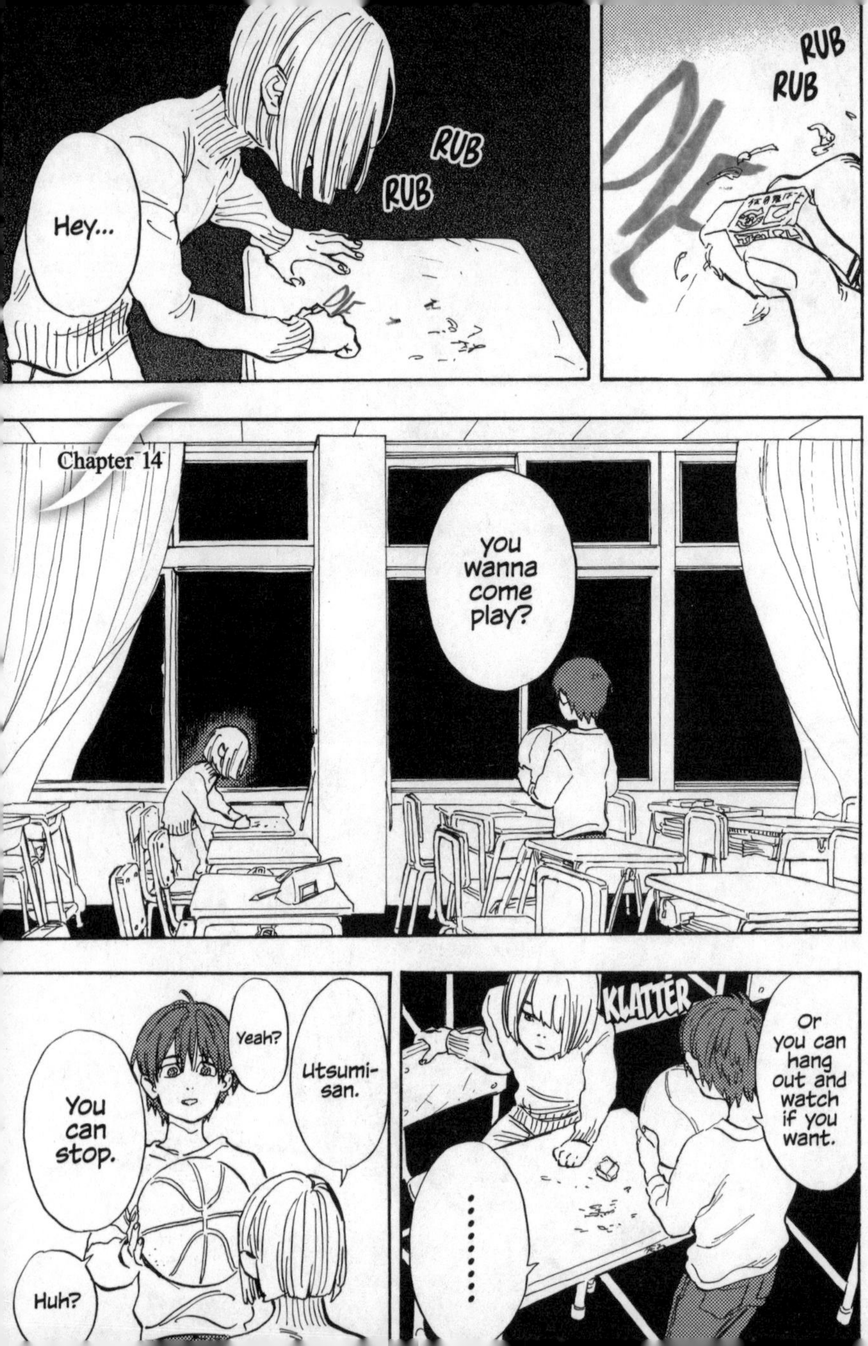
RUB
RUB
RUB
RUB
Hey...
Chapter 14
you wanna come play?
Or you can hang out and watch if you want.
KLATTER
......
Utsumi-san.
Yeah?
You can stop.
Huh?

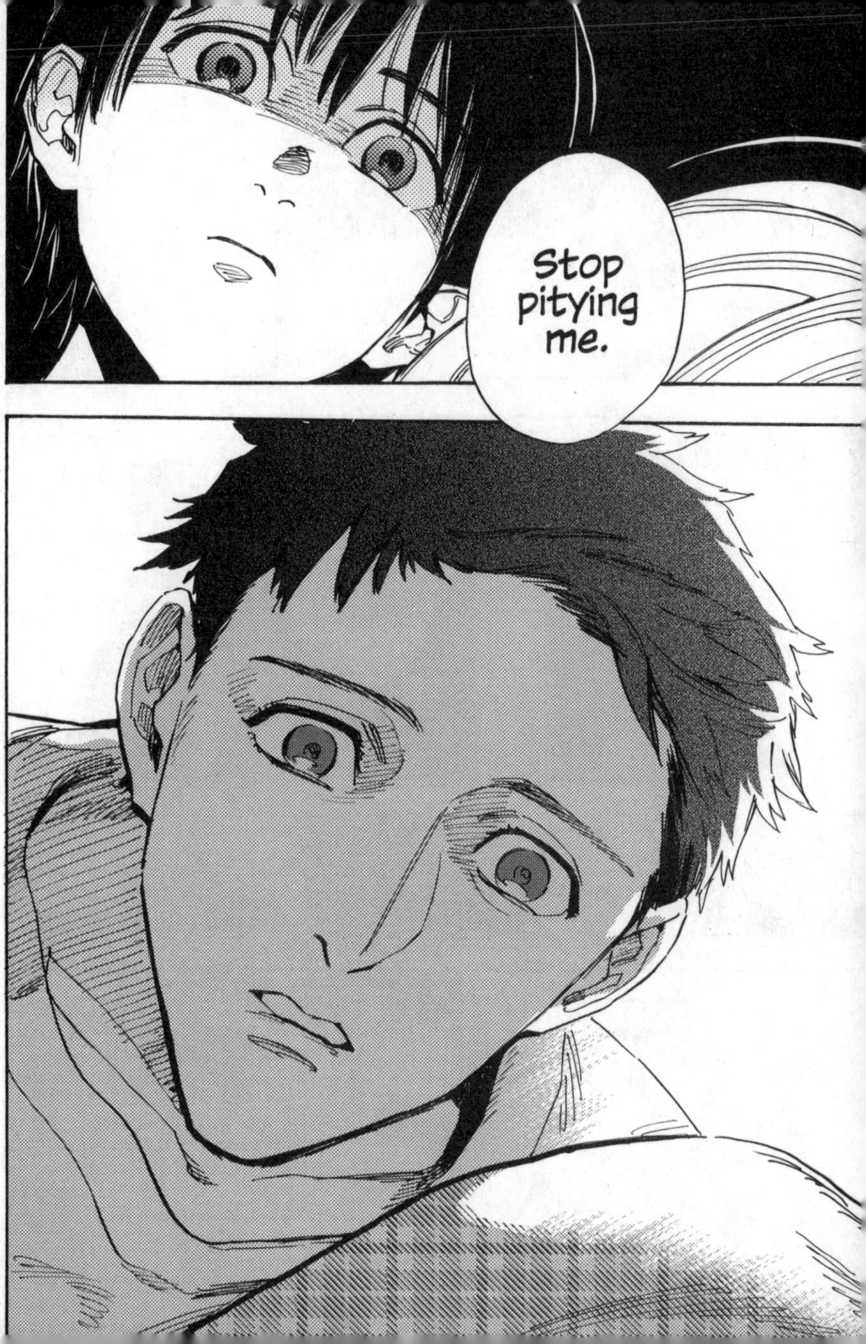
Stop pitying me.

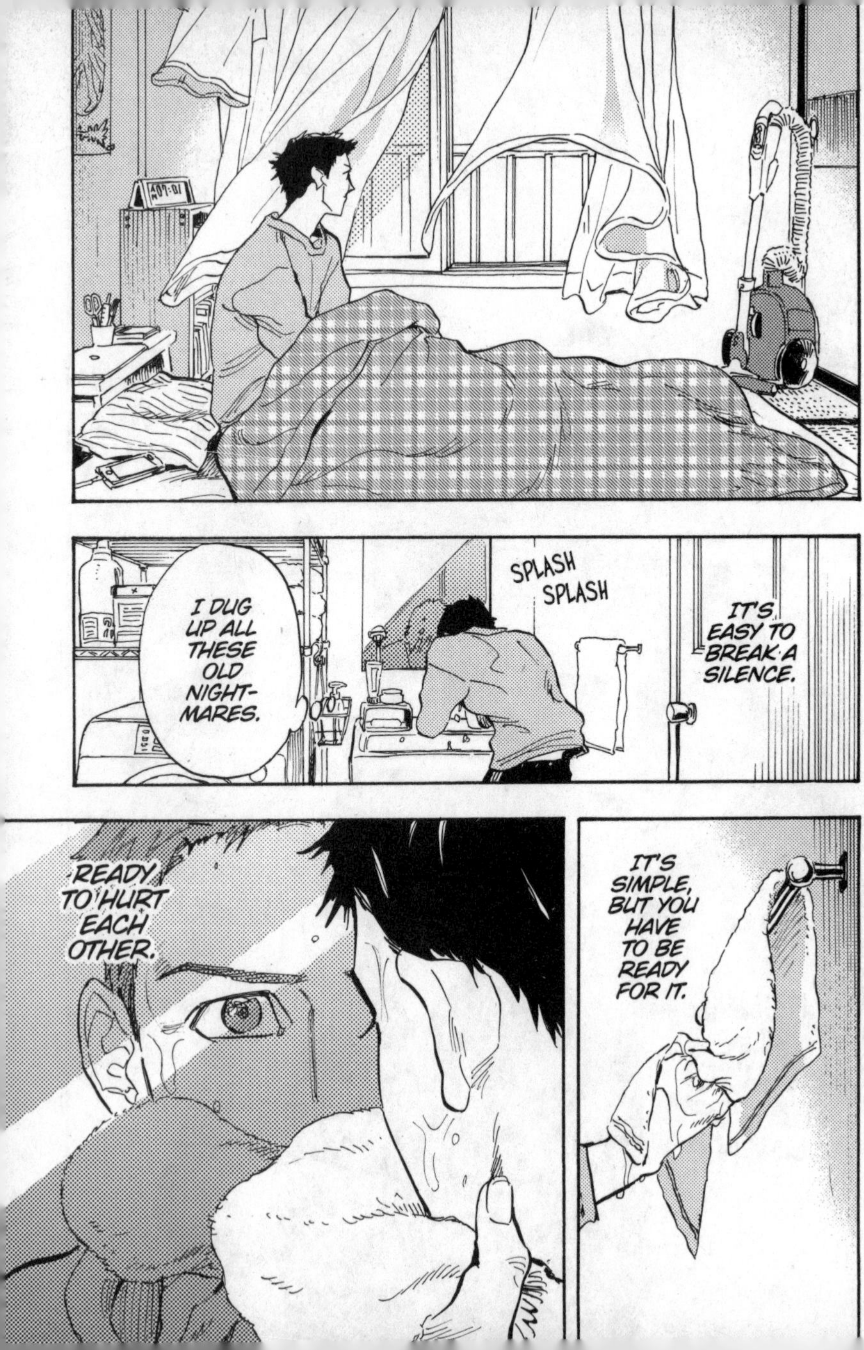
IT'S EASY TO BREAK A SILENCE.
SPLASH SPLASH
I DUG UP ALL THESE OLD NIGHT-MARES.
IT'S SIMPLE, BUT YOU HAVE TO BE READY FOR IT.
READY TO HURT EACH OTHER.

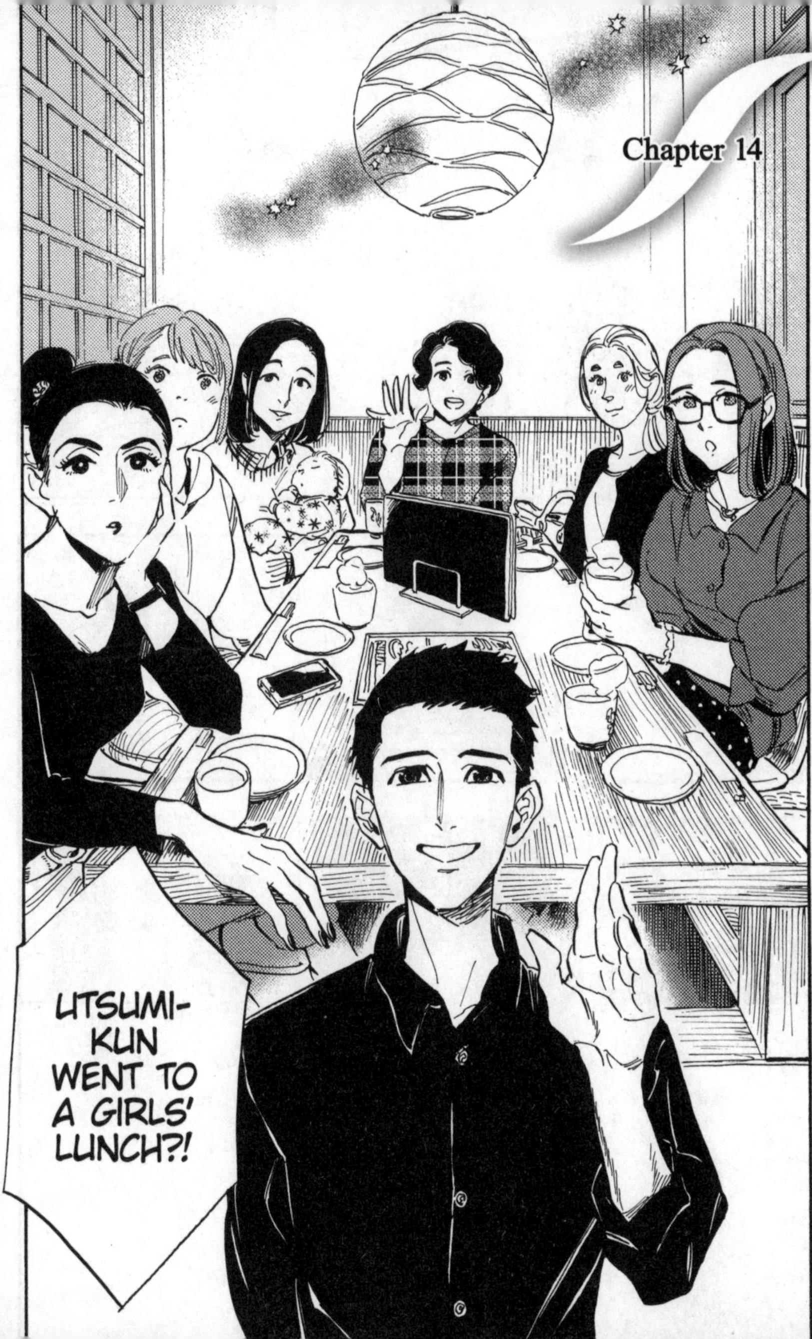
Chapter 14
UTSUMI-KUN WENT TO A GIRLS' LUNCH?!

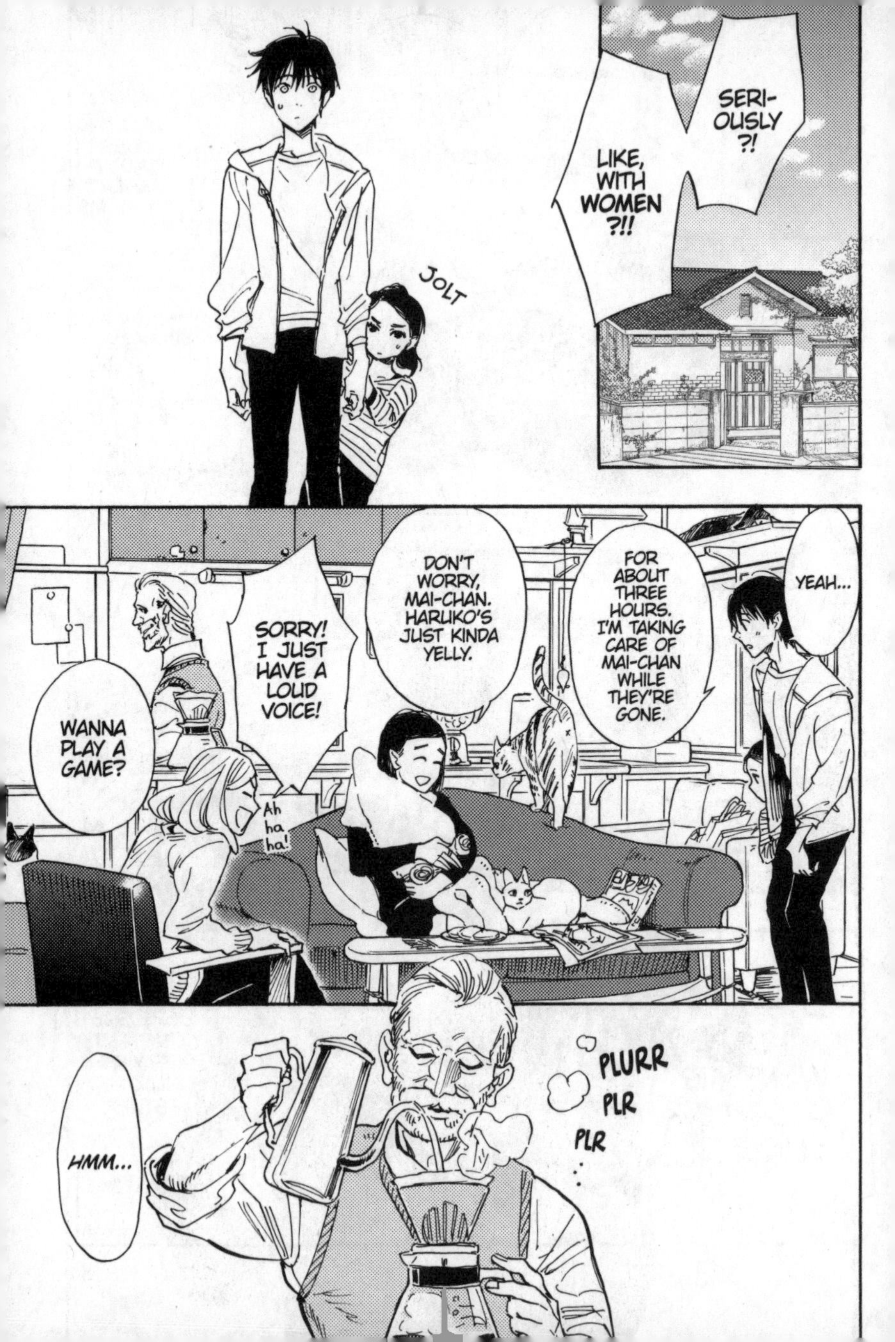
SERI-OUSLY?!
LIKE, WITH WOMEN?!!
JOLT
YEAH...
FOR ABOUT THREE HOURS. I'M TAKING CARE OF MAI-CHAN WHILE THEY'RE GONE.
DON'T WORRY, MAI-CHAN. HARUKO'S JUST KINDA YELLY.
SORRY! I JUST HAVE A LOUD VOICE!
Ah ha ha!
WANNA PLAY A GAME?
PLURR
PLR
PLR
HMM...

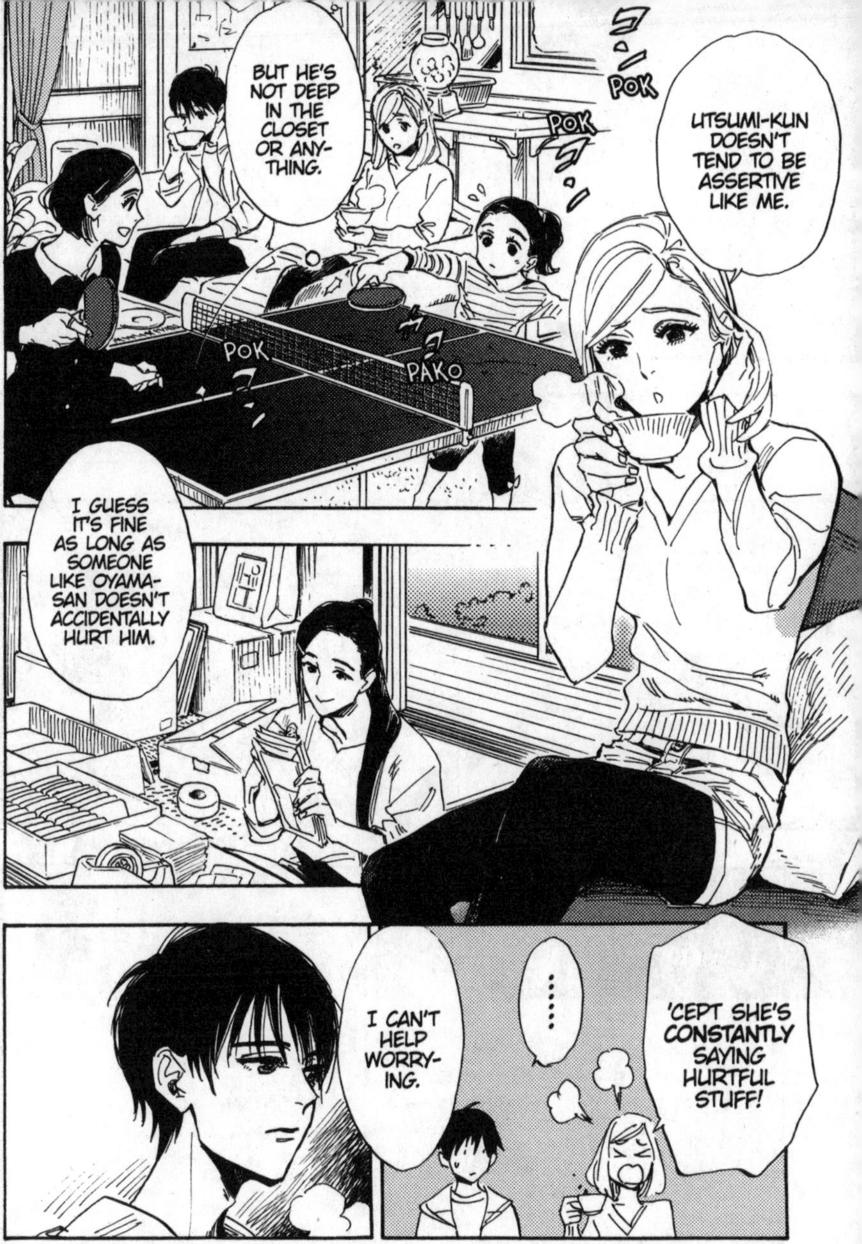
POK
POK
UTSUMI-KUN DOESN'T TEND TO BE ASSERTIVE LIKE ME.
BUT HE'S NOT DEEP IN THE CLOSET OR ANYTHING.
PAKO
POK
...
I GUESS IT'S FINE AS LONG AS SOMEONE LIKE OYAMA-SAN DOESN'T ACCIDENTALLY HURT HIM.
'CEPT SHE'S CONSTANTLY SAYING HURTFUL STUFF!
......
I CAN'T HELP WORRY-ING.

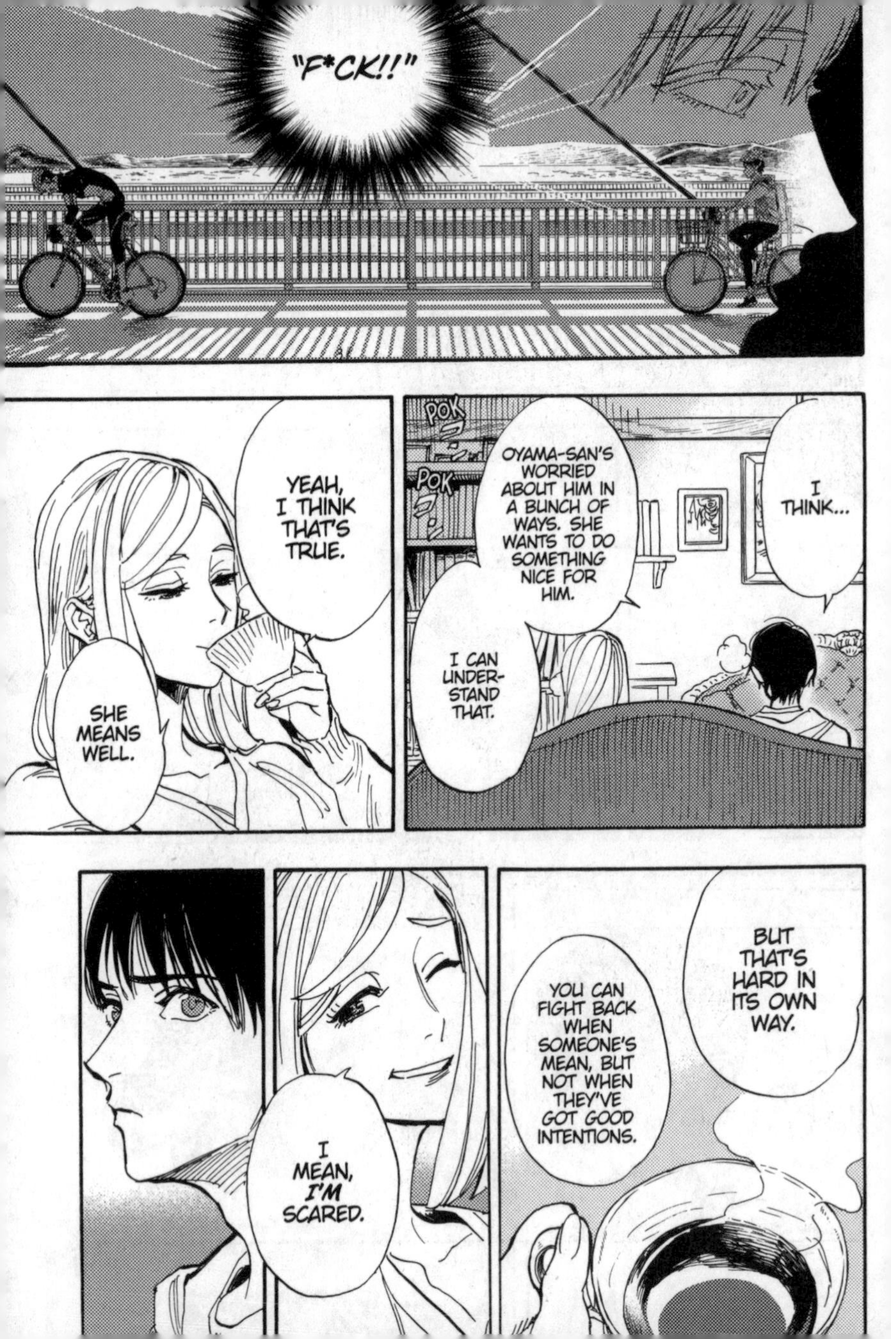
"F*CK!!"
I THINK...
OYAMA-SAN'S WORRIED ABOUT HIM IN A BUNCH OF WAYS. SHE WANTS TO DO SOMETHING NICE FOR HIM.
POK
POK
I CAN UNDERSTAND THAT.
YEAH, I THINK THAT'S TRUE.
SHE MEANS WELL.
BUT THAT'S HARD IN ITS OWN WAY.
YOU CAN FIGHT BACK WHEN SOMEONE'S MEAN, BUT NOT WHEN THEY'VE GOT GOOD INTENTIONS.
I MEAN, I'M SCARED.

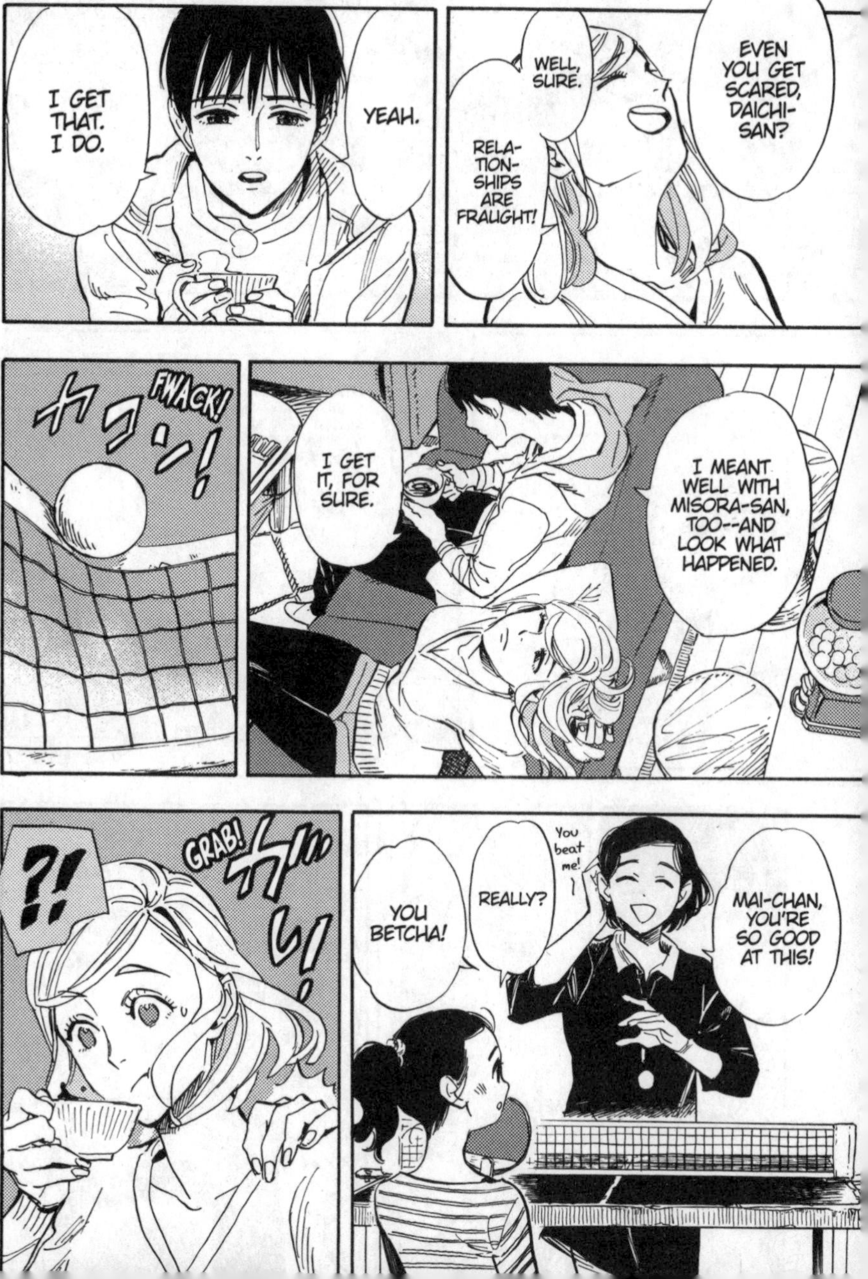
EVEN YOU GET SCARED, DAICHI-SAN?
WELL, SURE.
RELA-TION-SHIPS ARE FRAUGHT!
YEAH.
I GET THAT. I DO.
I MEANT WELL WITH MISORA-SAN, TOO--AND LOOK WHAT HAPPENED.
I GET IT, FOR SURE.
FWACK!
MAI-CHAN, YOU'RE SO GOOD AT THIS!
You beat me!
REALLY?
YOU BETCHA!
GRAB!
?!

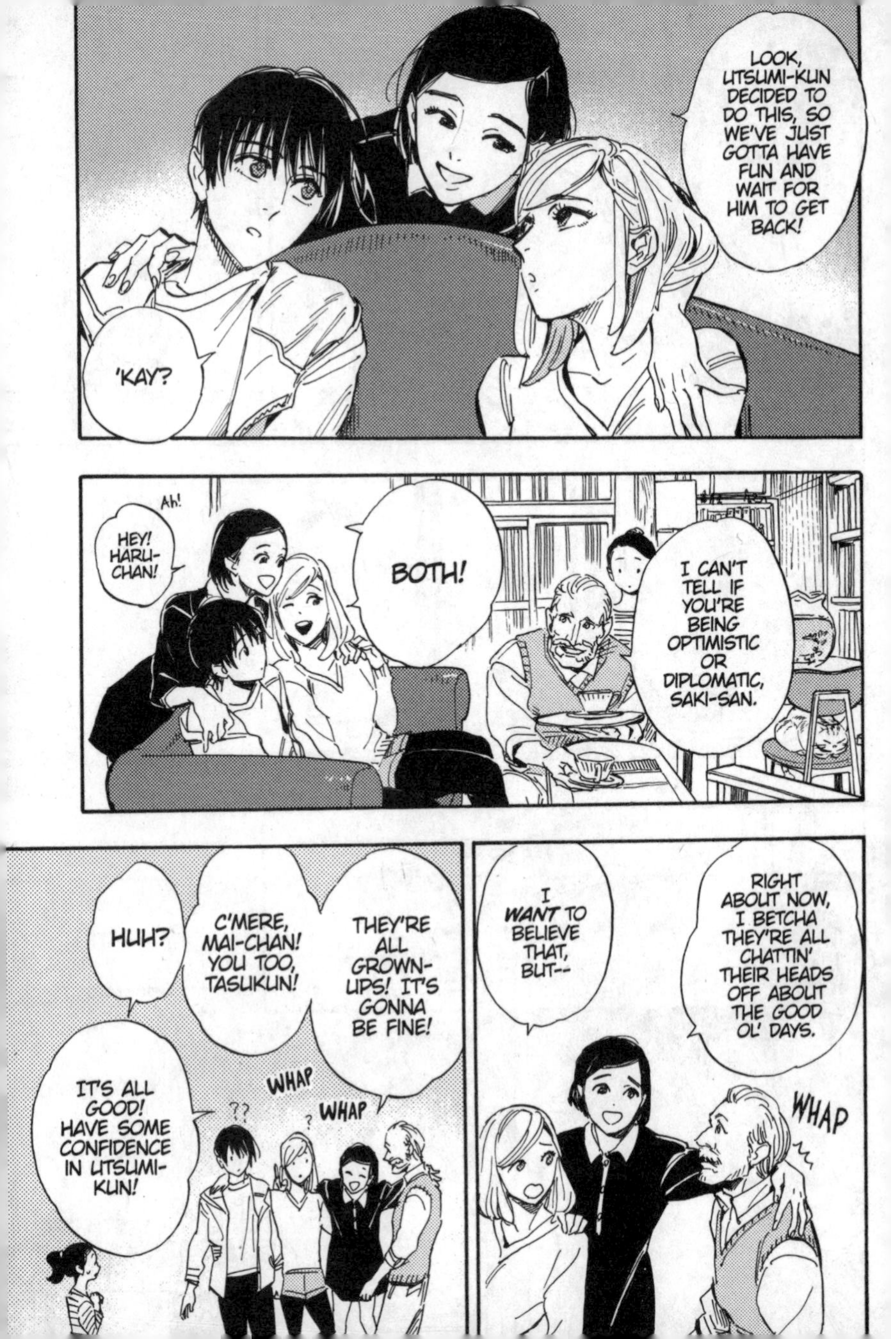
LOOK, UTSUMI-KUN DECIDED TO DO THIS, SO WE'VE JUST GOTTA HAVE FUN AND WAIT FOR HIM TO GET BACK!
'KAY?
I CAN'T TELL IF YOU'RE BEING OPTIMISTIC OR DIPLOMATIC, SAKI-SAN.
BOTH!
Ah!
HEY! HARU-CHAN!
RIGHT ABOUT NOW, I BETCHA THEY'RE ALL CHATTIN' THEIR HEADS OFF ABOUT THE GOOD OL' DAYS.
I *WANT* TO BELIEVE THAT, BUT--
WHAP
THEY'RE ALL GROWN-UPS! IT'S GONNA BE FINE!
C'MERE, MAI-CHAN! YOU TOO, TASUKUN!
HUH?
WHAP
WHAP
IT'S ALL GOOD! HAVE SOME CONFIDENCE IN UTSUMI-KUN!
??
?

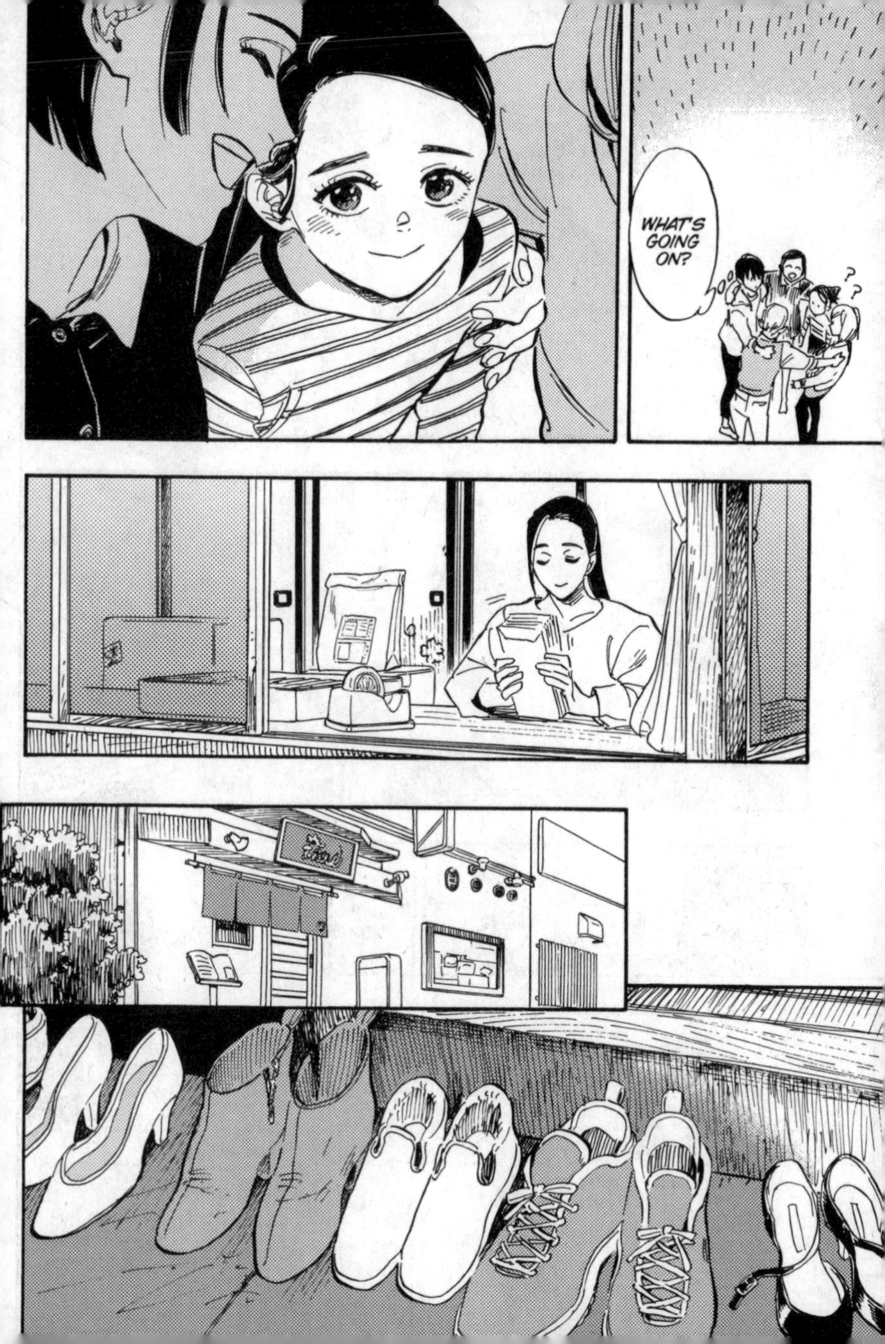
WHAT'S GOING ON?

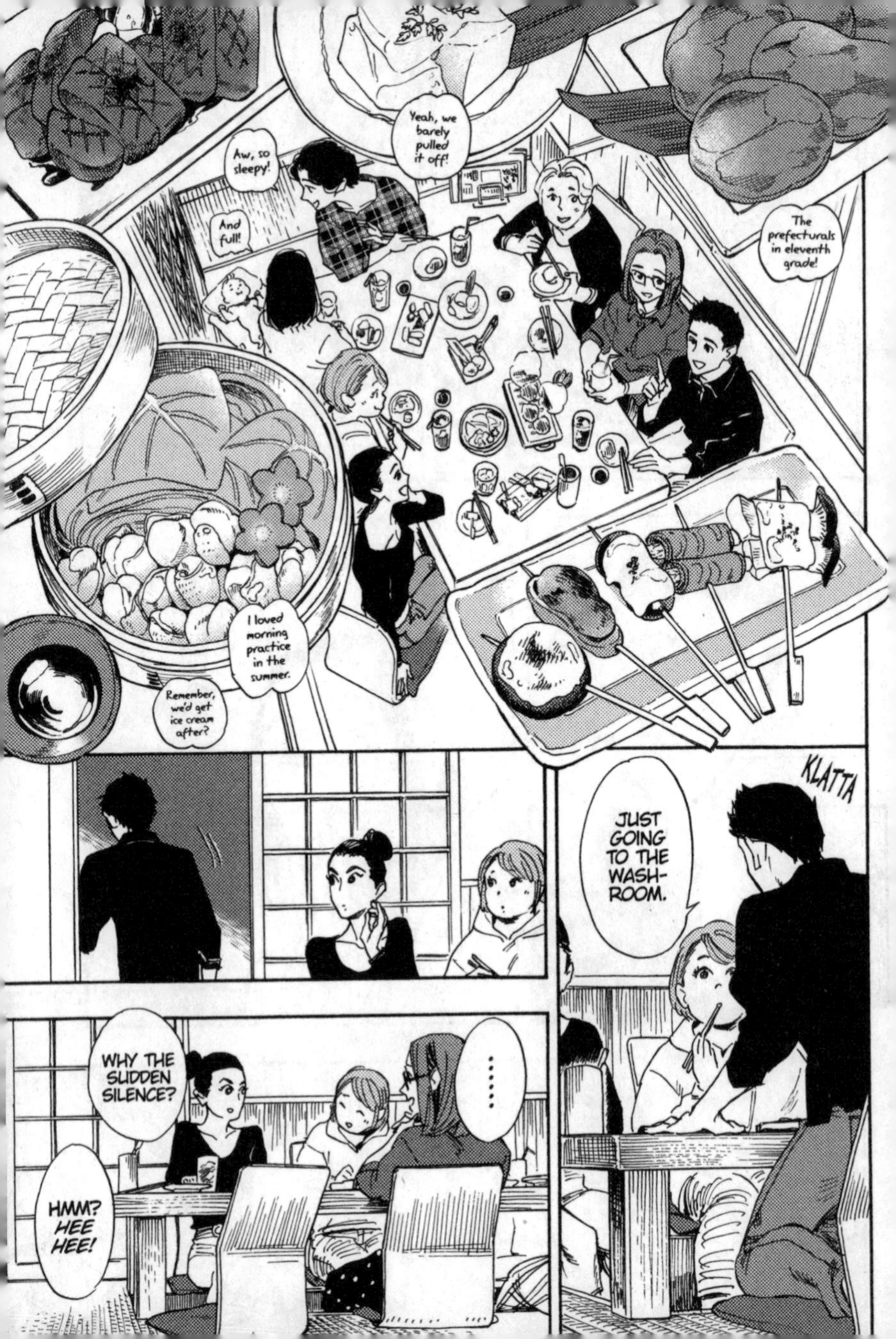
The prefecturals in eleventh grade!
Yeah, we barely pulled it off!
Aw, so sleepy!
And full!
I loved morning practice in the summer.
Remember, we'd get ice cream after?
KLATTA
JUST GOING TO THE WASH-ROOM.
.....
WHY THE SUDDEN SILENCE?
HMM? HEE HEE!

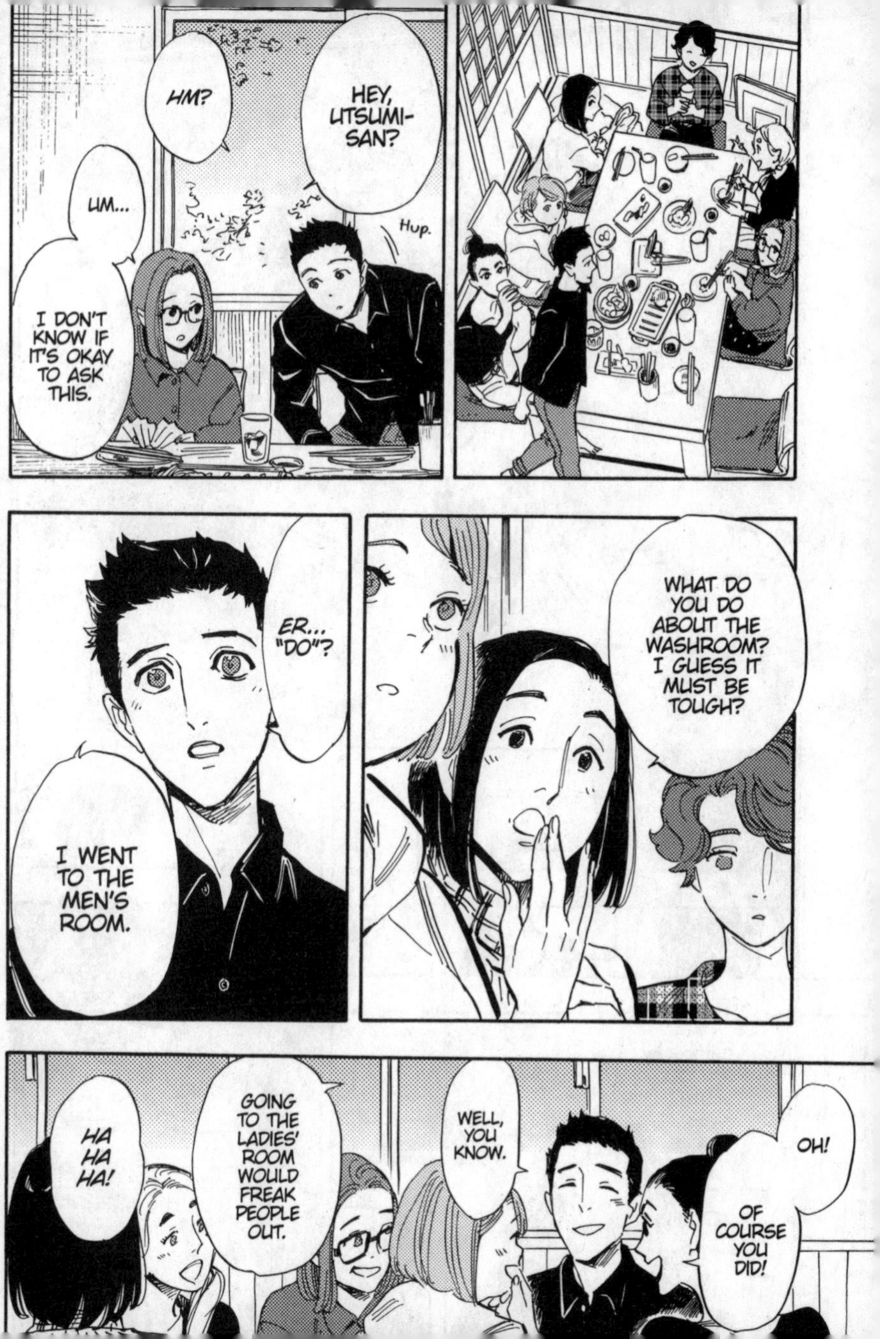
HEY, UTSUMI-SAN?
HM?
Hup.
UM...
I DON'T KNOW IF IT'S OKAY TO ASK THIS.
WHAT DO YOU DO ABOUT THE WASHROOM? I GUESS IT MUST BE TOUGH?
ER... "DO"?
I WENT TO THE MEN'S ROOM.
OH!
OF COURSE YOU DID!
WELL, YOU KNOW.
GOING TO THE LADIES' ROOM WOULD FREAK PEOPLE OUT.
HA HA HA!

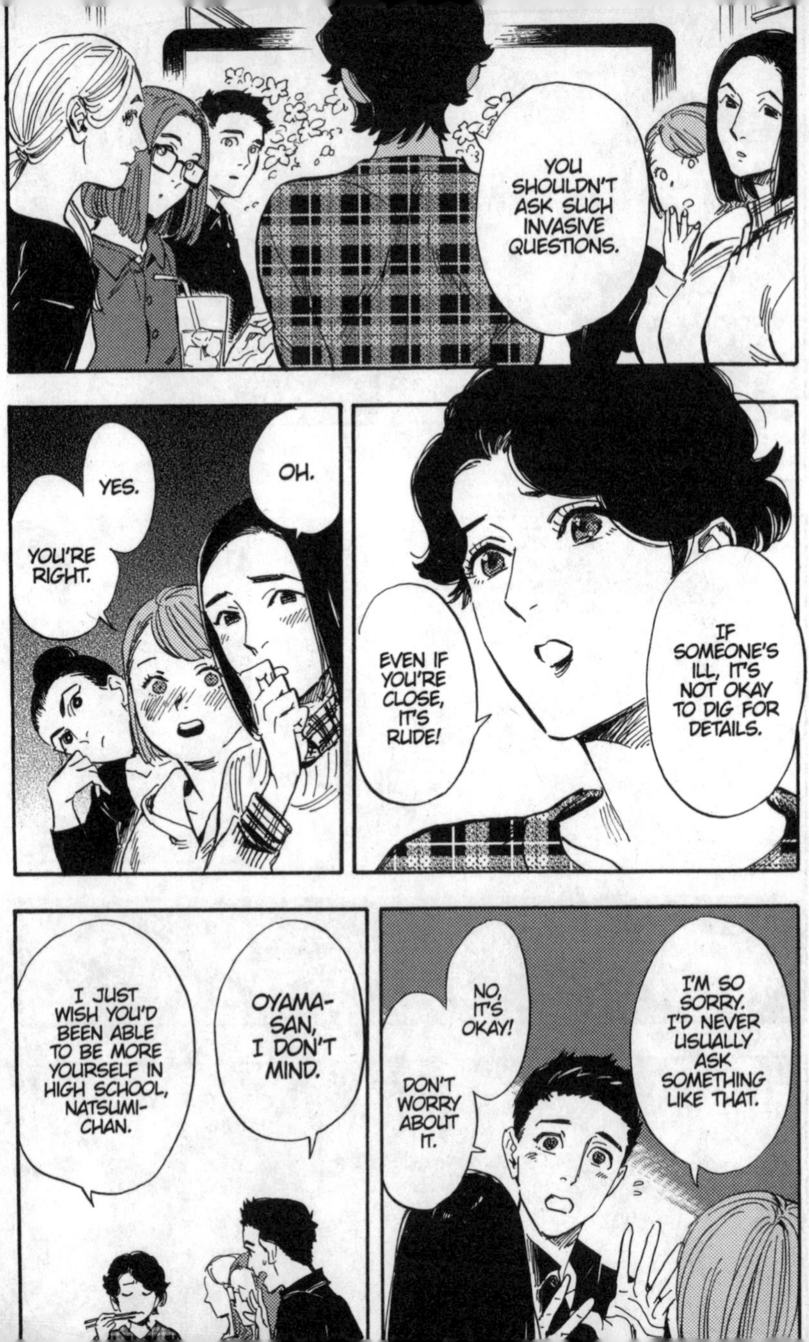
YOU SHOULDN'T ASK SUCH INVASIVE QUESTIONS.
IF SOMEONE'S ILL, IT'S NOT OKAY TO DIG FOR DETAILS.
EVEN IF YOU'RE CLOSE, IT'S RUDE!
OH.
YES.
YOU'RE RIGHT.
I'M SO SORRY. I'D NEVER USUALLY ASK SOMETHING LIKE THAT.
NO, IT'S OKAY!
DON'T WORRY ABOUT IT.
OYAMA-SAN, I DON'T MIND.
I JUST WISH YOU'D BEEN ABLE TO BE MORE YOURSELF IN HIGH SCHOOL, NATSUMI-CHAN.

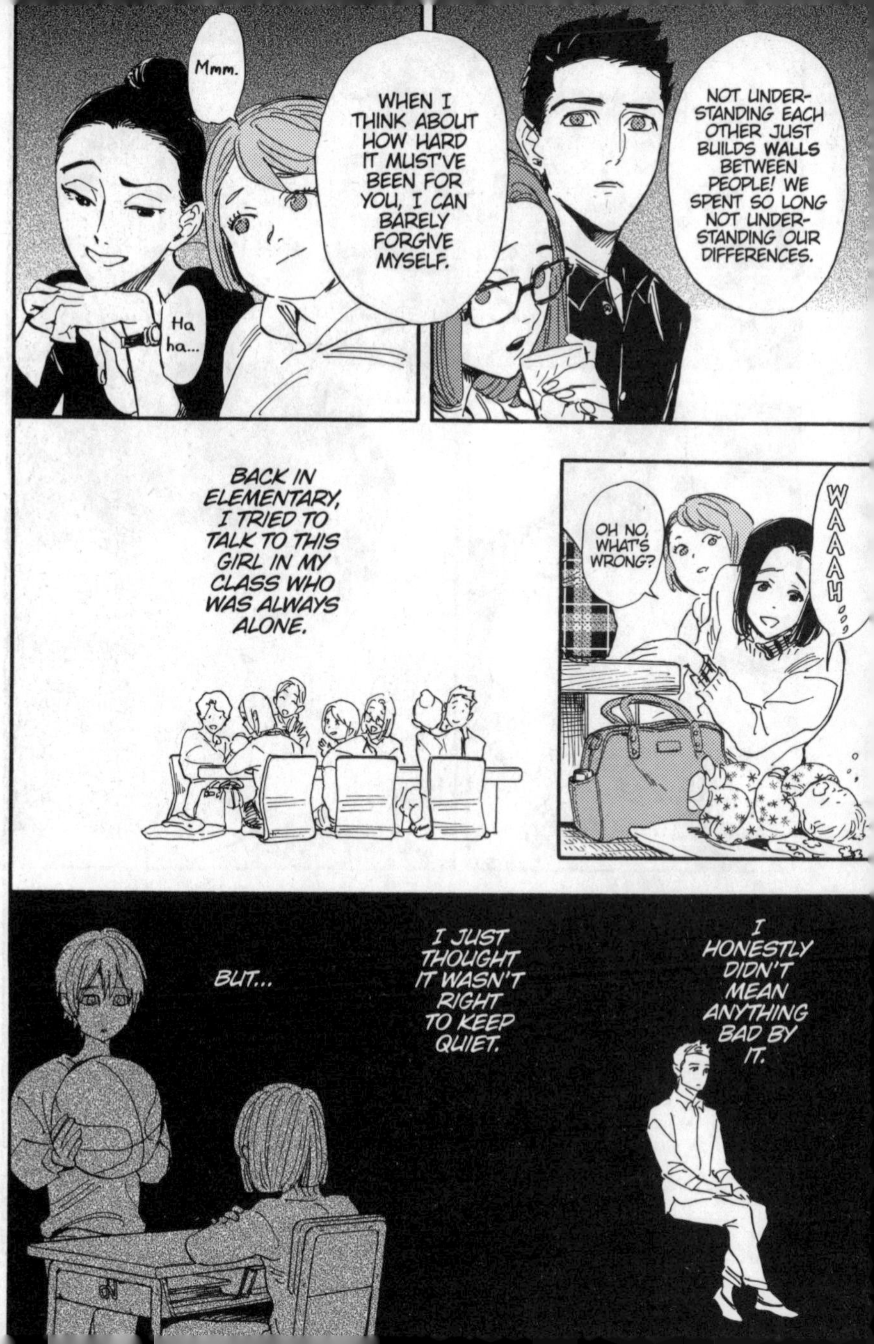
NOT UNDER-STANDING EACH OTHER JUST BUILDS WALLS BETWEEN PEOPLE! WE SPENT SO LONG NOT UNDER-STANDING OUR DIFFERENCES.
WHEN I THINK ABOUT HOW HARD IT MUST'VE BEEN FOR YOU, I CAN BARELY FORGIVE MYSELF.
Mmm.
Ha ha...
WAAAAH...
OH NO, WHAT'S WRONG?
BACK IN ELEMENTARY, I TRIED TO TALK TO THIS GIRL IN MY CLASS WHO WAS ALWAYS ALONE.
I HONESTLY DIDN'T MEAN ANYTHING BAD BY IT.
I JUST THOUGHT IT WASN'T RIGHT TO KEEP QUIET.
BUT...

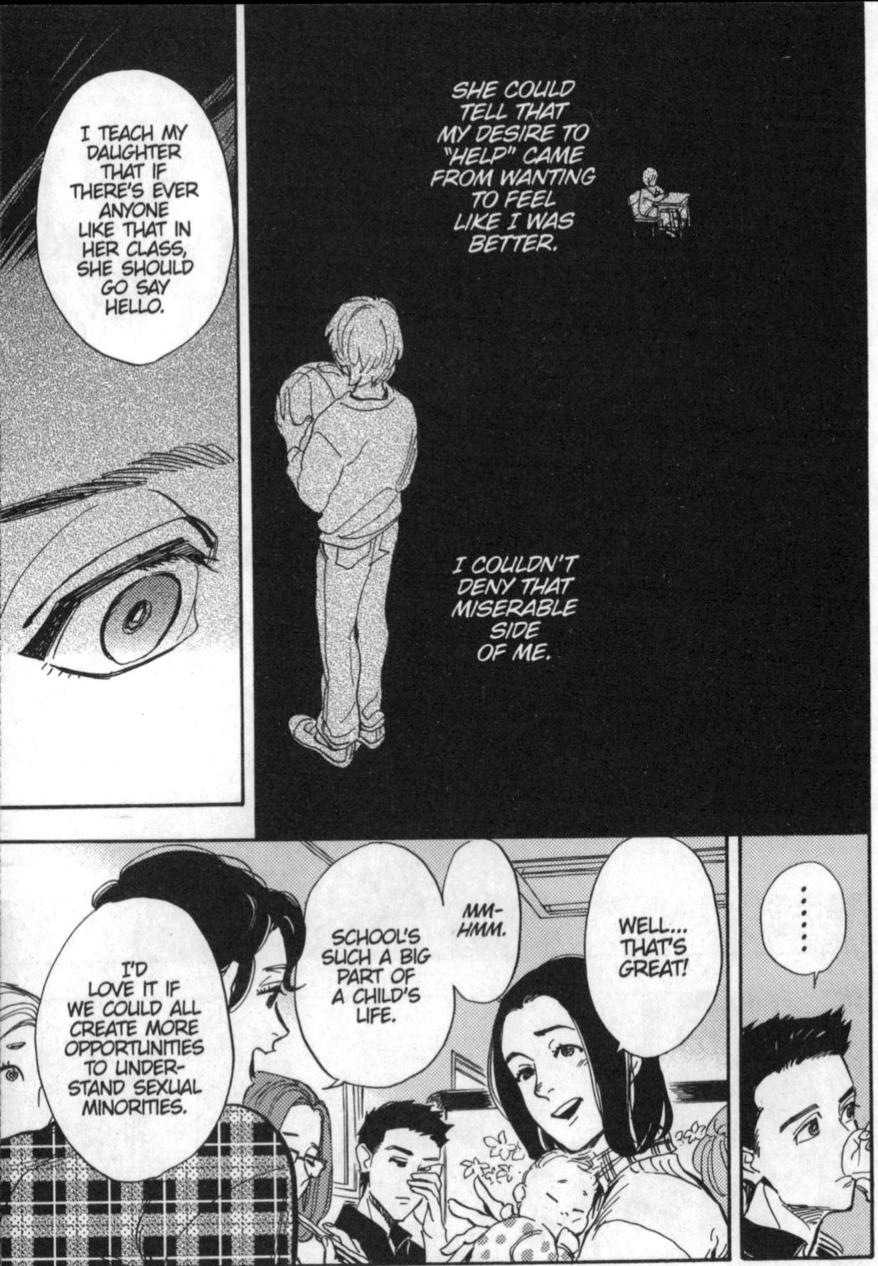
I TEACH MY DAUGHTER THAT IF THERE'S EVER ANYONE LIKE THAT IN HER CLASS, SHE SHOULD GO SAY HELLO.
SHE COULD TELL THAT MY DESIRE TO "HELP" CAME FROM WANTING TO FEEL LIKE I WAS BETTER.
I COULDN'T DENY THAT MISERABLE SIDE OF ME.
I'D LOVE IT IF WE COULD ALL CREATE MORE OPPORTUNITIES TO UNDER-STAND SEXUAL MINORITIES.
SCHOOL'S SUCH A BIG PART OF A CHILD'S LIFE.
MM-HMM.
WELL... THAT'S GREAT!
......

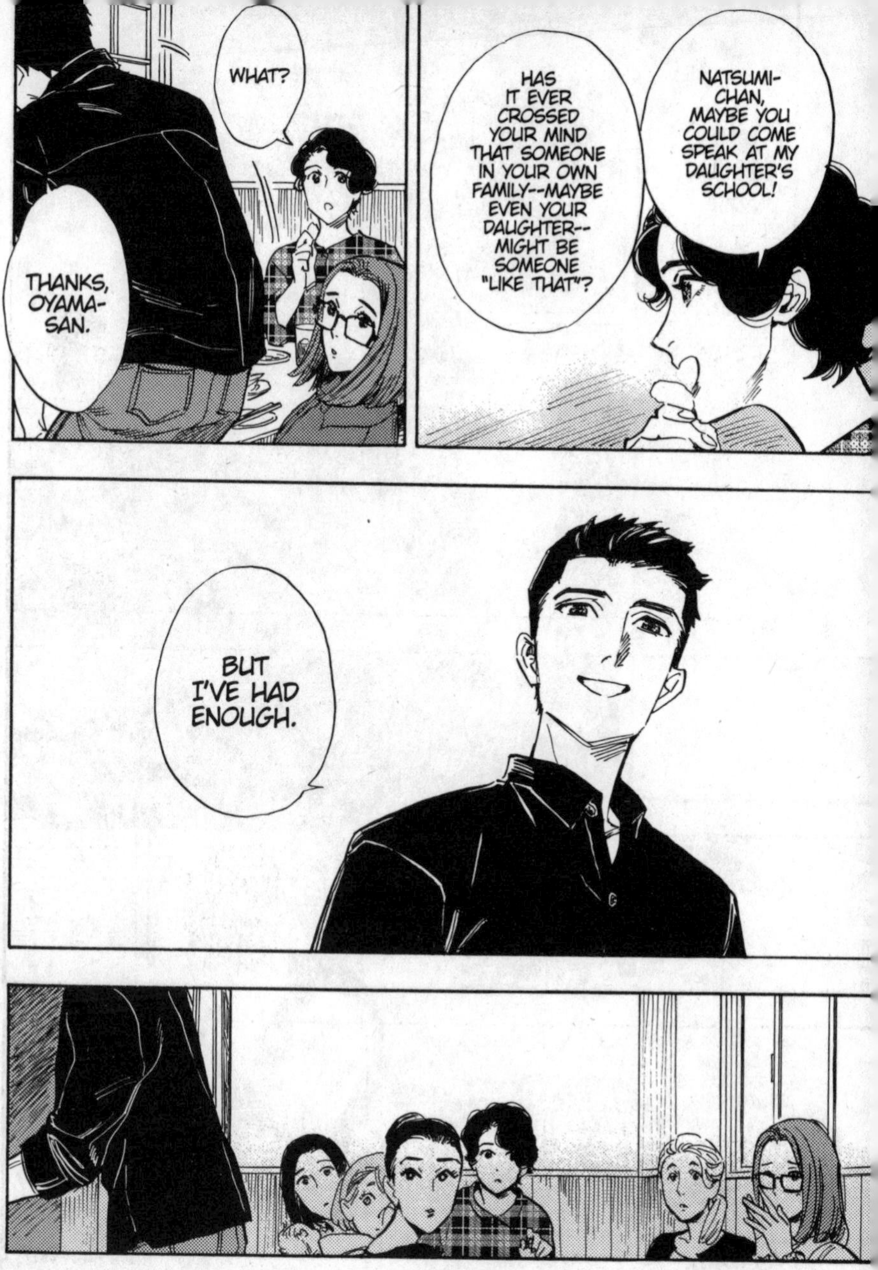
NATSUMI-CHAN, MAYBE YOU COULD COME SPEAK AT MY DAUGHTER'S SCHOOL!
HAS IT EVER CROSSED YOUR MIND THAT SOMEONE IN YOUR OWN FAMILY--MAYBE EVEN YOUR DAUGHTER--MIGHT BE SOMEONE "LIKE THAT"?
WHAT?
THANKS, OYAMA-SAN.
BUT I'VE HAD ENOUGH.

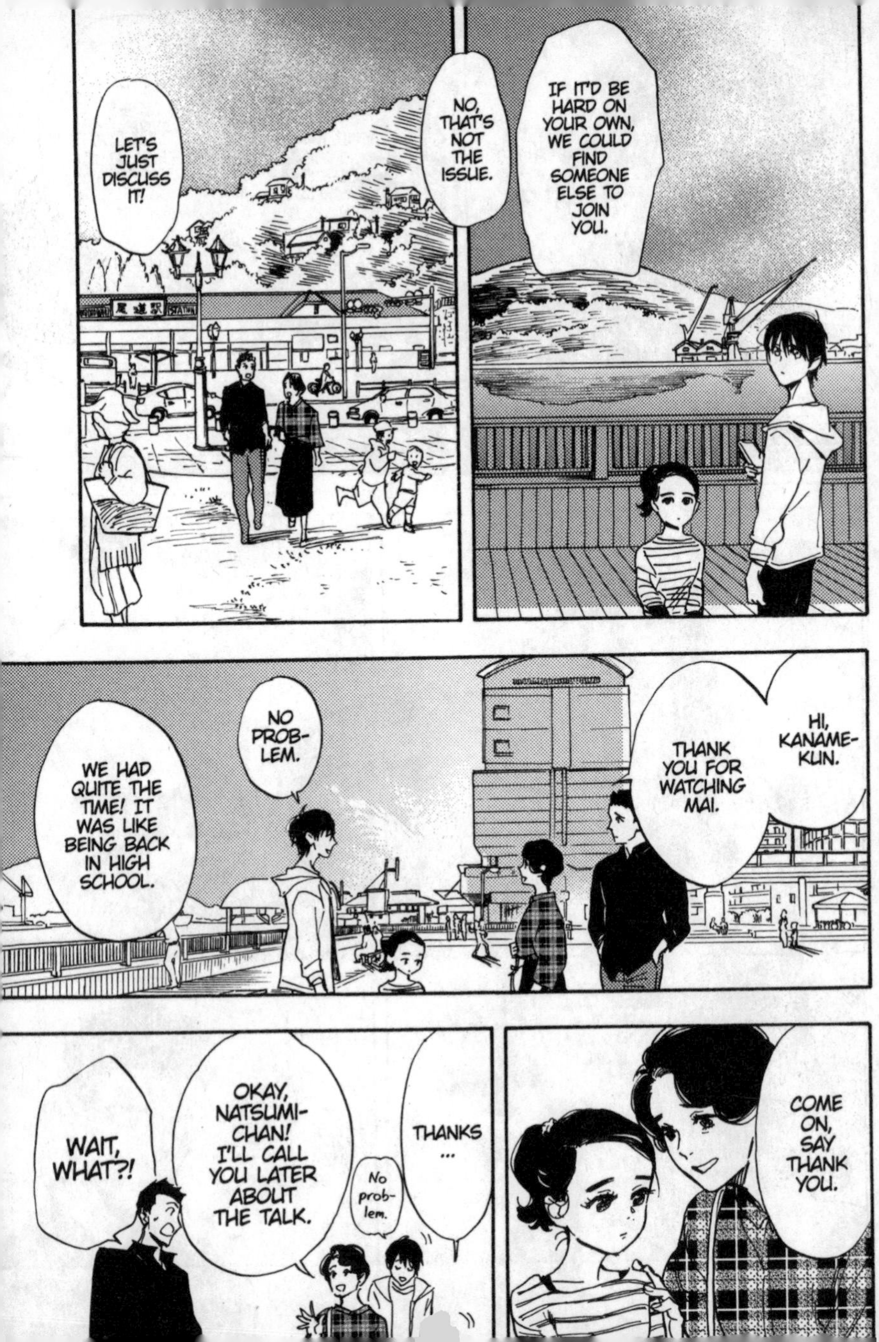
IF IT'D BE HARD ON YOUR OWN, WE COULD FIND SOMEONE ELSE TO JOIN YOU.
NO, THAT'S NOT THE ISSUE.
LET'S JUST DISCUSS IT!
HI, KANAME-KUN.
THANK YOU FOR WATCHING MAI.
NO PROB-LEM.
WE HAD QUITE THE TIME! IT WAS LIKE BEING BACK IN HIGH SCHOOL.
COME ON, SAY THANK YOU.
THANKS...
No prob-lem.
OKAY, NATSUMI-CHAN! I'LL CALL YOU LATER ABOUT THE TALK.
WAIT, WHAT?!

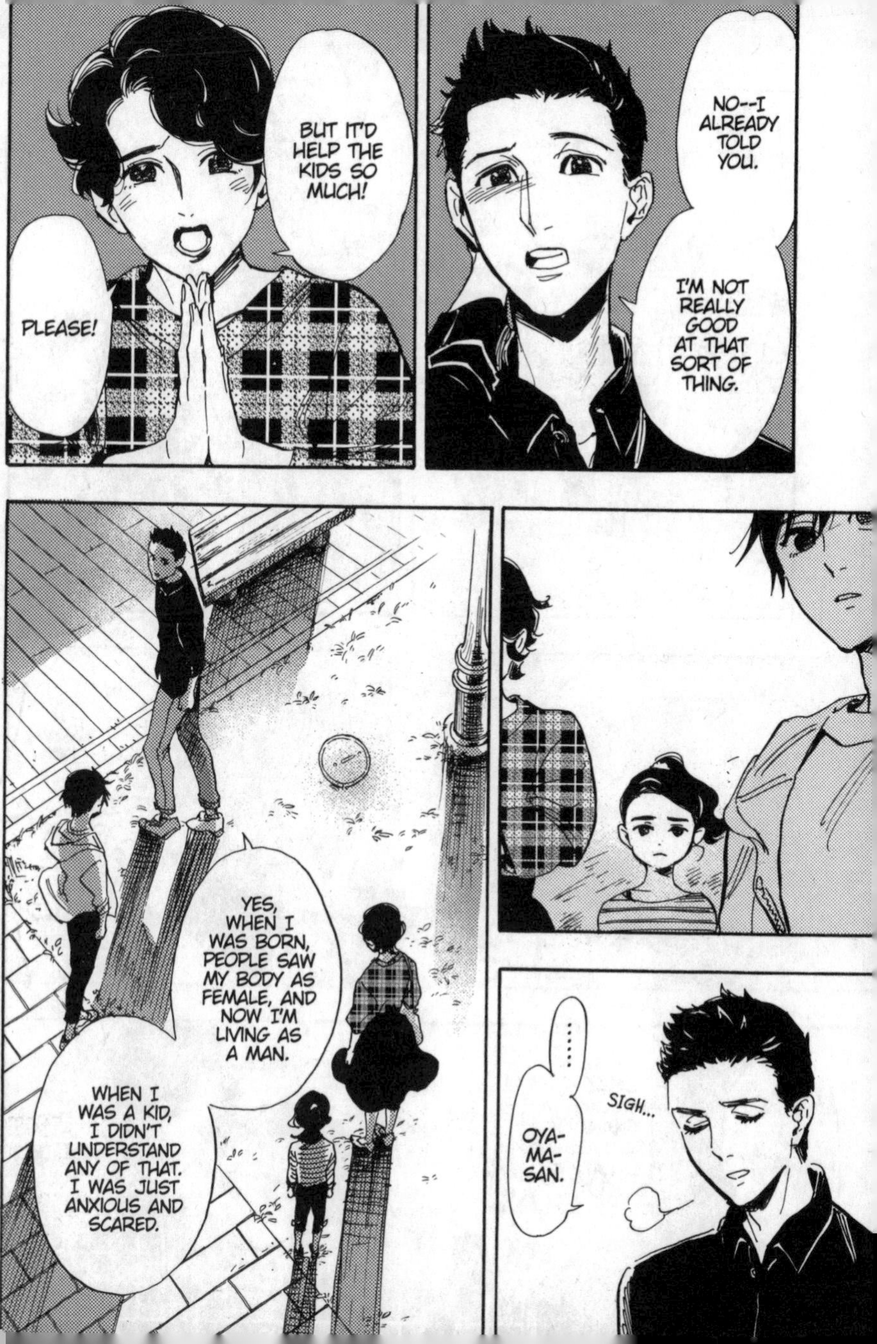
NO--I ALREADY TOLD YOU.
I'M NOT REALLY GOOD AT THAT SORT OF THING.
BUT IT'D HELP THE KIDS SO MUCH!
PLEASE!
......
OYA-MA-SAN.
SIGH...
YES, WHEN I WAS BORN, PEOPLE SAW MY BODY AS FEMALE, AND NOW I'M LIVING AS A MAN.
WHEN I WAS A KID, I DIDN'T UNDERSTAND ANY OF THAT. I WAS JUST ANXIOUS AND SCARED.

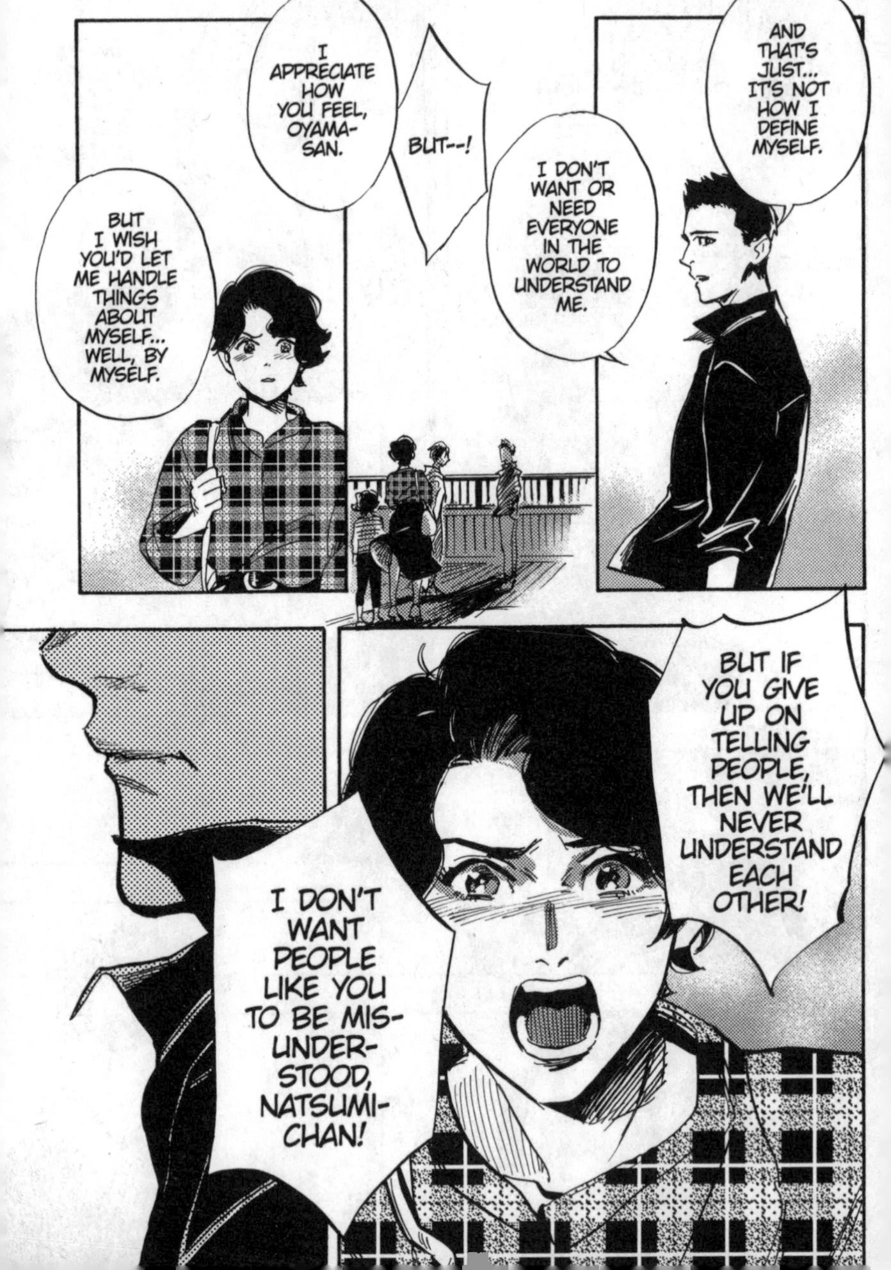
AND THAT'S JUST... IT'S NOT HOW I DEFINE MYSELF.
I DON'T WANT OR NEED EVERYONE IN THE WORLD TO UNDERSTAND ME.
BUT--!
I APPRECIATE HOW YOU FEEL, OYAMA-SAN.
BUT I WISH YOU'D LET ME HANDLE THINGS ABOUT MYSELF... WELL, BY MYSELF.
BUT IF YOU GIVE UP ON TELLING PEOPLE, THEN WE'LL NEVER UNDERSTAND EACH OTHER!
I DON'T WANT PEOPLE LIKE YOU TO BE MIS-UNDER-STOOD, NATSUMI-CHAN!

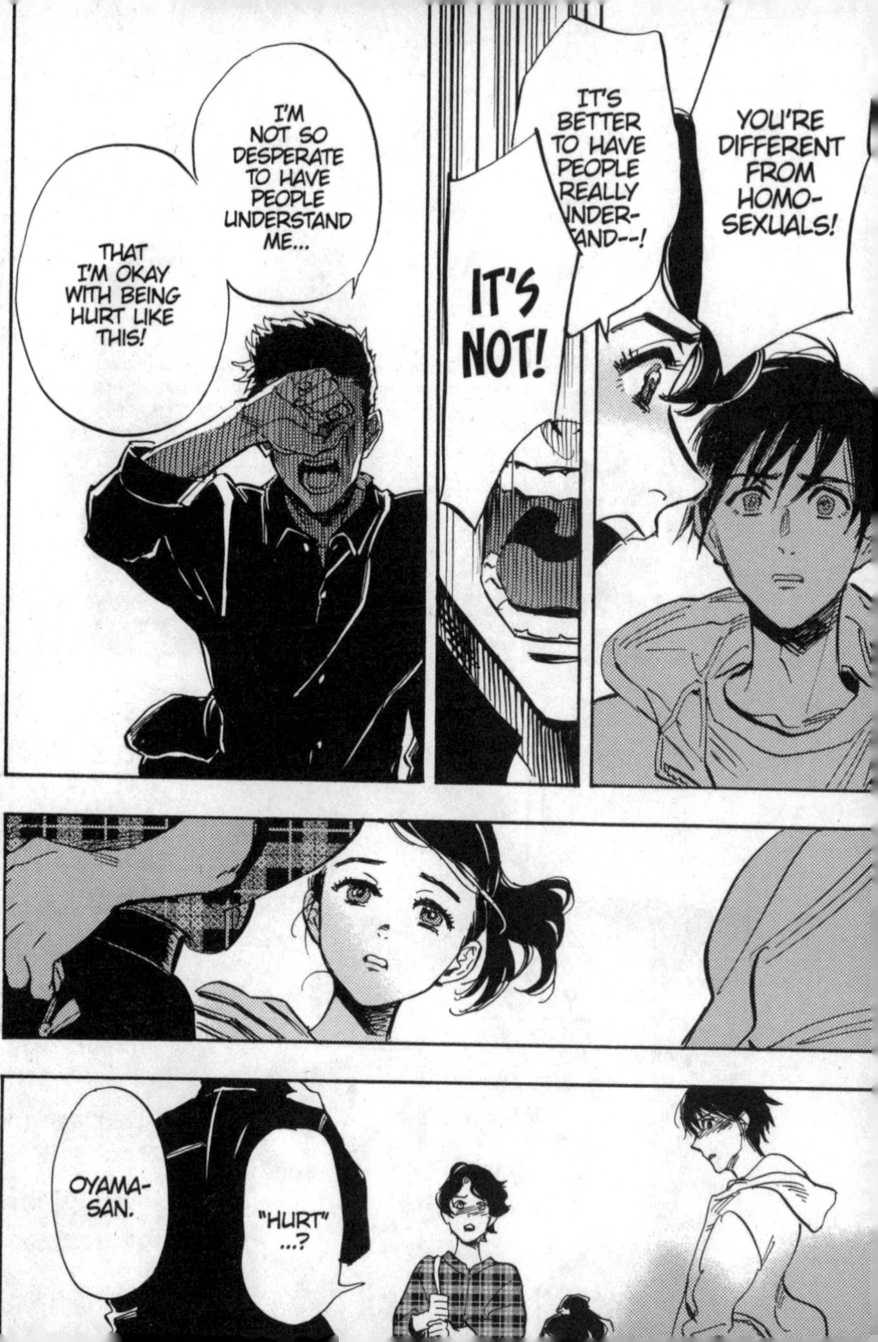
YOU'RE DIFFERENT FROM HOMO-SEXUALS!
IT'S BETTER TO HAVE PEOPLE REALLY UNDER-STAND--!
IT'S NOT!
I'M NOT SO DESPERATE TO HAVE PEOPLE UNDERSTAND ME...
THAT I'M OKAY WITH BEING HURT LIKE THIS!
"HURT" ...?
OYAMA-SAN.

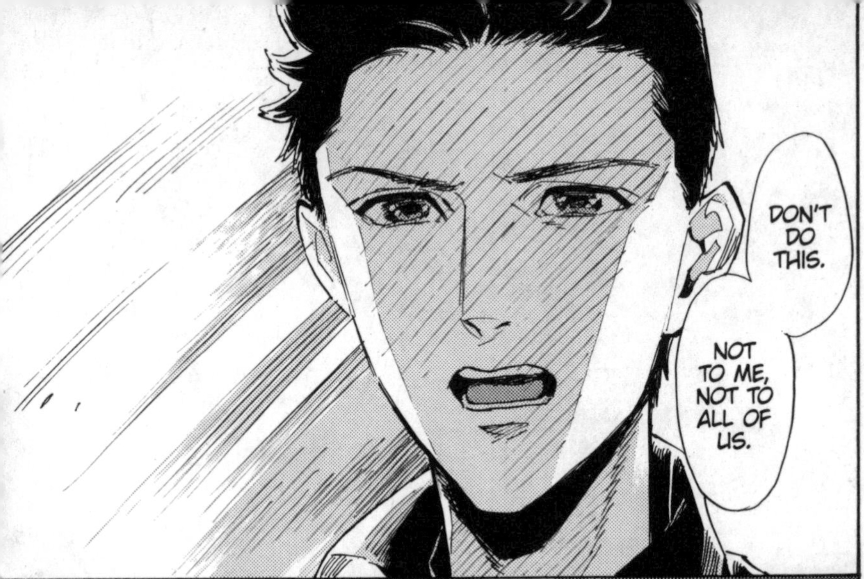
DON'T DO THIS.
NOT TO ME, NOT TO ALL OF US.

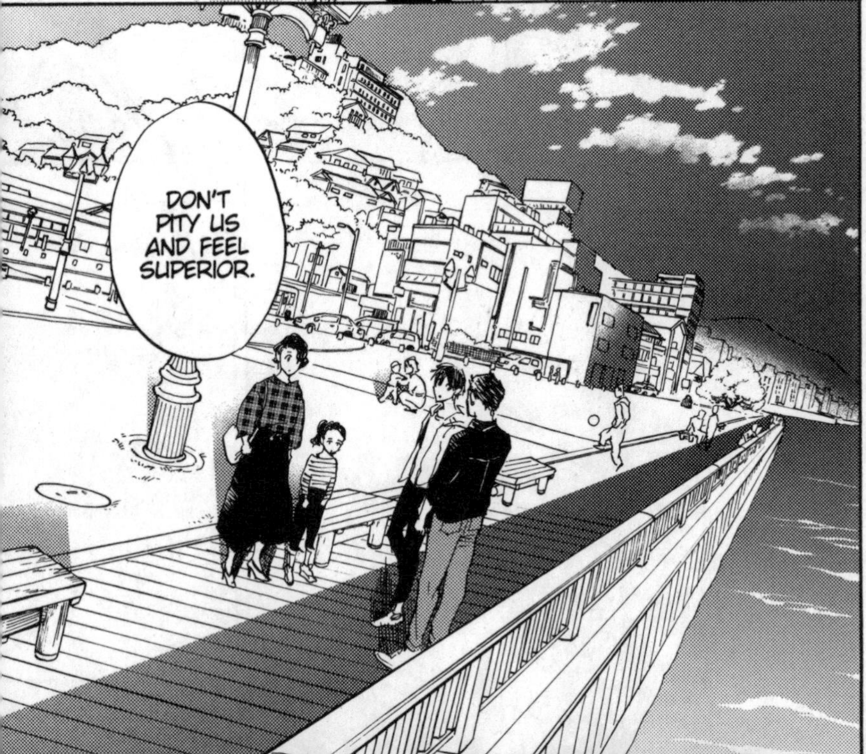
DON'T PITY US AND FEEL SUPERIOR.

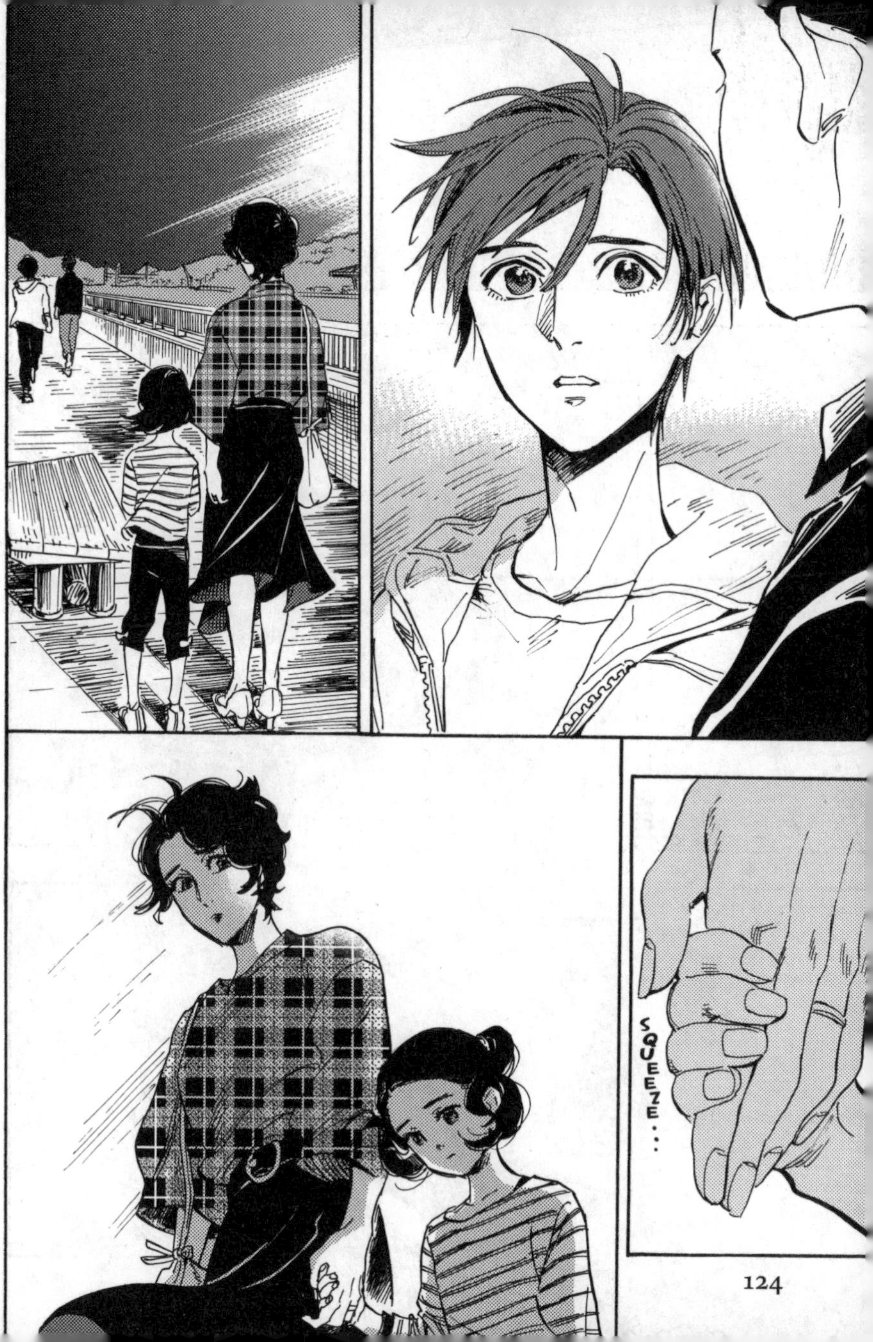
SQUEEZE...

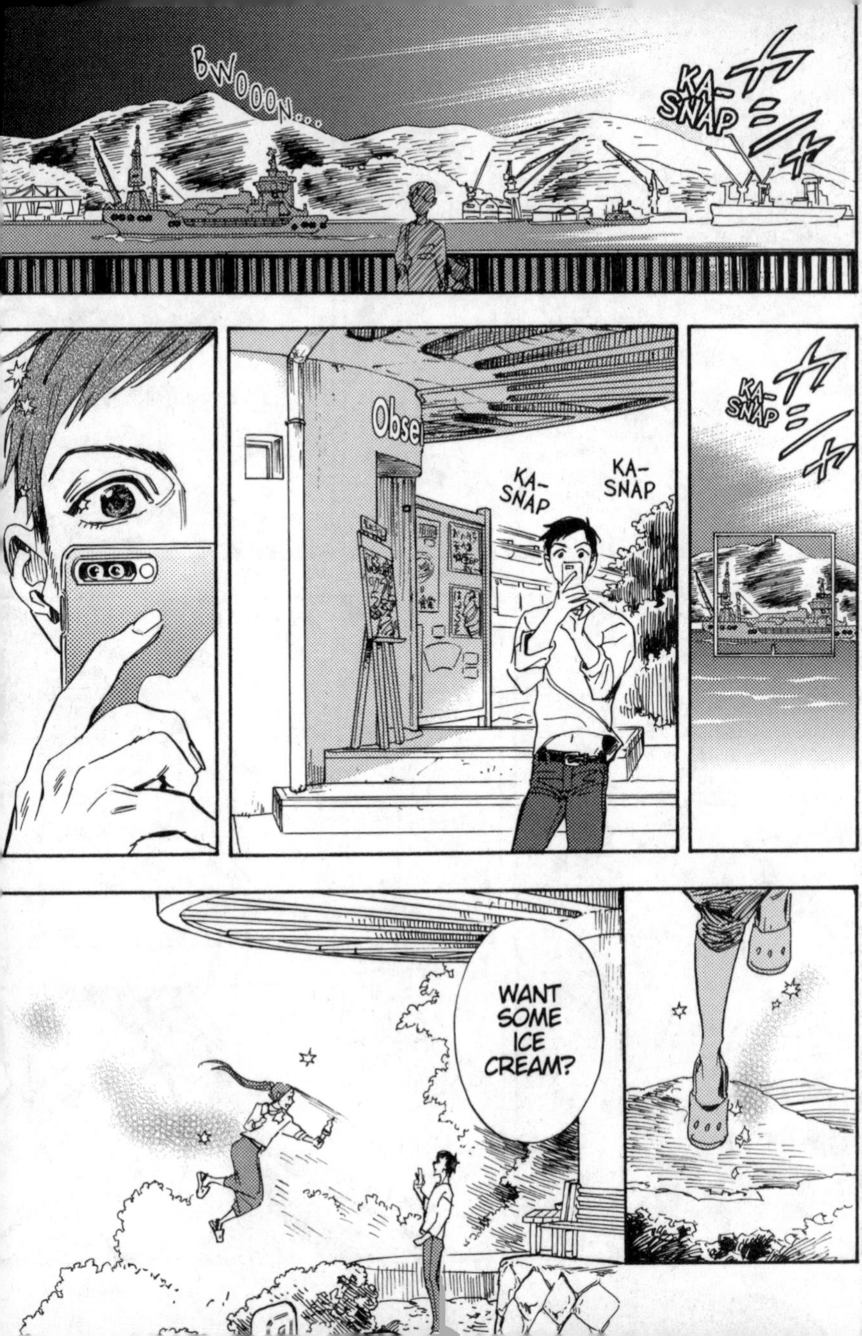
BWOOON...
KA-SNAP
KA-SNAP
KA-SNAP
KA-SNAP
WANT SOME ICE CREAM?

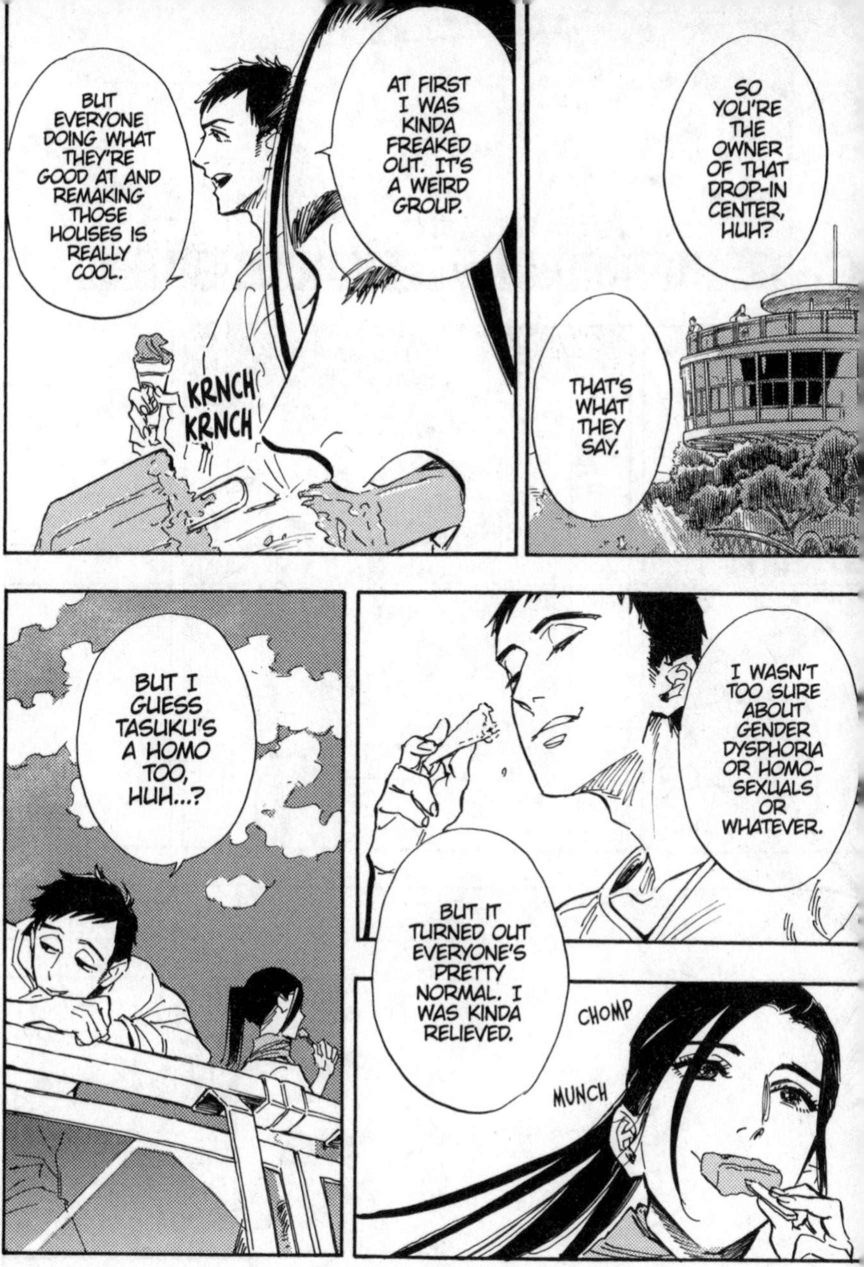
SO YOU'RE THE OWNER OF THAT DROP-IN CENTER, HUH?
THAT'S WHAT THEY SAY.
AT FIRST I WAS KINDA FREAKED OUT. IT'S A WEIRD GROUP.
BUT EVERYONE DOING WHAT THEY'RE GOOD AT AND REMAKING THOSE HOUSES IS REALLY COOL.
KRNCH KRNCH
I WASN'T TOO SURE ABOUT GENDER DYSPHORIA OR HOMO-SEXUALS OR WHATEVER.
BUT IT TURNED OUT EVERYONE'S PRETTY NORMAL. I WAS KINDA RELIEVED.
CHOMP
MUNCH
BUT I GUESS TASUKU'S A HOMO TOO, HUH...?

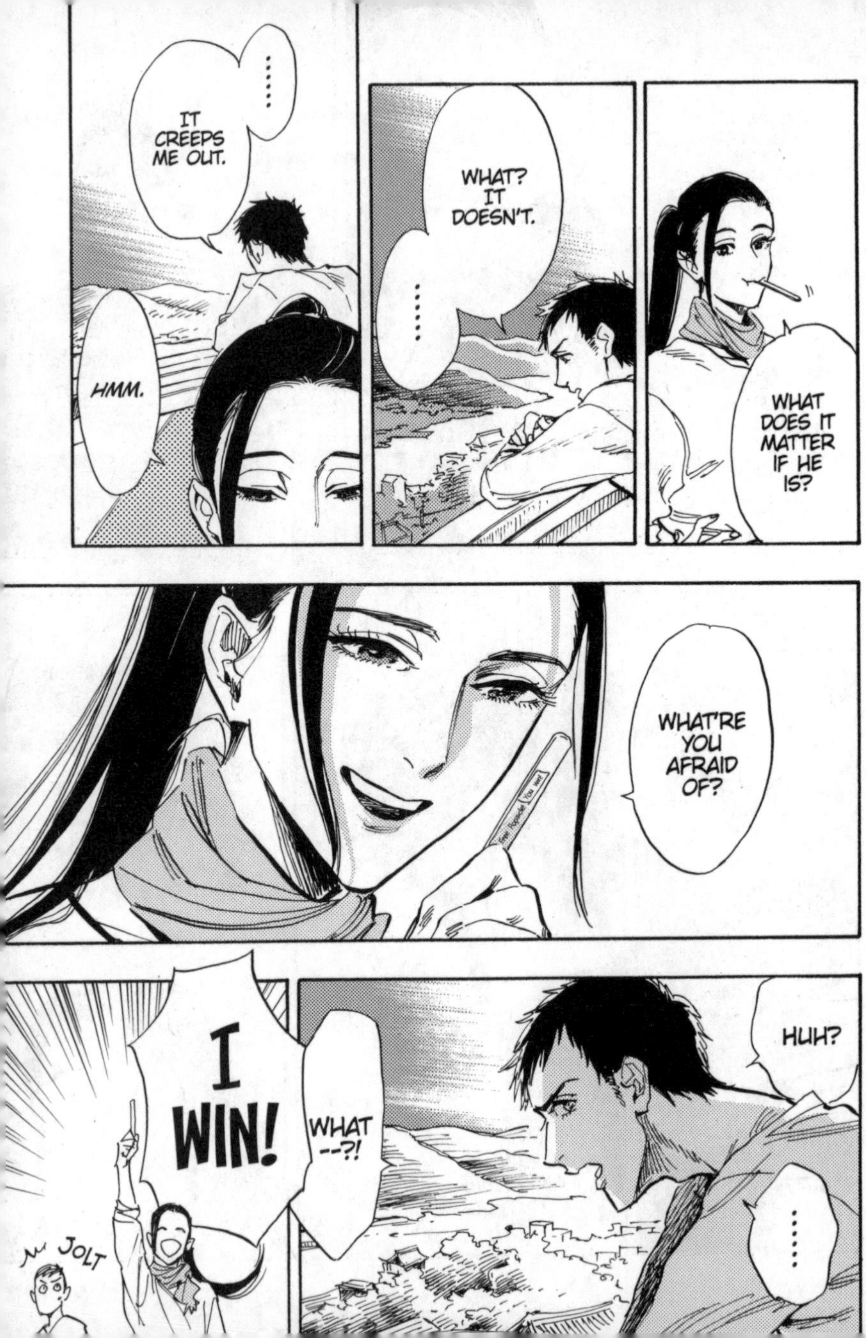
WHAT DOES IT MATTER IF HE IS?
WHAT? IT DOESN'T.
......
......
IT CREEPS ME OUT.
HMM.
WHAT'RE YOU AFRAID OF?
HUH?
......
I WIN!
WHAT --?!
JOLT

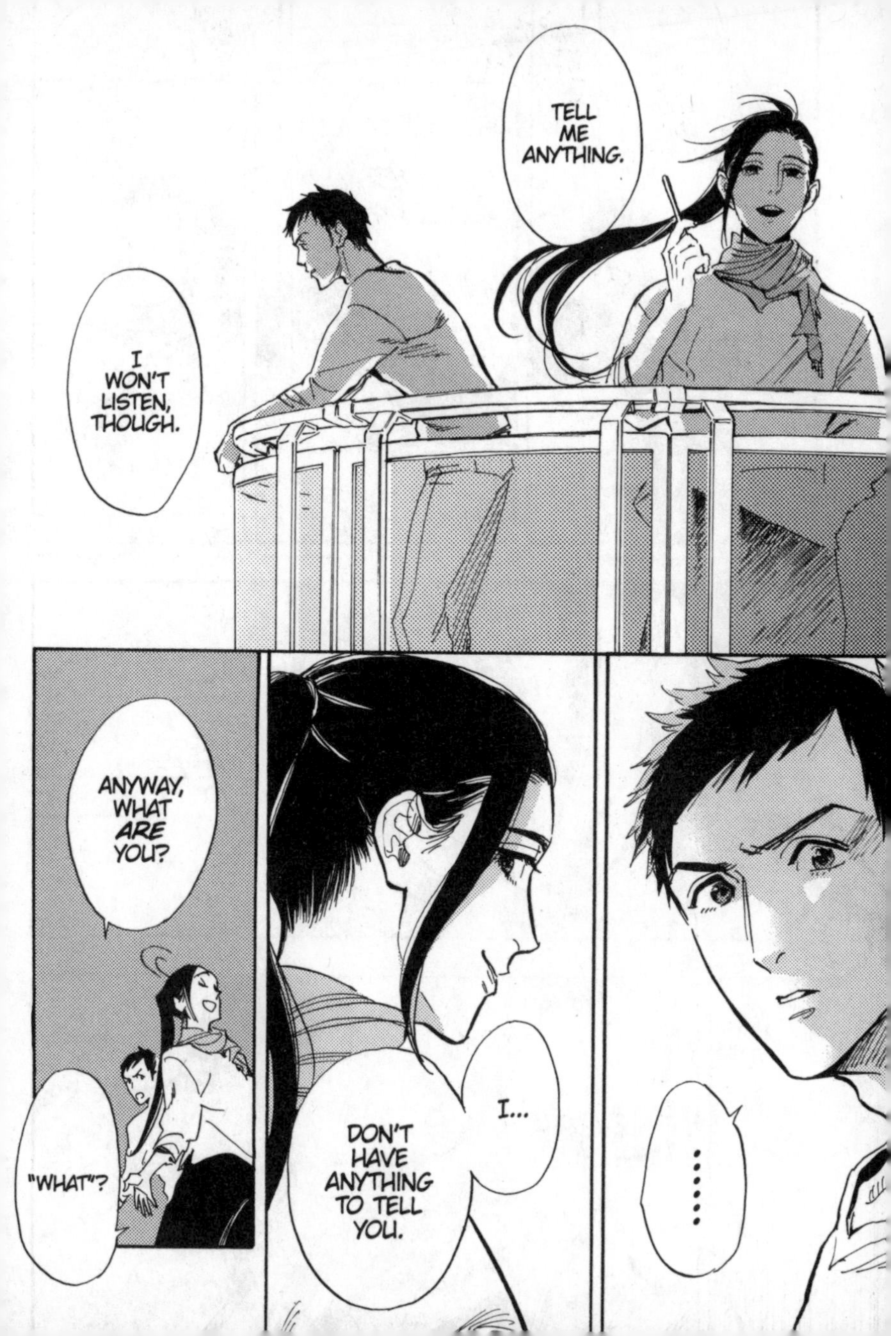
TELL ME ANYTHING.
I WON'T LISTEN, THOUGH.
......
I...
DON'T HAVE ANYTHING TO TELL YOU.
ANYWAY, WHAT *ARE* YOU?
"WHAT"?

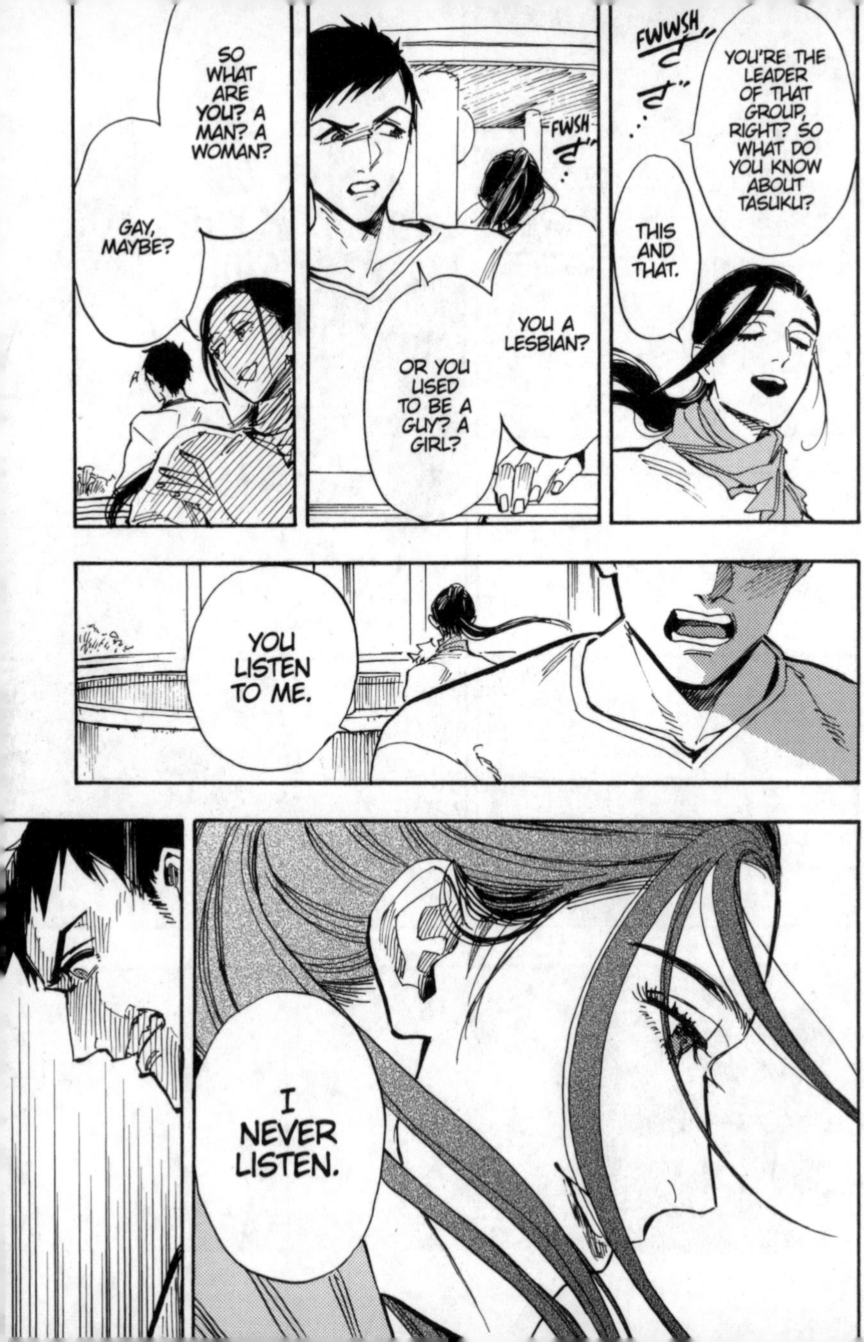
FWWSH
YOU'RE THE LEADER OF THAT GROUP, RIGHT? SO WHAT DO YOU KNOW ABOUT TASUKU?
THIS AND THAT.
FWSH
YOU A LESBIAN?
OR YOU USED TO BE A GUY? A GIRL?
SO WHAT ARE YOU? A MAN? A WOMAN?
GAY, MAYBE?
YOU LISTEN TO ME.
I NEVER LISTEN.

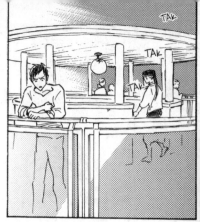

TAK

TAK

TAK

THEN
KEEP
YOUR
MOUTH
SHUT!!

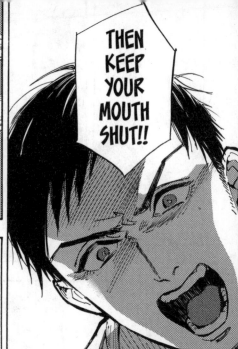

TAK

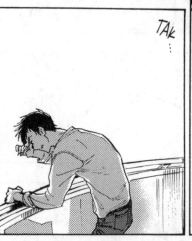

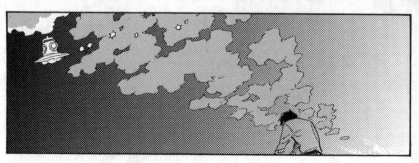

Our Dreams at Dusk

SHIMANAMI TASOGARE

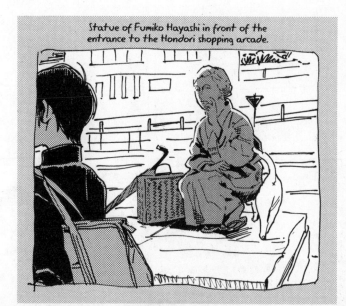

Statue of Fumiko Hayashi in front of the entrance to the Hondori shopping arcade.

Chapter 15

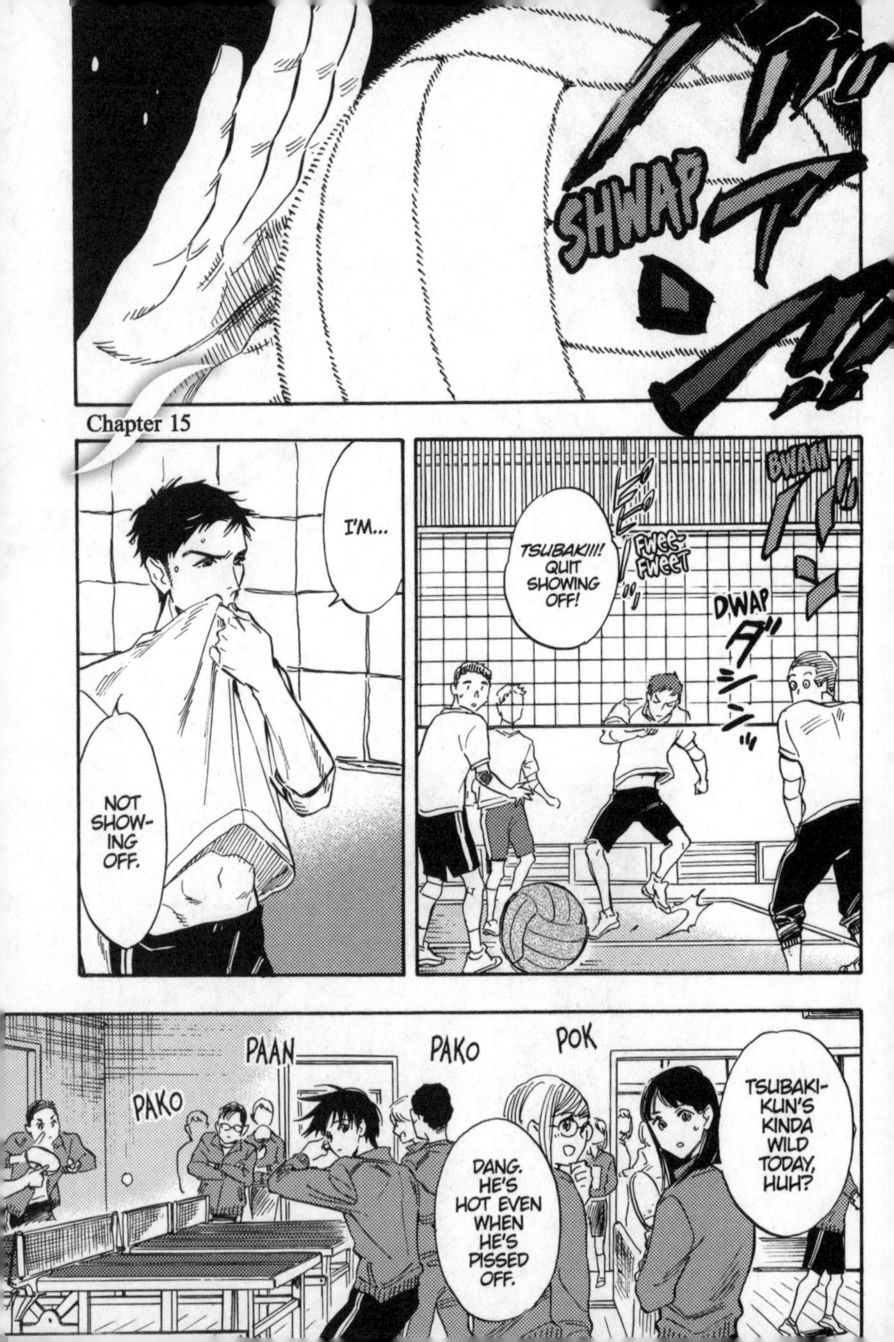
SHWAP
BWAM
TSUBAKIII! QUIT SHOWING OFF!
FWEE-FWEET
DWAP
I'M...
NOT SHOWING-ING OFF.
TSUBAKI-KUN'S KINDA WILD TODAY, HUH?
DANG. HE'S HOT EVEN WHEN HE'S PISSED OFF.
POK
PAKO
PAAN
PAKO

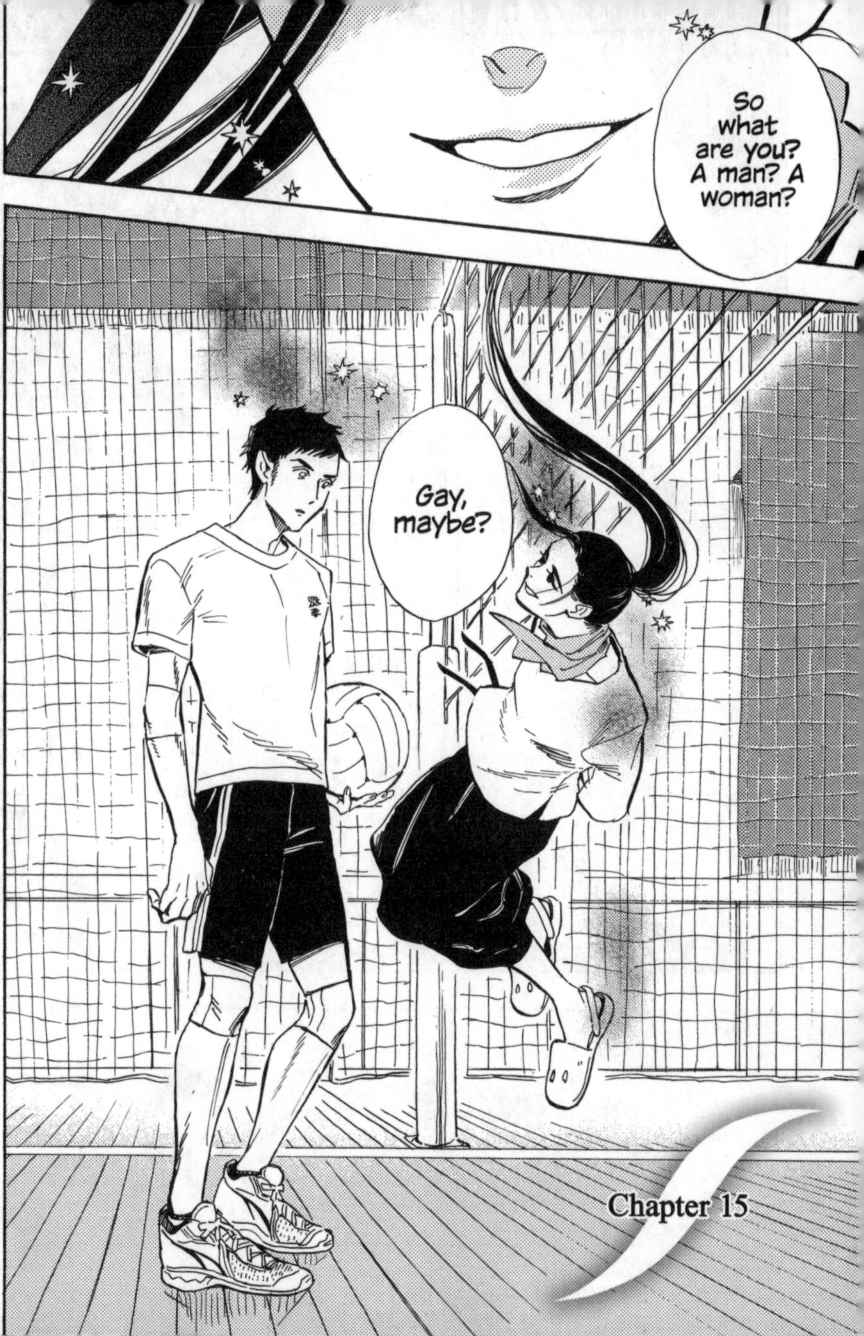
So what are you? A man? A woman?
Gay, maybe?
Chapter 15

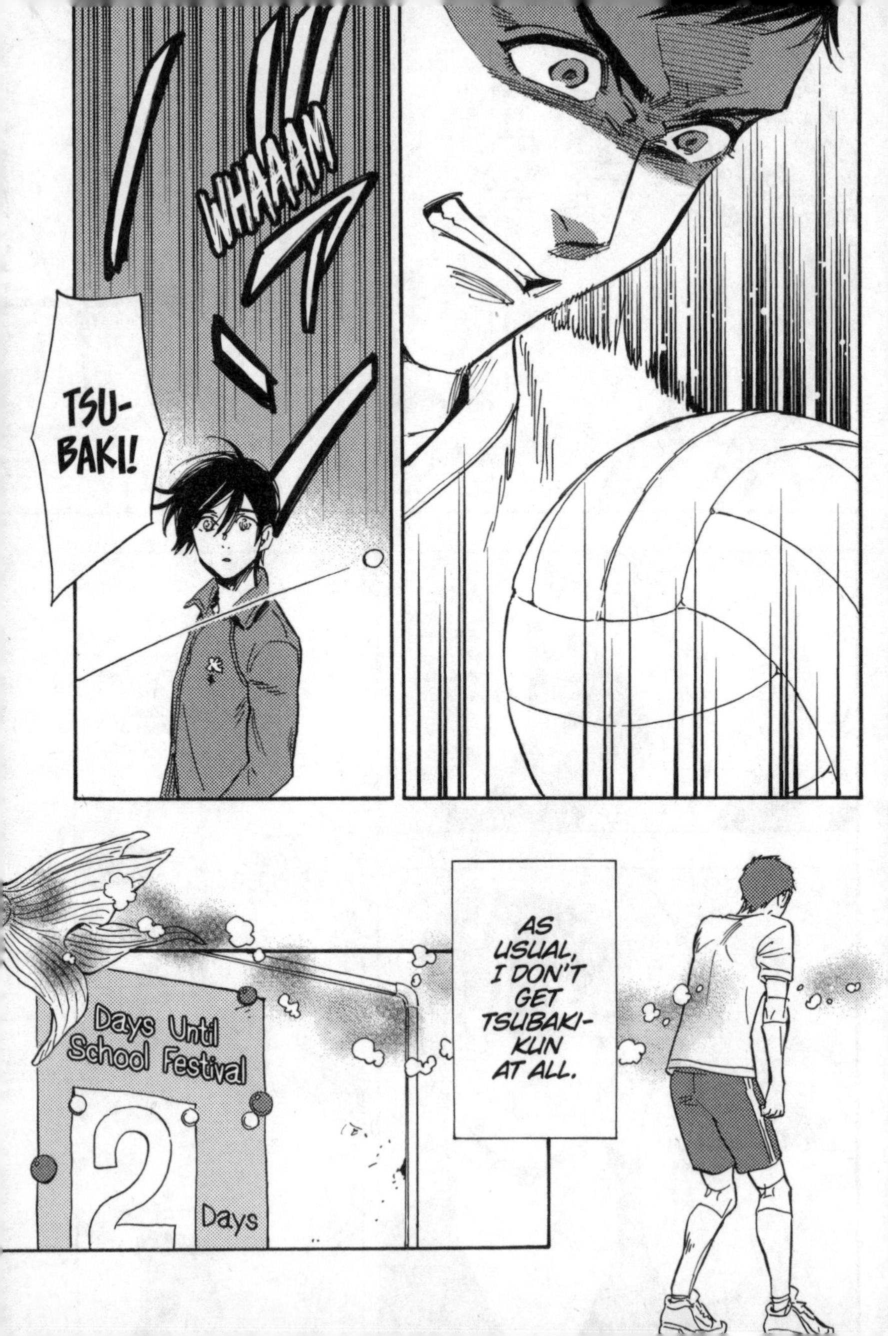
WHAAAM
TSU-BAKI!
AS USUAL, I DON'T GET TSUBAKI-KUN AT ALL.
Days Until School Festival
2 Days

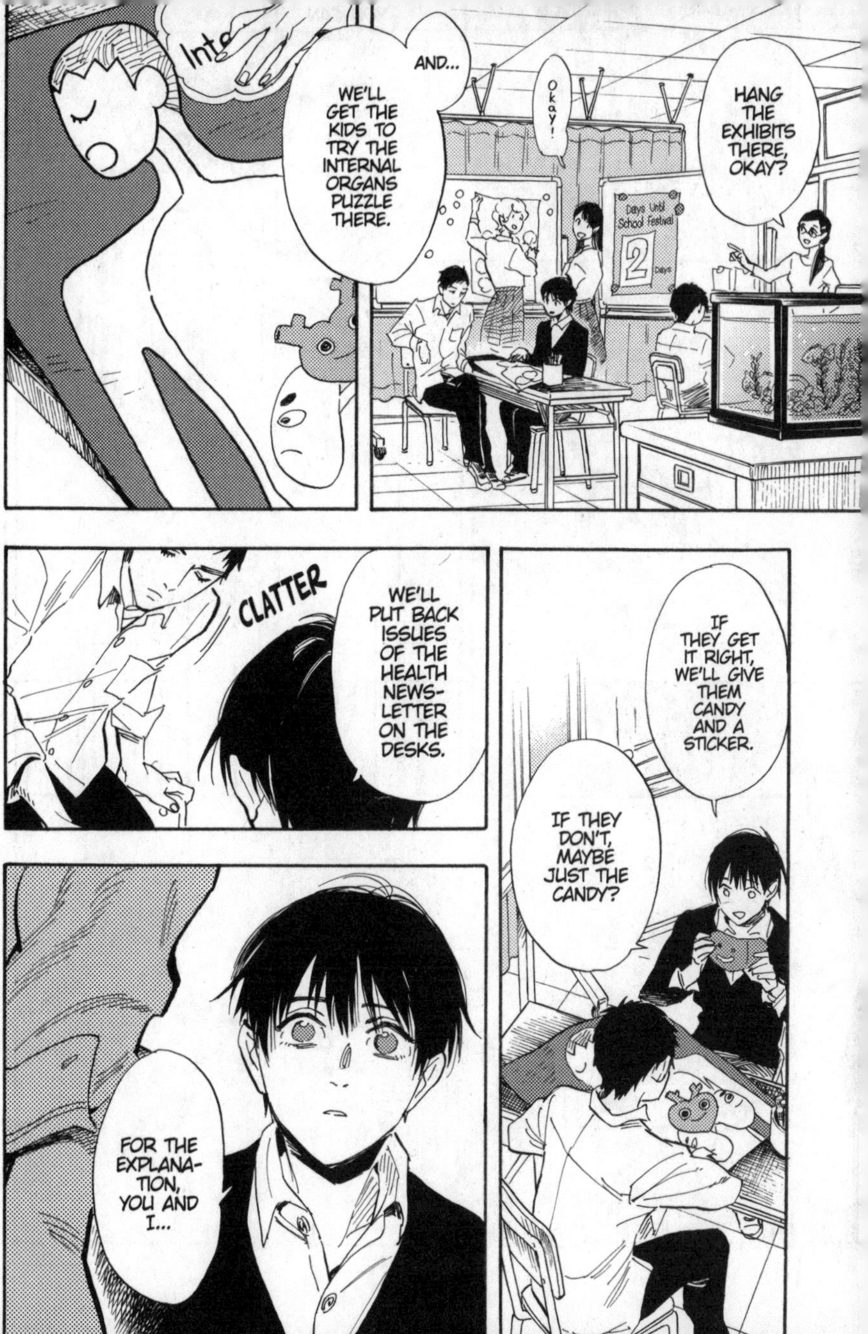
HANG THE EXHIBITS THERE, OKAY?
Okay!
Days Until School Festival
2
Days
AND...
WE'LL GET THE KIDS TO TRY THE INTERNAL ORGANS PUZZLE THERE.
Inte
IF THEY GET IT RIGHT, WE'LL GIVE THEM CANDY AND A STICKER.
IF THEY DON'T, MAYBE JUST THE CANDY?
WE'LL PUT BACK ISSUES OF THE HEALTH NEWS-LETTER ON THE DESKS.
CLATTER
FOR THE EXPLANA-TION, YOU AND I...

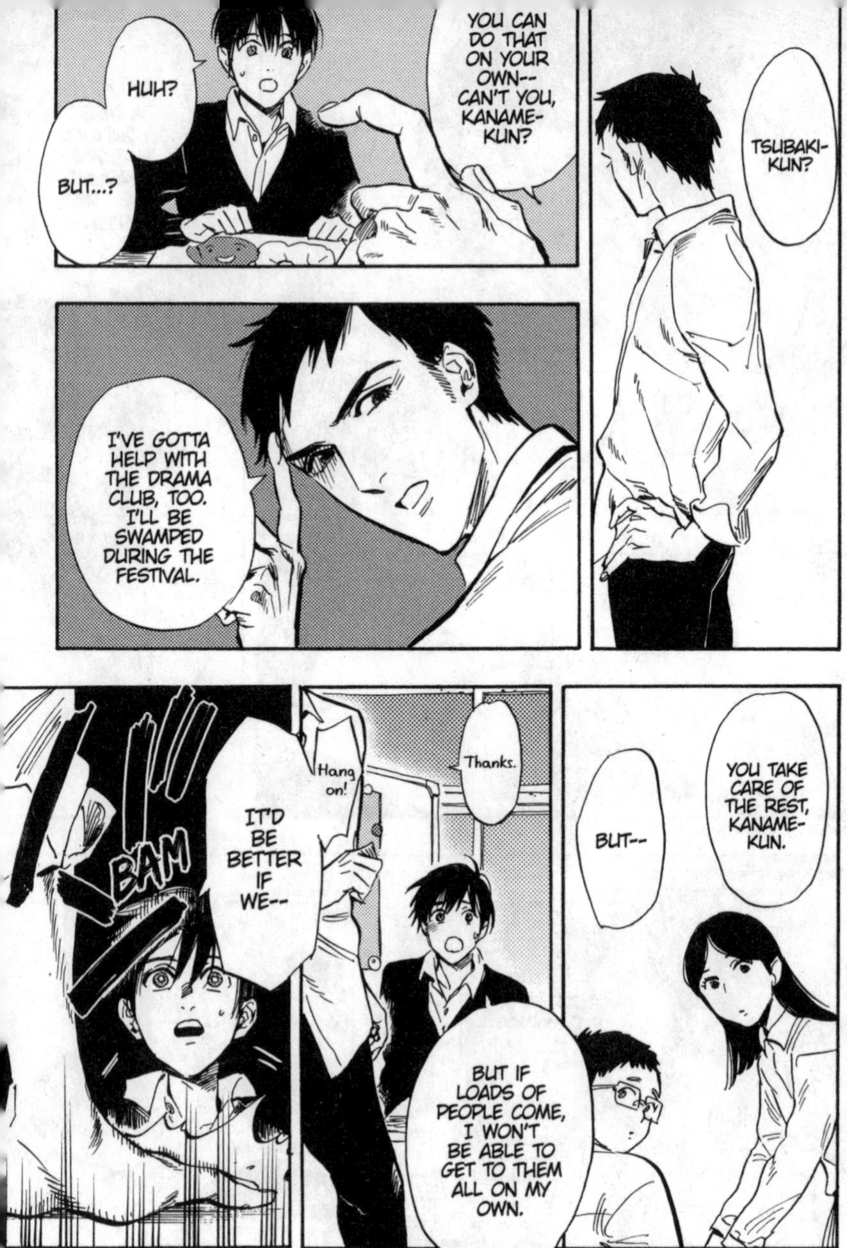
TSUBAKI-KUN?
YOU CAN DO THAT ON YOUR OWN-- CAN'T YOU, KANAME-KUN?
HUH?
BUT...?
I'VE GOTTA HELP WITH THE DRAMA CLUB, TOO. I'LL BE SWAMPED DURING THE FESTIVAL.
YOU TAKE CARE OF THE REST, KANAME-KUN.
BUT--
BUT IF LOADS OF PEOPLE COME, I WON'T BE ABLE TO GET TO THEM ALL ON MY OWN.
Thanks.
Hang on!
IT'D BE BETTER IF WE--
BAM

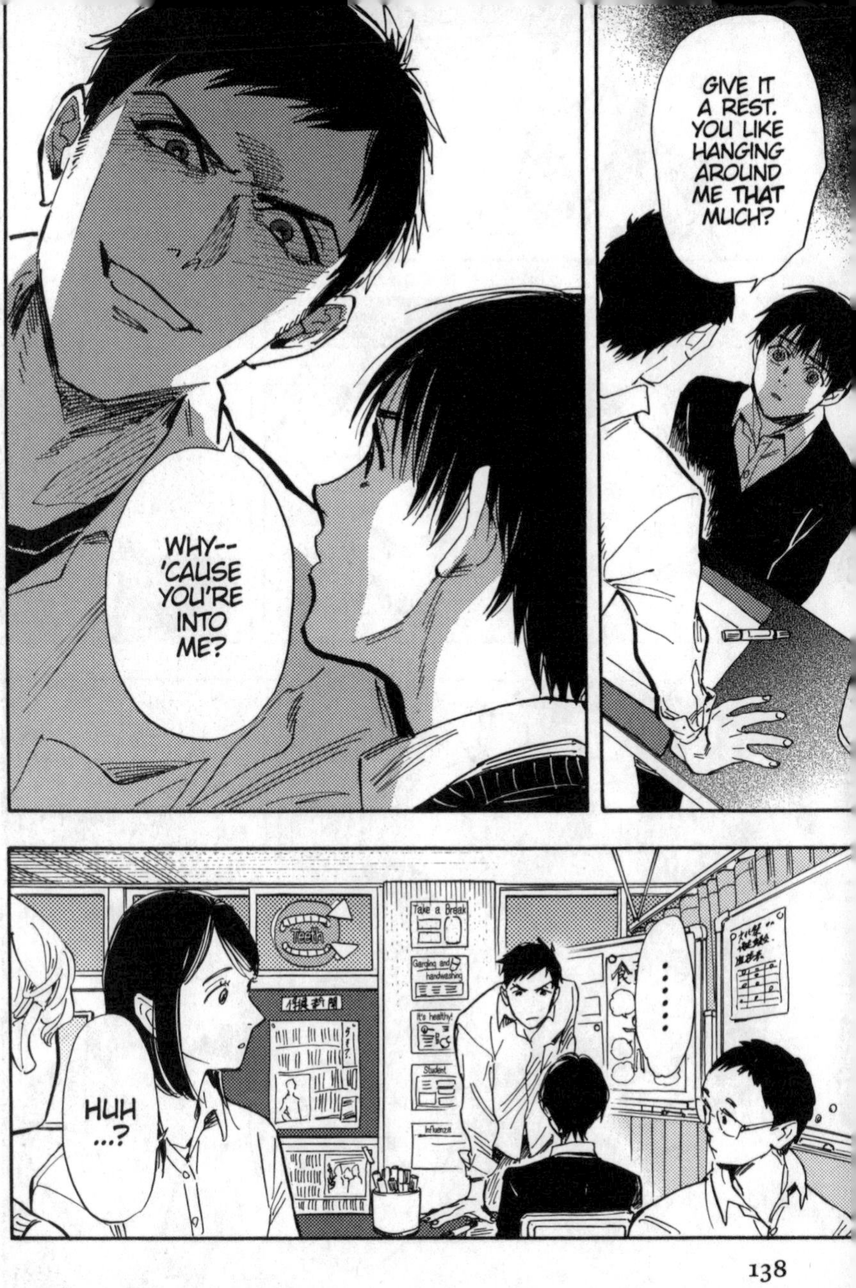
GIVE IT A REST. YOU LIKE HANGING AROUND ME THAT MUCH?
WHY-- 'CAUSE YOU'RE INTO ME?
Take a Break
Teeth
Gargling and handwashing
It's healthy!
Student
Influenza
......
HUH ...?

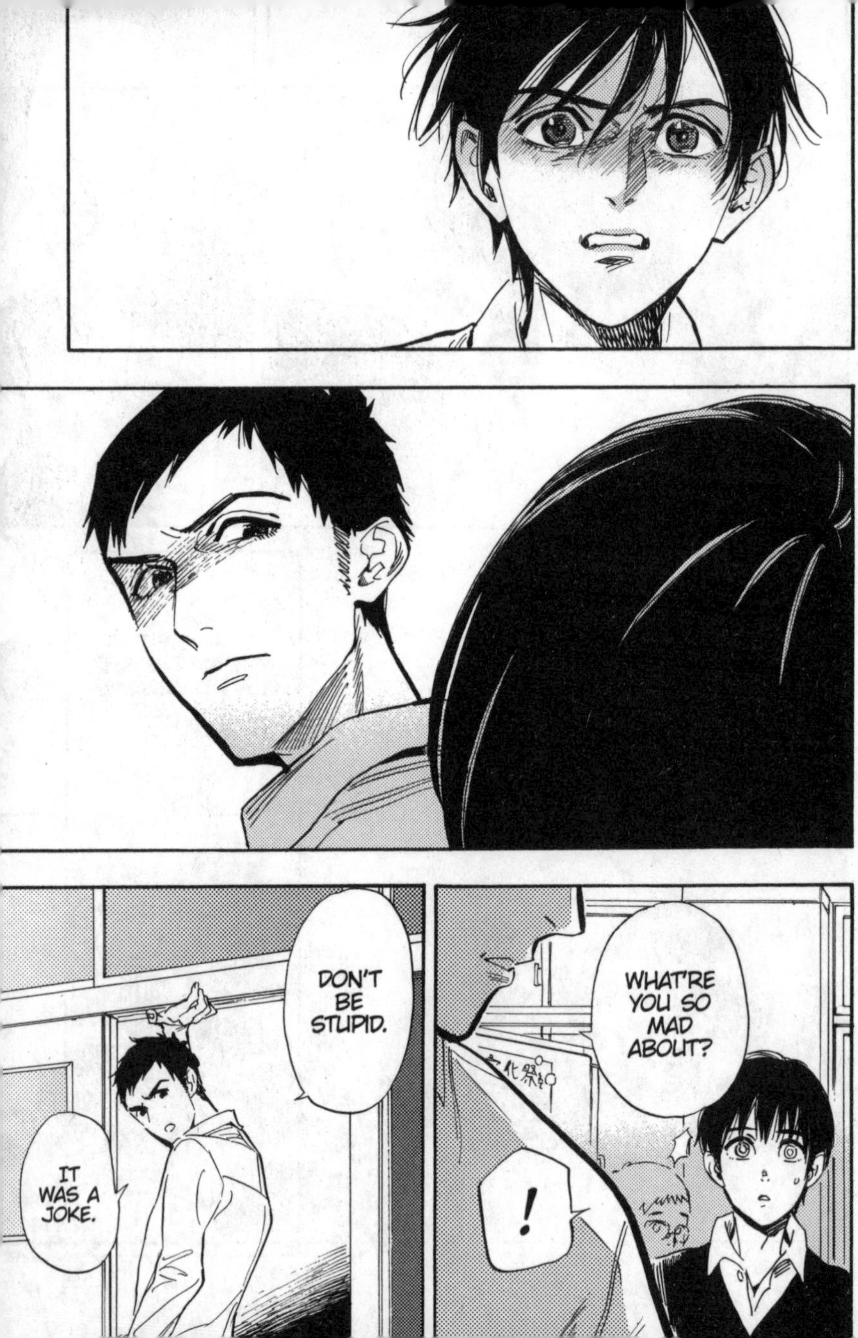
WHAT'RE YOU SO MAD ABOUT?
!
DON'T BE STUPID.
IT WAS A JOKE.

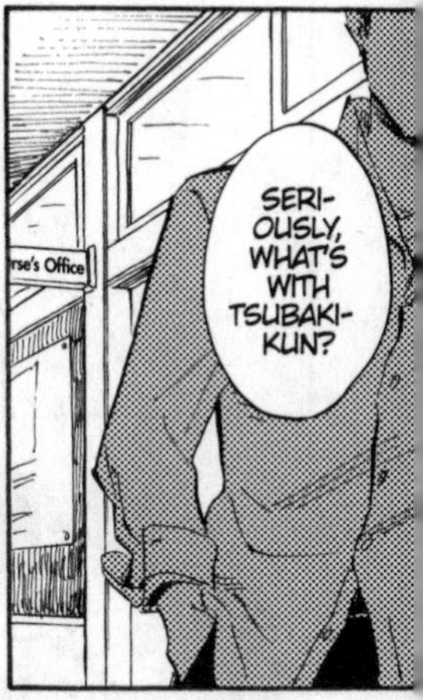
SERIOUSLY, WHAT'S WITH TSUBAKI-KUN?
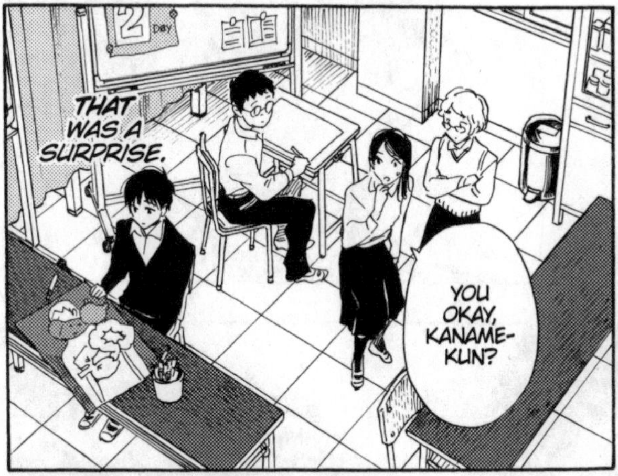
2 Day
THAT WAS A SURPRISE.
YOU OKAY, KANAME-KUN?
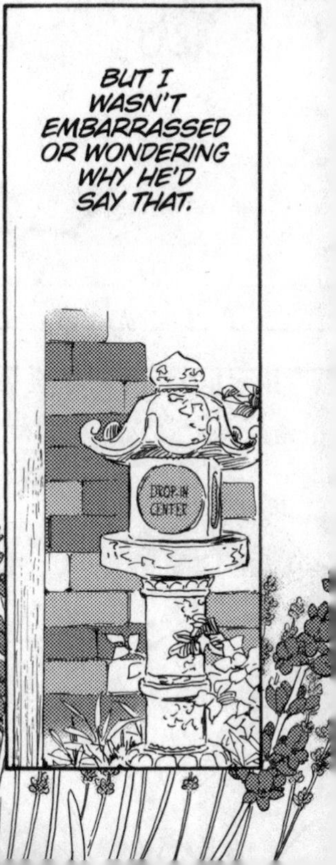
BUT I WASN'T EMBARRASSED OR WONDERING WHY HE'D SAY THAT.
DROP-IN CENTER
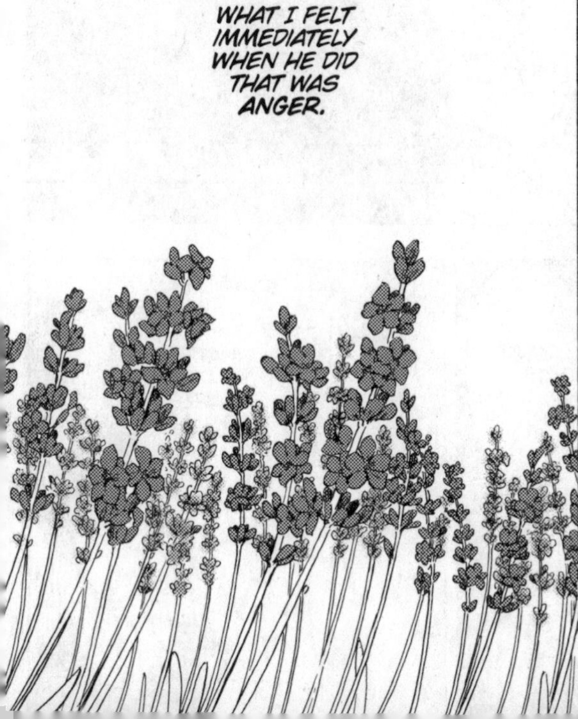
WHAT I FELT IMMEDIATELY WHEN HE DID THAT WAS ANGER.

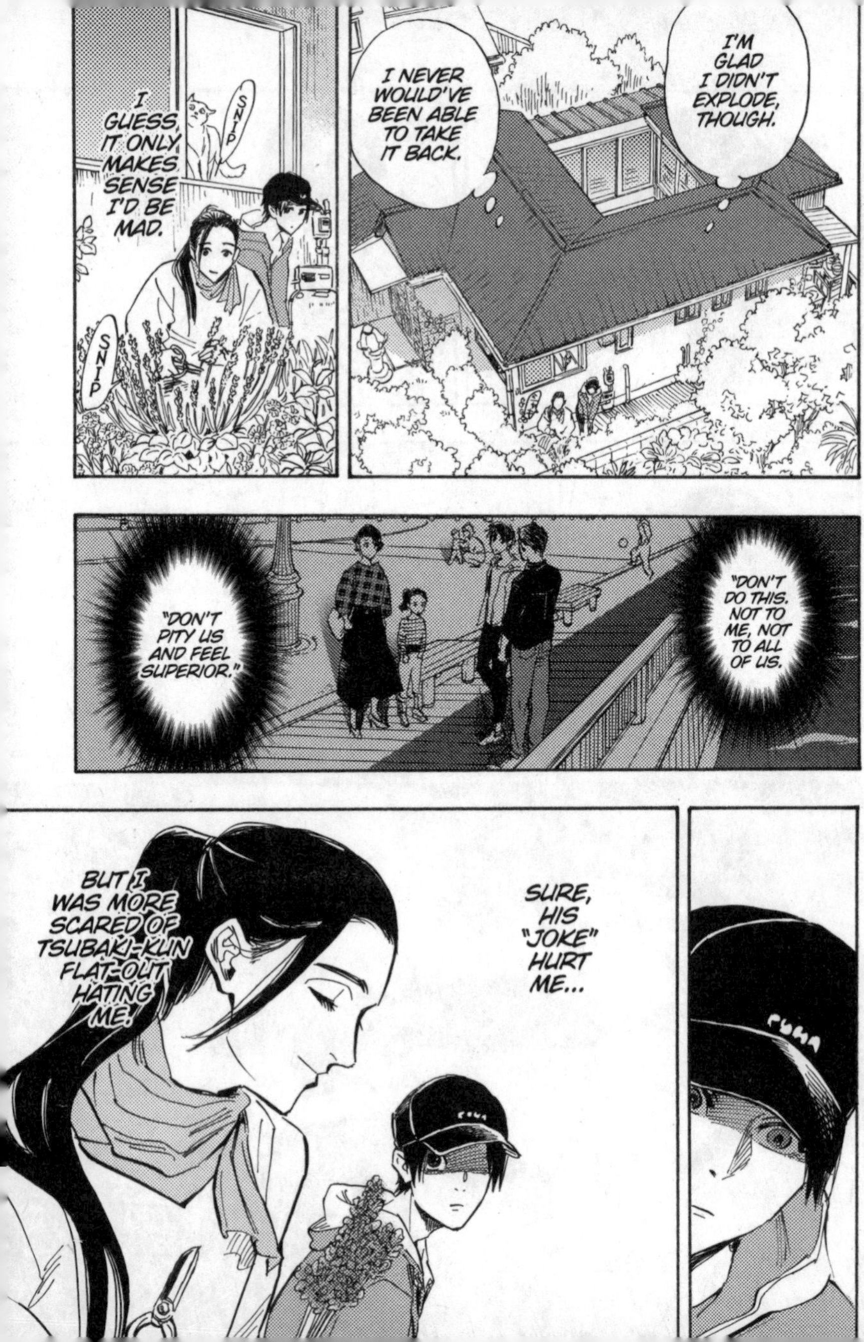
I'M GLAD I DIDN'T EXPLODE, THOUGH.
I NEVER WOULD'VE BEEN ABLE TO TAKE IT BACK.
SNIP
I GUESS, IT ONLY MAKES SENSE I'D BE MAD.
SNIP
"DON'T DO THIS. NOT TO ME, NOT TO ALL OF US.
"DON'T PITY US AND FEEL SUPERIOR."
PUMA
SURE, HIS "JOKE" HURT ME...
BUT I WAS MORE SCARED OF TSUBAKI-KUN FLAT-OUT HATING ME.

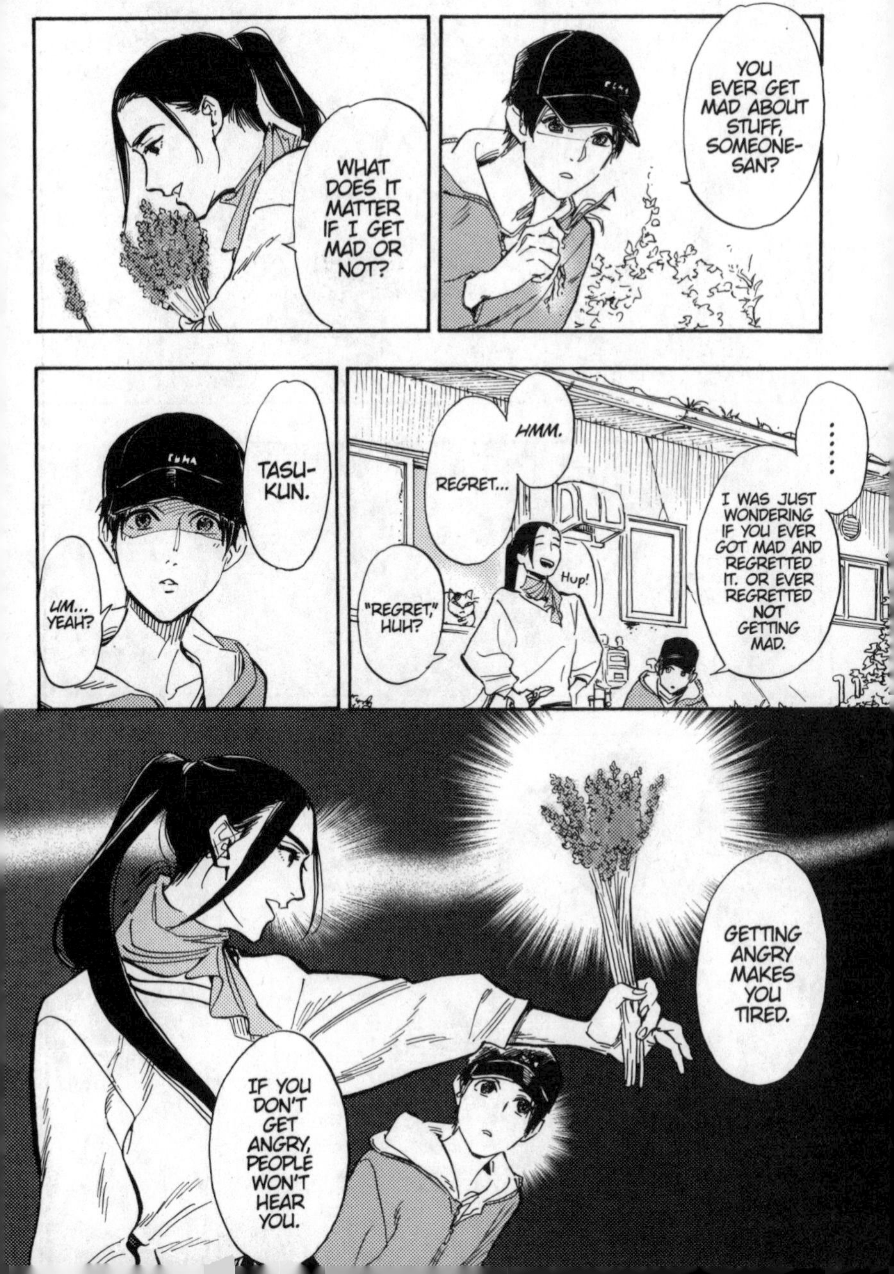
YOU EVER GET MAD ABOUT STUFF, SOMEONE-SAN?
WHAT DOES IT MATTER IF I GET MAD OR NOT?
......
I WAS JUST WONDERING IF YOU EVER GOT MAD AND REGRETTED IT. OR EVER REGRETTED NOT GETTING MAD.
HMM.
REGRET...
Hup!
"REGRET," HUH?
TASU-KUN.
UM... YEAH?
GETTING ANGRY MAKES YOU TIRED.
IF YOU DON'T GET ANGRY, PEOPLE WON'T HEAR YOU.

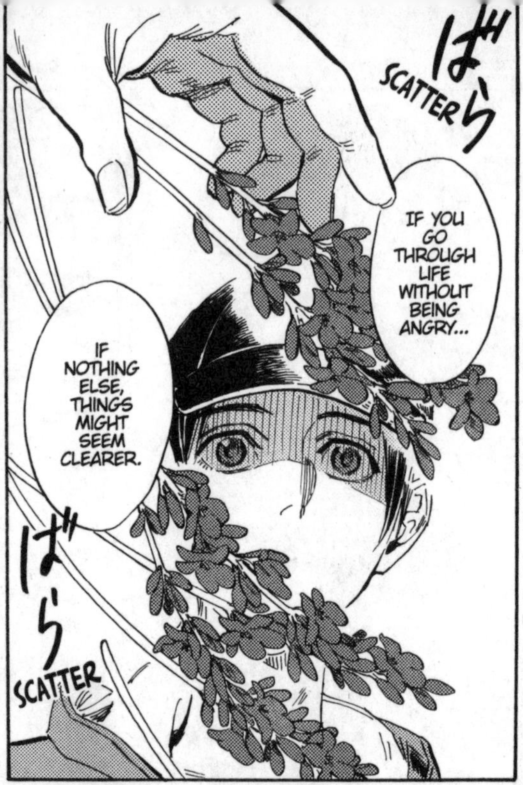
ばら
SCATTER
IF YOU GO THROUGH LIFE WITHOUT BEING ANGRY...
IF NOTHING ELSE, THINGS MIGHT SEEM CLEARER.
ばら
SCATTER

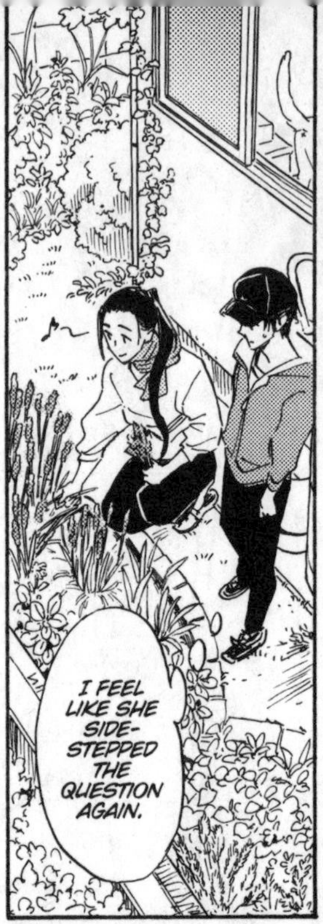
I FEEL LIKE SHE SIDE-STEPPED THE QUESTION AGAIN.

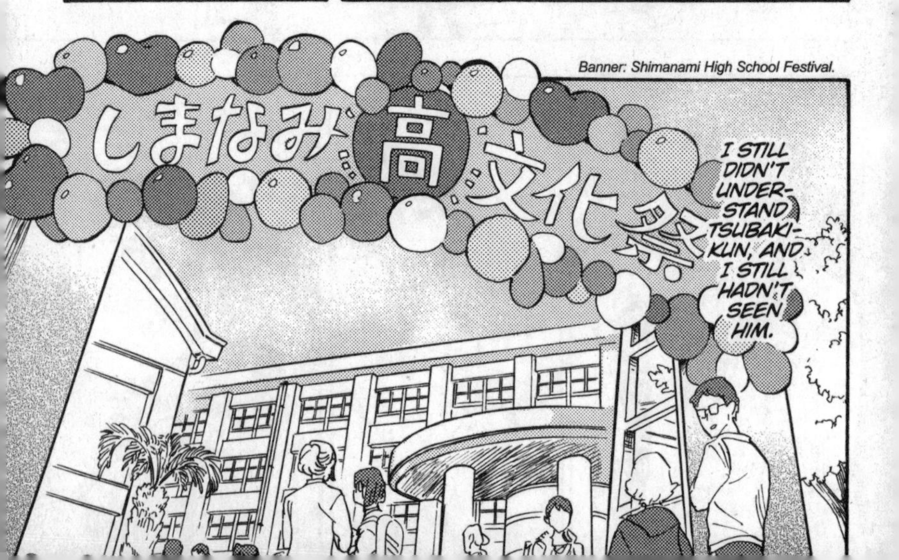
しまなみ高文化祭
I STILL DIDN'T UNDER-STAND TSUBAKI-KUN, AND I STILL HADN'T SEEN HIM.

Banner: Shimanami High School Festival.

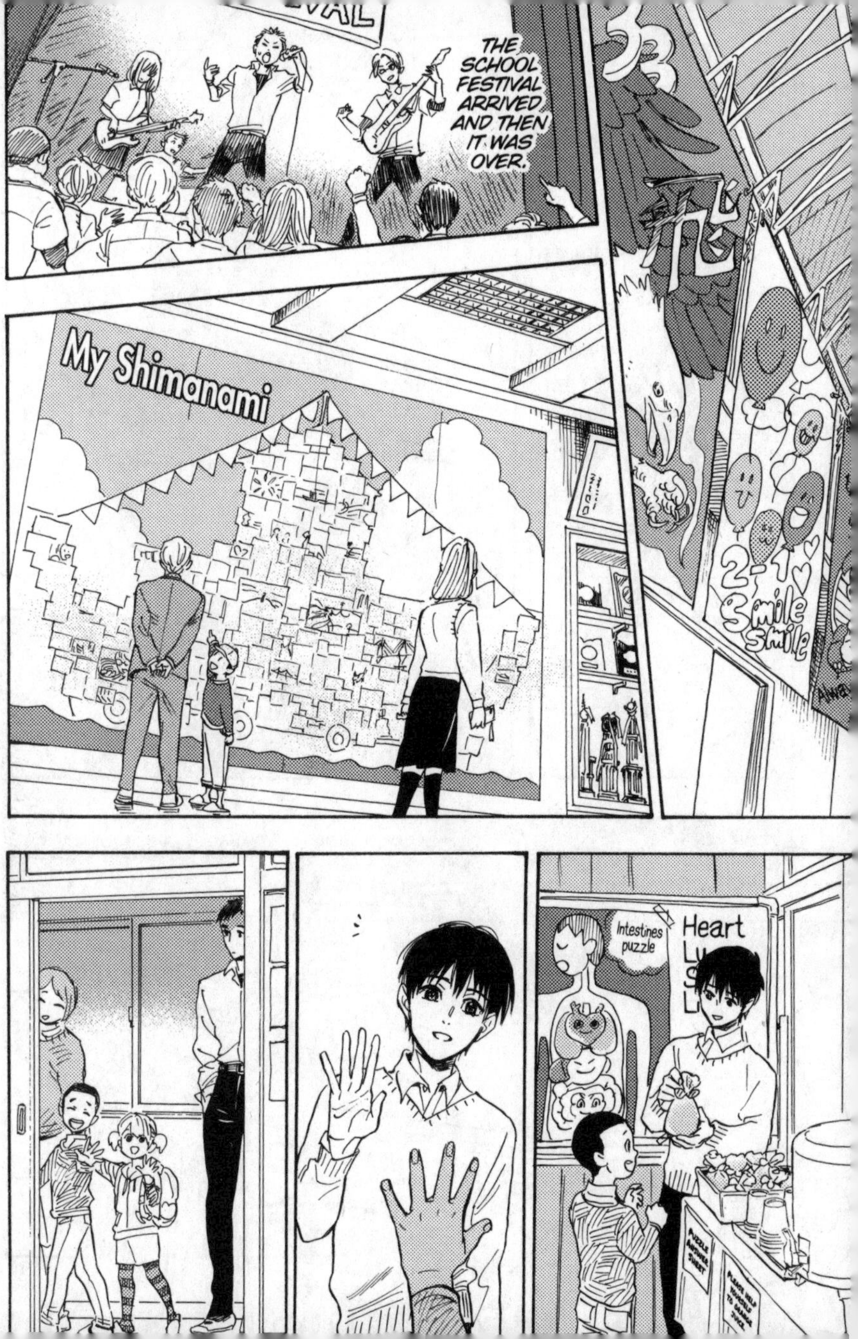

2-1 Smile Smile
THE SCHOOL FESTIVAL ARRIVED AND THEN IT WAS OVER.
My Shimanami
Intestines puzzle
Heart

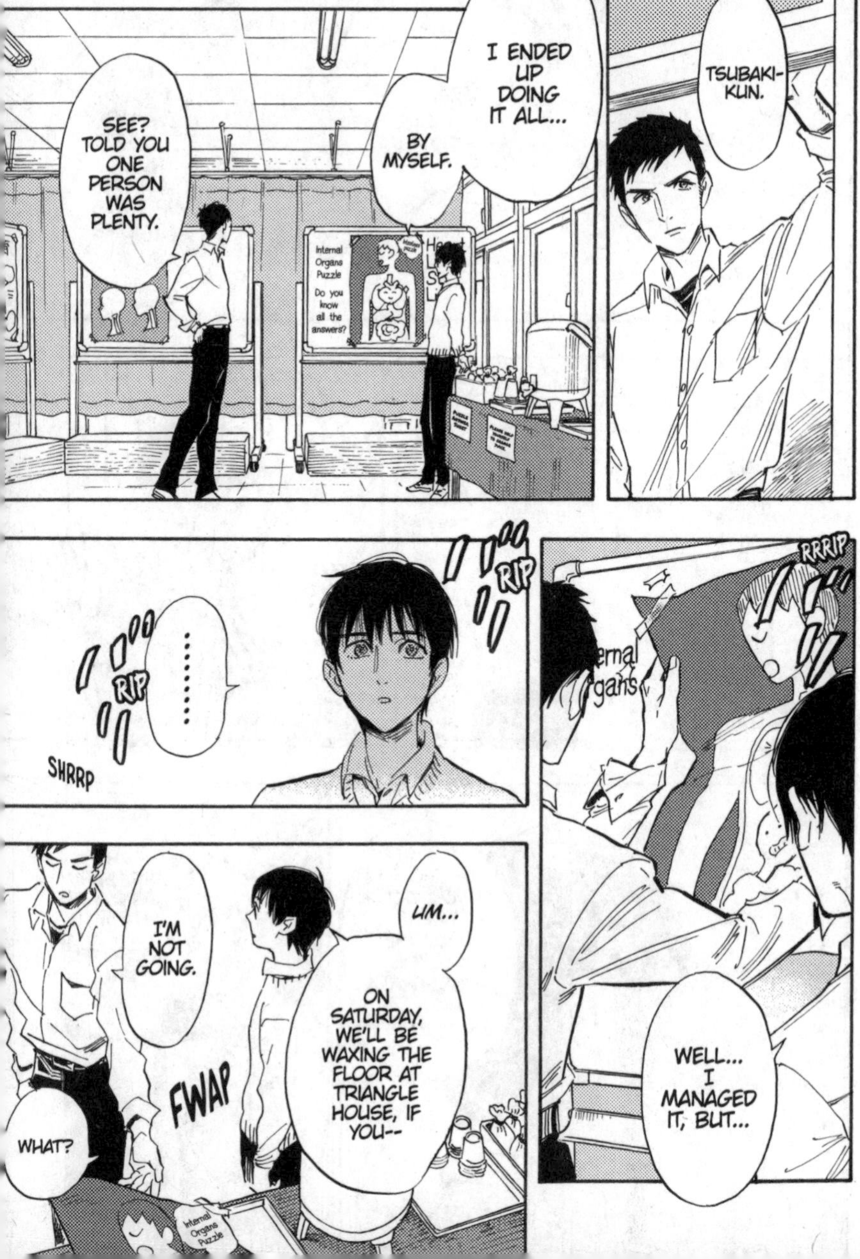
TSUBAKI-KUN.
I ENDED UP DOING IT ALL...
BY MYSELF.
SEE? TOLD YOU ONE PERSON WAS PLENTY.
Internal Organs Puzzle
Do you know all the answers?
RRRIP
ernal
gans
WELL... I MANAGED IT, BUT...
RIP
......
RIP
SHRRP
UM...
ON SATURDAY, WE'LL BE WAXING THE FLOOR AT TRIANGLE HOUSE, IF YOU--
I'M NOT GOING.
FWAP
WHAT?
Internal Organs Puzzle

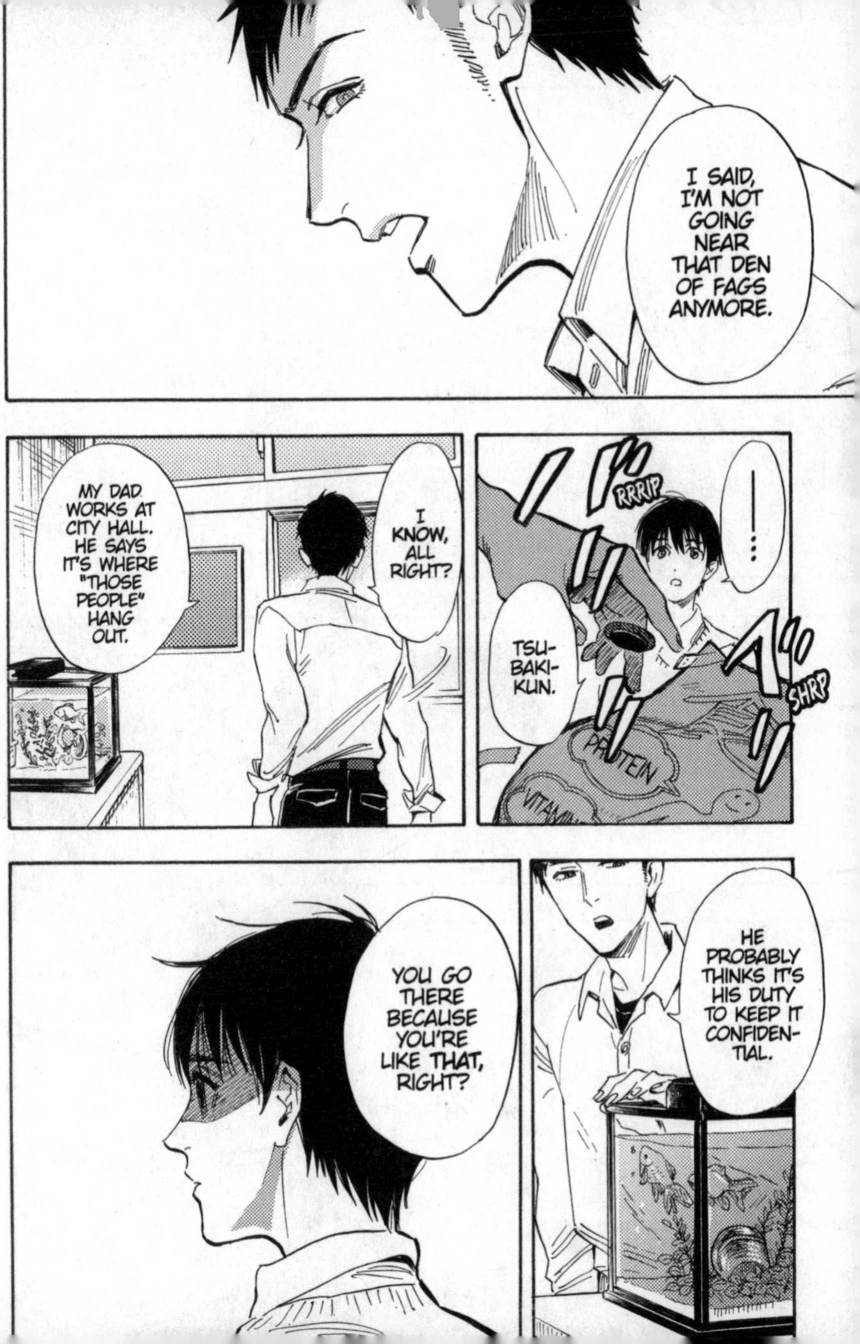
I SAID, I'M NOT GOING NEAR THAT DEN OF FAGS ANYMORE.
!...
RRRIP
SHRP
TSU-BAKI-KUN.
PROTEIN
I KNOW, ALL RIGHT?
MY DAD WORKS AT CITY HALL. HE SAYS IT'S WHERE "THOSE PEOPLE" HANG OUT.
HE PROBABLY THINKS IT'S HIS DUTY TO KEEP IT CONFIDEN-TIAL.
YOU GO THERE BECAUSE YOU'RE LIKE THAT, RIGHT?

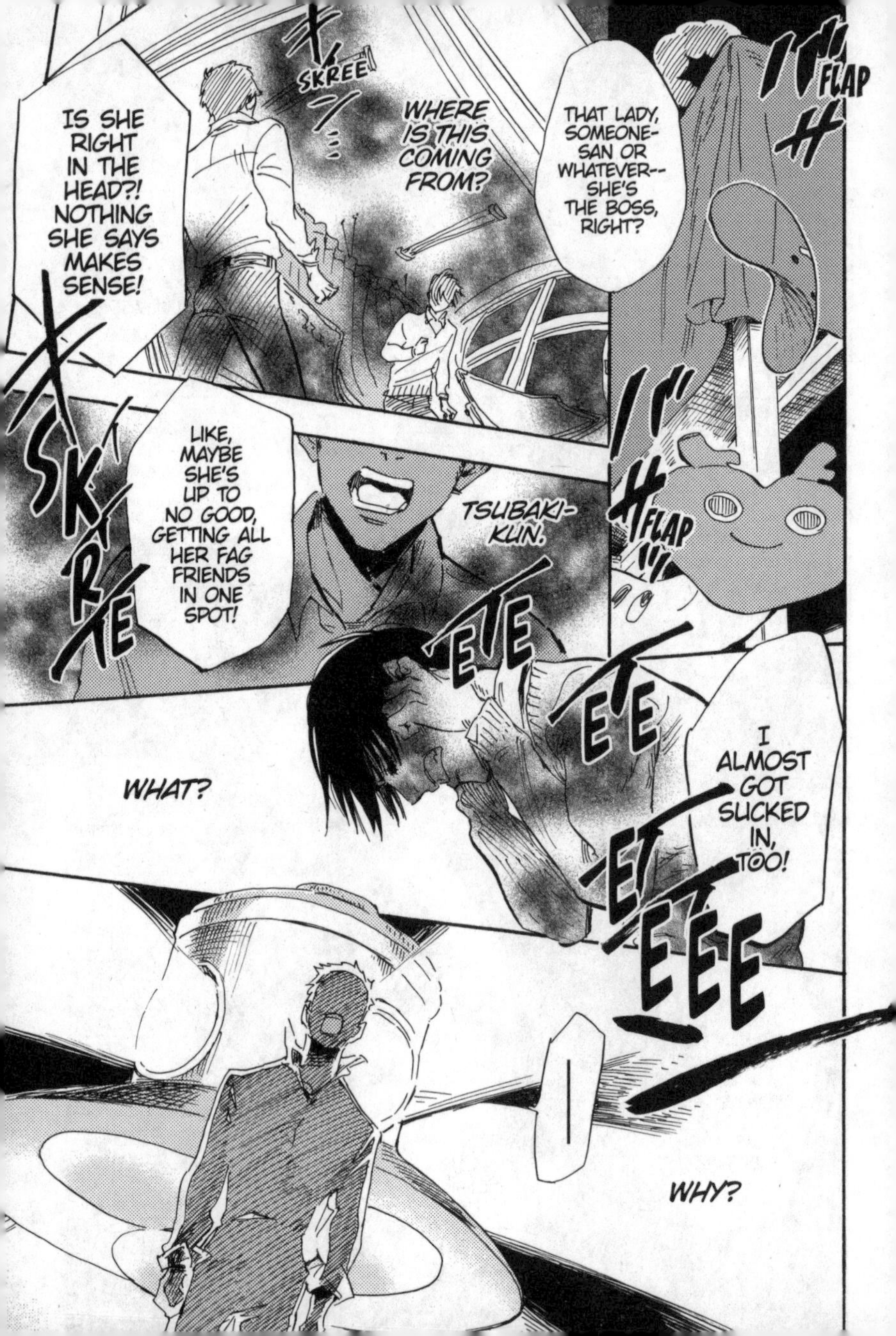
FLAP
THAT LADY, SOMEONE-SAN OR WHATEVER-- SHE'S THE BOSS, RIGHT?
WHERE IS THIS COMING FROM?
SKREE
IS SHE RIGHT IN THE HEAD?! NOTHING SHE SAYS MAKES SENSE!
FLAP
TSUBAKI-KUN.
LIKE, MAYBE SHE'S UP TO NO GOOD, GETTING ALL HER FAG FRIENDS IN ONE SPOT!
I ALMOST GOT SUCKED IN, TOO!
WHAT?
WHY?

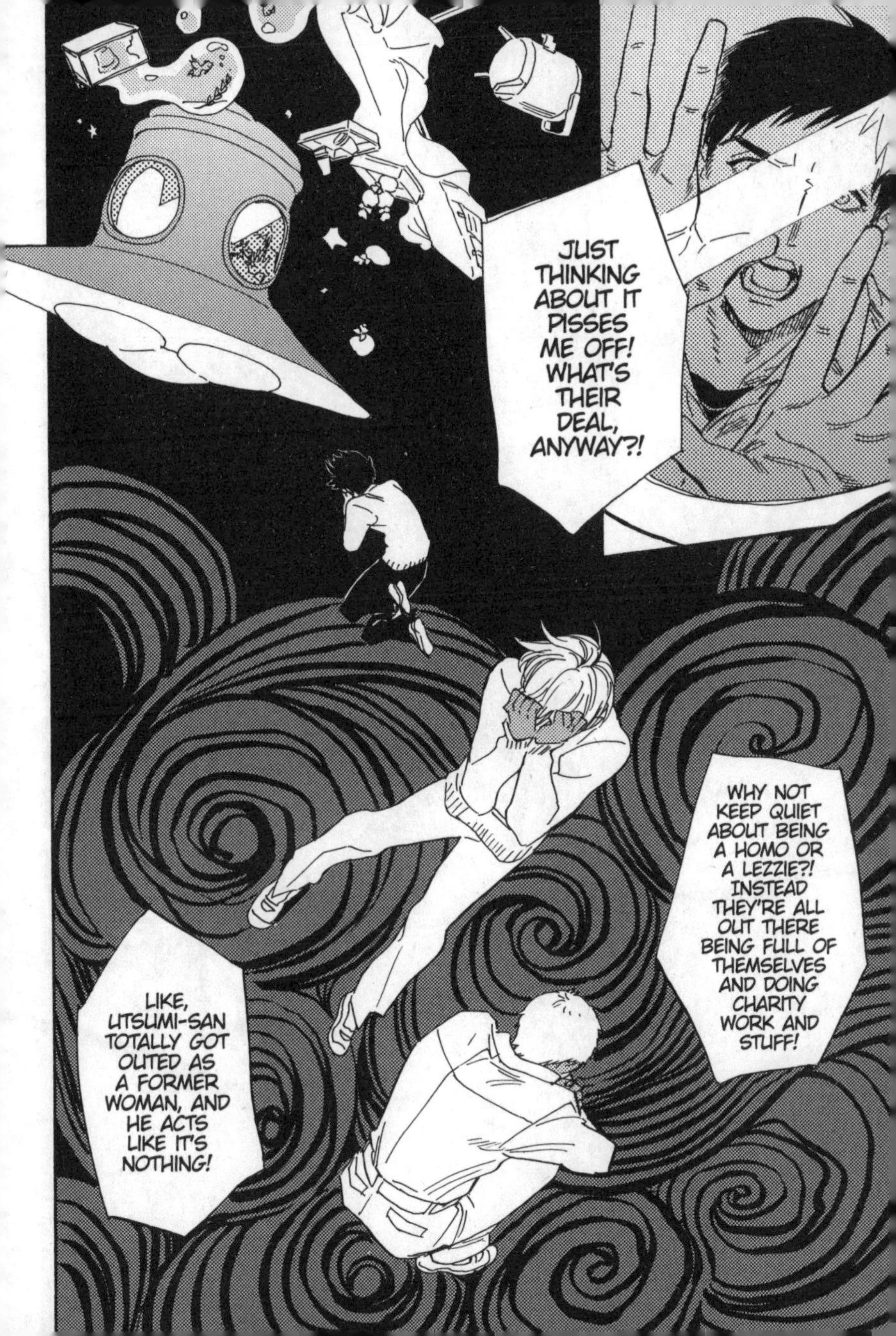
JUST THINKING ABOUT IT PISSES ME OFF! WHAT'S THEIR DEAL, ANYWAY?!
WHY NOT KEEP QUIET ABOUT BEING A HOMO OR A LEZZIE?! INSTEAD THEY'RE ALL OUT THERE BEING FULL OF THEMSELVES AND DOING CHARITY WORK AND STUFF!
LIKE, UTSUMI-SAN TOTALLY GOT OUTED AS A FORMER WOMAN, AND HE ACTS LIKE IT'S NOTHING!

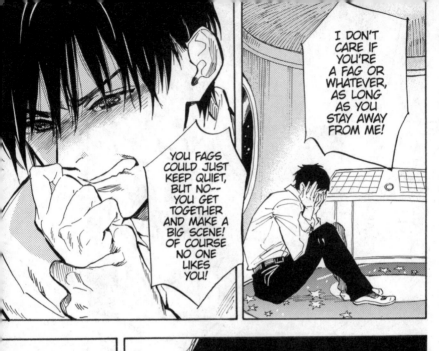

I DON'T CARE IF YOU'RE A FAG OR WHATEVER, AS LONG AS YOU STAY AWAY FROM ME!

YOU FAGS COULD JUST KEEP QUIET, BUT NO-- YOU GET TOGETHER AND MAKE A BIG SCENE! OF COURSE NO ONE LIKES YOU!

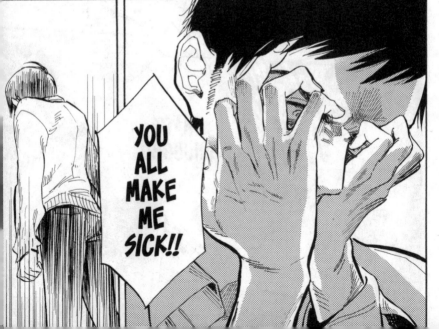

YOU ALL MAKE ME SICK!!

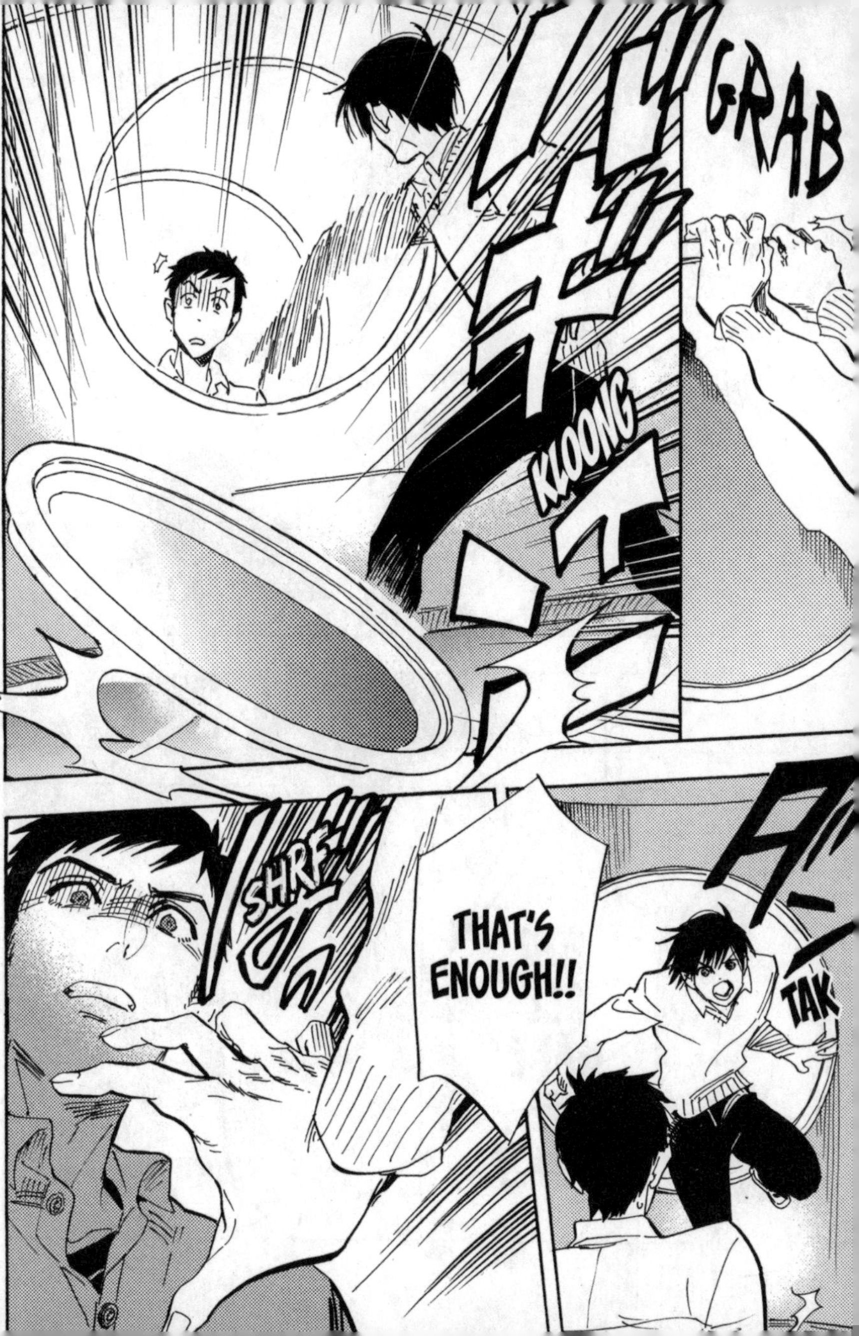
GRAB
KLOONG
TAK
THAT'S ENOUGH!!
SHRF

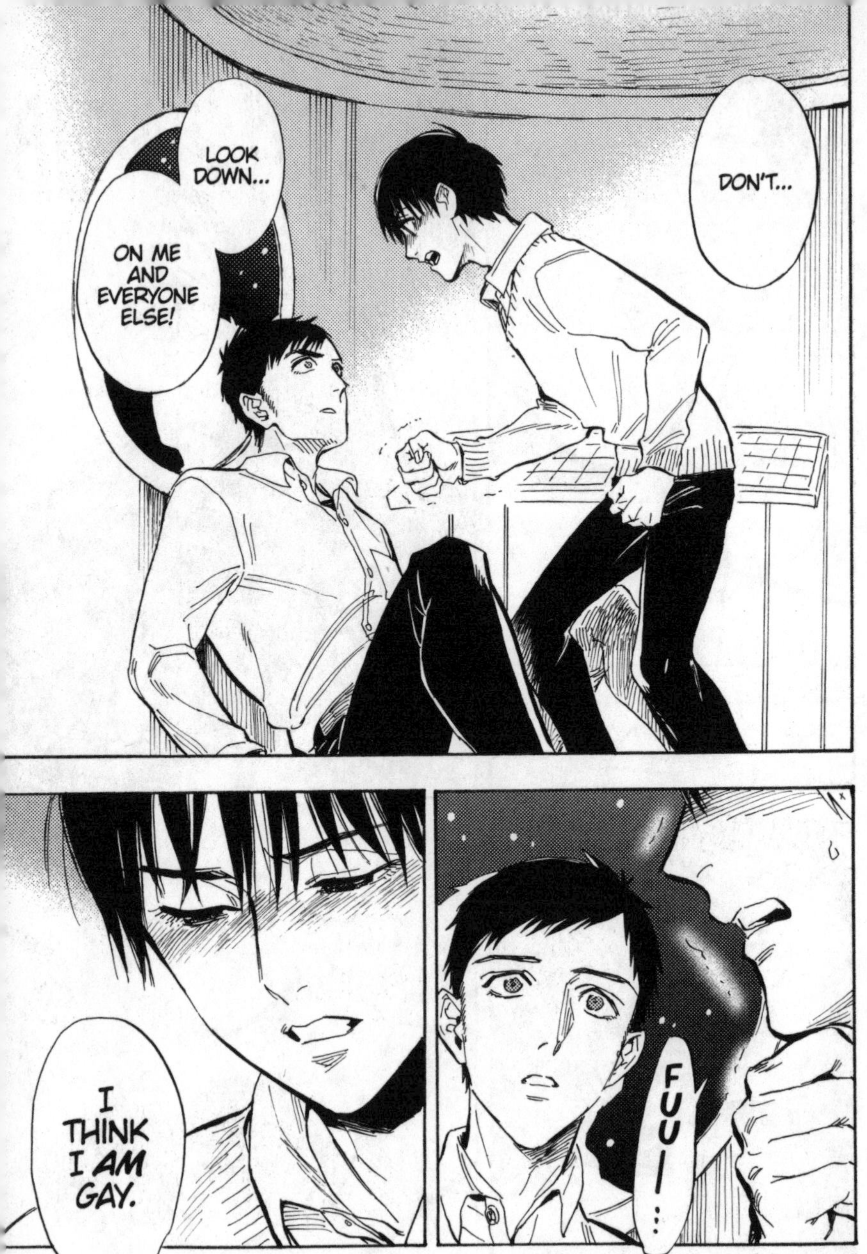
DON'T...
LOOK DOWN...
ON ME AND EVERYONE ELSE!
FUUU-...
I THINK I *AM* GAY.

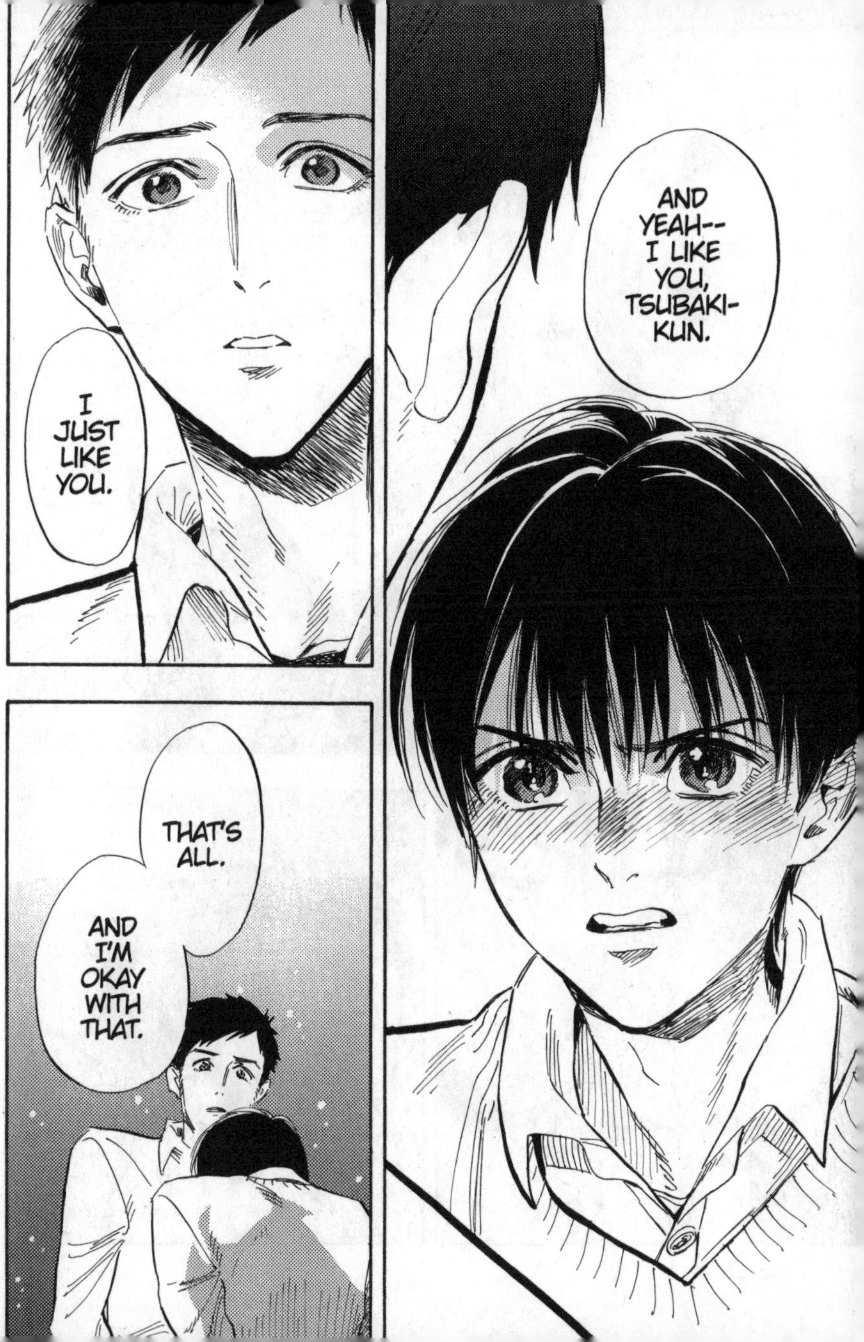
AND YEAH-- I LIKE YOU, TSUBAKI-KUN.
I JUST LIKE YOU.
THAT'S ALL.
AND I'M OKAY WITH THAT.

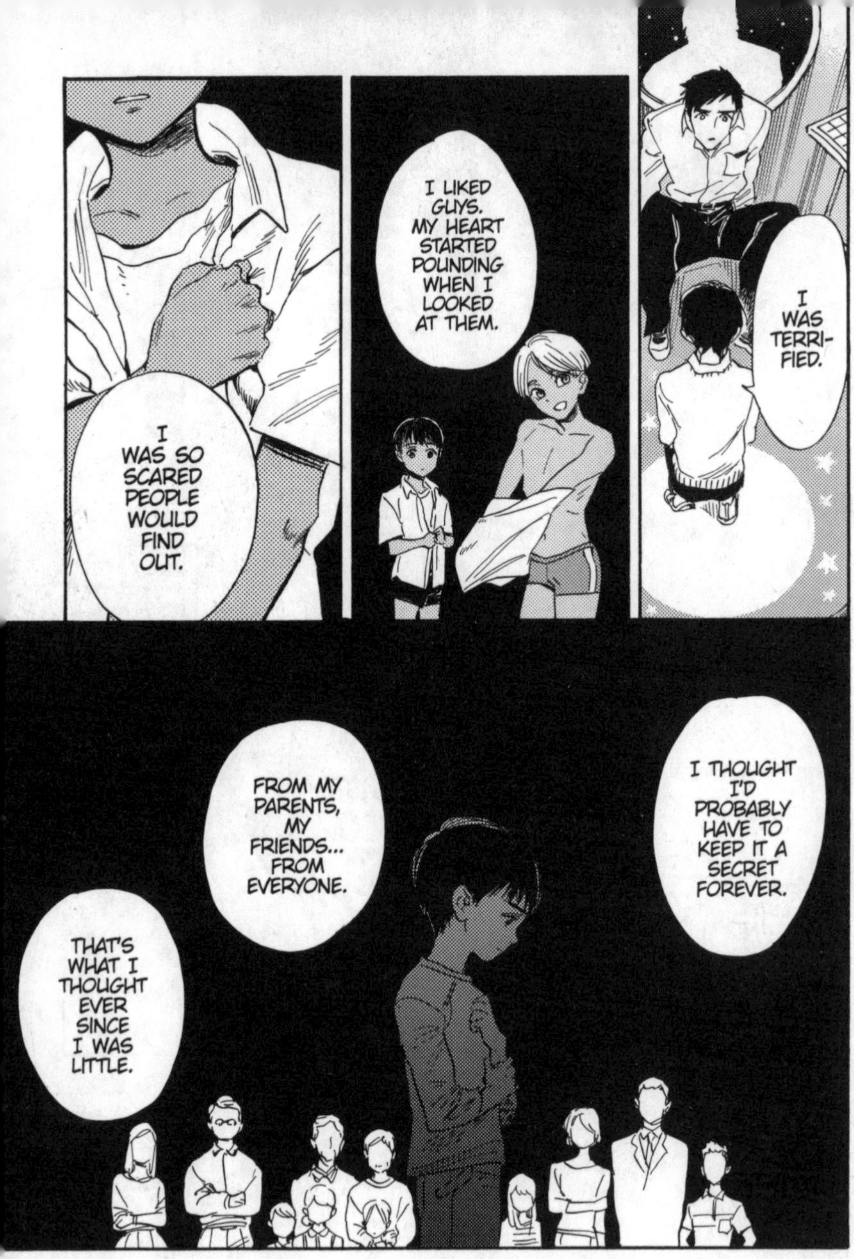
I WAS TERRI-FIED.
I LIKED GUYS. MY HEART STARTED POUNDING WHEN I LOOKED AT THEM.
I WAS SO SCARED PEOPLE WOULD FIND OUT.
I THOUGHT I'D PROBABLY HAVE TO KEEP IT A SECRET FOREVER.
FROM MY PARENTS, MY FRIENDS... FROM EVERYONE.
THAT'S WHAT I THOUGHT EVER SINCE I WAS LITTLE.

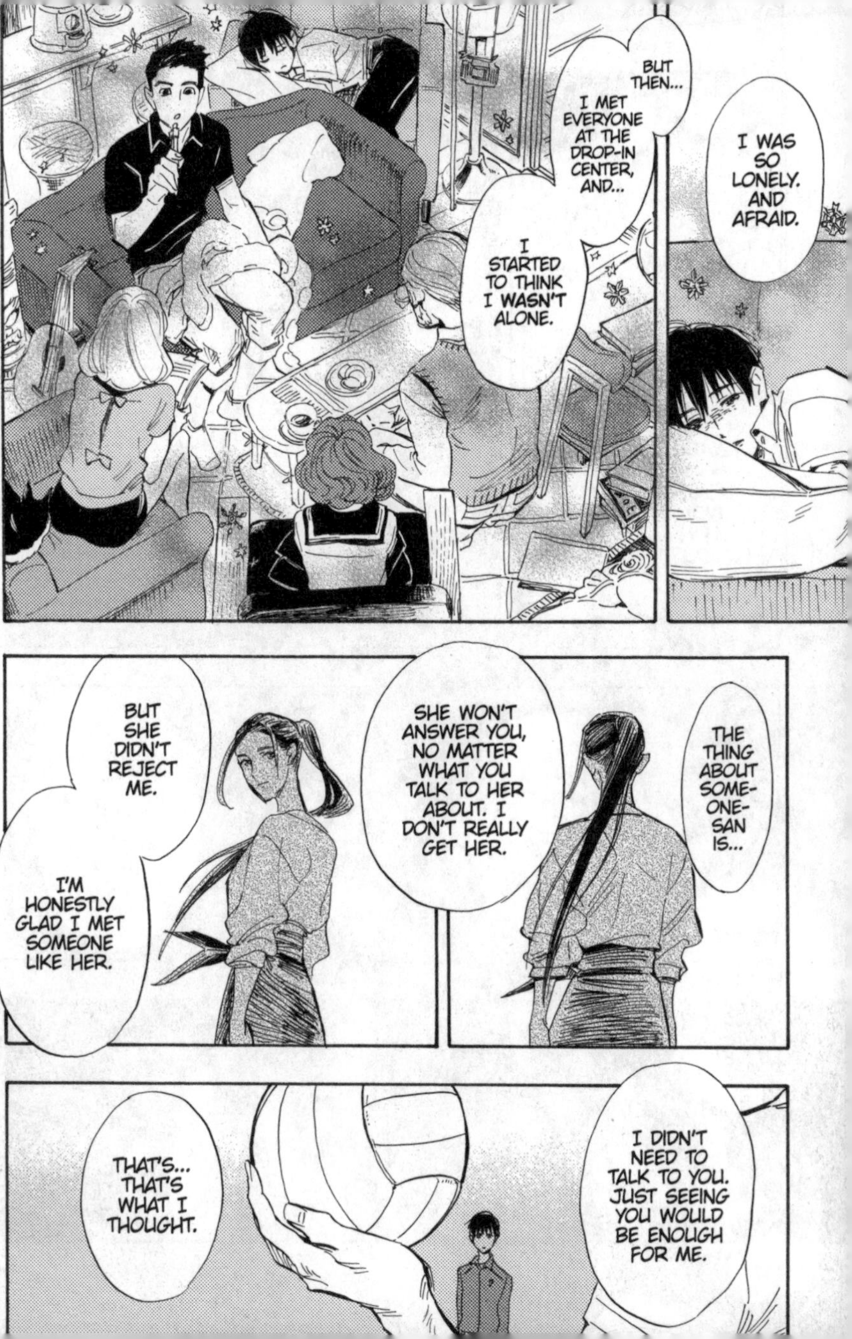
I WAS SO LONELY. AND AFRAID.
BUT THEN... I MET EVERYONE AT THE DROP-IN CENTER, AND...
I STARTED TO THINK I WASN'T ALONE.
THE THING ABOUT SOMEONE-SAN IS...
SHE WON'T ANSWER YOU, NO MATTER WHAT YOU TALK TO HER ABOUT. I DON'T REALLY GET HER.
BUT SHE DIDN'T REJECT ME.
I'M HONESTLY GLAD I MET SOMEONE LIKE HER.
I DIDN'T NEED TO TALK TO YOU. JUST SEEING YOU WOULD BE ENOUGH FOR ME.
THAT'S... THAT'S WHAT I THOUGHT.

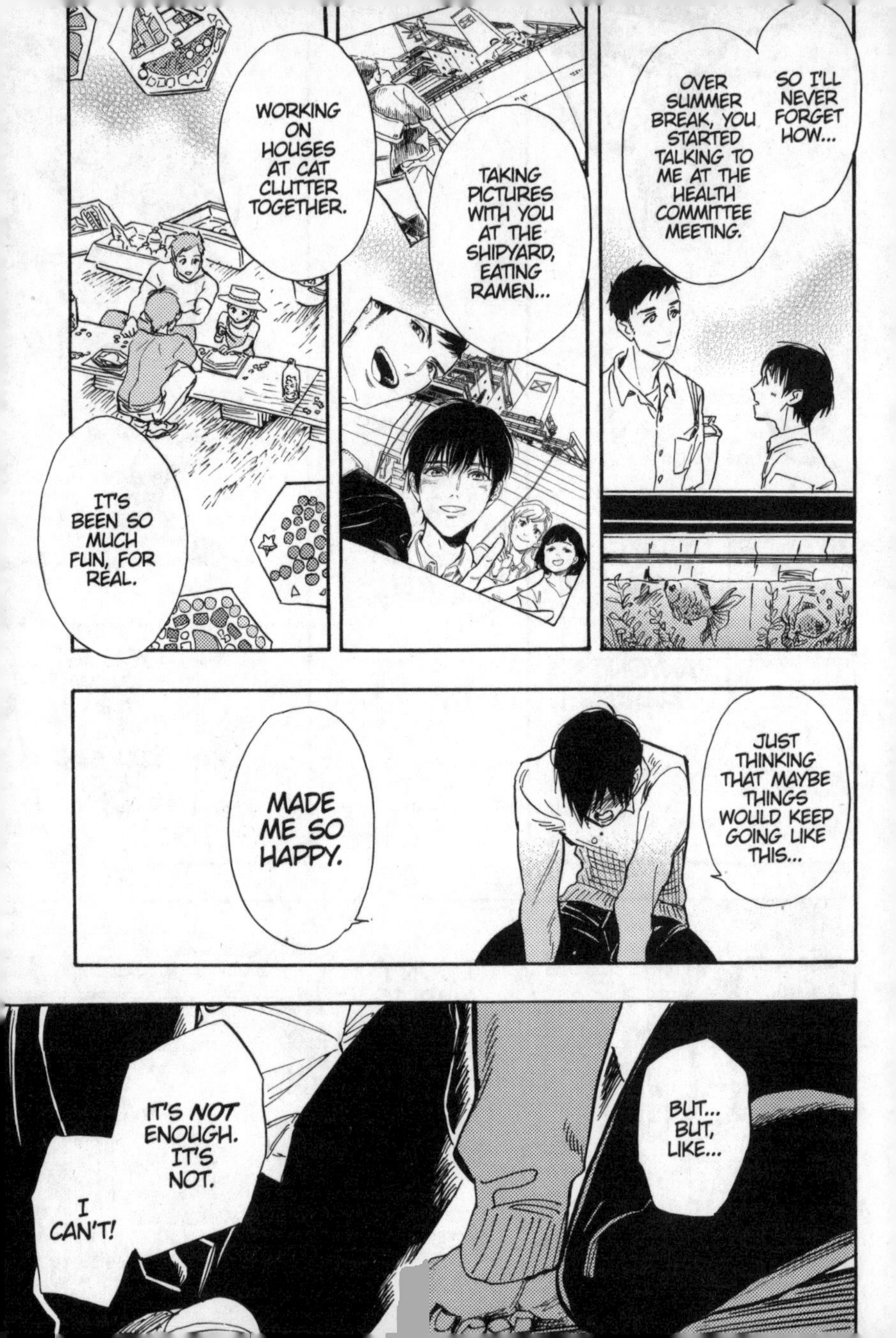
SO I'LL NEVER FORGET HOW...
OVER SUMMER BREAK, YOU STARTED TALKING TO ME AT THE HEALTH COMMITTEE MEETING.
TAKING PICTURES WITH YOU AT THE SHIPYARD, EATING RAMEN...
WORKING ON HOUSES AT CAT CLUTTER TOGETHER.
IT'S BEEN SO MUCH FUN, FOR REAL.
JUST THINKING THAT MAYBE THINGS WOULD KEEP GOING LIKE THIS...
MADE ME SO HAPPY.
BUT... BUT, LIKE...
IT'S *NOT* ENOUGH. IT'S NOT.
I CAN'T!

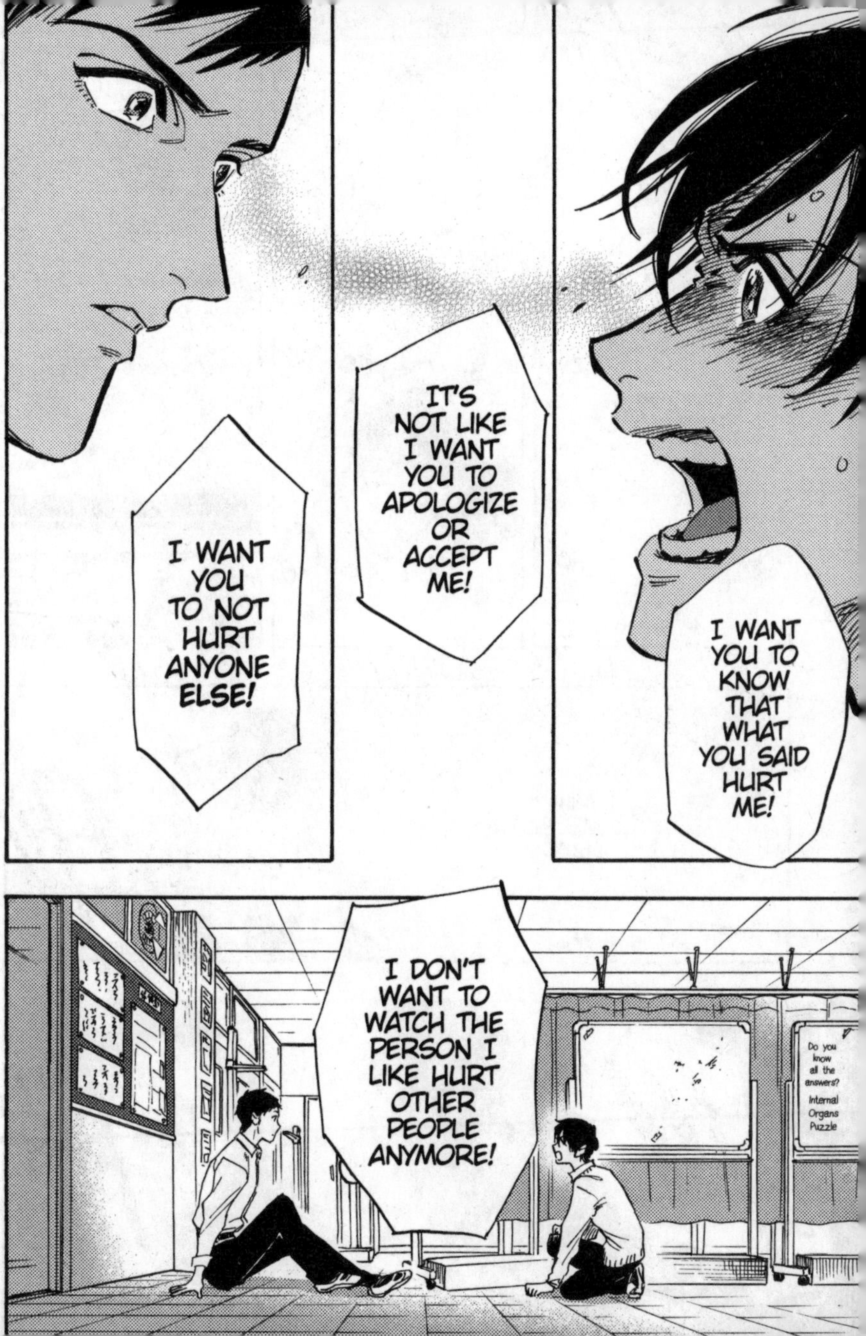
I WANT YOU TO KNOW THAT WHAT YOU SAID HURT ME!
IT'S NOT LIKE I WANT YOU TO APOLOGIZE OR ACCEPT ME!
I WANT YOU TO NOT HURT ANYONE ELSE!
I DON'T WANT TO WATCH THE PERSON I LIKE HURT OTHER PEOPLE ANYMORE!
Do you know all the answers? Internal Organs Puzzle

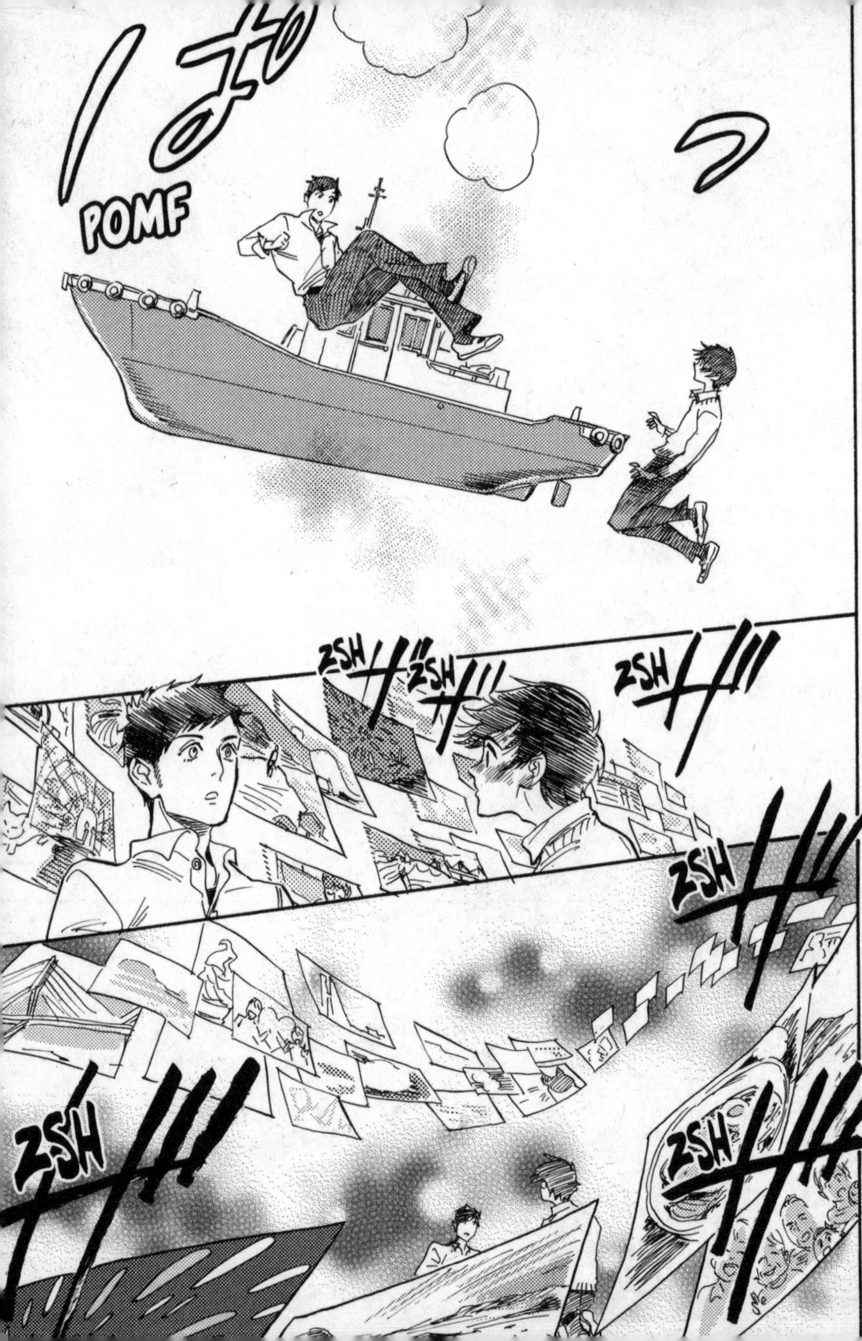

POMF
ZSH
ZSH
ZSH
ZSH
ZSH
ZSH

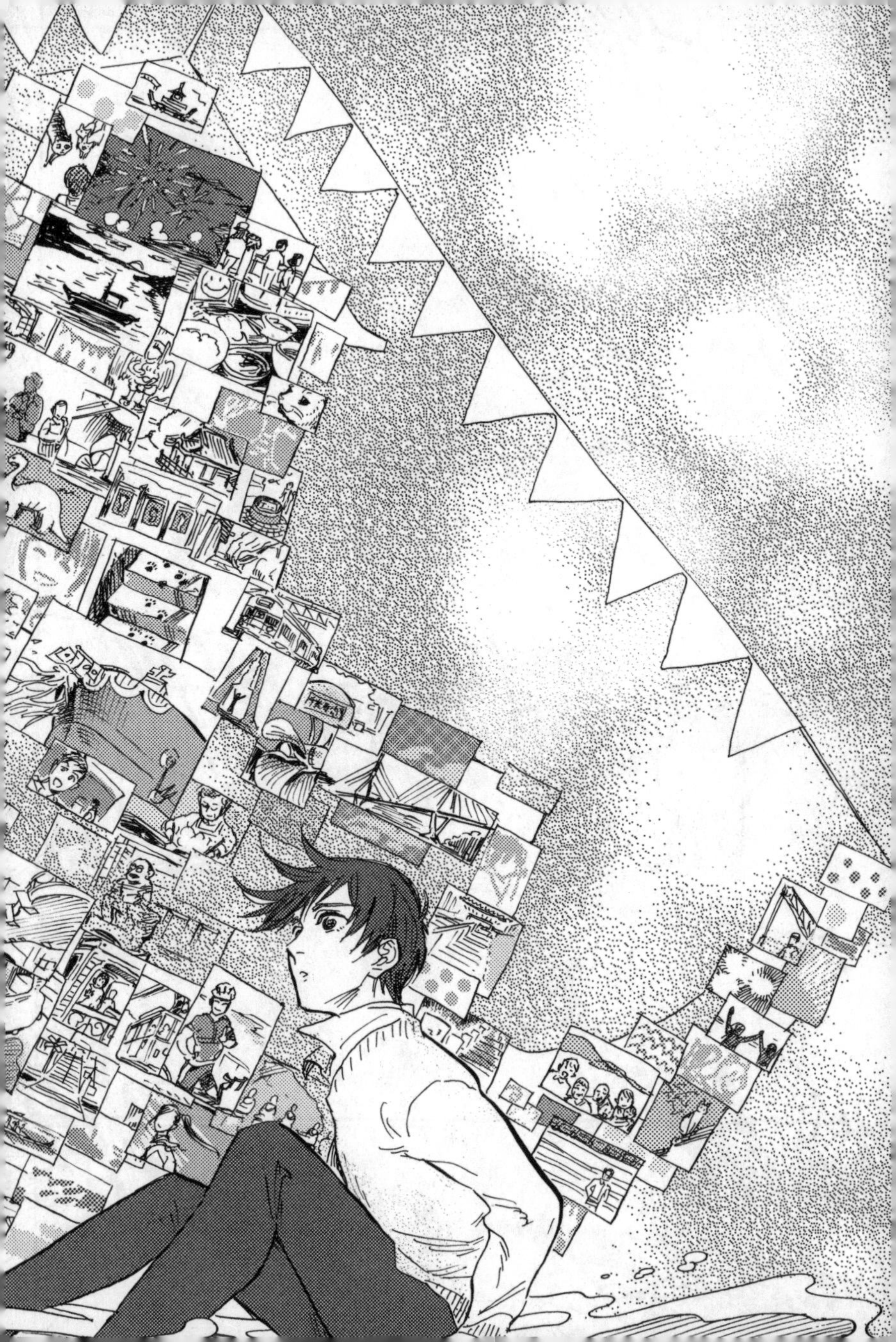

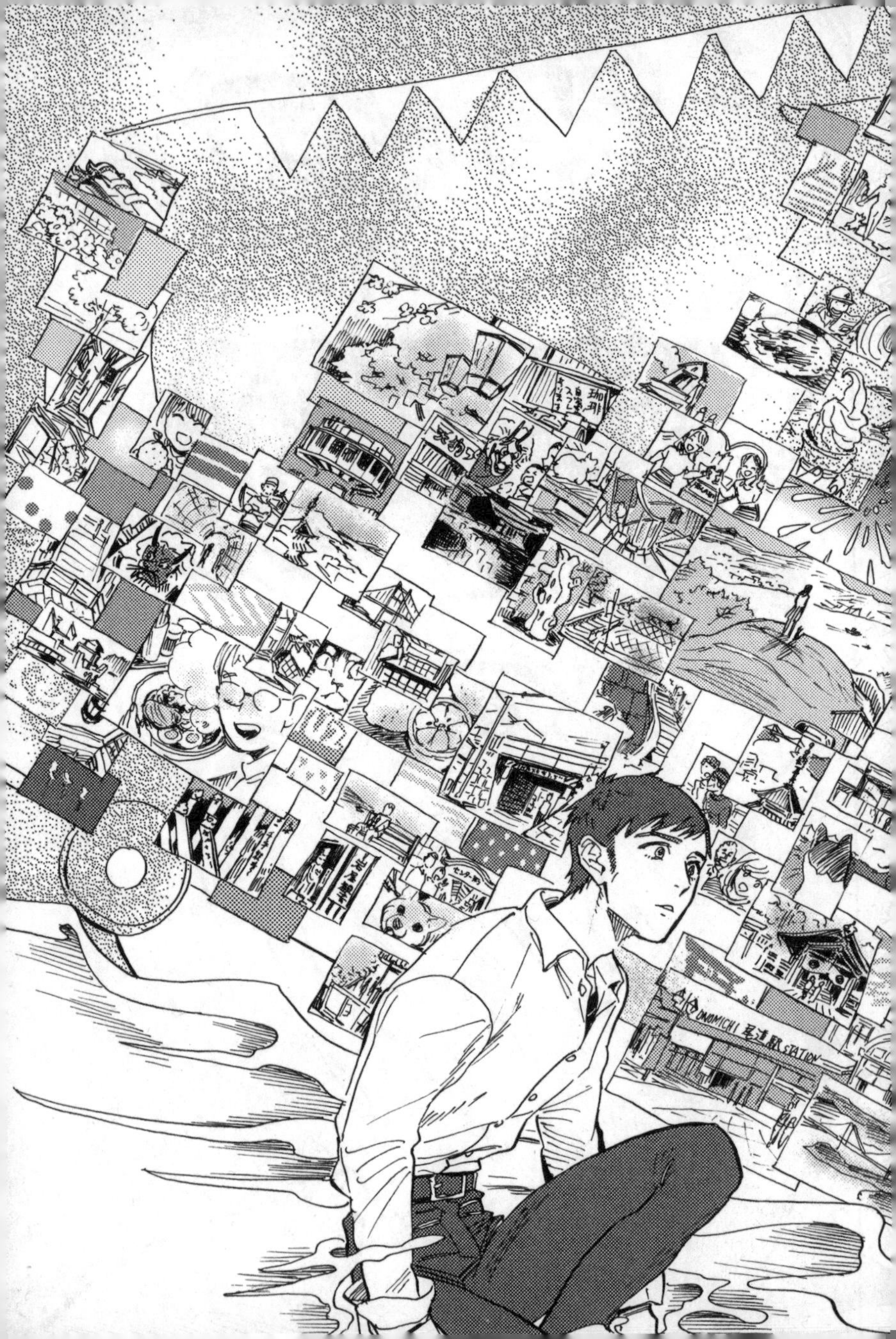
ONOMICHI 尾道駅 STATION

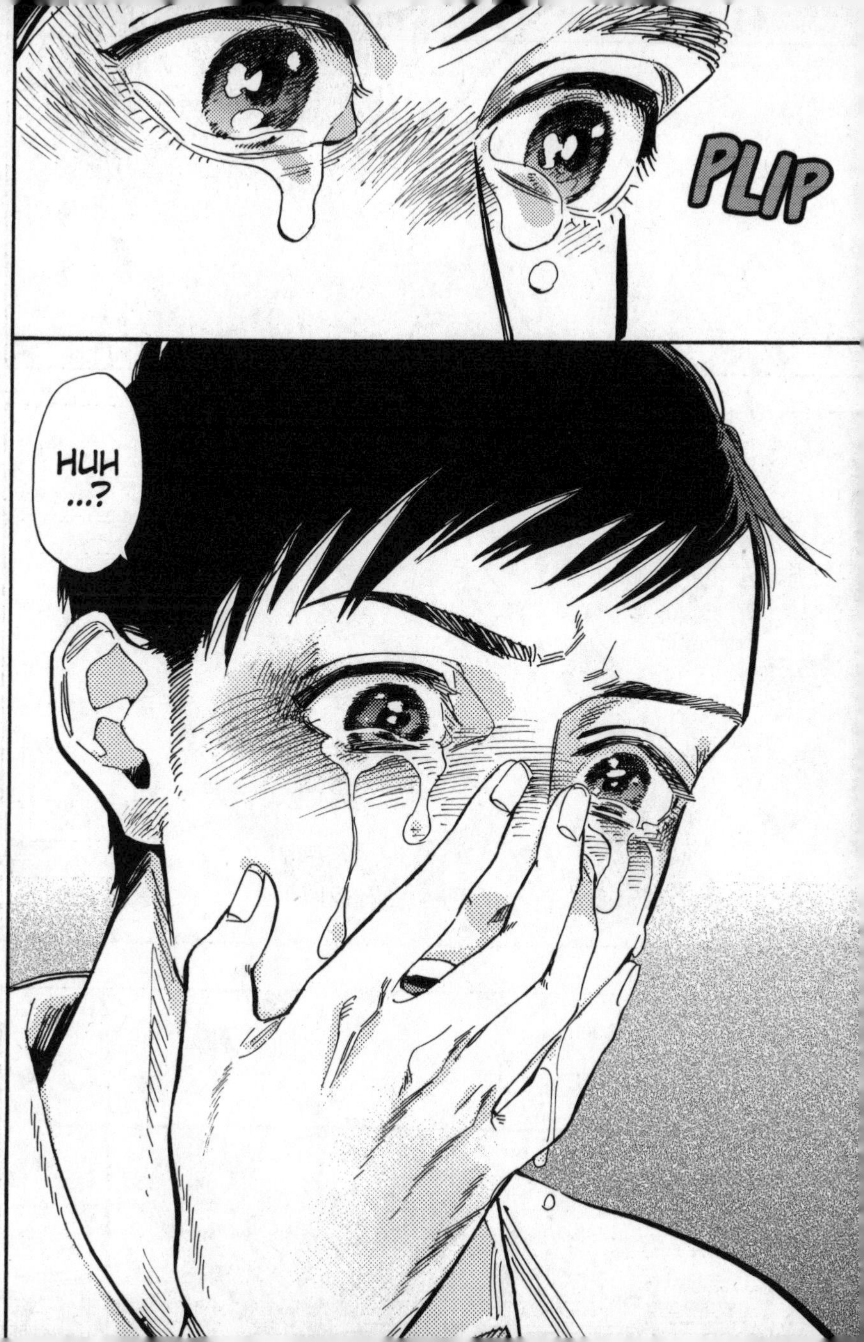
PLIP
HUH ...?

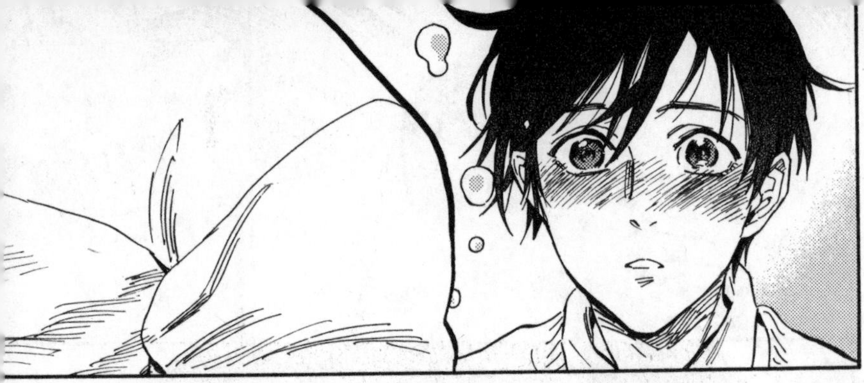

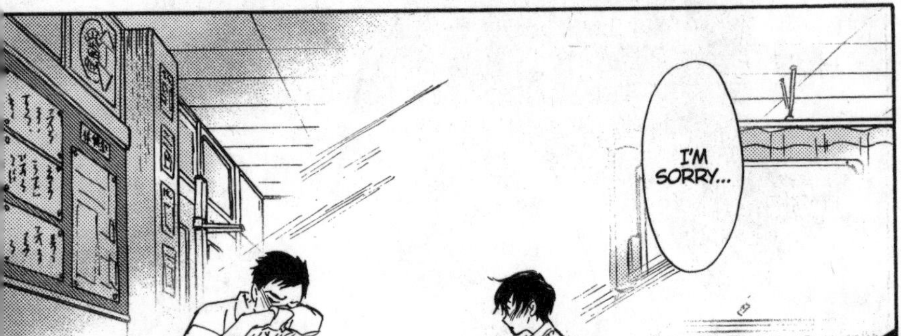
I'M SORRY...

Sign: Mukaishima Ferry Terminal.

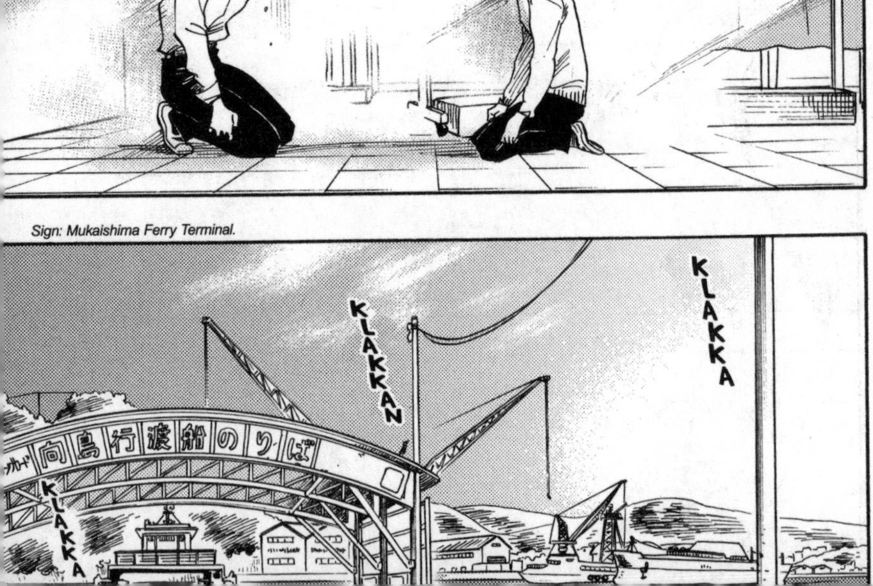
KLAKKA
KLAKKAN
向島行渡船のりば
KLAKKA

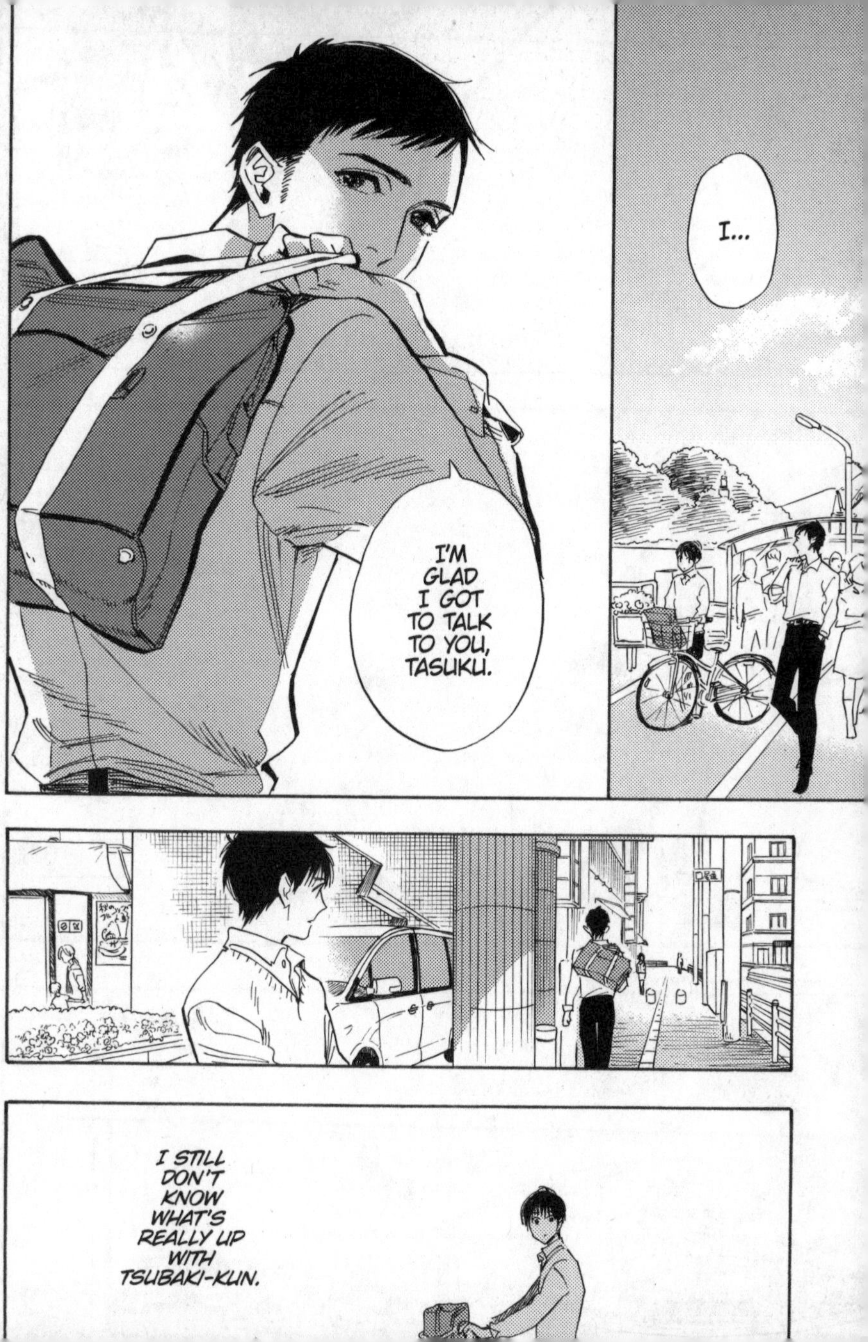
I...
I'M GLAD I GOT TO TALK TO YOU, TASUKU.
I STILL DON'T KNOW WHAT'S REALLY UP WITH TSUBAKI-KUN.

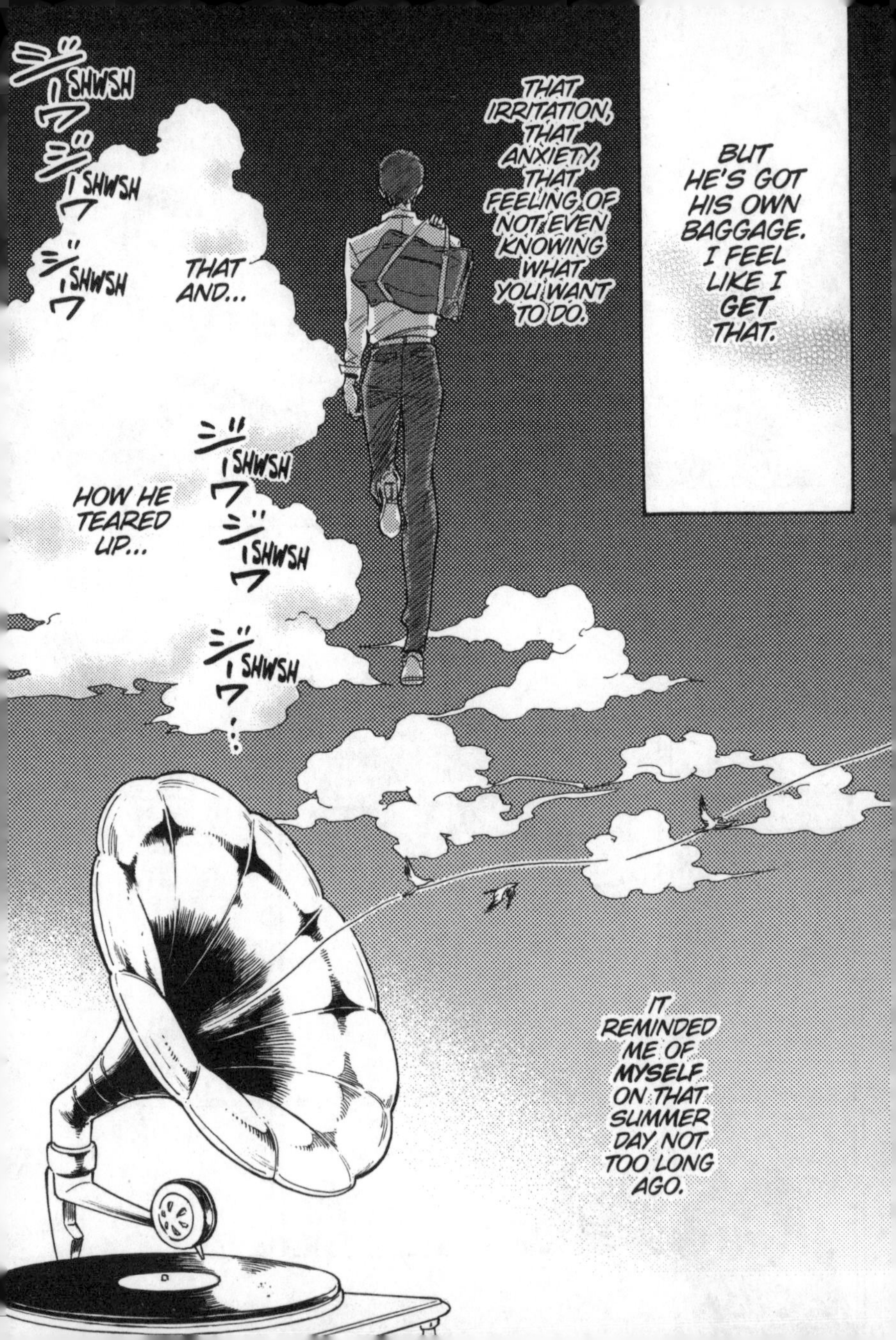
BUT HE'S GOT HIS OWN BAGGAGE. I FEEL LIKE I GET THAT.
THAT IRRITATION, THAT ANXIETY, THAT FEELING OF NOT EVEN KNOWING WHAT YOU WANT TO DO.
THAT AND...
SHWSH
SHWSH
SHWSH
SHWSH
HOW HE TEARED UP...
SHWSH
SHWSH
IT REMINDED ME OF MYSELF ON THAT SUMMER DAY NOT TOO LONG AGO.

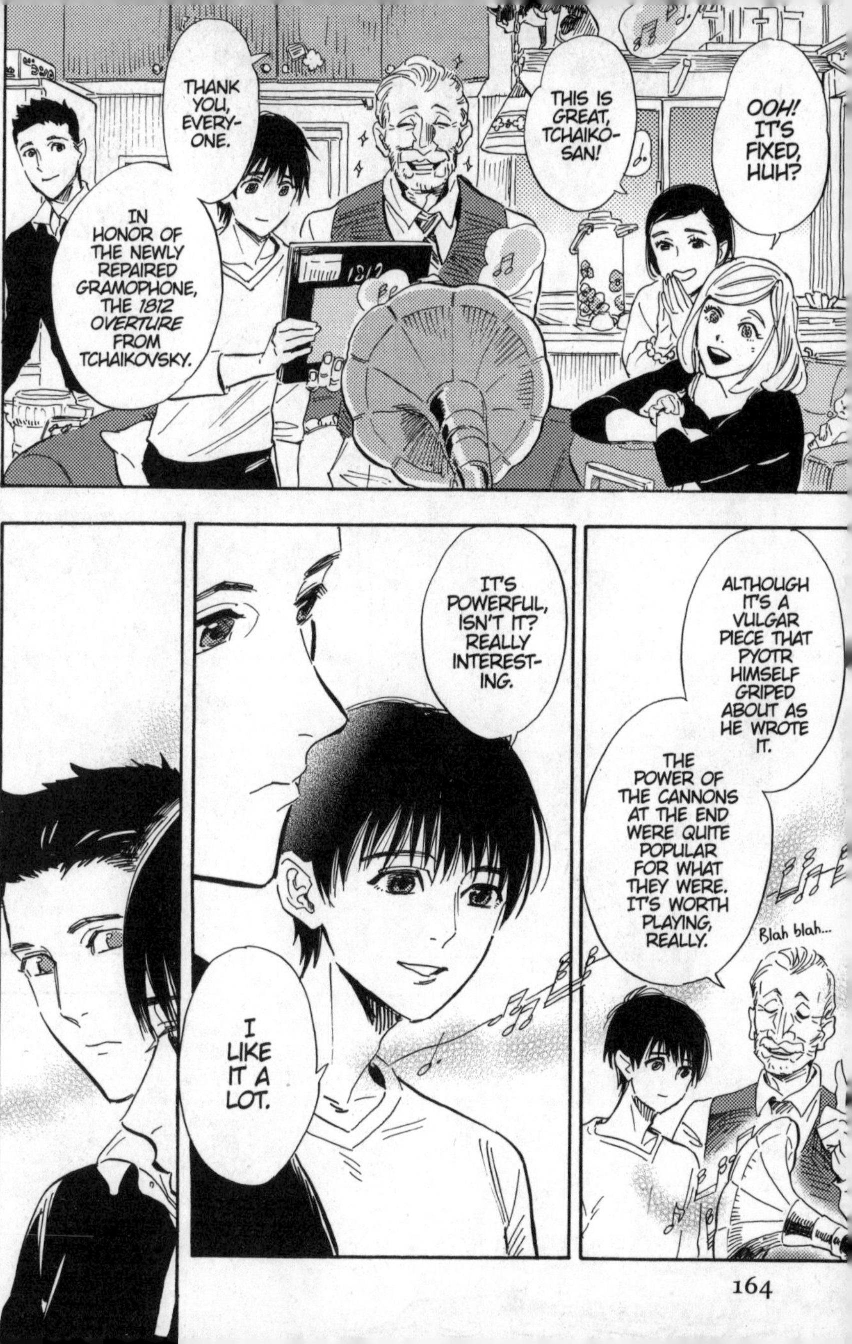
OOH! IT'S FIXED, HUH?
THIS IS GREAT, TCHAIKO-SAN!
THANK YOU, EVERYONE.
IN HONOR OF THE NEWLY REPAIRED GRAMOPHONE, THE 1812 OVERTURE FROM TCHAIKOVSKY.
ALTHOUGH IT'S A VULGAR PIECE THAT PYOTR HIMSELF GRIPED ABOUT AS HE WROTE IT.
THE POWER OF THE CANNONS AT THE END WERE QUITE POPULAR FOR WHAT THEY WERE. IT'S WORTH PLAYING, REALLY.
Blah blah...
IT'S POWERFUL, ISN'T IT? REALLY INTERESTING.
I LIKE IT A LOT.

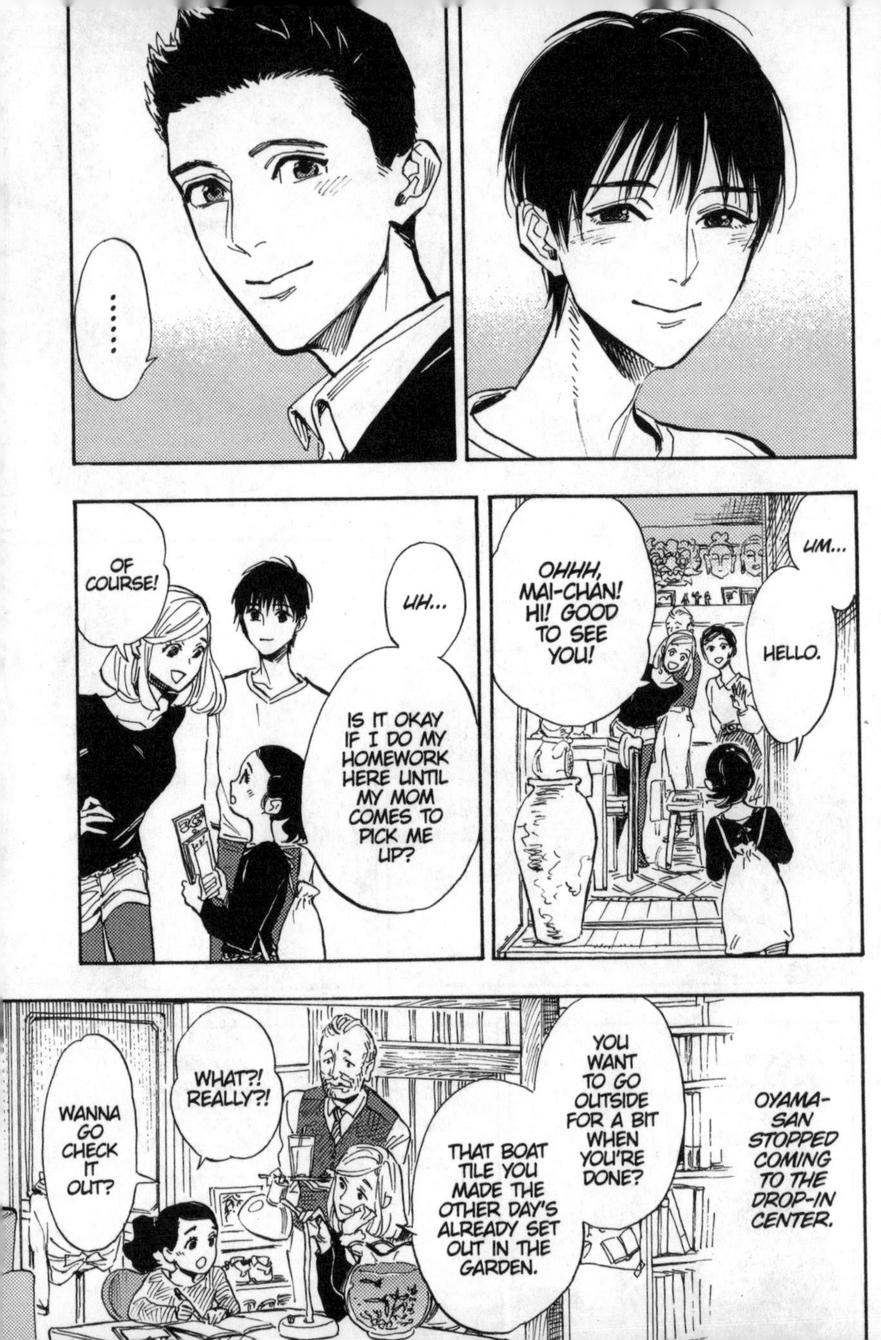
……
UM...
HELLO.
OHHH, MAI-CHAN! HI! GOOD TO SEE YOU!
UH...
IS IT OKAY IF I DO MY HOMEWORK HERE UNTIL MY MOM COMES TO PICK ME UP?
OF COURSE!
OYAMA-SAN STOPPED COMING TO THE DROP-IN CENTER.
YOU WANT TO GO OUTSIDE FOR A BIT WHEN YOU'RE DONE?
THAT BOAT TILE YOU MADE THE OTHER DAY'S ALREADY SET OUT IN THE GARDEN.
WHAT?! REALLY?!
WANNA GO CHECK IT OUT?

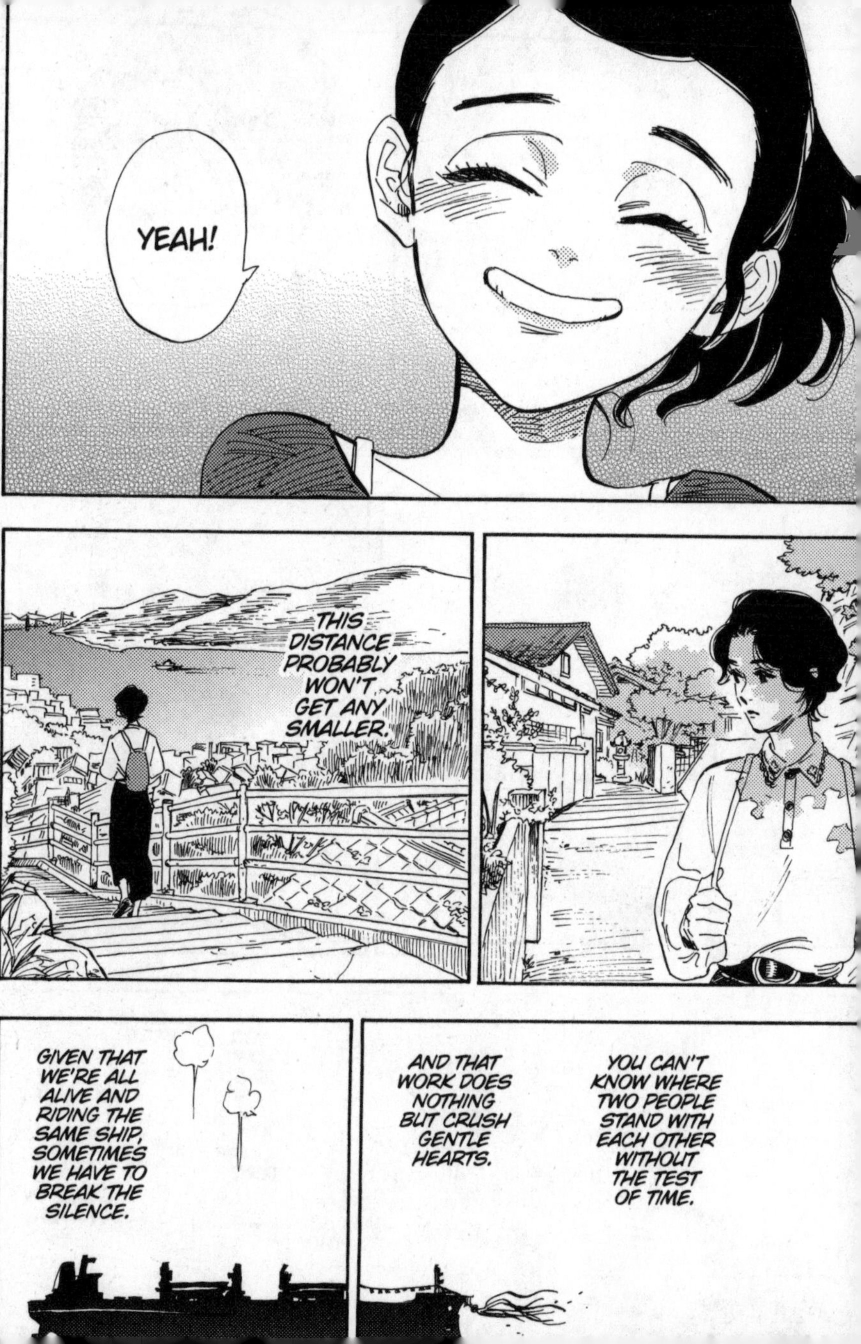
YEAH!
THIS DISTANCE PROBABLY WON'T GET ANY SMALLER.
GIVEN THAT WE'RE ALL ALIVE AND RIDING THE SAME SHIP, SOMETIMES WE HAVE TO BREAK THE SILENCE.
AND THAT WORK DOES NOTHING BUT CRUSH GENTLE HEARTS.
YOU CAN'T KNOW WHERE TWO PEOPLE STAND WITH EACH OTHER WITHOUT THE TEST OF TIME.

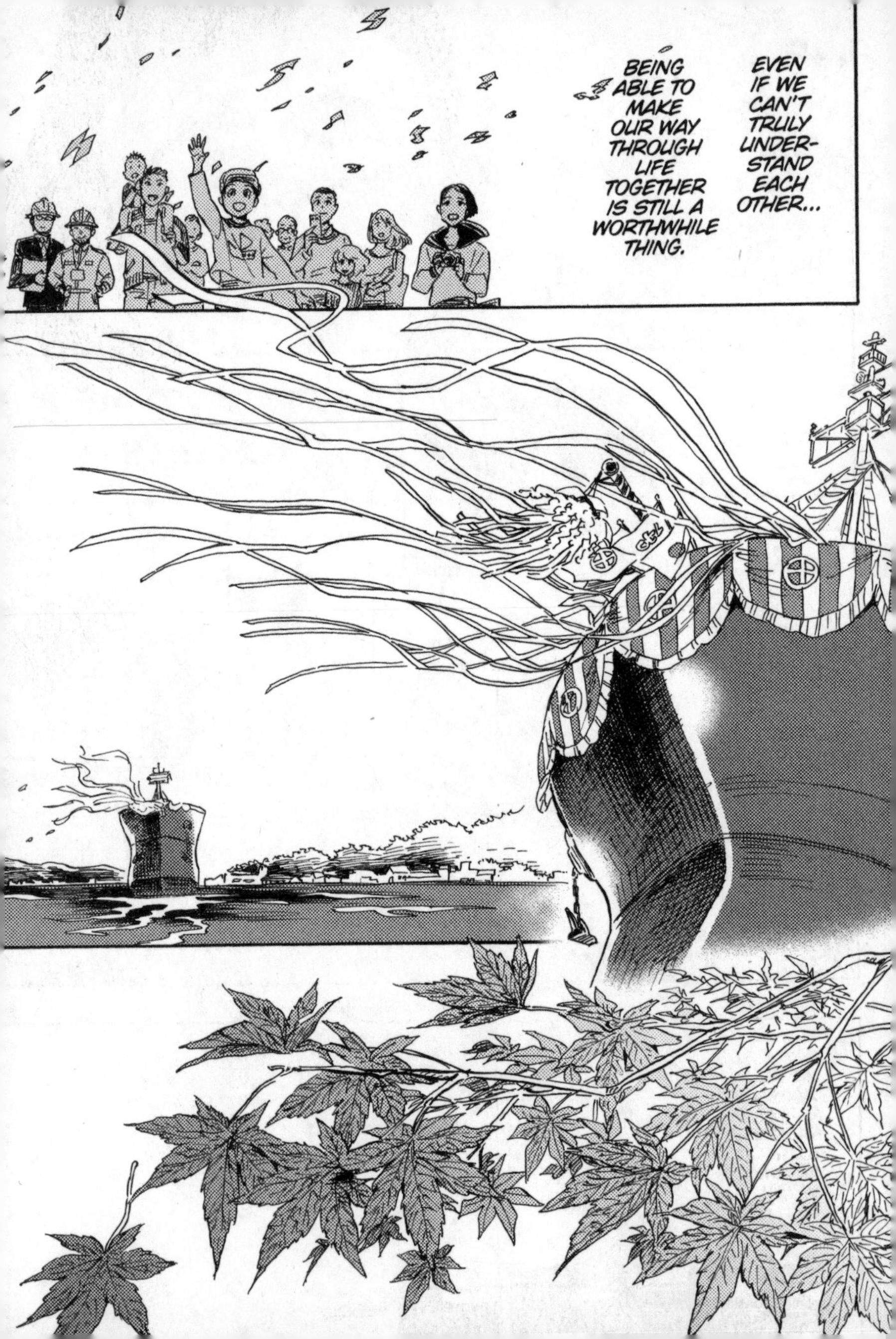
EVEN IF WE CAN'T TRULY UNDER-STAND EACH OTHER...
BEING ABLE TO MAKE OUR WAY THROUGH LIFE TOGETHER IS STILL A WORTHWHILE THING.

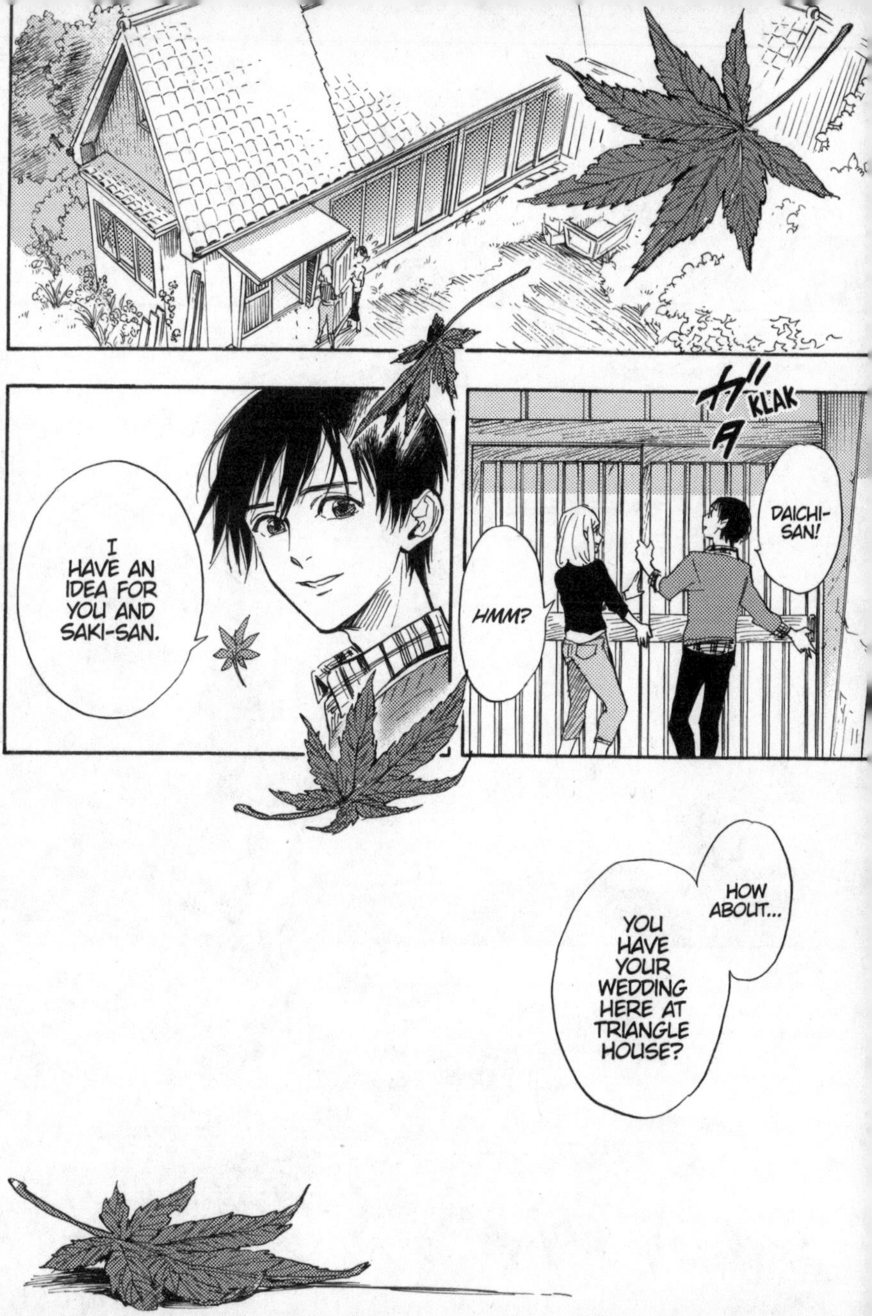
ガタ
KLAK
DAICHI-SAN!
HMM?
I HAVE AN IDEA FOR YOU AND SAKI-SAN.
HOW ABOUT...
YOU HAVE YOUR WEDDING HERE AT TRIANGLE HOUSE?

[Research Assistance]

NPO Onomichi Akiya Saisei Project
Masako Toyota

Trois Couleurs Co., Ltd.
Hiroko Masahara
Koyuki Higashi

Kentaro Tsuru
Mizuki Kunigi

Onomichi Municipal Tourism Department

SHIMANAMI **TASOGARE**

Our Dreams at Dusk (3) end

SEVEN SEAS ENTERTAINM

P9-DIG-643

Our Dreams at Dusk

SHIMANAMI **TASOGARE**   story and art by **YUHKI KAMATANI**   VOL. 3

TRANSLATION
Jocelyne Allen

ADAPTATION
Ysabet MacFarlane

LETTERING AND RETOUCH
Kaitlyn Wiley

COVER DESIGN
KC Fabellon

ORIGINAL EDITION DESIGNER
Hiroshi NIIGAMI (NARTI ; S)

PROOFREADER
Kurestin Armada
Danielle King

EDITOR
Jenn Grunigen

PRODUCTION MANAGER
Lissa Pattillo

EDITOR-IN-CHIEF
Adam Arnold

PUBLISHER
Jason DeAngelis

Seven Seas press and purchase enquiries can be sent to Marketing Manager
Lianne Sentar at press@gomanga.com. Information regarding the distribution
and purchase of digital editions is available from Digital Manager CK Russell
at digital@gomanga.com.

Seven Seas and the Seven Seas logo are trademarks of
Seven Seas Entertainment. All rights reserved.

ISBN: 978-1-64275-062-1

Printed in Canada

First Printing: September 2019

10 9 8 7 6 5 4 3 2 1

FOLLOW US ONLINE: **www.sevenseasentertainment.com**

READING DIRECTIONS

This book reads from *right to left*, Japanese style.
If this is your first time reading manga, you start
reading from the top right panel on each page and
take it from there. If you get lost, just follow the
numbered diagram here. It may seem backwards at
first, but you'll get the hang of it! Have fun!!

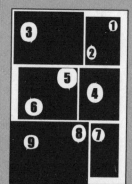